k_m	Market Return; Return on the Market Portfolio of Assets	PV	Present Value
k_p	• Cost of Preferred Stock	PVA_n	Present Value of an n-Year Annuity
	• Portfolio Return	$PVIF_{k,n}$	Present Value Interest Factor for a Single Amount Discounted at k Percent for n Periods
k_r	Cost of Retained Earnings	$PVIFA_{k,n}$	Present Value Interest Factor for an Annuity When Interest is Discounted Annually at k Percent for n Periods
k_s	Required Return on Common Stock		
m	Number of times per year interest is compounded		
M	Bond's Par Value	Q	• Order Quantity in Units
MACRS	Modified Accelerated Cost Recovery System		• Sales Quantity in Units
MNC	Multinational Company	R_F	Risk-Free Rate of Interest
MRP	Materials Requirement Planning	RADR	Risk-Adjusted Discount Rate
n	• Number of Outcomes Considered	ROA	Return on Total Assets
	• Number of Periods—Typically, Years	ROE	Return on Equity
	• Years to Maturity	S	Sources of Cash
N	Number of Days Payment Can Be Delayed by Giving up the Cash Discount	S	Inventory Usage in Units per Period
		SML	Security Market Line
N_d	Net Proceeds from the Sale of Debt (Bond)	t	Time
N_n	Net Proceeds from the Sale of New Common Stock	T	Firm's Marginal Tax Rate
		U	Uses of Cash
N_p	Net Proceeds from the Sale of the Preferred Stock	V	Value of an Asset or Firm
		VC	Variable Operating Cost per Unit
NPV	Net Present Value	w_j	• Proportion of the Portfolio's Total Dollar Value Represented by Asset j
O	Order Cost Per Order		
OC	Operating Cycle		• Proportion of a Specific Source of Financing j in the Firm's Capital Structure
P	Price (value) of Asset		
P_0	Value of Common Stock	WACC	Weighted Average Cost of Capital
PAC	Preauthorized Check	WMCC	Weighted Marginal Cost of Captial
PD	Preferred Stock Dividend	YTM	Yield to Maturity
P/E	Price/Earnings Ratio	α_t	Certainty Equivalent Factor in Year t
PMT	Amount of Payment	σ	Standard Deviation
Pr	Probability	Σ	Summation Sign

PRINCIPLES OF
MANAGERIAL
FINANCE BRIEF

THE ADDISON-WESLEY SERIES IN FINANCE

Chambers / Lacey
Modern Corporate Finance: Theory and Practice

Copeland
Exchange Rates and International Finance

Copeland / Weston
Financial Theory and Corporate Policy

Dufey / Giddy
Cases in International Finance

Eakins
Finance: Investments, Institutions, and Management

Eiteman / Stonehill / Moffett
Multinational Business Finance

Emery
Corporate Finance: Principles and Practice

Eng / Lees / Mauer
Global Finance

Gibson
International Finance

Gitman
Foundations of Managerial Finance

Gitman
Principles of Managerial Finance

Gitman
Principles of Managerial Finance, Brief Edition

Gitman / Joehnk
Fundamentals of Investing

Megginson
Corporate Finance Theory

Melvin
International Money and Finance

Mishkin / Eakins
Financial Markets and Institutions

Pinches
Essentials of Financial Management

Pinches
Financial Management

Radcliffe
Investment: Concepts-Analysis-Strategy

Rejda
Principles of Risk Management and Insurance

Rejda / McNamara
Personal Financial Planning

Solnik
International Investments

Thygerson
Management of Financial Institutions

Wagner
Financial Management with the Electronic Spreadsheet

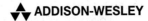 **ADDISON-WESLEY**

An Imprint of Addison Wesley Longman, Inc.

Reading, Massachusetts • Menlo Park, California • New York • Harlow, England
Don Mills, Ontario • Sydney • Mexico City • Madrid • Amsterdam

PRINCIPLES OF
MANAGERIAL FINANCE BRIEF

Second Edition

Lawrence J. Gitman
San Diego State University

Executive Editor: Denise Clinton
Sponsoring Editor: Julie Lindstrom
Development Editor: Ann Torbert
Managing Editor: Jim Rigney
Production Supervisor: Nancy Fenton
Marketing Manager: Amy Cronin
Supplements Editor: Deb Kiernan
Associate Media Producer: Jennifer Pelland
Editorial Assistant: Greta Brogna
Project Coordination, Text Design, Art Studio,
    and Electronic Page Makeup: Thompson Steele, Inc.
Design Manager: Rehina Hagen
Cover Designer: Leslie Haimes and Regina Hagen
Cover Photograph: Image ©1999 PhotoDisc Inc.
Manufacturing Coordinator: Tim McDonald
Printer and Binder: RR Donnelley & Sons Company
Cover Printer: The Lehigh Press

For permission to use copyrighted material, grateful acknowledgment is made to the copyright holders on p. S-1, which are hereby made part of this copyright page.

Library of Congress Cataloging-in-Publication Data

Gitman, Lawrence J.
    Principles of managerial finance : brief / Lawrence J. Gitman. —
2nd ed.
        p.   cm.
    ISBN 0-321-06081-4 (alk. paper)
    1. Corporations—Finance. 2. Business enterprises—Finance.
I. Title.
HG4011.G52   2000
658.15—dc21   99-29543
                                                                CIP

ISBN 0-321–06081–4

12345678910—DOW—0302010099

Dedicated to the memory
of my mother, Dr. Edith Gitman,
who instilled in me the importance
of education and hard work

BRIEF CONTENTS

DETAILED CONTENTS

PART 2   IMPORTANT FINANCIAL CONCEPTS   149

CHAPTER 6   150

TIME VALUE OF MONEY

PART ③ LONG-TERM INVESTMENT DECISIONS 267

PART ④   LONG-TERM FINANCIAL DECISIONS   353

CHAPTER 11   354

THE COST
OF CAPITAL

PART ⑤ SHORT-TERM FINANCIAL DECISIONS   459

CHAPTER 16   531

CASH AND MARKETABLE SECURITIES

TO THE INSTRUCTOR

Principles of Managerial Finance has consistently met the needs of the introductory finance course at the undergraduate level. This second Brief Edition continues to satisfy these market needs—and more—with a focused concentration on the fundamental concepts, techniques, and practices of managerial finance. It provides both instructors and students an introduction to managerial finance that is firmly grounded in the theory and practice of finance and at the same time is user-friendly.

The Brief Edition evolved from years of work on both *Principles of Managerial Finance* and *Foundations of Managerial Finance*. It incorporates the proven learning system from *Principles of Managerial Finance* with a more focused approach as to content, based on significant market feedback. Integrating pedagogy with the concepts and practical applications necessary for a solid understanding of managerial finance, this edition equips instructors and their students to concentrate on the concepts, techniques, and practices for keen financial decision making in an increasingly competitive business environment. The strong pedagogy and generous use of examples also make the text an easily accessible resource for long-distance learning and self-study programs. From classroom to boardroom, the second Brief Edition of *Principles of Managerial Finance* can help users get to where they want to be, efficiently and effectively.

DISTINGUISHING FEATURES OF THE SECOND BRIEF EDITION

Numerous features distinguish the second Brief Edition of *Principles of Managerial Finance* from its many excellent competitors. Among them are the book's length, its flexible organization, proven teaching/learning system, strong ties to practice, and important content improvements.

STREAMLINED PRESENTATION

This second Brief Edition has been sized to fit the one-term financial management course. It is intended for those professors who want to provide students with a thorough introduction to corporate finance that focuses on fundamental concepts, techniques, and practices of financial management. I've right-sized this book for the one-term course by eliminating from my longer book, *Principles of Managerial Finance*, ninth edition, topics that will be covered in subsequent courses. Specifically, I've eliminated the chapter on corporate mergers and the separate chapter on international managerial finance—although the integrated discussions and examples of international finance have been retained in appropriate chapter discussions throughout. In addition, the chapter in *Principles of*

Managerial Finance, ninth edition, that contains detailed discussions of leasing, convertibles, warrants, and options has been omitted from this Brief Edition. Also, coverage of capital budgeting in the Brief Edition continues to be presented in two chapters, whereas it has been expanded to three chapters in the longer book.

In the Brief Edition, a separate chapter on basic corporate securities (Chapter 3) describes the general features of corporate bonds of various types, contrasts the differences between debt and equity capital, and describes the rights and features associated with preferred and common stocks. This chapter sets the stage for subsequent discussion of the use of these financing sources in capital budgeting and capital structure decisions.

Finally, presentation of many topics has been streamlined throughout. The resulting book includes thorough coverage of all basic topics, yet is three chapters and about 300 pages shorter than *Principles of Managerial Finance,* ninth edition, on which it is based.

FLEXIBLE ORGANIZATION

The text's organization conceptually links the firm's actions and its value as determined in the securities markets. Each major decision area is presented in terms of both risk and return factors and their potential impact on the owners' wealth, as reflected by share value.

In organizing each chapter, I have adhered to a managerial decision-making perspective. That is, I have described a concept such as present value or operating leverage and have also related it to the financial manager's overall goal of wealth maximization. Once a particular concept has been developed, its application is illustrated by an example. The student is not left with just an abstract definition or discussion, but truly senses the related decision-making considerations and consequences.

The second Brief Edition of *Principles of Managerial Finance* contains 17 chapters, in 5 parts. Although the text is sequential, instructors can assign almost any chapter as a self-contained unit. This flexibility enables instructors to customize the text to various teaching strategies.

PROVEN TEACHING/LEARNING SYSTEM

The book's teaching/learning system is state-of-the-art. It is driven by a set of carefully developed learning goals that help guide and organize student reading and study. In addition, numerous other features reinforce student learning to promote achievement of the learning goals. Each of the system's key elements is described in what follows.

Learning Goals   The *PMF* Teaching/Learning System is anchored in a set of six proven Learning Goals (LGs) per chapter. Marked by a special icon, shown here in the margin, the learning goals are listed at the start of each chapter, tied to first-level headings, reviewed point by point at the chapter's end, and noted in assignment material and supplements such as the Test Bank and Study Guide.

These goals focus student attention on what material they need to learn, where they can find it in the chapter, and whether they've mastered it by the end of the chapter. In addition, instructors can easily build lectures and assignments around the LGs.

PMF **Toolbox**   A key visual aid in the *PMF* Teaching/learning System is the *PMF Toolbox*, a cluster of icons at the beginning of every major chapter section. Inside the Toolbox, students will find learning tools and resources that are available to them as they attempt to master each learning goal. These tools and resources consist of learning goals, software tutorials, problem-solving disk routines, and spreadsheet templates, where these apply to the topic at hand. An example of the Toolbox appears in Chapter 9 on capital budgeting and cash flow principles, next to the heading "Finding the Initial Investment" (page 278).

PMF **Example Method**   The *PMF Example Method* is an important component of the *PMF* Teaching/Learning System because it infuses practical demonstrations into the learning process. Seeing a financial concept or technique applied in a realistic example provides students with immediate reinforcement that helps cement their understanding of that concept or technique. Where applicable, the solution of each example shows the use of time lines, tables, and financial calculators. Calculator keystrokes of inputs, functions, and outputs are highlighted in discussions and examples of time value techniques in Chapter 6 and in the application of those techniques in subsequent chapters. Appendix A and the laminated table card included in all new books contain financial tables and note the basic calculator keystrokes for the most popular financial calculators.

Key Equations   Key equations are printed in green throughout the text to help students identify the most important mathematical relationships. The variables used in these equations are for convenience printed on the front endpapers of the book.

Marginal Glossary   Throughout the text, key terms and their definitions appear in the text margin when they are first introduced. In addition, these terms are **boldfaced** in the index for easy access to the glossary entry.

International Coverage   Discussions of international dimensions of chapter topics are integrated throughout the book. For example, Chapter 7 discusses the risks and returns associated with international diversification. Similarly, Chapter 9 addresses the international aspects of capital budgeting and long-term investments. In each chapter in which international coverage is included, the international material is integrated into chapter learning goals and the end-of-chapter summary and problem material.

Review Questions   *Review Questions* appear at the end of each section of the chapter (positioned before the next first-level heading) and are marked with a special design element. As students progress through the chapter, they can test their understanding of each key concept, technique, and practice before moving on to the next section.

Summary   End-of-chapter summaries are keyed to the learning goals, which are restated for reinforcement at the beginning of each *Summary* paragraph. The learning-goal-driven summary facilitates the student's review of the key material that was presented to support mastery of the given goal.

Self-Test Problems   At the end of most chapters, one or more *Self-Test Problems* are included. Each problem is keyed to the appropriate learning goal and the *PMF–Brief* CD-ROM Software icons from the Toolbox. Appendix B contains all worked-out solutions to Self-Test Problems in one location, marked with an easy-to-spot green stripe on the outsdie of the pages. These demonstration problems with solutions help to strengthen students' understanding of the topics and the techniques presented.

Chapter Problems   A comprehensive set of *Problems,* containing more than one problem for each concept or technique, provides students with multiple self-testing opportunities and give professors a wide choice of assignable material. A short descriptor at the beginning of every problem identifies the concept or technique that the problem has been designed to test. New in this edition, the problems are graded by difficulty level—warm-up, intermediate, and challenge—to indicate the amount of work that should be involved in solving each problem. Some of the end-of-chapter problems are graded "integrative" because they tie together related topics. All problems are keyed to the learning goals and the *PMF–Brief* CD-ROM Software using icons from the Toolbox. Guideline answers to selected end-of-chapter problems appear as in Appendix C.

Chapter Cases   Chapter *Cases* enable students to apply in realistic contexts what they've learned in the chapter. In Chapter 4, for example, students are asked to evaluate a firm's cash flows. In Chapter 8, students assess the impact of a proposed risky investment on a firm's bond and stock values. These end-of-chapter cases help strengthen practical understanding of financial tools and techniques without the added expense of a separate casebook.

Web Exercises   New in this second Brief Edition, a *Web Exercise* at the end of each chapter links the chapter topic to a related site on the Internet and asks students to use information located there to answer various questions. These exercises will capture student interest in using the Internet while educating them about finance-related sites.

Contemporary Design   A vibrant, contemporary design draws readers' attention to features of the learning system. Bars of data are shaded in tables and then graphed in the same shade so that visual learners can immediately see relationships among data.

STRONG TIES TO PRACTICE

A variety of features are used in the ninth edition to anchor student understanding in the operational aspects of topics presented. Many textual discussions present practical insights and applications of concepts and techniques. In addition, a number of special features are used both to ensure realism and to stimulate student interest.

Cross-Disciplinary Focus   Every chapter opens with an element that encourages students to understand the overall importance of the chapter material as well as its relationship to other major business disciplines. "Across the Disciplines" indicates the key benefits or interactions that those in accounting, information systems, management, marketing, and operations would likely have with regard to the financial management material covered in the chapter. This features allows students, regardless of their chosen business major, to understand the importance of the finance topics to that major and to that department within a company. In addition, it gives students a better appreciation for the numerous cross-disciplinary interactions that routinely occur in business.

Personal Finance Feature   To help students appreciate the pervasive nature of finance, a Personal Finance Perspective is included in each chapter. This example applies some aspect of the chapter material to the personal financial decisions of individuals. Chapter 2, for example, explains why it might be useful to look at the shape of the yield curve before making various personal finance decisions. Chapter 4 discusses how an understanding of depreciation can help the student make an informed decision when purchasing a car. Studying these examples should provide students with a solid understanding of the relationships between corporate and personal financial decisions.

IMPORTANT CONTENT IMPROVEMENTS

The publication of each new edition of a textbook offers the opportunity to update material in terms of important current and emerging issues, instruments, and techniques affecting the practice of financial management. Consistent exposure to current practical applications throughout the text enables students to walk away from the book and onto the job well-prepared with forward-looking, practical insight, rather than merely a conceptual grasp of the finance function. Each new edition also offers the opportunity to fine-tune material based on the considered comments of the book's users and potential users.

Because users and potential users often like to know where new material appears, here are the significant changes made in the second Brief Edition.

Chapter 1, which provides a newly streamlined overview of managerial finance, now includes the agency issue in a major text section of its own and a revised discussion of incentive and performance plans (in the compensation discussion).

Chapter 2 has been retitled "Institutions, Markets, and Interest Rates." The discussion of business taxation has been moved from this chapter into Chapter 4. In its place have been added sections on the basic corporate securities—bonds and stocks—and the difference between debt and equity capital. This new organization will give students a better understanding of these important securities from early in the course. In addition, the chapter now features streamlined coverage of investment banking, a new Personal Finance Perspective on what the yield curve might predict for personal financial decisions, and a new Self-Test Problem.

Chapter 3 presents the basic corporate securities. The discussion of common stock now precedes the discussion of preferred stock.

Chapter 4 now covers financial statements, taxes, depreciation, and cash flow. Taxes were moved from Chapter 2 in order to bring them closer to the related discussions of depreciation and cash flow. Chapter 4 now contains an updated Intel letter to stockholders, a new explanation of (and glossary entry for) double taxation, and a second Self-Test Problem on corporate taxes.

Chapter 5's coverage of financial statement analysis has a new Personal Finance Perspective on applying ratio analysis to personal finances.

Chapter 6 on time value of money has a revised discussion of nominal annual rate and effective annual rate (EAR) and simplified headings to improve understanding of chapter structure.

Chapter 7 on risk and return now contains a revised Personal Finance Perspective that better explains how to select from among the universe of mutual funds.

Chapter 8 on bond and stock valuation now includes a definition of interest-rate risk in the section on changing required returns.

Chapter 9 on capital budgeting and cash flow principles has been thoroughly updated.

Chapter 10 on capital budgeting techniques under certainty and risk includes a new format for decision criteria under the various capital budgeting techniques, and a new Personal Finance Perspective that demonstrates the application of capital budgeting analysis to a personal investment situation.

Chapter 11 on the cost of capital leads off a three-chapter part on long-term financing decisions. The primary change in Chapter 11 is a clearer explanation of the cost of retained earnings.

Chapter 12 on leverage and capital structure now includes a new, clearer illustration showing capital costs and the optimal capital structure.

Chapter 13 on dividend policy has a new Personal Finance Perspective on investors' reactions to stock splits.

Chapter 14 on financial planning is the first of four chapters on short-term financial decisions. It has been thoroughly updated, as has *Chapter 15* on working capital and short-term financing.

Chapter 16 on cash and marketable securities features a new Personal Finance Perspective that discusses online banking.

Chapter 17 on accounts receivable and inventory now includes a revised Personal Finance Perspective on managing personal credit.

SUPPLEMENTS TO THE *PMF* TEACHING/LEARNING SYSTEM

The *PMF* Teaching/learning System includes a variety of useful supplements for teachers and for students.

TEACHING TOOLS FOR INSTRUCTORS

The key teaching tools available to instructors are the *Instructor's Manual,* Testing Materials, and PowerPoint Lecture Presentations.

Instructor's Manual   *Compiled by Frederick P. Schadler, East Carolina University.* This comprehensive resource pulls together the teaching tools so that instructors can use the text easily and effectively in the classroom. Each chapter provides an overview of key topics and detailed answers and solutions to all Review Questions, end-of-chapter problems, and chapter cases. At the end of the manual are practice quizzes and solutions.

Testing Materials *Created by Hadi Salavitabar, SUNY–New Paltz.* Thoroughly revised to accommodate changes in the text, the Test Bank contains 2,500 questions made up of a mix of true/false, multiple-choice, and essay questions. For quick test selection and construction, each chapter features a handy chart for identifying type of question, skill tested by learning goal, and level of difficulty. Because the Test Bank is available in both printed and electronic formats—word processing files, and Windows or Macintosh *TestGen EQ* files— instructors should contact their Addison Wesley Longman sales representative to determine which format best meets their testing needs.

Instructors can download the *TestGen EQ* version of the Test Bank into *QuizMaster,* an on-line testing program for Windows and Macintosh that enables users to conduct timed or untimed exams at computer workstations. After completing tests, students can see their scores and view or print a diagnostic report of those topics or objectives requiring more attention. When installed on a local area network, *QuizMaster* allows instructors to save the scores on disk, print study diagnoses, and monitor progress of students individually or by class section and by all sections of the course.

PowerPoint Lecture Presentation *Created by Daniel Borgia, Florida Gulf Coast University.* Available for Windows or Macintosh on the Instructor's Resource CD–ROM, this presentation combines lecture notes with art from the textbook. The lecture presentations for each chapter can be viewed electronically in the classroom or can be printed as black-and-white transparency masters.

Instructor's Resource CD-ROM Electronic files of the Instructor's Manual, Test Bank, and PowerPoint Lecture Presentation are available on one convenient CD-ROM, compatible with both Windows and Macintosh computers. The electronic versions allow instructors to customize the support materials to their individual classroom needs.

LEARNING TOOLS FOR STUDENTS

Beyond the book itself, students have access to several resources for success in this course: the *PMF–Brief* CD-ROM, *Study Guide,* and the *Principles of Managerial Finance: Brief Second Edition* Web Site.

PMF Brief Second Edition CD-ROM Software Packaged with new copies of the text at no additional cost, the *PMF Brief Second Edition* CD-ROM Software, created by KMT Software, contains three state-of-the-art software tools: the *PMF Tutor,* the *PMF Problem Solver,* and the *PMF Excel Spreadsheet Templates.* Documentation and practical advice for using the *PMF Brief Second Edition* CD-ROM appears in Appendix D at the back of the textbook.

PMF Tutor The *PMF Tutor* extends self-testing opportunities beyond those of the printed page. The Tutor helps students to identify and solve various types of managerial finance problems. Part of the *PMF* Toolbox, the Tutor icon flags all the Tutor applications in the text. Through user-friendly menus, students can access over 55 different problem types, constructed by random-number generation for an inexhaustible supply of problems with little chance of repetition. Routines include financial ratios, time value of money, valuation, capital budgeting, and cost of capital.

PMF Problem-Solver   The *PMF Problem-Solver* contains seven short menu-driven programs to accelerate learning by providing an efficient way to perform financial computations. The Problem-Solver icon points out all related applications throughout the text of this popular provision of the *PMF* Toolbox. Referenced to specific text pages for quick review of techniques, the routines include financial ratios, time value of money, bond and stock valuation, capital budgeting cash flows and techniques, cost of capital, and cash budgets.

PMF Excel Spreadsheet Templates   The *PMF Excel Spreadsheet Templates* provide users with preprogrammed spreadsheet templates for inputting data and solving problems using perhaps the most popular and widely accepted practical software application. The template files correspond to selected end-of-chapter problems. The Excel Spreadsheet Template icon appears in the *PMF* Toolbox to note related applications throughout the text.

Study Guide   *Prepared by Gayle Russell of Eastern Connecticut State University.* The Study Guide is an integral component of the *PMF* Learning System. It offers many tools for studying finance. Each chapter contains the following features: chapter summary enumerated by learning goals; topical chapter outline, also broken down by learning goals for quick review; sample problem solutions; study tips; a full sample exam with the answers at the end of the chapter; and thumbnail printouts of the PowerPoint Lecture Presentations to facilitate classroom note taking.

Principles of Managerial Finance: Brief Second Edition Web Site   The Web site to accompany this textbook, located at **http://www.awlonline/gitman,** contains valuable links, self-assessment quizzes, threaded discussion boards, and much more. The site will be updated on a regular basis, so check frequently for new features.

TO MY COLLEAGUES, FRIENDS, AND FAMILY

No textbook can consistently meet market needs without continual feedback from colleagues, students, practitioners, and members of the publishing team. Once again, I invite colleagues to relate their classroom experiences using this book and its package to me at San Diego State University, or in care of the Acquisitions Editor in Finance, Addison Wesley Longman, One Jacob Way, Reading, Massachusetts 01867-3999. Your constructive criticism will help me to continue to improve the textbook and its Teaching/Learning System still further.

Addison Wesley Longman and former publisher HarperCollins sought the advice of a great many excellent reviewers, all of whom strongly influenced various aspects of both this book and the longer one on which it is based. Individuals who analyzed all or part of the manuscript of previous editions of *Principles of Managerial Finance* will find themselves thanked by name in the ninth edition of that book. My special thanks go to the following individuals who provided useful commentary on the development of the Brief Edition and its package:

Felix Ayadi
  Fayetteville State University
Stephen Beckenholdt
  College of Notre Dame of Maryland
Omar Benkato
  Ball State University
Jack Bower
  Eastern College
Janice Buddensick
  Wagner College
Samir P. Dagher
  Marywood College
Greg Filbeck
  University of Toledo
Wafica Ghoul
  Detroit College of Business
John Houston
  DePaul University
Joel Jankowski
  University of Tampa
Steve Johnson
  University of Texas at El Paso

Theodore T. Latz
  Lakeland Community College
Martin Laurence
  William Patterson College of New Jersey
Chan H. Lee
  Mankato State University
Pu Liu
  University of Arkansas
Narendar V. Rao
  Northeastern Illinois University
David L. Rayome
  Northern Michigan University
Marjorie A. Rubash
  Bradley University
George W. Trivoli
  Jacksonville State University
Paul Trogen
  East Tennessee State University
Theodore N. Wood
  Gordon College

Thanks, too, to reviewers whose input helped shape this edition of both texts:

Lewell F. Gunter, *University of Georgia*
Rick LeCompte, *Wichita State University*
John B. Mitchell, *Central Michigan University*
Lance Nail, *University of Alabama–Birmingham*
Prasad Padmanabahn, *San Diego State University*
Mary L. Piotrowski, *Northern Arizona University*
Gayle A. Russell, *Eastern Connecticut State University*
Patricia A. Ryan, *Drake University*
Richard W. Taylor, *Arkansas State University*
Emery A. Trahan, *Northeastern University*

My special thanks goes to all members of my book team whose vision, creativity, and ongoing support helped me to engineer all elements of the Teaching/Learning System: to Marlene G. Bellamy for the new Personal Finance Perspectives; to Daniel Borgia, Florida Gulf Coast University for preparation of the *PowerPoint Presentation* software; to Jim Kinlan, KMT Software for developing the *PMF Brief* CD-ROM Software; to Gayle Russell of Eastern

Connecticut State University for updating and revising the *Study Guide*; to Hadi Salavitabar of SUNY–New Paltz for cultivating the now-huge and reliable database of test items; to Fred Schadler of East Carolina University for updating the *Instructor's Manual*; and to Bernard W. Weinrich of St. Louis Community College, Forest Park Campus, for preparing the Web exercises. I'm pleased by and proud of all their efforts, and I'm confident that those who use the book—both instructors and students—will appreciate everything they've done to add new features of interest and to ensure accuracy, consistency, and accessibility throughout the package.

A standing ovation and hearty round of applause also go to the publishing team assembled by Addison Wesley—including Greta Brogna, Amy Cronin, Nancy Fenton, Deb Kiernan, Julie Lindstrom, Jennifer Pelland, and others who worked on the book—for the inspiration and the perspiration that define teamwork. Elinor Stapleton and all the people at Thompson Steele Production Services deserve an equally resounding ovation. Applause is also due Ann Torbert, whose development skills, creativity, expertise, and hard work have contributed to the book's standard of excellence. Also, special thanks to the formidable sales force in finance, whose ongoing efforts keep the business fun!

Finally, and most important, many thanks to my wife, Robin, and to our children, Zachary and Jessica, for patiently providing support, understanding, and good humor throughout the revision process. To them, I will be forever grateful.

—Lawrence J. Gitman

TO THE STUDENT

Because you have a good many options for getting your assigned reading materials, I appreciate your choosing this textbook as the best means for learning. You won't be disappointed. To meet your increasingly diverse needs and time constraints, my product team and I have put together in this textbook an effective learning system. It integrates a variety of learning tools with the concepts, techniques, and practical applications you'll need to learn about managerial finance. We have carefully listened to the compliments and complaints of professors and of students who have used earlier editions of this textbook in their coursework, and we have worked hard to present the most important concepts and practices of managerial finance in a clear and lively way.

Each chapter begins with a short paragraph that will give you a useful preview of the chapter topic. Next to that preview paragraph is a feature called "Across the Disciplines" that will help you understand the importance of the chapter material to your major, if it's not finance. After all, managerial finance is an essential component not just in the business curriculum or in professional training programs, but also in your daily job activities, *regardless of major*. Finance matters, plain and simple.

 Also at the beginning of the chapter you will find a list of six *Learning Goals*. Marked by a special icon, shown here in the margin, the learning goals are tied to first-level headings in the chapter and are reviewed point-by-point in the chapter-end summary. These goals will help you focus your attention on what material you need to learn, where you can find it in the chapter, and whether you've mastered it by the end of the chapter.

Other features are included to support your learning experience. At the end of each major text section are *Review Questions*. Although it may be tempting to rush past these questions, try to resist doing so. Pausing to test your understanding of the key concepts, techniques, and practices in the section you've just read will help you cement your understanding of that material.

Other features in the body of each chapter are intended to motivate and help organize your study. A *Personal Finance Perspective* is featured somewhere in each chapter. It provides an application of chapter concepts to typical personal financial situations, from the idea of depreciation on a used car purchase, to banking from home on a personal computer, to managing personal credit. In addition, key terms and their definitions appear in the margin when they are first introduced. Since these terms are the basic vocabulary of finance, you should be sure you know the key terms in any section of the text covered in your coursework. (They are boldfaced in the index for easy access to the glossary entry, in case you need to refer back to find a particular term.)

At the beginning of each major chapter section, you'll find a cluster of icons, which we call the *PMF Toolbox*. These icons represent learning tools and resources—learning goals, software tutorials, problem-solving disk routines, and spreadsheet templates—that are available to you in conjunction with the text section. We've already discussed the Learning Goals and how they work. The other items are described below:

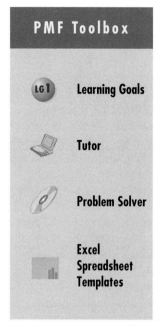

PMF Brief CD-ROM Software   Packaged with new copies of the text at no additional cost, your CD-ROM contains three useful tools: the *PMF Tutor*, the *PMF Problem-Solver*, and the *PMF Excel Spreadsheet Templates*. Documentation and practical advice for using the *PMF Brief* CD-ROM appears at the end of the book in Appendix D.

The *PMF Tutor* extends self-testing opportunities beyond those on the printed page. The Tutor helps you identify and solve various types of managerial finance problems. Part of the PMF Toolbox, the Tutor icon flags all Tutor applications in the text. Through user-friendly menus, you can access over fifty-five different problem types, constructed by random-number generation for an inexhaustible supply of problems with little chance of repetition. Taking the time to use the *PMF Tutor* should pay off for you in increased confidence when applying financial techniques.

The *PMF Problem-Solver* contains seven short menu-driven programs. These popular programs accelerate learning by providing an efficient way to perform financial computations. The Problem-Solver icon points out all related applications throughout the text of this popular provision of the *PMF* Toolbox. The routines are referenced to specific text pages for quick review of the technique.

The *PMF Excel Spreadsheet Templates* provide preprogrammed templates for inputting data and solving problems using Excel, one of the most popular and widely accepted practical applications. The template files correspond to selected end-of-chapter problems, and the template file names follow the chapter number and the problem number. Practice with this tool will increase your computer proficiency and add to your marketable business skills.

Lawrence Gitman

Study Guide (ISBN 0-321-06082-2)   *Created by Gayle Russell of Eastern Connecticut State University. The Study Guide to accompany Principles of Managerial Finance, Brief 2nd Edition,* is an integral component of the Learning System. It offers many good tools for studying finance. Each chapter includes the following features: chapter summary enumerated by learning goals; topical chapter outline, also broken down by learning goals for quick review; sample problem solutions; and a full sample exam with the answers at the end of the chapter; and thumbnail printouts of the PowerPoint Lecture Presentations to facilitate classroom note taking.

Given today's rapidly changing technology, who knows what might be available next semester? If you'd prefer electronic versions of texts—on disk or CD-ROM or any other platform—please let this publisher know by writing to the attention of the Acquisitions Editor in Finance, Addison Wesley Longman, One Jacob Way, Reading, Massachusetts 01867-3999. We are striving daily to keep apace of your needs and interests, and are interested in your ideas for improving the teaching and learning of finance.

We wish you all the best in both your academic and professional careers.

—Lawrence J. Gitman

PART 1 INTRODUCTION TO MANAGERIAL FINANCE

CHAPTERS IN THIS PART

1

OVERVIEW OF MANAGERIAL FINANCE

LEARNING GOALS

LG1 Define *finance* and its major areas and opportunities.

LG2 Review the basic forms of business organization.

LG3 Describe the managerial finance function and its relationship to economics and accounting.

LG4 Identify the financial manager's key activities.

LG5 Explain the wealth maximization goal of the financial manager and the role of ethics in the firm.

LG6 Discuss the agency issue.

ACROSS DISCIPLINES

The field of finance is broad and dynamic. It directly affects the lives of every person and every organization. Many areas for study and a large number of career opportunities are available in finance. The purpose of this chapter is to aquaint you with the study of finance and the role of the financial manager in the business organization. Finance will affect your working life in whatever area of study you choose to concentrate. Chapter 1 is important to:

- **accounting personnel** who will provide financial statements needed for financial analysis and planning and for making investment and financing decisions.

- **information systems analysts** who will design the information systems that provide historical data and projections to support investment and financing decisions.

- **management** because it defines the tasks that will be performed by finance personnel.

- **the marketing department** because sales volume will be critically affected by the cash and credit management policies of the finance department.

- **operations,** which will depend on the finance function to allocate funds for the purchase of equipment and raw materials and payment of employees.

WHAT IS FINANCE?

LG 1

finance
The art and science of managing money.

Finance can be defined as the art and science of managing money. Virtually all individuals and organizations earn or raise money and spend or invest money. Finance is concerned with the process, institutions, markets, and instruments involved in the transfer of money among and between individuals, businesses, and governments.

MAJOR AREAS AND OPPORTUNITIES IN FINANCE

The major areas of finance can be summarized by reviewing the career opportunities in finance. These opportunities broadly fall into two categories: financial services and managerial finance.

FINANCIAL SERVICES

financial services
The part of finance concerned with the delivery of advice and financial products.

Financial services is the area of finance concerned with the delivery of advice and financial products. It involves a variety of career opportunities in banking, personal financial planning, investments, real estate, and insurance. Career opportunities available in each of these areas are described briefly at this textbook's home page at www.awlonline.com/gitman.

MANAGERIAL FINANCE

managerial finance
Concerns the duties of the financial manager in the business firm.

financial manager
Actively manages the financial affairs of any type of business, whether private or public, large or small, profit-seeking or not-for-profit.

Managerial finance is concerned with the duties of the financial manager in the business firm. **Financial managers** actively manage the financial affairs of many types of business—financial and nonfinancial, private and public, large and small, profit-seeking and not-for-profit. They perform such varied financial tasks as planning, extending credit to customers, evaluating proposed large expenditures, and raising money to fund the firm's operations. In recent years the changing economic and regulatory environments have increased the importance and complexity of the financial manager's duties. As a result, many top executives in industry and government have come from the finance area.

Another important recent trend has been the globalization of business activity. U.S. corporations have dramatically increased their sales, purchases, investments, and fund raising in other countries, and foreign corporations have likewise increased these activities in the United States. These changes have created a need for financial managers who can help a firm manage cash flows in different currencies and protect against the risks that naturally arise from international transactions. Although the managerial finance function has become more complex, it remains a rewarding and fulfilling career.

THE STUDY OF MANAGERIAL FINANCE

An understanding of the concepts, techniques, and practices presented in this textbook will fully acquaint you with the financial manager's activities. Because most business decisions are measured in financial terms, the financial manager plays a key role in the operation of the firm. People in all areas of responsibility—

accounting, information systems, management, marketing, and operations—need a basic understanding of the managerial finance function.

All managers in the firm, regardless of their job descriptions, work with financial personnel to justify personnel requirements, negotiate operating budgets, deal with financial performance appraisals, and sell proposals based at least in part on their financial merits. Clearly, those managers who understand the financial decision-making process will be better able to address financial concerns, and will therefore more often get the resources they need to accomplish their own goals.

As you study this textbook, you will learn about career opportunities in managerial finance, briefly described in Table 1.1. Although this book focuses on profit-seeking firms, the principles presented here are equally applicable to public and nonprofit organizations. The decision-making principles developed in this text can also be applied to personal financial decisions. Occasional inserts, such as the one that follows, specifically provide a personal finance perspective. I hope that this first exposure to the exciting field of finance will provide the foundation and initiative for further study and possibly even a future career.

*P*ERSONAL FINANCE PERSPECTIVE

Personal Financial Managers Wear Many Hats

Just as the principles of finance can assist you in your job, they also can help you manage your personal finances. In fact, as manager of your own finances, you'll perform most of the jobs described in Table 1.1! As financial analyst, you will prepare personal financial statements and budgets, establish financial goals, and develop the short- and long-term financial plans to reach those goals. Before you make a major capital investment like a house or a car, you'll evaluate whether the initial cost is within your means and also determine how to finance it—in the case of a car, comparing alternatives like borrowing versus leasing. Cash man-

TABLE 1.1	Career Opportunities in Managerial Finance
Position	**Description**
Financial analyst	Primarily responsible for preparing the firm's financial plans and budgets. Other duties include financial forecasting, performing financial ratio analysis, and working closely with accounting.
Capital budgeting analyst/manager	Responsible for the evaluation and recommendation of proposed asset investments. May be involved in the financial aspects of implementing approved investments.
Project finance manager	In large firms, arranges financing for approved asset investments. Coordinates consultants, investment bankers, and legal counsel.
Cash manager	Responsible for maintaining and controlling the firm's daily cash balances. Frequently manages the firm's cash collection and disbursement activities and short-term investments, and coordinates short-term borrowing and banking relationships.
Credit analyst/manager	Administers the firm's credit policy by evaluating credit applications, extending credit, and monitoring and collecting accounts receivable.
Pension fund manager	In large companies, responsible for overseeing or managing the assets and liabilities of the employees' pension fund.

agement is another critical job: having sufficient funds to pay bills, choosing the right bank accounts, investing cash surpluses, and arranging for short-term borrowing (like credit cards and bank lines of credit). Finally, you're responsible for investment portfolio management and retirement ("pension") planning: saving and investing money to meet long-term goals like buying a house, sending your children to college, and having enough funds to retire comfortably. ●

? Review Questions

1-1   What is *finance?* Explain how this field affects every organization.

1-2   What is the *financial services* area of finance?

1-3   Describe the field of *managerial finance.* Compare and contrast this field with financial services.

1-4   Why is the study of managerial finance important regardless of the specific area of responsibility one has within the business firm?

BASIC FORMS OF BUSINESS ORGANIZATION

The three basic legal forms of business organization are the *sole proprietorship,* the *partnership,* and the *corporation.* Sole proprietorships are the most numerous. However, corporations are by far the dominant form with respect to receipts and net profits. Corporations are given primary emphasis in this textbook.

SOLE PROPRIETORSHIPS

sole proprietorship
A business owned by one person and operated for his or her own profit.

A **sole proprietorship** is a business owned by one person who operates it for his or her own profit. About 75 percent of all business firms are sole proprietorships. The typical sole proprietorship is a small business, such as a bike shop, a personal trainer, or a plumber. Typically, the proprietor, along with a few employees, runs the business. He or she normally raises capital from personal resources or by borrowing and is responsible for all business decisions. The sole proprietor has **unlimited liability**—his or her total wealth, not merely the amount originally invested, can be taken to satisfy business debts. The majority of sole proprietorships operate in the wholesale, retail, service, and construction industries. The key strengths and weaknesses of sole proprietorships are summarized in Table 1.2.

unlimited liability
The condition of a sole proprietorship (and general partnership) allowing the owner's total wealth to be taken to satisfy creditors.

PARTNERSHIPS

partnership
A business owned by two or more people and operated for profit.

A **partnership** consists of two or more owners doing business together for profit. Partnerships, which account for about 10 percent of all businesses, are typically larger than sole proprietorships. Finance, insurance, and real estate firms are the most common types of partnership. Public accounting and stock brokerage partnerships often have large numbers of partners.

articles of partnership
The written contract used to formally establish a business partnership.

Most partnerships are established by a written contract known as **articles of partnership.** In a *general (or regular) partnership,* all partners have unlimited liability, and each partner is legally liable for all of the debts of the partnership. Strengths and weaknesses of partnerships are summarized in Table 1.2.

TABLE 1.2	Strengths and Weaknesses of the Basic Legal Forms of Business Organization		
	Legal form		
	Sole proprietorship	Partnership	Corporation
Strengths	• Owner receives all profits • Low organizational costs • Income included and taxed on proprietor's personal tax return • Independence • Secrecy • Ease of dissolution	• Can raise more funds than sole proprietorships • Borrowing power enhanced by more owners • More available brain power and managerial skill • Income included and taxed on partner's tax return	• Owners have *limited liability*, which guarantees that they cannot lose more than they invested • Can achieve large size due to sale of stock • Ownership (stock) is readily transferable • Long life of firm • Can hire professional managers • Has better access to financing • Receives certain tax advantages
Weaknesses	• Owner has *unlimited liability*—total wealth can be taken to satisfy debts • Limited fund-raising power tends to inhibit growth • Proprietor must be jack-of-all-trades • Difficult to give employees long-run career opportunities • Lacks continuity when proprietor dies	• Owners have *unlimited liability* and may have to cover debts of other partners • Partnership is dissolved when a partner dies • Difficult to liquidate or transfer partnership	• Taxes generally higher, because corporate income is taxed and dividends paid to owners are also taxed • More expensive to organize than other business forms • Subject to greater government regulation • Lacks secrecy, because stockholders must receive financial reports

CORPORATIONS

corporation
An intangible business entity created by law (often called a "legal entity").

A **corporation** is an intangible business entity created by law. Often called a "legal entity," a corporation has the powers of an individual in that it can sue and be sued, make and be party to contracts, and acquire property in its own name. Although only about 15 percent of all businesses are incorporated, the corporation accounts for nearly 90 percent of business receipts and 80 percent of net profits. Although corporations are involved in all types of business, manufacturing corporations account for the largest portion of corporate business receipts and net profits. The key strengths and weaknesses of large corporations are summarized in Table 1.2.

It is important to recognize that there are many small private corporations in addition to the large corporations emphasized throughout this text. For many small corporations there is limited access to financing, and the requirement that the owner co-sign a loan moderates limited liability.

stockholders
The owners of a corporation, whose ownership or "equity" is evidenced by either *common stock* or *preferred stock*.

The owners of a corporation are its **stockholders**, whose ownership or "equity" is evidenced by either *common stock* or *preferred stock*.[1] These forms

---

[1]Some corporations do not have stockholders but rather have "members" who often have rights similar to those of stockholders—they are entitled to vote and receive dividends. Examples include mutual savings banks, credit unions, mutual insurance companies, and a whole host of charitable organizations.

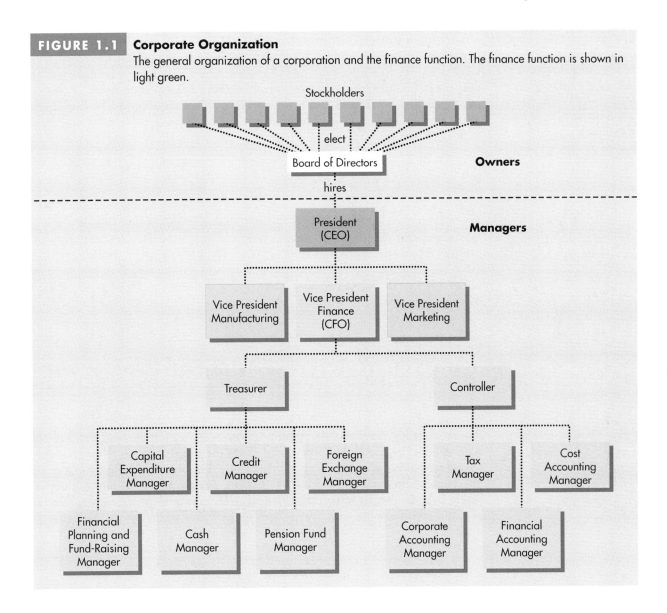

FIGURE 1.1   Corporate Organization
The general organization of a corporation and the finance function. The finance function is shown in light green.

common stock
The purest and most basic form of corporate ownership.

dividends
Periodic distributions of earnings to the stockholders of a firm.

board of directors
Group elected by the firm's stockholders and having ultimate authority to guide corporate affairs and make general policy.

of ownership are defined and discussed in Chapter 2. At this point it is enough to say that **common stock** is the purest and most basic form of corporate ownership. Stockholders expect to earn a return by receiving **dividends**—periodic distributions of earnings—or by realizing gains through increases in share price. As noted in the upper portion of Figure 1.1, the stockholders vote periodically to elect the members of the board of directors and to amend the firm's corporate charter.

The **board of directors** has the ultimate authority in guiding corporate affairs and in making general policy. The directors include key corporate personnel as well as outside individuals who typically are successful businesspeople. Outside directors for major corporations are typically paid an annual fee of $10,000 to $20,000 or more and are frequently granted options to buy a specified number of shares of the firm's stock at a stated—and often attractive—price.

president or chief executive officer (CEO)
Corporate official responsible for managing the firm's day-to-day operations and carrying out the policies established by the board of directors.

The **president or chief executive officer (CEO)** is responsible for managing day-to-day operations and carrying out the policies established by the board. The CEO is required to report periodically to the firm's directors. It is important to note the division between owners and managers in a large corporation, as shown by the dashed horizontal line in Figure 1.1. This separation and some of the issues surrounding it will be addressed in the discussion of *the agency issue* later in this chapter.

? Review Questions

1-5 What are the three basic forms of business organization? Which form is most common? Which form is dominant in terms of business receipts and net profits? Why?

1-6 Describe the role and basic relationship between the major parties in a corporation—stockholders, board of directors, and president. How are corporate owners compensated?

THE MANAGERIAL FINANCE FUNCTION

As noted earlier, people in all areas of responsibility within the firm will interact with finance personnel and procedures to get their jobs done. For financial personnel to make useful forecasts and decisions, they must be willing and able to talk to individuals in other areas of the firm. The managerial finance function can be broadly described by considering its role within the organization, its relationship to economics and accounting, and the key activities of the financial manager.

ORGANIZATION OF THE FINANCE FUNCTION

treasurer
The officer responsible for the firm's financial activities such as financial planning and fund raising, making capital expenditure decisions, and managing cash, credit, and the pension fund.

controller
The officer responsible for the firm's accounting activities, such as corporate accounting, tax management, and financial and cost accounting.

The size and importance of the managerial finance function depend on the size of the firm. In small firms, the finance function is generally performed by the accounting department. As a firm grows, the finance function typically evolves into a separate department linked directly to the company president or CEO through a vice president of finance, commonly called the chief financial officer (CFO). The lower portion of the organizational chart in Figure 1.1 shows the structure of the finance function in a typical medium-to-large-size firm, where the treasurer and the controller report to the vice president of finance. The **treasurer** is commonly responsible for handling financial activities, such as financial planning and fund raising, making capital expenditure decisions, and managing cash, credit, and the pension fund. The **controller** typically handles the accounting activities, such as corporate accounting, tax management, and financial and cost accounting. The treasurer's focus tends to be more external, whereas the controller's focus is more internal. *The activities of the treasurer, or financial manager, are the primary concern of this text.*

foreign exchange manager
The manager responsible for monitoring and managing the firm's exposure to loss from currency fluctuations.

If international sales or purchases are important to a firm, it may well employ one or more finance professionals whose job is to monitor and manage the firm's exposure to loss from currency fluctuations. A trained financial manager can "hedge," or protect against such a loss, at reasonable cost, using a variety of financial instruments. These **foreign exchange managers** (or traders) typically report to the firm's treasurer.

RELATIONSHIP TO ECONOMICS

marginal analysis
Economic principle that states that financial decisions should be made and actions taken only when the added benefits exceed the added costs.

The field of finance is closely related to economics. Financial managers must understand the economic framework and be alert to the consequences of varying levels of economic activity and changes in economic policy. They must also be able to use economic theories as guidelines for efficient business operation. The primary economic principle used in managerial finance is **marginal analysis,** the principle that financial decisions should be made and actions taken only when the added benefits exceed the added costs. Nearly all financial decisions ultimately come down to an assessment of their marginal benefits and marginal costs.

E x a m p l e ▼ Amy Chen is a financial manager for Strom Department Stores—a large chain of upscale department stores operating primarily in the western United States. She is currently trying to decide whether to replace one of the firm's computers with a new, more sophisticated one that would both speed processing time and handle a larger volume of transactions. The new computer would require a cash outlay of $80,000, and the old computer could be sold to net $28,000. The total benefits from the new computer (measured in today's dollars) would be $100,000, and the benefits over a similar time period from the old computer (measured in today's dollars) would be $35,000. Applying marginal analysis to this data, Amy finds:

Benefits with new computer	$100,000	
Less: Benefits with old computer	35,000	
(1) Marginal (added) benefits		$65,000
Cost of new computer	$180,000	
Less: Proceeds from sale of old computer	28,000	
(2) Marginal (added) costs		52,000
Net benefit [(1) − (2)]		$13,000

Because the marginal (added) benefits of $65,000 exceed the marginal (added) costs of $52,000, Amy recommends that the firm purchase the new computer to replace the old one. The firm will experience a net benefit of $13,000 as a result ▲ of this action.

RELATIONSHIP TO ACCOUNTING

The firm's finance (treasurer) and accounting (controller) activities are typically within the control of the financial vice president (CFO), as shown in the lower portion of Figure 1.1. These functions are closely related and generally overlap. Indeed, managerial finance and accounting are often not easily distinguishable.

In small firms the controller often carries out the finance function, and in large firms many accountants are closely involved in various finance activities. However, there are two basic differences between finance and accounting; one relates to the emphasis on cash flows and the other to decision making.

EMPHASIS ON CASH FLOWS

The accountant's primary function is to develop and provide data for measuring the performance of the firm, assessing its financial position, and paying taxes. Using certain generally accepted principles, the accountant prepares financial statements that recognize revenue at the point of sale and expenses when incurred. This approach is referred to as the **accrual basis.**

accrual basis
Recognizes revenue at the point of sale and recognizes expenses when incurred.

The financial manager, on the other hand, places primary emphasis on *cash flows,* the intake and outgo of cash. He or she maintains the firm's solvency by planning the cash flows necessary to satisfy its obligations and to acquire assets needed to achieve the firm's goals. The financial manager uses this **cash basis** to recognize the revenues and expenses only with respect to actual inflows and outflows of cash. Regardless of its profit or loss, a firm must have a sufficient flow of cash to meet its obligations as they come due.

cash basis
Recognizes revenues and expenses only with respect to actual inflows and outflows of cash.

Example ▼ Thomas Yachts, a small yacht dealer, in the calendar year just ended sold one yacht for $100,000; the yacht was purchased during the year at a total cost of $80,000. Although the firm paid in full for the yacht during the year, at year end it has yet to collect the $100,000 from the customer. The accounting view and the financial view of the firm's performance during the year are given by the following income and cash flow statements, respectively.

Accounting view (accrual-basis)		Financial view (cash-basis)	
Income Statement Thomas Yachts for the year ended 12/31		Cash Flow Statement Thomas Yachts for the year ended 12/31	
Sales revenue	$100,000	Cash inflow	$ 0
Less: Costs	80,000	Less: Cash outflow	80,000
Net profit	$ 20,000	Net cash flow	($80,000)

In an accounting sense Thomas Yachts is quite profitable, but it is a financial failure in terms of actual cash flow. Without adequate cash inflows to meet its obligations the firm will not survive, regardless of its level of profits. ▲

The preceding example shows that accrual accounting data do not fully describe the circumstances of a firm. Thus, the financial manager must look beyond financial statements to obtain insight into developing or existing problems. Of course, accountants are well aware of the importance of cash flows, and financial managers use and understand accrual-based financial statements. Nevertheless, the primary emphasis of accountants is on accrual methods, and the primary emphasis of financial managers is on cash flow methods.

DECISION MAKING

The second major difference between finance and accounting has to do with decision making. Accountants devote most of their attention to the collection and presentation of financial data. Financial managers evaluate the accounting statements, develop additional data, and make decisions based on their assessment of the associated returns and risks. Accountants provide consistently developed data about the firm's past, present, and future operations. Financial managers use these data, either in raw form or after certain adjustments and analyses, as an important input to the decision-making process. Of course, this does not mean that accountants never make decisions or that financial managers never gather data; rather, the primary focuses of accounting and finance are distinctly different.

KEY ACTIVITIES OF THE FINANCIAL MANAGER

The financial manager's primary activities are (1) performing financial analysis and planning, (2) making investment decisions, and (3) making financing decisions. Figure 1.2 relates each of these financial activities to the firm's balance sheet. Although investment and financing decisions can be conveniently viewed in terms of the balance sheet, these decisions are made on the basis of their cash flow effects. This focus on cash flow will become clearer in Chapter 4 as well as in later chapters.

PERFORMING FINANCIAL ANALYSIS AND PLANNING

Financial analysis and planning is concerned with (1) monitoring the firm's financial condition, (2) evaluating the need for increased (or reduced) productive capacity, and (3) determining what financing is required. Although this activity relies heavily on accrual-based financial statements, its underlying objective is to assess the firm's cash flows and develop plans that ensure adequate cash flow to support the firm's goals.

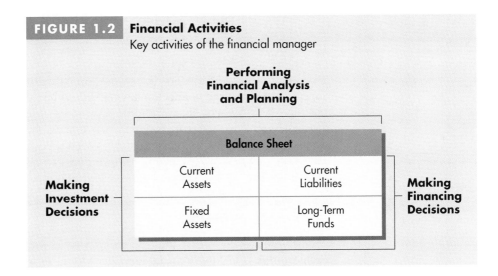

FIGURE 1.2   Financial Activities
Key activities of the financial manager

MAKING INVESTMENT DECISIONS

Investment decisions determine both the mix and the type of assets found on the left-hand side of the balance sheet. *Mix* refers to the number of dollars of current and fixed assets. Once the mix is established, the financial manager attempts to maintain optimal levels of each type of current asset. The financial manager also decides which fixed assets to acquire and when existing fixed assets need to be modified, replaced, or liquidated. These decisions are important because they affect the firm's success in achieving its goals.

MAKING FINANCING DECISIONS

Financing decisions deal with the right-hand side of the firm's balance sheet and involve two major areas. First, the most appropriate *mix* of short-term and long-term financing must be established. A second and equally important concern is which individual short-term or long-term sources of financing are best at a given point in time. Many of these decisions are dictated by necessity, but some require in-depth analysis of the financing alternatives, their costs, and their long-run implications. Again, it is the effect of these decisions on the firm's goal achievement that is most important.

? Review Questions

1-7   What financial activities does the treasurer, or financial manager, perform in the mature firm?
1-8   What is the primary economic principle used in managerial finance?
1-9   What are the major differences between accounting and finance with respect to emphasis on cash flows and decision making?
1-10   How are the three key activities of the financial manager related to the firm's balance sheet?

LG5 GOAL OF THE FINANCIAL MANAGER

As noted earlier, the owners of a corporation are normally distinct from its managers. Actions of the financial manager should be taken to achieve the objectives of the firm's owners, its stockholders. In most cases, if financial managers are successful in this endeavor, they will also achieve their own financial and professional objectives. So, financial managers need to know what *are* the objectives of the firm's owners. Many people believe that the owner's objective is always to maximize profits. Let's begin by looking at that goal.

MAXIMIZE PROFIT?

Some people believe that the firm's objective is always to maximize profits. To achieve this goal, the financial manager would take only those actions that are expected to make a major contribution to the firm's overall profits. For each

earnings per share (EPS)
The amount earned during the accounting period on each outstanding share of common stock, calculated by dividing the period's total earnings available for the firm's common stockholders by the number of shares of common stock outstanding.

alternative being considered, the financial manager would select the one that is expected to result in the highest monetary return.

Corporations commonly measure profits in terms of **earnings per share** (**EPS**), which represent the amount earned during the accounting period on each outstanding share of common stock. EPS are calculated by dividing the period's total earnings available for the firm's common stockholders by the number of shares of common stock outstanding.

Example ▼ Nick Bono, the financial manager of Harpers, Inc., a manufacturer of fishing gear, is choosing between two investments, X and Y. Each is expected to have the following EPS over its 3-year life.

	Earnings per share (EPS)			
Investment	Year 1	Year 2	Year 3	Total for years 1, 2, and 3
X	$1.40	$1.00	$ .40	$2.80
Y	.60	1.00	1.40	3.00

Based on the profit-maximization goal, investment Y would be preferred over investment X, because it results in higher total earnings per share over the 3-year period ($3.00 EPS for Y is greater than $2.80 EPS for X). ▲

But, is profit maximization a reasonable goal? No, it fails for several reasons: It ignores (1) the timing of returns, (2) cash flows available to stockholders, and (3) risk.

TIMING

Because the firm can earn a return on funds it receives, *the receipt of funds sooner rather than later is preferred.* In the preceding example, investment X provides much greater earnings per share in the first year. The larger returns in year 1 could be reinvested to provide greater future earnings.

CASH FLOWS

Profits do not necessarily represent *cash flows* available to the stockholders. Owners receive cash flow either in the form of cash dividends paid them or the proceeds from selling their shares for a higher price than initially paid. A greater EPS does not necessarily mean that a firm's board of directors will vote to increase dividend payments. Furthermore, a higher EPS does not necessarily translate into a higher stock price. Only when earnings increases are accompanied by the expectation of increased future cash flows would a higher stock price be expected.

RISK

risk
The chance that actual outcomes may differ from those expected.

Profit maximization also disregards **risk**—the chance that actual outcomes may differ from those expected. A basic premise in managerial finance is that a trade-off exists between return (cash flow) and risk. *Return and risk are in fact the key determinants of share price, which represents the wealth of the owners in the firm.*

risk-averse
Seeking to avoid risk.

Cash flow and risk affect share price differently: Higher cash flow is generally associated with a higher share price. Higher risk tends to result in a lower share price because the stockholder must be compensated for the greater risk. In general, stockholders are **risk-averse**—that is, they want to avoid risk. Where risk is involved, stockholders expect to earn higher rates of return on investments of higher risk and lower rates on lower-risk investments.

Because profit maximization does not achieve the objectives of the firm's owners, it should *not* be the goal of the financial manager.

MAXIMIZE SHAREHOLDER WEALTH

The goal of the firm, and therefore of all managers and employees, is *to maximize the wealth of the owners for whom it is being operated.* The wealth of corporate owners is measured by the share price of the stock, which in turn is based on the timing of returns (cash flows), their magnitude, and their risk. When considering each financial decision alternative in terms of its impact on the share price of the firm's stock, *financial managers should accept only those actions that are expected to increase share price.* (Figure 1.3 depicts this process.) Because share price represents the owners' wealth in the firm, share-price maximization is consistent with owner wealth maximization. Note that *return (cash flows) and risk are the key decision variables in the wealth maximization process.*

Two important issues related to share price maximization are economic value added (EVA) and the focus on stakeholders.

ECONOMIC VALUE ADDED (EVA)

economic value added
A measure used by many firms to determine whether an investment contributes positively to the owners' wealth; calculated by subtracting the cost of funds used to finance an investment from its after-tax operating profits.

Economic value added (EVA) is a measure used by many firms to determine whether an investment—proposed or existing—contributes positively to the owners' wealth.[2] EVA is calculated by subtracting the cost of funds used to finance an investment from its after-tax operating profits. Investments with posi-

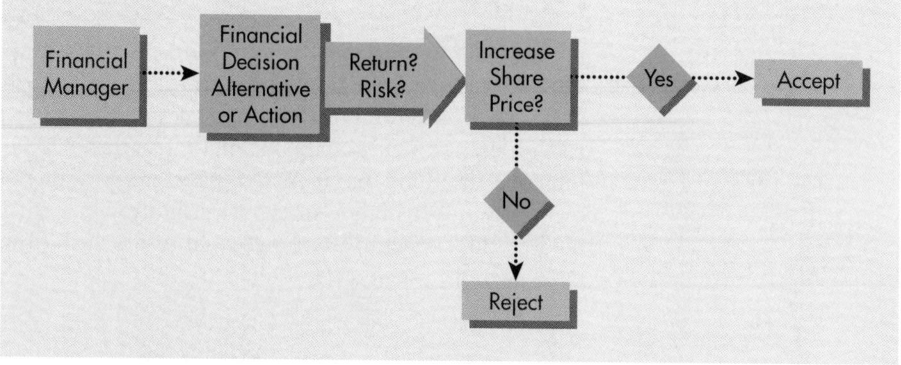

FIGURE 1.3 **Share Price Maximization**
Financial decisions and share price

[2]For a good summary of economic value added (EVA), see Shaun Tully, "The Real Key to Creating Wealth," *Fortune* (September 20, 1993), pp. 38–49.

tive EVAs increase shareholder value, and those with negative EVAs reduce shareholder value. Clearly, only those investments with positive EVAs are desirable. For example, the EVA of an investment with after-tax operating profits of $410,000 and associated financing costs of $375,000 would be $35,000 ($410,000 − $375,000). Because this EVA is positive, the investment is expected to increase owner wealth and is therefore acceptable. Of course, in practice numerous accounting and financial issues would be involved in making these estimates.

The growing popularity of EVA is due to both its relative simplicity and its strong link to owner wealth maximization. Advocates of EVA believe it exhibits a strong link to stock prices—positive EVAs are associated with increasing share prices, and vice versa. Many major firms, such as AT&T, Briggs & Stratton, Coca-Cola, and Quaker Oats, tout the effectiveness of this approach in isolating investments that create shareholder value. Although there is no denying the current popularity of EVA, it is simply a repackaged application of a standard investment decision-making technique called *net present value (NPV)*, which is described in detail in Chapter 10. What's important at this point is to recognize that useful tools, such as EVA, are available for measuring the owners' wealth maximization goal, particularly when making investment decisions.

WHAT ABOUT STAKEHOLDERS?

stakeholders
Groups such as employees, customers, suppliers, creditors, and owners who have a direct economic link to the firm.

Although shareholder wealth maximization is the primary goal, in recent years many firms have broadened their focus to include the interests of *stakeholders* as well as shareholders. **Stakeholders** are groups such as employees, customers, suppliers, creditors, and owners who have a direct economic link to the firm. Employees are paid for their labor, customers purchase the firm's products or services, suppliers are paid for the materials and services they provide, creditors provide debt financing, and owners provide equity financing. A firm with a *stakeholder focus* consciously avoids actions that would prove detrimental to stakeholders. The goal is not to maximize stakeholder well-being, but to preserve it.

The stakeholder view does not alter the shareholder wealth maximization goal. Such a view is often considered part of the firm's "social responsibility." It is expected to provide long-run benefit to shareholders by maintaining positive stakeholder relationships. Such relationships should minimize stakeholder turnover, conflicts, and litigation. Clearly, the firm can better achieve its goal of shareholder wealth maximization with the cooperation of—rather than conflict with—its other stakeholders.

THE ROLE OF ETHICS

In recent years, the actions taken by certain businesses have received major media attention. Examples include Liggett & Meyers' early 1999 agreement to fund the payment of more than $1 billion in smoking-related health claims; the late 1995 withdrawal in response to intense public pressure of Calvin Klein's advertising campaign that many believed bordered on "child pornography"; and Salomon Brothers' 1992 agreement to pay $122 million to the U.S. Treasury, create a $100 million restitution fund, and be temporarily banned from bidding in government security auctions as a consequence of making illegal bids in U.S. Treasury auctions.

ethics
Standards of conduct or moral judgment.

Clearly, these and other similar actions have raised the question of **ethics**—standards of conduct or moral judgment. Today, the business community in general and the financial community in particular are developing and enforcing ethical standards. The goal of these standards is to motivate business and market participants to adhere to both the letter and the spirit of laws and regulations concerned with business and professional practice.

An opinion survey of business leaders, business school deans, and members of Congress found that 63 percent of respondents felt that a business enterprise actually strengthens its competitive position by maintaining high ethical standards.[3] Respondents to the survey believed that the best way to encourage ethical business behavior is for firms to adopt a business code of ethics. These findings confirm the need for firms to proactively consider ethical issues relating to their interactions with stockholders, government, competitors, and the public at large.

CONSIDERING ETHICS

Robert A. Cooke, a noted ethicist, suggests that the following questions be used to assess the ethical viability of a proposed action.[4]

1. Is the action arbitrary or capricious? Does it unfairly single out an individual or group?
2. Does the action violate the moral or legal rights of any individual or group?
3. Does the action conform to accepted moral standards?
4. Are there alternative courses of action that are less likely to cause actual or potential harm?

Clearly, considering such questions before taking an action can help to ensure its ethical viability.

Today, more and more firms are directly addressing the issue of ethics by establishing corporate ethics policies and by requiring employee compliance with them. Frequently, employees are required to sign a formal pledge to uphold the firm's ethics policies. Such policies typically apply to employee actions in dealing with all corporate stakeholders, including the public. Many companies require employees to participate in ethics seminars and training programs.

ETHICS AND SHARE PRICE

An effective ethics program is believed to enhance corporate value. An ethics program can produce positive benefits: It can reduce potential litigation and judgment costs; maintain a positive corporate image; build shareholder confidence; and gain the loyalty, commitment, and respect of the firm's stakeholders. Such actions, by maintaining and enhancing cash flow and reducing perceived risk (as a result of greater investor confidence), can positively affect the firm's share price. *Ethical behavior is therefore viewed as necessary for achieving the firm's goal of owner wealth maximization.*[5]

---

[3]*Ethics in American Business* (New York: Touche Ross, 1987).

[4]Robert A. Cooke, "Business Ethics: A Perspective," in *Arthur Andersen Cases on Business Ethics* (Chicago: Arthur Andersen, September 1991), pp. 2 and 5.

[5]For an excellent discussion of this and related issues by a number of finance academics and practitioners who have given a lot of thought to financial ethics, see James S. Ang, "On Financial Ethics," *Financial Management* (Autumn 1993), pp. 32–59.

? Review Questions

1-11   List three reasons why profit maximization is not consistent with wealth maximization.

1-12   What is *risk?* Why must both risk and return be considered by the financial manager?

1-13   What is the goal of the firm and therefore of its managers and employees? How does one measure achievement of this goal?

1-14   What is *economic value added (EVA)?* How is it used?

1-15   Who are a firm's *stakeholders,* and what consideration is often given them in pursuing the firm's goal? Why?

1-16   Why is corporate ethics important? Discuss the relationship that is believed to exist between ethics and share price.

THE AGENCY ISSUE

We have seen that the goal of the financial manager should be to maximize the wealth of the owners of the firm. Thus management can be viewed as *agents* of the owners who have hired them and given them decision-making authority to manage the firm. Technically, any manager who owns less than 100 percent of the firm is to some degree an agent of the other owners. This separation of owners and managers is shown by the dashed horizontal line in Figure 1.1.

In theory, most financial managers would agree with the goal of owner wealth maximization. In practice, however, managers are also concerned with their personal wealth, job security, and fringe benefits, such as posh offices, country club memberships, and limousines, all provided at company expense. Such concerns may make managers reluctant or unwilling to take more than moderate risk if they perceive that too much risk might result in a loss of job and damage to personal wealth. The result is a less-than-maximum return and a potential loss of wealth for the owners.

RESOLVING THE AGENCY PROBLEM

agency problem
The likelihood that managers may place personal goals ahead of corporate goals.

From this conflict of owner and personal goals arises what has been called the **agency problem**—the likelihood that managers may place personal goals ahead of corporate goals. Two factors—market forces and *agency costs*—serve to prevent or minimize agency problems.

MARKET FORCES

One market force is *major shareholders,* particularly large institutional investors, such as mutual funds, life insurance companies, and pension funds. These holders of large blocks of a firm's stock have begun in recent years to exert pressure on management to perform. When necessary they exercise their voting rights as stockholders to replace underperforming management.

Another market force is the *threat of takeover* by another firm that believes that it can enhance the firm's value by restructuring its management, operations, and financing. The constant threat of takeover tends to motivate management to act in the best interest of the firm's owners by attempting to maximize share price.

AGENCY COSTS

agency costs
The costs borne by stockholders to minimize agency problems.

To minimize agency problems and contribute to the maximization of owners' wealth, stockholders incur **agency costs.** These are the costs of monitoring management behavior, ensuring against dishonest acts of management, and giving managers the financial incentive to maximize share price. The most popular, powerful, and expensive approach is to *structure management compensation* to correspond with share price maximization. The objective is to give managers incentives to act in the best interests of the owners. *Incentive plans* tend to tie management compensation to share price. The most popular incentive plan is the granting of **stock options** to management. These options allow managers to purchase stock at a set market price. If the market subsequently rises, managers will be rewarded by being able to resell the shares at the higher market price. More firms also are offering *performance plans*, which tie management compensation to measures such as earnings per share (EPS), growth in EPS, or other ratios of return. Use of incentive and performance plans appears to motivate managers to operate in a manner reasonably consistent with stock price maximization. In addition, well-structured compensation packages allow firms to hire the best managers available.

stock options
An incentive allowing management to purchase stock at the market price set at the time of the grant.

THE CURRENT VIEW

The execution of many management compensation plans has been closely scrutinized in recent years. Stockholders—both individuals and institutions—as well as the Securities and Exchange Commission (SEC) have publicly questioned the appropriateness of the multimillion-dollar compensation packages (including salary, bonus, and long-term compensation) that many corporate executives receive. For example, the three highest-paid CEOs in 1998 were (1) Michael Eisner, of Walt Disney, who earned $575.6 million; (2) Mel Karmazin, of CBS, who earned $201.9 million; and (3) Sanford Weill, of Citigroup, who earned $167.1 million. Tenth on the same list was M. Douglas Ivester of Coca-Cola, who earned $57.3 million. During 1998, the compensation of the average CEO of a major U.S. corporation rose by about 36 percent over 1997. CEOs of 365 of the largest U.S. companies surveyed by *Business Week*, using data from Standard & Poor's Compusat, earned an average of $10.6 million in total compensation; the average for the 20 highest paid CEOs was $101.2 million.

Recent studies have failed to find a strong relationship between CEO compensation and share price. The publicity surrounding these large compensation packages (without corresponding share price performance) is expected to drive down executive compensation in the future. Contributing to this publicity is the relatively recent SEC requirement that publicly traded companies disclose to shareholders and others both the amount of and method used to determine compensation to their highest paid executives. Unconstrained, managers may have other goals in addition to share price maximization, but much of the evidence suggests that share price maximization—the focus of this book—is the primary goal of most firms.

? R e v i e w   Q u e s t i o n s

1-17   What is the *agency problem?* How do market forces act to prevent or minimize this problem?

1-18   Define *agency costs,* and explain why firms incur them. How do firms attempt to structure management compensation to prevent or minimize agency problems?

USING THIS TEXT

The text's organization links the firm's activities to its value, as determined in the securities markets. The activities of the financial manager are described in five separate but related parts:

Part 1: Introduction to Managerial Finance
Part 2: Important Financial Concepts
Part 3: Long-Term Investment Decisions
Part 4: Long-Term Financial Decisions
Part 5: Short-Term Financial Decisions

Each major decision area is presented in terms of both return and risk factors and their potential impact on owners' wealth. Coverage of international topics is integrated into the chapter discussions.

The text has been developed around a group of 102 learning goals—6 per chapter. Mastery of these goals results in a broad understanding of the concepts, techniques, and practices of managerial finance. The goals have been carefully integrated into a learning system. Each chapter begins with a numbered list of learning goals. Next to each major text heading is a *toolbox,* which notes by number the specific learning goal(s) addressed in that section. At the end of each section of the chapter (positioned before the next major heading) are review questions that test the reader's understanding of key concepts, techniques, and practices in that section. At the end of each chapter, the chapter summaries, self-test problems, and problems are also keyed by number to each chapter's learning goals. By linking all elements to the learning goals, the integrated learning system facilitates the mastery of those goals.

Also keyed to various parts of the text is the *PMF Brief CD-ROM Software,* a disk for use with IBM PCs and compatible microcomputers. The disk contains three different sets of routines:

1. The *PMF Brief Tutor* is a user-friendly program that extends self-testing opportunities in the more quantitative chapters beyond those included in the end-of-chapter materials. It gives immediate feedback with detailed solutions and provides tutorial assistance (including text page references). Text

discussions and end-of-chapter problems with which the *PMF Brief Tutor* can be used are marked with a ⏷.

2. The *PMF Brief Problem-Solver* can be used as an aid in performing many of the routine financial calculations presented in the book. A CD-ROM symbol, ✐, identifies those text discussions and end-of-chapter problems that can be solved with the *PMF Brief Problem-Solver*.

3. The *PMF Brief Excel Spreadsheet Templates* can be used with Microsoft Excel to input data and carry out "what-if" types of analyses in selected chapters. These problems are marked by the symbol ▦.

A detailed discussion of how to use the *PMF Brief CD-ROM Software*—the *Tutor*, the *Problem-Solver*, and the *Excel Spreadsheet Templates*—is included in Appendix D, at the end of the book.

Each chapter ends with a case that integrates the chapter materials. Where applicable, the symbols for the *PMF Brief Problem-Solver* and/or the *PMF Brief Tutor* identify case questions that can be solved with the aid of these programs. The chapter-end cases can be used to synthesize and apply related concepts and techniques.

SUMMARY

LG1 **Define *finance* and its major areas and opportunities.** Finance, the art and science of managing money, affects the lives of every person and every organization. Major opportunities in financial services exist within banking and related institutions, personal financial planning, investments, real estate, and insurance. Managerial finance, concerned with the duties of the financial manager in the business firm, offers numerous career opportunities such as financial analyst, capital budgeting analyst/manager, project finance manager, cash manager, credit analyst/manager, and pension fund manager. The recent trend toward globalization of business activity has created new demands and opportunities in managerial finance.

LG2 **Review the basic forms of business organization.** The basic forms of business organization are the sole proprietorship, the partnership, and the corporation. Although there are more sole proprietorships than any other form of business organization, the corporation is dominant in terms of business receipts and net profits. The owners of a corporation are its stockholders, evidenced by either common stock or preferred stock. Stockholders expect to earn a return by receiving dividends or by realizing gains through

increases in share price. The key strengths and weaknesses of each form of business organization are summarized in Table 1.2.

LG3 **Describe the managerial finance function and its relationship to economics and accounting.** All areas of responsibility within a firm interact with finance personnel, processes, and procedures. In large firms, the managerial finance function might be handled by a separate department headed by the vice president of finance (CFO), to whom the treasurer and controller report; in small firms the finance function is generally performed by the accounting department. The financial manager must understand the economic environment and relies heavily on the economic principle of marginal analysis when making decisions. Financial managers use accounting data but differ from accountants, who devote primary attention to accrual methods and to gathering and presenting data, by concentrating on cash flows and decision making.

LG4 **Identify the financial manager's key activities.** The three key activities of the financial manager are (1) performing financial analysis and planning, (2) making investment decisions, and (3) making financing decisions.

Explain the wealth maximization goal of the financial manager and the role of ethics in the firm. The goal of the financial manager is to maximize the owners' wealth (dependent on stock price) rather than profits, because profit maximization ignores the timing of returns, does not directly consider cash flows, and ignores risk. Because return and risk are the key determinants of share price, both must be assessed by the financial manager when evaluating decision alternatives. EVA is a popular measure used to determine whether an investment positively contributes to the owners' wealth. The wealth-maximizing actions of financial managers should be consistent with the preservation of the wealth of *stakeholders,* groups such as employees, customers, suppliers, creditors, and owners who have a direct economic link to the firm. Positive ethical practices by the firm and its managers are believed to be necessary for achieving the firm's goal of owner wealth maximization.

 Discuss the agency issue. An agency problem results when managers, as agents for owners, place personal goals ahead of corporate goals. Market forces—both activism on the part of shareholders and the threat of takeover—tend to prevent or minimize agency problems. In addition, firms incur agency costs to monitor management behavior, ensure against dishonest acts of management, and provide incentives to management to act in the best interest of owners. Stock options and performance plans are examples of such agency costs.

PROBLEMS

WARM-UP   **1-1   Liability comparisons**   Merideth Harper has invested $25,000 in Southwest Development Company. The firm has recently declared bankruptcy and has $60,000 in unpaid debts. Explain the nature of payments, if any, by Ms. Harper in each of the following situations.

a. Southwest Development Company is a sole proprietorship owned by Ms. Harper.

b. Southwest Development Company is a 50–50 partnership of Ms. Harper and Christopher Black.

c. Southwest Development Company is a corporation.

WARM-UP   **1-2   Accrual income versus cash flow**   Thomas Book Sales, Inc., supplies textbooks to college and university bookstores. The books are shipped with a proviso that they must be paid for within 30 days, but can be returned for a full refund credit within 90 days. Thomas shipped and billed book titles totaling $760,000. Collections net of return credits during the year totaled $690,000. The company spent $300,000 acquiring the books that it shipped.

a. Using accrual-basis accounting and the figures above, show the firm's income for the past year.

b. Using cash-basis accounting and the figures above, show the firm's cash flow for the past year.

c. Which of these statements is more useful to the financial manager? Why?

INTERMEDIATE   **1-3   Identifying agency problems and costs**   Explain why each of the following situations is an agency problem and what costs to the firm might result from it. Suggest how the problem might be dealt with short of firing the individual(s) involved.

a. The front desk receptionist routinely takes an extra 20 minutes of lunch to take care of her personal errands.

b. Division managers are padding cost estimates in order to show short-term efficiency gains when the costs come in lower than the estimates.

c. The firm's chief executive officer has secret talks with a competitor about the possibility of a merger in which (s)he would become the CEO of the combined firms.

d. A branch manager lays off experienced full-time employees and staffs customer service positions with part-time or temporary workers to lower employment costs and raise this year's branch profit. The manager's bonus is based on profitability.

CASE   Chapter 1   **Assessing the Goal of Sports Products, Inc.**

Loren Seguara and Dale Johnson both work for Sports Products, Inc., a major producer of boating equipment and accessories. Loren works as a clerical assistant in the Accounting Department, and Dale works as a packager in the Shipping Department. During their lunch break one day, they began talking about the company. Dale complained that he had always worked hard, trying not to waste packing materials and to perform his job efficiently and cost-effectively. In spite of his efforts and those of his departmental co-workers, the firm's stock price had declined nearly $2 per share over the past 9 months. Loren indicated that she shared Dale's frustration, particularly because the firm's profits had been rising. Neither could understand why the firm's stock price was falling as profits rose.

Loren said that she had seen documents describing the firm's profit-sharing plan under which all managers were partially compensated on the basis of the firm's profits. She suggested that maybe it was profit that was important to management, because it directly affected their pay. Dale said, "That doesn't make sense, because the stockholders own the firm. Shouldn't management do what's best for stockholders? Something's wrong!" Loren responded, "Well, maybe that explains why the company hasn't concerned itself with the stock price. Look, the only profits stockholders receive are in the form of cash dividends, and this firm has never paid dividends during its 20-year history. We as stockholders therefore don't directly benefit from profits. The only way we benefit is for the stock price to rise." Dale chimed in, "That probably explains why the firm is being sued by state and federal environmental officials for dumping pollutants in the adjacent stream. Why spend money for pollution controls? It increases costs, lowers profits, and therefore lowers management's earnings!"

Loren and Dale realized that the lunch break had ended and they must quickly return to work. Before leaving, they decided to meet the next day to continue their discussion.

Required

a. What should the management of Sports Products, Inc., pursue as its overriding goal? Why?

b. Does the firm appear to have an *agency problem?* Explain.

c. Evaluate the firm's approach to pollution control. Does it seem to be *ethical?* Why might incurring the expense to control pollution be in the best interests of the firm's owners in spite of its negative impact on profits?

d. On the basis of the information provided, what specific recommendations would you offer the firm?

GOTO web site www.cob.ohio-state.edu/dept/fin/jobs/corpfin.htm and answer the following questions:

1. What are the highest-rated skill requirements for a typical position in corporate finance?
2. What are, according to Robert Half International, the key job areas in corporate finance?
3. What are the salary ranges in a small firm for the following positions in corporate finance: rookie financial analyst, credit manager, and chief financial officer?
4. According to the Salary Survey by the Treasury Management Association, what are the typical experience and education requirements for a division controller at General Motors or PepsiCo?

Now GOTO web site www.nyse.com and then click the JOBS icon; click the BUSINESS DIVISION icon on the bottom of the next screen. Answer the following questions:

5. What are the career opportunities the New York Securities Exchange has to offer within:
   a. Communications?
   b. the Equities Group?
   c. the Competitive Position Group and International?
   d. the Regulatory Group?

Now click the JOB SEARCH icon at the bottom of this screen.

6. What positions are now open with the NYSE? Where is each of these jobs located?

2 INSTITUTIONS, MARKETS, AND INTEREST RATES

LEARNING GOALS

LG1 Identify key participants in financial transactions and the basic activities and changing role of financial institutions.

LG2 Understand the relationship between financial institutions and markets, and the basic function and operation of the money market.

LG3 Describe the capital market, the securities traded there, and the role of the securities exchanges in the capital market.

LG4 Be able to interpret bond and stock price quotations.

LG5 Understand the role of the investment banker in securities offerings.

LG6 Describe the fundamentals of interest rates and required returns: inflation, term structure, risk premiums, and risk and return.

ACROSS *the* DISCIPLINES

Business firms operate in a complex environment, where financial institutions and markets affect investment opportunities and the cost and availability of financing. The activity of financial institutions and markets and the interactions of funds suppliers and funds demanders affect the cost of money (interest rates). This chapter acquaints you with the key aspects of the firm's environment—institutions, markets, and interest rates. Chapter 2 is important to:

- **accounting personnel** who will calculate the tax effects of various proposed transactions.

- **information systems analysts** who will design the database that gathers most of the data needed for determining the firm's tax liability.

- **management** because it will establish and maintain the firm's relationships with various financial institutions.

- **the marketing department** because top management will accept or reject some new products based on the risk-return trade-off.

- **operations,** which will rely on funding from various financial institutions to maintain and grow the firm's production capacity.

FINANCIAL INSTITUTIONS AND MARKETS: AN OVERVIEW

LG1   LG2

Firms that need funds from external sources can obtain them in three ways: One is through a *financial institution* that accepts savings and transfers them to those needing funds. Another is through *financial markets*, organized forums in which the suppliers and demanders of funds make transactions. A third is through *private placement*. In this section we focus primarily on financial institutions and financial markets. However, private placement of funds is not unusual, and we will consider this topic in a later section.

FINANCIAL INSTITUTIONS

financial institution
An intermediary that channels the savings of individuals, businesses, and governments into loans or investments.

Financial institutions are intermediaries that channel the savings of individuals, businesses, and governments into loans or investments. Many financial institutions pay savers interest on deposited funds; others provide services for a fee (for example, checking accounts for which customers pay service charges). Some financial institutions accept customers' deposits and lend this money to other customers; others invest customers' savings in earning assets such as real estate or stocks and bonds; and some do both. Financial institutions are required by the government to operate within established regulatory guidelines.

KEY PARTICIPANTS IN FINANCIAL TRANSACTIONS

The key suppliers and demanders of funds are individuals, businesses, and governments. The savings of individual consumers provide financial institutions with a large portion of their funds. Individuals not only supply funds to financial institutions but also demand funds from them in the form of loans. However, individuals as a group are the *net suppliers* for financial institutions: They save more money than they borrow.

Business firms also deposit some of their funds in financial institutions, primarily in checking accounts with commercial banks. Firms, like individuals, also borrow funds from these institutions. As a group, business firms are *net demanders* of funds: They borrow more money than they save.

Governments maintain deposits of temporarily idle funds, certain tax payments, and Social Security payments in commercial banks. They do not borrow funds *directly* from financial institutions, but by selling their securities to various institutions, governments indirectly borrow from them. The government also is typically a *net demander* of funds: It borrows more than it saves. We've all heard about the federal budget deficit.

MAJOR FINANCIAL INSTITUTIONS

The major financial institutions in the U.S. economy are commercial banks, savings and loans, credit unions, savings banks, life insurance companies, pension funds, and mutual funds. These institutions attract funds from individuals, businesses, and governments, combine them, and make loans available to individuals and businesses. A brief description of the major financial institutions is found in Table 2.1.

TABLE 2.1	Major Financial Institutions

Institution	Description
Commercial bank	Accepts both demand (checking) and time (savings) deposits. Also offers negotiable order of withdrawal (NOW) accounts, which are interest-earning savings accounts against which checks can be written, and money market deposit accounts. Makes loans directly to borrowers or through the financial markets.
Savings and loan	Similar to a commercial bank except that it may not hold demand (checking) deposits. Obtains funds from savings, NOW, and money market deposit accounts. Lends funds primarily to individuals and businesses for real estate mortgage loans.
Credit union	Deals primarily in transfer of funds between consumers. Membership is generally based on some common bond, such as working for a given employer. Accepts members' savings deposits, NOW account deposits, and money market deposit accounts. Lends funds to other members, typically to finance automotive or appliance purchases or home improvements.
Savings bank	Similar to a savings and loan in that it holds savings, NOW, and money market deposit accounts. Generally lends or invests funds through financial markets, but makes some mortgage loans. Located primarily in the Northeast.
Life insurance company	The largest type of financial intermediary handling individual savings. Receives premium payments and invests them to accumulate funds for future benefit payments. Lends funds to individuals or channels funds to business and governments, typically through the financial markets.
Pension fund	Set up so that employees can receive retirement income. Often employers match the contributions of their employees. The majority of funds is lent or invested via the financial markets.
Mutual fund	Pools funds from the sale of shares and uses them to acquire bonds and stocks of business and governmental units. Creates a professionally managed portfolio of securities to achieve a specified investment objective, such as liquidity with a high return. Hundreds of funds, with a variety of investment objectives, exist. Money market mutual funds provide competitive returns with very high liquidity.

THE CHANGING ROLE OF FINANCIAL INSTITUTIONS

Depository Institutions Deregulation and Monetary Control Act of 1980 (DIDMCA)
Signaled the beginning of the "financial services revolution" by eliminating interest-rate ceilings on all accounts and permitting certain institutions to offer new types of accounts and services.

A revolution in the delivery of financial services began with passage of the **Depository Institutions Deregulation and Monetary Control Act of 1980 (DIDMCA).** Nearly two decades later, financial institutions are today still reacting to this law. By eliminating interest-rate ceilings on all accounts and permitting certain institutions to offer new types of services, DIDMCA intensified competition and blurred traditional distinctions among financial institutions.

The trend today is toward the elimination of smaller financial institutions through acquisition or merger. In addition, mergers of large financial institutions, such as BankAmerica and NationsBank Corp. (now called BankAmerica), Bank One and First Chicago NBD (now called Bank One), Wells Fargo and Norwest Bank (now called Wells Fargo), and Washington Mutual, American Savings, and Ahmanson Corp. (now called Washington Mutual), are creating large national institutions that are rapidly displacing regional and local financial institutions. Contributing to this growth is new technology, particularly services such as ATMs, debit cards, checkless electronic banking, and Internet access. Large institutions that can afford to build and support the necessary technological infrastructure will be able to perpetuate their growth.

FINANCIAL MARKETS

financial markets
Provide a forum in which suppliers of funds and demanders of funds can transact business directly.

Financial markets provide a forum in which suppliers of funds and demanders of funds can transact business directly. Whereas the loans and investments of institutions are made without the direct knowledge of the suppliers of funds (savers), suppliers in the financial markets know where their funds are being lent or invested. The two key financial markets are the *money market* and the *capital market*. Transactions in short-term debt instruments, or marketable securities, take place in the money market. Long-term securities—bonds and stocks—are traded in the capital market.

primary market
Financial market in which securities are initially issued; the only market in which the issuer is directly involved in the transaction.

secondary market
Financial market in which pre-owned securities (those that are not new issues) are traded

All securities, whether in the money or capital market, are initially issued in the **primary market.** This is the only market in which the corporate or government issuer is directly involved in the transaction and receives direct benefit from the issue. That is, the company actually receives the proceeds from the sale of securities. Once the securities begin to trade between savers and investors, they become part of the **secondary market.** Whereas the primary market is the one in which "new" securities are sold, the secondary market can be viewed as a "used," or "preowned," securities market.

THE RELATIONSHIP BETWEEN INSTITUTIONS AND MARKETS

Financial institutions actively participate in the money market and the capital market as both suppliers and demanders of funds. Figure 2.1 depicts the general flow of funds in financial institutions and financial markets; private placement

FIGURE 2.1   Flow of Funds
Flow of funds for financial institutions and markets

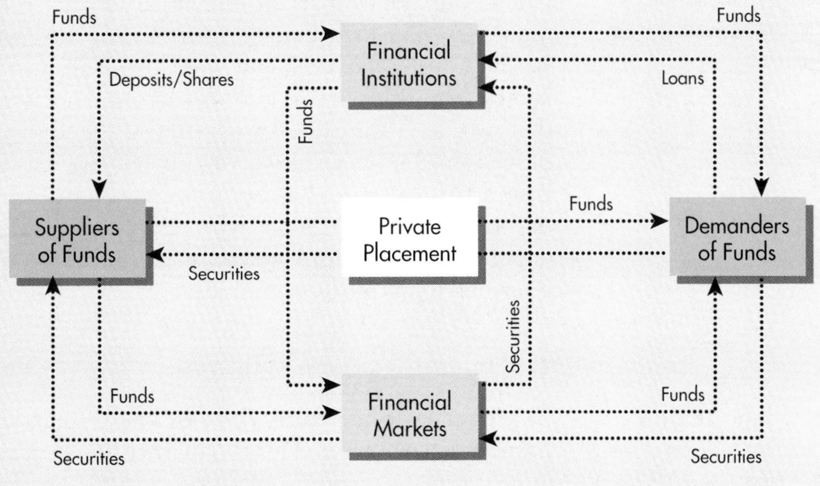

transactions are also shown. The individuals, businesses, and governments that supply and demand funds may be domestic or foreign. We end this section with a brief description of the money market, including its international equivalent—the *Eurocurrency market.* A later section of the chapter is devoted to discussion of the capital market because of its key importance to the firm.

THE MONEY MARKET

money market
A financial relationship created between suppliers and demanders of *short-term funds.*

The **money market** is created by a financial relationship between suppliers and demanders of *short-term funds,* which have maturities of one year or less. The money market exists because certain individuals, businesses, governments, and financial institutions have temporarily idle funds that they wish to place in some type of short-term, interest-earning instrument. At the same time, other individuals, businesses, governments, and financial institutions find themselves in need of seasonal or temporary financing. The money market thus brings together these suppliers and demanders of short-term liquid funds.

marketable securities
Short-term debt instruments, such as U.S. Treasury bills, commercial paper, and negotiable certificates of deposit issued by government, business, and financial institutions, respectively.

Most money market transactions are made in **marketable securities**—short-term debt instruments, such as U.S. Treasury bills, commercial paper, and negotiable certificates of deposit issued by government, business, and financial institutions, respectively. (Marketable securities are described in Chapter 16.)

THE OPERATION OF THE MONEY MARKET

The money market is not an actual organization housed in some central location. How, then, are suppliers and demanders of short-term funds brought together in the money market? Typically, they are matched through the facilities of large New York banks and through government securities dealers. A number of stock brokerage firms purchase various money market instruments for resale to customers. In addition, financial institutions such as banks and mutual funds purchase money market instruments for their portfolios to provide attractive returns on their customers' deposits and share purchases. Additionally, Federal Reserve banks may become involved in the money market in loans from one commercial bank to another; these loans are referred to as transactions in **federal funds.**

federal funds
Loan transactions between commercial banks in which the Federal Reserve banks become involved.

Individuals, businesses, governments, and financial institutions all participate in the money market. Individuals participate as purchasers and as sellers of money market instruments, but they are not initial issuers of these securities. Business firms, governments, and financial institutions both buy and sell marketable securities. They may be the primary issuers, or they may sell securities that they have purchased from others. Of course, each of these parties can issue only certain money market instruments; a business firm, for example, cannot issue a U.S. Treasury bill. Some financial institutions purchase marketable securities specifically for resale, whereas others purchase them as short-term investments. Businesses and governments purchase marketable securities to earn a return on temporarily idle funds.

THE EUROCURRENCY MARKET

Eurocurrency market
International equivalent of the domestic money market.

The international equivalent of the domestic money market is called the **Eurocurrency market.** This is a market for short-term bank deposits denominated in U.S. dollars or other easily convertible currencies. The Eurocurrency market has grown rapidly, primarily because it is an unregulated, wholesale, and global market that capably fills the needs of both borrowers and lenders.

Eurocurrency deposits arise when a corporation or individual makes a bank deposit in a currency other than the local currency of the country where the bank is located. If, for example, a multinational corporation deposits U.S. dollars in a London bank, this would create a Eurodollar deposit (a dollar deposit at a bank in Europe). Almost all Eurodollar deposits are *time deposits,* meaning that the bank would promise to repay the deposit, with interest, at a fixed date in the future—say, 6 months. During the interim the bank can lend this dollar deposit to creditworthy corporate or government borrowers. If the bank cannot find a borrower on its own, it may loan the deposit to another international bank. The rate charged on these "interbank loans" is called the **London Interbank Offered Rate (LIBOR),** and this is the base rate that is used to price all Eurocurrency loans.

London Interbank Offered Rate (LIBOR)
The base rate that is used to price all Eurocurrency loans.

? Review Questions

2-1   Who are the key participants in financial transactions? Who are net suppliers and who are net demanders?

2-2   What did the *Depository Institutions Deregulation and Monetary Control Act of 1980 (DIDMCA)* do to begin the "financial services revolution"? What appears to be the trend in terms of the size of financial institutions and the services they provide?

2-3   What role do *financial markets* play in our economy? What are *primary* and *secondary* markets? What relationship exists between financial institutions and financial markets?

2-4   What is the *money market?* How does it differ from the capital market?

2-5   What is the *Eurocurrency market?* What is the *London Interbank Offered Rate (LIBOR)* and how is it used in this market?

THE CAPITAL MARKET

capital market
A financial relationship created by institutions and arrangements that allows suppliers and demanders of *long-term funds* to make transactions.

The **capital market** is a financial relationship created by a number of institutions and arrangements that allows suppliers and demanders of *long-term funds*— funds with maturities of more than one year—to make transactions. Included among long-term funds are securities issues of business and government. The backbone of the capital market is formed by the various *securities exchanges* that provide a forum for bond and stock transactions. The smooth functioning of the capital market is important to the long-run growth of business.

bond
Long-term debt instrument used by business and government to raise large sums of money, generally from a diverse group of lenders.

KEY SECURITIES: BONDS AND STOCK

Major securities traded in the capital market include bonds (long-term debt) and both common and preferred stock (equity, or ownership). **Bonds** are long-term debt instruments used by business and government to raise large sums of money, generally from a diverse group of lenders. *Corporate bonds* typically pay interest *semiannually* (every 6 months) at a stated *coupon interest rate.* They have an initial *maturity* of from 10 to 30 years, and a *par,* or *face, value* of $1,000 that must be repaid at maturity. Bonds are described in detail in Chapter 3.

Example ▼ Lakeview Industries, a major microprocessor manufacturer, has issued a 12 percent coupon interest rate, 20-year bond with a $1,000 par value that pays interest semiannually. Investors who buy this bond receive the contractual right to $120 annual interest (12 percent coupon interest rate × $1,000 par value) distributed as $60 at the end of each 6 months ($\frac{1}{2}$ × $120) for 20 years, plus the
▲ $1,000 par value at the end of year 20.

common stock
Collectively, units of ownership interest, or equity, in a corporation.

preferred stock
A special form of ownership having a fixed periodic dividend that must be paid prior to payment of any common stock dividends.

As indicated in Chapter 1, shares of **common stock** are units of ownership interest, or equity, in a corporation. Common stockholders earn a return by receiving *dividends*—periodic distributions of earnings—or by realizing increases in share price. **Preferred stock** is a special form of ownership that has features of both a bond and common stock. Preferred stockholders are promised a fixed periodic dividend that must be paid prior to payment of any dividends to the common stockholders. In other words, preferred stock has "preference" over common stock. Preferred and common stock are described in detail in Chapter 3.

MAJOR SECURITIES EXCHANGES

securities exchanges
Organizations that provide the marketplace in which firms can raise funds through the sale of new securities and purchasers can resell securities.

efficient market
Market that allocates funds to their most productive uses as a result of competition among wealth-maximizing investors.

Securities exchanges provide the marketplace in which firms can raise funds through the sale of new securities and purchasers of securities can easily resell them when necessary. In addition, securities exchanges create **efficient markets**, which allocate funds to the most productive uses. This is especially true for securities that are actively traded on major exchanges where prices are believed to be close to their true value as a result of competition among wealth-maximizing investors.

Many people call securities exchanges "stock markets," but this label is misleading: Bonds, common stock, preferred stock, and a variety of other investment vehicles are all traded on these exchanges. The two key types of securities exchange are the organized exchange and the over-the-counter exchange. In addition, important capital markets exist outside the United States.

ORGANIZED SECURITIES EXCHANGES

organized securities exchanges
Tangible organizations that act as *secondary markets* where outstanding securities are resold.

Organized securities exchanges are tangible organizations that act as *secondary markets* where outstanding securities are resold. Organized exchanges account for about 59 percent of the *total dollar volume* of domestic shares traded. The best-known organized exchanges are the New York Stock Exchange (NYSE) and the American Stock Exchange (AMEX), both headquartered in New York City. There are also regional exchanges, such as the Chicago Stock Exchange and the Pacific Stock Exchange (co-located in Los Angeles and San Francisco).

Most exchanges are modeled after the New York Stock Exchange, which accounts for about 90 percent of the total annual dollar volume of shares traded on organized exchanges. In order for a firm's securities to be listed for trading on an organized exchange, the firm must file an application for listing and meet a number of requirements. For example, to be eligible for listing on the NYSE, a firm must have at least 2,000 stockholders owning 100 or more shares; a minimum of 1.1 million shares of publicly held stock; earnings of at least $15 million over the previous 3 years, with no loss in the previous 2 years; and a minimum of $100 million in stockholders' equity. Clearly, only large, widely held firms are candidates for listing on the NYSE.

To make transactions on the "floor" of the New York Stock Exchange, an individual or firm must own a "seat" on the exchange. There are a total of 1,366 seats on the NYSE, most of which are owned by brokerage firms. Trading is carried out on the floor of the exchange through an *auction process*. The goal of trading is to fill *buy orders* (orders to purchase securities) at the lowest price and to fill *sell orders* (orders to sell securities) at the highest price, thereby giving both purchasers and sellers the best possible deal.

Example ▼ Kathryn Blake, who has an account with Merrill Lynch, wishes to purchase 200 shares of the Microsoft Corporation at the prevailing market price. Kathryn calls her account executive,[1] Howard Kohn of Merrill Lynch, and places her order. Howard immediately has the order transmitted to the New York headquarters of Merrill Lynch, which forwards the order to the Merrill Lynch clerk on the floor of the exchange. The clerk dispatches the order to one of the firm's seat holders, who goes to the appropriate trading post and executes the order at the best possible price. The clerk then wires the execution price and confirmation of the transaction back to the brokerage office. Howard passes the relevant information along to Kathryn and completes the necessary paperwork. **▲**

Once placed, an order to buy or sell can be executed in minutes, thanks to sophisticated telecommunication devices. New Internet-based brokerage systems enable investors to electronically place their buy and sell orders. Information on the daily trading of securities is reported in various media, including financial publications such as the *Wall Street Journal*.

THE OVER-THE-COUNTER EXCHANGE

over-the-counter (OTC) exchange
Not an organization but an intangible market for the purchase and sale of securities not listed by the organized exchanges.

The **over-the-counter (OTC) exchange** is an intangible market for the purchase and sale of securities not listed by the organized exchanges. OTC traders, known as *dealers*, are linked with the purchasers and sellers of securities through the *National Association of Securities Dealers Automated Quotation (Nasdaq) System*. This sophisticated telecommunications network provides current bid and ask prices on thousands of actively traded OTC securities. The *bid price* is the highest price offered by a dealer to purchase a given security, and the *ask price* is the lowest price at which the dealer is willing to sell the security. The dealer in effect adds securities to his or her inventory by purchasing them at the bid price and sells securities from the inventory at the ask price, hoping to profit from the *spread* between the bid and ask price. Unlike the auction process on the organized securities exchanges, the prices at which securities are traded in the OTC market result from both competitive bids and negotiation.

Unlike the organized exchanges, the OTC handles *both* outstanding securities and new public issues, making it both a *secondary* and a *primary market*.

[1]The title *account executive* or *financial consultant* is often used to refer to an individual who traditionally has been called a *stockbroker*. These titles are believed to add respectability to the position and change the image of the stockbroker from that of a salesperson to that of a personal financial manager who provides diversified financial services to clients.

The OTC accounts for about 41 percent of the *total dollar volume* of domestic shares traded.

INTERNATIONAL CAPITAL MARKETS

Eurobond market
The oldest and largest international bond market, in which bonds, typically denominated in dollars, are issued and sold to investors outside the United States.

Although U.S. capital markets are by far the world's largest, there are important debt and equity markets outside the United States. In the **Eurobond market,** the oldest and largest international bond market, corporations and governments typically issue bonds denominated in dollars and sell them to investors located outside the United States. A U.S. corporation might, for example, issue dollar-denominated bonds that would be purchased by investors in Belgium, Germany, or Switzerland. Through the Eurobond market, issuing firms and governments can tap a much larger pool of investors than would be generally available in the local market.

foreign bond
Bond issued by a foreign corporation or government that is denominated in the investor's home currency and sold in the investor's home market.

The foreign bond market is another international market for long-term debt securities. A **foreign bond** is a bond issued by a foreign corporation or government that is denominated in the investor's home currency and sold in the investor's home market. A bond issued by a U.S. company that is denominated in Swiss francs and sold in Switzerland is an example of a foreign bond. Although the foreign bond market is much smaller than the Eurobond market, many issuers have found this to be an attractive way of tapping debt markets in Germany, Japan, Switzerland, and the United States.

international equity market
A vibrant equity market that emerged during the past decade to allow corporations to sell blocks of shares in several different countries simultaneously.

Finally, a vibrant **international equity market** has emerged in the past decade. Many corporations have discovered that they can sell blocks of shares to investors in a number of different countries simultaneously. This market has enabled corporations to raise far larger amounts of capital than they could have raised in any single national market. International equity sales have also proven indispensable to governments that have sold state-owned companies to private investors in recent years.

INTERPRETING BOND AND STOCK PRICE QUOTATIONS

The financial manager needs to stay abreast of the market values of the firm's outstanding bonds and stocks, whether they are traded on an organized exchange, over the counter, or in international markets. Similarly, existing and prospective bondholders and stockholders need to monitor the prices of the securities they own because these prices represent the current value of their investment. Information on bonds, stocks, and other securities is contained in **quotations,** which include current price data along with statistics on recent price behavior. Security price quotations are readily available for actively traded bonds and stocks. The most up-to-date "quotes" can be obtained electronically, via a personal computer. Price information is available from stockbrokers and is widely published in news media. Popular sources of daily security price quotations are financial newspapers, such as the *Wall Street Journal* and *Investor's Business Daily,* or the business sections of daily general newspapers.

quotations
Information on bonds, stocks, and other securities, including current price data and statistics on recent price behavior.

BOND QUOTATIONS

Part A of Figure 2.2 includes an excerpt from the New York Stock Exchange (NYSE) bond quotations reported in the April 2, 1999, *Wall Street Journal* for transactions through the close of trading on Thursday, April 1, 1999. We'll look

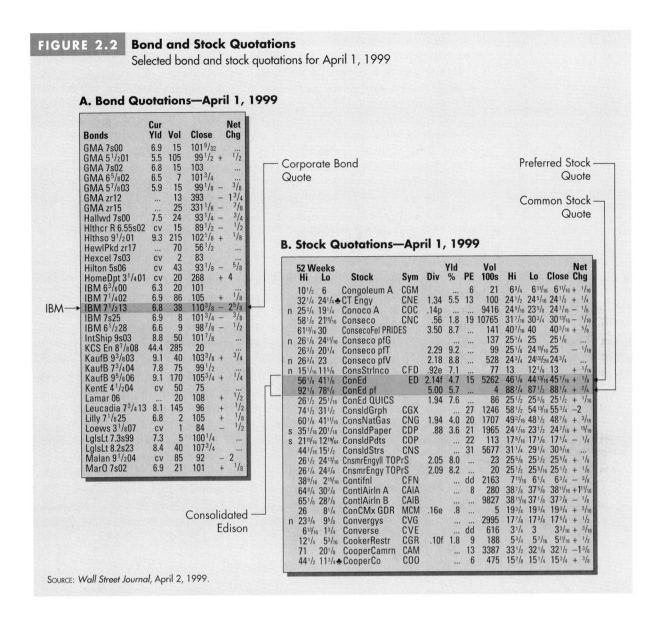

FIGURE 2.2   Bond and Stock Quotations
Selected bond and stock quotations for April 1, 1999

A. Bond Quotations—April 1, 1999

Corporate Bond Quote

Preferred Stock Quote

Common Stock Quote

B. Stock Quotations—April 1, 1999

IBM

Consolidated Edison

Source: *Wall Street Journal*, April 2, 1999.

at the corporate bond quotation for IBM, which is highlighted in Figure 2.2. The numbers following the company name—IBM—represent the bond's coupon interest rate and the year it matures: "$7\frac{1}{2}$ 13" means that the bond has a stated coupon interest rate of $7\frac{1}{2}$ percent and matures sometime in the year 2013. This information allows investors to differentiate between the various bonds issued by the corporation. Note that on the day of this quote IBM had five bonds listed. The next column, labeled "Cur Yld," gives the bond's *current yield*, which is found by dividing its annual coupon ($7\frac{1}{2}\%$, or 7.500%) by its closing price ($110\frac{3}{8}$), which in this case rounds to 6.8 percent ($7.500 \div 110.375 = .0679 \approx 6.8\%$).

The "Vol" column indicates the actual number of bonds that traded on the given day; 38 IBM bonds traded on Thursday, April 1, 1999. The final two columns include price information—the closing price and the net change in closing price from the prior trading day. Although most corporate bonds are issued with a *par,* or *face, value* of $1,000, *all bonds are quoted as a percentage of par.* A $1,000-par-value bond quoted at $92\frac{5}{8}$ is priced at $926.25 (92.625% × $1,000). Corporate bonds trade in fractions of $\frac{1}{8}$, which for $1,000-par-value bonds represents 1.25 *dollars.* Note that fractions are reduced to their lowest common denominator—$\frac{2}{8}$, $\frac{4}{8}$, and $\frac{6}{8}$ are expressed as $\frac{1}{4}$, $\frac{1}{2}$, and $\frac{3}{4}$, respectively. Thus, IBM's closing price of $110\frac{3}{8}$ for the day was $1,1103.75, that is, 110.375% × $1,000. Because a "Net Chg." of $-2\frac{5}{8}$ is given in the final column, the bond must have closed at 113 or $1,113.00 (113% × $1,000) on the prior day. Its price decreased by $2\frac{5}{8}$, or $26.00 ($2\frac{5}{8}$% × $1,000), on Thursday, April 1, 1999. Additional information may be included in a bond quotation, but we have looked at the basic elements.

STOCK QUOTATIONS

Part B of Figure 2.2 includes an excerpt from the NYSE stock quotations, also reported in the April 2, 1999, *Wall Street Journal* for transactions through the close of trading on Thursday, April 1, 1999. We'll look at both the common stock and preferred stock quotations for Consolidated Edison, highlighted in Figure 2.2. The quotations show that most stock prices are quoted in sixteenths of a dollar, with the fractions reduced to their lowest common denominator. The first two columns, labeled "Hi" and "Lo," contain the highest and lowest price at which the stock sold during the preceding 52 weeks. Consolidated Edison (abbreviated "ConEd") common stock, for example, traded between $56\frac{1}{8}$ and $41\frac{1}{8}$ during the 52-week period ending April 1, 1999. Listed to the right of the company's abbreviated name is its *stock symbol*—Consolidated Edison goes by "ED." The figure listed right after the stock symbol under "Div" is the annual cash dividend paid on each share of stock. The dividend for Consolidated Edison was $2.14 per share. The next item, labeled "Yld%," is the *dividend yield,* which is found by dividing the stated dividend by the closing share price. The dividend yield for Consolidated Edison is 4.7 percent (2.14 ÷ $45\frac{7}{16}$ = 2.14 ÷ 45.4375 = .0470 = 4.7%).

price/earnings (P/E) ratio
Measures the amount common stock investors are willing to pay for each dollar of the firm's earnings.

The **price/earnings (P/E) ratio**, labeled "PE," is next. It is calculated by dividing the closing market price by the firm's most recent annual earnings per share (EPS). The price/earnings (P/E) ratio measures the amount investors are willing to pay for each dollar of the firm's earnings. Consolidated Edison's P/E ratio was 15—the stock was trading at 15 times its earnings. The P/E ratio is believed to reflect investor expectations concerning the firm's future prospects: higher P/E ratios reflect investor optimism and confidence; lower P/E ratios reflect investor pessimism and concern.

The daily volume, labeled "Vol 100s," follows the P/E ratio. Here the day's sales are quoted in lots of 100 shares. The value 5262 for Consolidated Edison indicates that 526,200 shares of its common stock were traded on April 1, 1999. The "Hi," "Lo," and "Close" columns contain the highest, lowest, and closing (last) price, respectively, at which the stock sold on the given day. These values for Consolidated Edison were a high of $46.125, a low of $44.8125, and a closing price of $45.4375. The final column, "Net Chg," indicates the change in the closing price from that on the prior trading day. Consolidated Edison closed up $\frac{1}{8}$

($.125) from March 31, 1999, which means the closing price on that day was $45.3125 ($45\frac{5}{16}$).

Note that preferred stocks are listed with common stocks. For example, following Consolidated Edison's common stock in the quotes in part B of Figure 2.2 is its preferred stock, which is identified by the letters "pf." The quotation for preferred stock is nearly identical to that of common stock except that the value for the P/E ratio is left blank because it is irrelevant in the case of preferred stock.

Similar quotation systems are used for stocks that trade on other exchanges such as the American Stock Exchange (AMEX) and for the over-the-counter (OTC) exchange's Nasdaq national market issues. Also note that when a bond or stock issue is not traded on a given day it generally is not quoted in the financial and business press.

? R e v i e w   Q u e s t i o n s

2-6   What is the *capital market?* What role do securities exchanges play in the capital market?

2-7   How does the over-the-counter exchange operate? How does it differ from the organized securities exchanges?

2-8   Briefly describe the international capital markets, particularly the *Eurobond market* and the *international equity market.*

2-9   What information is found in a bond quotation? What unit of measurement is used to quote bond price data?

2-10   Describe the key items of information included in a stock quotation. What information does the stock's price/earnings (P/E) ratio provide? How are preferred stock quotations differentiated from those of common stock?

THE ROLE OF THE INVESTMENT BANKER

LG5

public offering
The sale of either bonds or stocks to the general public.

Long-term funds can be raised through a **public offering,** which is the sale of either bonds or stocks to the general public. As noted earlier, the initial public sale of bonds or stock occurs in the *primary market,* typically the *over-the-counter (OTC) exchange.* Once issued these securities trade on one of the securities exchanges. Here we take a brief look at the role of the *investment banker* in the initial sale of securities by the issuer.

Investment banking plays an important role in helping firms to raise long-term financing—both debt and equity—in the capital markets by finding buyers for new security issues. Investment bankers are neither investors nor bankers; they do not make long-term investments nor do they warehouse the savings of others. Instead, acting as an intermediary between the issuer and the buyers of new security issues, the investment banker purchases securities from corporate and government issuers and resells them to the general public. Many investment banking firms also operate in other areas as well. They may be securities brokerage firms, selling securities to the public. They may also perform an *advisory function* to firms by providing advice on mergers, acquisitions, and refinancing decisions.

investment banker
A financial intermediary that purchases securities from corporate and government issuers and resells them to the general public.

underwriting
The process in which an investment banker buys a security issue from the issuing firm at a lower price than the planned resale price, guaranteeing the issuer a specified amount from the issue and assuming the risk of price changes between purchase and sale.

UNDERWRITING

When **underwriting** a security issue, an investment banker guarantees the issuer that it will receive a specified amount from the issue. The banker buys the securities at a lower price than the planned resale price, thereby expecting to make a profit from the difference between the two prices—called the **spread.** The investment banker therefore bears the risk of price changes or a market collapse between the time of purchase and the time of sale of securities.

Example ▼

spread
The difference between the price paid for a security by the investment banker and the sale price.

Gigantica Corporation, a regional investment banking firm, is underwriting a $50 million common stock issue for Leader Electronics, an established manufacturer of consumer electronics. Gigantica has agreed to purchase the stock for $48 million. To recoup that amount, it must attempt to sell the stock for net proceeds of at least $48 million. If it can sell the stock for $50 million, it will earn a $2 million commission. Of course, there is also the risk that the investment banking firm might possibly lose part of the $48 million that it initially paid for the stock, if it fails to sell the stock for that amount.

▲

best efforts basis
A public offering in which the investment banker uses its resources to sell the security issue without taking on the risk of underwriting and is compensated on the basis of the number of securities sold.

In the case of some public offerings, the investment banker may not actually underwrite the issue, but may use its resources to sell the securities on a **best efforts basis.** In this case, the banker does not take on the financial risk associated with underwriting; compensation is based on the number of securities sold.

ORGANIZATION OF INVESTMENT BANKING ACTIVITY

competitive bidding
A method of choosing an investment banker in which the highest bidder for a security issue is awarded the issue.

negotiated offering
A security issue for which the investment banker is hired rather than awarded the issue through *competitive bidding.*

A firm that needs additional financing through the capital markets initiates the fund-raising process by selecting an investment banker to underwrite the new issue and provide advice. The investment banker may be selected through **competitive bidding,** in which the investment banker or group of bankers that bids the highest price for the issue is awarded it. If the investment banker is merely hired by the issuing firm, the security issue is called a **negotiated offering.** Once selected, the investment banker helps the firm determine how much capital should be raised and in what form—debt or equity. After an examination of certain legal aspects of the firm and its proposed offering, a tentative underwriting agreement is drawn up.

underwriting syndicate
A group of investment banking firms, each of which will underwrite a portion of a large security issue, thus lessening the risk of loss to any single firm.

selling group
A group of brokerage firms, each of which agrees to sell a portion of a security issue and expects to make a profit on the *spread* between the price at which they buy and sell the securities.

SYNDICATING THE UNDERWRITING

Due to the size of many new security issues, it is often necessary for the originating investment banker to form an **underwriting syndicate,** which is a group of investment banking firms. The use of an underwriting syndicate lessens the risk of loss to any single firm. Each underwriter in the syndicate must sell its portion of the issue. This is likely to result in a wider distribution of the new securities.

The originating underwriter with the assistance of syndicate members puts together a **selling group,** which distributes the new issue to the investing public. The selling group is normally made up of a large number of brokerage firms, each of which agrees to sell a certain portion of the issue. Members of the selling group, like underwriters, expect to make a profit on the *spread* between the price

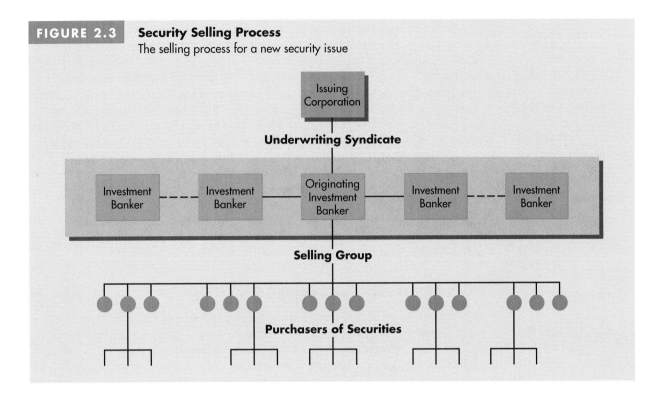

FIGURE 2.3   **Security Selling Process**
The selling process for a new security issue

at which they buy and sell the securities. Figure 2.3 depicts the selling process for a new security issue.

FULFILLING LEGAL REQUIREMENTS

Through the Securities and Exchange Commission (SEC), the federal government regulates the initial and subsequent trading of securities. Initial regulation tends to center on the public sale of new issues; subsequent regulation is concerned with the sale of securities in *secondary markets*—both organized and over-the-counter.

Before a *new security* can be issued, the issuer must obtain the approval of the SEC. The issuer is required to file a registration statement with the SEC, which must be on file for at least 20 days before approval is granted. The sale of the new security cannot begin until the registration statement is approved. One portion of the registration statement is the **prospectus;** it details the firm's operating and financial position. The prospectus may be issued to potential buyers during the pre-approval waiting period as long as a **red herring**—a statement indicating the tentative nature of the offering—is printed in red ink on the prospectus. Once the registration statement has been approved, the new security can be offered for sale if the prospectus is made available to all interested parties. *Approval of the registration statement by the SEC does not mean that the security is a good investment; it indicates only that the facts presented in the statement accurately reflect the firm's operating and financial position.*

prospectus
A portion of a security registration statement filed with the SEC that details the firm's operating and financial position; it must be made available to all interested parties.

red herring
On a prospectus, a statement, printed in red ink, indicating the tentative nature of a security offering while it is being reviewed by the SEC.

shelf registration
An SEC procedure that allows firms with more than $150 million in outstanding common stock to file a "master registration statement" covering a 2-year period and then, during that period, to sell securities that have already been approved under the master statement.

As an alternative to filing a lengthy registration statement, firms with more than $150 million in outstanding common stock can use a procedure known as **shelf registration.** This procedure allows a firm to file a "master registration statement"—a single document summarizing planned financing—covering a 2-year period. At any time during the 2 years, the firm, after filing a "short statement," can sell securities that have already been approved under the master statement. Under this procedure, the approved securities are effectively warehoused and kept "on the shelf" until the need exists or market conditions are appropriate. Shelf registration is popular with large firms that frequently need access to the capital markets to raise debt or equity funds.

Underwriting syndicates generally wait until the end of the registration period to price securities. The pricing decision is important because it affects the ease with which the issue can be sold and also the issuer's proceeds. The investment banker's "feel" for the mood of the market should result in a price that achieves the optimum mix of marketability and financial return.

COST OF INVESTMENT BANKING SERVICES

The overall cost of a security issue (the *flotation* cost) has two basic components—underwriting cost and administrative cost. The underwriting cost is the *spread*—the difference between what the investment banker pays for a security and its sale price in the market. The issuer also pays the administrative costs associated with the security issue, which include the SEC registration fee, printing costs, and accounting and legal fees. Generally, the larger the issue, the lower the overall cost in percentage terms. It is also generally true that the overall flotation cost for common stock is highest, followed by preferred stock and bonds in that order. Flotation costs can range from about 1.5 percent of the total proceeds on a large bond issue (more than $500 million) to 15 percent or more on a small common stock issue (around $6 million).

PRIVATE PLACEMENT

private placement
The direct sale of a new security issue to one or more purchasers.

As an alternative to a public offering, a firm can sometimes negotiate *private (or direct) placement* of a security issue. **Private placement** occurs when an investment banker arranges for the direct sale of a new security issue to one or more individuals or firms. The investment banker is paid a commission for acting as an intermediary in the transaction.

Private placement usually reduces administrative and issuance costs and provides flexibility, because the issuing firm need not file registration statements and is not required to obtain the approval of the SEC. In addition, the issuer has more flexibility in tailoring terms and later renegotiating them, should the need arise, than it does with a public offering. On the other hand, private placement poses a disadvantage to the *buyer* who at some future date may wish to sell the securities on the open market. SEC registration and approval would be required prior to public sale.

The trend in recent years is toward increasing use of public offerings and diminished use of private placements. Ordinarily, private placements are used primarily for bonds and preferred stock. Some large firms have in-house services for private placement of their short- and long-term debt. Common stock is sometimes directly placed when the firm believes that the existing shareholders might purchase the issue through an arrangement known as a *rights offering*, which is described in Chapter 3.

? Review Questions

2-11   What is an *investment banker?* What functions does it perform? Explain the sequence of events involved in the investment banking activity.

2-12   How is the investment banker compensated for its services? How are underwriting costs affected by the size and type of an issue?

2-13   What are the advantages of *private placements?*

INTEREST RATES AND REQUIRED RETURNS

Financial institutions and markets create the mechanism through which funds flow between savers (funds suppliers) and investors (funds demanders). The level of funds flow between suppliers and demanders can significantly affect economic growth. Growth results from the interaction of a variety of economic factors (such as the money supply, trade balances, and economic policies) that affect the cost of money—the interest rate or required return. The interest rate level acts as a regulating device that controls the flow of funds between suppliers and demanders. The *Board of Governors of the Federal Reserve System* regularly assesses economic conditions and, when necessary, initiates actions to raise or lower interest rates to control inflation and economic growth. Generally, the lower the interest rate, the greater the funds flow and therefore the greater the economic growth; the higher the interest rate, the lower the funds flow and economic growth. Interest rates and required returns are key variables that influence the actions of the financial manager.

INFLATION AND THE COST OF MONEY

interest rate
The compensation paid by the borrower of funds to the lender; from the borrower's point of view, the cost of borrowing funds.

required return
The cost of funds obtained by selling an ownership interest; it reflects the funds supplier's level of expected return.

risk-free rate of interest, R_F
The required return on a risk-free asset, typically a 3-month *U.S. Treasury bill.*

U.S. Treasury bill (T-bill)
Short-term IOUs issued by the U.S. Treasury; considered the risk-free asset.

The interest rate or required return represents the cost of money. It is the compensation that a demander of funds must pay a supplier. When funds are lent, the cost of borrowing the funds is the **interest rate.** When funds are obtained by selling an ownership interest—as in the sale of stock—the cost to the issuer is commonly called the **required return,** which reflects the funds supplier's level of expected return.

Ignoring risk factors, the cost of funds—the interest rate or required return—is closely tied to inflationary expectations. This can be demonstrated by using the **risk-free rate of interest, R_F,** which is defined as the required return on the risk-free asset. The risk-free asset is typically considered to be a 3-month **U.S. Treasury bill (T-bill),** which is a short-term IOU issued regularly by the U.S. Treasury. Figure 2.4 illustrates the movement of the rate of inflation and the risk-free rate of interest during the 20-year period 1978–1998. During this period the two rates tended to move in a similar fashion. Between 1978 and the early 1980s, inflation and interest rates were quite high, peaking at over 13 percent in 1980–1981. Since 1981 these rates have declined. The historic data clearly illustrate the significant impact of inflation on the actual rate of interest for the risk-free asset.

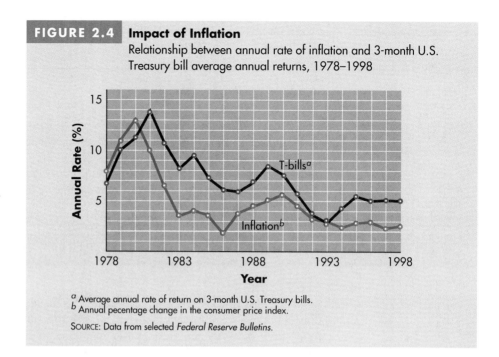

FIGURE 2.4   **Impact of Inflation**
Relationship between annual rate of inflation and 3-month U.S. Treasury bill average annual returns, 1978–1998

[a] Average annual rate of return on 3-month U.S. Treasury bills.
[b] Annual pecentage change in the consumer price index.
SOURCE: Data from selected *Federal Reserve Bulletins.*

---

term structure of interest rates
The relationship between the interest rate or rate of return and the time to maturity.

yield to maturity
Annual rate of interest earned on a security purchased on a given day and held to maturity.

yield curve
A graph of the *term structure of interest rates* that depicts the relationship between the *yield to maturity* of a security (*y* axis) and the time to maturity (*x* axis); it shows the pattern of interest rates on securities of equal quality and different maturity.

inverted yield curve
A downward-sloping yield curve that indicates generally cheaper long-term borrowing costs than short-term borrowing costs.

normal yield curve
An upward-sloping yield curve that indicates that short-term borrowing costs are below long-term borrowing costs.

TERM STRUCTURE OF INTEREST RATES

For any class of similar-risk securities, the **term structure of interest rates** relates the interest rate or rate of return to the time to maturity. For convenience we will use U.S. Treasury securities as a class, but other classes could include securities that have similar overall quality or risk ratings, as determined by independent agencies like Moody's and Standard & Poor's. The riskless nature of Treasury securities provides a laboratory in which to develop the term structure.

YIELD CURVES

The annual rate of interest earned on a security purchased on a given day and held to maturity is its **yield to maturity.** At any point in time the relationship between *yield to maturity* and the remaining time to maturity can be represented by a graph called the **yield curve.** The yield curve shows the pattern of interest rates on securities of equal quality and different maturity; it is a graphic depiction of the *term structure of interest rates.* Figure 2.5 shows three yield curves for all U.S. Treasury securities—one at May 22, 1981, a second one at September 29, 1989, and a third one at July 31, 1998.

Note that both the position and the shape of the yield curves change over time. The May 22, 1981, curve indicates high short-term interest rates and lower longer-term rates. This curve is described as *downward-sloping,* reflecting generally cheaper long-term borrowing costs than short-term borrowing costs. Historically, the downward-sloping yield curve, which is often called an **inverted yield curve,** has been the exception. More frequently, yield curves similar to that of July 31, 1998, have existed. These *upward-sloping* or **normal yield curves** indicate that short-term borrowing costs are below long-term borrowing costs.

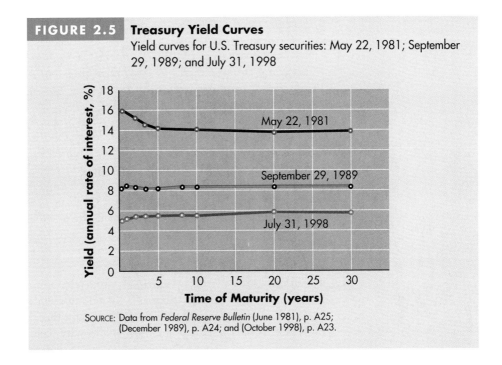

FIGURE 2.5 **Treasury Yield Curves**
Yield curves for U.S. Treasury securities: May 22, 1981; September 29, 1989; and July 31, 1998

SOURCE: Data from *Federal Reserve Bulletin* (June 1981), p. A25; (December 1989), p. A24; and (October 1998), p. A23.

flat yield curve
A yield curve that reflects relatively similar borrowing costs for both short- and longer-term loans.

Sometimes, a **flat yield curve**, similar to that of September 29, 1989, exists. It reflects relatively similar borrowing costs for both short- and longer-term loans.

The shape of the yield curve affects the firm's financing decisions. A financial manager who faces a downward-sloping yield curve is likely to rely more heavily on cheaper, long-term financing; when the yield curve is upward-sloping, the manager is more likely to use cheaper, short-term financing. Although a variety of other factors also influence the choice of loan maturity, the shape of the yield curve provides useful insights into future interest-rate expectations.

ⓟ*ERSONAL FINANCE PERSPECTIVE*

Watch the Curve!

As you make various personal finance decisions, from changing jobs to taking out education, car, and mortgage loans to starting your own business, you would be wise to watch the curve—the yield curve, that is—for what it can tell you about the financial future. In fall 1998 warning bells went off amongst economy-watchers, when the yield curve changed from the typical upward-sloping curve to a downward-sloping curve. Why was this a cause for alarm? The shape of the yield curve has been an excellent predictor of future economic growth. In general, sharp upward-sloping curves signal a substantial rise in economic activity within a year, while inverted yield curves preceded every recession since 1955. Most periods of flat or downward-sloping yield curves occur when the Federal Reserve increases short-term rates, tightening monetary policy to control inflation. These higher rates curtail business growth and eventually impact the various aspects of economic and financial well-being that Americans have come to enjoy.

However, analysis of 1998's downward-sloping yield curve revealed that it resulted not from increases in short-term rates but from falling long-term rates in the global economy. Financial turmoil in Asia, Latin America, and Russia pushed investors toward higher-quality, lower-risk, shorter-term securities. As global problems began affecting the United States, the Federal Reserve cut the discount rate from 5.50 to 5.25 percent. Two weeks later, the Fed again worked its economic magic, cutting the rate another .25 percent, to protect further weakening of the U.S. economy. As you enjoy the fruits of the extended period of steady economic growth that the United States has experienced over the last six years, you might whisper a word of thanks to the Federal Reserve and its chairman Alan Greenspan for staying ahead of the curve. ●

THEORIES OF TERM STRUCTURE

The dominance of the upward-sloping yield curve can be simply explained: Short-term securities are less risky than long-term securities because near-term events are more certain than future events, and therefore they have lower returns. However, this explanation fails to explain why yield curves often take on different shapes such as those shown in Figure 2.5. Three theories attempt to explain the general shape of the yield curve: the expectations hypothesis, liquidity preference theory, and market segmentation theory.

expectations hypothesis
Theory suggesting that the yield curve reflects investor expectations about future interest rates; an increasing inflation expectation results in an upward-sloping yield curve and a decreasing inflation expectation results in a downward-sloping yield curve.

Expectations Hypothesis   The **expectations hypothesis** suggests that the yield curve reflects investor expectations about future interest rates and inflation. Higher future rates of expected inflation will result in higher, long-term interest rates; the opposite occurs with lower future rates. This widely accepted explanation of the term structure can be applied to the securities of any issuer. Generally, under the expectations hypothesis, an increasing inflation expectation results in an upward-sloping yield curve; a decreasing inflation expectation results in a downward-sloping yield curve; and a stable inflation expectation results in a flat yield curve. Although, as we'll see, other theories exist, the observed strong relationship between inflation and interest rates (see Figure 2.4) supports this widely accepted theory.

liquidity preference theory
Theory suggesting that for any given issuer, long-term interest rates tend to be higher than short-term rates due to the lower liquidity and higher responsiveness to general interest rate movements of longer-term securities; causes the yield curve to be upward-sloping.

Liquidity Preference Theory   The tendency for yield curves to be upward-sloping can be further explained by **liquidity preference theory**. This theory indicates that for a given issuer, such as the U.S. Treasury, long-term rates tend to be higher than short-term rates. This belief is based on two behavioral facts:

1. Investors perceive less risk in short-term securities than in longer-term securities and are therefore willing to accept lower yields on them. The reason is that shorter-term securities are more liquid and less responsive to general interest rate movements.[2]

---

[2]Chapter 8 demonstrates that debt instruments with longer maturities are more sensitive to changing market interest rates. For a given change in market rates, the price or value of longer-term debts will be more significantly changed (up or down) than those with shorter maturities.

2. Borrowers are generally willing to pay a higher rate for long-term than for short-term financing. By locking in funds for a longer period of time, they can eliminate the potential of having to roll over short-term debt at unknown costs to obtain needed long-term financing.

Investors (lenders) tend to require a premium for tying up funds for longer periods, whereas borrowers are generally willing to pay a premium to obtain longer-term financing. These preferences of lenders and borrowers cause the yield curve to tend to be upward-sloping. Simply stated, longer maturities tend to have higher interest rates than shorter maturities.

market segmentation theory
Theory suggesting that the market for loans is segmented on the basis of maturity and that the sources of supply and demand for loans within each segment determine its prevailing interest rate; the slope of the yield curve is determined by the general relationship between the prevailing rates in each segment.

Market Segmentation Theory   The **market segmentation theory** suggests that the market for loans is segmented on the basis of maturity and that the supply of and demand for loans within each segment determine its prevailing interest rate. In other words, the equilibrium between suppliers and demanders of short-term funds, such as seasonal business loans, would determine prevailing short-term interest rates, and the equilibrium between suppliers and demanders of long-term funds, such as real estate loans, would determine prevailing long-term interest rates. The slope of the yield curve would be determined by the general relationship between the prevailing rates in each market segment. If supply of short-term rates is higher than demand for those rates at a time when supply of long-term rates is lower than demand for them, then short-term rates will be relatively low and long-term rates will be relatively high. Simply stated, low rates in the short-term segment and high rates in the long-term segment cause the yield curve to be upward-sloping. The opposite occurs for high short-term rates and low long-term rates.

All three theories of term structure have merit. From them we can conclude that at any time the slope of the yield curve is affected by (1) inflationary expectations, (2) liquidity preferences, and (3) the comparative equilibrium of supply and demand in the short- and long-term market segments. Upward-sloping yield curves result from higher future inflation expectations, lender preferences for shorter-maturity loans, and greater supply of short-term loans than of long-term loans relative to demand. The opposite behaviors would result in a downward-sloping yield curve. At any point in time, the interaction of these three forces will determine the prevailing slope of the yield curve.

RISK PREMIUMS: ISSUER AND ISSUE CHARACTERISTICS

risk premium
The amount by which the interest rate or required return on a security exceeds the risk-free rate of interest, R_F; it varies with specific issuer and issue characteristics.

So far we have considered only risk-free U.S. Treasury securities. We now add the element of risk, in order to assess what effect it has on the cost of funds. The amount by which the interest rate or required return exceeds the risk-free rate of interest, R_F, is a security's **risk premium**. The risk premium varies with specific issuer and issue characteristics. The specific issuer- and issue-related components of the risk premium include default risk, maturity risk, liquidity risk, contractual provisions, and tax risk. Each of these components is defined in Table 2.2. In

TABLE 2.2	Issuer- and Issue-Related Risk Components
Component	**Description**
Default risk	The possibility that the issuer of debt will not pay the contractual interest or principal as scheduled. The greater the uncertainty as to the borrower's ability to meet these payments, the greater the risk premium. High bond ratings reflect low default risk, and low bond ratings reflect high default risk.
Maturity risk (also called *interest rate risk*)	The fact that the longer the maturity, the more the value of a security will change in response to a given change in interest rates. If interest rates on otherwise similar-risk securities suddenly rise due to a change in the money supply, the prices of long-term bonds will decline by more than the prices of short-term bonds, and vice versa.[a]
Liquidity risk	The ease with which securities can be converted into cash without experiencing a loss in value. Generally, securities actively traded on major exchanges and over-the-counter have low liquidity risk, and less actively traded securities in a "thin market" have high liquidity risk.
Contractual provisions	Conditions that are often included in a debt agreement or a stock issue. Some of these reduce risk, whereas others may increase risk. For example, a provision allowing a bond issuer to retire its bonds prior to their maturity under favorable terms would increase the bond's risk.
Tax risk	The chance that Congress will make unfavorable changes in tax laws. The greater the potential impact of a tax law change on the return of a given security, the greater its tax risk. Generally, long-term securities are subject to greater tax risk than are those that are closer to their maturity dates.

[a]A detailed discussion of the effects of interest rates on the price or value of bonds and other fixed-income securities is presented in Chapter 8.

general, the highest risk premiums and therefore the highest returns are to be found in securities issued by firms with a high risk of default and in long-term maturities that are not actively traded, have unfavorable contractual provisions, and are not tax-exempt.

RISK AND RETURN

The fact that a positive relationship exists between risk and the actual or expected return should be evident. Investors tend to purchase those securities that are expected to provide a return commensurate with the perceived risk. The actual return earned on the security will affect whether investors sell, hold, or buy additional securities. In addition, most investors look to certain types of securities to provide a given range of risk-return behaviors.

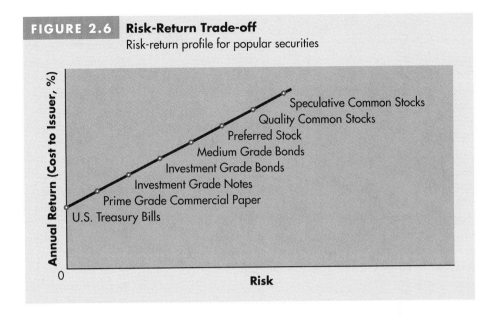

FIGURE 2.6   **Risk-Return Trade-off**
Risk-return profile for popular securities

risk-return trade-off
The fact that for accepting greater risk, investors must be compensated with the expectation of greater returns.

A **risk-return trade-off** exists: Investors must be compensated for accepting greater risk with the expectation of greater returns.[3] Figure 2.6 illustrates the typical relationship between risk and return for several popular securities. Clearly, greater risk results in higher costs to the issuer. Financial managers must attempt to keep revenues up and costs down, but they must also consider the risks associated with each investment and financing alternative. Decisions will ultimately rest on an analysis of the impact of risk and return on share price.

Review Questions

2-14   Define and differentiate between *interest rates* and *required returns*. Define the *risk-free rate of interest*, R_F, and a *U.S. Treasury bill (T-bill)*, and explain their relationship. What general relationship exists between inflationary expectations and the cost of money?

2-15   How does the *term structure of interest rates* relate to the *yield curve*? For a given class of similar-risk securities, what does each of the following yield curves reflect about interest rates: (**a**) downward-sloping; (**b**) upward-sloping; and (**c**) flat?

2-16   Briefly describe each of the following theories of the general shape of the yield curve: (**a**) expectations hypothesis; (**b**) liquidity preference theory; and (**c**) market segmentation theory.

2-17   Briefly describe the potential component risks that are embodied in the risk premium.

2-18   What is the *risk-return trade-off*? How should this relationship affect the actions of financial managers?

---

[3]The risk-return trade-off is discussed in detail in Chapter 7, where certain refinements are introduced to explain why investors are actually rewarded with higher returns for taking only certain types of "nondiversifiable" or inescapable risks.

SUMMARY

LG1 Identify key participants in financial transactions and the basic activities and changing role of financial institutions. Financial institutions, such as banks, savings and loans, and mutual funds, channel the savings of various individuals, businesses, and governments to demanders of these funds. Both the Depository Institutions Deregulation and Monetary Control Act of 1980 (DIDMCA) and the S&L crisis of the late 1980s have resulted in increased competition and a blurring of the distinction between various institutions. The trend today is toward a small number of very large national financial institutions that use the latest technology to efficiently offer a broad range of financial services.

LG2 Understand the relationship between financial institutions and markets, and the basic function and operation of the money market. The financial markets—the money market and the capital market—provide a forum in which suppliers and demanders of loans and investments can transact business directly. Financial institutions actively participate in the financial markets as both suppliers and demanders of funds. In the money market, marketable securities—short-term debt instruments— are traded. Individuals, businesses, governments, and financial institutions participate in the money market, which is created by the financial relationships between these suppliers and demanders of short-term funds. The Eurocurrency market is the international equivalent of the domestic money market.

LG3 Describe the capital market, the securities traded there, and the role of the securities exchanges in the capital market. In the capital market, long-term debt (bonds) and equity (preferred and common stock) transactions are made. The backbone of the capital market is the securities exchanges. The organized securities exchanges provide secondary markets for securities. The over-the-counter exchange, a telecommunications network linking active participants in this market, creates a secondary market for securities and is also a primary market in which new public issues are sold. Important debt and equity markets—the Eurobond market and the international equity market—exist outside of the United States.

LG4 Be able to interpret bond and stock price quotations. Information on bonds, stocks, and other securities is contained in their quotations, which include current price along with information on recent price behavior. Bond quotations show the bond's interest rate and year of maturity and the current yield, along with data on the previous trading session's volume, closing price, and net change. Closing price is quoted as a percentage of the bond's par value. Stock quotations show the high and low prices for the previous year, the annual cash dividend, the dividend yield, and the price/earnings ratio, along with data on the previous session's volume, high and low price, closing price, and net change. Preferred stocks are listed with common stocks.

LG5 Understand the role of the investment banker in securities offerings. Investment bankers act as financial intermediaries who purchase securities from corporate and government issuers and resell them to the general public. Their primary function is underwriting, which involves guaranteeing the issuer a specified amount from the issue. Some public offerings are, instead, sold on a best efforts basis. The investment banker may syndicate the underwriting, forms a selling group, fulfills legal requirements, and prices and distributes the issue. An alternative to public offerings is private placement of securities.

LG6 Discuss the fundamentals of interest rates and required returns; inflation, term structure, risk premiums, and risk and returns. The interest rate is the cost of borrowing, and the required return is the cost of obtaining ownership funds. The risk-free cost of funds, frequently measured using a 3-month U.S. Treasury bill, is closely tied to inflationary expectations. For similar-risk securities, the term structure of interest rates reflects the relationship between the interest rate and the time to maturity. Yield curves can be downward-sloping, upward-sloping (normal), or flat. Three theories—the expectations hypothesis, liquidity preference theory, and market segmentation theory—are cited to explain the general shape of the yield curve. The amount by which the interest rate or required return exceeds the risk-free rate of interest is the security's risk premium, which for similar-maturity securities varies with specific issuer- and issue-related characteristics. Each type of security offers a range of potential risk-return trade-offs.

SELF-TEST PROBLEM   (Solution in Appendix B)

ST 2-1   Given what you know about the general relationship between risk and return, locate each of the following securities on the graph below:

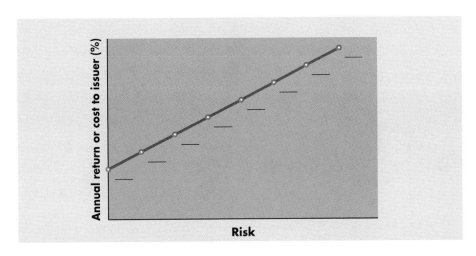

a. A 3-month U.S. Treasury bill paying 5.24%
b. A 30-year $30 million bond issue offered by Ford Motor Company
c. A 10-year U.S. Treasury bond
d. Coca-Cola common stock
e. Citicorp preferred stock
f. A $100,000 IOU from Mobil Oil (commercial paper), to be repaid in 90 days
g. An initial public offering of common stock in Night Flyer, a new high-tech company
h. A 12-month U.S. Treasury note

PROBLEMS

2-1   Bond quotation   Assume that the following quote for the Financial Management Corporation's $1,000-par-value bond was found in the Wednesday, November 8, issue of the *Wall Street Journal*.

Fin Mgmt 8¾ 05   8.7   558   100¼   −⅝

Given this information, answer the following questions:
a. On what day did the trading activity occur?
b. At what price did the bond close at the end of the day on November 7?
c. In what year does the bond mature?

    d. How many bonds were traded on the day quoted?
    e. What is the bond's coupon interest rate?
    f. What is the bond's *current yield?* Explain how this value was calculated.
    g. How much, if any, of a change in the bond's closing price took place between the day quoted and the day before? At what price did the bond close on the day before?

  2-2 Stock quotation   Assume that the following quote for the Advanced Business Machines stock (traded on the NYSE) was found in the Thursday, December 14, issue of the *Wall Street Journal.*

    $84\frac{1}{8}$ $51\frac{1}{4}$ **AdvBusMach ABM** 1.32 1.6 23 12432 $81\frac{3}{4}$ $80\frac{1}{8}$ $81\frac{3}{4} + 1\frac{5}{8}$

    Given this information, answer the following questions:
    a. On what day did the trading activity occur?
    b. At what price did the stock sell at the end of the day on Wednesday, December 13?
    c. What are the highest and lowest prices at which the stock sold on the day quoted?
    d. What is the firm's price/earnings ratio? What does it indicate?
    e. What is the last price at which the stock traded on the day quoted?
    f. How large a dividend is expected in the current year?
    g. What is the highest and lowest price at which the stock traded during the latest 52-week period?
    h. How many shares of stock were traded on the day quoted?
    i. How much, if any, of a change in stock price took place between the day quoted and the day before? What did the stock close at on the day before?

  2-3 Underwriting spread   Hildreth Recycling is interested in selling common stock to raise capital for plant expansion. The firm has consulted First Atlanta Company, a large underwriting firm, which believes that the stock can be sold for $80 per share. The underwriter, on investigation, has found that its administrative costs will be 2 percent of the sale price and its selling costs will be 1.5 percent of the sale price. If the underwriter requires a profit equal to 1 percent of the sale price, how much will the *spread* have to be *in dollars* to cover the underwriter's costs and profits?

  2-4 Bond underwriting analysis   RM International wishes to sell $100 million of bonds whose net proceeds will be used in the acquisition of Little Books. The company has estimated that the net proceeds after paying the underwriting costs should provide an amount sufficient to make the acquisition. The underwriter believes that the 100,000 bonds can be sold to the public at their $1,000 par value. The underwriter estimates that its administrative costs will be $3.5 million. It also must sell the bonds at a .75 percent discount from their par value to members of the selling group. The underwriting commission (in addition to recovery of its administrative costs) is 1 percent of the par value of the offering.
    a. Calculate the per-bond *spread* required by the underwriter to cover its costs.
    b. How much will RM International net from the issue?
    c. How much will the selling group receive? How much will the underwriter receive?

d. Assuming that this is a public offering, describe the nature of the underwriter's risk.

2-5   Yield curve   A firm wishing to evaluate interest rate behavior has gathered yield data on five U.S. Treasury securities, each having a different maturity and all measured at the same point in time. The summarized data follow:

U.S. Treasury security	Time to maturity	Yield
A	1 year	12.6%
B	10 years	11.2
C	6 months	13.0
D	20 years	11.0
E	5 years	11.4

a. Draw the yield curve associated with the data given.
b. Describe the resulting yield curve in **a,** and explain the general expectations embodied in it.

2-6   Term structure of interest rates   The following yield data for a number of highest quality corporate bonds existed at each of the three points in time noted.

Time to maturity (years)	Yield		
	5 years ago	2 years ago	Today
1	9.1%	14.6%	9.3%
3	9.2	12.8	9.8
5	9.3	12.2	10.9
10	9.5	10.9	12.6
15	9.4	10.7	12.7
20	9.3	10.5	12.9
30	9.4	10.5	13.5

a. On the same set of axes, draw the yield curve at each of the three given times.
b. Label each curve in **a** as to its general shape (downward-sloping, upward-sloping, flat).
c. Describe the general inflationary and interest rate expectation existing at each of the three times.

2-7   Risk-free rate and risk premiums   The risk-free rate of interest, R_F, and risk premiums for a number of securities follow:

Security	Risk-free rate of interest, R_F	Risk premium
A	6%	3%
B	9	2
C	8	2
D	5	4
E	11	1

a. Although not noted, what factor must be the cause of the differing risk-free rates shown above?

b. Find the actual rate of interest for each security.

  2-8   Risk premiums   Eleanor Burns is attempting to find the actual rate of interest for each of two securities—A and B—issued by different firms at the same point in time. She has gathered the data shown below.

Characteristic	Security A	Security B
Time to maturity	3 years	15 years
Risk-free rate, R_F	9.0%	6.0%
Risk premium for:		
Default risk	1.0%	2.0%
Maturity risk	0.5%	1.5%
Liquidity risk	1.0%	1.0%
Other risk	0.5%	1.5%

a. Find the total risk premium attributable to each security's issuer and issue characteristics.

b. Calculate the actual rate of interest for each security. Compare and discuss your findings.

C ASE   Chapter 2   **Helping a Friend Understand Yield Curves**

Carl Foster, a friend of yours, is working as a summer intern at an investment banking firm. During Carl's first morning on the job his boss showed him a graph of yield curves and asked what information it conveyed. The phone rang before Carl could answer, and then his boss rushed off to a lunch meeting. Anxious to make a good impression, Carl calls you on his lunch hour, asking you to help him before he sees his boss later in the day. Luckily for Carl, you were at your desk at the Federal Reserve District Bank and are willing to help him by answering the following questions.

Required

a. What does a downward-sloping yield curve indicate about long-term versus short-term borrowing costs?

b. What does an upward-sloping yield curve indicate about long-term versus short-term borrowing costs?

c. With which yield curve is the investment firm likely to get more business?

d. How would a believer in the *expectations hypothesis* explain the shapes of the yield curves?

e. What would a believer in the *liquidity preference theory* say about the effect of lenders' and borrowers' preferences on the shape of the yield curve?

f. What would a believer in the *market segmentation theory* say about the supply and demand for long-term versus short-term funding, given an upward-sloping yield curve?

Web Exercise

GOTO web site www.corpfinet.com. Click on Companies.

1. What are the headings in the left column under the title, Companies?

Now, click on Banks and then click on Top 25.

2. What are the five largest U.S. commercial banks, and what are their asset sizes?

3. Out of the list of top 25 banks, which bank is located geographically closest to you?

4. Prepare a bar graph that indicates how many of these 25 banks' principal offices are located in each state. Do not include in your graph states that have zero or one bank.

5. Which of these banks offer services to small businesses?

6. Name the banks that would help a business that has major international operations.

Under World Listings in the left column, click on Top 10.

7. How large are these banks compared to the banks in the U.S. top 25? *Hint:* Compare asset sizes.

8. How many of these banks have their principal offices in Japan? In the United States?

3

BASIC CORPORATE SECURITIES: BONDS AND STOCKS

LEARNING GOALS

LG1 Describe the legal aspects of bond financing and bond cost.

LG2 Discuss the general features, ratings, popular types, and international issues of corporate bonds.

LG3 Differentiate between debt and equity capital.

LG4 Review common stock ownership, par value, preemptive rights, and other important terminology.

LG5 Discuss common stock voting rights, dividends, and international issues.

LG6 Understand the rights, features, and special types of preferred stock.

ACROSS *the* DISCIPLINES

At some point, most businesses need to raise long-term funds in order to keep growing. By issuing bonds, corporations exchange a long-term IOU for needed funds. By issuing stock, corporations exchange ownership shares of the firm for the needed funds. The purpose of this chapter is to describe the key aspects of these two basic corporate securities. Chapter 3 is important to:

- **accounting personnel** who will estimate the effects on earnings per share of proposed bond and stock offerings.
- **information systems analysts** who will design systems that provide timely information that can be used to monitor and track the market behavior of the firm's outstanding securities.
- **management** because it will choose the appropriate security, its features, and the timing of its issuance.
- **the marketing department** because selling bonds or stock may provide the funds needed to support marketing research and new product development.
- **operations,** which will propose major expenditures that may require bond or stock financing.

CORPORATE BONDS

LG1 LG2

corporate bond
A debt instrument indicating that a corporation has borrowed a certain amount of money and promises to repay it in the future under clearly defined terms.

A **corporate bond** is a debt instrument indicating that a corporation has borrowed a certain amount of money and promises to repay it in the future under clearly defined terms. As described in Chapter 2, most bonds are issued with maturities of 10 to 30 years and with a par, or face, value of $1,000. The *coupon interest rate* on a bond represents the percentage of the bond's par value that will be paid annually, typically in two equal semiannual payments. The bondholders, who are the lenders, are promised the semiannual interest payments and, at maturity, repayment of the principal amount (par value).

LEGAL ASPECTS OF CORPORATE BONDS

Certain legal arrangements are required to protect purchasers of bonds. Bondholders are protected legally primarily through the indenture and the trustee.

BOND INDENTURE

bond indenture
A complex legal document stating the conditions under which a bond has been issued.

A **bond indenture** is a complex legal document stating the conditions under which a bond has been issued. It specifies both the rights of the bondholders and the duties of the issuing corporation. Included in the indenture are the interest and principal payments, various standard and restrictive provisions, and, frequently, sinking-fund requirements and security interest provisions.

standard debt provisions
Provisions in a *bond indenture* specifying certain criteria of satisfactory record keeping and general business maintenance on the part of the borrower (i.e., issuer); normally, they do not place a burden on the financially sound business.

Standard Provisions   The **standard debt provisions** included in the bond indenture specify certain criteria of satisfactory record keeping and general business maintenance on the part of the borrower (i.e., issuer). Standard debt provisions do not normally place a burden on a financially sound business.

Commonly included standard provisions require the borrower to:

1. *Maintain satisfactory accounting records* in accordance with generally accepted accounting principles (GAAP).
2. Periodically *supply audited financial statements,* which the bondholders use to monitor the firm.
3. *Pay taxes and other liabilities when due.*
4. *Maintain all facilities in good working order,* thereby behaving as a "going concern."

restrictive covenants
Contractual clauses in a *bond indenture* that place operating and financial constraints on the borrower.

Restrictive Provisions   Bond indentures normally include certain **restrictive covenants**—contractual clauses that place operating and financial constraints on the borrower. Restrictive covenants, coupled with standard debt provisions, help the bondholder protect itself against increases in borrower risk. Without these provisions, the borrower could "take advantage" of the bondholder by increasing the firm's risk, but not be required to pay the bondholder an increased return (interest). Restrictive covenants remain in force for the life of the bond issue.

The most common restrictive covenants:

1. Require the borrower to *maintain a minimum level of liquidity,* to ensure against loan default and ultimate failure.

2. *Prohibit borrowers from selling accounts receivable* to generate cash. Doing so could cause a long-run cash shortage if proceeds are used to meet current obligations.

3. Impose *fixed-asset restrictions* on the borrower. These constrain the firm with respect to the liquidation or encumbrance of fixed assets, because these actions could damage the firm's ability to repay the bonds.

4. *Constrain subsequent borrowing* by prohibiting additional long-term debt or by requiring that additional borrowing be *subordinated* to the original loan. **Subordination** means that subsequent creditors agree to wait until all claims of the *senior debt* are satisfied.

5. *Limits the firm's annual cash dividend payments* to a specified percentage or amount.

subordination
In a bond indenture, the stipulation that subsequent creditors agree to wait until all claims of the *senior debt* are satisfied.

Other restrictive covenants sometimes included in bond indentures prohibit or limit types of leases, business mergers, and large salary increases for certain employees; require continued employment of "key employees"; limit investment alternatives; or specify how borrowed funds can be used. All of these restrictive covenants are intended to protect bondholders' funds against increased risk.

The violation of any standard or restrictive provision by the borrower gives the bondholders the right to demand immediate repayment of the debt. Generally, the bondholders' representative will evaluate any violation to determine whether it is serious enough to jeopardize the loan. On the basis of such an evaluation, the bondholders may demand immediate repayment, continue the loan, or alter the terms of the bond indenture.

sinking-fund requirement
A restrictive provision that is often included in a bond indenture providing for the systematic retirement of bonds prior to their maturity.

Sinking-Fund Requirements   An additional restrictive provision often included in a bond indenture is a **sinking-fund requirement.** Its objective is to provide for the systematic retirement of bonds prior to their maturity. To carry out this requirement, the corporation makes semiannual or annual payments to a *trustee,* who uses these funds to retire bonds by purchasing them in the marketplace. This process is simplified by inclusion of a *call feature,* which permits the issuer to repurchase bonds at a stated price prior to maturity. The trustee will "call" bonds only when sufficient bonds cannot be purchased in the marketplace or when the market price of the bond is above the stated (call) price.

Security Interest   The bond indenture specifically identifies any collateral pledged against the bond. Usually, the title to the collateral is attached to the indenture, and the disposition of the collateral in various circumstances is specified. The protection of bond collateral is crucial to increase the safety of a bond issue.

trustee
A paid individual, corporation, or commercial bank trust department that acts as the third party to a bond indenture to ensure that the issuer does not default on its contractual responsibilities to the bondholders.

TRUSTEE

A **trustee** is a third party to a bond indenture. The trustee can be an individual, a corporation, or, most often, a commercial bank trust department. The trustee is paid to act as a "watchdog" on behalf of the bondholders, to ensure that the issuer does not default on its contractual responsibilities. The trustee is empowered to take specified actions on behalf of the bondholders if the terms of the indenture are violated.

COST OF BONDS

The cost of bond financing is generally greater than that of short-term borrowing. The bond indenture specifies the interest rate, the timing of payments, and the dollar amount of payments. The major factors affecting the cost, or interest rate, on a bond are its maturity, size of the offering, and, more important, issuer risk and the basic cost of money.

MATURITY

Generally, *long-term debt has higher interest rates than short-term debt.* As noted in Chapter 2, yield curves tend to be upward-sloping (long-term interest rates higher than short-term rates) as a result of several factors: (1) the general expectation of higher future rates of inflation; (2) lender preferences for shorter-term, more liquid loans; and (3) greater demand for long-term than for short-term loans relative to the supply of such loans. In a practical sense, the longer the maturity of a bond, the less accuracy there is in predicting future interest rates, and therefore the greater the bondholders' risk of giving up an opportunity to loan money at a higher rate. In addition, the longer the term, the greater the default risk associated with the bond. To compensate for all of these factors, bondholders typically demand higher interest rates on longer-term issues.

OFFERING SIZE

The *size of the bond offering* also affects the interest cost of borrowing, but in an inverse manner: Bond flotation and administration costs per dollar borrowed are likely to decrease with increasing offering size. On the other hand, the risk of the bondholders may increase, because larger offerings result in greater risk of default. The size of the offering must therefore be evaluated to determine the cost-risk trade-off.

ISSUER RISK

As noted in Chapter 2, the greater the firm's risk, the higher the interest rate. At a given point in time, the *risk premium* above the basic cost of money results from specific issuer- and issue-related components. The bondholders' primary concern is with the issuer's ability to fully repay the loan. The overall assessment of the issuer's risk, typically reflected in *bond ratings* provided by independent agencies (discussed later), is used to set the bond's coupon interest rate.

BASIC COST OF MONEY

The *cost of money in the capital market* is the basis for determining the coupon interest rate. Generally, the rate on U.S. Treasury securities with *equivalent maturities* is used as the basic (lowest-risk) cost of money. To determine the coupon interest rate, a risk premium reflective of the maturity, offering size, and most important, the issuer's default risk is added to the basic cost of money. Frequently, bond buyers rely on *bond ratings* to determine the issuer's overall risk and the required return. Instead of having to determine a risk premium, the bond buyer relies on the risk premium prevailing in the marketplace for similar-risk bonds.

GENERAL FEATURES OF A BOND ISSUE

Three common features of a bond issue are a conversion feature, a call feature, and stock purchase warrants. These features provide both the issuer and the purchaser with certain opportunities for replacing, retiring, and (or) supplementing the bond with some type of equity issue.

CONVERSION FEATURE

conversion feature
A feature of *convertible bonds* that allows bondholders to change each bond into a stated number of shares of common stock.

The **conversion feature** of *convertible bonds* allows bondholders to change each bond into a stated number of shares of common stock. Bondholders will convert their bonds only when the market price of the stock is greater than the conversion price, thus providing a profit.

CALL FEATURE

call feature
A feature that is included in almost all corporate bond issues that gives the issuer the opportunity to repurchase bonds at a stated *call price* prior to maturity.

call price
The stated price at which a bond may be repurchased, by use of a *call feature,* prior to maturity.

call premium
The amount by which a bond's call price exceeds its par value.

The **call feature** is included in almost all corporate bond issues. It gives the issuer the opportunity to repurchase bonds prior to maturity. The **call price** is the stated price at which bonds may be repurchased prior to maturity. Sometimes the call feature can be exercised only during a certain period. As a rule, the call price exceeds the par value of a bond by an amount equal to 1 year's interest. For example, a $1,000 bond with a 10 percent coupon interest rate would be callable for around $1,100 [$1,000 + (10% × $1,000)]. The amount by which the call price exceeds the bond's par value is commonly referred to as the **call premium.** This premium compensates bondholders for having the bond called away from them; to the issuer it is the cost of calling the bonds.

The call feature enables the issuer to retire outstanding debt prior to maturity. Thus, when interest rates fall, an issuer can call an outstanding bond and reissue a new bond at a lower interest rate. When interest rates rise, the call privilege will not be exercised, except possibly to meet sinking-fund requirements. Of course, to sell a callable bond, the issuer must pay a higher interest rate than on noncallable bonds of equal risk, to compensate bondholders for the risk of having the bonds called away from them and the risk of opportunity losses.

STOCK PURCHASE WARRANTS

stock purchase warrants
Instruments that give their holders the right to purchase a certain number of shares of the firm's common stock at a specified price over a certain period of time.

Bonds occasionally have stock purchase warrants attached as "sweeteners" to make them more attractive to prospective buyers. **Stock purchase warrants** are instruments that give their holders the right to purchase a certain number of shares of the firm's common stock at a specified price over a certain period of time. Their inclusion typically allows the firm to raise needed funds at a slightly lower coupon interest rate than would otherwise be required.

BOND RATINGS

Independent agencies such as Moody's and Standard & Poor's assess the riskiness of publicly traded bond issues. Moody's has 9 major ratings; Standard & Poor's has 10. These agencies derive the ratings by using financial ratio and cash flow analyses to assess the likelihood that the issuer will meet its obligations specified in the bond indenture. Table 3.1 summarizes these ratings. Normally an

TABLE 3.1	Moody's and Standard & Poor's Bond Ratings[a]			
Moody's	Interpretation	Standard & Poor's	Interpretation	
Aaa	Prime quality	AAA	Bank investment quality
Aa	High grade	AA	
A	Upper medium grade	A	
Baa	Medium grade	BBB	
Ba	Lower medium grade	BB	Speculative
	or speculative	B	
B	Speculative		
Caa	From very speculative	CCC	
Ca	to near or in default	CC	
C	Lowest grade	C	Income bond
		D	In default

[a]Some ratings may be modified to show relative standing within a major rating category; for example, Moody's uses numerical modifiers (1, 2, 3), whereas Standard & Poor's uses plus (+) and minus (−) signs.

Source: Moody's Investors Services, Inc., and Standard & Poor's Corporation.

inverse relationship exists between the quality or rating of a bond and the rate of return that it must provide bondholders. High-quality (high-rated) bonds provide lower returns than lower-quality (low-rated) bonds. This reflects the lender's risk-return trade-off. When considering bond financing, the financial manager must be concerned with the expected ratings of the bond issue, because these ratings affect salability and cost.

POPULAR TYPES OF BONDS

Bonds can be classified in a variety of ways. Here we break them into traditional bonds—the basic types that have been around for years—and contemporary bonds—newer, more innovative types. The traditional types of bonds are summarized in terms of their key characteristics and priority of lender's claim in Table 3.2. Note that the first three types—**debentures, subordinated debentures,** and **income bonds**—are unsecured, whereas the last three—**mortgage bonds, collateral trust bonds,** and **equipment trust certificates**—are secured.

Table 3.3 describes the key characteristics of five contemporary types of bonds—**zero** (or **low**) **coupon bonds, junk bonds, floating-rate bonds, extendible notes,** and **putable bonds.** These bonds can be either unsecured or secured. In recent years, changing capital market conditions and investor preferences, along with corporate financing needs, have spurred development of further innovations in bond financing.

TABLE 3.2	Characteristics and Priority of Lender's Claim of Traditional Types of Bonds	
Bond type	Characteristics	Priority of lender's claim
Unsecured Bonds		
Debentures	Unsecured bonds that only creditworthy firms can issue. Convertible bonds are normally debentures.	Claims are the same as those of any general creditor. May have other unsecured bonds subordinated to them.
Subordinated debentures	Claims are not satisfied until those of the creditors holding certain (senior) debts have been fully satisfied.	Claim is that of a general creditor but not as good as a senior debt claim.
Income bonds	Payment of interest is required only when earnings are available. Commonly issued in reorganization of a failing firm.	Claim is that of a general creditor. Are not in default when interest payments are missed, because they are contingent only on earnings being available.
Secured Bonds		
Mortgage bonds	Secured by real estate or buildings.	Claim is on proceeds from sale of mortgaged assets; if not fully satisfied, the lender becomes a general creditor. The *first-mortgage* claim must be fully satisfied before distribution of proceeds to *second-mortgage* holders, and so on. A number of mortgages can be issued against the same collateral.
Collateral trust bonds	Secured by stock and (or) bonds that are owned by the issuer. Collateral value is generally 25 to 35 percent greater than bond value.	Claim is on proceeds from stock and (or) bond collateral; if not fully satisfied, the lender becomes a general creditor.
Equipment trust certificates	Used to finance "rolling stock"— airplanes, trucks, boats, railroad cars. A trustee buys the asset with funds raised through the sale of trust certificates and then leases it to the firm, which, after making the final scheduled lease payment, receives title to the asset. A type of leasing.	Claim is on proceeds from the sale of the asset; if proceeds do not satisfy outstanding debt, trust certificate lenders become general creditors.

INTERNATIONAL BOND ISSUES

Companies and governments borrow internationally by issuing bonds in two principal financial markets: the Eurobond and the foreign bond. Both of these provide creditworthy borrowers the opportunity to obtain large amounts of long-term debt financing quickly, in their choice of currency and with flexible repayment terms.

EUROBONDS

Eurobond
A bond issued by an international borrower and sold to investors in countries with currencies other than the currency in which the bond is denominated.

A **Eurobond** is issued by an international borrower and sold to investors in countries with currencies other than the currency in which the bond is denominated. An example would be a dollar-denominated bond issued by a U.S. corporation and sold to Belgian investors.

From the founding of the Eurobond market in the 1960s until the mid-1980s, "blue chip" U.S. corporations were the largest single class of Eurobond issuers. Many of these companies were able to borrow in this market at interest rates below those the U.S. government paid on Treasury bonds it issued. As the

TABLE 3.3 Characteristics of Contemporary Types of Bonds

Bond type	Characteristics[a]
Zero (or low) coupon bonds	Issued with no (zero) or a very low coupon (stated interest) rate and sold at a large discount from par. A significant portion (or all) of the investor's return comes from gain in value (i.e., par value minus purchase price). Generally callable at par value. Because the issuer can annually deduct the current year's interest accrual without having to pay the interest until the bond matures (or is called), its cash flow each year is increased by the amount of the tax shield provided by the interest deduction.
Junk bonds	Debt rated Ba or lower by Moody's or BB or lower by Standard & Poor's. Commonly used during the 1980s by rapidly growing firms to obtain growth capital, most often as a way to finance mergers and takeovers. High-risk bonds with high yields—typically yielding 3 percent more than the best-quality corporate debt.
Floating-rate bonds	Stated interest rate is adjusted periodically within stated limits in response to changes in specified money or capital market rates. Popular when future inflation and interest rates are uncertain. Tend to sell at close to par due to the automatic adjustment to changing market conditions. Some issues provide for annual redemption at par at the option of the bondholder.
Extendible notes	Short maturities, typically 1 to 5 years, that can be renewed for a similar period at the option of holders. Similar to a floating-rate bond. An issue might be a series of 3-year renewable notes over a period of 15 years; every 3 years, the notes could be extended for another 3 years, at a new rate competitive with market interest rates at the time of renewal.
Putable bonds	Bonds that can be redeemed at par (typically, $1,000) at the option of their holder either at specific dates after the date of issue and every 1 to 5 years thereafter or when and if the firm takes specified actions such as being acquired, acquiring another company, or issuing a large amount of additional debt. In return for the right to "put the bond" at specified times or actions by the firm, the bond's yield is lower than that of a nonputable bond.

[a]The claims of lenders (i.e., bondholders) against issuers of each of these types of bonds vary, depending on their other features. Each of these bonds can be unsecured or secured.

market matured, issuers became able to choose the currency in which they borrowed, and European and Japanese borrowers rose to prominence. In more recent years, the Eurobond market has become much more balanced in terms of the mix of borrowers, total issue volume, and currency of denomination.

FOREIGN BONDS

foreign bond
A bond issued in a host country's financial market, in the host country's currency, by a foreign borrower.

Unlike a Eurobond, a **foreign bond** is issued in a host country's financial market, in the host country's currency, by a foreign borrower. A Deutsche-mark–denominated bond issued in Germany by a U.S. company is an example of a foreign bond. The three largest foreign bond markets are Japan, Switzerland, and the United States.

? Review Questions

3-1 What are typical maturities, denominations, and interest payments associated with a corporate bond? Describe the role of the *bond indenture* and the *trustee*.

3-2 Differentiate between *standard debt provisions* and *restrictive covenants* included in a bond indenture.

3-3   What are the consequences of violation of a standard or restrictive provision by the bond issuer?

3-4   What is a *conversion feature?* A *call feature? Stock purchase warrants?* How are bonds rated, and why?

3-5   How does the cost of bond financing typically relate to the cost of short-term borrowing? In addition to a bond's maturity, what other major factors affect its coupon interest rate?

3-6   Describe the basic characteristics of each of the following bond types: (**a**) debenture; (**b**) subordinated debenture; (**c**) income bond; (**d**) zero (or low) coupon bond; (**e**) junk bond; (**f**) floating-rate bond; (**g**) extendible note; and (**h**) putable bond.

3-7   Compare the basic features of the following secured bonds: (**a**) mortgage bond; (**b**) collateral trust bond; and (**c**) equipment trust certificate.

3-8   Describe and compare the basic characteristics of *Eurobonds* and *foreign bonds*.

DIFFERENCES BETWEEN DEBT AND EQUITY CAPITAL

capital
The long-term funds of a firm; all items on the right-hand side of the balance sheet, *excluding current liabilities*.

debt capital
All long-term borrowing, including bonds, incurred by the firm.

equity capital
The long-term funds provided by the firm's owners, the stockholders.

The term **capital** denotes the long-term funds of the firm. All items on the right-hand side of the firm's balance sheet, *excluding current liabilities*, are sources of capital. **Debt capital** includes all long-term borrowing, including bonds, incurred by the firm. **Equity capital** consists of long-term funds provided by the firm's owners, the stockholders. Equity capital can be raised *internally* through retained earnings, or *externally* by selling common or preferred stock. Here we begin with a brief discussion of equity capital, followed by discussions of common stock and preferred stock.

The key differences between debt and equity capital are summarized in Table 3.4. These differences relate to voice in management, claims on the firm's income and assets, maturity, and tax treatment.

TABLE 3.4 **Key Differences Between Debt and Equity Capital**

Characteristic	Type of capital	
	Debt	Equity
Voice in management[a]	No	Yes
Claims on income and assets	Senior to equity	Subordinate to debt
Maturity	Stated	None
Tax treatment	Interest deduction	No deduction

[a]In the event the issuer violates its stated contractual obligations to them, debtholders and preferred stockholders *may* receive a voice in management; otherwise, only common stockholders have voting rights.

VOICE IN MANAGEMENT

Unlike creditors (lenders), holders of equity capital (common and preferred stockholders) are owners of the firm. Holders of common stock have voting rights that permit them to select the firm's directors and to vote on special issues. In contrast, debtholders and preferred stockholders may receive voting privileges only when the firm has violated its stated contractual obligations to them.

CLAIMS ON INCOME AND ASSETS

Holders of equity have claims on both income and assets that are secondary to the claims of creditors. Their *claims on income* cannot be paid until the claims of all creditors, including both interest and scheduled principal payments, have been satisfied. Once these claims have been satisfied, the firm's board of directors decides whether to distribute dividends to the owners.

The equity holders' *claims on assets* of the firm also are secondary to the claims of creditors. If the firm fails, assets are sold, and the proceeds are distributed in this order: employees and customers, the government, creditors, and finally equity holders. Because equity holders are the last to receive any distribution of assets during bankruptcy proceedings, they expect greater returns from dividends and/or increases in stock price.

As will be explained in Chapter 11, the costs of the various forms of equity financing are generally higher than debt costs. One reason is that the suppliers of equity capital take more risk because of their subordinate claims on income and assets. Despite being more costly, equity capital is necessary for the firm to grow and mature. All firms must initially be financed with some common stock equity.

MATURITY

Unlike debt, equity capital is a *permanent form* of financing. It does not "mature," and therefore repayment is not required. Because equity does not mature and will be liquidated only during bankruptcy proceedings, the owners must recognize that although a ready market may exist for the firm's shares, the price that can be realized may fluctuate. This potential fluctuation of the market price of equity makes the overall returns to a firm's owners even more risky.

TAX TREATMENT

Interest payments to debtholders are treated as tax-deductible expenses on the firm's income statement, whereas dividend payments to common and preferred stockholders are not tax-deductible. The tax deductibility of interest lowers the cost of debt financing, thereby further causing the cost of debt financing to be lower than the cost of equity financing.

*P*ERSONAL FINANCE PERSPECTIVE
Bonds or Stocks?

As an investor, should you choose debt or equity instruments—bonds or stocks? As you might imagine, there's no simple answer, and the choice varies for each investor. From the investor's viewpoint, bonds offer steady interest income and relative safety of principal. Generally, the current income offered by bonds is higher than current income from stock dividends. Stocks, on the other hand, offer the potential for substantial—and even spectacular—capital gains, achieved through increases in stock prices, especially for stocks held over the long-term. Overall, stocks usually outperform bonds. The only time that stocks, in general, provide lower overall returns than bonds is in times of rising interest rates. Stock also offers a tax advantage: Because it typically generates greater capital gains than bonds, stock benefits more from the fact that gains are not taxed until the security is sold.

Many people who begin investing get swept up in the excitement of the "investment game" of buying and selling stocks based on tips from friends or their own intuition. (Few people get really excited about bonds.) Although you'll hear boasts from some investors who manage to make money from undisciplined stock speculation, many soon learn two important lessons about investing in stock or bonds: It requires careful thought—about your investment objectives, about where you are in your working and family life, and about how much risk you feel comfortable with. It also requires careful study—of the current and future state of the economy and of the prospects of individual companies that have debt and equity investments to offer you.

Most investors conclude that they do not need to make an either-or choice between bonds and stocks. Rather, most choose some asset allocation combination based on the financial objectives they identify for themselves—such as capital growth, current income needs, or preservation of capital. For example, a portfolio might be 20% invested in cash and cash equivalents, 30% invested in bonds, and 50% invested in stocks. Balancing your investments consistent with your financial goals is the key. As one investor put it, "As much as I love the thrill of playing the stock market, I recognize that holding bonds gives my portfolio the balance it needs at this stage in my life." ●

? R e v i e w Q u e s t i o n

3-9 What are *debt capital* and *equity capital*? What are the key differences between them with respect to voice in management, claims on income and assets, maturity, and tax treatment?

COMMON STOCK

LG4 LG5

The true owners of business firms are the common stockholders. A common stockholder is sometimes referred to as a *residual owner:* In essence he or she has no guarantee of receiving any cash inflows, but instead, receives what is left—the residual—after all other claims on the firm's income and assets have been satisfied. They are assured of only one thing: that they cannot lose any more than they have invested in the firm. As a result of this generally uncertain position, the common stockholder expects to be compensated with adequate dividends and, ultimately, capital gains. Here we discuss the fundamental aspects of common stock: ownership; par value; preemptive rights; authorized, outstanding, and issued shares; voting rights; dividends; and international stock issues.

privately owned (stock)
All common stock of a firm owned by a single individual.

closely owned (stock)
All common stock of a firm owned by a small group of investors (such as a family).

publicly owned (stock)
Common stock of a firm owned by a broad group of unrelated individual or institutional investors.

par value
A relatively useless value, arbitrarily placed on stock in the firm's corporate charter.

no par value
Describes stock that is issued without a *par value,* in which case the stock may be assigned a value or recorded on the firm's books at the price at which it is sold.

OWNERSHIP

The common stock of a firm can be **privately owned** by a single individual, **closely owned** by a small group of investors (such as a family), or **publicly owned** by a broad group of unrelated individual or institutional investors. Typically, small corporations are privately or closely owned, and if their shares are traded, this occurs infrequently and in small amounts. Large corporations, which are emphasized in the following discussions, are publicly owned, and their shares are generally actively traded on the organized or over-the-counter exchanges.

PAR VALUE

Unlike bonds, which always have a par value, common stock may be sold with or without a par value. The **par value** of a common stock is a relatively useless value, established in the firm's corporate charter. It is generally quite low, about $1. Firms often issue stock with **no par value,** in which case they may assign it a value or record it on the books at the price at which it is sold. A low par value may be advantageous in states where certain corporate taxes are based on the par value of stock; if a stock has no par value, the tax may be based on an arbitrarily determined per-share figure. The accounting entries resulting from the sale of common stock can be illustrated by a simple example.

Example ▼ Moxie Company, a soft drink manufacturer, has issued 1,000,000 shares of $2 par-value common stock, receiving proceeds of $50 per share. This results in the following entries on the firm's books:

Common stock (1,000,000 shares at $2 par)	$ 2,000,000
Paid-in capital in excess of par	48,000,000
Common stock equity	$50,000,000

Sometimes the entry "Paid-in capital in excess of par" is labeled "Capital surplus." This value is important because firms are usually prohibited by state law from distributing any paid-in capital as dividends. ▲

preemptive right
Allows common stockholders to maintain their *proportionate* ownership in the corporation when new shares are issued.

dilution of ownership
Occurs when a new stock issue results in each present shareholder having a claim on a *smaller* part of the firm's earnings than previously.

rights
Financial instruments that permit stockholders to purchase additional shares at a price below the market price, in direct proportion to their number of owned shares.

PREEMPTIVE RIGHTS

The **preemptive right** allows common stockholders to maintain their *proportionate* ownership in the corporation when new shares are issued. The preemptive right allows existing shareholders to maintain voting control and protect against the dilution of their ownership. **Dilution of ownership** usually results in the dilution of earnings, because each present shareholder has a claim on a *smaller* part of the firm's earnings than previously.

In a *rights offering,* the firm grants **rights** to its shareholders. These financial instruments permit stockholders to purchase additional shares at a price below the market price, in direct proportion to their number of owned shares. Rights are primarily used by smaller corporations whose shares are either *closely owned* or *publicly owned* and not actively traded. In these situations, rights are an important financing tool without which shareholders would run the risk of losing their proportionate control of the corporation. Rights are rarely used by large publicly owned corporations whose shares are widely held and actively traded because maintenance of proportionate control is not a major concern of their shareholders.

From the firm's viewpoint, the use of rights offerings to raise new equity capital may be less costly and generate more interest than a public offering of stock. An example may help to clarify the use of rights.

authorized shares
The number of shares of common stock that a firm's corporate charter allows without further shareholder approval.

outstanding shares
The number of shares of common stock held by the public.

treasury stock
The number of shares of outstanding stock that have been repurchased by the firm (shown as a deduction from stockholders' equity on the firm's balance sheet).

issued shares
The number of shares of common stock that have been put into circulation; they represent the sum of outstanding shares and treasury stock.

Example ▼ Dominic Company, a regional advertising firm, currently has 100,000 shares of common stock outstanding and is contemplating a rights offering of an additional 10,000 shares. Each existing shareholder will receive one right per share, and each right will entitle the shareholder to purchase one-tenth of a share of new common stock (10,000 ÷ 100,000), so 10 rights will be required to purchase one share of the stock. The holder of 1,000 shares (1 percent) of the outstanding common stock will receive 1,000 rights, each permitting the purchase of one-tenth of a share of new common stock, for a total of 100 new shares. If the shareholder exercises the rights, he or she will end up with a total of 1,100 shares of common stock, or 1 percent of the total number of shares then outstanding (110,000). Thus, the shareholder maintains the same proportion of ownership he or she had prior to the rights offering.   ▲

AUTHORIZED, OUTSTANDING, AND ISSUED SHARES

A firm's corporate charter defines the number of **authorized shares** that it can issue. The firm cannot sell more shares than the charter authorizes without obtaining approval through a shareholder vote. Because it is often difficult to amend the charter to authorize the issuance of additional shares, firms generally attempt to authorize more shares than they initially plan to issue. Authorized shares become **outstanding shares** when they are held by the public. If the *firm* repurchases any of its outstanding shares, these shares are recorded as **treasury stock** (and shown as a deduction from stockholders' equity on the firm's balance sheet). **Issued shares** are the shares of common stock that have been put into circulation; they represent the sum of outstanding shares and treasury stock.

Example ▼ Golden Enterprises, a producer of medical pumps, has the following stockholders' equity account on December 31:

Stockholders' equity	
Common stock—$.80 par value:	
Authorized 35,000,000 shares; issued 15,000,000 shares	$ 12,000,000
Paid-in capital in excess of par	63,000,000
Retained earnings	31,000,000
	$106,000,000
Less: Cost of treasury stock (1,000,000 shares)	4,000,000
Total stockholders' equity	$102,000,000

How many shares of additional common stock can Golden sell without gaining approval from its shareholders? The firm has 35 million authorized shares, 15 million issued shares, and 1 million shares of treasury stock. Thus, 14 million shares are outstanding (15 million issued shares − 1 million shares of treasury stock), and Golden can issue 21 million additional shares (35 million authorized shares − 14 million outstanding shares) without seeking shareholder approval.

⋮
▲ This total includes the treasury shares currently held, which the firm can reissue to the public without obtaining shareholder approval.

VOTING RIGHTS

Generally, each share of common stock entitles the holder to one vote in the election of directors and on special issues. Votes are generally assignable and must be cast at the annual stockholders' meeting.

In recent years, many firms have issued two or more classes of common stock, unequal voting rights being their key difference. The issuance of different classes of stock has been frequently used as a defense against a *hostile takeover* in which an outside group, without management support, tries to gain voting control of the firm by buying its shares in the marketplace. At other times, a class of **nonvoting common stock** is issued when the firm wishes to raise capital through the sale of common stock but does not want to give up its voting control. Issuing classes of stock with unequal voting rights results in some **supervoting shares,** which give their holders more votes per share than a regular share of common stock and allow them to better control the firm's future.

When different classes of common stock are issued on the basis of unequal voting rights, class A common is typically—but not universally—designated as nonvoting, and class B common would have voting rights. Generally, higher classes of shares are given preference in the distribution of earnings (dividends) and assets (in liquidation); lower-class shares, in exchange, receive voting rights. Treasury stock, which is held within the corporation, generally *does not* have voting rights, *does not* earn dividends, and *does not* have a claim on assets in liquidation. Two aspects of voting require special attention—proxies and voting systems.

PROXIES

Because most small stockholders do not attend the annual meeting to vote, they may sign a **proxy statement** giving their votes to another party. The solicitation of proxies from shareholders is closely controlled by the Securities and Exchange Commission, to protect against proxies being solicited on the basis of misleading information. Existing management generally receives the stockholders' proxies, because it is able to solicit them at company expense.

Occasionally, when the firm is widely owned, outsiders may wage a **proxy battle** to unseat the existing management and gain control. To win a corporate election, votes from a majority of the shares voted are required. Proxy battles generally occur when existing management is performing poorly; however, the odds of a nonmanagement group winning a proxy battle are generally slim.

VOTING SYSTEMS

Systems of voting shares may vary from company to company. The two dominant voting systems are majority voting and cumulative voting. Under the **majority voting system,** each stockholder is entitled to one vote for each share of stock owned. The stockholders vote for each position on the board of directors separately, and all stockholders are permitted to vote all of their shares for *each* director favored. The directors receiving the majority of the votes are elected. It is impossible for minority interests to select a director, because each shareholder

nonvoting common stock
Common stock that carries no voting rights; issued when the firm wishes to raise capital through the sale of common stock but does not want to give up its voting control.

supervoting shares
Stock that carries with it more votes per share than a regular share of common stock.

proxy statement
A statement giving the votes of a stockholder to another party.

proxy battle
The attempt by a nonmanagement group to gain control of the management of a firm by soliciting a sufficient number of proxy votes.

majority voting system
The system whereby, in the election of the board of directors, each stockholder is entitled to one vote for each share of stock owned, and he or she can vote all shares for *each* director favored.

cumulative voting system
The system under which each share of common stock is allotted a number of votes equal to the total number of corporate directors to be elected and votes can be given to *any* director(s).

can vote shares for as many candidates desired. As long as management controls a majority of the votes, it can elect all the directors.

Nearly half of all the states, including California, Illinois, and Michigan, require corporations chartered by them to use a **cumulative voting system** in the election of directors; other states permit cumulative voting as long as it is provided for in the corporation's charter. This system gives to each share of common stock a number of votes equal to the total number of directors to be elected. The votes can be given to *any* director(s) the stockholder desires. The advantage of this system is that it provides the minority shareholders with an opportunity to elect at least some directors.

DIVIDENDS

The payment of corporate dividends is at the discretion of the board of directors. Most corporations pay dividends quarterly. Dividends may be paid in cash, stock, or merchandise. Cash dividends are the most common; merchandise dividends are the least common. Common stockholders are not promised a dividend, but they come to expect certain payments based on the historical dividend pattern of the firm. Before dividends are paid to common stockholders, the claims of the government, all creditors, and preferred stockholders must be satisfied. Because of the importance of the dividend decision to the growth and valuation of the firm, detailed discussion of dividends is included in Chapter 13.

INTERNATIONAL STOCK ISSUES

Although the international market for common stock is not as large as the international market for debt securities, cross-border trading and issuance of common stock have increased dramatically in the past 20 years. Much of this increase is due to a growing desire on the part of securities investors to diversify their investment portfolios internationally.

STOCK ISSUED IN FOREIGN MARKETS

These days, corporations are discovering the benefits of issuing stock in foreign markets. For example, several top U.S. multinational companies have listed their stock in half a dozen or more stock markets—the London, Frankfurt, and Tokyo markets being the most popular. Issuing stock internationally both broadens the ownership base and helps a company to integrate itself into the local business scene. A listing on a foreign stock exchange both increases local business press coverage and serves as effective corporate advertising. Having locally traded stock can also facilitate corporate acquisitions because shares can be used as an acceptable method of payment.

FOREIGN STOCK IN U.S. MARKETS

Foreign corporations have also discovered the benefits of trading their stock in the United States. The disclosure and reporting requirements mandated by the U.S. Securities and Exchange Commission have historically discouraged all but the largest foreign firms from directly listing their shares on the New York or

American Stock Exchanges. For example, in 1993, Daimler-Benz became the first large German company to be listed on the NYSE. (Since then, Daimler-Benz and Chrysler have merged.)

Alternatively, most foreign companies tap the U.S. market through **American Depositary Receipts (ADRs)**. These are claims issued by U.S. banks representing ownership of shares of a foreign company's stock held on deposit by the U.S. bank in the foreign market. Because ADRs are issued, in dollars, by a U.S. bank to U.S. investors, they are subject to U.S. securities laws yet still give investors the opportunity to diversify their portfolios internationally.

American Depositary Receipts (ADRs)
Claims issued by U.S. banks representing ownership of shares of a foreign company's stock held on deposit by the U.S. bank in the foreign market and issued in dollars to U.S. investors.

? Review Questions

3-10 Why is the common stockholder considered the true owner of a firm? What risks do common stockholders take that other suppliers of long-term capital do not?

3-11 What is the *preemptive right?* How does it protect against *dilution of ownership?* What are *rights?*

3-12 Explain the relationships among the following: (**a**) authorized shares; (**b**) outstanding shares; (**c**) treasury stock; and (**d**) issued shares.

3-13 How are *proxies* used? Would a *majority* or a *cumulative* voting system be preferred by minority shareholders? Why?

3-14 What are the advantages, to both U.S.-based and foreign corporations, of issuing stock outside of their home markets? What are *American Depositary Receipts (ADRs)?*

LG6 PREFERRED STOCK

Preferred stock gives its holders certain privileges that make them senior to common stockholders. Because of this, firms generally do not issue large quantities of preferred stock. Preferred stockholders are promised a fixed periodic return, which is stated either as a percentage or as a dollar amount. In other words, a 5 percent preferred stock or a $5 preferred stock can be issued. The way the dividend is specified depends on whether the preferred stock has a par value. **Par-value preferred stock** has a stated face value, and its annual dividend is specified as a percentage. The annual dividend is stated in dollars on **no-par preferred stock**, which does not have a stated face value.

Preferred stock is most often issued by public utilities, by acquiring firms in merger transactions, or by firms that are experiencing losses and need additional financing. Public utilities issue preferred stock to increase their fixed-cost financing while increasing equity and avoiding the higher risk associated with debt financing. Preferred stock is used in connection with mergers to give the acquired firm's shareholders a fixed-income security that results in certain tax advantages. Preferred stock is frequently used by firms experiencing losses to raise needed funds. These firms can more easily sell preferred stock than common stock because it gives the preferred stockholder a claim senior to that of the common

par-value preferred stock
Preferred stock with a stated face value that is used with the specified dividend percentage to determine the annual dollar dividend.

no-par preferred stock
Preferred stock with no stated face value but with a stated annual dollar dividend.

stockholders, which therefore is less risky than common stock. Frequently, special features, such as a *conversion feature*, are included to enhance the attractiveness of the preferred stock and lower its cost to the issuer.

BASIC RIGHTS OF PREFERRED STOCKHOLDERS

The basic rights of preferred stockholders with respect to voting, the distribution of earnings, and the distribution of assets are somewhat more favorable than the rights of common stockholders.

VOTING RIGHTS

Preferred stock is often considered *quasi-debt* because, much like interest on debt, it specifies a fixed periodic (dividend) payment. Of course, as ownership, preferred stock is unlike debt in that it has no maturity date. Because their claim on the firm's income is fixed and takes precedence over the claim of common stockholders, preferred stockholders are not exposed to the same degree of risk as common stockholders. They are consequently *not normally given a voting right*.

DISTRIBUTION OF EARNINGS

Preferred stockholders have preference over common stockholders with respect to the *distribution of earnings*. If the stated preferred stock dividend is *passed* (not paid) by the board of directors, the payment of dividends to common stockholders is prohibited. It is this preference in dividend distribution that makes common stockholders the true risk takers with respect to receipt of periodic returns.

DISTRIBUTION OF ASSETS

Preferred stockholders are also usually given preference over common stockholders in the *liquidation of assets* as a result of a firm's bankruptcy, although they must "stand in line" behind creditors. The amount of the claim of preferred stockholders in liquidation is normally equal to the par, or stated, value of the preferred stock.

FEATURES OF PREFERRED STOCK

A number of features are generally included as part of a preferred stock issue. These features, along with a statement of the stock's par value, the amount of dividend payments, the dividend payment dates, and any restrictive covenants, are specified in an agreement similar to a *bond indenture*.

RESTRICTIVE COVENANTS

The restrictive covenants commonly found in a preferred stock issue are aimed at ensuring the continued existence of the firm and regular payment of the stated dividend. These covenants include provisions related to passing dividends, the sale of senior securities, mergers, sales of assets, minimum liquidity requirements, and the payment of common stock dividends or common stock repurchases. The violation of preferred stock covenants usually permits preferred stockholders either to obtain representation on the firm's board of directors or to force the retirement of their stock at or above its par value.

CUMULATION

cumulative preferred stock
Preferred stock for which all passed (unpaid) dividends in arrears must be paid along with the current dividend prior to the payment of dividends to common stockholders.

Most preferred stock is **cumulative** with respect to any dividends passed. That is, all dividends in arrears must be paid along with the current dividend prior to the payment of dividends to common stockholders. If preferred stock is **noncumulative,** passed (unpaid) dividends do not accumulate. In this case, only the current dividend must be paid prior to paying dividends to common stockholders. Because the common stockholders can receive dividends only after the dividend claims of preferred stockholders have been satisfied, it is in the firm's best interest to pay preferred dividends when they are due.[1] The following example will help to clarify the distinction between cumulative and noncumulative preferred stock.

noncumulative preferred stock
Preferred stock for which passed (unpaid) dividends do not accumulate.

Example ▼ Utley Corporation, a manufacturer of specialty automobiles, currently has outstanding an issue of $6 preferred stock on which quarterly dividends of $1.50 are to be paid. Because of a cash shortage, the last two quarterly dividends were passed. The directors of the company have been receiving a large number of complaints from common stockholders, who have, of course, not received any dividends in the past two quarters either. If the preferred stock is cumulative, the company will have to pay its preferred stockholders $4.50 per share ($3.00 of dividends in arrears plus the current $1.50 dividend) prior to paying dividends to its common stockholders. If the preferred stock is noncumulative, the firm must pay only the current $1.50 dividend to its preferred stockholders prior to paying ▲ dividends to its common stockholders.

PARTICIPATION

nonparticipating preferred stock
Preferred stock whose holders receive only the specified dividend payments.

Most issues of preferred stock are **nonparticipating,** which means that preferred stockholders receive only the specified dividend payments. Occasionally, **participating preferred stock** is issued, which allows preferred stockholders to participate with common stockholders in the receipt of dividends beyond a specified amount. This feature is included only when the firm considers it absolutely necessary to obtain badly needed funds.

participating preferred stock
Preferred stock that allows preferred stockholders to participate with common stockholders in the receipt of dividends beyond a specified amount.

CALL FEATURE

Preferred stock is generally *callable,* which means that the issuer can retire outstanding stock within a certain period of time at a specified price. The call option generally cannot be exercised until a specified date. The call price is normally set above the initial issuance price but may decrease according to a predetermined schedule as time passes. Making preferred stock callable provides the issuer with a method of bringing the fixed-payment commitment of the preferred issue to an end.

---

[1]Most preferred stock is cumulative, because it is difficult to sell noncumulative stock. Common stockholders obviously prefer issuance of noncumulative preferred stock, because it does not place them in quite as risky a position. But it is often in the best interest of the firm to sell *cumulative* preferred stock due to its lower cost.

C ONVERSION F EATURE

conversion feature
A feature of *convertible preferred stock* that allows its holders to change each share into a stated number of shares of common stock.

Preferred stock quite often contains a **conversion feature** that allows *holders of convertible preferred stock* to change each share into a stated number of shares of common stock. Sometimes the number of shares of common stock the preferred stock can be exchanged for changes according to a prespecified formula.

SPECIAL TYPES OF PREFERRED STOCK

adjustable-rate (or floating-rate) preferred stock (ARPS)
Preferred stock whose dividend rate is tied to interest rates on specific government securities.

Most preferred stock has a fixed dividend, but some firms issue **adjustable-rate (or floating-rate) preferred stock (ARPS)**. The dividend rate of such stock is tied to interest rates on specific government securities. Rate adjustments are commonly made quarterly, and typically the rate must be kept within preset limits. The appeal of ARPS is the protection that it offers investors against sharp rises in interest rates, because the dividend rate on ARPS will rise with interest rates. From the firm's perspective, adjustable-rate preferreds have appeal, because they can be sold at an initially lower dividend rate and the scheduled dividend rate will fall if interest rates decline.

payment-in-kind (PIK) preferred stock
Preferred stock that pays dividends in additional shares of preferred stock.

A relatively recent innovation in preferred stock financing, **payment-in-kind (PIK) preferred stock** pays dividends in additional shares of preferred stock, which pay dividends in even more preferred stock. After a stated time period, generally 5 or 6 years, PIK preferreds are supposed to begin paying cash dividends or provide holders with a chance to swap for another, more traditional security. These preferreds are essentially the equivalent of *junk bonds* and, like them, are issued to finance corporate takeovers. PIK preferreds are not viewed as a major corporate financing tool.

R e v i e w   Q u e s t i o n s

3–15 What is *preferred stock?* What claims do preferred stockholders have with respect to the distribution of earnings (dividends) and assets?

3–16 What are *cumulative* and *noncumulative* preferred stock? Which form is more common? Why?

3–17 What is a *call feature* in a preferred stock issue? What is an *adjustable-rate (or floating-rate) preferred stock (ARPS)?*

S UMMARY

LG1 **Describe the legal aspects of bond financing and bond cost.** Corporate bonds are debt instruments indicating that a corporation has borrowed a certain amount that it promises to repay in the future under clearly defined terms. Most bonds are issued with maturities of 10 to 30 years and a par value of $1,000. The bond indenture, enforced by a trustee, states all conditions of the bond issue. It contains both standard debt provisions and restrictive covenants, which may include a sinking-

fund requirement and/or a security interest. The interest rate on a bond depends on its maturity, offering size, issuer risk, and the basic cost of money.

LG2 **Discuss the general features, ratings, popular types, and international issues of corporate bonds.** A bond issue may include a conversion feature, a call feature, or stock purchase warrants. Bond ratings by independent agencies indicate the risk of a bond issue. A variety of traditional and contemporary types of bonds, some unsecured and others secured, are available; Tables 3.2 and 3.3 list them and summarize their characteristics. Eurobonds and foreign bonds enable established creditworthy companies and governments to borrow large amounts internationally.

LG3 **Differentiate between debt and equity capital.** Holders of equity capital (common and preferred stock) are owners of the firm. Typically only common stockholders have a voice in management through their voting rights. Equity holders have claims on income and assets that are secondary to the claims of creditors, have no maturity date, and do not receive tax benefits similar to those given to debtholders.

LG4 **Review common stock ownership, par value, preemptive rights, and other important terminology.** A common stockholder is a residual owner who receives what is left after all other claims have been satisfied. The common stock of a firm can be privately owned, closely owned, or publicly owned. It can be sold with or without a par value. Preemptive rights allow common stockholders to avoid dilution of ownership when new shares are issued. The firm grants rights to stockholders to purchase new shares in proportion to their number of owned shares at a price below the market price. Not all shares authorized in the corporate charter

are outstanding. If a firm has treasury stock, it will have issued more shares than are outstanding.

LG5 **Discuss common stock voting rights, dividends, and international issues.** Some firms have two or more classes of common stock, whose key difference is unequal voting rights. Proxies transfer voting rights from one party to another. Either majority voting or cumulative voting, which gives minority shareholders an opportunity to elect at least some directors, may be used by the firm to elect its directors. Dividend distributions to common stockholders are made at the sole discretion of the firm's board of directors. Firms can issue stock in foreign markets. Likewise, the stock of many foreign corporations is traded in the form of American Depositary Receipts (ADRs) in U.S. markets.

LG6 **Understand the rights, features, and special types of preferred stock.** Preferred stockholders have preference over common stockholders with respect to the distribution of earnings and assets and so are normally not given voting privileges. Preferred stock issues may have certain restrictive covenants, cumulative dividends, participation in earnings, a call feature, and a conversion feature. Special types of preferred stock include adjustable-rate (or floating-rate) preferred stock (ARPS) and payment-in-kind (PIK) preferred stock. Whereas most preferred stock is similar to debt in that it has stated fixed annual cash dividends, these special types do not.

PROBLEMS

  3-1 Bond interest payments   Charter Corp. has issued 2,5000 debentures with a total principal value of $2,500,000. The bonds have a coupon rate of 7 percent.
  a. What dollar amount of interest per bond can an investor expect to receive each year from Charter Corp.?
  b. What is Charter's total interest expense per year associated with this bond issue?

 3-2 Accounting for common stock   What accounting entries would be made on the firm's balance sheet in the following cases?
  a. A firm sells 10,000 shares of $1-par common stock at $13 per share.
  b. A firm sells 20,000 shares of $2-par common stock and receives $100,000.
  c. A firm sells 200,000 shares of no-par common stock for $8 million.
  d. A firm sells 14,000 shares of common stock for the par value of $5 per share.

3-3   Authorized and available shares   Aspin Corporation's charter authorizes issuance of 2,000,000 shares of common stock. Currently, 1,400,000 shares are outstanding and 100,000 shares are being held as treasury stock. The firm wishes to raise $48,000,000 for a plant expansion. Discussions with its investment bankers indicate that the sale of new common stock will net the firm $60 per share.

a. What is the maximum number of new shares of common stock the firm can sell without receiving further authorization from shareholders?

b. Based on the data given and your finding in **a**, will the firm be able to raise the needed funds without receiving further authorization?

c. What must the firm do to obtain authorization to issue more than the number of shares found in **a**?

3-4   Preferred dividends   Slater Lamp Manufacturing has an outstanding issue of preferred stock with an $80 par value and an 11 percent annual dividend.

a. What is the annual dollar dividend? If it is paid quarterly, how much will be paid each quarter?

b. If the preferred stock is *noncumulative* and the board of directors has passed the preferred dividend for the last 3 years, how much must be paid to preferred stockholders before dividends are paid to common stockholders?

c. If the preferred stock is *cumulative* and the board of directors has passed the preferred dividend for the last 3 years, how much must be paid to preferred stockholders before dividends are paid to common stockholders?

3-5   Preferred dividends   In each case in the following table, how many dollars of preferred dividends per share must be paid to preferred stockholders before common stock dividends are paid?

Case	Type	Par value	Dividend per share per period	Periods of dividends passed
A	Cumulative	$ 80	$5	2
B	Noncumulative	110	8%	3
C	Noncumulative	100	$11	1
D	Cumulative	60	8.5%	4
E	Cumulative	90	9%	0

3-6   Participating preferred stock   Union Shipping Company has outstanding an issue of 3,000 shares of participating preferred stock that has a $100 par value and an 8 percent annual dividend. The preferred stockholders participate fully (on an equal per-share basis) with common stockholders in annual dividends of more than $9 per share for common stock. The firm has 5,000 shares of common stock outstanding.

a. If the firm pays preferred stockholders their dividends and then declares an additional $100,000 in dividends, what is the total dividend per share for preferred and common stock?

b. If the firm pays preferred stockholders their dividends and then declares an additional $40,000 in dividends, what is the total dividend per share for each type of stockholder?

c. If the firm's preferred stock is *cumulative* and the past 2 years' dividends have been passed, what dividends will be received by each type of stockholder if the firm declares a *total* dividend of $30,000?

d. Rework **c** assuming that the total dividend payment is $20,000.

e. Rework **a** and **b** assuming that the preferred stock is nonparticipating.

CASE   Chapter 3   **Financing Lobo Enterprises' Expansion Program**

Lobo Enterprises, based in Dallas, began as a small radio station. In 1985 it used a sizable loan to purchase a much larger company involved in the exterminating business and has acquired other businesses since then. Net earnings have risen continuously through 2000, 12 years since Lobo Enterprises first went public. Currently, the firm's equity base is quite small in comparison to the amount of debt financing on its books. The company is also doing well in its media, wall-covering, and burglary and fire protection systems businesses. Most important, the exterminating business—benefiting from wider markets, new customers, and higher fees—is performing magnificently. In the fiscal year ended June 30, 2000, gross income at Lobo Enterprises rose 17 percent; profits were held down somewhat by startup costs in several new businesses. Lobo's capital outlays have approximated $11 million in each of the past two fiscal years, but higher expansion levels are likely in the near future and are expected to require an additional $23 million of financing.

A few years ago, Lobo's long-term debt equaled 85 percent of total capital, but debt has since been reduced to 70 percent of total capital. The debt carries an average interest rate of 11.7 percent before taxes. The debt reduction was partially financed through issuance of $7.7 million of 10 percent (annual dividend) preferred stock.

Currently, the directors must decide on a method of financing the $23 million expansion. They are primarily interested in an equity financing plan, because funds could be obtained without incurring added mandatory interest payments that would result in greater risk. Additional equity would allow Lobo Enterprises to avoid restrictive covenants that are often tied to bond financing and would provide a more flexible foundation from which bonds could be issued when interest rates fall. The decision, however, could result in lowering earnings per share (EPS) as well as diluting the current stockholders' control of the company. Rebecca Marks, the chief financial officer, has been charged with advising Lobo's board with regard to common and preferred stock financing alternatives.

Required

a. Discuss the overall advantages of equity financing for Lobo Enterprises at this time.

b. Discuss the advantages and disadvantages of selling common stock. Compare and contrast its use to the use of bond financing.

c. Discuss the advantages and disadvantages of selling preferred stock. Compare and contrast its use to the use of common stock financing.

d. In the event Lobo Enterprises decides to use common stock financing, discuss the advantages and disadvantages of using a rights offering rather than the public sale of new common stock.

e. Based solely on the nonquantitative factors discussed in **a** through **d,** what recommendation should Rebecca Marks make to Lobo's board about how to finance the firm's $23 million need? Justify your recommendation in light of the alternatives.

GOTO web site www.gap.com. Click on company and then on financials to find information to answer the following questions.

1. When was Gap stock initially offered for public sale? What was its price then?
2. What is Gap's current stock price?
3. What were Gap's sales for the most recent three months? What were its quarterly earnings?
4. How much was Gap's most recent dividend per share?
5. How many shares of stock does Gap have outstanding? Does the company have any preferred stock? (You'll have to look at the company's financial statements to answer this question.)

FINANCIAL STATEMENTS, TAXES, DEPRECIATION, AND CASH FLOW

LG1 Describe the purpose and basic components of the stockholders' report.

LG2 Review the purpose and key components of the income statement, the balance sheet, the statement of retained earnings, and the statement of cash flows.

LG3 Discuss the fundamentals of business taxation of ordinary income and capital gains.

LG4 Understand the effect of depreciation and other noncash charges on the firm's cash flows.

LG5 Determine the depreciable value of an asset, its depreciable life, and the amount of depreciation allowed each year for tax purposes.

LG6 Discuss the firm's cash flows and interpret the statement of cash flows.

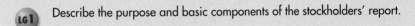

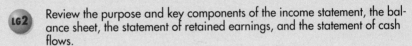

ACROSS *the* DISCIPLINES

All companies gather and analyze financial data about their operations, and report the resulting information to interested parties such as owners and managers. Most companies issue an annual stockholders' report in which they publish this information using, at minimum, four basic financial statements. The purpose of this chapter is to review the content of those four statements and to describe the impact of taxes and depreciation on the firm's cash flows—a relationship central to finance. Chapter 4 is important to:

- **accounting personnel** who calculate depreciation for tax purposes and determine the best depreciation method for financial reporting purposes.
- **information systems analysts** who will design the financial information system necessary to prepare the financial statements.
- **management** because it will maintain a dual focus on the company's cash flows and profit and loss.
- **the marketing department** because its decisions will have significant effects on the firm's cash flows and financial statements.
- **operations,** whose actions will significantly impact the company's cash flows and profit and loss.

THE STOCKHOLDERS' REPORT

Every corporation has many and varied uses for the standardized records and reports of its financial activities. Periodically, reports must be prepared for regulators, creditors (lenders), owners, and management. Regulators, such as federal and state securities commissions, enforce the accurate disclosure of corporate financial data. Creditors use financial data to evaluate the firm's ability to meet scheduled debt payments. Owners use financial data to decide whether to buy, sell, or hold a firm's stock. Management is concerned with regulatory compliance, satisfying creditors and owners, and monitoring the firm's performance.

The guidelines used to prepare and maintain financial records and reports are known as **generally accepted accounting principles (GAAP)**. These accounting practices and procedures are authorized by the accounting profession's rule-setting body, the **Financial Accounting Standards Board (FASB)**. *Publicly owned* corporations are required by the **Securities and Exchange Commission (SEC)**—the federal regulatory body that governs the sale and listing of securities—to provide their stockholders with an annual **stockholders' report.**[1] The annual report summarizes and documents the firm's financial activities during the past year. It begins with a letter to the stockholders from the firm's president and/or chairman of the board.

THE LETTER TO STOCKHOLDERS

The **letter to stockholders** is the primary communication from management to the firm's owners. It describes the events that are considered to have had the greatest impact on the firm during the year. In addition, the letter generally discusses management philosophy and strategies, as well as plans for the coming year and their anticipated effects on the firm's financial condition. Figure 4.1 includes the letter to the stockholders of Intel Corporation, a major supplier (1998 sales of about $26.3 billion) to the personal computing industry. The majority of the personal computers in use around the world today are based on Intel-architecture microprocessors. The letter discusses Intel's 1998 results, key research initiatives, growth strategy, and management realignment.

FINANCIAL STATEMENTS

Following the letter to stockholders will be, at minimum, the four key financial statements required by the SEC. These statements are (1) the income statement, (2) the balance sheet, (3) the statement of retained earnings, and (4) the statement of cash flows.[2] The annual corporate report must contain these statements

---

generally accepted accounting principles (GAAP)
The practice and procedure guidelines used to prepare and maintain financial records and reports; authorized by the *Financial Accounting Standards Board (FASB).*

Financial Accounting Standards Board (FASB)
The accounting profession's rule-setting body, which authorizes *generally accepted accounting principles (GAAP).*

Securities and Exchange Commission (SEC)
The federal regulatory body that governs the sale and listing of securities.

stockholders' report
Annual report required of *publicly owned* corporations that summarizes and documents for stockholders the firm's financial activities during the past year.

letter to stockholders
In the annual stockholders' report, the primary communication from management to the firm's owners.

---

[1]Although the Securities and Exchange Commission (SEC) does not have an official definition of "publicly owned," it requires informational reporting from corporations whose stock is traded on an organized exchange or over the counter and/or those with more than $5 million in assets and 500 or more stockholders, regardless of whether the firm publicly sells its securities. Firms that do not meet these requirements are commonly called "closely owned" firms.

[2]It is important to recognize that in practice, companies frequently use different statement titles. For example, General Electric uses "Statement of Earnings" rather than "Income Statement" and "Statement of Financial Position" rather than "Balance Sheet"; Bristol Myers Squibb uses "Statement of Earnings and Retained Earnings" rather than "Income Statement"; and Pfizer uses "Statement of Shareholders' Equity" rather than "Statement of Retained Earnings."

FIGURE 4.1   Letter to Stockholders of Intel Corporation

To our stockholders,

We faced extraordinary conditions in 1998. Competition in the value PC market segment, inventory corrections among some of our large customers in the first half of the year and an economic slowdown in some parts of the world all took their toll. As a consequence, our financial results in the first half of the year were not as strong as we would have liked. Revenues for the year were up 5%, with net income down 13% to $6.1 billion. At the same time, beneath these choppy waters, we were undergoing a fundamental sea change in how we see our business. The Internet is transforming the nature of the computing industry. As a leading provider of key computing and communications building blocks, we play a central role in this revolution. We are confident that our actions have helped us ride out the turbulence of 1998, and we are excited about our strategic plans to help drive the development of an increasingly connected computing world.

New products for all levels. With hindsight, it's clear that we were caught off guard by the increase in demand for low-cost PCs. We were late in recognizing the emergence of this value PC market segment—and the competition took advantage of our delay. While our global position remains strong, we lost market share in the U.S. retail segment of the market (which is about 10% of the worldwide PC market). We have redoubled our efforts to regain that share, with focused product development.

In response to the evolving computing marketplace, it was clear that we had to drive our business in a new way. We developed a broad game plan that would enable us to participate in every level of the newly segmented computing market. We revamped our microprocessor lineup with new products created specifically for each computing segment:

• Our Intel® Celeron™ microprocessor, introduced in April and followed in August by an enhanced version, offers entry-level PC buyers good value and reliable Intel technology. By the end of 1998, it was the second-highest volume PC microprocessor in the world, second only to the Pentium® II microprocessor.

• Our Pentium II microprocessor remains the heart of our business. Ideal for the performance desktop and entry-level servers and workstations, this powerful processor makes up the majority of units we sold worldwide in 1998.

• The powerhouse Pentium® II Xeon™ microprocessor, introduced in August, is specifically designed for mid- and high-range servers and workstations. Manufacturers can benefit by designing systems to harness the power of multiple high-performance processors. Demand for servers and workstations is increasing, and within both of these segments, sales of systems based on Intel architecture are growing much faster than the overall segment.

Our segmentation strategy is designed to allow us to participate profitably in various segments of the computing market and to pursue new growth opportunities in the high-end server and workstation market segments. Supported by our strong branding program, which conveys the benefits of Intel technology and the attributes of the products at each level, our segmentation strategy is working as intended.

1998 Geographic breakdown of revenues

Japan 7%
Asia-Pacific 20%
North America 45%
Europe 28%

Adjusting to a cost-competitive environment. 1998 found us operating in a more cost-competitive marketplace. We responded by setting aggressive new targets in cost management and manufacturing efficiency. With belt tightening in discretionary spending and some headcount reductions, we adjusted to an environment that demands leaner operations. We ended the year with headcount down 2% (excluding acquisitions) and our human resources employed in the areas of maximum return.

We also made great strides in manufacturing efficiency through a successful and rapid ramp to our new 0.25-micron process technology. With each new generation of our manufacturing process, the dimensions shrink on the finished chip, giving higher product yields as well as more powerful products.

In 1998, we also developed an innovative new packaging technology for our microprocessors, the Organic LAN Grid Array, that provides higher performance and versatility at lower cost for the final product. We are the only major chip maker using this packaging. We continue to invest in the state-of-the-art manufacturing facilities and R&D programs that make such innovations possible, spending $4 billion for capital additions and $2.7 billion for R&D in 1998.

The Internet drives an industry shift. Throughout the turbulence of the first half of the year, we were also adapting to a more fundamental shift in our business. Ten years ago, people bought PCs for personal productivity needs—spreadsheets, word processing and the like. Today, the number one reason people buy PCs is to get on the Internet. As the computing universe becomes connected, the demands on PCs and the entire computing infrastructure are expanding.

On a networked PC, every click of the mouse sets in motion a series of invisible and demanding tasks: compression and decompression of bulky downloads, encryption, virus scans and security checks, among others. These tasks have to be executed quickly and accurately behind the scenes, and they require powerful PCs. At the same time, behind the connected PCs is a large number of powerful servers, delivering data to the desktop and performing some of those compute-intensive functions. The number of servers is increasing as the Internet expands, providing a growing market segment for our products. We consider this opportunity so significant that more than half of Intel's microprocessor R&D investment is now committed to workstations and servers.

We also have a rapidly growing network products business, with software and hardware products designed to make it easier to connect and manage networked PCs for small businesses, large enterprises and home users. As part of our commitment to networking, we acquired Case Technology and Dayna Communications Inc. in 1997, and have entered into an agreement to acquire Shiva Corporation. These companies provide key technologies for improving Internet performance.

In addition to providing the powerful processors that are the key building blocks of the Internet and network products, we are engaging with other industry leaders in initiatives to expand Internet capabilities and product offerings. In 1998, our Corporate Business Development group made more than 100 new equity investments to help spur development of computer and Internet capabilities.

The Internet has stimulated the most intensely competitive cycle and development boom in the history of the computing industry. Being connected is now at the center of people's computing experience. The resulting opportunities have made our direction clear: to help drive the growth of the connected world. In 1999 and beyond, we will pursue our strategic intent to be a major force behind the Internet revolution.

Gordon E. Moore
Chairman Emeritus

Andrew S. Grove
Chairman

Craig R. Barrett
President and CEO

for at least the three most recent years of operation (2 years for balance sheets). Following the financial statements are Notes to Financial Statements—an important source of information on the accounting policies, procedures, calculations, and transactions underlying entries in the financial statements. Historical summaries of key operating statistics for the past 5 to 10 years are also commonly included with the financial statements.

OTHER FEATURES

The stockholders' reports of most widely held corporations also include discussions of the firm's activities, new products, research and development, and the like. Most companies view the annual report not only as a requirement, but also as an important vehicle for influencing owners' perceptions of the company.

? R e v i e w   Q u e s t i o n s

4-1   What are *generally accepted accounting principles (GAAP)* and who authorizes them? What role does the *Securities and Exchange Commission (SEC)* play in the financial reporting activities of U.S. corporations?
4-2   Describe the basic contents, including the key financial statements, of the stockholders' reports of publicly owned corporations.

THE FOUR KEY FINANCIAL STATEMENTS

Our chief concern in this section is to understand the factual information presented in the four required financial statements. We use the financial statements from the 2000 stockholders' report of a hypothetical firm, Elton Corporation.

INCOME STATEMENT

income statement
Provides a financial summary of the firm's operating results during a specified period.

The **income statement** provides a financial summary of the firm's operating results during a specified period. Most common are income statements covering a 1-year period ending at a specified date, ordinarily December 31 of the calendar year. Many large firms, however, operate on a 12-month financial cycle, or *fiscal year,* that ends at a time other than December 31. Monthly income statements are typically prepared for use by management, and quarterly statements must be made available to the stockholders of publicly owned corporations.

Table 4.1 presents Elton Corporation's income statement for the year ended December 31, 2000. The statement begins with *sales revenue*—the total dollar amount of sales during the period—from which the cost of goods sold is deducted. The resulting *gross profits* of $700,000 represent the amount remaining to satisfy operating, financial, and tax costs after meeting the costs of producing or purchasing the products sold.

TABLE 4.1	Elton Corporation Income Statement ($000) for the Year Ended December 31, 2000	
Sales revenue		$1,700
Less: Cost of goods sold		1,000
Gross profits		$ 700
Less: Operating expenses		
Selling expense	$ 80	
General and administrative expense	150	
Depreciation expense	100	
Total operating expense		330
Operating profits		$ 370
Less: Interest expense		70
Net profits before taxes		$ 300
Less: Taxes (rate = 40%)		120
Net profits after taxes		$ 180
Less: Preferred stock dividends		10
Earnings available for common stockholders		$ 170
Earnings per share (EPS)[a]		$ 1.70

[a]Calculated by dividing the earnings available for common stockholders by the number of shares of common stock outstanding ($170,000 ÷ 100,000 shares = $1.70 per share).

Next, *operating expenses,* which include selling expense, general and administrative expense, and depreciation expense, are deducted from gross profits.[3] The resulting *operating profits* of $370,000 represent the profits earned from producing and selling products; this amount does not consider financial and tax costs. (Operating profit is often called *earnings before interest and taxes,* or *EBIT.*) Next, the financial cost—*interest expense*—is subtracted from operating profits to find *net profits* (or *earnings*) *before taxes.* After subtracting $70,000 in 2000 interest, Elton Corporation had $300,000 of net profits before taxes.

After the appropriate tax rates have been applied to before-tax profits, taxes are calculated and deducted to determine *net profits* (or *earnings*) *after taxes.* Elton Corporation's net profits after taxes for 2000 were $180,000. Next, any preferred stock dividends must be subtracted from net profits after taxes to arrive at *earnings available for common stockholders.* This is the amount earned by the firm on behalf of the common stockholders during the period. Dividing earnings available for common stockholders by the number of shares of common stock outstanding results in *earnings per share (EPS).* EPS represents the amount earned during the accounting period on each outstanding share of common

---

[3]Depreciation expense can be, and frequently is, included in manufacturing costs—cost of goods sold—to calculate gross profits. Depreciation is shown as an expense in this text to isolate its impact on cash flows.

stock. In 2000, Elton Corporation earned $170,000 for its common stockholders, which represents $1.70 for each outstanding share.

BALANCE SHEET

balance sheet
Summary statement of the firm's financial position at a given point in time.

The **balance sheet** presents a summary statement of the firm's financial position at a given point in time. The statement balances the firm's *assets* (what it owns) against its financing, which can be either *debt* (what it owes) or *equity* (what was provided by owners). Elton Corporation's balance sheets on December 31 of 2000 and 1999 are presented in Table 4.2. They show a variety of asset, liability (debt), and equity accounts.

current assets
Short-term assets, expected to be converted into cash within 1 year or less.

An important distinction is made between short-term and long-term assets and liabilities. The **current assets** and **current liabilities** are *short-term* assets and liabilities. This means that they are expected to be converted into cash (current assets) or to be paid (current liabilities) within 1 year or less. All other assets and liabilities, along with stockholders' equity, which is assumed to have an infinite life, are considered *long-term*, or *fixed*, because they are expected to remain on the firm's books for 1 year or more.

current liabilities
Short-term liabilities, expected to be paid within 1 year or less.

As is customary, the assets are listed beginning with the most liquid down to the least liquid. Current assets therefore precede fixed assets. *Marketable securities* represent very liquid short-term investments, such as U.S. Treasury bills or certificates of deposit, held by the firm. Because of their highly liquid nature, marketable securities are frequently viewed as a form of cash. *Accounts receivable* represent the total monies owed the firm by its customers on credit sales made to them. *Inventories* include raw materials, work in process (partially finished goods), and finished goods held by the firm. The entry for *gross fixed assets* is the original cost of all fixed (long-term) assets owned by the firm.[4] *Net fixed assets* represent the difference between gross fixed assets and *accumulated depreciation*—the total expense recorded for the depreciation of fixed assets. (The net value of fixed assets is called their *book value*.)

Like assets, the liabilities and equity accounts are listed on the balance sheet from short-term to long-term. Current liabilities include *accounts payable*, amounts owed for credit purchases by the firm; *notes payable*, outstanding short-term loans, typically from commercial banks; and *accruals*, amounts owed for services for which a bill may not or will not be received. (Examples of accruals include taxes due the government and wages due employees.) *Long-term debt* represents debt for which payment is not due in the current year.

Stockholders' equity represents the owners' claims on the firm. The *preferred stock* entry shows the historic proceeds from the sale of preferred stock ($100,000 for Elton Corporation). Next, the amount paid in by the original purchasers of common stock is shown by two entries—common stock and paid-in capital in excess of par on common stock. The *common stock* entry reflects the *par value* of common stock. **Paid-in capital in excess of par** represents the amount of proceeds in excess of the par value received from the original sale of common stock. The sum of the common stock and paid-in capital accounts divided by the number of shares outstanding represents the original price per

paid-in capital in excess of par
The amount of proceeds in excess of the *par value* received from the original sale of common stock.

---

[4]For convenience the term *fixed assets* is used throughout this text to refer to what, in a strict accounting sense, is captioned "property, plant, and equipment." This simplification of terminology permits certain financial concepts to be more easily developed.

TABLE 4.2	Elton Corporation Balance Sheets ($000)		
		December 31	
Assets		2000	1999
Current assets			
Cash		$ 400	$ 300
Marketable securities		600	200
Accounts receivable		400	500
Inventories		600	900
Total current assets		$2,000	$1,900
Gross fixed assets (at cost)			
Land and buildings		$1,200	$1,050
Machinery and equipment		850	800
Furniture and fixtures		300	220
Vehicles		100	80
Other (includes certain leases)		50	50
Total gross fixed assets (at cost)		$2,500	$2,200
Less: Accumulated depreciation		1,300	1,200
Net fixed assets		$1,200	$1,000
Total assets		$3,200	$2,900
Liabilities and stockholders' equity			
Current liabilities			
Accounts payable		$ 700	$ 500
Notes payable		600	700
Accruals		100	200
Total current liabilities		$1,400	$1,400
Long-term debt		$ 600	$ 400
Total liabilities		$2,000	$1,800
Stockholders' equity			
Preferred stock		$ 100	$ 100
Common stock—$1.20 par, 100,000 shares outstanding in 2000 and 1999		120	120
Paid-in capital in excess of par on common stock		380	380
Retained earnings		600	500
Total stockholders' equity		$1,200	$1,100
Total liabilities and stockholders' equity		$3,200	$2,900

retained earnings
The cumulative total of all earnings, net of dividends, that have been retained and reinvested in the firm since its inception.

share received by the firm on a single issue of common stock. Elton Corporation therefore received $5.00 per share [($120,000 par + $380,000 paid-in capital in excess of par) ÷ 100,000 shares] from the sale of its common stock. Finally, **retained earnings** represent the cumulative total of all earnings, net of dividends, that have been retained and reinvested in the firm since its inception. It is important to recognize that retained earnings *are not cash* but rather have been utilized to finance the firm's assets.

Elton Corporation's balance sheets show that the firm's total assets increased from $2,900,000 in 1999 to $3,200,000 in 2000. The $300,000 increase was due primarily to the $200,000 increase in net fixed assets. The asset increase, in turn, appears to have been financed primarily by an increase of $200,000 in long-term debt. Better insight into these changes can be derived from the statement of cash flows, which we will discuss shortly.

STATEMENT OF RETAINED EARNINGS

statement of retained earnings
Reconciles the net income earned during a given year, and any cash dividends paid, with the change in retained earnings between the start and end of that year.

The **statement of retained earnings** reconciles the net income earned during a given year, and any cash dividends paid, with the change in retained earnings between the start and end of that year. Table 4.3 presents this statement for Elton Corporation for the year ended December 31, 2000. A review of the statement shows that the company began the year with $500,000 in retained earnings and had net profits after taxes of $180,000, from which it paid a total of $80,000 in dividends, resulting in year-end retained earnings of $600,000. Thus, the net increase for Elton Corporation was $100,000 ($180,000 net profits after taxes minus $80,000 in dividends) during 2000.

STATEMENT OF CASH FLOWS

statement of cash flows
Provides a summary of the firm's operating, investment, and financing cash flows during the period of concern.

The **statement of cash flows** provides a summary of the cash flows over the period of concern, typically, the year just ended. The statement, which is sometimes called a "source and use statement," provides insight into the firm's operating, investment, and financing cash flows. Elton Corporation's statement of cash flows for the year ended December 31, 2000, is presented in Table 4.9 on page 95. However, before we look at the development of this statement, it is helpful to understand various aspects of taxation and depreciation.

TABLE 4.3	Elton Corporation Statement of Retained Earnings ($000) for the Year Ended December 31, 2000		
Retained earnings balance (January 1, 2000)			$500
Plus: Net profits after taxes (for 2000)			180
Less: Cash dividends (paid during 2000)			
Preferred stock		($10)	
Common stock		(70)	
Total dividends paid			(80)
Retained earnings balance (December 31, 2000)			$600

? R e v i e w   Q u e s t i o n

4-3   What basic information is contained in: (a) the income statement; (b) the balance sheet; and (c) the statement of retained earnings? Briefly describe each.

BUSINESS TAXATION

LG3

Businesses, like individuals, must pay taxes on income. The income of sole proprietorships and partnerships is taxed as the income of the individual owners, whereas corporate income is subject to corporate taxes. Regardless of their legal form, all businesses can earn two types of income—ordinary and capital gains. Under current law, the tax treatment of these two types of income differs for those taxed as individuals; it does not differ for those subject to corporate taxes. Frequent amendments in the tax code, such as the *Internal Revenue Reconstructing and Reform Act of 1998*, which is reflected in the following discussions, make it likely that these rates will change before the next edition of this text is published. Because the corporation is financially dominant in our economy, *emphasis here is given to corporate taxation.*

ORDINARY INCOME

ordinary income
Income earned through the sale of a firm's goods or services.

The **ordinary income** of a corporation is income earned through the sale of a firm's goods or services. Ordinary income is currently taxed subject to the rates depicted in the corporate tax rate schedule in Table 4.4.

TABLE 4.4   Corporate Tax Rate Schedule

Range of taxable income	Base tax	+	(Rate × amount over base bracket)
			Tax calculation
$ 0 to $ 50,000	$ 0	+	(15% × amount over $ 0)
50,000 to 75,000	7,500	+	(25 × amount over 50,000)
75,000 to 100,000	13,750	+	(34 × amount over 75,000)
100,000 to 335,000[a]	22,250	+	(39 × amount over 100,000)
335,000 to 10,000,000	113,900	+	(34 × amount over 335,000)
Over $10,000,000[b]	3,400,000	+	(35 × amount over 10,000,000)

[a]Because corporations with taxable income in excess of $100,000 must increase their tax by the lesser of $11,750 or 5% of the taxable income in excess of $100,000, they will end up paying a 39% tax on taxable income between $100,000 and $335,000. The 5% surtax that raises the tax rate from 34% to 39% causes all corporations with taxable income between $335,000 and $10,000,000 to have an *average tax rate* of 34%.

[b]This bracket and its associated 35% tax rate was created with passage of the *Omnibus Budget Reconciliation Act of 1993,* which was signed into law by President Clinton on August 10, 1993, and was retroactive to its effective date of January 1, 1993.

Example ▼ Western Manufacturing, Inc., a small manufacturer of kitchen utensils, has before-tax earnings of $250,000. The tax on these earnings can be found by using the tax rate schedule given in Table 4.4:

$$\text{Total taxes due} = \$22,250 + [.39 \times (\$250,000 - \$100,000)]$$
$$= \$22,250 + (.39 \times \$150,000)$$
$$= \$22,250 + \$58,500 = \underline{\$80,750}$$

▲

From a financial point of view it is important to understand the difference between average and marginal tax rates, the treatment of interest and dividend income, and the effects of tax deductibility.

AVERAGE VERSUS MARGINAL TAX RATES

average tax rate
A firm's taxes divided by its taxable income.

The **average tax rate** paid on the firm's ordinary income can be calculated by dividing its taxes by its taxable income. For firms with taxable income of $10,000,000 or less, the average tax rate ranges from 15 to 34 percent, reaching 34 percent when taxable income equals or exceeds $335,000. For firms with taxable income in excess of $10,000,000, the average tax rate ranges between 34 and 35 percent. The average tax rate paid by Western Manufacturing, Inc., in the preceding example was 32.3 percent ($80,750 ÷ $250,000). As a corporation's income increases, its average tax rate approaches and finally reaches 34 percent. It remains at that level up to $10,000,000 of taxable income, beyond which it rises toward but never reaches 35 percent.

marginal tax rate
The rate at which additional income is taxed.

The **marginal tax rate** represents the rate at which additional income is taxed. In the current corporate tax structure, the marginal tax rate on income up to $50,000 is 15 percent; from $50,000 to $75,000 it is 25 percent; and so on, as shown in Table 4.4. To simplify calculations in the text, *a fixed 40 percent tax rate is assumed to be applicable to ordinary corporate income.*

Example ▼ If Western Manufacturing's earnings go up to $300,000, the marginal tax rate on the additional $50,000 of income will be 39 percent. The company will therefore have to pay additional taxes of $19,500 (.39 × $50,000). Total taxes on the $300,000, then, will be $100,250 ($80,750 + $19,500). To check this figure using the tax rate schedule in Table 4.4, we would get a total tax liability of $22,250 + [.39 × ($300,000 − $100,000)] = $22,250 + $78,000 = $100,250—the same value obtained by applying the marginal tax rate to the added income and adjusting the known tax liability.

▲

The *average tax rate* tends to be most useful in evaluating taxes historically, and the *marginal tax rate* is more frequently used in financial decision making. For example, it is often helpful to know the average tax rate at which taxes were paid over a given period. But in making decisions the important concern is the rate at which the earnings from alternative proposals will *actually* be taxed, that is, the marginal tax rate. With *progressive tax rates*—higher rates for higher levels of taxable income—the average tax rate is always less than or equal to the marginal tax rate. Given our focus on financial decision making, *the tax rates used throughout this text are assumed to represent marginal tax rates.*

INTEREST AND DIVIDEND INCOME

In the process of determining taxable income, any *interest received* by the corporation is included as ordinary income and is therefore taxed at the firm's applicable tax rates. Dividends, on the other hand, are treated differently due to **double taxation,** which occurs when the already once-taxed earnings of a corporation are distributed as cash dividends to stockholders, who must pay taxes on them. Therefore, dividends received on common and preferred stock held in other corporations, and representing less than 20 percent ownership in them, are subject to a 70 percent exclusion for tax purposes.[5] Because of the dividend exclusion, only 30 percent of these **intercorporate dividends** are included as ordinary income. The tax law provides this exclusion to avoid *triple taxation*—the first and second corporations are taxed on income before paying the dividend, and the dividend recipient must include the dividend in taxable income. This feature in effect eliminates most of the potential tax liability from the dividend received by the second and any subsequent corporations.

double taxation
Occurs when the already once-taxed earnings of a corporation are distributed as cash dividends to stockholders, who must pay taxes on them.

intercorporate dividends
Dividends received by one corporation on preferred and common stock held in other corporations.

Example ▼   Checker Industries, a major manufacturer of molds for the plastics industry, during the year just ended received $100,000 in interest on bonds it held and $100,000 in dividends on common stock it owned in other corporations. The firm is subject to a 40 percent marginal tax rate and is eligible for a 70 percent exclusion on its intercorporate dividend receipts. The after-tax income realized by Checker from each of these sources of investment income is found as follows:

	Interest income		Dividend income
(1) Before-tax amount	$100,000		$100,000
Less: Applicable exclusion	0	$(.70 \times \$100,000) =$	70,000
Taxable amount	$100,000		$ 30,000
(2) Tax (40%)	40,000		12,000
After-tax amount [(1) − (2)]	$ 60,000		$ 88,000

As a result of the 70 percent dividend exclusion, the after-tax amount is greater for the dividend income than for the interest income. Clearly, the dividend exclusion enhances the attractiveness of stock investments relative to bond investments made by one corporation in another corporation. ▲

TAX-DEDUCTIBLE EXPENSES

In calculating their taxes, corporations are allowed to deduct operating expenses, as well as interest expense. The tax deductibility of these expenses reduces their after-tax cost. The following example illustrates the benefit of tax deductibility.

---

[5]The exclusion is 80 percent if the corporation owns between 20 and 80 percent of the stock in the corporation paying it dividends; 100 percent of the dividends received are excluded if it owns more than 80 percent of the corporation paying it dividends. For convenience, we are assuming here that the ownership interest in the dividend-paying corporation is less than 20 percent.

Example ▼ Companies X and Y each expect in the coming year to have earnings before interest and taxes of $200,000. Company X during the year will have to pay $30,000 in interest; Company Y has no debt and therefore will have no interest expense. Calculation of the earnings after taxes for these two firms are as follows:

	Company X	Company Y
Earnings before interest and taxes	$200,000	$200,000
Less: Interest expense	30,000	0
Earnings before taxes	$170,000	$200,000
Less: Taxes (40%)	68,000	80,000
Earnings after taxes	$102,000	$120,000
Difference in earnings after taxes	$18,000	

Whereas Company X had $30,000 more interest expense than Company Y, Company X's earnings after taxes are only $18,000 less than those of Company Y ($102,000 versus $120,000). This difference is attributable to the fact that Company X's $30,000 interest expense deduction provided a tax savings of $12,000 ($68,000 for Company X versus $80,000 for Company Y). This amount can be calculated directly by multiplying the tax rate by the amount of ▲ interest expense (.40 × $30,000 = $12,000).

The tax deductibility of certain expenses reduces their actual (after-tax) cost to the profitable firm. Note that both for accounting and tax purposes *interest is a tax-deductible expense, whereas dividends are not.* Because dividends are not tax-deductible, their after-tax cost is equal to the amount of the dividend. Thus, a $30,000 cash dividend would have an after-tax cost of $30,000.

CAPITAL GAINS

capital gain
The amount by which the sale price of an asset exceeds the asset's initial purchase price.

If a firm sells a capital asset[6] such as stock held as an investment for more than its initial purchase price, the difference between the sale price and the purchase price is called a **capital gain.** For corporations, capital gains are added to ordinary corporate income and taxed at the regular corporate rates, with a maximum marginal tax rate of 39 percent.[7] To simplify the computations presented in later chapters of the text, as for ordinary income, *a fixed 40 percent tax rate is assumed to be applicable to corporate capital gains.*

Example ▼ The Loos Company, a manufacturer of pharmaceuticals, has operating earnings of $500,000 and has just sold for $40,000 an asset that was purchased 2 years ago for $36,000. Because the asset was sold for more than its initial purchase

---

[6]To simplify the discussion, only capital assets are considered here. The full tax treatment of gains and losses on depreciable assets is presented as part of the discussion of capital budgeting cash flows in Chapter 9.

[7]The *Omnibus Budget Reconciliation Act of 1993* included a provision that allows the capital gains tax to be halved on gains resulting from investments made after January 1, 1993, in startup firms with a value of less than $50 million that have been held for at least 5 years. This special provision, which is intended to help startup firms, is ignored throughout this text.

price, there is a capital gain of $4,000 ($40,000 sale price − $36,000 initial purchase price). The corporation's taxable income will total $504,000 ($500,000 ordinary income plus $4,000 capital gain). Because this total is above $335,000, the capital gain will be taxed at the 34 percent rate, resulting in a tax of $1,360 (.34 × $4,000).

? Review Questions

4-4   Briefly define ordinary corporate income and capital gains, and describe the tax treatments of each. What is the *average tax rate?* What is the *marginal tax rate?*

4-5   Why might the *intercorporate dividend* exclusion make corporate stock investments by one corporation in another more attractive than bond investments?

5-6   What benefit results from the tax deductibility of certain corporate expenses? Compare and contrast the tax treatment of corporate interest and dividend payments.

DEPRECIATION

LG4 LG5

depreciation
The systematic charging of a portion of the costs of fixed assets against annual revenues over time.

Business firms are permitted to systematically charge a portion of the costs of fixed assets against annual revenues. This allocation of historic cost over time is called **depreciation.** For tax purposes, the depreciation of business assets is regulated by the Internal Revenue Code, which experienced major changes under the *Tax Reform Act of 1986.* Because the objectives of financial reporting are sometimes different from those of tax legislation, a firm often will use different depreciation methods for financial reporting than those required for tax purposes. Tax laws are used to accomplish economic goals such as providing incentives for business investment in certain types of assets, whereas the objectives of financial reporting are of course quite different. Keeping two different sets of records for these two different purposes is legal.

modified accelerated cost recovery system (MACRS)
System used to determine the depreciation of assets for tax purposes.

Depreciation for tax purposes is determined by using the **modified accelerated cost recovery system (MACRS),**[8] whereas a variety of depreciation methods are available for financial reporting purposes. Before we discuss the methods of depreciating an asset, you must understand the relationship between depreciation and cash flows, the depreciable value of an asset, and the depreciable life of an asset.

DEPRECIATION AND CASH FLOWS

The financial manager is concerned with *cash flows* rather than net profits as reported on the income statement. To adjust the income statement to show *cash flow from operations,* all noncash charges must be *added back* to the firm's *net*

---

[8]This system, which was first established in 1981 with passage of the *Economic Recovery Tax Act,* was initially called the "accelerated cost recovery system (ACRS)." As a result of modifications to the system in the *Tax Reform Act of 1986,* it is now commonly called the "modified accelerated cost recovery system (MACRS)." Although some people continue to refer to this system as "ACRS," we correctly call it "MACRS" throughout this text.

noncash charges
Expenses deducted on the income statement that do not involve an actual outlay of cash during the period.

profits after taxes. **Noncash charges** are expenses that are deducted on the income statement but do not involve an actual outlay of cash during the period. Depreciation, amortization, and depletion allowances are examples. Because depreciation expenses are the most common noncash charges, we shall demonstrate their treatment. Amortization and depletion charges are treated in a similar fashion.

The general rule for adjusting net profits after taxes by adding back all non-cash charges is expressed as follows:

$$\text{Cash flow from operations} = \text{net profits after taxes} + \text{noncash charges} \qquad (4.1)$$

Applying Equation 4.1 to the 2000 income statement for Elton Corporation presented in Table 4.1 yields a cash flow from operations of $280,000 due to the noncash nature of depreciation:

Net profits after taxes	$180,000
Plus: Depreciation expense	100,000
Cash flow from operations	$280,000

Depreciation and other noncash charges shield the firm from taxes by lowering taxable income. Some people do not define depreciation as a source of funds; however, it is a source of funds in the sense that it represents a "nonuse" of funds. Table 4.5 shows Elton Corporation's income statement prepared on a *cash basis* to illustrate how depreciation shields income and enables nonuse of funds. Ignoring depreciation, except in determining the firm's taxes, results in cash flow from operations of $280,000—the value obtained before. Adjustment of the

TABLE 4.5	Elton Corporation Income Statement Calculated on a Cash Basis ($000) for the Year Ended December 31, 2000

Sales revenue		$1,700
Less: Cost of goods sold		1,000
Gross profits		$ 700
Less: Operating expenses		
Selling expense	$ 80	
General and administrative expense	150	
Depreciation expense (noncash charge)	0	
Total operating expense		230
Operating profits		$ 470
Less: Interest expense		70
Net profits before taxes		$ 400
Less: Taxes (from Table 4.1)		120
Cash flow from operations		$ 280

firm's net profits after taxes by adding back noncash charges such as depreciation will be used on a number of occasions in this text to estimate cash flow.

DEPRECIABLE VALUE OF AN ASSET

Under the basic MACRS procedures the depreciable value of an asset (the amount to be depreciated) is its *full* cost, including outlays for installation.[9] No adjustment is required for expected salvage value.

E x a m p l e ▼ Elton Corporation acquired a new machine at a cost of $38,000, with installation costs of $2,000. Regardless of its expected salvage value, the depreciable ▲ value of the machine is $40,000: $38,000 cost + $2,000 installation cost.

DEPRECIABLE LIFE OF AN ASSET

depreciable life
Time period over which an asset is depreciated.

The time period over which an asset is depreciated—its **depreciable life**—can significantly affect the pattern of cash flows. The shorter the depreciable life, the more quickly the cash flow created by the depreciation write-off will be received. Given the financial manager's preference for faster receipt of cash flows, a shorter depreciable life is preferred to a longer one. However, the firm must abide by certain Internal Revenue Service (IRS) requirements for determining depreciable life. These MACRS standards, which apply to both new and used assets, require the taxpayer to use as an asset's depreciable life the appropriate MACRS **recovery period.** There are six MACRS recovery periods—3, 5, 7, 10, 15, and 20 years—excluding real estate. It is customary to refer to the property classes (excluding real estate), in accordance with their recovery periods, as 3-, 5-, 7-, 10-, 15-, and 20-year property. The first four property classes—those routinely used by business—are defined in Table 4.6.

recovery period
The appropriate depreciable life of a particular asset as determined by MACRS.

TABLE 4.6	**First Four Property Classes Under MACRS**
Property class (recovery period)	**Definition**
3 years	Research equipment and certain special tools.
5 years	Computers, typewriters, copiers, duplicating equipment, cars, light-duty trucks, qualified technological equipment, and similar assets.
7 years	Office furniture, fixtures, most manufacturing equipment, railroad track, and single-purpose agricultural and horticultural structures.
10 years	Equipment used in petroleum refining or in the manufacture of tobacco products and certain food products.

[9]Land values are *not* depreciable. Therefore, to determine the depreciable value of real estate, the value of the land is subtracted from the cost of the real estate. In other words, only buildings and other improvements are depreciable.

*P*ERSONAL FINANCE PERSPECTIVE
Depreciation Counts When Buying a Car

If you understand how depreciation relates to car prices you can get a better deal on your next car. The average new car depreciates 28 percent as soon as you drive it away from the dealer. So, if you want a new car but can't afford the model you love, consider buying it "nearly new" instead—12 to 24 months old. With the increasing popularity of short-term car leases, you'll find a good supply of well-maintained late-model used cars, and you won't pay for the high depreciation in the early years.

Depreciation also plays a key role in the leasing process. When you lease a car, the payment is based on the amount the car depreciates in the time covered by the lease. To calculate your monthly lease payment, start with the cost of the car (which you negotiate as you would for a straight cash purchase). Then subtract the residual value, the estimated (depreciated) value of the car at the end of the lease period, to get the depreciation. Your total lease payments will equal the depreciation plus an interest factor. So with a higher residual value, you pay for less depreciation. ●

DEPRECIATION METHODS

For *financial reporting purposes* a variety of depreciation methods—straight-line, double-declining balance, and sum-of-the-years'-digits—can be used.[10] For *tax purposes,* using MACRS recovery periods, assets in the first four property classes are depreciated by the double-declining balance (200 percent) method using the half-year convention and switching to straight-line when advantageous. Although tables of depreciation percentages are not provided by law, the *approximate percentages* (i.e., rounded to nearest whole percent) written off each year for the first four property classes are given in Table 4.7. For purposes of this text we will use the MACRS depreciation percentages because they generally provide for the fastest write-off and therefore the best cash flow effects for the profitable firm.

Because MACRS requires use of the half-year convention, assets are assumed to be acquired in the middle of the year, and therefore only one-half of the first year's depreciation is recovered in the first year. As a result, the final half-year of depreciation is recovered in the year immediately following the asset's stated recovery period. In Table 4.7, the depreciation percentages for an *n*-year class asset are given for *n* + 1 years. For example, a 5-year asset is depreciated over 6 recovery years. (*Note:* The percentages in Table 4.7 have been rounded to the nearest whole percentage to simplify calculations while retaining realism.)

Because managerial finance focuses on cash flows, *only tax depreciation methods will be utilized throughout this textbook.* The application of the tax depreciation percentages in Table 4.7 can be demonstrated by a simple example.

Example ▼ Elton Corporation acquired, for an installed cost of $40,000, a machine having a recovery period of 5 years. Using the applicable percentages from Table 4.7, we can calculate the depreciation in each year as follows:

---

[10]For a review of these depreciation methods as well as other aspects of financial reporting, see any recently published financial accounting text.

| TABLE 4.7 | Rounded Depreciation Percentages by Recovery Year Using MACRS for First Four Property Classes |

	Percentage by recovery year[a]			
Recovery year	3 years	5 years	7 years	10 years
1	33%	20%	14%	10%
2	45	32	25	18
3	15	19	18	14
4	7	12	12	12
5		12	9	9
6		5	9	8
7			9	7
8			4	6
9				6
10				6
11				4
Totals	100%	100%	100%	100%

[a]These percentages have been rounded to the nearest whole percent to simplify calculations while retaining realism. To calculate the *actual* depreciation for tax purposes, be sure to apply the actual unrounded percentages or directly apply double-declining balance (200%) depreciation using the half-year convention.

Year	Cost (1)	Percentages (from Table 4.7) (2)	Depreciation [(1) × (2)] (3)
1	$40,000	20%	$ 8,000
2	40,000	32	12,800
3	40,000	19	7,600
4	40,000	12	4,800
5	40,000	12	4,800
6	40,000	5	2,000
Totals		100%	$40,000

Column 3 shows that the full cost of the asset is written off over 6 recovery years.

? Review Questions

4-7   In what sense does depreciation act as cash inflow? How can a firm's after-tax profits be adjusted to determine *cash flow from operations?*

4-8   Briefly describe the first four modified accelerated cost recovery system (MACRS) property classes and recovery periods. Explain how the depreciation percentages are determined by using the MACRS recovery periods.

ANALYZING THE FIRM'S CASH FLOW

The *statement of cash flows,* briefly described earlier, summarizes the firm's cash flow over a given period of time. Because it can be used to capture historic cash flow, the key aspects of the statement are discussed in this section. First, however, we need to discuss cash flow through the firm and the classification of sources and uses of cash.

THE FIRM'S CASH FLOWS

operating flows
Cash flows directly related to production and sale of the firm's products and services.

investment flows
Cash flows associated with purchase and sale of both fixed assets and business interests.

financing flows
Cash flows that result from debt and equity financing transactions; includes incurrence and repayment of debt, cash inflow from the sale of stock, and cash outflows to pay cash dividends or repurchase stock.

Figure 4.2 illustrates the firm's cash flows. Note that marketable securities, because of their highly liquid nature, are considered the same as cash. Both cash and marketable securities represent a reservoir of liquidity that is *increased by cash inflows* and *decreased by cash outflows.* Also note that the firm's cash flows have been divided into (1) operating flows, (2) investment flows, and (3) financing flows. The **operating flows** are cash inflows and outflows directly related to production and sale of the firm's products and services. **Investment flows** are cash flows associated with purchase and sale of both fixed assets and business interests. Clearly, purchase transactions would result in cash outflows, whereas sale transactions would generate cash inflows. The **financing flows** result from debt and equity financing transactions. Incurring and repaying either short-term debt (notes payable) or long-term debt would result in a corresponding cash inflow or outflow. Similarly, the sale of stock would result in a cash inflow; the payment of cash dividends or repurchase of stock would result in a financing outflow. In combination, the firm's operating, investment, and financing cash flows during a given period will affect the firm's cash and marketable securities balances.

CLASSIFYING SOURCES AND USES OF CASH

The statement of cash flows in effect summarizes the sources and uses of cash during a given period. Table 4.8 classifies the basic sources and uses of cash. For example, if a firm's accounts payable increased by $1,000 during the year, this change would be a *source of cash.* If the firm's inventory increased by $2,500, the change would be a *use of cash.*

A few additional points can be made with respect to the classification scheme in Table 4.8:

1. A *decrease* in an asset, such as the firm's cash balance, is a *source of cash flow* because cash that has been tied up in the asset is released and can be used for some other purpose, such as repaying a loan. On the other hand, an *increase* in the firm's cash balance is a *use of cash flow,* because additional cash is being tied up in the firm's cash balance.
2. Earlier, Equation 4.1 and the related discussion explained why depreciation and other noncash charges are considered cash inflows, or sources of cash. Adding noncash charges back to the firm's net profits after taxes gives cash flow from operations:

Cash flow from operations = net profits after taxes + noncash charges

FIGURE 4.2   Cash Flows
The firm's cash flows

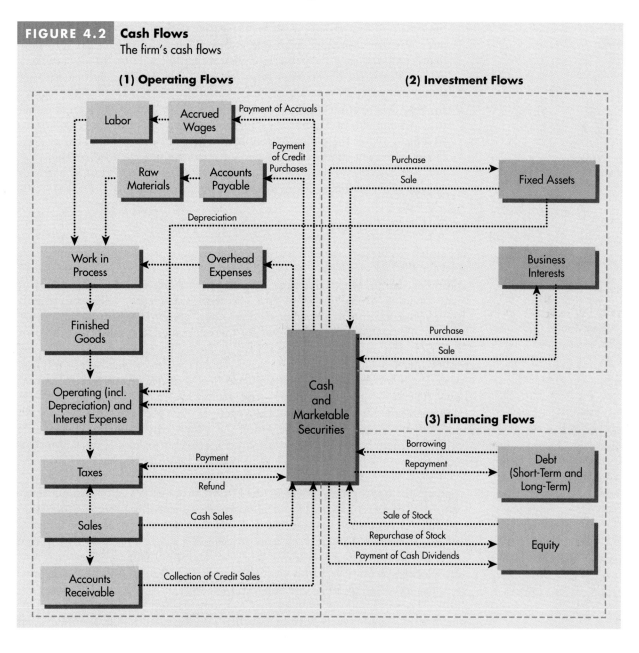

TABLE 4.8   The Sources and Uses of Cash

Sources	Uses
Decrease in any asset	Increase in any asset
Increase in any liability	Decrease in any liability
Net profits after taxes	Net loss
Depreciation and other noncash charges	Dividends paid
Sale of stock	Repurchase or retirement of stock

Note that a firm can have a *net loss* (negative net profits after taxes) and still have positive cash flow from operations when noncash charges (typically depreciation) during the period are greater than the net loss. In the statement of cash flows, net profits after taxes (or net losses) and noncash charges are therefore treated as separate entries.

3. Because depreciation is treated as a separate source of cash, only *gross* rather than *net* changes in fixed assets appear on the statement of cash flows. This treatment avoids the potential double counting of depreciation.

4. Direct entries of changes in retained earnings are not included on the statement of cash flows. Instead, entries for items that affect retained earnings appear as net profits or losses after taxes and dividends paid.

DEVELOPING THE STATEMENT OF CASH FLOWS

The statement of cash flows for a given period is developed using the income statement for the period, along with the beginning- and end-of-period balance sheets. The procedure involves classifying balance sheet changes as sources or uses of cash, obtaining income statement data, classifying the relevant values into operating, investment, and financing cash flows, and presenting them in the proper format.[11] The statement of cash flows for the year ended December 31, 2000, for Elton Corporation is presented in Table 4.9. Note that all sources as well as net profits after taxes and depreciation are treated as positive values—cash inflows. All uses, any losses, and dividends paid are treated as negative values—cash outflows. The items in each category—operating, investment, and financing—are totaled, and the three totals are added to get the "Net increase (decrease) in cash and marketable securities" for the period. As a check, this value should reconcile with the actual change in cash and marketable securities for the year, which is obtained from the beginning- and end-of-period balance sheets.

Example ▼ Applying the appropriate procedure to Elton Corporation's 2000 income statement (in Table 4.1) and 1999 and 2000 balance sheets (in Table 4.2), its 2000 statement of cash flows is presented in Table 4.9. This statement shows that the firm experienced a $500,000 increase in cash and marketable securities during 2000. Looking at Elton Corporation's 1999 and 2000 balance sheets in Table 4.2, we can see that the firm's cash increased by $100,000 and its marketable securities increased by $400,000 between December 31, 1999, and December 31, 2000. The $500,000 net increase in cash and marketable securities from the statement of cash flows therefore reconciles with the total change of $500,000 in these accounts during 2000. The statement of cash flows therefore reconciles ▲ with the actual balance sheet changes.

INTERPRETING THE STATEMENT

The statement of cash flows allows the financial manager and other interested parties to analyze the firm's cash flow. The manager should pay special attention to both the major categories of cash flow and the individual items of cash inflow

---

[11]For a description and demonstration of the detailed procedures for developing the statement of cash flows, see Lawrence J. Gitman, *Principles of Managerial Finance*, 9th ed. (Reading, MA: Addison Wesley Longman, 2000), Chapter 3, pp. 100–104.

TABLE 4.9	Elton Corporation Statement of Cash Flows ($000) for the Year Ended December 31, 2000

Cash Flow from Operating Activities

Net profits after taxes	$180	
Depreciation	100	
Decrease in accounts receivable	100	
Decrease in inventories	300	
Increase in accounts payable	200	
Decrease in accruals	$(100)^a$	
Cash provided by operating activities		$780

Cash Flow from Investment Activities

Increase in gross fixed assets	($300)	
Changes in business interests	0	
Cash provided by investment activities		(300)

Cash Flow from Financing Activities

Decrease in notes payable	($100)	
Increase in long-term debts	200	
Changes in stockholders' equity^b	0	
Dividends paid	(80)	
Cash provided by financing activities		20
Net increase in cash and marketable securities		$500

^{a}As is customary, parentheses are used to denote a negative number, which in this case is a cash outflow.

^{b}Retained earnings are excluded here, because their change is actually reflected in the combination of the net profits after taxes and dividends paid entries.

and outflow, to assess whether any developments have occurred that are contrary to the company's financial policies. In addition, the statement can be used to evaluate progress toward projected goals. This statement does not match specific cash inflows with specific cash outflows, but it can be used to isolate inefficiencies. For example, increases in accounts receivable and inventories resulting in major cash outflows may signal credit or inventory problems, respectively.

In addition, the financial manager can prepare a statement of cash flows developed from projected, or pro forma, financial statements. This approach can be used to determine whether planned actions are desirable in view of the resulting cash flows.

Example ▼ Analysis of Elton Corporation's statement of cash flows in Table 4.9 does not seem to indicate the existence of any major problems for the company. Its $780,000 of cash provided by operating activities plus the $20,000 provided by financing activities were used to invest an additional $300,000 in fixed assets and to increase cash and marketable securities by $500,000. The individual items of cash inflow and outflow seem to be distributed in a fashion consistent with prudent financial management. The firm seems to be growing: Less than half of its earnings ($80,000 out of $180,000) was paid to owners as dividends, and gross fixed assets increased by three times the amount of historic cost written off through depreciation expense ($300,000 increase in gross fixed assets versus $100,000 in depreciation expense). Major cash inflows were realized by decreasing inventories and increasing accounts payable. The major outflow of cash was to increase cash and marketable securities by $500,000 and thereby improve liquidity. Other inflows and outflows of Elton Corporation tend to support the fact that the firm was well managed financially during the period.

An understanding of the basic financial principles presented throughout this text is a prerequisite to the effective interpretation of the statement of cash flows.

? R e v i e w   Q u e s t i o n s

4-9   Describe the overall cash flow through the firm in terms of: (a) operating flows; (b) investment flows; and (c) financing flows.

4-10   List and describe *sources of cash* and *uses of cash*. Discuss why a decrease in cash is a source and an increase in cash is a use.

4-11   What statements are needed as inputs for preparing the statement of cash flows?

4-12   Describe the general format of the statement of cash flows. How are cash inflows differentiated from cash outflows on the statement? How can the accuracy of the final statement balance, "Net increase (decrease) in cash and marketable securities," be conveniently verified?

4-13   How is the statement of cash flows interpreted and used by the financial manager and other interested parties?

S UMMARY

LG1   **Describe the purpose and basic components of the stockholders' report.** The annual stockholders' report, which publicly owned corporations are required to provide to their stockholders, summarizes and documents the firm's financial activities during the past year. It includes the letter to stockholders and various subjective and factual information plus four key financial statements: (1) the income statement, (2) the balance sheet, (3) the statement of retained earnings, and (4) the statement of cash flows. Notes describing the technical aspects of the financial statements follow them.

LG2   **Review the purpose and key components of the income statement, the balance sheet, the statement of retained earnings, and the statement of cash flows.** The income statement summarizes operating results during the period of concern, by subtracting costs, expenses, and taxes from sales revenue to find the period's profits. The balance sheet summarizes the firm's financial position at a given point in time by balancing the firm's assets against its financing, which can be either debt (what it owes) or equity (what was provided by owners). The statement of retained earnings reconciles the net income earned during a given year, and any cash dividends paid, with the change in retained earnings between the start and end of that year. The statement of cash flows provides a summary of the cash flows over the period; the statement provides insight into the firm's operating, investment, and financing cash flows.

LG3   **Discuss the fundamentals of business taxation of ordinary income and capital gains.** Corporate income is subject to corporate taxes. Corporate tax rates are applicable to both ordinary income (after deduction of allowable expenses) and capital gains. The average tax rate paid by a corporation ranges from 15 to 35 percent. (For convenience, we assume a 40 percent marginal tax rate in this book.) Certain provisions in the tax code, such as intercorporate dividend exclusions and tax-deductible expenses, provide corporate taxpayers with opportunities to reduce their taxes.

 Understand the effect of depreciation and other noncash charges on the firm's cash flows. Depreciation, or the allocation of historic cost, is the most common type of noncash expenditure. To estimate cash flow from operations, depreciation and any other noncash charges are added back to net profits after taxes. Because they lower taxable income without an actual outflow of cash, noncash charges act as a source of funds to the firm.

Determine the depreciable value of an asset, its depreciable life, and the amount of depreciation allowed each year for tax purposes. The depreciable value of an asset and its depreciable life are determined by using the modified accelerated cost recovery system (MACRS) standards in the federal tax code. MACRS groups assets (excluding real estate) into six property classes based on length of recovery period—3, 5, 7, 10, 15, and 20 years—

and can be applied over the appropriate period by using a schedule of yearly depreciation percentages for each period.

Discuss the firm's cash flows and interpret the statement of cash flows. The statement of cash flows is divided into operating, investment, and financing flows. It can be developed using the income statement for the period, along with beginning- and end-of-period balance sheets. The procedure involves classifying balance sheet changes as sources or uses of cash, obtaining income statement data, classifying the relevant values into operating, investment, and financing cash flows, and presenting them in the proper format. The statement reconciles changes in the firm's cash flows with changes in cash and marketable securities for the period. Interpreting the statement of cash flows requires an understanding of basic financial principles and involves both the major categories of cash flow and the individual items of cash inflow and outflow.

SELF-TEST PROBLEMS   (Solutions in Appendix B)

ST 4–1   Corporate taxes   Montgomery Enterprises, Inc., had operating earnings of $280,000 for the year just ended. During the year the firm sold stock that it held in another company for $180,000, which was $30,000 above its original purchase price of $150,000, paid 1 year earlier.
a. What is the amount, if any, of capital gains realized during the year?
b. How much total taxable income did the firm earn during the year?
c. Use the corporate tax rate schedule given in Table 4.4 to calculate the firm's total taxes due.
d. Calculate both the *average tax rate* and the *marginal tax rate* based upon your findings.

ST 4–2   Depreciation and cash flow   A firm expects to have earnings before depreciation and taxes (EBDT) of $160,000 in each of the next 6 years. It is considering the purchase of an asset costing $140,000, requiring $10,000 in installation costs, and having a recovery period of 5 years.
a. Calculate the annual depreciation for the asset purchase using the MACRS depreciation percentages in Table 4.7 on page 91.
b. Calculate the annual operating cash flows for each of the 6 years. Assume that the new asset is the firm's only depreciable asset and that it is subject to a 40 percent ordinary tax rate.
c. Compare and discuss your findings in **a** and **b**.

PROBLEMS

   4-1 **Reviewing basic financial statements**   The income statement for the year ended December 31, 2000, the balance sheets for December 31, 2000 and 1999, and the statement of retained earnings for the year ended December 31, 2000, for Technica, Inc., are given on this and the following page. Briefly discuss the form and informational content of each of these statements.

Income Statement Technica, Inc. for the year ended December 31, 2000		
Sales revenue		$600,000
Less: Cost of goods sold		460,000
Gross profits		$140,000
Less: Operating expenses		
General and administrative expense	$30,000	
Depreciation expense	30,000	
Total operating expense		60,000
Operating profits		$ 80,000
Less: Interest expense		10,000
Net profits before taxes		$ 70,000
Less: Taxes		27,100
Earnings available for common stockholders		$ 42,900
Earnings per share (EPS)		$2.15

Balance Sheets Technica, Inc.		
	December 31	
Assets	**2000**	**1999**
Cash	$ 15,000	$ 16,000
Marketable securities	7,200	8,000
Accounts receivable	34,100	42,200
Inventories	82,000	50,000
Total current assets	$138,300	$116,200
Land and buildings	$150,000	$150,000
Machinery and equipment	200,000	190,000
Furniture and fixtures	54,000	50,000
Other	11,000	10,000
Total gross fixed assets	$415,000	$400,000
Less: Accumulated depreciation	145,000	115,000
Net fixed assets	$270,000	$285,000
Total assets	$408,300	$401,200
Liabilities and stockholders' equity		
Accounts payable	$ 57,000	$ 49,000
Notes payable	13,000	16,000
Accruals	5,000	6,000
Total current liabilities	$ 75,000	$ 71,000
Long-term debt	$150,000	$160,000
Stockholders' equity		
Common stock equity (shares outstanding: 19,500 in 2000 and 20,000 in 1999)	$110,200	$120,000
Retained earnings	73,100	50,200
Total stockholders' equity	$183,300	$170,200
Total liabilities and stockholders' equity	$408,300	$401,200

Statement of Retained Earnings Technica, Inc. for the year ended December 31, 2000	
Retained earnings balance (January 1, 2000)	$50,200
Plus: Net profits after taxes (for 2000)	42,900
Less: Cash dividends (paid during 2000)	(20,000)
Retained earnings balance (December 31, 2000)	$73,100

4-2 Financial statement account identification   Mark each of the accounts listed in the following table as follows:

a. In column (1), indicate in which statement—income statement (IS) or balance sheet (BS)—the account belongs.

b. In column (2), indicate whether the account is a current asset (CA), current liability (CL), expense (E), fixed asset (FA), long-term debt (LTD), revenue (R), or stockholders' equity (SE).

Account name	(1) Statement	(2) Type of account
Accounts payable	_____	_____
Accounts receivable	_____	_____
Accruals	_____	_____
Accumulated depreciation	_____	_____
Administrative expense	_____	_____
Buildings	_____	_____
Cash	_____	_____
Common stock (at par)	_____	_____
Cost of goods sold	_____	_____
Depreciation	_____	_____
Equipment	_____	_____
General expense	_____	_____
Interest expense	_____	_____
Inventories	_____	_____
Land	_____	_____
Long-term debts	_____	_____
Machinery	_____	_____
Marketable securities	_____	_____
Notes payable	_____	_____
Operating expense	_____	_____
Paid-in capital in excess of par	_____	_____
Preferred stock	_____	_____
Preferred stock dividends	_____	_____
Retained earnings	_____	_____
Sales revenue	_____	_____
Selling expense	_____	_____
Taxes	_____	_____
Vehicles	_____	_____

  4-3 Income statement preparation   Use the *appropriate items* from the following list to prepare in good form Perry Corporation's income statement for the year ended December 31, 2000.

Item	Values ($000) at or for year ended December 31, 2000
Accounts receivable	$350
Accumulated depreciation	205
Cost of goods sold	285
Depreciation expense	55
General and administrative expense	60
Interest expense	25
Preferred stock dividends	10
Sales revenue	525
Selling expense	35
Stockholders' equity	265
Taxes	rate = 40%

4-4   Income statement preparation   On December 31, 2000, Cathy Chen, a self-employed certified public accountant (CPA), completed her first full year in business. During the year she billed $180,000 for her accounting services. She had two employees: a bookkeeper and a clerical assistant. In addition to her *monthly* salary of $4,000, Ms. Chen paid *annual* salaries of $24,000 and $18,000 to the bookkeeper and the clerical assistant, respectively. Employment taxes and benefit costs for Ms. Chen and her employees totaled $17,300 for the year. Expenses for office supplies, including postage, totaled $5,200 for the year. In addition, Ms. Chen spent $8,500 during the year on tax-deductible travel and entertainment associated with client visits and new business development. Lease payments for the office space rented (a tax-deductible expense) were $1,350 *per month*. Depreciation expense on the office furniture and fixtures was $7,800 for the year. During the year, Ms. Chen paid interest of $7,500 on the $60,000 borrowed to start the business. She paid an average tax rate of 30 percent during 2000.

a. Prepare an income statement for Cathy Chen, CPA, for the year ended December 31, 2000.

b. How much *cash flow from operations* did Cathy realize during 2000?

c. Evaluate her 2000 financial performance.

4-5   Calculation of EPS and retained earnings   Philagem, Inc., ended 2000 with net profit *before* taxes of $218,000. The company is subject to a 40 percent tax rate and must pay $32,000 in preferred stock dividends before distributing any earnings on the 85,000 shares of common stock currently outstanding.

a. Calculate Philagem's 2000 earnings per share (EPS).

b. If the firm paid common stock dividends of $.80 per share, how many dollars would go to retained earnings?

4-6   Balance sheet preparation   Use the *appropriate items* from the following list to prepare in good form Owen Davis Company's balance sheet at December 31, 2000.

Item	Value ($000) at December 31, 2000
Accounts payable	$ 220
Accounts receivable	450
Accruals	55
Accumulated depreciation	265
Buildings	225
Cash	215
Common stock (at par)	90
Cost of goods sold	2,500
Depreciation expense	45
Equipment	140
Furniture and fixtures	170
General expense	320
Inventories	375
Land	100
Long-term debts	420
Machinery	420
Marketable securities	75
Notes payable	475
Paid-in capital in excess of par	360
Preferred stock	100
Retained earnings	210
Sales revenue	3,600
Vehicles	25

  4-7   Initial sale price of common stock   Beck Corporation has one issue of preferred stock and one issue of common stock outstanding. Given Beck's stockholders' equity account that follows, determine the original price per share at which the firm sold its single issue of common stock.

Stockholders' equity ($000)	
Preferred stock	$ 125
Common stock ($.75 par, 300,000 shares outstanding)	225
Paid-in capital in excess of par on common stock	2,625
Retained earnings	900
Total stockholders' equity	$3,875

4-8   Financial statement preparation   The balance sheet for Rogers Industries for December 31, 1999, follows. Information relevant to Rogers Industries' 2000 operations is given following the balance sheet. Using the data presented:

a. Prepare in good form an income statement for Rogers Industries for the year ended December 31, 2000. Be sure to show earnings per share (EPS).

b. Prepare in good form a balance sheet for Rogers Industries for December 31, 2000.

Balance Sheet ($000)
Rogers Industries
December 31, 1999

Assets		Liabilities and stockholders' equity	
Cash	$ 40	Accounts payable	$ 50
Marketable securities	10	Notes payable	80
Accounts receivable	80	Accruals	10
Inventories	100	Total current liabilities	$140
Total current assets	$230	Long-term debt	$270
Gross fixed assets	$890	Preferred stock	$ 40
Less: Accumulated		Common stock ($.75 par,	
depreciation	240	80,000 shares)	60
Net fixed assets	$650	Paid-in capital in excess of par	260
Total assets	$880	Retained earnings	110
		Total stockholders' equity	$470
		Total liabilities and stockholders' equity	$880

Relevant Information
Rogers Industries

1. Sales in 2000 were $1,200,000.
2. Cost of goods sold equals 60 percent of sales.
3. Operating expenses equal 15 percent of sales.
4. Interest expense is 10 percent of the total beginning balance of notes payable and long-term debts.
5. The firm pays 40 percent taxes on ordinary income.
6. Preferred stock dividends of $4,000 were paid in 2000.
7. Cash and marketable securities are unchanged.
8. Accounts receivable equal 8 percent of sales.
9. Inventory equals 10 percent of sales.
10. The firm acquired $30,000 of additional fixed assets in 2000.
11. Total depreciation expense in 2000 was $20,000.
12. Accounts payable equal 5 percent of sales.
13. Notes payable, long-term debt, preferred stock, common stock, and paid-in capital in excess of par remain unchanged.
14. Accruals are unchanged.
15. Cash dividends of $119,000 were paid to common stockholders in 2000.

4-9 **Statement of retained earnings**   Hayes Enterprises began 2000 with a retained earnings balance of $928,000. During 2000, the firm earned $377,000 after taxes. From this amount, preferred stockholders were paid $47,000 in dividends. At year-end 2000, the firm's retained earnings totaled $1,048,000. The firm had 140,000 shares of common stock outstanding during 2000.
   a. Prepare a statement of retained earnings for the year ended December 31, 2000, for Hayes Enterprises. (*Note:* Be sure to calculate and include the amount of cash dividends paid on common stock in 2000.)
   b. Calculate the firm's 2000 earnings per share (EPS).
   c. How large a per-share cash dividend did the firm pay on common stock during 2000?

  4-10 **Corporate taxes**   Tantor Supply, Inc., is a small corporation acting as the exclusive distributor of a major line of sporting goods. During 2000 the firm earned $92,500 before taxes.
   a. Calculate the firm's tax liability using the corporate tax rate schedule given in Table 4.4.
   b. How much is Tantor Supply's 2000 after-tax earnings?
   c. What was the firm's *average tax rate,* based on your findings in **a?**
   d. What is the firm's *marginal tax rate,* based on your findings in **a?**

  4-11 **Average corporate tax rates**   Using the corporate tax rate schedule given in Table 4.4, perform the following:
   a. Calculate the tax liability, after-tax earnings, and average tax rates for the following levels of corporate earnings before taxes: $10,000; $80,000; $300,000; $500,000; $1.5 million; $10 million; and $15 million.
   b. Plot the average tax rates (measured on the *y* axis) against the pretax income levels (measured on the *x* axis). What generalization can be made concerning the relationship between these variables?

4-12 **Marginal corporate tax rates**   Using the corporate tax rate schedule given in Table 4.4, perform the following:
   a. Find the marginal tax rate for the following levels of corporate earnings before taxes: $15,000; $60,000; $90,000; $200,000; $400,000; $1 million; and $20 million.
   b. Plot the marginal tax rates (measured on the *y* axis) against the pretax income levels (measured on the *x* axis). Explain the relationship between these variables.

INTERMEDIATE

4-13 Interest versus dividend income   During the year just ended, Shering Distributors, Inc., had pretax earnings from operations of $490,000. In addition, during the year it received $20,000 in income from interest on bonds it held in Zig Manufacturing and received $20,000 in income from dividends on its 5 percent common stock holding in Tank Industries, Inc. Shering is in the 40 percent tax bracket and is eligible for a 70 percent dividend exclusion on its Tank Industries stock.

a. Calculate the firm's tax on its operating earnings only.
b. Find the tax and after-tax amount attributable to the interest income from Zig Manufacturing bonds.
c. Find the tax and after-tax amount attributable to the dividend income from the Tank Industries, Inc., common stock.
d. Compare, contrast, and discuss the after-tax amounts resulting from the interest income and dividend income calculated in b and c.
e. What is the firm's total tax liability for the year?

INTERMEDIATE

4-14 Interest versus dividend expense   Michaels Corporation expects earnings before interest and taxes to be $40,000 for this period. Assuming an ordinary tax rate of 40 percent, compute the firm's earnings after taxes and earnings available for common stockholders (earnings after taxes and preferred stock dividends, if any) under the following conditions:

a. The firm pays $10,000 in interest.
b. The firm pays $10,000 in preferred stock dividends.

WARM-UP

4-15 Capital gains taxes   Perkins Manufacturing is considering the sale of two nondepreciable assets, X and Y. Asset X was purchased for $2,000 and will be sold today for $2,250. Asset Y was purchased for $30,000 and will be sold today for $35,000. The firm is subject to a 40 percent tax rate on capital gains.

a. Calculate the amount of capital gain, if any, realized on each of the assets.
b. Calculate the tax on the sale of each asset.

WARM-UP

4-16 Capital gains taxes   The following table contains purchase and sale prices for the nondepreciable assets of a major corporation. The firm paid taxes of 40 percent on capital gains.

Asset	Purchase price	Sale price
A	$ 3,000	$ 3,400
B	12,000	12,000
C	62,000	80,000
D	41,000	45,000
E	16,500	18,000

a. Determine the amount of capital gain realized on each of the five assets.
b. Calculate the amount of tax paid on each of the assets.

WARM-UP

4-17 Cash flow   A firm had earnings after taxes of $50,000 in 2000. Depreciation charges were $28,000, and a $2,000 charge for amortization of a bond discount was incurred. What was the firm's *cash flow from operations* during 2000?

4-18   **Depreciation**   On January 1, 2000, Norton Systems acquired two new assets. Asset A was research equipment costing $17,000 and having a 3-year recovery period. Asset B was duplicating equipment having an installed cost of $45,000 and a 5-year recovery period. Using the MACRS depreciation percentages in Table 4.7 on page 91, prepare a depreciation schedule for each of these assets.

  4-19   **Depreciation and cash flow**   A firm in the third year of depreciating its only asset, originally costing $180,000 and having a 5-year MACRS recovery period, has gathered the following data relative to the current year's operations.

Accruals	$ 15,000
Current assets	120,000
Interest expense	15,000
Sales revenue	400,000
Inventory	70,000
Total costs before depreciation, interest, and taxes	290,000
Tax rate on ordinary income	40%

a. Use the *relevant data* to determine the *cash flow from operations* for the current year.
b. Explain the impact that depreciation, as well as any other noncash charges, has on a firm's cash flows.

  4-20   **Classifying sources and uses**   Classify each of the following items as a source (S) or a use (U) of funds, or as neither (N).

Item	Change ($)	Item	Change ($)
Cash	+100	Accounts receivable	−700
Accounts payable	−1,000	Net profits	+600
Notes payable	+500	Depreciation	+100
Long-term debt	−2,000	Repurchase of stock	+600
Inventory	+200	Cash dividends	+800
Fixed assets	+400	Sale of stock	+1,000

CASE   Chapter 4

Evaluating Cline Custom Bicycles' Cash Flows

Darin Cline, formerly an internationally renowned professional bicycle racer, owns and operates Cline Custom Bicycles—a firm that builds and markets custom bicycles to shops throughout the United States. Darin has just received his firm's 2000 income statement, 2000 and 1999 balance sheets, and 2000 statement of retained earnings, shown on the following pages. Although he is quite pleased to have achieved record earnings of $106,000 in 2000, Darin is concerned about the firm's cash flows. Specifically, he is finding it more and more difficult to pay the firm's bills in a timely manner.

To gain insight into the firm's cash flow problems, Darin instructed the firm's senior accountant to prepare the firm's 2000 statement of cash flows, which he planned to evaluate. Unfortunately, the senior accountant abruptly resigned prior to completing preparation of the firm's statement of cash flows. Darin has hired you to complete the partially prepared statement shown in the middle of page 109 and to use it to evaluate the firm's 2000 cash flows.

Income Statement ($000) Cline Custom Bicycles for the year ended December 31, 2000		
Sales revenue		$2,200
Less: Cost of goods sold		1,420
Gross profits		$ 780
Less: Operating expenses		
Selling expense	$300	
General and administrative expense	270	
Depreciation expense	30	
Total operating expense		600
Operating profits		$ 180
Less: Interest expense		29
Net profits before taxes		$ 151
Less: Taxes (30%)		45
Net profits after taxes		$ 106

Balance Sheets ($000) Cline Custom Bicycles		
	December 31	
Assets	2000	1999
Current assets		
Cash	$ 30	$ 50
Marketable securities	10	20
Accounts receivable	320	350
Inventories	460	320
Total current assets	$ 820	$ 740
Gross fixed assets	$ 560	$ 520
Less: Accumulated depreciation	180	150
Net fixed assets	$ 380	$ 370
Total assets	$1,200	$1,110
Liabilities and stockholders' equity		
Current liabilities		
Accounts payable	$ 390	$ 320
Notes payable	110	90
Accruals	20	20
Total current liabilities	$ 520	$ 430
Long-term debt	$ 320	$ 350
Total liabilities	$ 840	$ 780
Stockholders' equity		
Common stock (500,000 shares at $.20 par value)	$ 100	$ 100
Paid-in capital in excess of par	150	150
Retained earnings	110	80
Total stockholders' equity	$ 360	$ 330
Total liabilities and stockholders' equity	$1,200	$1,110

Statement of Retained Earnings ($000)
Cline Custom Bicycles
for the year ended December 31, 2000

Retained earnings balance (January 1, 2000)	$ 80
Plus: Net profits after taxes (for 2000)	106
Less: Cash dividends on common stock	
(paid during 2000)	(76)
Retained earnings balance (December 31, 2000)	$110

Statement of Cash Flows
Cline Custom Bicycles
for the year ended December 31, 2000

Cash Flow from Operating Activities			
Net profits after taxes	$106,000		
Depreciation	?		
Decrease in accounts receivable	?		
Increase in inventories	(140,000)		
Increase in accounts payable	?		
Cash provided by operating activities		$?	
Cash Flow from Investment Activities			
Increase in gross fixed assets	$?		
Cash provided by investment activities		?	
Cash Flow from Financing Activities			
Increase in notes payable	$?		
Decrease in long-term debt	?		
Change in stockholders' equity	0		
Dividends paid	?		
Cash provided by financing activities		?	
Net increase (decrease) in cash and			
marketable securities		$?	

Required

a. Use the financial data presented to complete Cline Custom Bicycles' statement of cash flows for the year ended December 31, 2000. [*Note:* The question marks above the rules indicate the need to calculate and insert the missing entries. Be sure to properly use parentheses to differentiate cash outflows (uses of funds) from cash inflows (sources of funds).]

b. Evaluate the statement prepared in **a** in light of Cline's current cash flow difficulties.

c. On the basis of your evaluation in **b,** what recommendations might you offer Darin Cline?

Web Exercise

GOTO web site www.hoovers.com. In the toolbox in the left column, click ticker symbol and enter LUV—the stock symbol for Southwest Airlines—into the search box; then click GO>>.

1. Who are the top competitors to Southwest Airlines?
2. Who is the CFO of Southwest Airlines?

At the top of the page, click Financials.

3. Which two financial statements are given for Southwest Airlines?
4. How many years of data are given here?

FINANCIAL STATEMENT ANALYSIS

5

LEARNING GOALS

LG1 Understand the parties interested in performing financial ratio analysis and the common types of ratio comparisons.

LG2 Describe some of the cautions that should be considered in performing financial ratio analysis.

LG3 Use popular ratios to analyze a firm's liquidity and the activity of inventory, accounts receivable, accounts payable, and total assets.

LG4 Discuss the relationship between debt and financial leverage and the ratios that can be used to assess the firm's degree of indebtedness and its ability to meet interest payments associated with debt.

LG5 Evaluate a firm's profitability relative to its sales, asset investment, and owners' equity investment.

LG6 Use the DuPont system and a summary of financial ratios to perform a complete ratio analysis.

ACROSS *the* DISCIPLINES

Financial statements contain important information on a company's operating results and financial position. Because these statements are widely standardized, the data they contain can be used to make comparisons between firms and over time. The relationship between certain items of financial data can be used to identify areas where the firm excels and, more importantly, areas of opportunity for improvement. This chapter explains four categories of financial ratios and their use. Chapter 5 is important to:

- **accounting personnel** who will calculate and interpret the financial ratios.
- **information systems analysts** who will design financial information systems that provide most of the data for ratio calculations.
- **management** because it must assess market reaction to the changes in financial ratios that result from its decisions.
- **the marketing department** because its activities will be evaluated by financial ratio analysis; and, inventories may be lowered and credit-granting policies tightened to better conform to industry averages.
- **operations,** which may be denied new equipment or facilities requests because of their adverse effect on the financial ratios.

USING FINANCIAL RATIOS

ratio analysis
Involves the methods of calculating and interpreting financial ratios to assess the firm's performance.

In the preceding chapter, we reviewed the firm's four basic financial statements. The information contained in these statements is of major significance to various interested parties who need to have relative measures of the company's operating efficiency. *Relative* is the key word here, because the analysis of financial statements is based on the knowledge and use of *ratios* or *relative values*.

Ratio analysis involves methods of calculating and interpreting financial ratios to assess the firm's performance. The basic inputs to ratio analysis are the firm's income statement and balance sheet.

INTERESTED PARTIES

Ratio analysis of a firm's financial statements is of interest to shareholders, creditors, and the firm's own management. Both present and prospective shareholders are interested in the firm's current and future level of risk and return, which directly affect share price. The firm's creditors are primarily interested in the short-term liquidity of the company and in its ability to make interest and principal payments. A secondary concern of creditors is the firm's profitability; they want assurance that the business is healthy and will continue to be successful. Management, like stockholders, is concerned with all aspects of the firm's financial situation. Thus, it attempts to produce financial ratios that will be considered favorable by both owners and creditors. In addition, management uses ratios to monitor the firm's performance from period to period. Any unexpected changes are examined to isolate developing problems.

TYPES OF RATIO COMPARISONS

Ratio analysis is not merely the application of a formula to financial data to calculate a given ratio. More important is the *interpretation* of the ratio value. To answer such questions as, Is it too high or too low? Is it good or bad?, a meaningful basis for comparison is needed. Two types of ratio comparisons can be made: cross-sectional and time-series.

cross-sectional analysis
Comparison of different firms' financial ratios at the same point in time; involves comparing the firm's ratios to those of other firms in its industry or to industry averages.

CROSS-SECTIONAL ANALYSIS

Cross-sectional analysis involves comparison of different firms' financial ratios at the same point in time. The typical business is interested in how well it has performed in relation to other firms in its industry. Often, the reported financial statements of competing firms will be available for analysis. Frequently, a firm will compare its ratio values to those of a key competitor or group of competitors that it wishes to emulate. This type of cross-sectional analysis, called **benchmarking,** has become very popular in recent years. By comparing the firm's ratios to those of the *benchmark company,* it can identify areas in which it excels and, more importantly, areas of opportunity for improvement.

benchmarking
A type of *cross-sectional analysis* in which the firm's ratio values are compared to those of a key competitor or group of competitors, primarily to identify areas of opportunity for improvement.

Another popular type of comparison is to industry averages. These figures can be found in the *Almanac of Business and Industrial Financial Ratios, Dun &*

Bradstreet's Industry Norms and Key Business Ratios, Business Month, FTC Quarterly Reports, Robert Morris Associates Statement Studies, and other sources such as industry association publications. A sample from one available source of industry averages is given in Table 5.1.

Comparing a particular ratio to the standard should uncover any *deviations from the norm.* Many people mistakenly believe that as long as the firm has a value "better than" the industry average, it can be viewed favorably. However, this "better than average" viewpoint can be misleading. Quite often a ratio value that is far better than the norm can indicate problems. It is therefore important for the analyst to investigate *significant deviations to either side* of the industry standard.

The analyst must also recognize that ratios with large deviations from the norm are only the *symptoms* of a problem. Further analysis is typically required to isolate the *causes* of the problem. Once the reason for the problem is known, management can develop prescriptive actions for eliminating it. The fundamental point is this: *Ratio analysis merely directs attention to potential areas of concern; it does not provide conclusive evidence as to the existence of a problem.*

Example ▼ In early 2001, Marie Sanchez, the chief financial analyst at Dwiggans Manufacturing, a producer of refrigeration equipment, gathered data on the firm's financial performance during 2000, the year just ended. She calculated a variety of ratios and obtained industry averages. She was especially interested in the inventory turnover, which reflects the speed with which the firm moves its inventory from raw materials through production into finished goods and to the customer as a completed sale. Generally, higher values of this ratio are preferred, because they indicate a quicker turnover of inventory. Dwiggans Manufacturing's calculated inventory turnover for 2000 and the industry average inventory turnover were, respectively:

	Inventory turnover, 2000
Dwiggans Manufacturing	14.8
Industry average	19.7

Marie's initial reaction to these data was that the firm had managed its inventory significantly *better than* the average firm in the industry. The turnover was in fact nearly 53 percent faster than the industry average. Upon reflection, however, she realized that a very high inventory turnover could also mean very low levels of inventory. The consequence of low inventory could be excessive stockouts (insufficient inventory). Discussions with people in the manufacturing and marketing departments did in fact uncover such a problem: Inventories during the year were extremely low, the result of numerous production delays that hindered the firm's ability to meet demand and resulted in lost sales. What had initially appeared to reflect extremely efficient inventory management was actually the symptom of a major problem.

TABLE 5.1 Industry Average Ratios for Selected Lines of Business[a]

Line of business (number of concerns reporting)[b]	Current ratio (X)	Quick ratio (X)	Sales to inventory (X)	Collection period (days)	Total assets to sales (%)	Total liabilities to net worth (%)	Return on sales (%)	Return on total assets (%)	Return on net worth (%)
Department	6.4	1.7	5.7	3.2	33.5	20.0	4.0	8.6	16.1
stores	3.1	0.8	4.4	11.2	48.3	68.2	1.5	3.8	6.8
(242)	1.9	0.3	3.0	35.1	64.0	145.3	(0.1)	0.8	1.8
Electronic	3.0	1.8	20.7	33.3	28.2	44.5	5.4	10.1	28.4
computers	1.9	1.1	10.5	54.0	58.0	106.9	1.2	4.6	11.7
(142)	1.3	0.7	6.1	90.9	96.4	243.7	(1.0)	0.4	0.4
Grocery	3.1	1.2	27.8	1.1	14.5	37.8	3.0	13.4	30.5
stores	1.7	0.5	18.7	3.3	20.6	88.3	1.5	5.5	12.6
(965)	1.1	0.3	12.5	6.2	32.4	206.4	0.5	1.7	4.9
Motor	2.4	1.1	11.7	19.4	26.5	76.3	4.6	8.2	20.4
vehicles	1.7	0.7	6.1	33.6	42.8	135.9	1.8	3.1	9.2
(51)	1.3	0.4	4.3	50.7	70.6	233.6	0.5	0.7	1.9

[a]These 1998 values are given for each ratio for each line of business. The center value is the median, and the values immediately above and below it are the upper and lower quartiles, respectively.

[b]Standard Industrial Classification (SIC) codes for the lines of business shown are, respectively: SIC #5311, SIC #3571, SIC #5411, SIC #3711.

Source: "Industry Norms and Key Business Ratios," Copyright © 1999 Dun & Bradstreet, Inc. Reprinted with permission.

TIME-SERIES ANALYSIS

time-series analysis
Evaluation of the firm's financial performance over time using financial ratio analysis.

Time-series analysis evaluates performance over time. Comparison of current to past performance, using ratios, allows the firm to determine whether it is progressing as planned. Developing trends can be seen by using multiyear comparisons, and knowledge of these trends can assist the firm in planning future operations. As in cross-sectional analysis, any significant year-to-year changes should be evaluated to assess whether they are symptomatic of a major problem. Time-series analysis also is often helpful in checking the reasonableness of a firm's projected (pro forma) financial statements. A comparison of *current* and *past* ratios to those resulting from an analysis of *projected* statements may reveal discrepancies or overoptimism.

COMBINED ANALYSIS

The most informative approach to ratio analysis is one that combines cross-sectional and time-series analyses. A combined view permits assessment of a trend in the behavior of a ratio in relation to the trend for the industry. Figure 5.1 depicts this type of approach using the average collection period ratio of Alcott Company, a small manufacturer of patio furniture, over the years 1997–2000. This ratio reflects the average amount of time it takes the firm to collect bills, and lower values of this ratio generally are preferred. The figure quickly discloses that (1) Alcott's effectiveness in collecting its receivables is poor in comparison to the industry, and (2) Alcott's trend is toward longer collection periods. Clearly, Alcott needs to shorten its collection period.

CAUTIONS ABOUT RATIO ANALYSIS

Before discussing specific ratios, we should consider the following cautions:

1. A single ratio does not generally provide sufficient information from which to judge the *overall* performance of the firm. Only when a group of ratios is

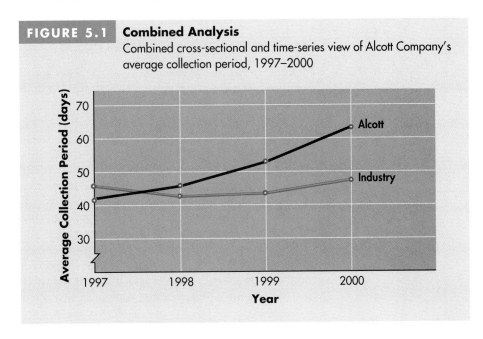

FIGURE 5.1   Combined Analysis
Combined cross-sectional and time-series view of Alcott Company's average collection period, 1997–2000

used can reasonable judgments be made. However, if an analysis is concerned only with certain *specific* aspects of a firm's financial position, one or two ratios may be sufficient.

2. The financial statements being compared should be dated at the same point in time during the year. If they are not, the effects of *seasonality* may produce erroneous conclusions and decisions. For example, comparison of the inventory turnover of a toy manufacturer at the end of June with its end-of-December value can be misleading. Clearly the seasonal impact of the December holiday selling season would skew any conclusions about the firm's inventory management drawn from such a comparison. Erroneous conclusions such as this can be avoided by comparing results for June of the current year to June of the prior year, December to December, and so forth, to eliminate the effects of seasonality.

3. It is preferable to use audited financial statements for ratio analysis. If the statements have not been audited, the data contained in them may not reflect the firm's true financial condition.

4. The financial data being compared should have been developed in the same way. The use of differing accounting treatments—especially relative to inventory and depreciation—can distort the results of ratio analysis, regardless of whether cross-sectional or time-series analysis is used.

5. When the ratios of one firm are compared with those of another, or with those of the firm itself over time, results can be distorted due to inflation. Inflation can cause the book values of inventory and depreciable assets to differ greatly from their true (replacement) values. Additionally, inventory costs and depreciation write-offs can differ from their true values, thereby distorting profits. These inflationary effects typically have greater impact the larger the differences in the ages of the assets of the firms being compared. Without adjustment, inflation tends to cause older firms (older assets) to appear more efficient and profitable than newer firms (newer assets). Clearly, care must be taken in comparing ratios of older to newer firms or a firm to itself over a long period of time.

CATEGORIES OF FINANCIAL RATIOS

Financial ratios can be divided for convenience into four basic categories: liquidity ratios, activity ratios, debt ratios, and profitability ratios. Liquidity, activity, and debt ratios primarily measure risk; profitability ratios measure return. In the near term the important categories are liquidity, activity, and profitability, because these provide the information that is critical to the short-run operation of the firm. (If a firm cannot survive in the short run, we need not be concerned with its longer-term prospects.) Debt ratios are useful primarily when the analyst is sure that the firm will successfully weather the short run.

As a rule, the necessary inputs to an effective financial analysis include, at minimum, the income statement and the balance sheet. We will use the 2000 and 1999 income statements and balance sheets for Alcott Company, presented in Tables 5.2 and 5.3, to demonstrate ratio calculations. Note, though, that the ratios presented in the remainder of this chapter can be applied to nearly any company. Of course, companies in different industries use ratios that are particularly focused on aspects peculiar to their industry.

TABLE 5.2	**Alcott Company Income Statements ($000)**	
		For the years ended December 31
	2000	**1999**
Sales revenue	$3,074	$2,567
Less: Cost of goods sold	2,088	1,711
Gross profits	$ 986	$ 856
Less: Operating expenses		
Selling expense	$ 100	$ 108
General and administrative expenses	229	222
Depreciation expense	239	223
Total operating expense	$ 568	$ 553
Operating profits	$ 418	$ 303
Less: Interest expense	93	91
Net profits before taxes	$ 325	$ 212
Less: Taxes (rate = 29%)[a]	94	64
Net profits after taxes	$ 231	$ 148
Less: Preferred stock dividends	10	10
Earnings available for common stockholders	$ 221	$ 138
Earnings per share (EPS)[b]	$ 2.90	$ 1.81

[a]The 29% tax rate for 2000 results because the firm has certain special tax write-offs that do not show up directly on its income statement.

[b]Calculated by dividing the earnings available for common stockholders by the number of shares of common stock outstanding—76,262 in 2000 and 76,244 in 1999. Earnings per share in 2000: $221,000 ÷ 76,262 = $2.90; in 1999: $138,000 ÷ 76,244 = $1.81.

? Review Questions

5-1   With regard to financial ratio analyses of a firm, how do the viewpoints held by the firm's present and prospective shareholders, creditors, and management differ?

5-2   How can ratio analysis be used for *cross-sectional* and *time-series* comparisons? What is *benchmarking?* Which type of ratio comparison would be more common for internal analysis?

5-3   To what types of deviations from the norm should the analyst devote primary attention when performing cross-sectional ratio analysis? Why?

5-4   Why is it preferable to compare financial statements that are dated at the same point in time during the year?

TABLE 5.3	Alcott Company Balance Sheets ($000)		
		December 31	
Assets		2000	1999
Current assets			
Cash		$ 363	$ 288
Marketable securities		68	51
Accounts receivable		503	365
Inventories		289	300
Total current assets		$1,223	$1,004
Gross fixed assets (at cost)			
Land and buildings		$2,072	$1,903
Machinery and equipment		1,866	1,693
Furniture and fixtures		358	316
Vehicles		275	314
Other (includes financial leases)		98	96
Total gross fixed assets (at cost)		$4,669	$4,322
Less: Accumulated depreciation		2,295	2,056
Net fixed assets		$2,374	$2,266
Total assets		$3,597	$3,270
Liabilities and stockholders' equity			
Current liabilities			
Accounts payable		$ 382	$ 270
Notes payable		79	99
Accruals		159	114
Total current liabilities		$ 620	$ 483
Long-term debt		$1,023	$ 967
Total liabilities		$1,643	$1,450
Stockholders' equity			
Preferred stock—cumulative 5%, $100 par, 2,000 shares authorized and issued[a]		$ 200	$ 200
Common stock—S2.50 par, 100,000 shares authorized, shares issued and outstanding in 2000: 76,262; in 1999: 76,244		191	190
Paid-in capital in excess of par on common stock		428	418
Retained earnings		1,135	1,012
Total stockholders' equity		$1,954	$1,820
Total liabilities and stockholders' equity		$3,597	$3,270

[a]The annual preferred stock dividend would be $5 per share (5% × $100 par), or a total of $10,000 annually ($5 per share × 2,000 shares).

ANALYZING LIQUIDITY

liquidity
A firm's ability to satisfy its short-term obligations *as they come due.*

The **liquidity** of a business firm is measured by its ability to satisfy its short-term obligations *as they come due.* Liquidity refers to the solvency of the firm's *overall* financial position—the ease with which it can pay its bills. The three basic measures of liquidity are (1) net working capital, (2) the current ratio, and (3) the quick (acid-test) ratio.

NET WORKING CAPITAL

net working capital
A measure of liquidity calculated by subtracting current liabilities from current assets.

Net working capital, although not actually a ratio, is a common measure of a firm's overall liquidity. It is calculated as follows:

$$\text{Net working capital} = \text{current assets} - \text{current liabilities}$$

The net working capital for Alcott Company in 2000 is:

$$\text{Net working capital} = \$1,223,000 - \$620,000 = \$603,000$$

This figure is *not* useful for comparing the performance of different firms, but it is quite useful for internal control.[1] Often a *restrictive covenant* included in a *bond indenture* (see Chapter 3) will specify a minimum level of net working capital that the firm must maintain. This requirement protects creditors by forcing the firm to maintain adequate liquidity. A time-series comparison of the firm's net working capital is often helpful in evaluating its operations.

CURRENT RATIO

current ratio
A measure of liquidity calculated by dividing the firm's current assets by its current liabilities.

The **current ratio,** one of the most commonly cited financial ratios, measures the firm's ability to meet its short-term obligations. It is expressed as follows:

$$\text{Current ratio} = \frac{\text{current assets}}{\text{current liabilities}}$$

The current ratio for Alcott Company in 2000 is:

$$\frac{\$1,223,000}{\$620,000} = 1.97$$

A current ratio of 2.0 is occasionally cited as acceptable, but a value's acceptability depends on the industry in which the firm operates. For example, a current ratio of 1.0 would be considered acceptable for a utility but might be unacceptable for a manufacturing firm. The more predictable a firm's cash flows, the

---

[1] To make cross-sectional as well as better time-series comparisons, *net working capital as a percent of sales* can be calculated. For Alcott Company in 2000, this ratio would be 19.6 percent ($603,000 ÷ $3,074,000). In general, the larger this value, the greater the firm's liquidity, and the smaller this value, the lesser the firm's liquidity. Because of the relative nature of this measure, it is often used to make liquidity comparisons.

lower the acceptable current ratio. Because Alcott Company is in a business with a relatively predictable annual cash flow, its current ratio of 1.97 should be quite acceptable.

It is useful to note that whenever a firm's current ratio is 1.0, its net working capital is zero. If a firm has a current ratio of less than 1.0, it will have negative net working capital. Net working capital is useful only in comparing the liquidity of the same firm over time. It should not be used to compare the liquidity of different firms; the current ratio should be used instead.

QUICK (ACID-TEST) RATIO

quick (acid-test) ratio
A measure of liquidity calculated by dividing the firm's current assets minus inventory by current liabilities.

The **quick (acid-test) ratio** is similar to the current ratio except that it excludes inventory, which is generally the least liquid current asset. The generally low liquidity of inventory results from two factors: (1) many types of inventory cannot be easily sold because they are partially completed items, special-purpose items, and the like; and (2) inventory is typically sold on credit, which means that it becomes an account receivable before being converted into cash. The quick ratio is calculated as follows:

$$\text{Quick ratio} = \frac{\text{current assets} - \text{inventory}}{\text{current liabilities}}$$

The quick ratio for Alcott Company in 2000 is:

$$\frac{\$1,223,000 - \$289,000}{\$620,000} = \frac{\$934,000}{\$620,000} = 1.51$$

A quick ratio of 1.0 or greater is occasionally recommended, but as with the current ratio, an acceptable value depends largely on the industry. The quick ratio provides a better measure of overall liquidity only when a firm's inventory cannot be easily converted into cash. If inventory is liquid, the current ratio is a preferred measure of overall liquidity.

? R eview **Q** uestion

5-5   Why is net working capital useful only in time-series comparisons of overall liquidity, whereas the current and quick ratios can be used for both cross-sectional and time-series analysis?

ANALYZING ACTIVITY

activity ratios
Measure the speed with which various accounts are converted into sales or cash.

Activity ratios measure the speed with which various accounts are converted into sales or cash. With regard to current accounts, measures of liquidity are generally inadequate, because differences in the *composition* of a firm's current accounts can significantly affect its "true" liquidity. For example, consider the current assets and liabilities on the balance sheets of firms A and B, below:

Firm A			
Cash	$ 0	Accounts payable	$ 0
Marketable securities	0	Notes payable	10,000
Accounts receivable	0	Accruals	0
Inventories	20,000	Total current liabilities	$10,000
Total current assets	$20,000		

Firm B			
Cash	$ 5,000	Accounts payable	$ 5,000
Marketable securities	5,000	Notes payable	3,000
Accounts receivable	5,000	Accruals	2,000
Inventories	5,000	Total current liabilities	$10,000
Total current assets	$20,000		

Both firms appear to be equally liquid, because their current ratios are both 2.0 ($20,000 ÷ $10,000). However, a closer look at the differences in the composition of current assets and liabilities suggests that *firm B is more liquid than firm A*. This is true for two reasons: (1) Firm B has more liquid assets in the form of cash and marketable securities than firm A, which has only a single, relatively illiquid asset in the form of inventories, and (2) firm B's current liabilities are in general more flexible than the single current liability—notes payable—of firm A.

It is therefore important to look beyond measures of overall liquidity and to assess the activity (liquidity) of specific current accounts. A number of ratios are available for measuring the activity of the most important current accounts, which include inventory, accounts receivable, and accounts payable.[2] The activity (efficiency of utilization) of total assets can also be assessed.

INVENTORY TURNOVER

inventory turnover
Measures the activity, or liquidity, of a firm's inventory.

Inventory turnover commonly measures the activity, or liquidity, of a firm's inventory. It is calculated as follows:

$$\text{Inventory turnover} = \frac{\text{cost of goods sold}}{\text{inventory}}$$

[2]For convenience, the activity ratios involving these current accounts assume that their end-of-period values are good approximations of the average account balance during the period—typically 1 year. Technically, when the month-end balances of inventory, accounts receivable, or accounts payable vary during the year, the average balance, calculated by summing the 12 month-end account balances and dividing the total by 12, should be used instead of the year-end value. Because the data needed to find averages are generally unavailable to the external analyst, year-end values are frequently used to calculate activity ratios for current accounts.

Applying this relationship to Alcott Company in 2000 yields:

$$\text{Inventory turnover} = \frac{\$2,088,000}{\$289,000} = 7.2$$

The resulting turnover is meaningful only when it is compared with that of other firms in the same industry or to the firm's past inventory turnover. An inventory turnover of 20.0 would not be unusual for a grocery store, whereas a common inventory turnover for an aircraft manufacturer would be 4.0.

average age of inventory
Average length of time inventory is held by the firm.

Inventory turnover can easily be converted into an **average age of inventory** by dividing it into 360—the number of days in a year.[3] For Alcott Company, the average age of inventory would be 50.0 days (360 ÷ 7.2). This value can also be viewed as the average number of days' sales in inventory.

AVERAGE COLLECTION PERIOD

average collection period
The average amount of time needed to collect accounts receivable.

The **average collection period,** or average age of accounts receivable, is useful in evaluating credit and collection policies.[4] It is arrived at by dividing the average daily sales[5] into the accounts receivable balance:

$$\text{Average collection period} = \frac{\text{accounts receivable}}{\text{average sales per day}}$$

$$= \frac{\text{accounts receivable}}{\dfrac{\text{annual sales}}{360}}$$

The average collection period for Alcott Company in 2000 is:

$$\frac{\$503,000}{\dfrac{\$3,074,000}{360}} = \frac{\$503,000}{\$8,539} = 58.9 \text{ days}$$

On the average it takes the firm 58.9 days to collect an account receivable.

The average collection period is meaningful only in relation to the firm's credit terms. If Alcott Company extends 30-day credit terms to customers, an average collection period of 58.9 days may indicate a poorly managed credit or collection department, or both. Or, the lengthened collection period could be the result of an intentional relaxation of credit-term enforcement in response to competitive pressures. If the firm had extended 60-day credit terms, the 58.9-day average collection period would be quite acceptable. Clearly, additional information would be required in order to evaluate the effectiveness of the firm's credit and collection policies.

---

[3]Unless otherwise specified, a 360-day year consisting of twelve 30-day months is assumed throughout this textbook. This assumption allows some simplification of the calculations used to illustrate key concepts.

[4]The average collection period is sometimes called the *days' sales outstanding (DSO)*. The evaluation and establishment of credit and collection policies are discussed in Chapter 17.

[5]The formula as presented assumes, for simplicity, that all sales are made on a credit basis. If such is not the case, *average credit sales per day* would be substituted for average sales per day.

AVERAGE PAYMENT PERIOD

average payment period
The average amount of time needed to pay accounts payable.

The **average payment period**, or average age of accounts payable, is calculated in the same manner as the average collection period:

$$\text{Average payment period} = \frac{\text{accounts payable}}{\text{average purchases per day}}$$

$$= \frac{\text{accounts payable}}{\dfrac{\text{annual purchases}}{360}}$$

The difficulty in calculating this ratio stems from the need to find annual purchases—a value not available in published financial statements. Ordinarily, purchases are estimated as a given percentage of cost of goods sold. If we assume that Alcott Company's purchases equaled 70 percent of its cost of goods sold in 2000, its average payment period is:

$$\frac{\$382,000}{\dfrac{.70 \times \$2,088,000}{360}} = \frac{\$382,000}{\$4,060} = 94.1 \text{ days}$$

This figure is meaningful only in relation to the average credit terms extended to the firm. If Alcott Company's suppliers, on the average, have extended 30-day credit terms, an analyst would give it a low credit rating. If the firm has been generally extended 90-day credit terms, its credit would be acceptable. Prospective lenders and suppliers of trade credit are especially interested in the average payment period, because it provides them with a sense of the bill-paying patterns of the firm.

TOTAL ASSET TURNOVER

total asset turnover
Indicates the efficiency with which the firm uses its assets to generate sales.

The **total asset turnover** indicates the efficiency with which the firm uses its assets to generate sales. Generally, the higher a firm's total asset turnover, the more efficiently its assets have been used. This measure is probably of greatest interest to management, because it indicates whether the firm's operations have been financially efficient. Total asset turnover is calculated as follows:

$$\text{Total asset turnover} = \frac{\text{sales}}{\text{total assets}}$$

The value of Alcott Company's total asset turnover in 2000 is:

$$\frac{\$3,074,000}{\$3,597,000} = .85$$

This means the company turns an amount equal to its total assets .85 times a year.

One caution with respect to use of this ratio: It cannot always be used for comparative purposes because it is based on the *historical costs* of total assets. Because some firms have significantly newer or older assets than others, comparing total asset turnovers of those firms can be misleading. Firms with newer assets will tend to have lower turnovers than those with older assets. The differences in these turnover measures could result from more costly assets rather than from operating efficiencies. The financial manager, therefore, should be cautious when using this ratio for cross-sectional comparisons.

? Review Question

5-6   To assess the reasonableness of the firm's average collection period and average payment period ratios, what additional information is needed in each instance? Explain why.

ANALYZING DEBT

The *debt position* of a firm indicates the amount of other people's money being used in attempting to generate profits. In general, the financial analyst is most concerned with long-term debts, because these commit the firm to paying interest, and eventually the principal, over the long run. Because creditors' claims must be satisfied before earnings can be distributed to shareholders, present and prospective shareholders pay close attention to the ability to repay debts. Lenders are also concerned about the firm's indebtedness, because the more indebted the firm, the more likely it will be unable to satisfy the claims of all its creditors. Management obviously must be concerned with indebtedness because of the attention paid to it by other parties and in the interest of keeping the firm solvent.

financial leverage
The magnification of risk and return introduced through the use of fixed-cost financing such as debt and preferred stock.

In general, the more debt a firm uses in relation to its total assets, the greater its *financial leverage.* **Financial leverage** is the magnification of risk and return introduced through the use of fixed-cost financing such as debt and preferred stock. The more fixed-cost debt, or financial leverage, a firm uses, the greater will be its risk and its expected return.

Example ▼ Michael Karp and Amy Parsons are incorporating a new business venture they have formed. After much analysis they have determined that an initial investment of $50,000—$20,000 of current assets and $30,000 of fixed assets—is necessary. These funds can be obtained in either of two ways. The first is the *no-debt plan,* under which they would together invest the full $50,000 without borrowing. The other alternative, the *debt plan,* involves making a combined investment of $25,000 and borrowing the balance of $25,000 at 12 percent annual interest. Regardless of which alternative they choose, Michael and Amy expect sales to average $30,000, costs and operating expenses to average $18,000, and earnings to be taxed at a 40 percent rate. The balance sheets and income statements associated with the two plans are summarized in Table 5.4.

The no-debt plan results in after-tax profits of $7,200, which represent a 14.4 percent rate of return on the partners' $50,000 investment. The debt plan results in $5,400 of after-tax profits, which represent a 21.6 percent rate of return on their combined investment of $25,000. The debt plan provides Michael and Amy with a higher rate of return, but the risk of this plan is also greater, because the ▲ annual $3,000 of interest must be paid before they receive earnings.

TABLE 5.4	Financial Statements Associated with Michael and Amy's Alternatives		
Balance Sheets		No-debt plan	Debt plan
Current assets		$20,000	$20,000
Fixed assets		30,000	30,000
Total assets		$50,000	$50,000
Debt (12% interest)		$ 0	$25,000
(1) Equity		50,000	25,000
Total liabilities and equity		$50,000	$50,000
Income Statements			
Sales		$30,000	$30,000
Less: Costs and operating expenses		18,000	18,000
Operating profits		$12,000	$12,000
Less: Interest expense		0	$.12 \times \$25,000 =$ 3,000
Net profit before taxes		$12,000	$ 9,000
Less: Taxes (rate = 40%)		4,800	3,600
(2) Net profit after taxes		$ 7,200	$ 5,400
Return on equity [(2) ÷ (1)]		$\dfrac{\$7,200}{\$50,000} = 14.4\%$	$\dfrac{\$5,400}{\$25,000} = 21.6\%$

This example it makes it clear that *with increased debt comes greater risk as well as higher potential return.* Therefore, the greater the financial leverage, the greater the potential risk and return. A detailed discussion of the impact of debt on the firm's risk, return, and value is included in Chapter 12. Here, we emphasize the use of financial debt ratios to assess externally the degree of a firm's indebtedness and its ability to meet interest payments associated with debt.

DEBT RATIO

debt ratio
Measures the proportion of total assets financed by the firm's creditors.

The **debt ratio** measures the proportion of total assets financed by the firm's creditors. The higher this ratio, the greater the amount of other people's money being used in an attempt to generate profits. The ratio is calculated as follows:

$$\text{Debt ratio} = \frac{\text{total liabilities}}{\text{total assets}}$$

The debt ratio for Alcott Company in 2000 is:

$$\frac{\$1,643,000}{\$3,597,000} = .457 = 45.7\%$$

This indicates that the company has financed close to half of its assets with debt. The higher this ratio, the greater the firm's degree of indebtedness and the more financial leverage it has.

TIMES INTEREST EARNED RATIO

times interest earned ratio
Measures the firm's ability to make contractual interest payments; also called the *interest coverage ratio.*

The **times interest earned ratio,** sometimes called the *interest coverage ratio,* measures the firm's ability to make contractual interest payments—that is, *service* its debt. The higher the value of this ratio, the better able the firm is to fulfill its interest obligations. The times interest earned ratio is calculated as follows:

$$\text{Times interest earned} = \frac{\text{earnings before interest and taxes}}{\text{interest}}$$

The value of *earnings before interest and taxes* is the same as the figure for operating profits shown in the income statement. Applying this ratio to Alcott Company yields the following 2000 value:

$$\text{Times interest earned} = \frac{\$418,000}{\$93,000} = 4.5$$

Alcott Company's times interest earned ratio seems acceptable. It has a good margin of safety. As a rule, a value of at least 3.0—and preferably closer to 5.0—is suggested. The lower the ratio, the greater the risk to both lenders and owners. This risk results because if the firm were unable to meet scheduled interest payments, it could be driven into bankruptcy. This ratio therefore allows owners, creditors, and managers to assess the firm's ability to meet additional interest obligations on debt.

Review Question

5-7   What is *financial leverage?* What ratio can be used to measure a firm's *degree of indebtedness?* What ratio can be used to assess the firm's *ability to meet interest payments* associated with debt?

LG5 ANALYZING PROFITABILITY

There are many measures of profitability, which relate the returns of the firm to its sales, assets, or equity. As a group, these measures evaluate the firm's earnings with respect to a given level of sales, a certain level of assets, or the owners' investment. Without profits, a firm could not attract outside capital. Moreover, present owners and creditors would become concerned about the company's future and attempt to recover their funds. Owners, creditors, and management pay close attention to boosting profits due to the great importance placed on earnings in the marketplace.

COMMON-SIZE INCOME STATEMENTS

common-size income statement
An income statement in which each item is expressed as a percentage of sales.

A popular tool for evaluating profitability in relation to sales is the **common-size income statement.** On this statement, each item is expressed as a percentage of sales, thus highlighting the relationship between sales and specific costs, expenses, and forms of income. Common-size income statements are especially useful in comparing performance across years. Three frequently cited ratios of profitability

TABLE 5.5	Alcott Company Common-Size Income Statements		
	For the years ended December 31		Evaluation[a]
	2000	1999	1999–2000
Sales revenue	100.0%	100.0%	same
Less: Cost of goods sold	67.9	66.7	worse
(1) Gross profit margin	32.1%	33.3%	worse
Less: Operating expenses			
Selling expense	3.3%	4.2%	better
General and administrative expenses	6.3	7.3	better
Lease expense	1.1	1.3	better
Depreciation expense	7.8	8.7	better
Total operating expense	18.5%	21.5%	better
(2) Operating profit margin	13.6%	11.8%	better
Less: Interest expense	3.0	3.5	better
Net profits before taxes	10.6%	8.3%	better
Less: Taxes	3.1	2.5	worse[b]
(3) Net profit margin	7.5%	5.8%	better

[a]Subjective assessments based on data provided.

[b]Taxes as a percent of sales increased noticeably between 1999 and 2000 due to differing costs and expenses, whereas the average tax rates (taxes ÷ net profits before taxes) for 1999 and 2000 remained about the same—30 and 29 percent, respectively.

that can be read directly from the common-size income statement are (1) the gross profit margin, (2) the operating profit margin, and (3) the net profit margin.

Common-size income statements for 2000 and 1999 for Alcott Company are presented and evaluated in Table 5.5. The statements reveal that the firm's cost of goods sold increased from 66.7 percent of sales in 1999 to 67.9 percent in 2000, resulting in a worsening gross profit margin. However, thanks to a decrease in total operating expenses, the firm's net profit margin rose from 5.8 percent of sales in 1999 to 7.5 percent in 2000. The decrease in 2000 expenses more than compensated for the increase in the cost of goods sold. A decrease in the firm's 2000 interest expense (3.0 percent of sales versus 3.5 percent in 1999) added to the increase in 2000 profits.

GROSS PROFIT MARGIN

gross profit margin
Measures the percentage of each sales dollars remaining after the firm has paid for its goods.

The **gross profit margin** measures the percentage of each sales dollar remaining after the firm has paid for its goods. The higher the gross profit margin, the better, and the lower the relative cost of merchandise sold. Of course, the opposite case is also true, as the Alcott Company example shows. The gross profit margin is calculated as follows:

$$\text{Gross profit margin} = \frac{\text{sales} - \text{cost of goods sold}}{\text{sales}} = \frac{\text{gross profits}}{\text{sales}}$$

The value for Alcott Company's gross profit margin for 2000 is:

$$\frac{\$3,074,000 - \$2,088,000}{\$3,074,000} = \frac{\$986,000}{\$3,074,000} = 32.1\%$$

This value is labeled (1) on the common-size income statement in Table 5.5.

OPERATING PROFIT MARGIN

operating profit margin
Measures the percentage of each sales dollar remaining after all costs and expenses *other than* interest and taxes are deducted; the *pure profits* earned on each sales dollar.

The **operating profit margin** measures the percentage of each sales dollar remaining after all costs and expenses *other than* interest and taxes are deducted. It represents the *pure profits* earned on each sales dollar. Operating profits are "pure" because they measure only the profits earned on operations and ignore any financial and government charges (interest and taxes). A high operating profit margin is preferred. The operating profit margin is calculated as follows:

$$\text{Operating profit margin} = \frac{\text{operating profits}}{\text{sales}}$$

The value for Alcott Company's operating profit margin for 2000 is:

$$\frac{\$418,000}{\$3,074,000} = 13.6\%$$

This value is labeled (2) on the common-size income statement in Table 5.5.

NET PROFIT MARGIN

net profit margin
Measures the percentage of each sales dollar remaining after all costs and expenses, *including* interest and taxes, have been deducted.

The **net profit margin** measures the percentage of each sales dollar remaining after all costs and expenses, *including* interest and taxes, have been deducted. The higher the firm's net profit margin, the better. The net profit margin is a commonly cited measure of the firm's success with respect to earnings on sales. "Good" net profit margins differ considerably across industries. A net profit margin of 1 percent or less would not be unusual for a grocery store, whereas a net profit margin of 10 percent would be low for a retail jewelry store. The net profit margin is calculated as follows:

$$\text{Net profit margin} = \frac{\text{net profits after taxes}}{\text{sales}}$$

Alcott Company's net profit margin for 2000 is:

$$\frac{\$231,000}{\$3,074,000} = 7.5\%$$

This value is labeled (3) on the common-size income statement in Table 5.5.

RETURN ON TOTAL ASSETS (ROA)

return on total assets (ROA)
Measures the firm's overall effectiveness in generating profits with its available assets; also called the *return on investment (ROI)*.

The **return on total assets (ROA)**, also called the *return on investment (ROI)*, measures the firm's overall effectiveness in generating profits with its available assets. The higher the firm's return on total assets, the better. The return on total assets is calculated as follows:

$$\text{Return on total assets} = \frac{\text{net profits after taxes}}{\text{total assets}}$$

Alcott Company's return on total assets in 2000 is:

$$\frac{\$231,000}{\$3,597,000} = 6.4\%$$

To assess Alcott's 6.4 percent return on total assets, appropriate cross-sectional and time-series data would be needed.

RETURN ON EQUITY (ROE)

return on equity (ROE)
Measures the return earned on the owners' investment in the firm.

The **return on equity (ROE)** measures the return earned on the owners' investment in the firm.[6] Generally, the higher this return, the better off are the owners. Return on equity is calculated as follows:

$$\text{Return on equity} = \frac{\text{net profits after taxes}}{\text{stockholders' equity}}$$

This ratio for Alcott Company in 2000 is:

$$\frac{\$231,000}{\$1,954,000} = 11.8\%$$

To evaluate Alcott's 11.8 percent return on equity, appropriate cross-sectional and time-series data would be needed.

ⓅERSONAL FINANCE PERSPECTIVE
Self-Analysis

Can you apply ratio analysis to your personal finances? You bet! Personal financial ratios assume that you have prepared personal financial statements—a balance sheet that monitors your net worth (the amount by which your total assets exceed your total liabilities) and an income and expenditures statement that serves as a general budget. To learn how to prepare such statements, you should consult a standard personal finance textbook.

You can calculate a liquidity ratio using data from your balance sheet. This measure shows how long you could continue to pay current liabilities with your existing liquid assets if an unexpected event curtailed your income. It is calculated by dividing liquid assets by total current debts (any amounts that must be paid within one year). A liquidity ratio of say, 20 percent, would indicate that you could cover about a fifth of your year's obligations with what you have on hand. Put another way, a 20 percent ratio would indicate that you'd have about two and a half months' coverage (one month is 1/12, or 8.3 percent). There is no hard-and-fast rule as to what this ratio should be, although a standard guideline is to have a reserve fund of three to six months of after-tax income.

---

[6]This ratio measures the returns earned by both preferred and common stockholders. It includes preferred stock dividends in the profit figure and preferred stock in the equity value, but because the amount of preferred stock and its impact on a firm are generally quite small or nonexistent, this formula is a reasonably good approximation of the true owners'—that is, the common stockholders'—return.

The most important measure made from your income statement is the bottom line, *which shows the cash surplus (or deficit) from the period's activities. You can use this number to find your* savings ratio, *calculated as cash surplus divided by your after-tax income. As a benchmark against which to evaluate your own performance, U.S. families on average have savings ratios of about 5 to 8 percent.*

As is true of corporate financial ratios, you can use personal financial ratios to track your own financial progress over time. Lenders also will use these (or similar) ratios to compare your financial performance with that of other potential borrowers. ●

? R e v i e w Q u e s t i o n s

5-8 What is a *common-size income statement?* Which three ratios of profitability are found on this statement?

5-9 What would explain a firm's having a high *gross profit margin* and a low *net profit margin?*

5-10 Define and differentiate between *return on total assets (ROA)* and *return on equity (ROE)*. Which measure is probably of greatest interest to owners? Why?

A COMPLETE RATIO ANALYSIS

Analysts frequently wish to take an overall look at a firm's financial performance. As noted earlier, no single ratio is adequate for assessing all aspects of a firm's financial condition. Here we consider two popular approaches to a complete ratio analysis: (1) the DuPont system of analysis, and (2) the summary analysis of a large number of ratios. Each of these approaches has merit. The DuPont system acts as a *diagnostic tool* with which to assess the key areas responsible for the firm's financial condition. The summary analysis approach tends to view *all aspects* of the firm's financial activities to isolate key areas of responsibility.

DUPONT SYSTEM OF ANALYSIS

DuPont system of analysis
System used by management to dissect the firm's financial statements and to assess its financial condition.

The **DuPont system of analysis** is named for the DuPont Corporation, which originally popularized its use. It is used by financial managers to dissect the firm's financial statements and to assess its financial condition. The DuPont system merges the income statement and balance sheet into two summary measures of profitability: return on total assets (ROA) and return on equity (ROE). Figure 5.2 depicts the basic DuPont system with Alcott Company's 2000 monetary and ratio values. The upper portion of the chart summarizes the income statement activities; the lower portion summarizes the balance sheet activities.

The DuPont system links the *net profit margin* (which measures the firm's profitability on sales) with its *total asset turnover* (which indicates how efficient-

FIGURE 5.2   **DuPont System**
The DuPont system of analysis with application to Alcott Company (2000)

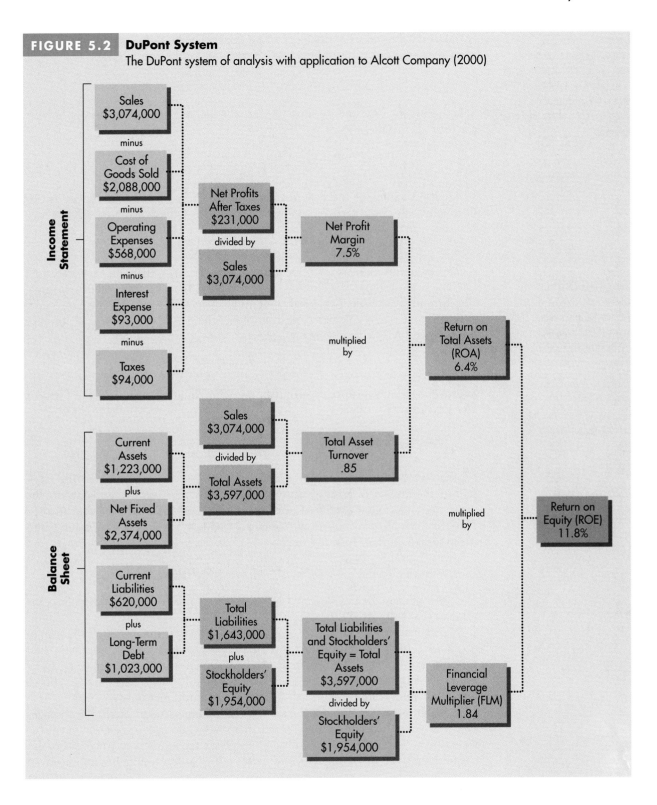

DuPont formula
Relates the firm's net profit margin and total asset turnover to its return on total assets (ROA). ROA is the product of the net profit margin and the total asset turnover.

modified DuPont formula
Relates the firm's return on total assets (ROA) to its return on equity (ROE) using the *financial leverage multiplier (FLM)*.

financial leverage multiplier (FLM)
The ratio of the firm's total assets to stockholders' equity.

ly the firm has used its assets to generate sales). The **DuPont formula** then multiplies these two ratios to find the firm's *return on total assets (ROA):*

$$\text{ROA} = \text{net profit margin} \times \text{total asset turnover}$$

Substituting the appropriate formulas into the equation and simplifying produces the formula given earlier:

$$\text{ROA} = \frac{\text{net profits after taxes}}{\text{sales}} \times \frac{\text{sales}}{\text{total assets}} = \frac{\text{net profits after taxes}}{\text{total assets}}$$

If the 2000 values of the net profit margin and total asset turnover for Alcott Company, calculated earlier, are substituted into the DuPont formula, the result is:

$$\text{ROA} = 7.5\% \times .85 = 6.4\%$$

As expected, this value is the same as that calculated directly in an earlier section.

The second step in the DuPont system employs the **modified DuPont formula.** This formula relates the firm's return on total assets (ROA) to the return on equity (ROE). The latter is calculated by multiplying the ROA by the **financial leverage multiplier (FLM)**, which is the ratio of total assets to stockholders' equity:

$$\text{ROE} = \text{ROA} \times \text{FLM}$$

Substituting the appropriate formulas into the equation produces the formula given earlier:

$$\text{ROE} = \frac{\text{net profits after taxes}}{\text{total assets}} \times \frac{\text{total assets}}{\text{stockholders' equity}} = \frac{\text{net profits after taxes}}{\text{stockholders' equity}}$$

Use of the financial leverage multiplier to convert the ROA to the ROE reflects the impact of leverage (use of debt) on owners' return. Substituting the values for Alcott Company's ROA of 6.4 percent, calculated earlier, and Alcott's FLM of 1.84 ($3,597,000 total assets ÷ $1,954,000 stockholders' equity) into the modified DuPont formula yields:

$$\text{ROE} = 6.4\% \times 1.84 = 11.8\%$$

The 11.8 percent ROE calculated by using the modified DuPont formula is the same as that calculated directly.

The considerable advantage of the DuPont system is that it allows the firm to break its return on equity into three parts: a profit-on-sales component (net profit margin), an efficiency-of-asset-use component (total asset turnover), and a use-of-leverage component (financial leverage multiplier). The total return to owners therefore can be analyzed in these important dimensions.

As an illustration, look at the ratio values summarized in Table 5.6 on pages 134 and 135. Alcott Company's net profit margin and total asset turnover increased between 1999 and 2000 to levels above the industry average. In combination, improved profit on sales and better use of assets resulted in an improved ROA. Increased asset return, coupled with the increased use of debt reflected in the increased financial leverage multiplier (not shown), caused the owners' return (ROE) to increase. Simply stated, the DuPont system of analysis shows that the improvement in Alcott Company's 2000 ROE resulted from greater profit on sales, better use of assets, and increased leverage. Of course, it is important to recognize that the increased return reflected in the ROE may be due to the increased risk caused by the higher leverage.

SUMMARIZING ALL RATIOS

Ratio values calculated for 1998 through 2000 for Alcott Company, along with the industry average ratios for 2000, are summarized in Table 5.6. The table shows the formula for each ratio. Using these data, we can discuss the four key aspects of Alcott's performance—(1) liquidity, (2) activity, (3) debt, and (4) profitability—on a cross-sectional and time-series basis.

LIQUIDITY

The overall liquidity of the firm seems to exhibit a reasonably stable trend, having been maintained at a level that is relatively consistent with the industry average in 2000. The firm's liquidity seems to be good.

ACTIVITY

Alcott Company's inventory appears to be in good shape. Its inventory management seems to have improved, and in 2000 it performed at a level above that of the industry. The firm may be experiencing some problems with accounts receivable. The average collection period seems to have crept up above that of the industry. Alcott also appears to be slow in paying its bills; it is nearly 30 days later than the industry average. Payment procedures should be examined to ensure that the company's credit standing is not adversely affected. Although overall liquidity appears to be good, some attention should be given to the management of receivables and payables. Alcott's total asset turnover reflects a sizable decline in the efficiency of asset utilization between 1998 and 1999. Although in 2000 the total asset turnover rose to a level considerably above the industry average, it appears that the pre-1999 level of efficiency has not yet been achieved.

DEBT

Alcott Company's indebtedness increased over the 1998–2000 period and is currently above the industry average. Although the increase in the debt ratio could be cause for alarm, the firm's ability to meet interest obligations improved from 1999 to 2000 to a level that outperforms the industry. The firm's increased indebtedness in 1999 apparently caused a deterioration in its ability to pay interest adequately, but improved income in 2000 enabled the firm to meet its fixed-payment obligations consistent with the average firm in the industry. In summary, it appears that although 1999 was an off year, the company's ability to service its debts in 2000 adequately compensates for the increased degree of indebtedness.

TABLE 5.6 Summary of Alcott Company Ratios (1998–2000, Including 2000 Industry Averages)

Ratio	Formula	Year 1998[a]	Year 1999[b]	Year 2000[b]	Industry average 2000[c]	Evaluation[d] Cross-sectional 2000	Evaluation[d] Time-series 1998–2000	Evaluation[d] Overall
Liquidity								
Net working capital	current assets − current liabilities	$583,000	$521,000	$603,000	$427,000	good	good	good
Current ratio	$\dfrac{\text{current assets}}{\text{current liabilities}}$	2.04	2.08	1.97	2.05	OK	OK	OK
Quick (acid-test) ratio	$\dfrac{\text{current assets} - \text{inventory}}{\text{current liabilities}}$	1.32	1.46	1.51	1.43	OK	good	good
Activity								
Inventory turnover	$\dfrac{\text{cost of goods sold}}{\text{inventory}}$	5.1	5.7	7.2	6.6	good	good	good
Average collection period	$\dfrac{\text{accounts receivable}}{\text{average sales per day}}$	43.9 days	51.2 days	58.9 days	44.3 days	poor	poor	poor
Average payment period	$\dfrac{\text{accounts payable}}{\text{average purchases per day}}$	75.8 days	81.2 days	94.1 days	66.5 days	poor	poor	poor
Total asset turnover	$\dfrac{\text{sales}}{\text{total assets}}$	.94	.79	.85	.75	OK	OK	OK
Debt								
Debt ratio	$\dfrac{\text{total liabilities}}{\text{total assets}}$	36.8%	44.3%	45.7%	40.0%	OK	OK	OK
Times interest earned ratio	$\dfrac{\text{earnings before interest and taxes}}{\text{interest}}$	5.6	3.3	4.5	4.3	good	OK	OK

Ratio	Formula	Year			Industry average 2000[c]	Evaluation[d]		
		1998[a]	1999[b]	2000[b]		Cross-sectional 2000	Time-series 1998–2000	Overall
Profitability								
Gross profit margin	$\dfrac{\text{gross profits}}{\text{sales}}$	31.4%	33.3%	32.1%	30.0%	OK	OK	OK
Operating profit margin	$\dfrac{\text{operating profits}}{\text{sales}}$	14.6%	11.8%	13.6%	11.0%	good	OK	good
Net profit margin	$\dfrac{\text{net profits after taxes}}{\text{sales}}$	8.8%	5.8%	7.5%	6.4%	good	OK	good
Return on total assets (ROA)	$\dfrac{\text{net profits after taxes}}{\text{total assets}}$	8.3%	4.5%	6.4%	4.8%	good	OK	good
Return on equity (ROE)	$\dfrac{\text{net profits after taxes}}{\text{stockholders' equity}}$	13.1%	8.1%	11.8%	8.0%	good	OK	good

[a]Calculated from data not included in the chapter.
[b]Calculated by using the financial statements presented in Tables 5.2 and 5.3.
[c]Obtained from sources not included in this chapter.
[d]Subjective assessments based on data provided.

PROFITABILITY

Alcott's profitability relative to sales in 2000 was better than the average company in the industry, although it did not match the firm's 1998 performance. Although the *gross* profit margin in 1999 and 2000 was better than in 1998, higher levels of operating and interest expenses in 1999 and 2000 appear to have caused the 2000 *net* profit margin to fall below that of 1998. However, Alcott Company's 2000 net profit margin is quite favorable when compared to the industry average. The firm's return on total assets and return on equity behaved similar to its net profit margin over the 1998–2000 period. Alcott appears to have experienced either a sizable drop in sales between 1998 and 1999 or a rapid expansion in assets during that period. The owners' return, as evidenced by the high 2000 level of return on equity, suggests that the firm is performing quite well. Of course, as was noted in the discussion of the DuPont analysis of Alcott's 2000 results, the firm's increased ROE actually resulted from increased returns and increased risk. This can be seen in the firm's increased debt ratios and financial leverage multiplier (FLM). The firm's above-average returns—net profit margin, ROA, and ROE—appear to be consistent with its above-average risk.

In summary, the firm appears to be growing and has recently expanded its assets, financed primarily through the use of debt. The 1999–2000 period seems to reflect a phase of adjustment and recovery from the rapid growth in assets. Alcott's sales, profits, and other performance factors seem to be growing with the increase in the size of the operation. In short, the firm appears to have done quite well in 2000.

? R e v i e w   Q u e s t i o n s

5-11   Financial ratio analysis is often divided into four categories: *liquidity, activity, debt,* and *profitability* ratios. Differentiate each of these areas of analysis from the others. Which is of the greatest relative concern to present and prospective creditors?

5-12   What three areas of analysis are combined in using the *modified DuPont formula?* How are they combined to explain the firm's return on equity (ROE)? How is risk from financial leverage captured using this system?

5-13   Describe how you would approach a complete ratio analysis of the firm by summarizing a large number of ratios.

SUMMARY

LG1 **Understand the parties interested in performing financial ratio analysis and the common types of ratio comparisons.** Ratio analysis allows present and prospective stockholders and lenders and the firm's management to evaluate the firm's financial performance. It can be performed on a cross-sectional or a time-series basis. Benchmarking is a popular type of cross-sectional analysis.

LG2 **Describe some of the cautions that should be considered in performing financial ratio analysis.** (1) A single ratio does not generally provide sufficient information. (2) Financial statements being compared should be dated at the same point in time during the year. (3) Audited financial statements should be used. (4) Data should be checked for consistency of accounting treatment. (5) Inflation and different asset ages can distort ratio comparisons.

LG3 **Use popular ratios to analyze a firm's liquidity and the activity of inventory, accounts receivable, accounts payable, and total assets.** The liquidity, or ability of the firm to pay its bills as they come due, can be measured by net working capital, the current ratio, or the quick (acid-test) ratio. Activity ratios measure the speed with which accounts are converted into sales or cash. The activity of inventory can be measured by its turnover, that of accounts receivable by the average collection period, and that of accounts payable by the average payment period. Total asset turnover measures the efficiency with which the firm uses its assets to generate sales. Formulas for these liquidity and activity ratios are summarized in Table 5.6.

LG4 **Discuss the relationship between debt and financial leverage and the ratios that can be used to assess the firm's degree of indebtedness and its ability to meet interest payments associated with debt.** The more debt a firm uses, the greater its financial leverage, which magnifies both risk and return. Financial debt ratios measure both the degree of indebtedness and the ability to service debts. A common measure of indebtedness is the debt ratio. The ability to make contractual interest payments can be measured by times interest earned. Formulas for these debt ratios are summarized in Table 5.6.

LG5 **Evaluate a firm's profitability relative to its sales, asset investment, and owners' equity investment.** Measures of profitability can be made in various ways. The common-size income statement, which shows all items as a percentage of sales, can be used to determine gross profit margin, operating profit margin, and net profit margin. Other measures of profitability include return on total assets and return on equity. Formulas for these profitability ratios are summarized in Table 5.6.

LG6 **Use the DuPont system and a summary of financial ratios to perform a complete ratio analysis of a firm.** The DuPont system of analysis is a diagnostic tool used to find the key areas responsible for the firm's financial performance. It allows the firm to break the return on equity into three components: profit on sales, efficiency of asset use, and use of leverage. The DuPont system of analysis, summarized in Figure 5.2, makes it possible to assess all aspects of the firm's activities in order to isolate key areas of responsibility.

SELF-TEST PROBLEMS   (Solutions in Appendix B)

LG3 LG4 LG5 ST 5-1 Ratio formulas and interpretations Without referring to the text, indicate for each of the following ratios the formula for its calculation and the kinds of problems, if any, the firm is likely to have if these ratios are too high relative to the industry average. What if they are too low relative to the industry? Create a table similar to the one that follows and fill in the empty blocks.

Ratio	Too high	Too low
Current ratio =		
Inventory turnover =		
Times interest earned =		
Gross profit margin =		
Return on total assets =		

ST 5-2 ...

OK

ST 5-2 **Balance sheet completion using ratios**   Complete the 2000 balance sheet for O'Keefe Industries using the information that follows it.

Balance Sheet O'Keefe Industries December 31, 2000			
Cash	$ 30,000	Accounts payable	$120,000
Marketable securities	25,000	Notes payable	
Accounts receivable	_____	Accruals	20,000
Inventories	_____	Total current liabilities	_____
Total current assets	_____	Long-term debt	
Net fixed assets	_____	Stockholders' equity	$600,000
Total assets	_____	Total liabilities and stockholders' equity	_____

The following financial data for 2000 are also available:
(1) Sales totaled $1,800,000.
(2) The gross profit margin was 25 percent.
(3) Inventory turnover was 6.0.
(4) There are 360 days in the year.
(5) The average collection period was 40 days.
(6) The current ratio was 1.60.
(7) The total asset turnover ratio was 1.20.
(8) The debt ratio was 60 percent.

PROBLEMS

5-1 **Liquidity management**   Bauman Company's total current assets, net working capital, and inventory for each of the past 4 years follow:

Item	1997	1998	1999	2000
Total current assets	$16,950	$21,900	$22,500	$27,000
Net working capital	7,950	9,300	9,900	9,600
Inventory	6,000	6,900	6,900	7,200

a. Calculate the firm's current and quick ratios for each year. Compare the resulting time series of each measure of liquidity (i.e., net working capital, the current ratio, and the quick ratio).
b. Comment on the firm's liquidity over the 1997–2000 period.
c. If you were told that Bauman Company's inventory turnover for each year in the 1997–2000 period and the industry averages were as follows, would this support or conflict with your evaluation in b? Why?

Inventory turnover	1997	1998	1999	2000
Bauman Company	6.3	6.8	7.0	6.4
Industry average	10.6	11.2	10.8	11.0

5-2 Inventory management   Wilkins Manufacturing has sales of $4 million and a gross profit margin of 40 percent. Its *end-of-quarter inventories* are as follows:

Quarter	Inventory
1	$ 400,000
2	800,000
3	1,200,000
4	200,000

a. Find the average quarterly inventory and use it to calculate the firm's inventory turnover and the average age of inventory.
b. Assuming that the company is in an industry with an average inventory turnover of 2.0, how would you evaluate the activity of Wilkins' inventory?

5-3 Accounts receivable management   An evaluation of the books of Blair Supply, shown in the following table, gives the end-of-year accounts receivable balance, which is believed to consist of amounts originating in the months indicated. The company had annual sales of $2.4 million. The firm extends 30-day credit terms.

Month of origin	Amounts receivable
July	$ 3,875
August	2,000
September	34,025
October	15,100
November	52,000
December	193,000
Year-end accounts receivable	$300,000

a. Use the year-end total to evaluate the firm's collection system.
b. If 70 percent of the firm's sales occur between July and December, would this affect the validity of your conclusion in a? Explain.

5-4 Debt analysis   Springfield Bank is evaluating Creek Enterprises, which has requested a $4,000,000 loan, to assess the firm's financial leverage and financial risk. On the basis of the debt ratios for Creek, along with the industry averages and Creek's recent financial statements (which follow), evaluate and recommend appropriate action on the loan request.

Income Statement Creek Enterprises for the year ended December 31, 2000		
Sales revenue		$30,000,000
Less: Cost of goods sold		21,000,000
Gross profits		$ 9,000,000
Less: Operating expenses		
Selling expense	$3,000,000	
General and administrative expenses	2,000,000	
Depreciation expense	1,000,000	
Total operating expense		6,000,000
Operating profits		$ 3,000,000
Less: Interest expense		1,000,000
Net profits before taxes		$ 2,000,000
Less: Taxes (rate = 40%)		800,000
Net profits after taxes		$ 1,200,000

Balance Sheet Creek Enterprises December 31, 2000			
Assets		**Liabilities and stockholders' equity**	
Current assets		Current liabilities	
Cash	$ 1,000,000	Accounts payable	$ 8,000,000
Marketable securities	3,000,000	Notes payable	8,000,000
Accounts receivable	12,000,000	Accruals	500,000
Inventories	7,500,000	Total current liabilities	$16,500,000
Total current assets	$23,500,000	Long-term debt	$20,000,000
Gross fixed assets (at cost)		Stockholders' equity	
Land and buildings	$11,000,000	Preferred stock (25,000 shares,	
Machinery and equipment	20,500,000	$4 dividend)	$ 2,500,000
Furniture and fixtures	8,000,000	Common stock (1 million shares at $5 par)	5,000,000
Gross fixed assets	$39,500,000	Paid-in capital in excess of par value	4,000,000
Less: Accumulated depreciation	13,000,000	Retained earnings	2,000,000
Net fixed assets	$26,500,000	Total stockholders' equity	$13,500,000
Total assets	$50,000,000	Total liabilities and stockholders' equity	$50,000,000

Industry averages	
Debt ratio	.51
Times interest earned ratio	7.30

 INTERMEDIATE **LG5** 5-5 Common-size statement analysis A common-size income statement for Creek Enterprises' 1999 operations follows. Using the firm's 2000 income statement presented in Problem 5-4, develop the 2000 common-size income statement and compare it to the 1999 statement. Which areas require further analysis and investigation?

Common-Size Income Statement Creek Enterprises for the year ended December 31, 1999		
Sales revenue ($35,000,000)		100.0%
Less: Cost of goods sold		65.9
Gross profits		34.1%
Less: Operating expenses		
Selling expense	12.7%	
General and administrative expenses	6.9	
Depreciation expense	3.6	
Total operating expense		23.2
Operating profits		10.9%
Less: Interest expense		1.5
Net profits before taxes		9.4%
Less: Taxes (rate = 40%)		3.8
Net profits after taxes		5.6%

5-6   DuPont system of analysis   Use the following ratio information for Johnson International and the industry averages for Johnson's line of business to:
a. Construct the DuPont system of analysis for both Johnson and the industry.
b. Evaluate Johnson (and the industry) over the 3-year period.
c. In which areas does Johnson require further analysis? Why?

Johnson	1998	1999	2000
Financial leverage multiplier	1.75	1.75	1.85
Net profit margin	.059	.058	.049
Total asset turnover	2.11	2.18	2.34
Industry averages			
Financial leverage multiplier	1.67	1.69	1.64
Net profit margin	.054	.047	.041
Total asset turnover	2.05	2.13	2.15

5-7   Cross-sectional ratio analysis   Use the following financial statements for Fox Manufacturing Company for the year ended December 31, 2000, along with the industry average ratios also given in what follows, to:
a. Prepare and interpret a ratio analysis of the firm's 2000 operations.

b. Summarize your findings and make recommendations.

Income Statement Fox Manufacturing Company for the year ended December 31, 2000		
Sales revenue		$600,000
Less: Cost of goods sold		460,000
Gross profits		$140,000
Less: Operating expenses		
General and administrative expenses	$30,000	
Depreciation expense	30,000	
Total operating expense		60,000
Operating profits		$ 80,000
Less: Interest expense		10,000
Net profits before taxes		$ 70,000
Less: Taxes		27,100
Net profits after taxes (earnings available for common stockholders)		$ 42,900
Earnings per share (EPS)		$ 2.15

Balance Sheet Fox Manufacturing Company December 31, 2000	
Assets	
Cash	$ 15,000
Marketable securities	7,200
Accounts receivable	34,100
Inventories	82,000
Total current assets	$138,300
Net fixed assets	$270,000
Total assets	$408,300
Liabilities and stockholders' equity	
Accounts payable	$ 57,000
Notes payable	13,000
Accruals	5,000
Total current liabilities	$ 75,000
Long-term debt	$150,000
Stockholders' equity	
Common stock equity (20,000 shares outstanding)	$110,200
Retained earnings	73,100
Total stockholders' equity	$183,300
Total liabilities and stockholders' equity	$408,300

Ratio	Industry average, 2000
Net working capital	$125,000
Current ratio	2.35
Quick ratio	.87
Inventory turnover[a]	4.55
Average collection period[a]	35.3 days
Total asset turnover	1.09
Debt ratio	.300
Times interest earned ratio	12.3
Gross profit margin	.202
Operating profit margin	.135
Net profit margin	.091
Return on total assets (ROA)	.099
Return on equity (ROE)	.167

[a]Based on a 360-day year and on end-of-year figures.

INTERMEDIATE

5-8   **Financial statement analysis**   The financial statements of Zach Industries for the year ended December 31, 2000, follow.

Income Statement Zach Industries for the year ended December 31, 2000	
Sales revenue	$160,000
Less: Cost of goods sold	106,000
Gross profits	$ 54,000
Less: Operating expenses	
Selling expense	$ 16,000
General and administrative expenses	11,000
Depreciation expense	10,000
Total operating expense	$ 37,000
Operating profits	$ 17,000
Less: Interest expense	6,100
Net profits before taxes	$ 10,900
Less: Taxes	4,360
Net profits after taxes	$ 6,540

Balance Sheet Zach Industries December 31, 2000	
Assets	
Cash	$ 500
Marketable securities	1,000
Accounts receivable	25,000
Inventories	45,500
Total current assets	$ 72,000
Land	$ 26,000
Buildings and equipment	90,000
Less: Accumulated depreciation	38,000
Net fixed assets	$ 78,000
Total assets	$150,000
Liabilities and stockholders' equity	
Accounts payable	$ 22,000
Notes payable	47,000
Total current liabilities	$ 69,000
Long-term debt	$ 22,950
Common stock	$ 31,500
Retained earnings	$ 26,550
Total liabilities and stockholders' equity	$150,000

a. Use the preceding financial statements to complete the following table. Assume that the industry averages given in the table are applicable for both 1999 and 2000.
b. Analyze Zach Industries' financial condition as it relates to (1) liquidity, (2) activity, (3) debt, and (4) profitability. Summarize the company's overall financial condition.

Ratio	Industry average	Actual 1999	Actual 2000
Current ratio	1.80	1.84	_____
Quick ratio	.70	.78	_____
Inventory turnover[a]	2.50	2.59	_____
Average collection period[a]	37 days	36 days	_____
Debt ratio	65%	67%	_____
Times interest earned ratio	3.8	4.0	_____
Gross profit margin	38%	40%	_____
Net profit margin	3.5%	3.6%	_____
Return on total assets	4.0%	4.0%	_____
Return on equity	9.5%	8.0%	_____

[a]Based on a 360-day year and on end-of-year figures.

5-9 **Integrative—Complete ratio analysis**   Given the following financial statements, historical ratios, and industry averages, calculate the Sterling Company's financial ratios for the most recent year. Analyze its overall financial situation from both a cross-sectional and a time-series viewpoint. Break your analysis into an evaluation of the firm's liquidity, activity, debt, and profitability.

Income Statement Sterling Company for the year ended December 31, 2000		
Sales revenue		$10,000,000
Less: Cost of goods sold		7,500,000
Gross profits		$ 2,500,000
Less: Operating expenses		
Selling expense	$300,000	
General and administrative expenses	700,000	
Depreciation expense	200,000	
Total operating expense		1,200,000
Operating profits		$ 1,300,000
Less: Interest expense		200,000
Net profits before taxes		$ 1,100,000
Less: Taxes (rate = 40%)		440,000
Net profits after taxes		$ 660,000
Less: Preferred stock dividends		50,000
Earnings available for common stockholders		$ 610,000
Earnings per share (EPS)		$3.05

Balance Sheet Sterling Company December 31, 2000					
Assets			**Liabilities and stockholders' equity**		
Current assets			Current liabilities		
Cash		$ 200,000	Accounts payable[a]		$ 900,000
Marketable securities		50,000	Notes payable		200,000
Accounts receivable		800,000	Accruals		100,000
Inventories		950,000	Total current liabilities		$ 1,200,000
Total current assets		$ 2,000,000	Long-term debt		$ 3,000,000
Gross fixed assets (at cost)	$12,000,000		Stockholders' equity		
Less: Accumulated depreciation	3,000,000		Preferred stock (25,000 shares, $2 dividend)		$ 1,000,000
Net fixed assets		$ 9,000,000	Common stock (200,000 shares at $3 par)		600,000
Other assets		$ 1,000,000	Paid-in capital in excess of par value		5,200,000
Total assets		$12,000,000	Retained earnings		1,000,000
			Total stockholders' equity		$ 7,800,000
			Total liabilities and stockholders' equity		$12,000,000

[a]Annual credit purchases of $6,200,000 were made during the year.

Historical and Industry Average Ratios for Sterling Company

Ratio	Actual 1998	Actual 1999	Industry average 2000
Net working capital	$760,000	$720,000	$1,600,000
Current ratio	1.40	1.55	1.85
Quick ratio	1.00	.92	1.05
Inventory turnover	9.52	9.21	8.60
Average collection period	45.0 days	36.4 days	35.0 days
Average payment period	58.5 days	60.8 days	45.8 days
Total asset turnover	.74	.80	.74
Debt ratio	.20	.20	.30
Times interest earned ratio	8.2	7.3	8.0
Gross profit margin	.30	.27	.25
Operating profit margin	.12	.12	.10
Net profit margin	.067	.067	.058
Return on total assets (ROA)	.049	.054	.043
Return on equity (ROE)	.066	.073	.072

CASE   Chapter 5

Assessing Martin Manufacturing's Current Financial Position

Terry Spiro, an experienced budget analyst at Martin Manufacturing Company, has been asked to assess the firm's financial performance during 2000 and its financial position at year-end. To complete this assignment, she gathered the firm's 2000 financial statements, which follow. In addition, Terry obtained the firm's ratio values for 1998 and 1999, along with the 2000 industry average ratios (also applicable to 1998 and 1999). These are presented in the table at the bottom of page 147.

Income Statement
Martin Manufacturing Company
for the year ended December 31, 2000

Sales revenue		$5,075,000
Less: Cost of goods sold		3,704,000
Gross profits		$1,371,000
Less: Operating expenses		
Selling expense	$650,000	
General and administrative expenses	416,000	
Depreciation expense	152,000	
Total operating expense		1,218,000
Operating profits		$ 153,000
Less: Interest expense		93,000
Net profits before taxes		$ 60,000
Less: Taxes (rate = 40%)		24,000
Net profits after taxes		$ 36,000

Balance Sheets Martin Manufacturing Company		
	December 31	
Assets	2000	1999
Current assets		
Cash	$ 25,000	$ 24,100
Accounts receivable	805,556	763,900
Inventories	700,625	763,445
Total current assets	$1,531,181	$1,551,445
Gross fixed assets (at cost)	$2,093,819	$1,691,707
Less: Accumulated depreciation	500,000	348,000
Net fixed assets	$1,593,819	$1,343,707
Total assets	$3,125,000	$2,895,152
Liabilities and stockholders' equity		
Current liabilities		
Accounts payable	$ 230,000	$ 400,500
Notes payable	311,000	370,000
Accruals	75,000	100,902
Total current liabilities	$ 616,000	$ 871,402
Long-term debt	$1,165,250	$ 700,000
Total liabilities	$1,781,250	$1,571,402
Stockholders' equity		
Preferred stock	$ 50,000	$ 50,000
Common stock (at par)	100,000	100,000
Paid-in capital in excess of par value	193,750	193,750
Retained earnings	1,000,000	980,000
Total stockholders' equity	$1,343,750	$1,323,750
Total liabilities and stockholders' equity	$3,125,000	$2,895,152

Historical and Industry Average Ratios Martin Manufacturing Company				
Ratio	Actual 1998	Actual 1999	Actual 2000	Industry average 2000
Current ratio	1.7	1.8	_____	1.5
Quick ratio	1.0	.9	_____	1.2
Inventory turnover (times)	5.2	5.0	_____	10.2
Average collection period	50 days	55 days	_____	46 days
Total asset turnover (times)	1.5	1.5	_____	2.0
Debt ratio	45.8%	54.3%	_____	24.5%
Times interest earned ratio	2.2	1.9	_____	2.5
Gross profit margin	27.5%	28.0%	_____	26.0%
Net profit margin	1.1%	1.0%	_____	1.2%
Return on total assets (ROA)	1.7%	1.5%	_____	2.4%
Return on equity (ROE)	3.1%	3.3%	_____	3.2%

Required

a. Calculate the firm's 2000 financial ratios, and then fill in the preceding table.
b. Analyze the firm's current financial position from both a cross-sectional and a time-series viewpoint. Break your analysis into an evaluation of the firm's liquidity, activity, debt, and profitability.
c. Summarize the firm's overall financial position based on your findings in **b.**

Web Exercise

GOTO web site www.yahoo.com. On the left side of the Yahoo home page screen, click BFC. On the right side of the next screen, click Y! Finance. Enter the stock symbol LUV in the QUOTES box. Click on Ratio Comparisons.

1. Whose are the three groups of standards to which Southwest Airlines ratios are compared?
2. Which of the financial ratios that were covered in this chapter are given for Southwest Airlines Companies, Inc.?
3. When compared to the industry standards, which two ratios does Southwest Airlines seem to be doing very well? Which two ratios does Southwest Airlines seem to be doing *not* so well?
4. Where does LUV rank in the airline industry in total market capitalization?

PART 2

IMPORTANT FINANCIAL CONCEPTS

CHAPTERS IN THIS PART

6 TIME VALUE OF MONEY

ACROSS *the* DISCIPLINES

Because we view the firm as a going concern, we assess the decisions of its financial managers, and ultimately the value of the firm itself, in light of its cash flows. The opportunity to earn interest on the firm's funds makes the timing of its cash flows important, because a dollar received in the future is not the same as a dollar received today. Thus, money has a time value, which affects everyone—individuals, businesses, and government. In this chapter we explore the concepts related to the time value of money. Chapter 6 is important to:

- **accounting personnel** who will frequently employ time value of money calculations when accounting for certain transactions.
- **information systems analysts** who will design systems that optimize the firm's use of its cash flow.
- **management** because it plans cash collections and disbursements so that the firm will get the greatest value from its money.
- **the marketing department** because funding for new programs and products must be justified financially using time value of money techniques.
- **operations,** which could face small production quantities and low inventories because of the time value of money.

THE ROLE OF TIME VALUE IN FINANCE

Firms are always confronted with opportunities to earn positive rates of return on their funds, either through investment in attractive projects or in interest-bearing securities or deposits. Therefore, the timing of cash flows—both out-flows and inflows—has important economic consequences, which financial managers explicitly recognize as the *time value of money*. Time value is based on the idea that a dollar today is worth more than a dollar that will be received at some future date. We begin our study of time value in finance by considering two views of time value—future value and present value—and the computational aids commonly used to streamline time value calculations.

FUTURE VERSUS PRESENT VALUE

Financial values and decisions can be assessed by using either future value or present value techniques. Although these techniques will result in the same deci-sions, they view the decision differently. Future value techniques typically mea-sure cash flows at the *end* of a project's life; present value techniques measure cash flows at the *start* of a project's life (time zero). *Future value* is cash you will receive at a given future date, and *present value* is just like cash in hand today.

time line
Depicts investment cash flows on a horizontal line on which time zero is at the leftmost end and future periods are marked from left to right.

A **time line** can be used to depict the cash flows associated with a given investment. It is a horizontal line on which time zero appears at the leftmost end and future periods are marked from left to right. A time line covering five periods (in this case, years) is given in Figure 6.1. The cash flow occurring at time zero and at the end of each year is shown above the line; the negative values represent *cash outflows* ($10,000 at time zero) and the positive values represent *cash inflows* ($3,000 inflow at the end of year 1, $5,000 inflow at the end of year 2, and so on).

Because money has a time value, all of the cash flows associated with an investment, such as those depicted in Figure 6.1, must be measured at the same point in time. Typically, that point is either the end or the beginning of the investment's life. The future value technique uses *compounding* to find the future value of each cash flow at the end of the investment's life and then sums those values to find the investment's future value. This approach is depicted above the time line in Figure 6.2, which shows that the future value of each cash flow is

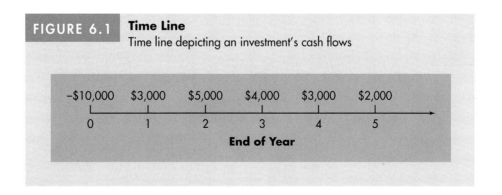

FIGURE 6.1   Time Line
Time line depicting an investment's cash flows

–$10,000	$3,000	$5,000	$4,000	$3,000	$2,000
0	1	2	3	4	5

End of Year

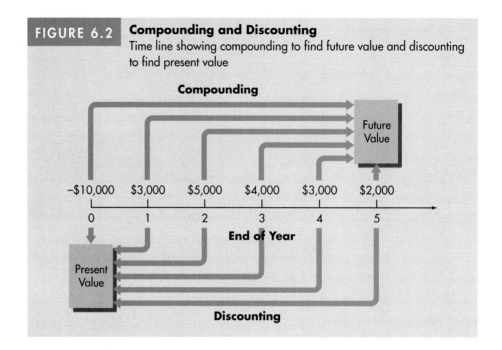

FIGURE 6.2 **Compounding and Discounting**
Time line showing compounding to find future value and discounting to find present value

measured at the end of the investment's 5-year life. Alternatively, the present value technique uses *discounting* to find the present value of each cash flow at time zero and then sums those values to find the investment's value today. Application of this approach is depicted below the time line in Figure 6.2.

The meaning and mechanics of both compounding to find future value and discounting to find present value are covered later in this chapter. Although future value and present value result in the same decisions, *financial managers— because they make decisions at time zero—tend to rely primarily on present value techniques.*

COMPUTATIONAL AIDS

Time-consuming calculations are often involved in finding future and present values. Although you should understand the concepts and mathematics underlying these calculations, the practical application of these important time value techniques can be streamlined. Here we focus on the use of financial tables and financial calculators as computational aids. Personal computers can also be used to simplify time value calculations.

FINANCIAL TABLES

Financial tables, easily developed from formulas, include various future and present value interest factors that simplify time value calculations. Although the degree of decimal precision (rounding) varies, the tables are typically indexed by the interest rate (in columns) and the number of periods (in rows). Figure 6.3 shows this general layout. If we wished to use this table to find the interest factor at a 20 percent interest rate for 10 years, its value would be found at the intersection of the 20% column and the 10-year row, as shown in the white box. A full

FIGURE 6.3 **Financial Tables**
Layout and use of a financial table

Period				Interest Rate	$\downarrow$			
	1%	2%	⋯	10%	⋯	**20%**	⋯	50%
1			⋯		⋯	⋮	⋯	
2			⋯		⋯	⋮	⋯	
3			⋯		⋯	⋮	⋯	
⋮	⋮	⋮	⋯	⋮	⋯	⋮	⋯	⋮
→ 10	⋯	⋯	⋯	⋯	⋯	**X.XXX**	⋯	⋯
⋮	⋮	⋮	⋯	⋮	⋯	⋮	⋯	⋮
20			⋯		⋯		⋯	
⋮	⋮	⋮	⋯	⋮	⋯	⋮	⋯	⋮
50			⋯		⋯		⋯	

set of the four basic financial tables is included in Appendix A, at the end of the book. These tables are described more fully later in this chapter and are used to demonstrate the application of time value techniques.

FINANCIAL CALCULATORS

During the past 15 years, the power of the financial calculator has improved dramatically and its cost has declined. Today, a powerful financial calculator can be purchased for $20 to $30. Generally, *financial calculators* include numerous preprogrammed, often menu-driven financial routines. This chapter and those that follow show the keystrokes for calculating interest factors and making other financial computations. For convenience, we use the important financial keys, labeled in a fashion consistent with most major financial calculators.

We focus primary attention on the keys pictured and defined in Figure 6.4. We typically use the compute key (CPT) and only four of the five keys in the second

FIGURE 6.4 **Calculator Keys**
Important financial keys on the typical calculator

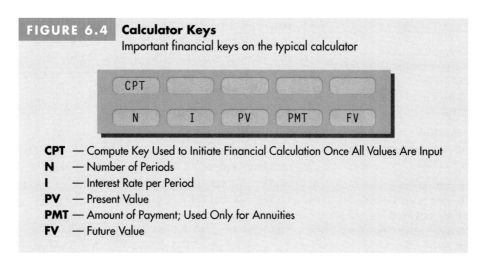

CPT — Compute Key Used to Initiate Financial Calculation Once All Values Are Input
N — Number of Periods
I — Interest Rate per Period
PV — Present Value
PMT — Amount of Payment; Used Only for Annuities
FV — Future Value

row, with one of the four keys representing the unknown value being calculated. (Occasionally, all five of the keys, with one representing the unknown value, are used.) The keystrokes on some of the more sophisticated calculators are menu-driven, so that after you select the appropriate routine, the calculator prompts you to input each value; on these calculators, a compute key is not needed to obtain a solution. Regardless, any calculator with the basic future and present value functions can be used in lieu of financial tables. The keystrokes of other financial calculators are explained in the reference guides that accompany them.

Although this text demonstrates the use of both financial tables and financial calculators, you are strongly urged to use a calculator to streamline routine financial calculations *once you understand the basic underlying concepts*. With a little practice, both the speed and accuracy of financial computations using a calculator can be greatly enhanced. Note that because of a calculator's greater precision, slight differences are likely to exist between values calculated using financial tables and those found with a financial calculator. Remember, conceptual understanding of the material is the objective. An ability to solve problems with the aid of a calculator does not necessarily reflect such an understanding, so don't settle just for answers. Work with the material until you are sure you also understand the concepts.

Review Questions

6-1   What is a *time line,* and how does it depict cash flows?
6-2   What is the difference between *future value* and *present value?* Which approach is preferred by financial managers? Why?
6-3   How are financial tables laid out and accessed?

FUTURE VALUE OF A SINGLE AMOUNT

compound interest
Interest earned on a given deposit that has become part of the principal at the end of a specified period.

principal
The amount of money on which interest is paid.

future value
The value of a present amount at a future date found by applying compound interest over a specified period of time.

Imagine that at age 25 you begin making annual cash deposits of $2,000 into a savings account that pays 5 percent annual interest. At the end of 40 years, at age 65, you would have made deposits totaling $80,000 (40 years × $2,000 per year). Assuming that you have made no withdrawals, what do you think your account balance would be? $100,000? $150,000? $200,000? No, your $80,000 would have grown to $242,000! Why? Because the time value of money allowed the deposits to earn interest, and interest on interest, that was compounded over the 40 years.

THE CONCEPT OF FUTURE VALUE

We speak of **compound interest** to indicate that the amount of interest earned on a given deposit has become part of the principal at the end of a specified period. The term **principal** refers to the amount of money on which the interest is paid. Annual compounding is the most common type.

The **future value** of a present amount is found by applying *compound interest* over a specified period of time. Savings institutions advertise compound interest returns at a rate of x percent or x percent interest compounded annually, semiannually, quarterly, monthly, weekly, daily, or even continuously. The concept of future value with annual compounding can be illustrated by a simple example.

E x a m p l e ▼ If Fred Moreno places $100 in a savings account paying 8 percent interest compounded annually, at the end of 1 year he will have $108 in the account—the initial principal of $100 plus 8 percent ($8) in interest. The future value at the end of the first year is calculated by using Equation 6.1:

$$\text{Future value at end of year 1} = \$100 \times (1 + .08) = \$108 \tag{6.1}$$

If Fred were to leave this money in the account for another year, he would be paid interest at the rate of 8 percent on the new principal of $108. At the end of this second year there would be $116.64 in the account—the principal at the beginning of year 2 ($108) plus 8 percent of the $108 ($8.64) in interest. The future value at the end of the second year is calculated by using Equation 6.2:

$$\begin{aligned}\text{Future value at end of year 2} &= \$108 \times (1 + .08) \\ &= \$116.64\end{aligned} \tag{6.2}$$

Substituting the expression between the equal signs in Equation 6.1 for the $108 figure in Equation 6.2 gives us Equation 6.3:

$$\begin{aligned}\text{Future value at end of year 2} &= \$100 \times (1 + .08) \times (1 + .08) \\ &= \$100 \times (1 + .08)^2 \\ &= \$116.64\end{aligned} \tag{6.3}$$

▲ This equation leads to a more general formula for calculating future value.

THE EQUATION FOR FUTURE VALUE

The basic relationship in Equation 6.3 can be generalized to find the future value after any number of periods. Let

FV_n = future value at the end of period n
PV = initial principal, or present value
k = annual rate of interest paid. (*Note:* On financial calculators, **I** is typically used to represent this rate.)
n = number of periods—typically years—the money is left on deposit

By using this notation, a general equation for the future value at the end of period n can be formulated:

$$FV_n = PV \times (1 + k)^n \tag{6.4}$$

The application of Equation 6.4 can be illustrated by a simple example.

E x a m p l e ▼ Jane Farber placed $800 in a savings account paying 6 percent interest compounded annually. She wishes to determine how much money will be in the account at the end of 5 years. Substituting $PV = \$800$, $k = .06$, and $n = 5$ into Equation 6.4 gives the amount at the end of year 5:

$$FV_5 = \$800 \times (1 + .06)^5 = \$800 \times (1.338) = \$1,070.40$$

Jane will have $1,070.40 in the account at the end of the fifth year.

Time-Line Use   This analysis can be depicted on a time line as shown:

Time line for future value of a single amount ($800 initial principal, earning 6 percent, at the end of 5 years)

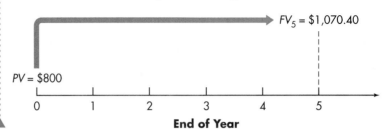

USING TABLES AND CALCULATORS TO FIND FUTURE VALUE

Solving the equation in the preceding example is time-consuming, because one must raise 1.06 to the fifth power. Using a future value interest table or a financial calculator greatly simplifies the calculations, as we will demonstrate in this section. The table that provides values for $(1 + k)^n$ in Equation 6.4 is included near the back of the book in Appendix Table A-1.[1] The value in each cell of the table is called the **future value interest factor.** This factor is the multiplier used to calculate at a specified interest rate the future value of a present amount as of a given time. The future value interest factor for an initial principal of $1 compounded at k percent for n periods is referred to as $FVIF_{k,n}$:

future value interest factor for an annuity
The multiplier used to calculate the future value of an annuity at a specified interest rate over a given period of time.

$$\text{Future value interest factor} = FVIF_{k,n} = (1 + k)^n \qquad (6.5)$$

By finding the intersection of the annual interest rate, k, and the appropriate periods, n, you will find the future value interest factor relevant to a particular problem.[2] By letting $FVIF_{k,n}$ represent the appropriate factor, we can rewrite Equation 6.4 as follows:

$$FV_n = PV \times (FVIF_{k,n}) \qquad (6.6)$$

This expression indicates that to find the future value, FV_n, at the end of period n of an initial deposit, we have merely to multiply the initial deposit, PV, by the appropriate future value interest factor. An example will illustrate this calculation using both a table and a calculator.

Example ▼ In the preceding example, Jane Farber placed $800 in her savings account at 6 percent interest compounded annually and wishes to find out how much will be in the account at the end of 5 years.

Table Use   The future value interest factor for an initial principal of $1 on deposit for 5 years at 6 percent interest compounded annually, $FVIF_{6\%,5\text{yrs}}$, found

---

[1]This table is commonly referred to as a "compound interest table" or a "table of the future value of one dollar." As long as the reader understands the source of the table values, the various names attached to it should not create confusion, because one can always make a trial calculation of a value for one factor as a check.

[2]Although we commonly deal with years rather than periods, financial tables are frequently presented in terms of periods to provide maximum flexibility.

in Table A-1, is 1.338. Multiplying the initial principal of $800 by this factor results in a future value at the end of year 5 of $1,070.40.

Calculator Use[3]   The preprogrammed financial functions in the financial calculator can be used to calculate the future value directly.[4] First, punch in $800 and depress **PV**; next, punch in 5 and depress **N**; then, punch in 6 and depress **I** (which is equivalent to "*k*" in our notation)[5]; finally, to calculate the future value, depress **CPT** and then **FV**. The future value of $1,070.58 should appear on the calculator display. On many calculators, this value will be preceded by a minus sign (i.e., −1,070.58). *If a minus sign appears on your calculator, ignore it here, as well as in all other "Calculator Use" illustrations in this text.*[6]

Inputs:	800	5	6		
Functions:	PV	N	I	CPT	FV
Outputs:					1070.58

Because the calculator is more accurate than the future value factors, which have been rounded to the nearest .001, a slight difference—in this case, $.18—will frequently exist between the values found by these alternative methods. Clearly, the improved accuracy and ease of calculation tend to favor the use of the calculator when making financial calculations such as this. *Note: In future examples of calculator use, we will use only a display similar to that shown above. If you need a reminder of the procedures involved, go back and review the paragraph just before this display.*

A GRAPHIC VIEW OF FUTURE VALUE

Remember that we measure future value at the *end* of the given period. The relationship between various interest rates, the number of periods interest is earned, and the future value of one dollar are illustrated in Figure 6.5. It clearly shows that: (1) the higher the interest rate, the higher the future value, and (2) the longer the period of time, the higher the future value. Note that for an interest rate of 0 percent, the future value always equals the present value ($1.00). But

---

[3]Many calculators allow the user to set the number of payments per year. Most of these calculators are preset for monthly payments—12 payments per year. Because we work primarily with annual payments—one payment per year—it is important to *make sure that your calculator is set for one payment per year*. Although most calculators are preset to recognize that all payments occur at the end of the period, it is important to *make sure that your calculator is correctly set on the* END *mode*. Consult the reference guide that accompanies your calculator for instructions for setting these values.

[4]To avoid including previous data in current calculations, *always clear all registers of your calculator before inputting values and making each computation.*

[5]The known values *can be punched into the calculator in any order;* the order specified in this as well as other calculator use demonstrations included in this text results merely from convenience and personal preference.

[6]The calculator differentiates inflows from the outflows by preceding outflows with a negative sign. For example, in the problem just demonstrated, the $800 present value (PV), because it was keyed as a positive number (i.e., 800), is considered an inflow or deposit. Therefore, the calculated future value (FV) of −1070.58 is preceded by a minus sign to show that it is the resulting outflow or withdrawal. Had the $800 present value been keyed in as a negative number (i.e., −800), the future value of $1,070.58 would be displayed as a positive number (i.e., 1070.58). Simply stated, *the cash flows—present value (PV) and future value (FV)—will have opposite signs.*

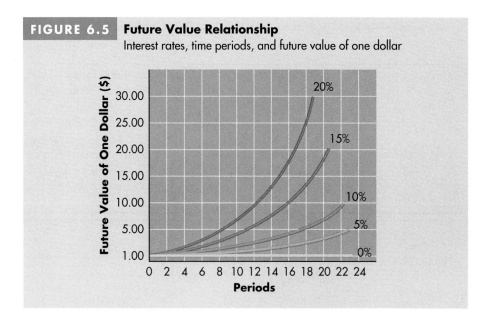

FIGURE 6.5   Future Value Relationship
Interest rates, time periods, and future value of one dollar

for any interest rate greater than zero, the future value is greater than the present value of $1.00.

COMPOUNDING MORE FREQUENTLY THAN ANNUALLY

Interest is often compounded more frequently than once a year. Savings institutions compound interest semiannually, quarterly, monthly, weekly, daily, or even continuously. This section discusses various issues and techniques relating to compounding more frequently than annually.

SEMIANNUAL COMPOUNDING

semiannual compounding
Compounding of interest over two periods within the year.

Semiannual compounding of interest involves two compounding periods within the year. Instead of the stated interest rate being paid once a year, one-half of the stated interest rate is paid twice a year.

Example ▼ Fred Moreno has decided to invest $100 in a savings account paying 8 percent interest *compounded semiannually*. If he leaves his money in the account for 2 years, he will be paid 4 percent interest compounded over four periods, each of which is 6 months long. Table 6.1 uses interest factors to show that at the end of 1 year, with 8 percent semiannual compounding, Fred will have $108.16. At the ▲ end of 2 years, he will have $116.99.

QUARTERLY COMPOUNDING

quarterly compounding
Compounding of interest over four periods within the year.

Quarterly compounding of interest involves four compounding periods within the year. One-fourth of the stated interest rate is paid four times a year.

Example ▼ Fred Moreno has found an institution that will pay him 8 percent interest *compounded quarterly*. If he leaves his money in this account for 2 years, he will be

TABLE 6.1	The Future Value from Investing $100 at 8 Percent Interest Compounded Semiannually Over 2 Years

Period	Beginning principal (1)	Future value interest factor (2)	Future value at end of period [(1) × (2)] (3)
6 months	$100.00	1.04	$104.00
1 year	104.00	1.04	108.16
18 months	108.16	1.04	112.49
2 years	112.49	1.04	116.99

TABLE 6.2	The Future Value from Investing $100 at 8 Percent Interest Compounded Quarterly Over 2 Years

Period	Beginning principal (1)	Future value interest factor (2)	Future value at end of period [(1) × (2)] (3)
3 months	$100.00	1.02	$102.00
6 months	102.00	1.02	104.04
9 months	104.04	1.02	106.12
1 year	106.12	1.02	108.24
15 months	108.24	1.02	110.40
18 months	110.40	1.02	112.61
21 months	112.61	1.02	114.86
2 years	114.86	1.02	117.16

TABLE 6.3	The Future Value from Investing $100 at 8 Percent Interest for Years 1 and 2 Given Various Compounding Periods

End of year	Compounding period		
	Annual	Semiannual	Quarterly
1	$108.00	$108.16	$108.24
2	116.64	116.99	117.16

paid 2 percent interest compounded over eight periods, each of which is 3 months long. Table 6.2 uses interest factors to show the amount Fred will have at the end of 2 years. At the end of 1 year, with 8 percent interest quarterly compounding, Fred will have $108.24. At the end of 2 years, he will have $117.16.

Table 6.3 compares values for Fred Moreno's $100 at the end of years 1 and 2 given annual, semiannual, and quarterly compounding at the 8 percent rate. As shown, *the more frequently interest is compounded, the greater the amount of money accumulated.* This is true for any interest rate for any period of time.

A General Equation for Compounding More Frequently Than Annually

It should be clear from the preceding examples that if *m* equals the number of times per year interest is compounded, Equation 6.4 (our formula for annual compounding) can be rewritten as:

$$FV_n = PV \times \left(1 + \frac{k}{m}\right)^{m \times n} \tag{6.7}$$

If *m* = 1, Equation 6.7 reduces to Equation 6.4. Thus, if interest is compounded annually (once a year), Equation 6.7 will provide the same result as Equation 6.4. The general use of Equation 6.7 can be illustrated with a simple example.

Example ▼ The preceding examples calculated the amount that Fred Moreno would have at the end of 2 years if he deposited $100 at 8 percent interest compounded semiannually and quarterly. For semiannual compounding, *m* would equal 2 in Equation 6.7; for quarterly compounding, *m* would equal 4. Substituting the appropriate values for semiannual and quarterly compounding into Equation 6.7:

1. *For semiannual compounding:*

$$FV_2 = \$100 \times \left(1 + \frac{.08}{2}\right)^{2 \times 2} = \$100 \times (1 + .04)^4 = \$116.99$$

2. *For quarterly compounding:*

$$FV_2 = \$100 \times \left(1 + \frac{.08}{4}\right)^{4 \times 2} = \$100 \times (1 + .02)^8 = \$117.16$$

▲ These results agree with the values for FV_2 in Tables 6.1 and 6.2.

If the interest were compounded monthly, weekly, or daily, *m* would equal 12, 52, or 365, respectively.

Using Tables and Calculators

We can use the future value interest factors for one dollar, given in Table A-1, to find the future value when interest is compounded *m* times each year. Instead of indexing the table for *k* percent and *n* years, as we do when interest is compounded annually, we index it for (*k* ÷ *m*) percent and (*m* × *n*) periods. However, the table is less useful, because it includes only selected rates for a limited number of periods. Instead, a financial calculator or personal computer is typically required. The following example demonstrates the use of both a table and a calculator.

Example ▼ Fred Moreno wished to find the future value of $100 invested at 8 percent compounded both semiannually and quarterly for 2 years. The number of compounding periods, *m*, the interest rate, and number of periods used in each case, along with the future value interest factor, are as follows:

Compounding period	m	Interest rate ($k \div m$)	Periods ($m \times n$)	Future value interest factor from Table A-1
Semiannual	2	8% ÷ 2 = 4%	2 × 2 = 4	1.170
Quarterly	4	8% ÷ 4 = 2%	4 × 2 = 8	1.172

Table Use   Multiplying each of the future value interest factors by the initial $100 deposit results in a value of $117.00 (1.170 × $100) for semiannual compounding and a value of $117.20 (1.172 × $100) for quarterly compounding.

Calculator Use   If the calculator were used for the semiannual compounding calculation, the number of periods would be 4 and the interest rate would be 4 percent. The future value of $116.99 should appear on the calculator display.

Inputs: 100   4   4

Functions: PV   N   I   CPT   FV

Outputs: 116.99

For the quarterly compounding case, the number of periods would be 8 and the interest rate would be 2 percent. The future value of $117.17 should appear on the calculator display.

Inputs: 100   8   2

Functions: PV   N   I   CPT   FV

Outputs: 117.17

Comparing the calculator and table values, we can see that the calculator values generally agree with those values given in Table 6.3 but are more precise because the table factors have been rounded.

CONTINUOUS COMPOUNDING

continuous compounding
Compounding of interest an infinite number of times per year at intervals of microseconds.

In the extreme case, interest can be compounded continuously. **Continuous compounding** involves compounding over every microsecond—the smallest time period imaginable. In this case, m in Equation 6.7 would approach infinity, and through the use of calculus, the equation would become:

$$FV_n \text{ (continuous compounding)} = PV \times (e^{k \times n}) \qquad (6.8)$$

where e is the exponential function, which has a value of 2.7183.[7] The future value interest factor for continuous compounding is therefore:

$$FVIF_{k,n} \text{ (continuous compounding)} = e^{k \times n} \qquad (6.9)$$

---

[7]Most calculators have the exponential function, typically noted by e^x, built into them. The use of this key is especially helpful in calculating future value when interest is compounded continuously.

Example ▼ To find the value at the end of 2 years ($n = 2$) of Fred Moreno's $100 deposit ($PV$ = 100) into an account paying 8 percent annual interest ($k = .08$) compounded continuously, we can substitute into Equation 6.8:

$$FV_2 \text{ (continuous compounding)} = \$100 \times e^{.08 \times 2} = \$100 \times 2.7183^{.16}$$
$$= \$100 \times 1.1735 = \$117.35$$

Calculator Use   To find this value using the calculator, first, find the value of $e^{.16}$ by punching in .16 and then pressing **2nd** and then e^x to get 1.1735. Next multiply this value by $100 to get the future value of $117.35. (*Note:* On some calculators, **2nd** may not have to be pressed before pressing e^x.)

Inputs:	.16		100
Functions:	2nd e^x		X =
Outputs:	1.1735		117.35

The future value with continuous compounding therefore equals $117.35, which, as expected, is larger than the future value of interest compounded semi-annually ($116.99) or quarterly ($117.16). As was noted earlier, continuous compounding offers the largest amount that would result from compounding interest more frequently than annually.

▲

℗ERSONAL FINANCE PERSPECTIVE

The Rewards of Compounding

Compound interest can work its magic for your personal finances, too. When they were in their early 30s, Lou and Cathy Hayward decided to invest 10 percent of their salaries every year. Now in their mid-40s, the couple has a nest egg of $180,000. If the Haywards continue to save at their current rate of $6,500 a year and earn 8.7 percent after taxes, their annual retirement income will be $50,000 in today's dollars, including Social Security.

Think you can't find any money to save in an already tight budget? Put just $25 a month in a mutual fund that earns 8.4 percent annually—the average after-inflation stock return between 1975 and 1995—and in 20 years your account will have $15,500. Increase the monthly amount to $100 and you'll be $62,000 richer. If you don't have the discipline to invest regularly, set up an automatic investment program with a mutual fund that moves money directly from your bank account to an investment account each month or quarter. ●

NOMINAL AND EFFECTIVE ANNUAL RATES OF INTEREST

nominal (stated) annual rate
Contractual rate of interest charged by a lender or promised by a borrower.

Both consumers and businesses need to make objective comparisons of loan costs or investment returns over different compounding periods. In order to put interest rates on a common basis, to allow comparison, we distinguish between nominal and effective annual rates. The **nominal,** or **stated, annual rate** is the contractual annual rate charged by a lender or promised by a borrower. The

effective (true) annual rate
The rate of interest actually paid or earned.

effective, or **true, annual rate (EAR)** is the annual rate of interest actually paid or earned. The effective annual rate reflects the impact of compounding frequency, whereas the nominal annual rate does not.

Using the notation introduced earlier, we can calculate the effective annual rate, EAR, by substituting values for the nominal annual rate, k, and the compounding frequency, m, into Equation 6.10.

$$EAR = \left(1 + \frac{k}{m}\right)^m - 1 \qquad (6.10)$$

We can apply this equation using data from preceding examples.

Example ▼ Fred Moreno wishes to find the effective annual rate associated with an 8 percent nominal annual rate ($k = .08$) when interest is compounded (1) annually ($m = 1$); (2) semiannually ($m = 2$); and (3) quarterly ($m = 4$). Substituting these values into Equation 6.10, we get the following:

1. *For annual compounding:*

$$EAR = \left(1 + \frac{.08}{1}\right)^1 - 1 = (1 + .08)^1 - 1 = 1 + .08 - 1 = .08 = 8\%$$

2. *For semiannual compounding:*

$$EAR = \left(1 + \frac{.08}{2}\right)^2 - 1 = (1 + .04)^2 - 1 = 1.0816 - 1 = .0816 = 8.16\%$$

3. *For quarterly compounding:*

$$EAR = \left(1 + \frac{.08}{4}\right)^4 - 1 = (1 + .02)^4 - 1 = 1.0824 - 1 = .0824 = 8.24\%$$

These values demonstrate two important points: (1) The nominal and effective rates are equivalent for annual compounding, and (2) the effective annual rate increases with increasing compounding frequency.[8]

annual percentage rate (APR)
The *nominal annual rate* of interest, found by multiplying the periodic rate by the number of periods in 1 year, that must be disclosed to consumers on credit cards and on other loans as a result of "truth-in-lending laws."

annual percentage yield (APY)
The *effective annual rate* of interest that must be disclosed to consumers by banks on their savings products as a result of "truth-in-savings laws."

At the consumer level, "truth-in-lending laws" require disclosure on credit cards and other loans of the **annual percentage rate (APR)**. The APR is the *nominal annual rate* found by multiplying the periodic rate by the number of periods in 1 year. For example, a bank credit card that charges 1½ percent per month would have an APR of 18 percent (1.5 percent per month × 12 months per year). "Truth-in-savings laws," on the other hand, require banks to quote on their savings products the **annual percentage yield (APY)**. The APY is the *effective annual rate* a savings product pays. For example, a savings account that pays .5 percent per month would have an APY of 6.17 percent [$(1.005)^{12} - 1$]. Quoting loan interest rates at their lower nominal annual rate—the APR—and

---

[8]The *maximum* effective annual rate for a given nominal annual rate occurs when interest is compounded *continuously*. The effective annual rate for this extreme case can be found by using the following equation:

$$EAR \text{ (continuous compounding)} = e^k - 1 \qquad (6.10a)$$

For the 8 percent nominal annual rate ($k = .08$), substitution into Equation 6.10a results in an effective annual rate of

$$e^{.08} - 1 = 1.0833 - 1 = .0833 = 8.33\%$$

in the case of continuous compounding. This is the highest effective annual rate attainable with an 8 percent nominal rate.

savings interest rates at the higher effective annual rate—the APY—offers two advantages: It tends to standardize disclosure to consumers, and it allows financial institutions to quote the most attractive interest rates—low loan rates and high savings rates.

R e v i e w   Q u e s t i o n s

6-4   How is the *compounding process* related to the payment of interest on savings? What is the general equation for the future value, FV_n, in period n if PV dollars are deposited in an account paying k percent annual interest?

6-5   What effect would (**a**) a *decrease* in the interest rate or (**b**) an *increase* in the holding period of a deposit have on its future value? Why?

6-6   What effect does compounding interest more frequently than annually have on (**a**) the future value generated by a beginning principal and (**b**) the *effective annual rate (EAR)*? Why?

6-7   What is *continuous compounding*? How does the future value of a given deposit at a given rate of interest using continuous compounding compare to the value obtained by using annual or any other compounding period?

6-8   Differentiate between a *nominal annual rate* and an *effective annual rate (EAR)*. Under what compounding period are they equivalent?

LG3

FUTURE VALUE OF AN ANNUITY

annuity
A stream of equal annual cash flows. These cash flows can be *inflows* of returns earned on investments or *outflows* of funds invested to earn future returns.

An **annuity** is a stream of equal annual cash flows. These cash flows can be *inflows* of returns earned on investments or *outflows* of funds invested to earn future returns. The calculations required to find the future value of an annuity on which interest is paid at a specified rate compounded annually can be illustrated by the following example.

Example ▼   Mollie Carr wishes to determine how much money she will have at the end of 5 years if she deposits $1,000 annually at the *end of each* of the next 5 years into a savings account paying 7 percent annual interest. Table 6.4 presents the calculations required to find the future value of this annuity at the end of year 5.

Time-Line Use   This situation is depicted on the following time line:

Time line for future value of an annuity ($1,000 end-of-year deposit, earning 7 percent, at the end of 5 years)

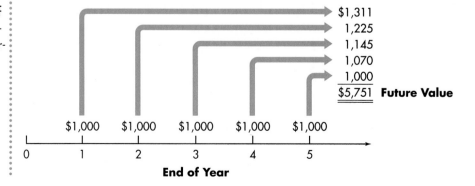

TABLE 6.4	The Future Value of a $1,000 5-Year Annuity Compounded at 7 Percent			
End of year	Amount deposited (1)	Number of years compounded (2)	Future value interest factors from Table A-1 (3)	Future value at end of year [(1) × (3)] (4)
1	$1,000	4	1.311	$1,311
2	1,000	3	1.225	1,225
3	1,000	2	1.145	1,145
4	1,000	1	1.070	1,070
5	1,000	0	1.000	1,000
		Future value of annuity at end of year 5		$5,751

As the table and figure show, at the end of year 5, Mollie will have $5,751 in her account. Column 2 of the table indicates that because the deposits are made at the end of the year, the first deposit will earn interest for 4 years, the second for 3 years, and so on. The future value interest factors in column 3 correspond to these interest-earning periods and the 7 percent rate of interest.

USING TABLES AND CALCULATORS TO FIND FUTURE VALUE OF AN ANNUITY

Annuity calculations can be simplified by using an interest table for the future value of an annuity or a financial calculator. A table for the future value of a $1 *annuity* is given in Appendix Table A-2. The factors included in the table are based on the assumption that every deposit is made at the *end of the period*.[9] The formula for the **future value interest factor for an annuity** when interest is compounded annually at k percent for n periods, $FVIFA_{k,n}$, is:[10]

future value interest factor for an annuity
The multiplier used to calculate the future value of an annuity at a specified interest rate over a given period of time.

$$FVIFA_{k,n} = \sum_{t=1}^{n}(1 + k)^{t-1} \tag{6.11}$$

This factor is the multiplier used to calculate the future value of an annuity at a specified interest rate over a given period of time.

By letting FVA_n equal the future value of an n-year annuity, PMT equal the amount to be deposited annually at the end of each year, and $FVIFA_{k,n}$ represent the appropriate *future value interest factor for a one-dollar annuity compounded*

---

[9]The discussions of annuities throughout this text concentrate on the more common form of annuity—the *ordinary annuity*, which is an annuity that occurs at the *end* of each period. An annuity that occurs at the *beginning* of each period is called an *annuity due*. The financial tables for annuities included in this book are prepared for use with ordinary annuities.

[10]This formula merely states that the future value interest factor for an n-year annuity is found by adding the sum of the first $n - 1$ future value interest factors to 1.000; that is:

$$FVIFA_{k,n} = 1.000 + \sum_{t=1}^{n-1} FVIF_{k,t}$$

at k *percent for* n *years,* the relationship among these variables can be expressed as follows:

$$FVA_n = PMT \times (FVIFA_{k,n})$$ (6.12)

An example will illustrate this calculation using both a table and a calculator.

Example ▼ As noted earlier, Mollie Carr wishes to find the future value *(FVA_n)* at the end of 5 years *(n)* of an annual *end-of-year deposit* of $1,000 *(PMT)* into an account paying 7 percent annual interest *(k)* during the next 5 years.

Table Use The appropriate future value interest factor for a 5-year annuity at 7 percent *(FVIFA_{7%,5 yrs})*, found in Table A-2, is 5.751. By using Equation 6.12, the $1,000 deposit $\times$ 5.751 results in a future value for the annuity of $5,751.

Calculator Use Using the calculator inputs shown below, you should find the future value of the annuity to be $5,750.74—a slightly more precise answer than that found using the table.

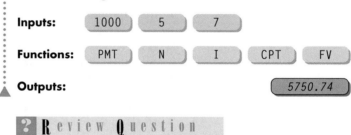

Inputs: | 1000 | 5 | 7 |

Functions: | PMT | N | I | CPT | FV |

Outputs: | 5750.74 |

? R e v i e w   Q u e s t i o n

6-9 Explain how to conveniently determine the future value of an annuity that provides a stream of *end-of-period* cash inflows.

PRESENT VALUE OF A SINGLE AMOUNT

present value
The current dollar value of a future amount; the amount of money that would have to be invested today at a given interest rate over a specified period to equal the future amount.

It is often useful to determine the value today of a future amount of money. **Present value** is the current dollar value of a future amount—the amount of money that would have to be invested today at a given interest rate over a specified period to equal the future amount. Present value depends largely on the investment opportunities of the recipient and the point in time at which the amount is to be received. This section explores the present value of a single amount.

THE CONCEPT OF PRESENT VALUE

discounting cash flows
The process of finding present values; the inverse of compounding interest.

The process of finding present values is often referred to as **discounting cash flows.** It is concerned with answering the question: "If I can earn *k* percent on my money, what is the most I would be willing to pay now for an opportunity to receive *FV_n* dollars *n* periods from today?" This process is actually the inverse of compounding interest. Instead of finding the future value of present dollars invested at a given rate, discounting determines the present value of a future amount, assuming the opportunity to earn a certain return, k, on the money. This annual rate of return is variously referred to as the *discount rate, required return, cost of capital,* or *opportunity cost.* These terms will be used interchangeably in this text. The discounting process can be illustrated by a simple example.

Example ▼ Mr. Cotter has an opportunity to receive $300 one year from now. If he can earn 6 percent on his investments in the normal course of events, what is the most he should pay now for this opportunity? To answer this question, he must determine how many dollars would have to be invested at 6 percent today to have $300 one year from now. By letting PV equal this unknown amount and using the same notation as in the future value discussion, the situation can be expressed as follows:

$$PV \times (1 + .06) = \$300 \tag{6.13}$$

Solving Equation 6.13 for PV gives us Equation 6.14:

$$PV = \frac{\$300}{(1 + .06)} \tag{6.14}$$
$$= \$283.02$$

The "present value" of $300 received one year from today, given an opportunity cost of 6 percent, is $283.02. Mr. Cotter should be indifferent to whether he receives $283.02 today or $300.00 one year from now. That is, investment of $283.02 today at the 6 percent opportunity cost would result in $300 at the end ▲ of 1 year.

THE EQUATION FOR PRESENT VALUE

The present value of a future amount can be found mathematically by solving Equation 6.4 for PV. In other words, one merely wants to obtain the present value, PV, of some future amount, FV_n, to be received n periods from now, assuming an opportunity cost of k. Solving Equation 6.4 for PV gives us Equation 6.15, which is the general equation for the present value of a future amount:

$$PV = \frac{FV_n}{(1 + k)^n} = FV_n \times \left[\frac{1}{(1 + k)^n}\right] \tag{6.15}$$

Note the similarity between this general equation for present value and the equation in the preceding example (Equation 6.14). The use of this equation can be illustrated by a simple example.

Example ▼ Pam Valenti wishes to find the present value of $1,700 that will be received 8 years from now. Pam's opportunity cost is 8 percent. Substituting $FV_8 = \$1,700$, $n = 8$, and $k = .08$ into Equation 6.15 yields:

$$PV = \frac{\$1,700}{(1 + .08)^8} \tag{6.16}$$

To solve Equation 6.16, the term $(1 + .08)$ must be raised to the eighth power. The value resulting from this time-consuming calculation is 1.851. Dividing this value into $1,700 yields a present value for the $1,700 of $918.42.

Time-Line Use   This analysis can be depicted on the following time line:

Time line for present value of a single amount ($1,700 future amount, discounted at 8 percent, from the end of 8 years)

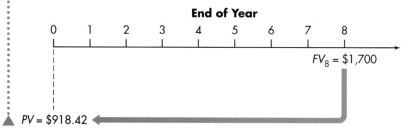

USING TABLES AND CALCULATORS TO FIND PRESENT VALUE

present value interest factor
The multiplier used to calculate at a specified discount rate the present value of an amount to be received in a future period.

The present value calculation can be simplified by using a **present value interest factor.** This factor is the multiplier used to calculate at a specified discount rate the present value of an amount to be received in a future period. The present value interest factor for the present value of $1 discounted at k percent for n periods is referred to as $PVIF_{k,n}$:

$$\text{Present value interest factor} = PVIF_{k,n} = \frac{1}{(1 + k)^n} \qquad (6.17)$$

Appendix Table A–3 presents present value interest factors for $1. By letting $PVIF_{k,n}$ represent the appropriate factor, we can rewrite Equation 6.15 as follows:

$$PV = FV_n \times (PVIF_{k,n}) \qquad (6.18)$$

This expression indicates that to find the present value, PV, of an amount to be received in a future period, n, we have merely to multiply the future amount, FV_n, by the appropriate present value interest factor. An example will illustrate this calculation using both a table and a calculator.

Example ▼ As noted, Pam Valenti wishes to find the present value of $1,700 to be received 8 years from now, assuming an 8 percent opportunity cost.

Table Use   The present value interest factor for 8 percent and 8 years, $PVIF_{8\%,8\,yrs}$, found in Table A-3, is .540. Multiplying the $1,700 future value by this factor results in a present value of $918.

Calculator Use   Using the calculator's financial functions and the inputs shown below, you should find the present value to be $918.46.

Inputs: [1700] [8] [8]

Functions: [FV] [N] [I] [CPT] [PV]

Outputs: [918.46]

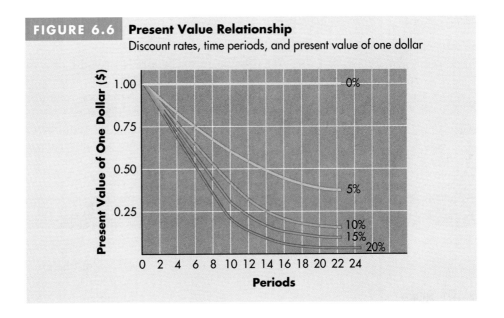

FIGURE 6.6 **Present Value Relationship**
Discount rates, time periods, and present value of one dollar

Because of rounding in the calculation in Equation 6.16 and of the factors in Table A-3, the value obtained with the calculator—$918.46—is more accurate, although for purposes of this text, these differences are insignificant.

A GRAPHIC VIEW OF PRESENT VALUE

Remember that present value calculations assume that the future values are measured at the *end* of the given period. The relationship among various discount rates, time periods, and the present value of one dollar is illustrated in Figure 6.6. Everything else being equal, the figure clearly shows that: (1) the higher the discount rate, the lower the present value, and (2) the longer the period of time, the lower the present value. Also note that given a discount rate of 0 percent, the present value always equals the future value ($1.00). But for any discount rate greater than zero, the present value is less than the future value of $1.00.

COMPARING PRESENT VALUE AND FUTURE VALUE

We will close this section with a couple of important observations about present values. One is that the expression for the present value interest factor for k percent and n periods, $1/(1 + k)^n$, is the *inverse* of the future value interest factor for k percent and n periods, $(1 + k)^n$. This fact can be confirmed by dividing a present value interest factor for k percent and n periods, $PVIF_{k,n}$, into 1.0 and comparing the resulting value to the future value interest factor given in Table A-1 for k percent and n periods, $FVIF_{k,n}$. The two values should be equivalent.

Second, because of the relationship between present value interest factors and future value interest factors, we can find the present value interest factors given a table of future value interest factors, and vice versa. For example, the future value interest factor from Table A–1 for 10 percent and 5 periods is 1.611. Dividing this value into 1.0 yields .621, which is the present value interest factor given in Table A-3 for 10 percent and 5 periods.

Review Questions

6-10 What is meant by "the present value of a future amount"? What is the equation for the present value, *PV*, of a future amount, FV_n, to be received in period *n*, assuming that the firm requires a minimum return of *k* percent? How are present value and future value calculations related?

6-11 What effect does *increasing* (**a**) the required return and (**b**) the time period have on the present value of a future amount? Why?

PRESENT VALUE OF CASH FLOW STREAMS

mixed stream
A stream of cash flows that reflects no particular pattern.

Quite often in finance there is a need to find the present value of a *stream* of cash flows to be received in various future periods. Two basic types of cash flow streams are possible: the mixed stream and the annuity. A **mixed stream** of cash flows reflects no particular pattern; an *annuity,* as stated earlier, is a pattern of equal annual cash flows. Because certain shortcuts are possible in finding the present value of an annuity, we will discuss mixed streams and annuities separately. In addition, the present value of a perpetuity is considered in this section.

PRESENT VALUE OF A MIXED STREAM

To find the present value of a mixed stream of cash flows, we determine the present value of each future amount, as described in the preceding section, and then add together all the individual present values, to find the total present value of the stream. An example will illustrate this procedure using a table or a calculator.

Example ▼ QTD Company, a shoe manufacturer, has been offered an opportunity to receive the following mixed stream of cash flows over the next 5 years:

Year	Cash flow
1	$400
2	800
3	500
4	400
5	300

If the firm must earn at least 9 percent on its investments, what is the most it should pay for this opportunity?

Table Use To solve this problem, determine the present value of each cash flow discounted at 9 percent for the appropriate number of years. The sum of these individual values is the present value of the total stream. The present value interest factors required are those shown in Table A-3. Table 6.5 presents the calcula-

	Cash flow	$PVIF_{9\%,n}$[a]	Present value [(1) × (2)]
Year (n)	(1)	(2)	(3)
1	$400	.917	$ 366.80
2	800	.842	673.60
3	500	.772	386.00
4	400	.708	283.20
5	300	.650	195.00
	Present value of mixed stream		$1,904.60

TABLE 6.5 The Present Value of a Mixed Stream of Cash Flows

[a]Present value interest factors at 9 percent are from Table A-3.

tions needed to find the present value of the cash flow stream, which turns out to be $1,904.60.

Calculator Use You can use a calculator to find the present value of each individual cash flow, as demonstrated earlier, and then sum the present values, to get the present value of the stream of cash flows. However, most financial calculators have a function that allows you to punch in *all cash flows*, specify the discount rate, and then directly calculate the present value of the entire cash flow stream. Because calculators provide more precise solutions than those based on rounded table factors, the present value of QTD Company's cash flow stream found using a calculator will be a value that is close, but not precisely equal, to the $1,904.60 value calculated before.

Paying $1,904.60 would provide exactly a 9 percent return. QTD should not pay more than that amount for the opportunity to receive these cash flows.

Time-Line Use This situation is depicted on the following time line:

Time line for present value of a mixed stream (end-of-year cash flows, discounted at 9 percent, over the corresponding number of years)

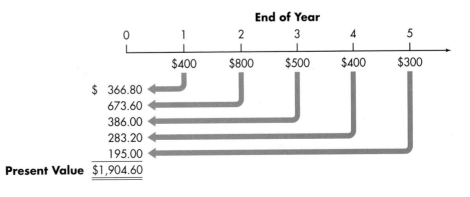

TABLE 6.6	The Long Method for Finding the Present Value of an Annuity		
Year (n)	Cash flow (1)	$PVIF_{8\%,n}{}^{a}$ (2)	Present value [(1) × (2)] (3)
1	$700	.926	$ 648.20
2	700	.857	599.90
3	700	.794	555.80
4	700	.735	514.50
5	700	.681	476.70
		Present value of annuity	$2,795.10

^{a}Present value interest factors at 8 percent are from Table A-3.

PRESENT VALUE OF AN ANNUITY

The method for finding the present value of an annuity is similar to that used for a mixed stream, but can be simplified somewhat.

Example ▼ Labco Company, a small producer of plastic toys, wants to determine the most it should pay to purchase a particular annuity. The firm requires a minimum return of 8 percent on all investments, and the annuity consists of cash flows of $700 per year for 5 years. Table 6.6 shows the long method for finding the present value of the annuity—which is the same as the method used for the mixed stream. This procedure yields a present value of $2,795.10.

Time-Line Use   Similarly, this situation is depicted on the following time line:

Time line for present value of an annuity ($700 end-of-year cash flows, discounted at 8 percent, over 5 years)

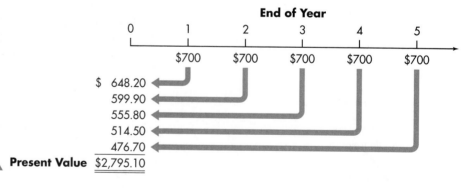

USING TABLES AND CALCULATORS TO FIND PRESENT VALUE OF AN ANNUITY

Annuity calculations can be simplified by using an interest table for the present value of an annuity or a calculator. The values for the present value of a $1 annuity are given in Appendix Table A-4. The interest factors in Table A-4 actually represent the sum of the first *n* present value interest factors in Table A-3 for a given discount rate. The formula for the **present value interest factor for an**

present value interest factor for an annuity
The multiplier used to calculate the present value of an annuity at a specified discount rate over a given period of time.

annuity with end-of-year cash flows that are discounted at k percent for n periods, $PVIFA_{k,n}$, is:[11]

$$PVIFA_{k,n} = \sum_{t=1}^{n} \frac{1}{(1 + k)^t} \qquad (6.19)$$

This factor is the multiplier used to calculate the present value of an annuity at a specified discount rate over a given period of time.

By letting PVA_n equal the present value of an n-year annuity, PMT equal the amount to be received annually at the end of each year, and $PVIFA_{k,n}$ represent the appropriate value for the *present value interest factor for a one-dollar annuity discounted at* k *percent for* n *years,* the relationship among these variables can be expressed as follows:

$$PVA_n = PMT \times (PVIFA_{k,n}) \qquad (6.20)$$

An example will illustrate this calculation for both a table and a calculator.

Example ▼ Labco Company, as noted, wants to find the present value of a 5-year annuity of $700 assuming an 8 percent opportunity cost.

Table Use   The present value interest factor for an annuity at 8 percent for 5 years ($PVIFA_{8\%,5\text{yrs}}$), found in Table A-4, is 3.993. By using Equation 6.20, the $700 annuity $\times$ 3.993 results in a present value of $2,795.10.

Calculator Use Using the calculator's financial functions and the inputs shown below, you should find the present value of the annuity to be $2,794.90.

Inputs: [700]   [5]   [8]

Functions: [PMT]   [N]   [I]   [CPT]   [PV]

Outputs: [2794.90]

Because of rounding in the calculation in Table 6.6 and of the factors in Table A-4, the value obtained with the calculator—$2,794.90—is most accurate, although for purposes of this text these differences are insignificant. ▲

PRESENT VALUE OF A PERPETUITY

perpetuity
An annuity with an infinite life, providing continual annual cash flows.

A **perpetuity** is an annuity with an infinite life—in other words, an annuity that never stops providing its holder with a cash flow at the end of each year. It is sometimes necessary to find the present value of a perpetuity. The present value interest factor for a perpetuity discounted at the rate k is:

$$PVIFA_{k,\infty} = \frac{1}{k} \qquad (6.21)$$

---

[11]This formula merely states that the present value interest factor for an n-year annuity is found by summing the first n present value interest factors at the given rate; that is:

$$PVIFA_{k,n} = \sum_{t=1}^{n} PVIF_{k,t}$$

As the equation shows, the appropriate factor, $PVIFA_{k,\infty}$, is found merely by dividing the discount rate, k (stated as a decimal), into 1. The validity of this method can be seen by looking at the factors in Table A-4 for 8, 10, 20, and 40 percent: As the number of periods (typically years) approaches 50, the values of these factors approach 12.500 (1 ÷ .08), 10.000 (1 ÷ .10), 5.000 (1 ÷ .20), and 2.500 (1 ÷ .40), respectively. An example will help to clarify the application of the factor given in Equation 6.21.

Example ▼ Fanny May wishes to determine the present value of a $1,000 perpetuity discounted at 10 percent. The appropriate present value interest factor can be found by dividing 1 by .10, as noted in Equation 6.21. Substituting the resulting factor, 10, and the amount of the perpetuity, $PMT = \$1,000$, into Equation 6.20 results in a present value of $10,000 for the perpetuity. In other words, the receipt of $1,000 every year for an indefinite period is worth only $10,000 today if Fanny May can earn 10 percent on her investments. If she had $10,000 and earned 10 percent interest on it each year, $1,000 a year could be withdrawn indefinitely without touching the initial $10,000, which would never be drawn upon. ▲

❓ Review Questions

6-12   How is the present value of a mixed stream of cash flows calculated? How can the calculations required to find the present value of an annuity be streamlined?

6-13   What is a *perpetuity?* How can the present value interest factor for such a stream of cash flows be determined?

LG6

SPECIAL APPLICATIONS OF TIME VALUE

Future value and present value techniques have a number of important applications. We will study three of these in this section: (1) the calculation of the deposits needed to accumulate a future sum, (2) the calculation of amortization on loans, and (3) the determination of interest or growth rates.

DEPOSITS TO ACCUMULATE A FUTURE SUM

People often wish to determine the annual deposit necessary to accumulate a certain amount of money so many years hence. Suppose you want to buy a house 5 years from now and estimate that an initial down payment of $20,000 will be required at that time. You wish to make equal annual end-of-year deposits in an account paying annual interest of 6 percent, so you must determine what size annuity will result in a lump sum equal to $20,000 at the end of year 5. The solution to this problem is closely related to the process of finding the future value of an annuity.

Earlier in the chapter, we found the future value of an n-year annuity, FVA_n, by multiplying the annual deposit, PMT, by the appropriate interest factor,

$FVIFA_{k,n}$. The relationship of the three variables has been defined by Equation 6.12, which is rewritten here as Equation 6.22:

$$FVA_n = PMT \times (FVIFA_{k,n}) \tag{6.22}$$

We can find the annual deposit required to accumulate FVA_n dollars, given a specified interest rate, k, and a certain number of years, n, by solving Equation 6.22 for PMT. Isolating PMT on the left side of the equation gives us:

$$PMT = \frac{FVA_n}{FVIFA_{k,n}} \tag{6.23}$$

Once this is done, we have only to substitute the known values of FVA_n and $FVIFA_{k,n}$ into the right side of the equation to find the annual deposit required. An example will demonstrate this calculation.

Example ▼ As just stated, you want to determine the equal annual end-of-year deposits required to accumulate $20,000 at the end of 5 years given an interest rate of 6 percent.

Table Use Table A-2 indicates that the future value interest factor for an annuity at 6 percent for 5 years ($FVIFA_{6\%,5yrs}$), is 5.637. Substituting $FVA_5 = \$20,000$ and $FVIFA_{6\%,5yrs} = 5.637$ into Equation 6.23 yields an annual required deposit, PMT, of $3,547.99. Thus, if $3,547.99 is deposited at the end of each year for 5 years, at 6 percent interest, there will be $20,000 in the account at the end of the 5 years.

Calculator Use Using the calculator inputs shown below, you should find the annual deposit amount to be $3,547.93. Note that this value, except for a slight rounding difference, agrees with the value found by using Table A-2.

Inputs: 20000   5   6

Functions: FV   N   I   CPT   PMT

Outputs: 3547.93

LOAN AMORTIZATION

loan amortization
The determination of the equal annual loan payments necessary to provide a lender with a specified interest return and to repay the loan principal over a specified period.

loan amortization schedule
A schedule of equal payments to repay a loan. It shows the allocation of each loan payment to interest and principal.

The term **loan amortization** refers to the determination of the equal annual loan payments necessary to provide a lender with a specified interest return and to repay the loan principal over a specified period. The loan amortization process involves finding the future payments (over the term of the loan) whose present value at the loan interest rate equals the amount of initial principal borrowed. Lenders use a **loan amortization schedule** to determine these payment amounts and the allocation of each payment to interest and principal. In the case of home mortgages, these tables are used to find the equal *monthly* payments necessary to *amortize*, or pay off, the mortgage at a specified interest rate over a 15- to 30-year period.

Amortizing a loan actually involves creating an annuity out of a present amount. For example, say you borrow $6,000 at 10 percent and agree to make equal annual end-of-year payments over 4 years. To find the size of the payments, the lender determines the amount of a 4-year annuity discounted at 10 percent that has a present value of $6,000. This process is actually the inverse of finding the present value of an annuity.

Earlier in the chapter, we found the present value, PVA_n, of an n-year annuity of PMT dollars by multiplying the annual amount, PMT, by the present value interest factor for an annuity ($PVIFA_{k,n}$). This relationship, which was originally expressed as Equation 6.20, is rewritten here as Equation 6.24:

$$PVA_n = PMT \times (PVIFA_{k,n}) \qquad (6.24)$$

To find the equal annual payment required to pay off, or amortize, the loan, PVA_n, over a certain number of years at a specified interest rate, we need to solve Equation 6.24 for PMT. Isolating PMT on the left side of the equation gives:

$$PMT = \frac{PVA_n}{PVIFA_{k,n}} \qquad (6.25)$$

Once this is done, we have only to substitute the known values of PVA_n and $PVIFA_{k,n}$ into the right side of the equation to find the annual payment required.

Example ▼ As just stated, you want to determine the equal annual end-of-year payments necessary to amortize fully a $6,000, 10 percent loan over 4 years.

Table Use Table A-4 indicates that the present value interest factor for an annuity corresponding to 10 percent and 4 years ($PVIFA_{10\%,4yrs}$) is 3.170. Substituting $PVA_4 = \$6,000$ and $PVIFA_{10\%,4yrs} = 3.170$ into Equation 6.25 and solving for PMT yields an annual loan payment of $1,892.74. Thus, to repay the interest and principal on a $6,000, 10 percent, 4-year loan, equal annual end-of-year payments of $1,892.74 are necessary.

Calculator Use Using the calculator inputs shown below, you should find the annual payment amount to be $1,892.82. Except for a slight rounding difference, this value agrees with the one found using Table A-4.

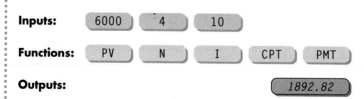

The allocation of each loan payment to interest and principal can be seen in columns 3 and 4 of the *loan amortization schedule* in Table 6.7. The portion of each payment representing interest (column 3) declines over the repayment period, and the portion going to principal repayment (column 4) increases. This pattern is typical of amortized loans; with level payments, as the principal is reduced, the interest component declines, leaving a larger portion of each subsequent payment to repay principal.

TABLE 6.7	Loan Amortization Schedule ($6,000 Principal, 10 Percent Interest, 4-Year Repayment Period)

End of year (1)	Loan payment (1)	Beginning-of-year principal (2)	Payments — Interest [.10 × (2)] (3)	Payments — Principal [(1) − (3)] (4)	End-of-year principal [(2) − (4)] (5)
1	$1,892.74	$6,000.00	$600.00	$1,292.74	$4,707.26
2	1,892.74	4,707.26	470.73	1,422.01	3,285.25
3	1,892.74	3,285.25	328.53	1,564.21	1,721.04
4	1,892.74	1,721.04	172.10	1,720.64	—[a]

[a]Due to rounding, a slight difference ($.40) exists between the beginning-of-year-4 principal (in column 2) and the year-4 principal payment (in column 4).

INTEREST OR GROWTH RATES

It is often necessary to calculate the compound annual interest or *growth rate* (i.e., the annual rate of change in value) of a series of cash flows. In doing this, either future value or present value interest factors can be used. The approach using present value interest factors is described in this section. The simplest situation is one in which a person wishes to find the rate of interest or growth in a series of cash flow.[12] This can be illustrated by the following example.

Example ▼ Al Taylor wishes to find the rate of interest or growth of the following series of cash flows:

Year	Cash flow	
2000	$1,520	4
1999	1,440	3
1998	1,370	2
1997	1,300	1
1996	1,250	

By using the first year (1996) as a base year, we see that interest has been earned (or growth experienced) for 4 years.

---

[12]Because the calculations required for finding interest rates and growth rates, given certain cash flow streams, are the same, this section refers to the calculations as those required to find interest *or* growth rates.

Table Use   The first step in finding the interest or growth rate is to divide the amount received in the earliest year by the amount received in the latest year. This gives the present value interest factor for a *single amount* for 4 years, $PVIF_{k,4yrs}$, which is .822 ($1,250 ÷ $1,520). The interest rate in Table A-3 associated with the factor closest to .822 for 4 years is the interest or growth rate of Al's cash flows. In the row for year 4 in Table A-3, the factor for 5 percent is .823—almost exactly the .822 value. Therefore, the interest or growth rate of the given cash flows is approximately (to the nearest whole percent) 5 percent.[13]

Calculator Use   Using the calculator for this application, we treat the earliest value as a present value, PV, and the latest value as a future value, FV_n. (*Note:* Most calculators require *either* the PV or FV value to be input as a negative number in order to calculate an unknown interest or growth rate. That approach is used here.) Using the inputs shown below, you should find the interest or growth rate to be 5.01 percent, which is consistent with, but more precise than, the value found using Table A-3.

Inputs:	1250	-1520	4		
Functions:	PV	FV	N	CPT	I
Outputs:				5.01	

Another type of interest rate problem involves finding the interest rate associated with an *annuity*, or equal-payment loan. The procedure for doing so can be demonstrated with the following example:

Example ▼ Jan Jong can borrow $2,000 to be repaid in equal annual end-of-year amounts of $514.14 for the next 5 years. She wants to find the interest rate on this loan.

Table Use   Substituting PVA_5 = $2,000 and PMT = $514.14 into Equation 6.24 and rearranging the equation to solve for $PVIFA_{k,5yrs}$, we get:

$$PVIFA_{k,5yrs} = \frac{PVA_5}{PMT} = \frac{\$2,000}{\$514.14} = 3.890 \tag{6.26}$$

The interest rate for 5 years associated with the annuity factor closest to 3.890 in Table A-4 is 9 percent. Therefore, the interest rate on the loan is approximately (to the nearest whole percent) 9 percent.

Calculator Use   (*Note:* Most calculators require either the PMT or PV value to be input as a negative number in order to calculate an unknown interest rate on an equal-payment loan. That approach is used here.) Using the inputs shown

---

[13]Rounding of interest or growth rate estimates to the nearest whole percent is assumed throughout this text. To obtain more precise estimates, *interpolation*—a mathematical technique for estimating unknown intermediate values—can be applied.

below, you should find the interest rate to be 9.00 percent, which is consistent with, but more precise than, the approximate value found by using Table A-4.

Inputs: 514.14   -2000   5

Functions: PMT   PV   N   CPT   I

Outputs: 9.00

? Review Questions

6-14   How can the size of the equal annual end-of-year deposits necessary to accumulate a certain future sum in a specified future period be determined?

6-15   Describe the procedure used to amortize a loan into a series of equal annual payments. What is a *loan amortization schedule?*

6-16   Which present value interest factors would be used to find **(a)** the growth rate associated with a series of cash flows, and **(b)** the interest rate associated with an equal-payment loan?

SUMMARY

LG1   Discuss the role of time value in finance and the use of computational aids to simplify its application. Financial managers use time value of money techniques to explicitly recognize their opportunities to earn positive returns when assessing the value of the expected cash flow streams associated with decision alternatives. Alternatives can be assessed by either compounding to find future value or discounting to find present value. Because they are at time zero when making decisions, financial managers rely primarily on present value techniques. Both financial tables and financial calculators can streamline the practical application of time value techniques.

LG2   Understand the concept of future value, its calculation for a single amount, and the effects of compounding interest more frequently than annually. Future value relies on compound interest to measure future amounts: the initial principal or deposit in one period, along with the interest earned on it, becomes the beginning principal of the following period. Interest can be compounded at intervals ranging from annually to daily, and even continuously. The more frequently interest is compounded, the larger the future amount that will

be accumulated and the higher the effective annual rate (EAR). The annual percentage rate (APR)—a nominal annual rate—is quoted on credit cards and loans, and the annual percentage yield (APY)—an effective annual rate—is quoted on savings products. The interest factor formulas and basic equation for the future value of a single amount are given in Table 6.8.

LG3   Find the future value of an annuity. An annuity is a pattern of equal annual cash flows. The future value of an annuity can be found by using the future value interest factor for an annuity. The product of the annual amount of the annuity and the future value interest factor for the appropriate rate of interest and number of periods is the future value of the annuity. Alternatively, a calculator can be used to calculate quickly the future value of an annuity. The interest factor formula and basic equation for the future value of an annuity are given in Table 6.8.

LG4   Understand the concept of present value, its calculation for a single amount, and the relationship of present to future value. Present value is the inverse of future value. The present value of a

TABLE 6.8	Summary of Key Definitions, Formulas, and Equations for Time Value of Money

Variable definitions

e = exponential function = 2.7183
EAR = effective annual rate
FV_n = future value or amount at the end of period n
FVA_n = future value of an n-year annuity
k = annual rate of interest
m = number of times per year interest is compounded
n = number of periods—typically, years—over which money earns a return
PMT = amount deposited or received annually at the end of each year
PV = initial principal or present value
PVA_n = present value of an n-year annuity
t = period number index

Interest factor formulas

Future value of a single amount:

$$FVIF_{k,n} = \left(1 + \frac{k}{m}\right)^{m \times n} \qquad \text{[Eq. 6.7]}$$

for annual compounding, $m = 1$,

$$FVIF_{k,n} = (1 + k)^n \qquad \text{[Eq. 6.5; factors in Table A-1]}$$

for continuous compounding, $m = \infty$,

$$FVIF_{k,n} = e^{k \times n} \qquad \text{[Eq. 6.9]}$$

to find the effective annual rate,

$$EAR = \left(1 + \frac{k}{m}\right)^m - 1 \qquad \text{[Eq. 6.10]}$$

Future value of an annuity:

$$FVIFA_{k,n} = \sum_{t=1}^{n} (1 + k)^{t-1} \qquad \text{[Eq. 6.11; factors in Table A-2]}$$

Present value of a single amount:

$$PVIF_{k,n} = \frac{1}{(1 + k)^n} \qquad \text{[Eq. 6.17; factors in Table A-3]}$$

Present value of an annuity:

$$PVIFA_{k,n} = \sum_{t=1}^{n} \frac{1}{(1 + k)^t} \qquad \text{[Eq. 6.19; factors in Table A-4]}$$

Present value of a perpetuity:

$$PVIFA_{k,\infty} = \frac{1}{k} \qquad \text{[Eq. 6.21]}$$

Basic equations

Future value (single amount):	$FV_n = PV \times (FVIF_{k,n})$	[Eq. 6.6]
Future value (annuity):	$FVA_n = PMT \times (FVIFA_{k,n})$	[Eq. 6.12]
Present value (single amount):	$PV = FV_n \times (PVIF_{k,n})$	[Eq. 6.18]
Present value (annuity):	$PVA_n = PMT \times (PVIFA_{k,n})$	[Eq. 6.20]

future amount is the amount of money today that is equivalent to the given future amount, considering the return that can be earned on the current money. The present value of a single amount can be found using either the present value interest factor for one dollar or a calculator. The interest factor formula and basic equation for the present value of a single amount are given in Table 6.8.

 Calculate the present value of a mixed stream of cash flows, an annuity, and a perpetuity. The present value of a mixed stream of cash flows is the sum of the present values of each individual cash flow. The present value of an annuity can be found by using the present value interest factor for an annuity. The product of the annual amount of the annuity and the present value interest factor for the appropriate rate of interest and number of periods is the present value of the annuity. The present

value of a perpetuity—an infinite-lived annuity—is found by dividing 1 by the discount rate to represent the present value interest factor. The interest factor formulas and basic equation for the present value of an annuity are given in Table 6.8.

 Describe the procedures involved in (1) determining deposits to accumulate a future sum, (2) loan amortization, and (3) finding interest or growth rates. The annual deposit to accumulate a given future sum can be found by solving the equation for the future value of an annuity for the annual payment. A loan can be amortized into equal annual payments by solving the equation for the present value of an annuity for the annual payment. Interest or growth rates can be estimated by finding the unknown interest rate in the equation for the present value of a single amount, an annuity, or a mixed stream.

SELF-TEST PROBLEMS   (Solutions in Appendix B)

ST 6-1   Future values   Delia Martin has $10,000 that she can deposit in any of three savings accounts for a 3-year period. Bank A compounds interest on an annual basis, bank B compounds interest twice each year, and bank C compounds interest each quarter. All three banks have a stated annual interest rate of 4 percent.
  a. What amount would Ms. Martin have at the end of the third year, leaving all interest paid on deposit, in each bank?
  b. What effective annual rate (EAR) would she earn in each of the banks?
  c. On the basis of your findings in **a** and **b**, which bank should Ms. Martin deal with? Why?
  d. If a fourth bank—Bank D, also with a 4 percent stated interest rate—compounds interest continuously, how much would Ms. Martin have at the end of the third year? Does this alternative change your recommendation in **c?** Explain why or why not.

ST 6-2   Future values of annuities   Ramesh Abdul wishes to choose the better of two equally costly cash flow streams—annuity X and annuity Y. X provides cash inflow of $9,000 at the end of each of the next 6 years. Y provides cash inflow of $10,000 at the end of each of the next 6 years. Assume that Ramesh can earn 15 percent on annuity X and 11 percent on annuity Y.
  a. On a purely subjective basis, which annuity do you think is more attractive? Why?
  b. Find the future value at the end of year 6, FVA_6, for both annuities—X and Y.
  c. Use your finding in **b** to indicate which annuity is more attractive. Compare your finding to your subjective response in **a.**

   ST 6-3   Present values   You have a choice of accepting either of two 5-year cash flow streams or lump-sum amounts. One cash flow stream is an annuity, and the other is a mixed stream. You may accept alternative A or B—either as a cash flow stream or as a lump sum. Given the cash flow stream and lump-sum amounts associated with each, and assuming a 9 percent opportunity cost, which alternative (A or B) and in which form (cash flow stream or lump-sum amount) would you prefer?

	Cash flow stream	
End of year	Alternative A	Alternative B
1	$700	$1,100
2	700	900
3	700	700
4	700	500
5	700	300
	Lump-sum amount	
At time zero	$2,825	$2,800

   ST 6-4   Deposits to accumulate a future sum   Judi Jordan wishes to accumulate $8,000 by the end of 5 years by making equal annual end-of-year deposits over the next 5 years. If Judi can earn 7 percent on her investments, how much must she deposit at the *end of each year* to meet this goal?

PROBLEMS

   6-1   Using a time line   The financial manager at Starbuck Industries is considering an investment that requires an initial outlay of $25,000 and is expected to result in cash inflows of $3,000 at the end of year 1, $6,000 at the end of years 2 and 3, $10,000 at the end of year 4, $8,000 at the end of year 5, and $7,000 at the end of year 6.
   a. Draw and label a time line depicting the cash flows associated with Starbuck Industries' proposed investment.
   b. Use arrows to demonstrate, on the time line in **a**, how compounding to find future value can be used to measure all cash flows at the end of year 6.
   c. Use arrows to demonstrate, on the time line in **b**, how discounting to find present value can be used to measure all cash flows at time zero.
   d. Which of the approaches—future value or present value—is most often relied on by the financial manager for decision-making purposes? Why?

   6-2   Future value calculation   *Without referring to tables or the preprogrammed function of your financial calculator,* use the basic formula for future value along with the given interest rate, k, and number of periods, n, to calculate the future value interest factor in each of the cases shown in the following table. Compare the calculated value to the table value in Appendix Table A-1.

Case	Interest rate, k	Number of periods, n
A	12%	2
B	6	3
C	9	2
D	3	4

6-3 **Future value tables** Use the future value interest factors in Appendix Table A-1 in each of the cases shown in the following table to estimate, to the nearest year, how long it would take an initial deposit, assuming no withdrawals,
a. To double.
b. To quadruple.

Case	Interest rate
A	7%
B	40
C	20
D	10

6-4 **Future values** For each of the cases shown in the table below, calculate the future value of the single cash flow deposited today that will be available at the end of the deposit period if the interest is compounded annually at the rate specified over the given period.

Case	Single cash flow	Interest rate	Deposit period
A	$ 200	5%	20 years
B	4,500	8	7
C	10,000	9	10
D	25,000	10	12
E	37,000	11	5
F	40,000	12	9

6-5 **Future value** You have $1,500 to invest today at 7 percent interest compounded annually.
a. How much will you have accumulated in the account at the end of:
   (1) 3 years?
   (2) 6 years?
   (3) 9 years?
b. Use your findings in **a** to calculate the amount of interest earned in:
   (1) the first 3 years (years 1 to 3).
   (2) the second 3 years (years 4 to 6).

(3) the third 3 years (years 7 to 9).

c. Compare and contrast your findings in **b.** Explain why the amount of interest earned increases in each succeeding 3-year period.

6-6 **Inflation and future value**   As part of your financial planning you wish to purchase a new car exactly 5 years from today. The car you wish to purchase costs $14,000 today, and your research indicates that its price will increase by 2 to 4 percent per year over the next 5 years.

a. Estimate the price of the car at the end of 5 years if inflation is:

(1) 2 percent per year.

(2) 4 percent per year.

b. How much more expensive will the car be if the rate of inflation is 4 percent rather than 2 percent?

6-7 **Future value and time**   You can deposit $10,000 into an account paying 9 percent annual interest either today or exactly 10 years from today. How much better off will you be at the end of 40 years if you decide to make the initial deposit today rather than 10 years from today?

6-8 **Single-payment loan repayment**   A person borrows $200 to be repaid in 8 years with 14 percent annually compounded interest. The loan may be repaid at the end of any earlier year with no prepayment penalty.

a. What amount would be due if the loan is repaid at the end of year 1?

b. What is the repayment at the end of year 4?

c. What amount is due at the end of the eighth year?

6-9 **Changing compounding frequency**   Using annual, semiannual, and quarterly compounding periods, for each of the following: (1) calculate the future value if $5,000 is initially deposited, and (2) determine the effective annual rate (EAR):

a. At 12 percent annual interest for 5 years.

b. At 16 percent annual interest for 6 years.

c. At 20 percent annual interest for 10 years.

6-10 **Compounding frequency, future value, and effective annual rates**   For each of the cases in the table below:

Case	Amount of initial deposit	Nominal interest rate, k	Compounding frequency, m (times/year)	Deposit period
A	$ 2,500	6%	2	5 years
B	50,000	12	6	3
C	1,000	5	1	10
D	20,000	16	4	6

a. Calculate the future value at the end of the specified deposit period.

b. Determine the effective annual rate, EAR.

c. Compare the nominal annual rate, k, to the effective annual rate, EAR. What relationship exists between compounding frequency and the nominal and effective annual rates?

6-11   Continuous compounding   For each of the following cases, find the future value at the end of the deposit period, assuming that interest is compounded continuously at the given nominal annual rate.

Case	Amount of initial deposit	Nominal interest rate, k	Deposit period
A	$1,000	9%	2 years
B	600	10	10
C	4,000	8	7
D	2,500	12	4

 6-12   Compounding frequency and future value   You plan to invest $2,000 in an individual retirement arrangement (IRA) today at a *nominal annual rate* of 8 percent, which is expected to apply to all future years.

    a. How much will you have in the account at the end of 10 years if interest is compounded:
      (1) annually?
      (2) semiannually?
      (3) daily (assume a 360-day year)?
      (4) continuously?
    b. What is the *effective annual rate, EAR,* for each compounding period in **a**?
    c. How much greater will your IRA account balance be at the end of 10 years if interest is compounded continuously rather than annually?
    d. How does the compounding frequency affect the future value and effective annual rate for a given deposit? Explain in terms of your findings in **a** through **c**.

 6-13   Comparing compounding periods   Reed Levin wishes to determine the future value at the end of 2 years of a $15,000 deposit made today into an account paying a nominal annual rate of 12 percent.

    a. Find the future value of Reed's deposit assuming that interest is compounded:
      (1) annually.
      (2) quarterly.
      (3) monthly.
      (4) continuously.
    b. Compare your findings in **a,** and use them to demonstrate the relationship between compounding frequency and future value.
    c. What is the maximum future value obtainable given the $15,000 deposit, 2-year time period, and 12 percent nominal annual rate? Use your findings in **a** to explain.

   6-14   Future value of an annuity   For each of the cases shown in the following table, calculate the future value of the annuity at the end of the deposit period, assuming that the annuity cash flows occur at the end of each year.

Case	Amount of annuity	Interest rate	Deposit period
A	$ 2,500	8%	10 years
B	500	12	6
C	30,000	20	5
D	11,500	9	8
E	6,000	14	30

6-15   Future value of annuities   Marian Kirk wishes to select the better of two 10-year annuities—C and D—as described.

>   **Annuity C** $2,500 per year for 10 years, earning an 8 percent annual return.
>   **Annuity D** $2,200 per year for 10 years, earning an 11 percent annual return.

a. Find the future value of both annuities at the end of year 10, assuming no withdrawals are made during the period.
b. Use your findings in **a** to indicate which annuity Marian should select.

6-16   Future value of a retirement annuity   Kip Thomas, a 25-year-old college graduate, wishes to retire at age 65. To supplement other sources of retirement income he can deposit $2,000 each year into a tax-deferred individual retirement arrangement (IRA). The IRA will be invested to earn an annual return of 10 percent, which is assumed attainable over the next 40 years.

a. If Kip makes annual end-of-year $2,000 deposits into the IRA, how much would he have accumulated by the end of his 65th year?
b. If Kip decides to wait until age 35 to begin making annual end-of-year $2,000 deposits into the IRA, how much would he have accumulated by the end of his 65th year?
c. Using your findings in **a** and **b**, discuss the impact of delaying making deposits into the IRA for 10 years (age 25 to age 35) on the amount accumulated by the end of Kip's 65th year.

6-17   Annuities and compounding   Janet Boyle intends to deposit $300 per year in a credit union for the next 10 years, and the credit union pays an annual interest rate of 8 percent.

a. Determine the future value that Janet will have at the end of 10 years given that end-of-period deposits are made and no interest is withdrawn if:
   (1) $300 is deposited annually and the credit union pays interest annually.
   (2) $150 is deposited semiannually and the credit union pays interest semiannually.
   (3) $75 is deposited quarterly and the credit union pays interest quarterly.
b. Use your finding in **a** to discuss the effect of more frequent deposits and compounding of interest on the future value of an annuity.

6-18   Future value of a mixed stream   For each of the mixed streams of cash flows shown in the following table, determine the future value at the end of the final year if deposits are made at the *beginning of each year* into an account paying annual interest of 12 percent, assuming that no withdrawals are made during the period.

	Cash flow stream		
Year	A	B	C
1	$ 900	$30,000	$1,200
2	1,000	25,000	1,200
3	1,200	20,000	1,000
4		10,000	1,900
5		5,000	

6-19 **Future value of lump sum versus a mixed stream**   Gina Vitale has just contracted to sell a small parcel of land that she inherited a few years ago. The buyer is
willing to pay $24,000 at closing of the transaction or will pay the amounts
shown in the following table at the *beginning* of each of the next 5 years.
Because Gina doesn't really need the money today, she plans to let it accumulate
in an account that earns 7 percent annual interest. Given her desire to buy a
house at the end of 5 years after closing on the sale of the lot, she decides to
choose the payment alternative—$24,000 lump sum or mixed stream of pay-
ments in the following table—that provides the highest future value at the end
of 5 years.

Mixed stream	
Beginning of year	Cash flow
1	$ 2,000
2	4,000
3	6,000
4	8,000
5	10,000

a. What is the future value of the lump sum at the end of year 5?
b. What is the future value of the mixed stream at the end of year 5?
c. Based on your findings in **a** and **b,** which alternative should Gina take?
d. If Gina could earn 10 rather than 7 percent on the funds, would your recommendation in **c** change? Explain.

6-20 **Present value calculation**   *Without referring to tables or the preprogrammed
function of your financial calculator,* use the basic formula for present value
along with the given opportunity cost, k, and number of periods, n, to calculate
the present value interest factor in each of the cases shown in the following
table. Compare the calculated value to the table value.

Case	Opportunity cost, k	Number of periods, n
A	2%	4
B	10	2
C	5	3
D	13	2

6-21 Present values For each of the cases shown in the following table, calculate the present value of the cash flow, discounting at the rate given and assuming that the cash flow is received at the end of the period noted.

Case	Single cash flow	Discount rate	End of period
A	$ 7,000	12%	4 years
B	28,000	8	20
C	10,000	14	12
D	150,000	11	6
E	45,000	20	8

6-22 Present value concept Answer each of the following questions.
a. What single investment, made today, earning 12 percent annual interest, will be worth $6,000 at the end of 6 years?
b. What is the present value of $6,000 to be received at the end of 6 years if the discount rate is 12 percent?
c. What is the most you would pay today for a promise to repay you $6,000 at the end of 6 years if your opportunity cost is 12 percent?
d. Compare, contrast, and discuss your findings in **a** through **c**.

6-23 Present value Terry Murphy has been offered a future payment of $500 three years from today. If his opportunity cost is 7 percent compounded annually, what value should he place on this opportunity today? What is the most he should pay to purchase this payment today?

6-24 Present value An Ohio state savings bond can be converted to $100 at maturity 6 years from purchase. If the state bonds are to be competitive with U.S. Savings Bonds, which pay 8 percent annual interest (compounded annually), at what price must the state sell its bonds? Assume no cash payments on savings bonds prior to redemption.

6-25 Present value and discount rates You just won a lottery that promises to pay you $1,000,000 exactly 10 years from today. Because the $1,000,000 payment is guaranteed by the state in which you live, opportunities exist to sell the claim today for an immediate lump-sum cash payment.
a. What is the least you will sell your claim for if you could earn the following rates of return on similar-risk investments during the 10-year period?
(1) 6 percent

(2) 9 percent
(3) 12 percent
b. Rework **a** under the assumption that the $1,000,000 payment will be received in 15 rather than 10 years.
c. Based on your findings in **a** and **b**, discuss the effect of both the size of the rate of return and the time until receipt of payment on the present value of a future sum.

INTERMEDIATE

6-26 Present value comparisons of lump sums In exchange for a $20,000 payment today, a well-known company will allow you to choose *one* of the alternatives shown in the following table. Your opportunity cost is 11 percent.

Alternative	Lump-sum amount
A	$28,500 at end of 3 years
B	$54,000 at end of 9 years
C	$160,000 at end of 20 years

a. Find the value today of each alternative.
b. Are all the alternatives acceptable, i.e., worth $20,000 today?
c. Which alternative, if any, would you take?

INTERMEDIATE

6-27 Cash flow investment decision Jerry Carney has an opportunity to purchase any of the investments shown in the following table. The purchase price, the amount of the single cash inflow, and its year of receipt are given for each investment. Which purchase recommendations would you make, assuming that Jerry can earn 10 percent on his investments?

Investment	Price	Single cash inflow	Year of receipt
A	$18,000	$30,000	5
B	600	3,000	20
C	3,500	10,000	10
D	1,000	15,000	40

INTERMEDIATE

6-28 Relationship between future value and present value Using *only* the information in the following table:

Year (t)	Cash flow	Future value interest factor at 5 percent ($FVIF_{5\%,t}$)
1	$ 800	1.050
2	900	1.102
3	1,000	1.158
4	1,500	1.216
5	2,000	1.276

a. Determine the *present value* of the mixed stream of cash flows using a 5 percent discount rate.
b. How much would you be willing to pay for an opportunity to buy this stream, assuming that you can at best earn 5 percent on your investments?
c. What effect, if any, would a 7 percent rather than a 5 percent opportunity cost have on your analysis? (Explain verbally.)

6-29 Present value—Mixed streams   Find the present value of the streams of cash flows shown in the following table. Assume that the firm's opportunity cost is 12 percent.

A		B		C	
Year	Cash flow	Year	Cash flow	Year	Cash flow
1	−$2,000	1	$10,000	1–5	$10,000/yr.
2	3,000	2–5	5,000/yr.	6–10	8,000/yr.
3	4,000	6	7,000		
4	6,000				
5	8,000				

6-30 Present value—Mixed streams   Given the mixed streams of cash flows shown in the following table:

	Cash flow stream	
Year	A	B
1	$ 50,000	$ 10,000
2	40,000	20,000
3	30,000	30,000
4	20,000	40,000
5	10,000	50,000
Totals	$150,000	$150,000

a. Find the present value of each stream using a 15 percent discount rate.
b. Compare the calculated present values and discuss them in light of the fact that the undiscounted cash flows total $150,000 in each case.

6-31 Funding budget shortfalls   As part of your personal budgeting process, you have determined that in each of the next 5 years you will have budget shortfalls. In other words, you will need the amounts shown in the following table at the end of the given year to balance your budget, i.e., inflows = outflows. You expect to be able to earn 8 percent on your investments during the next 5 years and wish to fund the budget shortfalls over the next 5 years with a single lump sum.

End of year	Budget shortfall
1	$ 5,000
2	4,000
3	6,000
4	10,000
5	3,000

    a. How large must the lump-sum deposit today into an account paying 8 percent annual interest be to provide for full coverage of the anticipated budget shortfalls?

    b. What effect would an increase in your earnings rate have on the amount calculated in **a**? Explain.

6-32   Present value of an annuity   For each of the cases shown in the table below, calculate the present value of the annuity, assuming that the annuity cash flows occur at the end of each year.

Case	Amount of annuity	Interest rate	Period
A	$ 12,000	7%	3 years
B	55,000	12	15
C	700	20	9
D	140,000	5	7
E	22,500	10	5

6-33   Present value of a retirement annuity   An insurance agent is trying to sell you an immediate retirement annuity, which for a lump-sum fee paid today will provide you with $12,000 per year for the next 25 years. You currently earn 9 percent on low-risk investments comparable to the retirement annuity. Ignoring taxes, what is the most you would pay for this annuity?

6-34   Funding your retirement   You plan to retire in exactly 20 years. Your goal is to create a fund that will allow you to receive $20,000 per year for the 30 years between retirement and death (a psychic told you would die after 30 years). You know that you will be able to earn 11 percent per year during the 30-year retirement period.

    a. How large a fund will you need *when you retire* in 20 years to provide the 30-year, $20,000 retirement annuity?

    b. How much would you need *today* as a lump sum to provide the amount calculated in **a** if you earn only 9 percent per year during the 20 years preceding retirement?

    c. What effect would an increase in the rate you can earn both during and prior to retirement have on the values found in **a** and **b**? Explain.

6-35 **Present value of an annuity versus a lump sum** Assume that you just won the state lottery. Your prize can be taken either in the form of $40,000 at the end of each of the next 25 years (i.e., $1,000,000 over 25 years) or as a lump sum of $500,000 paid immediately.

    a. If you expect to be able to earn 5 percent annually on your investments over the next 25 years, ignoring taxes and other considerations, which alternative should you take? Why?

    b. Would your decision in **a** be altered if you could earn 7 rather than 5 percent on your investments over the next 25 years? Why?

    c. On a strict economic basis, at approximately what earnings rate would you be indifferent in choosing between the two plans?

6-36 **Perpetuities** Given the data in the following table, determine for each of the perpetuities:

Perpetuity	Annual amount	Discount rate
A	$ 20,000	8%
B	100,000	10
C	3,000	6
D	60,000	5

    a. The appropriate present value interest factor.

    b. The present value.

6-37 **Creating an endowment** Upon completion of her introductory finance course, Marla Lee was so pleased with the amount of useful and interesting knowledge she gained that she convinced her parents, who were wealthy alums of the university she was attending, to create an endowment. The endowment would allow three needy students to take the introductory finance course each year into perpetuity. The guaranteed annual cost of tuition and books for the course was $600 per student. The endowment would be created by making a lump-sum payment to the university. The university expected to earn exactly 6 percent per year on these funds.

    a. How large an initial lump-sum payment must Marla's parents make to the university to fund the endowment?

    b. What amount would be needed to fund the endowment if the university could earn 9 percent rather than 6 percent per year on the funds?

6-38 **Deposits to accumulate future sums** For each of the cases shown in the following table, determine the amount of the equal annual end-of-year deposit required to accumulate the given sum at the end of the specified period, assuming the stated annual interest rate.

Case	Sum to be accumulated	Accumulation period	Interest rate
A	$ 5,000	3 years	12%
B	100,000	20	7
C	30,000	8	10
D	15,000	12	8

6-39 **Creating a retirement fund**   To supplement your planned retirement in exactly 42 years, you estimate that you need to accumulate $220,000 by the end of 42 years from today. You plan to make equal annual end-of-year deposits into an account paying 8 percent annual interest.
INTERMEDIATE
   a. How large must the annual deposits be to create the $220,000 fund by the end of 42 years?
   b. If you can afford to deposit only $600 per year into the account, how much will you have accumulated by the end of the 42nd year?

6-40 **Accumulating a growing future sum**   A retirement home at Deer Trail Estates now costs $85,000. Inflation is expected to cause this price to increase at 6 percent per year over the 20 years before J. R. Rogers retires. How large an equal annual end-of-year deposit must be made each year into an account paying an annual interest rate of 10 percent for Rogers to have the cash to purchase a home at retirement?
INTERMEDIATE

6-41 **Deposits to create a perpetuity**   You have decided to endow your favorite university with a scholarship. It is expected to cost $6,000 per year to attend the university into perpetuity. You expect to give the university the endowment in 10 years and will accumulate it by making annual (end-of-year) deposits into an account. The rate of interest is expected to be 10 percent for all future time periods.
INTERMEDIATE
   a. How large must the endowment be?
   b. How much must you deposit at the end of each of the next 10 years to accumulate the required amount?

6-42 **Loan amortization**   Determine the equal annual end-of-year payment required each year over the life of the loans shown in the following table to repay them fully during the stated term of the loan.

WARM-UP

Loan	Principal	Interest rate	Term of loan
A	$12,000	8%	3 years
B	60,000	12	10
C	75,000	10	30
D	4,000	15	5

6-43 **Loan amortization schedule**   Val Hawkins borrowed $15,000 at a 14 percent annual rate of interest to be repaid over 3 years. The loan is amortized into three equal annual end-of-year payments.
INTERMEDIATE

a. Calculate the annual end-of-year loan payment.
b. Prepare a loan amortization schedule showing the interest and principal breakdown of each of the three loan payments.
c. Explain why the interest portion of each payment declines with the passage of time.

CHALLENGE

6-44   Loan interest deductions   Liz Rogers just closed a $10,000 business loan that is to be repaid in three equal annual end-of-year payments. The interest rate on the loan is 13 percent. As part of her firm's detailed financial planning, Liz wishes to determine the annual interest deduction attributable to the loan. (Because it is a business loan, the interest portion of each loan payment is tax-deductible to the business.)
a. Determine the firm's annual loan payment.
b. Prepare an amortization schedule for the loan.
c. How much interest expense will Liz's firm have in *each* of the next three years as a result of this loan?

6-45   Growth rates   You are given the series of cash flows shown in the following table:

WARM-UP

	Cash flows		
Year	A	B	C
1	$500	$1,500	$2,500
2	560	1,550	2,600
3	640	1,610	2,650
4	720	1,680	2,650
5	800	1,760	2,800
6		1,850	2,850
7		1,950	2,900
8		2,060	
9		2,170	
10		2,280	

a. Calculate the compound annual growth rate associated with each cash flow stream.
b. If year 1 values represent initial deposits in a savings account paying annual interest, what is the annual rate of interest earned on each account?
c. Compare and discuss the growth rate and interest rate found in **a** and **b**, respectively.

INTERMEDIATE

6-46   Rate of return   Carlos Cordero has $1,500 to invest. His investment counselor suggests an investment that pays no stated interest but will return $2,000 at the end of 3 years.
a. What annual rate of return will Mr. Cordero earn with this investment?
b. Mr. Cordero is considering another investment, of equal risk, which earns an annual return of 8 percent. Which investment should he take, and why?

6-47   Rate of return and investment choice   Clare Jaccard has $5,000 to invest. Because she is only 25 years old, she is not concerned about the length of the investment's life. What she is sensitive to is the rate of return she will earn on the investment. With the help of her financial adviser Clare has isolated the four equally risky investments, each providing a lump-sum return, shown in the following table. All of the investments require an initial $5,000 payment.

Investment	Lump-sum return	Investment life
A	$ 8,400	6 years
B	15,900	15
C	7,600	4
D	13,000	10

a. Calculate to the nearest 1 percent the rate of return on each of the four investments available to Clare.
b. Which investment would you recommend to Clare given her goal of maximizing the rate of return?

6-48   Rate of return—Annuity   What is the rate of return on an investment of $10,606 if the company expects to receive $2,000 each year for the next 10 years?

6-49   Choosing the best annuity   Raina Herzig wishes to choose the best of four immediate retirement annuities available to her. In each case, in exchange for paying a single premium today, she will receive equal annual end-of-year cash benefits for a specified number of years. She considers the annuities to be equally risky and is not concerned about their differing lives. Her decision will be based solely on the rate of return she will earn on each annuity. The key terms of each of the four annuities are shown in the following table.

Annuity	Premium paid today	Annual benefit	Life
A	$30,000	$3,100	20 years
B	25,000	3,900	10
C	40,000	4,200	15
D	35,000	4,000	12

a. Calculate to the nearest 1 percent the rate of return on each of the four annuities being considered by Raina.
b. Given Raina's stated decision criterion, which annuity would you recommend?

6-50   Loan rates of interest   David Pearson has been shopping for a loan to finance the purchase of a used car. He has found three possibilities that seem attractive and wishes to select the one having the lowest interest rate. The information available with respect to each of the three $5,000 loans is shown in the following table:

Loan	Principal	Annual payment	Term
A	$5,000	$1,352.81	5 years
B	5,000	1,543.21	4
C	5,000	2,010.45	3

a. Determine the interest rate associated with each of the loans.
b. Which loan should David take?

CASE   Chapter 6   Funding Jill Moran's Retirement Annuity

Sunrise Industries wishes to accumulate funds to provide a retirement annuity for its vice president of research, Jill Moran. Ms. Moran by contract will retire at the end of exactly 12 years. Upon retirement, she is entitled to receive an annual end-of-year payment of $42,000 for exactly 20 years. If she dies prior to the end of the 20-year period, the annual payments will pass to her heirs. During the 12-year "accumulation period" Sunrise wishes to fund the annuity by making equal annual end-of-year deposits into an account earning 9 percent interest. Once the 20-year "distribution period" begins, Sunrise plans to move the accumulated monies into an account earning a guaranteed 12 percent per year. At the end of the distribution period, the account balance will equal zero. Note that the first deposit will be made at the end of year 1 and the first distribution payment will be received at the end of year 13.

Required

a. Draw a time line depicting all of the cash flows associated with Sunrise's view of the retirement annuity.

b. How large a sum must Sunrise accumulate by the end of year 12 to provide the 20-year, $42,000 annuity?

c. How large must Sunrise's equal annual end-of-year deposits into the account be over the 12-year accumulation period to fund fully Ms. Moran's retirement annuity?

d. How much would Sunrise have to deposit annually during the accumulation period if it could earn 10 percent rather than 9 percent during the accumulation period?

e. How much would Sunrise have to deposit annually during the accumulation period if Ms. Moran's retirement annuity was a perpetuity and all other terms were the same as initially described?

Web Exercise

GOTO web site www.arachnoid.com/lutusp/finance_old.html. Page down to the portion of this screen that contains the financial calculator.

1. To determine the FV of a fixed amount enter the following:
    Into PV, enter −1000; into np, enter 1; into pmt, enter 0; and, into ir, enter 8. Now click on Calculate FV, and 1080.00 should appear in the FV window.
2. Determine FV for each of the following compounding periods by changing *only* the following:
    a. np to 2, and ir to 8/2
    b. np to 12, and ir to 8/12
    c. np to 52, and ir to 8/52
3. To determine the PV of a fixed amount enter the following:
    Into FV, 1080; into np, 1; into pmt, 0; and, into ir, 8.
    Now click on Calculate PV. What is the PV?
4. To determine the FV of an annuity enter the following:
    Into PV, 0; into FV, 0; into np, 12; into pmt, 1000; and, into ir, 8.
    Now click on Calculate FV. What is the FV?
5. To determine the PV of an annuity, change only the FV setting to 0; keep the other entries the same as in question 4.
    Click on Calculate PV. What is the PV?
6. Check your answers for questions 4 and 5 by using the techniques discussed in this chapter.

GOTO web site www.homeowners.com/. Click Calculators in the left column. Click Mortgage Calculator.

7. Enter the following into the mortgage calculator: Loan amount, 100000; duration in years, 30; and interest rate, 10.
    Click on compute payment. What is the monthly payment?
8. Calculate the monthly payment for $100,000 loans for 30 years at 8%, 6%, 4%, and 2%.
9. Calculate the monthly payment for $100,000 loans at 8% for 30 years, 20 years, 10 years, and 5 years.

7 RISK AND RETURN

ACROSS *the* DISCIPLINES

The concept that return should increase if risk increases is fundamental to modern management and finance. This relationship is regularly observed in the financial markets, and important clarification of it has led to Nobel prizes. In this chapter we discuss these two key factors in finance—risk and return—and introduce some quantitative tools and techniques used to measure risk and return for individual assets and for groups of assets. Chapter 7 is important to:

- **accounting personnel** who will decide if it is best to employ accounting practices that stabilize the firm's annual net income.
- **information systems analysts** who will build decision packages that help management do sensitivity and correlation analyses.
- **management** because it adds and cancels product groups so that the firm's portfolio of products will have an acceptable level of risk.
- **the marketing department** because an aggressive marketing strategy might not be the best choice if it produces an erratic earnings pattern.
- **operations,** which can enter into long-term contracts with suppliers so as to reduce the fluctuations in raw material prices.

RISK AND RETURN FUNDAMENTALS

LG1

To maximize share price, the financial manager must learn to assess the two key determinants of share price: risk and return. Each financial decision presents certain risk and return characteristics, and the unique combination of these characteristics has an impact on share price. Risk can be viewed as it relates either to a single asset or to a **portfolio**—a collection, or group, of assets. We will look at both, beginning with the general concept of risk in terms of a single asset. First, though, it is important to understand the fundamentals of risk, return, and risk aversion.

portfolio
A collection, or group, of assets.

RISK DEFINED

risk
The chance of financial loss or, more formally, the variability of returns associated with a given asset.

In the most basic sense, **risk** is the chance of financial loss. Assets having greater chances of loss are viewed as more risky than those with lesser chances of loss. More formally, the term *risk* is used interchangeably with *uncertainty* to refer to the *variability of returns associated with a given asset*. A government bond that guarantees its holder $100 interest after 30 days has no risk, because there is no variability associated with the return. An equivalent $100 investment in a firm's common stock, which over the same period may earn anywhere from $0 to $200, is very risky due to the high variability of its return. The more certain the return from an asset, the less variability and therefore the less risk.

RETURN DEFINED

return
The total gain or loss experienced on an investment over a given period of time; calculated by dividing the asset's change in value plus any cash distributions during the period by its beginning-of-period investment value.

Obviously, if we are going to assess risk based on variability of return, we need to be certain we know what *return* is, and how to measure it. **Return** is the total gain or loss experienced on an investment over a given period of time. It is commonly measured as the change in value plus any cash distributions during the period, expressed as a percentage of the beginning-of-period investment value. The expression for calculating the rate of return earned on any asset over period t, k_t, is commonly defined as:

$$k_t = \frac{P_t - P_{t-1} + C_t}{P_{t-1}} \tag{7.1}$$

where

k_t = actual, expected, or required rate of return during period t
P_t = price (value) of asset at time t
P_{t-1} = price (value) of asset at time $t - 1$
C_t = cash (flow) received from the asset investment in the time period $t - 1$ to t

The return, k_t, reflects the combined effect of changes in value, $P_t - P_{t-1}$, and cash flow, C_t, realized over period t. Equation 7.1 is used to determine the rate of return over a time period as short as 1 day or as long as 10 years or more. However, in most cases, t is equal to 1 year, and k therefore represents an annual rate of return.

Example ▼ Roberta's Gameroom, a video arcade, wishes to determine the return on two of its video machines, Conqueror and Demolition. Conqueror was purchased exactly 1 year ago for $20,000 and currently has a market value of $21,500. During the year, it generated $800 of after-tax cash receipts. Demolition was purchased 4 years ago; its value in the year just completed declined from $12,000 to $11,800. During the year, it generated $1,700 of after-tax cash receipts. Substituting into Equation 7.1, we can calculate the annual rate of return, k, for each video machine:

Conqueror (C):

$$k_C = \frac{\$21,500 - \$20,000 + \$800}{\$20,000} = \frac{\$2,300}{\$20,000} = \underline{\underline{11.5\%}}$$

Demolition (D):

$$k_D = \frac{\$11,800 - \$12,000 + \$1,700}{\$12,000} = \frac{\$1,500}{\$12,000} = \underline{\underline{12.5\%}}$$

Although the market value of Demolition declined during the year, its cash flow caused it to earn a higher rate of return than that earned by Conqueror during the same period. Clearly, the combined impact of changes in value and cash flow measured by the rate of return is important. ▲

RISK AVERSION

risk-averse
The attitude toward risk in which an increased return is required for an increase in risk.

Financial managers generally seek to avoid risk. Most managers are **risk-averse—** for a given increase in risk they require an increase in return. This attitude is believed consistent with that of the owners for whom the firm is being managed. Managers generally tend to be conservative rather than aggressive when accepting risk. Accordingly, *a risk-averse financial manager requiring higher returns for greater risk is assumed throughout this text.*

Review Questions

7-1 Define *risk* as it relates to financial decision making. Do any assets have perfectly certain returns?
7-2 Define *return*. Describe the basic calculation involved in finding the return on an investment.
7-3 Describe the attitude toward risk of a *risk-averse* financial manager. Do many managers exhibit this behavior?

RISK OF A SINGLE ASSET

The risk of a single asset is measured in much the same way as the risk of an entire portfolio of assets, although certain benefits accrue to holders of portfolios. For both single assets and for portfolios, we can assess risk by looking at expected return behaviors, and we can measure the risk using statistics.

RISK ASSESSMENT

Risk can be assessed using sensitivity analysis and probability distributions to look at the behavior of returns. These approaches provide a feel for the level of risk embodied in a given asset.

SENSITIVITY ANALYSIS

sensitivity analysis
An approach for assessing risk that uses a number of possible return estimates to obtain a sense of the variability among outcomes.

range
A measure of an asset's risk, which is found by subtracting the pessimistic (worst) outcome from the optimistic (best) outcome.

Sensitivity analysis uses a number of possible return estimates to obtain a sense of the variability among outcomes. One common method involves estimating the pessimistic (worst), the most likely (expected), and the optimistic (best) returns associated with a given asset. In this case, the asset's risk can be measured by the **range**, which is found by subtracting the pessimistic outcome from the optimistic outcome. The greater the range for a given asset, the more variability, or risk, it is said to have.

Example ▼ Alfred Company, a custom golf equipment manufacturer, wants to choose the better of two alternative investments, A and B. Each requires an initial outlay of $10,000 and each has a *most likely* annual rate of return of 15 percent. To evaluate the riskiness of these assets, management has made *pessimistic* and *optimistic* estimates of the returns associated with each. The three estimates for each asset, along with its range, are given in Table 7.1. Asset A appears to be less risky than asset B, because its range of 4 percent (17% − 13%) is less than the range of 16 percent (23% − 7%) for asset B. The risk-averse decision maker would prefer asset A over asset B, because A offers the same most likely return as B ▲ (15%) but with lower risk (smaller range).

Although the use of sensitivity analysis and the range is rather crude, it does provide the decision maker with a feel for the behavior of returns. This insight can be used as a rough assessment of the risk involved.

PROBABILITY DISTRIBUTIONS

probability
The *chance* that a given outcome will occur.

Probability distributions provide a more quantitative insight into an asset's risk. The **probability** of a given outcome is its *chance* of occurring. If an outcome has an 80 percent probability of occurrence, the given outcome would be expected to occur 8 out of 10 times. If an outcome has a probability of 100 percent, it is certain to occur. Outcomes having a probability of zero will never occur.

TABLE 7.1	Assets A and B	
	Asset A	Asset B
Initial investment	$10,000	$10,000
Annual rate of return		
Pessimistic	13%	7%
Most likely	15%	15%
Optimistic	17%	23%
Range	4%	16%

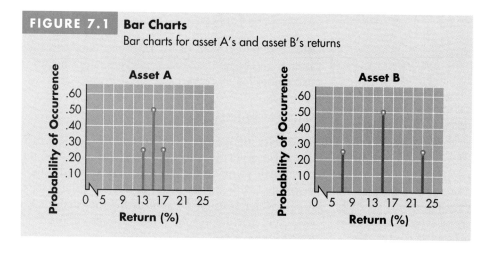

FIGURE 7.1   **Bar Charts**
Bar charts for asset A's and asset B's returns

E x a m p l e ▼   Alfred Company's past estimates indicate that the probabilities of the pessimistic, most likely, and optimistic outcomes occurring are 25, 50, and 25 percent, respectively. The sum of these probabilities must equal 100 percent; that is, they must be based on all the alternatives considered.

probability distribution
A model that relates probabilities to the associated outcomes.

bar chart
The simplest type of probability distribution; shows only a limited number of outcomes and associated probabilities for a given event.

continuous probability distribution
A probability distribution showing all the possible outcomes and associated probabilities for a given event.

A **probability distribution** is a model that relates probabilities to the associated outcomes. The simplest type of probability distribution is the **bar chart,** which shows only a limited number of outcome-probability coordinates. The bar charts for Alfred Company's assets A and B are shown in Figure 7.1. Although both assets have the same most likely return, the range of return is much more dispersed for asset B than for asset A—16 percent versus 4 percent.

If we knew all the possible outcomes and associated probabilities, we could develop a **continuous probability distribution.** This type of distribution can be thought of as a bar chart for a very large number of outcomes. Figure 7.2 presents continuous probability distributions for assets A and B. Note in Figure 7.2 that although assets A and B have the same most likely return (15 percent), the distribution of returns for asset B has much greater *dispersion* than the distribution for asset A. Clearly, asset B is more risky than asset A.

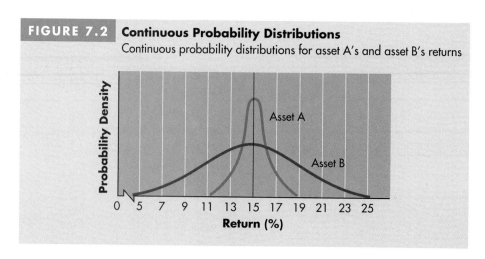

FIGURE 7.2   **Continuous Probability Distributions**
Continuous probability distributions for asset A's and asset B's returns

RISK MEASUREMENT

In addition to its *range*, the risk of an asset can be measured quantitatively using statistics. Here we consider two statistics—the standard deviation and the coefficient of variation—that can be used to measure the risk (i.e., variability) of asset returns.

STANDARD DEVIATION

standard deviation (σ_k)
The most common statistical indicator of an asset's risk; it measures the dispersion around the *expected value*.

expected value of a return ($\bar{k}$)
The most likely return on a given asset.

The most common statistical indicator of an asset's risk is the **standard deviation**, **σ_k**, which measures the dispersion around the *expected* value. The **expected value of a return**, **$\bar{k}$**, is the most likely return on an asset. This value can be calculated by using Equation 7.2:[1]

$$\bar{k} = \sum_{i=1}^{n} k_i \times Pr_i \tag{7.2}$$

where

k_i = return for the *i*th outcome
Pr_i = probability of occurrence of the *i*th outcome
n = number of outcomes considered

Example ▼

The expected values for Alfred Company's assets A and B are presented in Table 7.2. Column 1 gives the Pr_i's and column 2 gives the k_i's. In each case n equals 3. The expected value for each asset's return is 15 percent.

The expression for the *standard deviation of returns*, σ_k, is given in Equation 7.3:[2]

$$\sigma_k = \sqrt{\sum_{i=1}^{n} (k_i - \bar{k})^2 \times Pr_i} \tag{7.3}$$

In general, the higher the standard deviation, the greater the risk.

---

[1] The formula for finding the expected value of return, $\bar{k}$, when all of the outcomes, k_i, are known and their related probabilities are assumed to be equal, is a simple arithmetic average:

$$k = \frac{\sum_{i=1}^{n} k_i}{n} \tag{7.2a}$$

where n is the number of observations. Equation 7.2 is emphasized in this chapter because returns and related probabilities are often available.

[2] The formula that is commonly used to find the standard deviation of returns, σ_k, in a situation in which *all* outcomes are known *and* their related probabilities are assumed equal, is

$$\sigma_k = \sqrt{\frac{\sum_{i=1}^{n} (k_i - k)^2}{n-1}} \tag{7.3a}$$

where n is the number of observations. Equation 7.3 is emphasized in this chapter because returns and related probabilities are often available.

Possible outcomes	Probability (1)	Returns (2)	Weighted value [(1) × (2)] (3)
TABLE 7.2 Expected Values of Returns for Assets A and B			
Asset A			
Pessimistic	.25	13%	3.25%
Most likely	.50	15	7.50
Optimistic	.25	17	4.25
Total	1.00	Expected return	15.00%
Asset B			
Pessimistic	.25	7%	1.75%
Most likely	.50	15	7.50
Optimistic	.25	23	5.75
Total	1.00	Expected return	15.00%

Example ▼ Table 7.3 on the following page presents the standard deviations for Alfred Company's assets A and B, based on the data presented earlier. The standard deviation for asset A is 1.41 percent, and the standard deviation for asset B is 5.66 percent. The higher risk of asset B is clearly reflected in its higher standard **▲** deviation.

COEFFICIENT OF VARIATION

coefficient of variation (CV)
A measure of relative dispersion that is useful in comparing the risk of assets with differing expected returns.

The **coefficient of variation, CV,** is a measure of relative dispersion that is useful in comparing the risk of assets with differing expected returns. Equation 7.4 gives the expression for the coefficient of variation:

$$CV = \frac{\sigma_k}{\bar{k}} \qquad (7.4)$$

The higher the coefficient of variation, the greater the risk.

Example ▼ When the standard deviation (in Table 7.3) and the expected returns (in Table 7.2) for assets A and B are substituted into Equation 7.4, the coefficients of variation for A and B are .094 (1.41% ÷ 15%) and .377 (5.66% ÷ 15%), respectively. Asset B has the higher coefficient of variation and is therefore more risky than asset A—which we already knew from the standard deviation. Because both assets have the same expected return, the coefficient of variation has not provid- **▲** ed any new information.

The real utility of the coefficient of variation comes in comparing the risk of assets that have *different* expected returns. A simple example will illustrate this point.

TABLE 7.3	The Calculation of the Standard Deviation of the Returns for Assets A and B

Asset A

i	k_i	$\bar{k}$	$k_i - \bar{k}$	$(k_i - \bar{k})^2$	Pr_i	$(k_i - \bar{k})^2 \times Pr_i$
1	13%	15%	−2%	4%	.25	1%
2	15	15	0	0	.50	0
3	17	15	2	4	.25	1

$$\sum_{i=1}^{3}(k_i - \bar{k})^2 \times Pr_i = 2\%$$

$$\sigma_{k_A} = \sqrt{\sum_{i=1}^{3}(k_i - \bar{k})^2 \times Pr_i} = \sqrt{2}\% = \underline{1.41\%}$$

Asset B

i	k_i	$\bar{k}$	$k_i - \bar{k}$	$(k_i - \bar{k})^2$	Pr_i	$(k_i - \bar{k})^2 \times Pr_i$
1	7%	15%	−8%	64%	.25	16%
2	15	15	0	0	.50	0
3	23	15	8	64	.25	16

$$\sum_{i=1}^{3}(k_i - \bar{k})^2 \times Pr_i = 32\%$$

$$\sigma_{k_B} = \sqrt{\sum_{i=1}^{3}(k_i - \bar{k})^2 \times Pr_i} = \sqrt{32}\% = \underline{5.66\%}$$

Example ▼ A firm wants to select the less risky of two alternative assets—X and Y. The expected return, standard deviation, and coefficient of variation for each of these assets' returns are:

Statistics	Asset X	Asset Y
(1) Expected return	12%	20%
(2) Standard deviation	9%[a]	10%
(3) Coefficient of variation [(2) ÷ (1)]	.75	.50[a]

[a]Preferred asset using the given risk measure.

Based solely on their standard deviations, the firm would prefer asset X, which has a lower standard deviation than asset Y (9 percent versus 10 percent). However, management would be making a serious error in choosing asset X over asset Y, because the relative dispersion—the risk—of the assets as reflected in the coefficient of variation is lower for Y than for X (.50 versus .75). Clearly, the use of the coefficient of variation to compare asset risk is effective because it also considers the relative size, or expected return, of the assets.

? Review Questions

7-4 How can *sensitivity analysis* be used to assess asset risk? Define and describe the role of the *range* in sensitivity analysis.

7-5 What does a plot of the *probability distribution* of outcomes show a decision maker about an asset's risk? What is the difference between a *bar chart* and a *continuous probability distribution*?

7-6 What does the *standard deviation* of asset returns indicate? What relationship exists between the size of the standard deviation and the degree of asset risk?

7-7 What is the *coefficient of variation*? How is it calculated? When is it preferred over the standard deviation for comparing asset risk?

LG4 RISK OF A PORTFOLIO

efficient portfolio
A portfolio that maximizes return for a given level of risk or minimizes risk for a given level of return.

correlation
A statistical measure of the relationship, if any, between series of numbers representing data of any kind.

positively correlated
Descriptive of two series that move in the same direction.

negatively correlated
Descriptive of two series that move in opposite directions.

correlation coefficient
A measure of the degree of correlation between two series.

perfectly positively correlated
Describes two *positively correlated* series that have a *correlation coefficient* of +1.

perfectly negatively correlated
Describes two *negatively correlated* series that have a *correlation coefficient* of −1.

The risk of any single proposed asset investment should not be viewed independent of other assets. New investments must be considered in light of their impact on the risk and return of the *portfolio* of assets. The financial manager's goal is to create an **efficient portfolio**, one that maximizes return for a given level of risk or minimizes risk for a given level of return. The statistical concept of *correlation* underlies the process of diversification that is used to develop an efficient portfolio.

CORRELATION

Correlation is a statistical measure of the relationship, if any, between series of numbers representing data of any kind, from returns to test scores. If two series move in the same direction, they are **positively correlated**. If the series move in opposite directions, they are **negatively correlated**.

The degree of correlation is measured by the **correlation coefficient**, which ranges from +1 for **perfectly positively correlated** series to −1 for **perfectly negatively correlated** series. These two extremes are depicted for series M and N in Figure 7.3. The perfectly positively correlated series move exactly together; the perfectly negatively correlated series move in exactly opposite directions.

DIVERSIFICATION

The concept of correlation is essential to developing an efficient portfolio. To reduce overall risk, it is best to combine or add to the portfolio assets that have a negative (or a low positive) correlation. Combining negatively correlated assets can reduce the overall variability of returns. Figure 7.4 shows that a portfolio containing the negatively correlated assets F and G, both having the same expected return, $\bar{k}$, also has the return $\bar{k}$ but has less risk (variability) than either of the

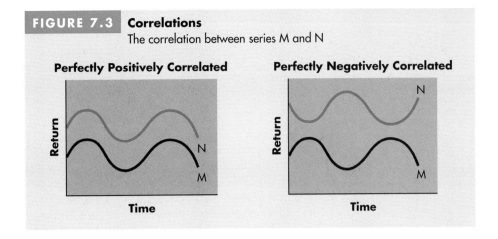

FIGURE 7.3 **Correlations**
The correlation between series M and N

individual assets. Even if assets are not negatively correlated, the lower the positive correlation between them, the lower the resulting risk.

Some assets are **uncorrelated**—that is, there is no interaction between their returns. Combining uncorrelated assets can reduce risk—not as effectively as combining negatively correlated assets, but more effectively than combining positively correlated assets. The correlation coefficient for uncorrelated assets is close to zero and acts as the midpoint between perfect positive and perfect negative correlation.

The creation of a portfolio by combining two assets with perfectly positively correlated returns *cannot* reduce the portfolio's overall risk below the risk of the least risky asset. Alternatively, a portfolio combining two assets with less than perfectly positive correlation *can* reduce total risk to a level below that of either of the components, which in certain situations may be zero. For example, assume that you manufacture machine tools. The business is very *cyclical*, with high sales when the economy is expanding and low sales during a recession. If you acquired another machine-tool company, with sales positively correlated with those of your firm, the combined sales would still be cyclical, and risk would remain the

uncorrelated

Describes two series that lack any interaction between their returns and therefore have a *correlation coefficient* close to zero.

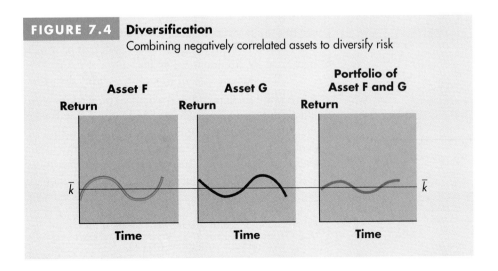

FIGURE 7.4 **Diversification**
Combining negatively correlated assets to diversify risk

same. Alternatively, however, you could acquire a sewing-machine manufacturer, which is *countercyclical.* It typically has low sales during economic expansion and high sales during recession (when consumers are more likely to make their own clothes). Combination with the sewing-machine manufacturer, which has negatively correlated sales, should reduce the firm's risk. A numeric example will provide a better understanding of the role of correlation in the diversification process.

E x a m p l e ▼ Table 7.4 presents the forecasted returns from three different assets—X, Y, and Z—over the next 5 years, along with their expected values and standard deviations. Each of the assets has an expected value of return of 12 percent and a standard deviation of 3.16 percent. The assets therefore have equal return and equal risk, although their return patterns are not necessarily identical. The return patterns of assets X and Y are perfectly negatively correlated, moving in exactly opposite directions over time. Assets X and Z are perfectly positively correlated, moving in precisely the same direction. (*Note:* The returns for X and Z are identical.)[3]

Portfolio XY   Portfolio XY (shown in Table 7.4) is created by combining equal portions of assets X and Y—the perfectly negatively correlated assets. The risk in this portfolio, as reflected by its standard deviation, is reduced to 0 percent, and the expected return value remains at 12 percent. Because both assets have the same expected return values, are combined in equal parts, and are perfectly negatively correlated, the combination results in the complete elimination of risk. Whenever assets are perfectly negatively correlated, an optimum combination (similar to the 50–50 mix in the case of assets X and Y) exists for which the resulting standard deviation will equal 0.

Portfolio XZ   Portfolio XZ (shown in Table 7.4) is created by combining equal portions of assets X and Z—the perfectly positively correlated assets. The risk in this portfolio, as reflected by its standard deviation, is unaffected by this combination: Risk remains at 3.16 percent, and the expected return value remains at 12 percent. Whenever perfectly positively correlated assets such as X and Z are combined, the standard deviation of the resulting portfolio cannot be reduced *below that of the least risky asset;* the maximum portfolio standard deviation will be that of the riskiest asset. Because assets X and Z have the same standard deviation (3.16 percent), the minimum and maximum standard deviations are the same (3.16 percent), which is the only value that could be taken on by a combination of these assets. This result can be attributed to the unlikely situation
▲ that X and Z are identical assets.

Although detailed statistical explanations can be given for the behaviors illustrated in Table 7.4, the important point is that assets can be combined so that the resulting portfolio has less risk than that of either of the assets independently—and this can be achieved without any loss of return. Portfolio XY illustrates such behavior. The more negative (or less positive) the correlation between asset returns, the greater the risk-reducing benefits of diversification. In no case

---

[3]Identical return streams are used in this example to permit clear illustration of the concepts, but it is *not* necessary for return streams to be identical for them to be perfectly positively correlated. Any return streams that move (i.e., vary) exactly together—regardless of the relative magnitude of the returns—are perfectly positively correlated.

TABLE 7.4 Forecasted Returns, Expected Values, and Standard Deviations for Assets X, Y, and Z and Portfolios XY and XZ

| | Assets | | | Portfolios | |
| | | | | XY[a] (50%X + 50%Y) | XZ[b] (50%X + 50%Z) |
Year	X	Y	Z		
2001	8%	16%	8%	12%	8%
2002	10	14	10	12	10
2003	12	12	12	12	12
2004	14	10	14	12	14
2005	16	8	16	12	16
Statistics:					
Expected value[c]	12%	12%	12%	12%	12%
Standard deviation[d]	3.16%	3.16%	3.16%	0%	3.16%

[a]Portfolio XY, which consists of 50 percent of asset X and 50 percent of asset Y, illustrates *perfect negative correlation* because these two return streams behave in completely opposite fashion over the 5-year period. Its return values are calculated as shown in the following table.

| | Forecasted Return | | | Expected Portfolio |
| | Asset X | Asset Y | Portfolio Return Calculation | Return, k_p |
Year	(1)	(2)	(3)	(4)
2001	8%	16%	$(.50 \times 8\%) + (.50 \times 16\%) =$	12%
2002	10	14	$(.50 \times 10\ ) + (.50 \times 14\ ) =$	12
2003	12	12	$(.50 \times 12\ ) + (.50 \times 12\ ) =$	12
2004	14	10	$(.50 \times 14\ ) + (.50 \times 10\ ) =$	12
2005	16	8	$(.50 \times 16\ ) + (.50 \times 8\ ) =$	12

[b]Portfolio XZ, which consists of 50 percent of asset X and 50 percent of asset Z, illustrates *perfect positive correlation* because these two return streams behave identically over the 5-year period. Its return values are calculated using the same method demonstrated in note *a* above for portfolio XY.

[c]Because the probabilities associated with the returns are not given, the general equation, Equation 7.2a in footnote 1, is used to calculate the expected values as demonstrated below for portfolio XY.

$$k_{xy} = \frac{12\% + 12\% + 12\% + 12\% + 12\%}{5} = \frac{60\%}{5} = \underline{\underline{12\%}}$$

The same formula is applied to find the expected value of return for assets X, Y, and Z, and portfolio XZ.

[d]Because the probabilities associated with the returns are not given, the general equation, Equation 7.3a in footnote 2, is used to calculate the standard deviations as demonstrated below for portfolio XY.

$$\sigma_{k_{xy}} = \sqrt{\frac{(12\% - 12\%)^2 + (12\% - 12\%)^2 + (12\% - 12\%)^2 + (12\% - 12\%)^2 + (12\% - 12\%)^2}{5 - 1}}$$

$$= \sqrt{\frac{0\% + 0\% + 0\% + 0\% + 0\%}{4}} = \sqrt{\frac{0}{4}}\% = \underline{\underline{0\%}}$$

The same formula is applied to find the standard deviation of returns for assets X, Y, and Z, and portfolio XZ.

does creating portfolios of assets result in greater risk than that of the riskiest asset included in the portfolio. It is important to recognize that these relationships apply when considering the addition of an asset to an existing portfolio.

INTERNATIONAL DIVERSIFICATION

The ultimate example of portfolio diversification involves including foreign assets in a portfolio. The inclusion of assets from countries that are less sensitive to the U.S. business cycle (i.e., that are negatively correlated) reduces the portfolio's responsiveness to market movements and to foreign currency fluctuations.

RETURNS FROM INTERNATIONAL DIVERSIFICATION

Over long periods, returns from internationally diversified portfolios tend to be superior to those of purely domestic ones. This is particularly so if the U.S. economy is performing relatively poorly and the dollar is depreciating in value against most foreign currencies. At such times the dollar returns to U.S. investors on a portfolio of foreign assets can be very attractive indeed. However, over any single short or intermediate period, international diversification can yield subpar returns—particularly during periods when the dollar is appreciating in value relative to other currencies. Overall, though, the logic of international portfolio diversification assumes that these fluctuations in currency values and relative performance will average out over long periods and that an internationally diversified portfolio will tend to yield a comparable return at a lower level of risk than will similar purely domestic portfolios.

RISKS OF INTERNATIONAL DIVERSIFICATION

political risk
Risk that arises from the possibility that a host government might take actions harmful to foreign investors or that political turmoil in a country might endanger investments made in that country.

U.S. investors should, however, also be aware of the potential dangers of international investing. In addition to the risk induced by currency fluctuations, several other financial risks are unique to international investing. Most important is **political risk,** which arises from the possibility that a host government might take actions harmful to foreign investors or that political turmoil in a country might endanger investments made in that country. Political risks are particularly acute in developing countries, where unstable or ideologically motivated governments may attempt to block return of profits by foreign investors or even seize (nationalize) their assets in the host country. An example of political risk was the heightened concern after Desert Storm in the early 1990s that Saudi Arabian fundamentalists would take over and nationalize the U.S. oil facilities located there.

Even where governments do not impose exchange controls or seize assets, international investors may suffer if a shortage of hard currency prevents payment of dividends or interest to foreigners. When governments must allocate scarce foreign exchange, they rarely give top priority to the interests of foreign investors. Instead, hard currency reserves are typically used to pay for necessary imports such as food and industrial materials and to pay interest on the government's debts. Because most of the debt of developing countries is held by banks rather than individuals, foreign investors are often badly harmed when a country experiences political or economic problems.

❓ R e v i e w   Q u e s t i o n s

7-8   Why must assets be evaluated in a portfolio context? What is an *efficient portfolio?*

7-9   Why is the *correlation* between asset returns important? How does diversification allow risky assets to be combined so that the risk of the portfolio is less than the risk of the individual assets in it?

7-10   How does international diversification enhance risk reduction? When might international diversification result in subpar returns? What are *political risks,* and how do they affect international diversification?

RISK AND RETURN: THE CAPITAL ASSET PRICING MODEL (CAPM)

capital asset pricing model (CAPM)
The basic theory that links together risk and return for all assets.

The most important aspect of risk is the *overall risk* of the firm as viewed by investors in the marketplace. Overall risk significantly affects investment opportunities—and even more important, the owners' wealth. The basic theory that links together risk and return for all assets is the **capital asset pricing model (CAPM)**.[4] Here we will use CAPM to understand the basic risk-return trade-offs involved in all types of financial decisions.

TYPES OF RISK

To understand the basic types of risk, consider what happens to the risk of a portfolio consisting of a single security (asset), to which we add securities randomly selected from, say, the population of all actively traded securities. Using the standard deviation of return, σ_k, to measure the total portfolio risk, Figure 7.5 depicts the behavior of the total portfolio risk (*y* axis) as more securities are added (*x* axis). With the addition of securities, the total portfolio risk declines, and tends to approach a limit, due to the effects of diversification (as explained in the previous section). Research has shown that, on average, most of the risk-reduction benefits of diversification can be gained by forming portfolios containing 15 to 20 randomly selected securities.[5]

---

[4]The initial development of this theory is generally attributed to William F. Sharpe, "Capital Asset Prices: A Theory of Market Equilibrium Under Conditions of Risk," *Journal of Finance* 19 (September 1964), pp. 425–442, and John Lintner, "The Valuation of Risk Assets and the Selection of Risky Investments in Stock Portfolios and Capital Budgets," *Review of Economics and Statistics* 47 (February 1965), pp. 13–37. A number of authors subsequently advanced, refined, and tested this now widely accepted theory.

[5]See, for example, W. H. Wagner and S. C. Lau, "The Effect of Diversification on Risk," *Financial Analysts Journal* 26 (November–December 1971), pp. 48–53, and Jack Evans and Stephen H. Archer, "Diversification and the Reduction of Dispersion: An Empirical Analysis," *Journal of Finance* 23 (December 1968), pp. 761–767. A more recent study, Gerald D. Newbould and Percy S. Poon, "The Minimum Number of Stocks Needed for Diversification," *Financial Practice and Education* (Fall 1993), pp. 85–87, shows that because an investor holds but one of a large number of possible *x*-security portfolios, it is unlikely that he or she will experience the average outcome. As a consequence, the study suggests that a minimum of 40 stocks is needed to fully diversify a portfolio. This study tends to support the widespread popularity of mutual fund investments.

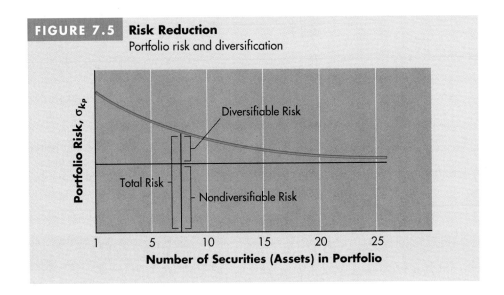

FIGURE 7.5 **Risk Reduction**
Portfolio risk and diversification

Number of Securities (Assets) in Portfolio

---

total risk
The combination of a security's nondiversifiable and diversifiable risk.

diversifiable risk
The portion of an asset's risk that is attributable to firm-specific, random causes; can be eliminated through diversification.

nondiversifiable risk
The relevant portion of an asset's risk attributable to market factors that affect all firms; cannot be eliminated through diversification.

The **total risk** of a security can be viewed as consisting of two parts:

$$\text{Total security risk} = \text{nondiversifiable risk} + \text{diversifiable risk} \qquad (7.5)$$

Diversifiable risk, sometimes called *unsystematic risk,* represents the portion of an asset's risk that is associated with random causes that can be eliminated through diversification. It is attributable to firm-specific events, such as strikes, lawsuits, regulatory actions, and loss of a key account. **Nondiversifiable risk,** also called *systematic risk,* is attributable to market factors that affect all firms, and it cannot be eliminated through diversification. Factors such as war, inflation, international incidents, and political events account for nondiversifiable risk.

Because any investor can create a portfolio of assets that will eliminate virtually all diversifiable risk, *the only relevant risk is nondiversifiable risk.* Any investor or firm therefore must be concerned solely with an asset's nondiversifiable risk. The measurement of nondiversifiable risk is thus of primary importance in selecting assets with the most desired risk-return characteristics.

THE MODEL: CAPM

The capital asset pricing model (CAPM) links together nondiversifiable risk and return for all assets. We will discuss the model in four sections. The first defines, derives, and describes the beta coefficient, which is a measure of nondiversifiable risk. The second section presents an equation of the model itself, and the third graphically describes the relationship between risk and return. The final section offers some general comments on CAPM.

beta coefficient (*b*)
A measure of nondiversifiable risk. An *index* of the degree of movement of an asset's return in response to a change in the *market return.*

market return
The return on the market portfolio of all traded securities.

BETA COEFFICIENT

The **beta coefficient,** *b,* measures nondiversifiable risk. It is an *index* of the degree of movement of an asset's return in response to a change in the *market return.* The beta coefficient for an asset can be found by examining the asset's historical returns relative to the returns for the market. The **market return** is the return on the market portfolio of all traded securities. The *Standard & Poor's 500 Stock Composite Index* or some similar stock index is commonly used as the market return. Although betas for actively traded stocks can be obtained from a variety of sources, you should understand how they are derived and interpreted and how they are applied to portfolios.

Deriving Beta from Return Data   The relationship between an asset's return and the market return and its use in deriving beta can be demonstrated graphically. Figure 7.6 plots the relationship between the returns of two assets— R and S—and the market return. Note that the horizontal (*x*) axis measures the market return and the vertical (*y*) axis measures the individual asset's returns. The first step in deriving beta involves plotting the coordinates for the market return and asset returns from various points in time. Such annual market return–asset return coordinates are shown in Figure 7.6 *for asset S only* for the years 1993 through 2000. For example, in 2000, asset S's return was 20 percent when the market return was 10 percent. By use of statistical techniques, the "characteristic line" that best explains the relationship between the asset return and the market return coordinates is fit to the data points. The slope of this line is *beta*. The beta for asset R is about .80 and that for asset S is about 1.30. Asset S's higher beta (steeper characteristic line slope) indicates that its return is more responsive to changing market returns. *Therefore it is more risky* than asset R.

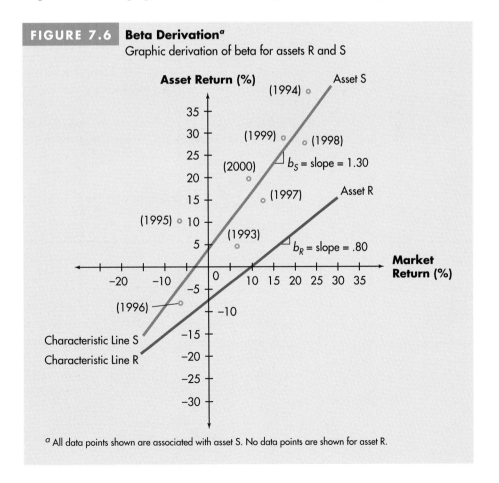

FIGURE 7.6   Beta Derivation[a]
Graphic derivation of beta for assets R and S

[a] All data points shown are associated with asset S. No data points are shown for asset R.

TABLE 7.5	Selected Beta Coefficients and Their Interpretations	
Beta	**Comment**	**Interpretation**
2.0	} Move in same direction as market	Twice as responsive, or risky, as the market
1.0		Same response or risk as the market (i.e., average risk)
.5		Only half as responsive, or risky, as the market
0		Unaffected by market movement
− .5	} Move in opposite direction to market	Only half as responsive, or risky, as the market
−1.0		Same response or risk as the market (i.e., average risk)
−2.0		Twice as responsive, or risky, as the market

Interpreting Betas   The beta coefficient for the market is considered to be equal to 1.0; all other betas are viewed in relation to this value. Asset betas may take on values that are either positive or negative, but positive betas are the norm. The majority of beta coefficients fall between .5 and 2.0. The return of a stock that is half as responsive as the market ($b = .5$) is expected to change by ½ percent for each 1 percent change in the return of the market portfolio. A stock that is twice as responsive as the market ($b = 2.0$) is expected to experience a 2 percent change in its return for each 1 percent change in the return of the market portfolio. Table 7.5 provides some selected beta values and their associated interpretations. Beta coefficients can be obtained for actively traded stocks from published sources, such as *Value Line Investment Survey,* or through brokerage firms. Betas for some selected stocks are given in Table 7.6.

Portfolio Betas   The beta of a portfolio can be easily estimated by using the betas of the individual assets it includes. Letting w_j represent the proportion of

TABLE 7.6	Beta Coefficients for Selected Stocks (April 9, 1999)		
Stock	**Beta**	**Stock**	**Beta**
Anheuser-Busch	.70	Merrill Lynch & Company	2.00
Apple Computer	.95	Microsoft Corp.	1.10
Callaway Golf	1.75	Procter & Gamble	.90
Cascade Natural Gas	.55	Occidental Petroleum	.85
Delta Air Lines	1.25	Seagram Company	1.05
Exxon Corporation	.80	Sempra Energy	.60
General Motors	1.10	Sony Corporation	.90
Harley-Davidson	1.20	Tandy Corporation	1.35
Intel Corp.	1.00	Universal Foods	.75
IBM	1.10	Xerox Corporation	1.00

Source: Value Line Investment Survey (New York: Value Line Publishing, April 9, 1999).

the portfolio's total dollar value represented by asset j and b_j equal the beta of asset j, we can use Equation 7.6 to find the portfolio beta, b_p:

$$b_p = (w_1 \times b_1) + (w_2 \times b_2) + \cdots + (w_n \times b_n) = \sum_{j=1}^{n} w_j \times b_j \qquad (7.6)$$

Of course, $\sum_{j=1}^{n} w_j = 1$, which means that 100 percent of the portfolio's assets must be included in this computation.

Portfolio betas are interpreted in the same way as individual asset betas. They indicate the degree of responsiveness of the *portfolio's* return to changes in the market return. For example, when the market return increases by 10 percent, a portfolio with a beta of .75 will experience a 7.5 percent increase in its return (.75 × 10%); a portfolio with a beta of 1.25 will experience a 12.5 percent increase in its return (1.25 × 10%). Low-beta portfolios are less responsive and therefore less risky than high-beta portfolios.

Example ▼ The Austin Fund, a large investment company, wishes to assess the risk of two portfolios—V and W. Both portfolios contain five assets, with the proportions and betas shown in Table 7.7. The betas for the two portfolios, b_v and b_w, can be calculated by substituting data from the table into Equation 7.6 as follows:

$$b_v = (.10 \times 1.65) + (.30 \times 1.00) + (.20 \times 1.30) + (.20 \times 1.10) + (.20 \times 1.25)$$
$$= .165 + .300 + .260 + .220 + .250 = 1.195 \approx \underline{\underline{1.20}}$$

$$b_w = (.10 \times .80) + (.10 \times 1.00) + (.20 \times .65) + (.10 \times .75) + (.50 \times 1.05)$$
$$= .080 + .100 + .130 + .075 + .525 = \underline{\underline{.91}}$$

Portfolio V's beta is 1.20, and portfolio W's is .91. These values make sense, because portfolio V contains relatively high-beta assets and portfolio W contains relatively low-beta assets. Clearly, portfolio V's returns are more responsive to changes in market returns and are therefore more risky than portfolio W's.

TABLE 7.7   **Austin Fund's Portfolios V and W**

	Portfolio V		Portfolio W	
Asset	Proportion	Beta	Proportion	Beta
1	.10	1.65	.10	.80
2	.30	1.00	.10	1.00
3	.20	1.30	.20	.65
4	.20	1.10	.10	.75
5	.20	1.25	.50	1.05
Totals	1.00		1.00	

THE EQUATION

Using the beta coefficient, *b*, to measure nondiversifiable risk, the *capital asset pricing model (CAPM)* is given in Equation 7.7:

$$k_j = R_F + [b_j \times (k_m - R_F)] \tag{7.7}$$

where

$$
\begin{aligned}
k_j &= \text{required return on asset } j \\
R_F &= \text{risk-free rate of return, commonly measured by the} \\
&\quad\ \text{return on a U.S. Treasury bill} \\
b_j &= \text{beta coefficient or index of nondiversifiable risk for} \\
&\quad\ \text{asset } j \\
k_m &= \text{market return; return on the market portfolio of} \\
&\quad\ \text{assets}
\end{aligned}
$$

The required return on an asset, k_j, is an increasing function of beta, b_j, which measures nondiversifiable risk. In other words, the higher the risk, the higher the required return, and the lower the risk, the lower the required return.

The model can be divided into two parts: (1) the *risk-free rate,* and (2) the *risk premium.* These are, respectively, the two elements on either side of the addition sign in Equation 7.7. The $(k_m - R_F)$ portion of the risk premium is called the *market risk premium,* because it represents the premium the investor must receive for taking the average amount of risk associated with holding the market portfolio of assets.[6] Let us look at an example.

Example ▼ Herbst Corporation, a growing computer-software developer, wishes to determine the required return on an asset Z, which has a beta of 1.5. The risk-free rate of return is found to be 7 percent; the return on the market portfolio of assets is 11 percent. Substituting $b_z = 1.5$, $R_F = 7$ percent, and $k_m = 11$ percent into the capital asset pricing model given in Equation 7.7 yields a required return:

$$k_z = 7\% + [1.5 \times (11\% - 7\%)] = 7\% + 6\% = \underline{\underline{13\%}}$$

The market risk premium of 4 percent ($11\% - 7\%$), when adjusted for the asset's index of risk (beta) of 1.5, results in a risk premium of 6 percent ($1.5 \times 4\%$). That risk premium, when added to the 7 percent risk-free rate, results in a 13 percent required return. Other things being equal, the higher the beta, the higher the required return, and the lower the beta, the lower the required return. ▲

---

[6]Although CAPM has been widely accepted, a broader theory, *arbitrage pricing theory (APT),* first described by Stephen A. Ross, "The Arbitrage Theory of Capital Asset Pricing," *Journal of Economic Theory* (December 1976), pp. 341–360, has in recent years received a great deal of attention in the financial literature. The theory suggests that the risk premium on securities may be better explained by a number of factors underlying and in place of the market return used in CAPM. The CAPM in effect can be viewed as being derived from APT. Although testing of APT theory confirms the importance of the market return, it has thus far failed to clearly identify other risk factors. As a result of this failure as well as APT's lack of practical acceptance and usage, we concentrate our attention here on CAPM.

*P*ERSONAL FINANCE PERSPECTIVE

Risky Business

Mutual funds are investment companies that offer ownership in a diversified and professionally managed portfolio of investments. With more than 8,500 publicly traded mutual funds to choose from, how can you decide which fund(s) to buy?

The first thing to do is to narrow down the list of funds to two or three types of funds that best match your investment needs. Every fund has a particular investment objective, and funds typically are categorized based on that goal. A few of the alternatives are growth funds (aimed at capital gains and long-term growth), equity-income funds (for current income and capital preservation), bond funds (current income through investment in bonds), money market funds (high liquidity through investment in short-term money market instruments), index funds (which capture market volatility by holding a portfolio equivalent to that of a specific market index), and international funds (foreign securities). When you have your short-list of possible funds, you would look at the performance of the remaining choices.

Standard deviation and beta (found in fund reports from Morningstar and Value Line) can help in the selection of mutual funds. Standard deviation measures volatility of returns: The higher the number, the more returns stray from a fund's average return. Because standard deviation is not tied to an index, it helps when comparing different types of funds. For example, U.S. diversified equity funds over a recent 3-year period had a standard deviation of 9.85, compared to bond funds at 5.15. A fund's beta shows how it moves relative to an index—the S&P 500 for stock funds, a bond index for bond funds. This measure is useful for funds that move with the capital markets, less so for specialized funds.

As is generally true for any investment, the more you know about a mutual fund's risk and return profile, the more likely you will be to pick a winner! ●

THE GRAPH: THE SECURITY MARKET LINE (SML)

security market line (SML)
The depiction of the *capital asset pricing model (CAPM)* as a graph that reflects the required return in the marketplace for each level of nondiversifiable risk (beta).

When the capital asset pricing model (Equation 7.7) is depicted graphically, it is called the **security market line** (SML). The SML will, in fact, be a straight line. It reflects the required return in the marketplace for each level of nondiversifiable risk (beta). In the graph, risk as measured by beta, b, is plotted on the x axis, and required returns, k, are plotted on the y axis. The risk-return tradeoff is clearly represented by the SML. Let us look at an illustration.

E x a m p l e ▼
In the preceding example for Herbst Corporation, the risk-free rate, R_F, was 7 percent, and the market return, k_m, was 11 percent. The betas associated with R_F and k_m, b_{R_F} and b_m, are by definition 0^7 and 1, respectively, and the SML can be plotted by using these two sets of coordinates (i.e., $b_{R_F} = 0$, $R_F = 7\%$; and $b_m = 1.0$, $k_m = 11\%$). Figure 7.7 presents the resulting security market line. As traditionally shown, the security market line in Figure 7.7 presents the required return

---

[7]Because R_F is the rate of return on a risk-free asset, the beta associated with the risk-free asset, b_{R_F}, would equal 0. The 0 beta on the risk-free asset reflects not only its absence of risk but also that the asset's return is unaffected by movements in the market return.

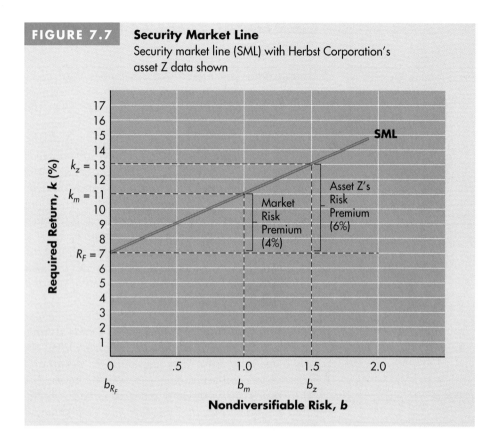

FIGURE 7.7   **Security Market Line**
Security market line (SML) with Herbst Corporation's asset Z data shown

associated with all positive betas. The market risk premium of 4 percent (k_m of 11% − R_F of 7%) has been highlighted. For a beta for asset Z, b_z, of 1.5, its corresponding required return, k_z, is 13 percent. Also shown in the figure is asset Z's risk premium of 6 percent (k_z of 13% − R_F of 7%). It should be clear that for assets with betas greater than 1, the risk premium is greater than that for the market; for assets with betas less than 1, the risk premium is less than that for the market.

SOME COMMENTS ON CAPM

The capital asset pricing model generally relies on historical data. The betas, which are developed using data for the given asset as well as for the market, may or may not actually reflect the *future* variability of returns. Therefore the required returns specified by the model can be viewed only as rough approximations. Users of betas commonly make subjective adjustments to the historically determined betas to reflect their expectations of the future.

The CAPM was developed to explain the behavior of security prices and provide a mechanism whereby investors could assess the impact of a proposed security investment on their portfolio's overall risk and return. It is based on an assumed **efficient market**—a market in which there are many small investors, each having the same information and expectations with respect to securities; no restrictions on investment, no taxes, and no transaction costs; and rational investors, who view securities similarly and are risk-averse, preferring higher

efficient market
An assumed "perfect" market in which there are many small investors, each having the same information and expectations with respect to securities; no restrictions on investment, no taxes, and no transaction costs; and rational investors, who view securities similarly and are risk-averse, preferring higher returns and lower risk.

returns and lower risk. Although the perfect world of the efficient market appears to be unrealistic, studies have provided support for the existence of the expectational relationship described by CAPM in active markets such as the New York Stock Exchange.[8]

In spite of the fact that the risk-return tradeoff described by CAPM is not generally applicable to all assets, it provides a useful conceptual framework for evaluating and linking risk and return. An awareness of this tradeoff and an attempt to consider risk as well as return in financial decision making should aid the financial manager in achieving the goal of owner wealth maximization.

? Review Questions

7-11   What is the relationship of total risk, nondiversifiable risk, and diversifiable risk? Why is nondiversifiable risk the *only relevant risk?*

7-12   What is *beta* and what risk does it measure? How are asset betas derived? How can you find the beta of a portfolio?

7-13   What is the equation for the *capital asset pricing model (CAPM)?* Explain the meaning of each variable. Assuming a risk-free rate of 8 percent and a market return of 12 percent, draw the *security market line (SML).*

7-14   Why do financial managers have difficulty applying CAPM in decision making? Generally, what benefit does CAPM provide them?

SUMMARY

 Understand the meaning and fundamentals of risk, return, and risk aversion. Risk is the chance of loss or, more formally, the variability of returns. Return is the change in value plus any cash distributions expressed as a percentage of the initial value. The variable definitions and equation for the rate of return are given in Table 7.8. Most financial decision makers are risk-averse: They require higher expected returns as compensation for taking greater risk.

Describe procedures for measuring the risk of a single asset. The risk of a single asset is measured in much the same way as the risk

of a portfolio, or collection, of assets. Sensitivity analysis and probability distributions can be used to assess risk. Sensitivity analysis uses a number of possible return estimates to assess the variability of outcomes. Probability distributions, both bar charts and continuous distributions, provide a more quantitative insight into an asset's risk.

Discuss risk measurement for a single asset using the standard deviation and coefficient of variation. In addition to the range, which is the optimistic (best) outcome minus the pessimistic (worst) outcome, the standard deviation and the

---

[8]A study by Eugene F. Fama and Kenneth R. French, "The Cross-Section of Expected Stock Returns," *Journal of Finance* 47 (June 1992), pp. 427–465, raised serious questions about the validity of CAPM. The study failed to find a significant relationship between the *historic* betas and *historic* returns on over 2,000 stocks during 1963–1990. In other words, they found that the magnitude of a stock's *historical* beta had no relationship to the level of its *historical* return. Although Fama and French's study continues to receive attention, CAPM has not been abandoned because its rejection as a *historical* model fails to reject its validity as an *expectational* model. Therefore, in spite of this challenge, CAPM continues to be viewed as a logical and useful framework—both conceptually and operationally—for linking *expected* nondiversifiable risk and return.

TABLE 7.8	Summary of Key Definitions and Formulas for Risk and Return

Variable definitions

b_j = beta coefficient or index of nondiversifiable risk for asset j

b_p = portfolio beta

C_t = cash received from the asset investment in the time period $t - 1$ to t

CV = coefficient of variation

$\bar{k}$ = expected value of a return

k_i = return for the ith outcome

k_j = required return on asset j

k_m = market return; the return on the market portfolio of assets

k_t = actual, expected, or required rate of return during period t

n = number of outcomes considered

P_t = price (value) of asset at time t

P_{t-1} = price (value) of asset at time $t - 1$

Pr_i = probability of occurrence of the ith outcome

R_F = risk-free rate of return

σ_k = standard deviation of returns

w_j = proportion of total portfolio dollar value represented by asset j

Risk and return formulas

Rate of return during period t:

$$k_t = \frac{P_t - P_{t-1} + C_t}{P_{t-1}} \qquad \text{[Eq. 7.1]}$$

Expected value of a return:
for probabilistic data,

$$\bar{k} = \sum_{i=1}^{n} k_i \times Pr_i \qquad \text{[Eq. 7.2]}$$

general formula,

$$\bar{k} = \frac{\sum_{i=1}^{n} k_i}{n} \qquad \text{[Eq. 7.2a]}$$

Standard deviation of return:
for probabilistic data,

$$\sigma_k = \sqrt{\sum_{i=1}^{n} (k_i - \bar{k})^2 \times Pr_i} \qquad \text{[Eq. 7.3]}$$

general formula,

$$\sigma_k = \sqrt{\frac{\sum_{i=1}^{n} (k_i - \bar{k})^2}{n - 1}} \qquad \text{[Eq. 7.3a]}$$

Coefficient of variation:

$$CV = \frac{\sigma_k}{\bar{k}} \qquad \text{[Eq. 7.4]}$$

Total security risk = nondiversifiable
risk + diversifiable risk [Eq. 7.5]

Portfolio beta:

$$b_p = \sum_{i=1}^{n} w_j \times b_j \qquad \text{[Eq. 7.6]}$$

Capital asset pricing model
(CAPM):

$$k_j = R_F + [b_j \times (k_m - R_F)] \qquad \text{[Eq. 7.7]}$$

coefficient of variation can be used to measure risk quantitatively. The standard deviation measures the dispersion around an asset's expected value, and the coefficient of variation uses the standard deviation to measure dispersion on a relative basis. The key variable definitions and equations for the expected value of a return, standard deviation of return, and the coefficient of variation are summarized in Table 7.8.

LG4 **Understand the risk and return characteristics of a portfolio in terms of correlation and diversification and the impact of international assets on a portfolio.** The financial manager's goal is to create an efficient portfolio that maximizes return for a given level of risk or minimizes risk for a given level of return. The risk of a portfolio of assets may be reduced through diversification. New investments must be considered in light of their effect on the risk and return of the portfolio. Correlation, which is the statistical relationship between asset returns, affects the diversification process. The more negative (or less positive) the correlation between asset returns, the greater the risk-reducing benefits of diversification. International diversification involves including foreign assets in a portfolio and can be used to further reduce a portfolio's risk.

LG5 **Review the two types of risk and the derivation and role of beta in measuring the rele-**
vant **risk of both an individual security and a portfolio.** The total risk of a security consists of nondiversifiable and diversifiable risk. Nondiversifiable risk is the only relevant risk because diversifiable risk can be easily eliminated through diversification. Nondiversifiable risk can be measured by the beta coefficient, which reflects the relationship between an asset's return and the market return. Beta is derived by using statistical techniques to find the slope of the "characteristic line" that best explains the historic relationship between the asset's return and the market return. The beta of a portfolio is a weighted average of the betas of the individual assets that it includes. The variable definitions and equations for total risk and the portfolio beta are given in Table 7.8.

LG6 **Explain the capital asset pricing model (CAPM) and its relationship to the security market line (SML).** The capital asset pricing model (CAPM) uses beta to relate an asset's risk relative to the market to the asset's required return. The variable definitions and equation for CAPM are summarized in Table 7.8. The graphic depiction of CAPM is the security market line (SML). Although it has some shortcomings, CAPM provides a useful conceptual framework for evaluating and linking risk and return.

SELF-TEST PROBLEMS   **(Solutions in Appendix B)**

ST 7–1   Portfolio analysis   You have been asked for your advice in selecting a portfolio of assets and have been supplied with the following data:

| | Expected return | | |
Year	Asset A	Asset B	Asset C
2001	12%	16%	12%
2002	14	14	14
2003	16	12	16

No probabilities have been supplied. You have been told that you can create two portfolios—one consisting of assets A and B and the other consisting of assets A and C—by investing equal proportions (i.e., 50 percent) in each of the two component assets.

a. What is the expected return for each asset over the 3-year period?

b. What is the standard deviation for each asset's return?

c. What is the expected return for each of the two portfolios?

d. How would you characterize the correlations of returns of the two assets making up each of the two portfolios identified in **c?**

e. What is the standard deviation for each portfolio?

f. Which portfolio do you recommend? Why?

ST 7-2   Beta and CAPM   Currently under consideration is a project with a beta, *b*, of 1.50. At this time, the risk-free rate of return, R_F, is 7 percent, and the return on the market portfolio of assets, k_m, is 10 percent. The project is actually *expected* to earn an annual rate of return of 11 percent.

a. If the return on the market portfolio were to increase by 10 percent, what would be expected to happen to the project's *required return?* What if the market return were to decline by 10 percent?

b. Use the capital asset pricing model (CAPM) to find the *required return* on this investment.

c. On the basis of your calculation in **b,** would you recommend this investment? Why or why not?

d. Assume that as a result of investors becoming less risk-averse, the market return drops by 1 percent to 9 percent. What impact would this change have on your responses in **b** and **c?**

PROBLEMS

7-1   Rate of return   Douglas Keel, a financial analyst for Orange Industries, wishes to estimate the rate of return for two similar-risk investments—X and Y. Keel's research indicates that the immediate past returns will act as reasonable estimates of future returns. A year earlier, investment X had a market value of $20,000 and investment Y, of $55,000. During the year, investment X generated cash flow of $1,500 and investment Y generated cash flow of $6,800. The current market values of investments X and Y are $21,000 and $55,000, respectively.

a. Calculate the expected rate of return on investments X and Y using the most recent year's data.

b. Assuming that the two investments are equally risky, which one should Keel recommend? Why?

7-2   Return calculations   For each of the investments shown in the table at the top of the following page, calculate the rate of return earned over the unspecified time period.

Investment	Beginning-of-period value	End-of-period value	Cash flow during period
A	$ 800	$ 1,100	$ −100
B	120,000	118,000	15,000
C	45,000	48,000	7,000
D	600	500	80
E	12,500	12,400	1,500

INTERMEDIATE **7-3 Risk preference** Oren Wells, the financial manager for Winston Enterprises, wishes to evaluate three prospective investments—X, Y, and Z. Currently, the firm earns 12 percent on its investments, which have a risk index of 6 percent. The three investments under consideration are profiled in the following table in terms of expected return and expected risk. If Oren Wells is risk-averse, which investment, if any, will he select? Explain why.

Investment	Expected return	Expected risk index
X	14%	7%
Y	12	8
Z	10	9

INTERMEDIATE **7-4 Risk analysis** Babb Products is considering an investment in an expanded product line. Two possible types of expansion are being considered. After investigating the possible outcomes, the company made the estimates shown in the following table:

	Expansion A	Expansion B
Initial investment	$12,000	$12,000
Annual rate of return		
Pessimistic	16%	10%
Most likely	20%	20%
Optimistic	24%	30%

a. Determine the range of the rates of return for each of the two projects.
b. Which project is less risky? Why?
c. If you were making the investment decision, which one would you choose? Why? What does this imply about your feelings toward risk?
d. Assume that expansion B's most likely outcome is 21 percent per year and all other facts remain the same. Does this change your answer to part **c**? Why?

 7-5 Risk and probability Blue Book Publishers is considering the purchase of one of two microfilm cameras—R or S. Both should provide benefits over a 10-year period, and each requires an initial investment of $4,000. Management has constructed the following table of estimates of rates of return and probabilities for pessimistic, most likely, and optimistic results:

	Camera R		Camera S	
	Amount	Probability	Amount	Probability
Initial investment	$4,000	1.00	$4,000	1.00
Annual rate of return				
Pessimistic	20%	.25	15%	.20
Most likely	25%	.50	25%	.55
Optimistic	30%	.25	35%	.25

a. Determine the range for the rate of return for each of the two cameras.
b. Determine the expected value of return for each camera.
c. Which camera is riskier? Why?

 7-6 **Bar charts and risk**   David's Sportswear is considering bringing out a line of designer jeans. Currently, it is negotiating with two different well-known designers. Because of the highly competitive nature of the industry, the two designs have been given code names. After market research, the firm has established the expectations shown in the following table about the annual rates of return:

		Annual rate of return	
Market acceptance	Probability	Line J	Line K
Very poor	.05	.0075	.010
Poor	.15	.0125	.025
Average	.60	.0850	.080
Good	.15	.1475	.135
Excellent	.05	.1625	.150

Use the table to:
a. Construct a bar chart for each line's annual rate of return.
b. Calculate the expected value of return for each line.
c. Evaluate the relative riskiness for each jean line's rate of return using the bar charts.

  7-7 **Coefficient of variation**   Ferrous Manufacturing has isolated four alternatives for meeting its need for increased production capacity. The data gathered relative to each of these alternatives is summarized in the following table:

Alternative	Expected return	Standard deviation of return
A	20%	7.0%
B	22	9.5
C	19	6.0
D	16	5.5

    a. Calculate the coefficient of variation for each alternative.
    b. If the firm wishes to minimize risk, which alternative do you recommend? Why?

7-8 **Assessing return and risk**   Newby Tool must choose between two asset purchases. The annual rate of return and the related probabilities given in the following table summarize the firm's analysis to this point:

CHALLENGE

Project 257		Project 432	
Rate of return	Probability	Rate of return	Probability
−10%	.01	10%	.05
10	.04	15	.10
20	.05	20	.10
30	.10	25	.15
40	.15	30	.20
45	.30	35	.15
50	.15	40	.10
60	.10	45	.10
70	.05	50	.05
80	.04		
100	.01		

    a. For each project, compute:
       (1) The range of possible rates of return.
       (2) The expected value of return.
       (3) The standard deviation of the returns.
       (4) The coefficient of variation.
    b. Construct a bar chart of each distribution of rates of return.
    c. Which project would you consider less risky? Why?

 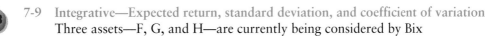

7-9 Integrative—Expected return, standard deviation, and coefficient of variation
Three assets—F, G, and H—are currently being considered by Bix

Manufacturing. The probability distributions of expected returns for these assets are shown in the following table.

	Asset F		Asset G		Asset H	
i	Pr_i	Return, k_i	Pr_i	Return, k_i	Pr_i	Return, k_i
1	.10	40%	.40	35%	.10	40%
2	.20	10	.30	10	.20	20
3	.40	0	.30	−20	.40	10
4	.20	−5			.20	0
5	.10	−10			.10	−20

a. Calculate the expected value of return, $\bar{k}$, for each of the three assets. Which provides the largest expected return?
b. Calculate the standard deviation, σ_k, for each of the three assets' returns. Which appears to have the greatest risk?
c. Calculate the coefficient of variation, CV, for each of the three assets. Which appears to have the largest *relative* risk?

CHALLENGE **7–10** **Portfolio return and standard deviation**   Jamie Wong is considering building a portfolio containing two assets, L and M. Asset L will represent 40 percent of the dollar value of the portfolio, and asset M will account for the other 60 percent. The expected returns over the next 6 years, 2001–2006, for each of these assets, are shown in the following table:

	Expected return	
Year	Asset L	Asset M
2001	14%	20%
2002	14	18
2003	16	16
2004	17	14
2005	17	12
2006	19	10

a. Calculate the expected portfolio return, k_p, for *each* of the 6 years.
b. Calculate the expected value of portfolio returns, $\bar{k}_p$, over the 6-year period.
c. Calculate the standard deviation of expected portfolio returns, σ_{k_p}, over the 6-year period.
d. How would you characterize the correlation of returns of the two assets L and M?
e. Discuss any benefits of diversification achieved through creation of the portfolio.

CHALLENGE 7-11   Portfolio analysis   You have been given the return data shown in the first table on three assets—F, G, and H—over the period 2001–2004:

	Expected return		
Year	Asset F	Asset G	Asset H
2001	16%	17%	14%
2002	17	16	15
2003	18	15	16
2004	19	14	17

Using these assets, you have isolated the three investment alternatives shown in the following table:

Alternative	Investment
1	100% of asset F
2	50% of asset F and 50% of asset G
3	50% of asset F and 50% of asset H

a. Calculate the expected return over the 4-year period for each of the three alternatives.
b. Calculate the standard deviation of returns over the 4-year period for each of the three alternatives.
c. Use your findings in **a** and **b** to calculate the coefficient of variation for each of the three alternatives.
d. On the basis of your findings, which of the three investment alternatives do you recommend? Why?

INTERMEDIATE 7-12   Correlation, risk, and return   Matt Peters wishes to evaluate the risk and return behaviors associated with various combinations of assets V and W under three assumed degrees of correlation—perfect positive, uncorrelated, and perfect negative. The expected return and risk values calculated for each of the assets are shown in the following table:

Asset	Expected return, $\bar{k}$	Risk (standard deviation), σ_k
V	8%	5%
W	13	10

a. If the returns of assets V and W are *perfectly positively correlated* (correlation coefficient = +1), describe the *range* of (1) expected return and (2) risk associated with all possible portfolio combinations.

b. If the returns of assets V and W are *uncorrelated* (correlation coefficient = 0), describe the *approximate range* of (1) expected return and (2) risk associated with all possible portfolio combinations.

c. If the returns of assets V and W are *perfectly negatively correlated* (correlation coefficient = −1), describe the *range* of (1) expected return and (2) risk associated with all possible portfolio combinations.

  7-13 Total, nondiversifiable, and diversifiable risk   Allen Ferris randomly selected securities from all those listed on the New York Stock Exchange for his portfolio. He began with one security and added securities one by one until a total of 20 securities were held in the portfolio. After each security was added, Allen calculated the portfolio standard deviation, σ_{k_p}. The calculated values are shown in the following table:

Number of securities	Portfolio risk, σ_{k_p}	Number of securities	Portfolio risk, σ_{k_p}
1	14.50%	11	7.00%
2	13.30	12	6.80
3	12.20	13	6.70
4	11.20	14	6.65
5	10.30	15	6.60
6	9.50	16	6.56
7	8.80	17	6.52
8	8.20	18	6.50
9	7.70	19	6.48
10	7.30	20	6.47

a. On a set of number of securities in portfolio (*x* axis)-portfolio risk (*y* axis) axes, plot the portfolio risk data given in the preceding table.

b. Divide the total portfolio risk in the graph into its *nondiversifiable* and *diversifiable* risk components and label each of these on the graph.

c. Describe which of the two risk components is the *relevant risk*, and explain why it is relevant. How much of this risk exists in Allen Ferris's portfolio?

  7-14 Graphic derivation of beta   A firm wishes to graphically estimate the betas for two assets—A and B. It has gathered the return data shown in the table at the top of the following page for the market portfolio and both assets over the last ten years, 1991–2000.

	Actual return		
Year	Market portfolio	Asset A	Asset B
1991	6%	11%	16%
1992	2	8	11
1993	−13	−4	−10
1994	−4	3	3
1995	−8	0	−3
1996	16	19	30
1997	10	14	22
1998	15	18	29
1999	8	12	19
2000	13	17	26

a. On a set of market return (*x* axis)–asset return (*y* axis) axes, use the data given to draw the characteristic line for asset A and for asset B (on the same set of axes).
b. Use the characteristic lines from **a** to estimate the betas for assets A and B.
c. Use the betas found in **b** to comment on the relative risks of assets A and B.

WARM-UP **7-15** Interpreting beta   A firm wishes to assess the impact of changes in the market return on an asset that has a beta of 1.20.
a. If the market return increased by 15 percent, what impact would this change be expected to have on the asset's return?
b. If the market return decreased by 8 percent, what impact would this change be expected to have on the asset's return?
c. If the market return did not change, what impact, if any, would be expected on the asset's return?
d. Would this asset be considered more or less risky than the market? Explain.

WARM-UP **7-16** Betas   Answer the following questions for assets A to D shown in the table.

Asset	Beta
A	.50
B	1.60
C	−.20
D	.90

a. What impact would a *10 percent increase* in the market return be expected to have on each asset's return?
b. What impact would a *10 percent decrease* in the market return be expected to have on each asset's return?
c. If you were certain that the market return would *increase* in the near future, which asset would you prefer? Why?

d. If you were certain that the market return would *decrease* in the near future, which asset would you prefer? Why?

 7-17 Betas and risk rankings Stock A has a beta of .80, stock B has a beta of 1.40, and stock C has a beta of −.30.

a. Rank these stocks from the most risky to the least risky.
b. If the return on the market portfolio increases by 12 percent, what change would you expect in the return for each of the stocks?
c. If the return on the market portfolio declines by 5 percent, what change would you expect in the return for each of the stocks?
d. If you felt that the stock market was just ready to experience a significant decline, which stock would you likely add to your portfolio? Why?
e. If you anticipated a major stock market rally, which stock would you add to your portfolio? Why?

 7-18 Portfolio betas Rose Berry is attempting to evaluate two possible portfolios—both consisting of the same five assets but held in different proportions. She is particularly interested in using beta to compare the risk of the portfolios and in this regard has gathered the data shown in the following table:

		Portfolio weights	
Asset	Asset beta	Portfolio A	Portfolio B
1	1.30	10%	30%
2	.70	30	10
3	1.25	10	20
4	1.10	10	20
5	.90	40	20
Totals		100%	100%

a. Calculate the betas for portfolios A and B.
b. Compare the risk of each portfolio to the market as well as to each other. Which portfolio is more risky?

 7-19 Capital asset pricing model (CAPM) For each of the cases shown in the following table, use the capital asset pricing model to find the required return:

Case	Risk-free rate, R_F	Market return, k_m	Beta, b
A	5%	8%	1.30
B	8	13	.90
C	9	12	−.20
D	10	15	1.00
E	6	10	.60

7-20 Manipulating CAPM   Use the basic equation for the capital asset pricing model (CAPM) to work each of the following:

a. Find the *required return* for an asset with a beta of .90 when the risk-free rate and market return are 8 and 12 percent, respectively.

b. Find the *risk-free rate* for a firm with a required return of 15 percent and a beta of 1.25 when the market return is 14 percent.

c. Find the *market return* for an asset with a required return of 16 percent and a beta of 1.10 when the risk-free rate is 9 percent.

d. Find the *beta* for an asset with a required return of 15 percent when the risk-free rate and market return are 10 and 12.5 percent, respectively.

  7-21 Security market line, SML   Assume that the risk-free rate, R_F, is currently 9 percent and that the market return, k_m, is currently 13 percent.

a. Draw the security market line (SML) on a set of nondiversifiable risk (*x* axis)–required return (*y* axis) axes.

b. Calculate and label the *market risk premium* on the axes in **a.**

c. Given the previous data, calculate the required return on asset A having a beta of .80 and asset B having a beta of 1.30.

d. Draw in the betas and required returns from **c** for assets A and B on the axes in **a.** Label the *risk premium* associated with each of these assets, and discuss them.

  7-22 Integrative—Risk, return, and CAPM   Jessup Box Company must consider several investment projects, A through E, using the capital asset pricing model (CAPM) and its graphic representation, the security market line (SML). Relevant information is presented in the following table.

Item	Rate of return	Beta, *b*
Risk-free asset	9%	0
Market portfolio	14	1.00
Project A	—	1.50
Project B	—	.75
Project C	—	2.00
Project D	—	0
Project E	—	−.50

a. Calculate the required return and risk premium for each project, given its level of nondiversifiable risk.

b. Use your findings in **a** to draw the security market line (required return relative to nondiversifiable risk).

c. Discuss the relative nondiversifiable risk of projects A through E.

| CASE | Chapter 7 | Analyzing Risk and Return on Chargers Products' Investments |

Junior Sayou, a financial analyst for Chargers Products, a manufacturer of stadium benches, must evaluate the risk and return of two assets—X and Y. The firm is considering adding these assets to its diversified asset portfolio. To assess the return and risk of each asset, Junior gathered data on the annual cash flow and beginning- and end-of-year values of each asset over the immediately preceding 10 years, 1991–2000. These data are summarized in the following table. Junior's investigation suggests that both assets, on average, will tend to perform in the future just as they have during the past 10 years. He therefore believes that the expected annual return can be estimated by finding the average annual return for each asset over the past 10 years.

Junior believes that each asset's risk can be assessed in two ways: in isolation and as part of the firm's diversified portfolio of assets. The risk of the assets in isolation can be found by using the standard deviation and coefficient of variation of returns over the past 10 years. The capital asset pricing model (CAPM) can be used to assess the asset's risk as part of the firm's portfolio of assets. Applying some sophisticated quantitative techniques, Junior estimated betas for assets X and Y of 1.60 and 1.10, respectively. In addition, he found that the risk-free rate is currently 7 percent and the market return is 10 percent.

Return Data for Assets X and Y, 1991–2000

| | | Asset X | | | Asset Y | |
| | | Value | | | Value | |
Year	Cash flow	Beginning	Ending	Cash flow	Beginning	Ending
1991	$1,000	$20,000	$22,000	$1,500	$20,000	$20,000
1992	1,500	22,000	21,000	1,600	20,000	20,000
1993	1,400	21,000	24,000	1,700	20,000	21,000
1994	1,700	24,000	22,000	1,800	21,000	21,000
1995	1,900	22,000	23,000	1,900	21,000	22,000
1996	1,600	23,000	26,000	2,000	22,000	23,000
1997	1,700	26,000	25,000	2,100	23,000	23,000
1998	2,000	25,000	24,000	2,200	23,000	24,000
1999	2,100	24,000	27,000	2,300	24,000	25,000
2000	2,200	27,000	30,000	2,400	25,000	25,000

Required

a. Calculate the annual rate of return for each asset in *each* of the 10 preceding years, and use those values to find the average annual return for each asset over the 10-year period.

    b. Use the returns calculated in **a** to find (1) the standard deviation and (2) the coefficient of variation of the returns for each asset over the 10-year period 1991–2000.

    c. Use your findings in **a** and **b** to evaluate and discuss the return and risk associated with each asset. Which asset appears to be preferable? Explain.

    d. Use the CAPM to find the required return for each asset. Compare this value with the average annual returns calculated in **a**.

    e. Compare and contrast your findings in **c** and **d**. What recommendations would you give Junior with regard to investing in either of the two assets? Explain to Junior why he is better off using beta rather than the standard deviation and coefficient of variation to assess the risk of each asset.

Web Exercise

GOTO web site www.stern.nyu.edu/~adamodar/New_Home_Page/datafile/histret.html.

1. Compute the arithmetic average for the annual return for stocks, T-bills, and T-bonds for the last 10 years of data.
2. Compute the standard deviation for the averages calculated in question 1.
3. Which has the highest arithmetic average—stocks, T-bills, or T-bonds?
4. Which has the largest standard deviation?
5. How much money would you have if you had invested $100 into stocks in 1926? If you had invested $100 in T-bills in 1926? And, if you had invested $100 in T-bonds in 1926?
6. Using the arithmetic average data given on this web site, what is the risk premium of stocks versus T-bills for the shortest time period given in the charts?
7. Using the arithmetic average data given on this web site, what is the risk premium of stocks versus T-bonds for the shortest time period given in the charts?
8. Explain the difference between your answer to question 6 and your answer to question 7.

BOND AND STOCK VALUATION

LG1 Describe the key inputs and basic model used in the valuation process.

LG2 Apply the bond valuation model and describe the impact of required return and time to maturity on bond values.

LG3 Explain yield to maturity, its calculation, and the procedure used to value bonds that pay interest semiannually.

LG4 Perform basic common stock valuation using both the zero-growth and constant-growth models.

LG5 Discuss the use of book value, liquidation value, and price/earnings multiples to estimate common stock values.

LG6 Understand the relationships among financial decisions, return, risk, and the firm's value.

ACROSS *the* DISCIPLINES

All major financial decisions must be viewed in terms of expected risk, expected return, and their combined impact on share price. In this chapter, we link the concepts of risk and return learned in the previous chapter in order to find the value of the two basic corporate securities—bonds and stocks. This process, called valuation, can be used to find the value of any asset. Here the primary focus is on stock value—the value the financial manager attempts to maximize. Chapter 8 is important to:

- **accounting personnel** who will prepare external financial statements that influence outsiders' perceptions of the firm.
- **information systems analysts** who will design information systems that help forecast cash flows easily and accurately.
- **management** because it will determine the policies that directly affect the value of the firm's stock.
- **the marketing department** because good product development, promotion, and sales activities will positively impact cash flows, risk, and value.
- **operations,** which must maintain good purchasing, inventory, production, and distribution practices to stabilize cash flows and keep the firm's required rate of return as low as possible.

LG 1

VALUATION FUNDAMENTALS

valuation
The process that links risk and return to determine the worth of an asset.

Valuation is the process that links risk and return to determine the worth of an asset. It is a relatively simple process that can be applied to *expected* streams of benefits from bonds, stocks, income properties, oil wells, and so on. To determine their worth at a given point in time, the manager uses time value of money techniques presented in Chapter 6 and the concepts of risk and return developed in Chapter 7.

KEY INPUTS

The key inputs to the valuation process include cash flows (returns), timing, and the required return (risk). Each is discussed below.

CASH FLOWS (RETURNS)

The value of any asset depends on the cash flow(s) it is *expected* to provide over the ownership period. To have value, an asset does not have to provide an annual cash flow; it can provide an intermittent cash flow or even a single cash flow over the period.

E x a m p l e ▼ Nancy Dorr, financial analyst for Kemp Industries, a diversified holding company, wishes to estimate the value of three of its assets—common stock in Wortz United, an interest in an oil well, and an original painting by a well-known artist. Her cash flow estimates for each were as follows.

Stock in Wortz United   *Expect* to receive cash dividends of $300 per year indefinitely.

Oil well   *Expect* to receive cash flow of $2,000 at the end of 1 year, $4,000 at the end of 2 years, and $10,000 at the end of 4 years, when the well is to be sold.

Original painting   *Expect* to be able to sell the painting in 5 years for $85,000.

With these cash flow estimates, Nancy has taken the first step toward placing a
▲ value on each of these assets.

TIMING

In addition to making cash flow estimates, we must know the timing of the cash flows.[1] For example, the cash flows of $2,000, $4,000, and $10,000 for the oil well in the example were expected to occur at the end of years 1, 2, and 4,

---

[1]Although cash flows can occur at any time during a year, for computational convenience as well as custom, we will assume they occur at the end of the year unless otherwise noted.

respectively. In combination, the cash flow and its timing fully define the return expected from the asset.

REQUIRED RETURN (RISK)

The level of risk associated with a given cash flow can significantly affect its value. In general, the greater the risk of (or the less certain) a cash flow, the lower its value. Greater risk can be incorporated into an analysis by using a higher required return or discount rate. Recall that in the capital asset pricing model (CAPM) (see Equation 7.7), the greater the risk as measured by beta, b, the higher the required return, k. In the valuation process, too, the required return is used to incorporate risk into the analysis: The higher the risk, the greater the required return; the lower the risk, the less the required return.

E x a m p l e ▼   Let's return to Nancy Dorr's task of placing a value on Kemp Industries' original painting, which is expected to provide a single cash flow of $85,000 at the end of 5 years, and consider two scenarios:

Scenario 1—Certainty   A major art gallery has contracted to buy the painting for $85,000 at the end of 5 years. Because this is considered a certain situation, Nancy views this asset as "money in the bank." She thus would use the prevailing risk-free rate, R_F, of 9 percent as the required return when calculating the value of the painting.

Scenario 2—High Risk   The value of original paintings by this artist has fluctuated widely over the past 10 years. Although Nancy expects to be able to get $85,000 for the painting, she realizes that its sale price in 5 years could range between $30,000 and $140,000. Due to the high uncertainty surrounding the painting's value, Nancy believes that a 15 percent required return is appropriate.

These two estimates of the appropriate required return illustrate how this rate captures risk. The often subjective nature of such estimates is also clear. ▲

THE BASIC VALUATION MODEL

Simply stated, the value of any asset is *the present value of all future cash flows it is expected to provide over the relevant time period.* The time period can be as short as 1 year or as long as infinity. The value of an asset is therefore determined by discounting the expected cash flows back to their present value, using the required return commensurate with the asset's risk as the appropriate discount rate. Utilizing the present value techniques presented in Chapter 6, we can express the value of any asset at time zero, V_0, as:

$$V_0 = \frac{CF_1}{(1+k)^1} + \frac{CF_2}{(1+k)^2} + \cdots + \frac{CF_n}{(1+k)^n} \tag{8.1}$$

where

V_0 = value of the asset at time zero

CF_t = cash flow *expected* at the end of year t

k = appropriate required return (discount rate)

n = relevant time period

Using present value interest factor notation, $PVIF_{k,n}$ from Chapter 6, Equation 8.1 can be rewritten as:

$$V_0 = [CF_1 \times (PVIF_{k,1})] + [CF_2 \times (PVIF_{k,2})] + \cdots + [CF_n \times (PVIF_{k,n})] \qquad (8.2)$$

Substituting the expected cash flows, CF_t, over the relevant time period, n, and the appropriate required return, k, into Equation 8.2, we can determine the value of any asset.

E x a m p l e ▼ Nancy Dorr, using appropriate required returns and Equation 8.2, calculated the value of each asset (using present value interest factors from Table A-3), as shown in Table 8.1. Wortz United stock has a value of $2,500, the oil well's value is $9,262, and the original painting has a value of $42,245. Had she instead used a calculator, the values of the oil well and original painting would

| TABLE 8.1 | Valuation of Kemp Industries' Assets by Nancy Dorr |

Asset	Cash flow, CF		Appropriate required return	Valuation
Wortz United stock[a]	$300/year indefinitely		12%	$V_0 = \$300 \times (PVIFA_{12\%,\infty})$ $= \$300 \times \dfrac{1}{.12} = \underline{\underline{\$2,500}}$
Oil well[b]	Year (t) 1 2 3 4	CF_t $ 2,000 4,000 0 10,000	20%	$V_0 = [\$2,000 \times (PVIF_{20\%,1})]$ $+ [\$4,000 \times (PVIF_{20\%,2})]$ $+ [\$0 \times (PVIF_{20\%,3})]$ $+ [\$10,000 \times (PVIF_{20\%,4})]$ $= [\$2,000 \times (.833)]$ $+ [\$4,000 \times (.694)]$ $+ [\$0 \times (.579)]$ $+ [\$10,000 \times (.482)]$ $= \$1,666 + \$2,776$ $+ \$0 + \$4,820$ $= \underline{\underline{\$9,262}}$
Original painting[c]	$85,000 at end of year 5		15%	$V_0 = \$85,000 \times (PVIF_{15\%,5})$ $= \$85,000 \times (.497)$ $= \underline{\underline{\$42,245}}$

[a]This is a perpetuity (infinite-lived annuity), and therefore the present value interest factor given in Equation 6.21 is applied.

[b]This is a mixed stream of cash flows and therefore requires a number of $PVIF$s, as noted.

[c]This is a lump-sum cash flow and therefore requires a single $PVIF$.

have been $9,266.98 and $42,260.03, respectively. Note that regardless of the pattern of the expected cash flow from an asset, the basic valuation equation can be used to determine its value.

? Review Questions

8-1   What is *valuation*, and why is it important for the financial manager to understand the valuation process?

8-2   Briefly describe the three key inputs to the valuation process. Does the valuation process apply only to assets providing an annual cash flow? Explain.

8-3   Define and specify the general equation for the value of any asset, V_0, in terms of its *expected* cash flow in each year and the appropriate required return.

BOND VALUATION

The basic valuation equation can be customized for use in valuing specific securities—bonds, preferred stock, and common stock. Bonds and preferred stock are similar, because they have stated contractual interest and dividend cash flows. The dividends on common stock, on the other hand, are not known in advance. Bond valuation is described in this section, and common stock valuation is discussed in the following section.[2]

BOND FUNDAMENTALS

As discussed in Chapter 3, *bonds* are long-term debt instruments used by business and government to raise large sums of money, typically from a diverse group of lenders. Most corporate bonds pay interest *semiannually* at a stated *coupon interest rate*, have an initial *maturity* of 10 to 30 years, and have a *par*, or *face*, *value* of $1,000 that must be repaid at maturity. An example will illustrate the terms of a corporate bond.

Example ▼ Stills Company, a large defense contractor, on January 1, 2001, issued a 10 percent coupon interest rate, 10-year bond with a $1,000 par value that pays interest semiannually. Investors who buy this bond receive the contractual right to two cash flows: (1) $100 annual interest (10 percent coupon interest rate × $1,000 par value) distributed as $50 (½ × $100) at the end of each 6 months ▲ and (2) the $1,000 par value at the end of the tenth year.

We will use data presented for Stills Company's bond issue to look at basic bond valuation and other issues.

---

[2]Because the procedures are identical, the valuation of preferred stock is demonstrated as a special case in the discussion of valuing common stock.

BASIC BOND VALUATION

The value of a bond is the present value of the payments its issuer is contractually obligated to make, from the current time until it matures. The basic equation for the value, B_0, of a bond is given by Equation 8.3:

$$B_0 = I \times \left[\sum_{t=1}^{n} \frac{1}{(1+k_d)^t} \right] + M \times \left[\frac{1}{(1+k_d)^n} \right] \tag{8.3}$$

$$= I \times (PVIFA_{k_d,n}) + M \times (PVIF_{k_d,n}) \tag{8.3a}$$

where

B_0 = value of the bond at time zero
I = *annual* interest paid in dollars[3]
n = number of years to maturity
M = par value in dollars
k_d = required return on a bond

We calculate bond value using Equation 8.3a and the appropriate financial tables (A-3 and A-4) or by using a financial calculator.

Example ▼ *Assuming that interest on the Stills Company's new issue is paid annually* and that the required return is equal to the bond's coupon interest rate, I = $100, k_d = 10 percent, M = $1,000, and n = 10 years.

Table Use   Substituting the values noted above into Equation 8.3a yields

$$B_0 = \$100 \times (PVIFA_{10\%,10\text{yrs}}) + \$1,000 \times (PVIF_{10\%,10\text{yrs}})$$
$$= \$100 \times (6.145) + \$1,000 \times (.386)$$
$$= \$614.50 + \$386.00 = \underline{\underline{\$1,000.50}}$$

The bond therefore has a value of approximately $1,000.[4]

Calculator Use   Using the Stills Company's inputs shown below, you should find the bond value to be exactly $1,000.

Inputs: ⬭ 10 ⬭   ⬭ 10 ⬭   ⬭ 100 ⬭   ⬭ 1000 ⬭

Functions: ⬭ N ⬭   ⬭ I ⬭   ⬭ PMT ⬭   ⬭ FV ⬭   ⬭ CPT ⬭   ⬭ PV ⬭

Outputs: ⬭ *1000* ⬭

---

[3]The payment of annual rather than semiannual bond interest is assumed throughout the following discussion. This assumption simplifies the calculations involved while maintaining the conceptual accuracy of the valuation procedures presented.

[4]Note that a slight rounding error ($.50) results here due to the use of the table factors, which are rounded to the nearest thousandth.

Note that the bond value calculated in the example is equal to its par value; *this will always be the case when the required return is equal to the coupon interest rate.*

Time-Line Use The computations involved in finding the bond value are depicted graphically on the following time line.

Graphic depiction of bond valuation (Stills Company's 10 percent coupon interest rate, 10-year maturity, $1,000 par, January 1, 2000, issue paying annual interest; required return = 10 percent)

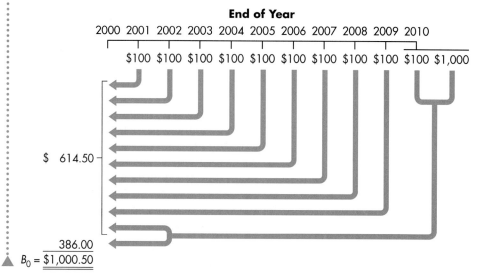

End of Year

2000 2001 2002 2003 2004 2005 2006 2007 2008 2009 2010

$100 $100 $100 $100 $100 $100 $100 $100 $100 $100 $1,000

$ 614.50

386.00

$B_0 = \underline{\$1,000.50}$

BOND VALUE BEHAVIOR

In practice, the value of a bond in the marketplace is rarely equal to its par value. As was seen in the bond quotations in Figure 2.2, part A on page 33, the closing prices of bonds often differ from their par values of 100 (100 percent of par). Some are valued below par (quoted below 100) and others are valued above par (quoted above 100). A variety of forces in the economy as well as the passage of time tend to affect value. Although these external forces are really in no way controlled by bond issuers or investors, it is useful to understand the impact that required return and time to maturity have on bond value.

REQUIRED RETURNS AND BOND VALUES

Whenever the required return on a bond differs from the bond's coupon interest rate, the bond's value will differ from its par value. The required return is likely to differ from the coupon interest rate because either (1) economic conditions have changed, causing a shift in the basic cost of long-term funds, or (2) the firm's risk has changed. Increases in the basic cost of long-term funds or in risk will raise the required return; decreases in the cost of funds or in risk will lower the required return.

discount
The amount by which a bond sells at a value that is less than its par value.

Regardless of the exact cause, what is important is the relationship between the required return and the coupon interest rate: When the required return is greater than the coupon interest rate, the bond value, B_0, will be less than its par value, M. In this case, the bond is said to sell at a **discount**, which will equal $M -$

premium
The amount by which a bond sells at a value that is greater than its par value.

B_0. On the other hand, when the required return falls below the coupon interest rate, the bond value will be greater than par. In this case, the bond is said to sell at a **premium**, which will equal $B_0 - M$. An example will illustrate this point.

E x a m p l e ▼ In the preceding example, we saw that when the required return equaled the coupon interest rate, the bond's value equaled its $1,000 par value. If for the same bond the required return were to rise to 12 percent, its value would be found as follows (using Equation 8.3a):

Table Use

$$B_0 = \$100 \times (PVIFA_{12\%,10\text{yrs}}) + \$1,000 \times (PVIF_{12\%,10\text{yrs}})$$
$$= \$100 \times (5.650) + \$1,000 \times (.322) = \underline{\underline{\$887.00}}$$

Calculator Use Using the inputs shown below, you should find the value of the bond with a 12 percent required return to be $887.00.

Inputs: | 10 | 12 | 100 | 1000 |

Functions: | N | I | PMT | FV | CPT | PV |

Outputs: | 887.00 |

The bond would therefore sell at a *discount* of $113.00 ($1,000 par value − $887.00 value).

If, on the other hand, the required return fell to, say, 8 percent, the bond's value would be found as follows:

Table Use

$$B_0 = \$100 \times (PVIFA_{8\%,10\text{yrs}}) + \$1,000 \times (PVIF_{8\%,10\text{yrs}})$$
$$= \$100 \times (6.710) + \$1,000 \times (.463) = \underline{\underline{\$1,134.00}}$$

Calculator Use Using the inputs shown below, you should find the value of the bond with an 8 percent required return to be $1,134.20. Note that this value is more precise than the $1,134 value calculated using the rounded financial table factors.

Inputs: | 10 | 8 | 100 | 1000 |

Functions: | N | I | PMT | FV | CPT | PV |

Outputs: | 1134.20 |

The bond would therefore sell for a *premium* of about $134.00 ($1,134.00 value − $1,000 par value). The results of this and earlier calculations for Stills Company's bond values are summarized in Table 8.2 and graphically depicted in Figure 8.1.

TABLE 8.2	Bond Values for Various Required Returns (Stills Company's 10 Percent Coupon Interest Rate, 10-Year Maturity, $1,000 Par, January 1, 2001, Issue Paying Annual Interest)

Required return, k_d	Bond value, B_0	Status
12%	$ 887.00	Discount
10	1,000.00	Par value
8	1,134.00	Premium

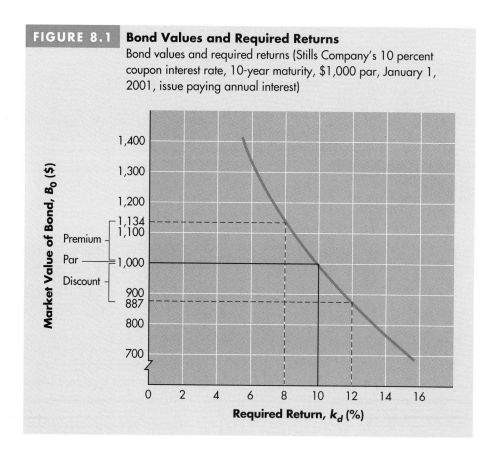

FIGURE 8.1 Bond Values and Required Returns
Bond values and required returns (Stills Company's 10 percent coupon interest rate, 10-year maturity, $1,000 par, January 1, 2001, issue paying annual interest)

TIME TO MATURITY AND BOND VALUES

Whenever the required return is different from the coupon interest rate, the amount of time to maturity affects bond value. An additional factor is whether required returns are constant or changing over the life of the bond.

Constant Required Returns   When the required return is different from the coupon interest rate and is assumed to be *constant until maturity*, the value of

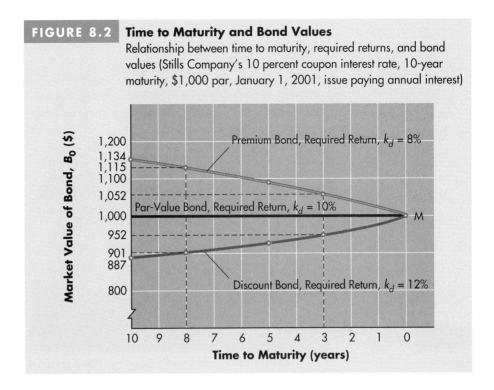

FIGURE 8.2   Time to Maturity and Bond Values
Relationship between time to maturity, required returns, and bond values (Stills Company's 10 percent coupon interest rate, 10-year maturity, $1,000 par, January 1, 2001, issue paying annual interest)

the bond will approach its par value as the passage of time moves the bond's value closer to maturity. (Of course, when the required return *equals* the coupon interest rate, the bond's value will remain at par until it matures.)

Example ▼ Figure 8.2 depicts the behavior of the bond values calculated earlier and presented in Table 8.2 for Stills Company's 10 percent coupon interest rate bond paying annual interest and having 10 years to maturity. Each of the three required returns, 12, 10, and 8 percent—is assumed to remain constant over the 10 years to the bond's maturity. The bond's value in each case approaches and ultimately equals the bond's $1,000 par value at its maturity.

At the 12 percent required return, the bond's discount declines with the passage of time, as the bond's value increases from $887 to $1,000. When the 10 percent required return equals the bond's coupon interest rate, its value remains unchanged at $1,000 over its maturity. Finally, at the 8 percent required return, the bond's premium will decline as its value drops from $1,134 to $1,000 at maturity. With the required return assumed to be constant to maturity, the bond's value approaches its $1,000 par or maturity value as the time to maturity declines. ▲

interest-rate risk
The chance that interest rates will change and thereby change the required return and bond value. Rising rates, which result in decreasing bond values, are of greatest concern.

Changing Required Returns   The chance that interest rates will change and thereby change the required return and bond value is called **interest-rate risk.** Because a rise in interest rates, and therefore the required return, results in a decrease in bond value, bondholders are typically more concerned with rising interest rates. The shorter the amount of time until a bond's maturity, the less responsive is its market value to a given change in the required return. In other words, short maturities have less interest-rate risk than do long maturities when all other features—coupon interest rate, par value, and interest-payment frequency—are the same.

Example ▼ The effect of changing required returns on bonds of differing maturity can be illustrated by using Stills Company's bond and Figure 8.2. If, as denoted by the dashed line at 8 years to maturity, the required return rises from 10 percent to 12 percent, the bond's value falls from $1,000 to $901—a 9.9 percent decrease. If the same change in required return had occurred with only 3 years to maturity, as denoted by the dashed line, the bond's value would have dropped to just $952—only a 4.8 percent decrease. Similar types of responses can be seen for the change in bond value associated with decreases in required returns. The shorter the time to maturity, the smaller the impact on bond value caused by a given **▲** change in the required return.

YIELD TO MATURITY (YTM)

yield to maturity (YTM)
The rate of return investors earn if they buy a bond at a specific price and hold it until maturity. Assumes that the issuer makes all scheduled interest and principal payments as promised.

When investors evaluate bonds, they commonly consider **yield to maturity (YTM),** which is the rate of return investors earn if they buy the bond at a specific price and hold it until maturity. The measure assumes, of course, that the issuer makes all scheduled interest and principal payments as promised. The yield to maturity on a bond with a current price equal to its par value (i.e., $B_0 = M$) will always equal the coupon interest rate. When the bond value differs from par, the yield to maturity will differ from the coupon interest rate.

Assuming that interest is paid annually, the yield to maturity on a bond can be found by solving Equation 8.3 for k_d. In other words, the current value, B_0, the annual interest, I, the par value, M, and the years to maturity, n, are known, and the required return must be found. The required return is the bond's yield to maturity. The YTM can be found by trial and error or by use of a financial calculator. The calculator provides accurate YTM values with minimum effort. Finding YTM is demonstrated in the following example.

Example ▼ The Stills Company bond, which currently sells for $1,080, has a 10 percent coupon interest rate and $1,000 par value, pays interest annually, and has 10 years to maturity. Because $B_0 = \$1,080$, $I = \$100$ (.10 × $1,000), $M = \$1,000$, and $n = 10$ years, substituting into Equation 8.3a, we get

$$\$1,080 = \$100 \times (PVIFA_{k_d,10\text{yrs}}) + \$1,000 \times (PVIF_{k_d,10\text{yrs}})$$

Our objective is to solve the equation for k_d—the YTM.

Trial and Error   Because we know that a required return, k_d, of 10 percent (which equals the bond's 10 percent coupon interest rate) would result in a value of $1,000, the discount rate that would result in $1,080 must be less than 10 percent. (Remember that the lower the discount rate, the higher the present value, and the higher the discount rate, the lower the present value.) Trying 9 percent, we get:

$$\$100 \times (PVIFA_{9\%,10\text{yrs}}) + \$1,000 \times (PVIF_{9\%,10\text{yrs}}) = \$100 \times (6.418) + \$1,000 \times (.422)$$
$$= \$641.80 + \$422.00 = \$1,063.80$$

Because the 9 percent rate is not quite low enough to bring the value up to $1,080, we next try 8 percent and get:

$$\$100 \times (PVIFA_{8\%,10\text{yrs}}) + \$1,000 \times (PVIF_{8\%,10\text{yrs}}) = \$100 \times (6.710) + \$1,000 \times (.463)$$
$$= \$671.00 + \$463.00 = \$1,134.00$$

Because the value at the 8 percent rate is too high and the value at the 9 percent rate is too low, the bond's yield to maturity must be between 8 and 9 percent. Because $1,063.80 is closer to $1,080, the YTM to the nearest whole percent is 9 percent. (By using *interpolation,* we could eventually find the more precise YTM value to be 8.77 percent.)

Calculator Use   [*Note:* Most calculators require *either* the present (B_0 in this case) or future (I and M in this case) values to be input as a negative number to calculate yield to maturity. That approach is used here.] Using the inputs shown below, you should find the YTM to be 8.766. Note that this number is more precise than the YTM value found before by using the trial-and-error approach.

Inputs:	10	-1080	100	1000		
Functions:	N	PV	PMT	FV	CPT	I
Outputs:						8.766

SEMIANNUAL INTEREST AND BOND VALUES

The procedure used to value bonds paying interest semiannually is similar to that shown in Chapter 6 for compounding interest more frequently than annually—except that here we need to find present value instead of future value. It involves:

1. Converting annual interest, I, to semiannual interest by dividing I by 2.
2. Converting the number of years to maturity, n, to the number of 6-month periods to maturity by multiplying n by 2.
3. Converting the required return for similar-risk bonds that also pay semiannual interest from an annual rate, k_d, to a semiannual rate by dividing k_d by 2.

Substituting these three changes into Equation 8.3 yields:

$$B_0 = \frac{I}{2} \times \left[\sum_{i=1}^{2n} \frac{1}{\left(1 + \frac{k_d}{2}\right)^t} \right] + M \times \left[\left(\frac{1}{1 + \frac{k_d}{2}}\right)^{2n} \right] \tag{8.4}$$

$$= \frac{I}{2} \times \left(PVIFA_{\frac{k_d}{2},2n} \right) + M \times \left(PVIF_{\frac{k_d}{2},2n} \right) \tag{8.4a}$$

An example will illustrate the application of this equation.

Example ▼ Assuming that the Stills Company bond pays interest semiannually and that the required return, k_d, is 12 percent for similar-risk bonds that also pay semiannual interest, substituting these values into Equation 8.4a yields:

$$B_0 = \frac{\$100}{2} \times \left(PVIFA_{\frac{12\%}{2},2 \times 10\text{yrs}} \right) + \$1,000 \times \left(PVIF_{\frac{12\%}{2},2 \times 10\text{yrs}} \right)$$

Table Use

$$B_0 = \$50 \times (PVIFA_{6\%,20 \text{ periods}}) + \$1,000 \times (PVIF_{6\%,20 \text{ periods}})$$
$$= \$50 \times (11.470) + \$1,000 \times (.312) = \underline{\underline{\$885.50}}$$

Calculator Use   When using a calculator to find bond value when interest is paid semiannually, we must double the number of periods and divide both the required return and the annual interest by 2. For the Stills Company bond, we would use 20 periods (2 × 10 years), a required return of 6 percent (12 percent ÷ 2), and an interest payment of $50 ($100 ÷ 2). Using those inputs, you should find the bond value with semiannual interest to be $885.30. Note that this value is more precise than the value calculated using the rounded financial table factors.

Inputs: `20`   `6`   `50`   `1000`

Functions: `N`   `I`   `PMT`   `FV`   `CPT`   `PV`

▲ Outputs: `885.30`

Comparing this result with the $887.00 value found earlier for annual compounding (see Table 8.2), we can see that the bond's value is lower when semiannual interest is paid. *This will always occur when the bond sells at a discount.* For bonds selling at a premium, the opposite will occur: The value with semiannual interest will be greater than with annual interest.

? Review **Q**uestions

8-4   Describe the basic procedure used to value a bond that pays *annual* interest. What procedure is used to value bonds paying interest *semiannually?*

8-5   What relationship between the required return and coupon interest rate will cause a bond to sell (**a**) at a discount? (**b**) at a premium? and (**c**) at its par value? Explain.

8-6   If the required return on a bond differs from its coupon interest rate and is assumed to be constant until maturity, describe the behavior of the bond value over the passage of time as the bond moves toward maturity.

8-7   As a risk-averse investor, to protect against the potential impact of rising interest rates on bond value, would you prefer bonds with short or long periods until maturity? Explain why.

8-8   What is meant by a bond's *yield to maturity (YTM)?*

COMMON STOCK VALUATION

Common stockholders expect to be rewarded through periodic cash dividends and an increasing—or at least nondeclining—share value. Like current owners, prospective owners frequently estimate the firm's value. They purchase the stock when they believe that it is *undervalued*—that its true value is greater than its market price. They sell the stock when they feel that it is *overvalued*—that its market price is greater than its true value. Here we consider some of the most popular stock valuation techniques.

ꝑERSONAL FINANCE PERSPECTIVE

Buy or Sell When Disaster Strikes?

In the month after agricultural giant Archer-Daniels-Midland was accused of price-fixing, its stock price dropped 15 percent. Faced with the company's uncertain future, many investors promptly sold their stock. But they should have looked instead at how similar disasters affected other large companies— like Exxon after the Valdez *oil spill, Philip Morris with its tobacco problems, and Intel's flawed Pentium chip. Big companies typically have the financial resources to recover, and despite setbacks, most eventually rebound. Investors who ride out the disaster or have the courage to buy in at a low price can earn rich rewards. Intel shareholders who bought after the stock fell 12 percent in late 1994 earned over 120 percent by the middle of 1995 and even more as technology stocks rode to new highs by late 1995.*

Individual investors should be cautious before buying on bad news, advise professional money managers. It's not easy to predict whether a company will turn itself around or be ruined by its misfortunes, but buying a company whose fundamentals are still solid can pay off over time. ●

THE BASIC STOCK VALUATION EQUATION

Like bonds, the value of a share of common stock is equal to the present value of all future benefits (dividends) it is expected to provide. Although a stockholder can earn capital gains by selling stock at a price above that originally paid, what is really sold is the right to all future dividends. Even stocks that are not expected to pay dividends in the foreseeable future have a value attributable to a distant dividend expected to result from sale of the company or liquidation of its assets. Therefore, from a valuation viewpoint *only dividends are relevant.*

By redefining terms, the basic valuation model in Equation 8.1 can be specified for common stock, as given in Equation 8.5:

$$P_0 = \frac{D_1}{(1+k_s)^1} + \frac{D_2}{(1+k_s)^2} + \cdots + \frac{D_\infty}{(1+k_s)^\infty} \tag{8.5}$$

where

P_0 = value of common stock
D_t = per-share dividend expected at the end of year t
k_s = required return on common stock

The equation can be simplified somewhat by redefining each year's dividend, D_t, in terms of anticipated growth. We will consider two cases here: zero growth and constant growth.

ZERO GROWTH

zero-growth model
An approach to dividend valuation that assumes a constant, nongrowing dividend stream.

The simplest approach to dividend valuation, the **zero-growth model**, assumes a constant, nongrowing dividend stream. In terms of the notation already introduced:

$$D_1 = D_2 = \cdots = D_\infty$$

Letting D_1 represent the amount of the annual dividend, Equation 8.5 under zero growth would reduce to:

$$P_0 = D_1 \times \sum_{t=1}^{\infty} \frac{1}{(1+k_s)^t} = D_1 \times (PVIFA_{k_s,\infty}) = D_1 \times \frac{1}{k_s} = \frac{D_1}{k_s} \tag{8.6}$$

The equation shows that with zero growth, the value of a share of stock would equal the present value of a perpetuity of D_1 dollars discounted at a rate k_s. Let's look at an example.

Example ▼ The dividend of Addison Company, an established textile producer, is expected to remain constant at $3 per share indefinitely. If the required return on its stock is 15 percent, the stock's value is $20 ($3 ÷ .15).

Preferred Stock Valuation Because preferred stock typically provides its holders with a fixed annual dividend over its assumed infinite life, *Equation 8.6 can be used to find the value of preferred stock.* The value of preferred stock can be estimated by substituting the stated dividend on the preferred stock for D_1 and the required return on the preferred stock for k_s, in Equation 8.6. For example, a preferred stock paying a $5 stated annual dividend and having a required return of 13 percent would have a value of $38.46 ($5 ÷ .13).

constant-growth model
A widely cited dividend valuation approach that assumes that dividends will grow at a constant rate that is less than the required return.

CONSTANT GROWTH

The most widely cited dividend valuation approach, the **constant-growth model**, assumes that dividends will grow at a constant rate, g, that is less than the required return, k_s. (The assumption that $k_s > g$ is a necessary mathematical condition for deriving this model.) By letting D_0 represent the most recent dividend, Equation 8.5 can be rewritten as follows:

$$P_0 = \frac{D_0 \times (1+g)^1}{(1+k_s)^1} + \frac{D_0 \times (1+g)^2}{(1+k_s)^2} + \cdots + \frac{D_0 \times (1+g)^\infty}{(1+k_s)^\infty} \qquad (8.7)$$

If we simplify Equation 8.7, it can be rewritten as follows:[5]

$$P_0 = \frac{D_1}{k_s - g} \qquad (8.8)$$

Gordon model
A common name for the *constant-growth model* that is widely cited in dividend valuation.

The constant-growth model in Equation 8.8 is commonly called the **Gordon model.** An example will show how it works.

E x a m p l e ▼ Honee Company, a small cosmetics company, from 1995 through 2000 paid the following per-share dividends:

Year	Dividend per share
2000	$1.40
1999	1.29
1998	1.20
1997	1.12
1996	1.05
1995	1.00

The annual growth rate of dividends is assumed to equal the expected constant rate of dividend growth, *g*. Using Appendix Table A-3 for the present value interest factor, *PVIF*, or a financial calculator in conjunction with the technique described for finding growth rates in Chapter 6, we find that the annual growth

---

[5]The calculations necessary to derive Equation 8.8 from Equation 8.7 follow. The first step is to multiply each side of Equation 8.7 by $(1 + k_s)/(1 + g)$ and subtract Equation 8.7 from the resulting expression. This yields

$$\frac{P_0 \times (1+k_s)}{1+g} - P_0 = D_0 - \frac{D_0 \times (1+g)^\infty}{(1+k_s)^\infty} \qquad (1)$$

Because k_s is assumed to be greater than *g*, the second term on the right side of Equation 1 should be zero. Thus,

$$P_0 \times \left(\frac{1+k_s}{1+g} - 1 \right) = D_0 \qquad (2)$$

Equation 2 is simplified as follows:

$$P_0 \times \left[\frac{(1+k_s) - (1+g)}{1+g} \right] = D_0 \qquad (3)$$

$$P_0 \times (k_s - g) = D_0 \times (1+g) \qquad (4)$$

$$P_0 = \frac{D_1}{k_s - g} \qquad (5)$$

Equation 5 equals Equation 8.8.

rate of dividends equals 7 percent.[6] The company estimates that its dividend in 2001, D_1, will equal $1.50. The required return, k_s, is assumed to be 15 percent. By substituting these values into Equation 8.8, the value of the stock is:

$$P_0 = \frac{\$1.50}{.15 - .07} = \frac{\$1.50}{.08} = \underline{\underline{\$18.75 \text{ per share}}}$$

Assuming that the values of D_1, k_s, and g are accurately estimated, Honee Company's stock value is $18.75 per share.

OTHER APPROACHES TO COMMON STOCK VALUATION

Many other approaches to common stock valuation exist. The more popular approaches include book value, liquidation value, and some type of a price/earnings multiple.

book value per share
The amount per share of common stock that would be received if all of the firm's assets were sold for their *exact book value* and if the proceeds remaining after paying all liabilities (including preferred stock) were divided among the common stockholders.

BOOK VALUE

Book value per share is simply the amount per share of common stock that would be received if all of the firm's assets were *sold for their exact book (accounting) value* and the proceeds remaining after paying all liabilities (including preferred stock) were divided among the common stockholders. This method lacks sophistication, and its reliance on historical balance sheet data ignores the firm's expected earnings potential. Further, it generally lacks any true relationship to the firm's value in the marketplace. Let us look at an example.

Example ▼ At year-end 2000, Honee Company's balance sheet shows total assets of $6 million, total liabilities including preferred stock of $4.5 million, and 100,000 shares of common stock outstanding. Its book value per share therefore would be:

$$\frac{\$6,000,000 - \$4,500,000}{100,000 \text{ shares}} = \underline{\underline{\$15 \text{ per share}}}$$

---

[6]The technique involves solving the following equation for g:

$$D_{2000} = D_{1995} \times (1 + g)^5$$

$$\frac{D_{1995}}{D_{2000}} = \frac{1}{(1 + g)^5} = PVIF_{g,5}$$

Two basic steps can be followed using the present value table. First, by dividing the earliest dividend ($D_{1995} = \$1.00$) by the most recent dividend ($D_{2000} = \$1.40$), a factor for the present value of one dollar, $PVIF$, of .714 ($\$1.00 \div \$1.40$) results. Although six dividends are shown, *they reflect only 5 years of growth*. The number of years of growth can alternatively be found by subtracting the earliest year from the most recent year, i.e., $2000 - 1995 = 5$ *years of growth*. By looking across the table at the present value interest factors, $PVIF$, for 5 years, the factor closest to .714 occurs at 7 percent (.713). Therefore, the growth rate of the dividends, rounded to the nearest whole percentage, is 7 percent.

Alternatively, a financial calculator can be used. (*Note:* Most calculators require either the PV or FV value to be input as a negative number to calculate an unknown interest or growth rate. That approach is used here.) Using the inputs shown below, you should find the growth rate to be 6.96 percent, which we round to 7 percent.

Inputs:	1.00	−1.40	5	
Functions:	PV	FV	N	CPT	I
Outputs:				6.96

Because this value assumes that assets could be sold for their book value, it may not represent the minimum price at which shares are valued in the marketplace. As a matter of fact, although most stocks sell above book value, it is not unusual to find stocks selling below book value when investors believe either that assets are overvalued or the firm's liabilities are understated. Therefore, book value is not a reliable basis on which to value stock.

LIQUIDATION VALUE

liquidation value per share
The *actual amount* per share of common stock to be received if all of the firm's assets were sold for their *market value,* liabilities (including preferred stock) were paid, and any remaining money were divided among the common stockholders.

Liquidation value per share is the *actual amount* per share of common stock that would be received if all of the firm's assets were sold for their *market value,* liabilities (including preferred stock) were paid, and any remaining money were divided among the common stockholders.[7] This measure is more realistic than book value—because it is based on current market values of the firm's assets—but it still fails to consider the earning power of those assets. An example will illustrate.

Example ▼ Honee Company found upon investigation that it could obtain only $5.25 million if it sold its assets today. The firm's liquidation value per share therefore would be:

$$\frac{\$5,250,000 - \$4,500,000}{100,000 \text{ shares}} = \$7.50 \text{ per share}$$

Ignoring liquidation expenses, this amount would be the firm's minimum value.

PRICE/EARNINGS (P/E) MULTIPLES

The *price/earnings (P/E) ratio,* introduced in Chapter 2, reflects the amount investors are willing to pay for each dollar of earnings. The average P/E ratio in a particular industry can be used as the guide to a firm's value—if it is assumed that investors value the earnings of that firm as they do the "average" firm in the industry. The **price/earnings multiple approach** is a popular technique to estimate the firm's share value, by multiplying the firm's expected earnings per share (EPS) by the average price/earnings (P/E) ratio for the industry. The average P/E ratio for the industry can be obtained from a source such as *Standard & Poor's Industrial Ratios.*

price/earnings multiple approach
A technique to estimate the firm's share value; calculated by multiplying the firm's expected earnings per share (EPS) by the average price/earnings (P/E) ratio for the industry.

    The use of P/E multiples is especially helpful in valuing firms that are not publicly traded, whereas market price quotations can be used to value a publicly traded firm. In any case, the price/earnings multiple approach is considered superior to the use of book or liquidation values because it considers *expected* earnings. An example will demonstrate the use of a price/earnings multiple.

Example ▼ Honee Company is expected to earn $2.60 per share next year (2001), based on an analysis of the firm's earnings trend and expected economic and industry conditions. The average price/earnings (P/E) ratio for firms in the same industry is 7.

---

[7]In the event of liquidation, creditors' claims must be satisfied first, then those of the preferred stockholders. Anything left goes to common stockholders.

Multiplying Honee's expected earnings per share (EPS) of $2.60 by this ratio gives us a value for the firm's shares of $18.20, assuming that investors will continue to measure the value of the average firm at 7 times its earnings.

So how much is Honee Company's stock "really" worth? That's a trick question, because there's no one right answer. It is important to recognize that the answer depends on the assumptions made and the techniques used. Professional securities analysts typically use a variety of models and techniques to value stocks. For example, an analyst might use the constant-growth model, liquidation value, and price/earnings (P/E) multiple to estimate the worth of a given stock. If the analyst feels comfortable with the estimates, he or she would value the stock at no more than the largest estimate. If the firm's estimated liquidation value per share exceeds its "going concern" value per share, estimated using one of the valuation models (zero- or constant-growth) or the P/E multiple approach, the firm would be viewed as "worth more dead than alive." In that case, the firm would lack sufficient earning power to justify its existence and should probably be liquidated.

? R e v i e w Q u e s t i o n s

8–9 Describe, compare, and contrast the *zero-growth* and *constant-growth* models that are frequently used to estimate common stock value.

8–10 Which common stock valuation model can be used to find the value of *preferred stock?* Describe its application in this case.

8–11 Explain each of the three other approaches to common stock valuation: (a) book value; (b) liquidation value; and (c) price/earnings (P/E) multiples. Which of these is considered the best?

DECISION MAKING AND COMMON STOCK VALUE

LG6

Valuation equations measure the stock value at a point in time based on expected return and risk. Any decisions of the financial manager that affect these variables can cause the value of the firm to change. Figure 8.3 depicts the relationship among financial decisions, return, risk, and stock value.

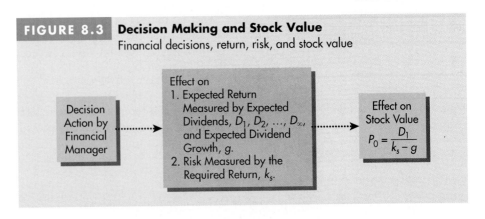

FIGURE 8.3 **Decision Making and Stock Value**
Financial decisions, return, risk, and stock value

Decision Action by Financial Manager

Effect on
1. Expected Return Measured by Expected Dividends, $D_1, D_2, \ldots, D_\infty$, and Expected Dividend Growth, g.
2. Risk Measured by the Required Return, k_s.

Effect on Stock Value
$$P_0 = \frac{D_1}{k_s - g}$$

CHANGES IN EXPECTED RETURN

Assuming that economic conditions remain stable, any management action that would cause current and prospective stockholders to raise their dividend expectations should increase the firm's value. In Equation 8.8, we can see that P_0 will increase for any increase in D_1 or g. Any action of the financial manager that will increase the level of expected returns without changing risk (the required return) should be undertaken, because it will positively affect owners' wealth. An example will illustrate.

Example ▼ Under the constant-growth model, Honee Company was found to have a share value of $18.75. On the following day, the firm announced a major technological breakthrough that would revolutionize its industry. Current and prospective stockholders would not adjust their required return of 15 percent as a result of this new information, but they would expect future dividends to increase. Specifically, they could expect that although the dividend next year, D_1, would remain at $1.50, the expected rate of growth thereafter would increase from 7 to 9 percent. If we substitute $D_1 = \$1.50$, $k_s = .15$, and $g = .09$ into Equation 8.8, the resulting value equals $25 [i.e., $1.50 ÷ (.15 − .09)]. The increased value therefore resulted from the higher expected future dividends reflected in the increase ▲ in the growth rate.

CHANGES IN RISK

Although k_s is defined as the required return, it is (as pointed out in Chapter 7) directly related to the nondiversifiable risk, which can be measured by beta. The *capital asset pricing model (CAPM)* given in Equation 7.7 is restated as Equation 8.9:

$$k_s = R_F + [b \times (k_m - R_F)] \tag{8.9}$$

With the risk-free rate, R_F, and the market return, k_m, held constant, the required return, k_s, depends directly on beta. In other words, any action taken by the financial manager that increases risk will also increase the required return. In Equation 8.8 we can see that with all else constant, an increase in the required return, k_s, will reduce share value, P_0. Likewise, a decrease in the required return will increase share value. Thus, any action of the financial manager that increases risk contributes toward a reduction in value, and any action that decreases risk contributes toward an increase in value. An example will illustrate.

Example ▼ Assume that Honee Company's 15 percent required return resulted from a risk-free rate of 9 percent, a market return of 13 percent, and a beta of 1.50. Substituting into the capital asset pricing model, Equation 8.9, we get a required return, k_s, of 15 percent:

$$k_s = 9\% + [1.50 \times (13\% - 9\%)] = \underline{\underline{15\%}}$$

With this return, the value of the firm, P_0, was calculated to be $18.75 in the earlier example (on pages 249–50).

Now imagine that the financial manager makes a decision that, without changing expected dividends, increases the firm's beta to 1.75. Assuming that R_F

and k_m remain at 9 and 13 percent, respectively, the required return will increase to 16 percent (i.e., 9% + [1.75 × (13% − 9%)]) to compensate stockholders for the increased risk. Substituting D_1 = \$1.50, k_s = .16, and g = .07 into the valuation equation, Equation 8.8, results in a share value of \$16.67 [i.e., \$1.50 ÷ (.16 − .07)]. As expected, raising the required return, without any corresponding increase in expected return, causes the firm's stock value to decline. Clearly, the financial manager's action was not in the owners' best interest.

COMBINED EFFECT

A financial decision rarely affects return and risk independently; most decisions affect both factors. In terms of the measures presented, with an increase in risk (beta, b) one would expect an increase in return (D_1 or g, or both), assuming that R_F and k_m remain unchanged. Depending on the size of the changes in these variables, the net effect on value can be assessed.

Example ▼ If we assume that the two changes illustrated for Honee Company in the preceding examples occur simultaneously, key variable values would be D_1 = \$1.50, k_s = .16, and g = .09. Substituting into the valuation model, we obtain a share price of \$21.43 [i.e., \$1.50 ÷ (.16 − .09)]. The net result of the decision, which increased return (g from 7 to 9 percent) as well as risk (b from + 1.50 to 1.75 and k_s from 15 to 16 percent), is positive, because the share price increased from \$18.75 to \$21.43. Assuming that the key variables are accurately measured, the decision appears to be in the best interest of the firm's owners, because it increases their wealth. ▲

? Review Questions

8-12   Explain the linkages among financial decisions, return, risk, and stock value. How do the *capital asset pricing model (CAPM)* and the *Gordon model* fit into this basic framework? Explain.

8-13   Assuming that all other variables remain unchanged, what impact would *each* of the following have on stock price? (a) The firm's beta increases. (b) The firm's required return decreases. (c) The dividend expected next year decreases. (d) The rate of growth in dividends is expected to increase. Explain your answers.

SUMMARY

LG1 **Describe the key inputs and basic model used in the valuation process.** Key inputs to the valuation process include cash flows (returns), timing, and the required return (risk). The value, or worth, of any asset is equal to the present value of all future cash flows it is *expected* to provide over the relevant time period. The key variable defini-

tions and the basic valuation model for any asset are summarized in Table 8.3.

LG2 **Apply the bond valuation model and describe the impact of required return and time to maturity on bond values.** The value of a bond is the present value of its interest payments plus the pres-

TABLE 8.3	Summary of Key Valuation Definitions and Formulas

Variable definitions

B_0 = bond value

CF_t = cash flow *expected* at the end of year t

D_1 = per-share dividend expected at the end of year *1*

g = constant rate of growth in dividends

I = annual interest on a bond

k = appropriate required return (discount rate)

k_d = required return on a bond

k_s = required return on common stock

M = par, or face, value of a bond

n = relevant time period, or number of years to maturity

P_0 = value of common stock

V_0 = value of the asset at time zero

Valuation formulas

Value of any asset:

$$V_0 = \frac{CF_1}{(1+k)^1} + \frac{CF_2}{(1+k)^2} + \cdots + \frac{CF_n}{(1+k)^n} \qquad \text{[Eq. 8.1]}$$

$$= [CF_1 \times (PVIF_{k,1})] + [CF_2 \times (PVIF_{k,2})] + \cdots + [CF_n \times (PVIF_{k,n})] \qquad \text{[Eq. 8.2]}$$

Bond value:

$$B_0 = I \times \left[\sum_{t=1}^{n} \frac{1}{(1+k_d)^t} \right] + M \times \left[\frac{1}{(1+k_d)^n} \right] \qquad \text{[Eq. 8.3]}$$

$$= I \times (PVIFA_{k_d,n}) + M \times (PVIF_{k_d,n}) \qquad \text{[Eq. 8.3a]}$$

Common stock value:

$$\text{Zero growth:} \qquad P_0 = \frac{D_1}{k_s} \quad \text{(also used to value preferred stock)} \qquad \text{[Eq. 8.6]}$$

$$\text{Constant growth:} \qquad P_0 = \frac{D_1}{k_s - g} \qquad \text{[Eq. 8.8]}$$

ent value of its par value. The key variable definitions and the basic valuation formula for a bond are summarized in Table 8.3. The discount rate used to determine bond value is the required return, which may differ from the bond's coupon interest rate. A bond can sell at a discount, at par, or at a premium, depending upon whether the required return is greater than, equal to, or less than its coupon interest rate. The amount of time to maturity affects bond values. Even if required return remains constant, the value of a bond will approach its par value as the passage of time moves the bond closer to maturity. The shorter the amount of time until a bond's maturity, the less responsive is its market value to a given change in the required return.

LG3 **Explain yield to maturity, its calculation, and the procedure used to value bonds that pay interest semiannually.** Yield to maturity (YTM) is the rate of return investors earn if they buy a bond at a specific price and hold it until maturity, assuming that the issuer makes all scheduled interest and principal payments as promised. YTM can be calculated by trial and error or by use of a financial calculator. Bonds that pay interest semiannually are valued by using the same procedure used to value bonds paying annual interest except that the interest payments are one-half of the annual interest payments, the number of periods is twice the number of years to maturity, and the required return is one-half of the stated annual required return on similar-risk bonds.

LG4 **Perform basic common stock valuation using both the zero-growth and constant-growth models.** The value of a share of common stock is the present value of all future dividends it is expected to provide over an infinite time horizon. Two cases of dividend growth—zero-growth and constant-growth—can be considered in common stock valuation. The key variable definitions and the basic valuation formulas for each of these cases are summarized in Table 8.3. The most widely cited model is the constant-growth (Gordon) model.

LG5 **Discuss the use of book value, liquidation value, and price/earnings multiples to estimate common stock values.** Book value per share is the amount per share of common stock that would be received if the firm sold all of its assets for their exact book (accounting) value, paid off its liabilities (including preferred stock), and divided the remaining funds among the common stockholders.

Liquidation value per share is the amount received by each shareholder if the firm sold its assets at their market value, paid off liabilities (including preferred stock), and distributed the remaining funds among the common stockholders. The price/earnings (P/E) multiple approach estimates stock value by multiplying the firm's expected earnings per share (EPS) by the average price/earnings (P/E) ratio for the industry. Of these three approaches, P/E multiples are the most popular in practice because, unlike book and liquidation value, they view the firm as a going concern whose value lies in its earning power rather than its asset values.

LG6 **Understand the relationships among financial decisions, return, risk, and the firm's value.** In a stable economy, any action of the financial manager that increases the level of expected return without changing risk should increase share value, and any action that reduces the level of expected return without changing risk should reduce share value. Similarly, any action that increases risk (required return) will reduce share value, and any action that reduces risk will increase share value. In the constant-growth model, returns are measured by next year's dividend and its growth rate, and risk is measured by the required return. Because most financial decisions affect both return and risk, an assessment of their combined effect on value must be part of the financial decision-making process.

SELF-TEST PROBLEMS   (Solutions in Appendix B)

ST 8-1   **Bond valuation**   Lahey Industries has a $1,000 par value bond with an 8 percent coupon interest rate outstanding. The bond has 12 years remaining to its maturity date.
    a. If interest is paid *annually*, what is the value of the bond when the required return is (1) 7 percent, (2) 8 percent, and (3) 10 percent?
    b. Indicate for each case in **a** whether the bond is selling at a discount, at a premium, or at its par value.
    c. Using the 10 percent required return, find the bond's value when interest is paid *semiannually*.

ST 8-2   **Yield to maturity**   Elliot Enterprises' bonds currently sell for $1,150, have an 11 percent coupon interest rate and a $1,000 par value, pay interest *annually*, and have 18 years to maturity.

a. Calculate the bonds' yield to maturity (YTM).

b. Compare the YTM calculated in **a** to the bonds' coupon interest rate, and use a comparison of the bonds' current price and their par value to explain this difference.

ST 8-3   Common stock valuation   Perry Motors' common stock currently pays an annual dividend of $1.80 per share. The required return on the common stock is 12 percent. Estimate the value of the common stock under each of the following dividend-growth-rate assumptions.

a. Dividends are expected to grow at an annual rate of 0 percent to infinity.

b. Dividends are expected to grow at a constant annual rate of 5 percent to infinity.

PROBLEMS

WARM-UP   LG1   8-1   Valuation fundamentals   Imagine that you are trying to evaluate the economics of purchasing an automobile. You expect the car to provide annual after-tax cash benefits of $1,200 and that you can sell the car for after-tax proceeds of $5,000 at the end of the planned 5-year ownership period. All funds for purchasing the car will be drawn from your savings, which are currently earning 6 percent after taxes.

a. Identify the cash flows, their timing, and the required return applicable to valuing the car.

b. What is the maximum price you would be willing to pay to acquire the car? Explain.

WARM-UP   LG1   8-2   Valuation of assets   Using the information provided in the table at the top of the next page, find the value of each asset.

Asset	Cash flow		Appropriate required return
	End of year	Amount	
A	1	$ 5,000	18%
	2	5,000	
	3	5,000	
B	1 through ∞	$ 300	15%
C	1	$ 0	16%
	2	0	
	3	0	
	4	0	
	5	35,000	
D	1 through 5	$ 1,500	12%
	6	8,500	
E	1	$ 2,000	14%
	2	3,000	
	3	5,000	
	4	7,000	
	5	4,000	
	6	1,000	

INTERMEDIATE **8-3** **Asset valuation and risk**   Dora Hayes wishes to estimate the value of an asset expected to provide cash inflows of $3,000 per year at the end of years 1 through 4 and $15,000 at the end of year 5. Her research indicates that she must earn 10 percent on low-risk assets, 15 percent on average-risk assets, and 22 percent on high-risk assets.

a. What is the most Dora should pay for the asset if it is classified as (1) low risk, (2) average risk, and (3) high risk?

b. If Dora is unable to assess the risk of the asset and wants to be certain she's making a good deal, based on your findings in **a,** what is the most she should pay? Why?

c. All else being the same, what effect does increasing risk have on the value of an asset? Explain in light of your findings in **a.**

INTERMEDIATE **8-4** **Basic bond valuation**   Redenour Supply has an issue of $1,000-par-value bonds with a 12 percent coupon interest rate outstanding. The issue pays interest *annually* and has 16 years remaining to its maturity date.

a. If bonds of similar risk are currently earning a 10 percent rate of return, how much should the Redenour Supply bond sell for today?

b. Describe the *two* possible reasons that similar-risk bonds are currently earning a return below the coupon interest rate on the Redenour Supply bond.

c. If the required return were at 12 instead of 10 percent, what would the current value of Redenour's bond be? Contrast this finding with your findings in **a** and discuss.

8-5   Bond valuation—Annual interest   Calculate the value of each of the bonds shown in the following table, all of which pay interest *annually.*

Bond	Par value	Coupon interest rate	Time to maturity	Required return
A	$1,000	14%	20 years	12%
B	1,000	8	16	8
C	100	10	8	13
D	500	16	13	18
E	1,000	12	10	10

8-6   Bond value and changing required returns   National Telephone has outstanding a bond issue that will mature to its $1,000 par value in 12 years. The bond has a coupon interest rate of 11 percent and pays interest *annually.*
   a. Find the value of the bond if the required return is (1) 11 percent, (2) 15 percent, and (3) 8 percent.
   b. Plot your findings in **a** on a set of required return (*x* axis)–market value of bond (*y* axis) axes.
   c. Use your findings in **a** and **b** to discuss the relationship between the coupon interest rate on a bond and the required return and the market value of the bond relative to its par value.
   d. What two reasons cause the required return to differ from the coupon interest rate?

8-7   Bond value and time—Constant required returns   Pecos Manufacturing has just issued a 15-year, 12 percent coupon interest rate, $1,000-par bond that pays interest *annually.* The required return is currently 14 percent, and the company is certain it will remain at 14 percent until the bond matures in 15 years.
   a. Assuming that the required return does remain at 14 percent until maturity, find the value of the bond with (1) 15 years, (2) 12 years, (3) 9 years, (4) 6 years, (5) 3 years, and (6) 1 year to maturity.
   b. Plot your findings on a set of time to maturity (*x* axis)–market value of bond (*y* axis) axes constructed similarly to Figure 8.2.
   c. All else remaining the same, when the required return differs from the coupon interest rate and is assumed to be constant to maturity, what happens to the bond value as time moves toward maturity? Explain in light of the graph in **b**.

8-8   Bond value and time—Changing required returns   Lynn Parsons is considering investing in either of two outstanding bonds. The bonds both have $1,000 par values and 11 percent coupon interest rates and pay *annual* interest. Bond A has exactly 5 years to maturity, and bond B has 15 years to maturity.
   a. Calculate the value of bond A if the required return is (1) 8 percent, (2) 11 percent, and (3) 14 percent.

b. Calculate the value of bond B if the required return is (1) 8 percent, (2) 11 percent, and (3) 14 percent.

c. From your findings in **a** and **b,** complete the following table, and discuss the relationship between time to maturity and changing required returns.

Required return	Value of bond A	Value of bond B
8%	?	?
11	?	?
14	?	?

d. If Lynn wanted to minimize interest-rate risk, which bond should she purchase? Why?

   8-9 **Yield to maturity** The Salem Company bond currently sells for $955, has a 12 percent coupon interest rate and $1,000 par value, pays interest *annually,* and has 15 years to maturity.
INTERMEDIATE
a. Calculate the yield to maturity (YTM) on this bond.
b. Explain the relationship that exists between the coupon interest rate and yield to maturity and the par value and market value of a bond.

 8-10 **Yield to maturity** Each of the bonds shown in the table below pays interest *annually.*
INTERMEDIATE

Bond	Par value	Coupon interest rate	Time to maturity	Current value
A	$1,000	9%	8 years	$ 820
B	1,000	12	16	1,000
C	500	12	12	560
D	1,000	15	10	1,120
E	1,000	5	3	900

a. Calculate the yield to maturity (YTM) for each bond.
b. What relationship exists between the coupon interest rate and yield to maturity and the par value and market value of a bond? Explain.

   8-11 **Bond valuation—Semiannual interest** Find the value of a bond maturing in 6 years, with a $1,000 par value and a coupon interest rate of 10 percent (5 percent paid semiannually) if the required return on similar-risk bonds is 14 percent annual interest (7 percent paid semiannually).
INTERMEDIATE

  8-12 **Bond valuation—Semiannual interest** Calculate the value of each of the bonds shown in the following table, all of which pay interest *semiannually.*
INTERMEDIATE

Bond	Par value	Coupon interest rate	Time to maturity	Required return
A	$1,000	10%	12 years	8%
B	1,000	12	20	12
C	500	12	5	14
D	1,000	14	10	10
E	100	6	4	14

8-13 **Bond valuation—Quarterly interest**   Calculate the value of a $5,000-par-value bond paying quarterly interest at an annual coupon interest rate of 10 percent and having 10 years until maturity if the required return on similar-risk bonds is currently a 12 percent annual rate paid *quarterly.*

8-14 **Common stock valuation—Zero growth**   Cable Enterprises is a mature firm in the machine-tool-component industry. The firm's most recent common stock dividend was $2.40 per share. Due to its maturity as well as stable sales and earnings, the firm's management feels that dividends will remain at the current level for the foreseeable future.

a. If the required return is 12 percent, what will be the value of Cable Enterprises' common stock?

b. If the firm's risk as perceived by market participants suddenly increases, causing the required return to rise to 20 percent, what will be the common stock value?

c. Based on your findings in **a** and **b,** what impact does risk have on value? Explain.

8-15 **Preferred stock valuation**   Poltak Stamping wishes to estimate the value of its outstanding preferred stock. The preferred issue has an $80 par value and pays an annual dividend of $6.40 per share. Similar-risk preferred stocks are currently earning a 9.3 percent annual rate of return.

a. What is the market value of the outstanding preferred stock?

b. If an investor purchases the preferred stock at the value calculated in **a,** how much does she gain or lose per share if she sells the stock when the required return on similar-risk preferreds has risen to 10.5 percent? Explain.

8-16 **Common stock value—Constant growth**   Use the constant-growth model (Gordon model) to find the value of each firm in the following table.

Firm	Dividend expected next year	Dividend growth rate	Required return
A	$1.20	8%	13%
B	4.00	5	15
C	.65	10	14
D	6.00	8	9
E	2.25	8	20

INTERMEDIATE

8-17 **Common stock value—Constant growth** Moody Boiler Company has paid the dividends shown in the following table over the past 6 years:

Year	Dividend per share
2000	$2.87
1999	2.76
1998	2.60
1997	2.46
1996	2.37
1995	2.25

The firm's dividend per share next year is expected to be $3.02.

a. If you can earn 13 percent on similar-risk investments, what is the most you would pay per share for this firm?

b. If you can earn only 10 percent on similar-risk investments, what is the most you would be willing to pay per share?

c. Compare and contrast your findings in **a** and **b,** and discuss the impact of changing risk on share value.

CHALLENGE

8-18 **Common stock value—Both growth models** You are evaluating the potential purchase of a small business currently generating $42,500 of after-tax cash flow $(D_0 = \$42,500)$. Based on a review of similar-risk investment opportunities, you must earn an 18 percent rate of return on the proposed purchase. Because you are relatively uncertain about future cash flows, you decide to estimate the firm's value using two possible cash flow, growth rate assumptions.

a. What is the firm's value if cash flows are expected to grow at an annual rate of 0 percent to infinity?

b. What is the firm's value if cash flows are expected to grow at a constant annual rate of 7 percent to infinity?

INTERMEDIATE

8-19 **Book and liquidation value** The balance sheet for Grannis Mill Company is as follows.

Balance Sheet Grannis Mill Company December 31			
Assets		**Liabilities and stockholders' equity**	
Cash	$ 40,000	Accounts payable	$100,000
Marketable securities	60,000	Notes payable	30,000
Accounts receivable	120,000	Accrued wages	30,000
Inventories	160,000	Total current liabilities	$160,000
Total current assets	$380,000	Long-term debt	$180,000
Land and buildings (net)	$150,000	Preferred stock	$ 80,000
Machinery and equipment	250,000	Common stock (10,000 shares)	360,000
Total fixed assets (net)	$400,000		
Total assets	$780,000	Total liabilities and stockholders' equity	$780,000

Additional information with respect to the firm is available:
(1) Preferred stock can be liquidated at book value.
(2) Accounts receivable and inventories can be liquidated at 90 percent of book value.
(3) The firm has 10,000 shares of common stock outstanding.
(4) All interest and dividends are currently paid up.
(5) Land and buildings can be liquidated at 130 percent of book value.
(6) Machinery and equipment can be liquidated at 70 percent of book value.
(7) Cash and marketable securities can be liquidated at book value.

Given this information, answer the following:
a. What is Grannis Mill's book value per share?
b. What is its liquidation value per share?
c. Compare, contrast, and discuss the values found in **a** and **b**.

  8-20   **Valuation with price/earnings multiples**   For each of the firms shown in the following table, use the data given to estimate their common stock value employing price/earnings (P/E) multiples.

Firm	Expected EPS	Price/earnings multiple
A	$3.00	6.2
B	4.50	10.0
C	1.80	12.6
D	2.40	8.9
E	5.10	15.0

 8-21   **Management action and stock value**   Blanding Enterprises' most recent dividend was $3 per share, its expected annual rate of dividend growth is 5 percent, and the required return is now 15 percent. A variety of proposals are being considered by management to redirect the firm's activities. For each of the following proposed actions, determine the impact on share price and indicate the best alternative.
a. Do nothing, which will leave the key financial variables unchanged.
b. Invest in a new machine that will increase the dividend growth rate to 6 percent and lower the required return to 14 percent.
c. Eliminate an unprofitable product line, which will increase the dividend growth rate to 7 percent and raise the required return to 17 percent.
d. Merge with another firm, which will reduce the growth rate to 4 percent and raise the required return to 16 percent.
e. Acquire a subsidiary operation from another manufacturer. The acquisition should increase the dividend growth rate to 8 percent and increase the required return to 17 percent.

  8-22   **Integrative—Valuation and CAPM formulas**   Given the information on the next page for the stock of Foster Company, calculate its beta.

Current price per share of common	$50.00
Expected dividend per share next year	$ 3.00
Constant annual dividend growth rate	9%
Risk-free rate of return	7%
Return on market portfolio	10%

CHALLENGE

8-23 Integrative—Risk and valuation RPM Enterprises has a beta of 1.20, the risk-free rate of return is currently 10 percent, and the market return is 14 percent. The company, which plans to pay a dividend of $2.60 per share in the coming year, anticipates that its future dividends will increase at an annual rate consistent with that experienced over the 1994–2000 period, when the following dividends were paid:

Year	Dividend per share	Year	Dividend per share
2000	$2.45	1996	$1.82
1999	2.28	1995	1.80
1998	2.10	1994	1.73
1997	1.95		

a. Use the capital asset pricing model (CAPM) to determine the required return on RPM Enterprises' stock.
b. Using the constant-growth model and your finding in a, estimate the value of RPM Enterprises' stock.
c. Explain what effect, if any, a decrease in beta would have on the value of RPM's stock.

CHALLENGE

8-24 Integrative—Valuation and CAPM Pickney Steel Company wishes to determine the value of Acme Foundry, a firm that it is considering acquiring for cash. Pickney wishes to use the capital asset pricing model (CAPM) to determine the applicable discount rate to use as an input to the constant growth valuation model. Acme's stock is not publicly traded. After studying the betas of firms similar to Acme that are publicly traded, Pickney believes that an appropriate beta for Acme's stock would be 1.25. The risk-free rate is currently 9 percent, and the market return is 13 percent. Acme's historic dividend per share for each of the past 6 years is shown in the following table.

Year	Dividend per share
2000	$3.44
1999	3.28
1998	3.15
1997	2.90
1996	2.75
1995	2.45

a. Given that Acme is expected to pay a dividend of $3.68 next year, determine the maximum cash price Pickney should pay for each share of Acme.
b. Discuss the use of the CAPM for estimating the value of common stock, and describe the effect on the resulting value of Acme of:
   (1) A decrease in its dividend growth rate of 2 percent from that exhibited over the 1995–2000 period.
   (2) A decrease in its beta to 1.

CASE   Chapter 8   **Assessing the Impact of Suarez Manufacturing's Proposed Risky Investment on its Bond and Stock Values**

Early in 2001, Inez Marcus, the chief financial officer for Suarez Manufacturing, was given the task of assessing the impact of a proposed risky investment on the firm's bond and stock values. To perform the necessary analysis, Inez gathered the following relevant data on the firm's bonds and stock.

Bonds   The firm has one bond issue currently outstanding. It has a $1,000 par value, a 9 percent coupon interest rate, and 18 years remaining to maturity. Interest on the bond is paid *annually,* and the bond's required return is currently 8 percent. After a great deal of research and consultation, Inez concluded that the proposed investment would not violate any of the bond's numerous provisions. Because the proposed investment will increase the overall risk of the firm, she expects that if it is undertaken, the required return on these bonds will increase to 10 percent.

Stock   During the immediate past 5 years (1996–2000) the annual dividends paid on the firm's common stock were as follows:

Year	Dividend per share
2000	$1.90
1999	1.70
1998	1.55
1997	1.40
1996	1.30

The firm expects that without the proposed investment the dividend in 2001 will be $2.09 per share and the historic annual rate of growth (rounded to the nearest whole percent) will continue in the future. Currently, the required return on the common stock is 14 percent. Inez's research indicates that if the proposed investment is undertaken, the 2001 dividend will rise to $2.15 per share and the annual rate of dividend growth will increase to 13 percent. As a result of the increased risk associated with the proposed risky investment, the required return on the common stock is expected to increase by 2 percent to an annual rate of 16 percent.

Armed with the preceding data, Inez must now assess the impact of the proposed risky investment on the market value of Suarez's bonds and stock. To simplify her calculations, she plans to round the historic growth rate in common stock dividends to the nearest whole percent.

Required

a. Find the *current* value of each of Suarez Manufacturing's bonds.

b. Find the *current* value per share of Suarez Manufacturing's common stock.

c. Find the value of Suarez's bonds in the event that it *undertakes the proposed risky investment*. Compare this value to that found in **a.** What effect would the proposed investment have on the firm's bondholders? Explain.

d. Find the value of Suarez's common stock in the event that it *undertakes the proposed risky investment* and assuming that the dividend growth rate increases to 13 percent. Compare this value to that found in **b.** What effect would the proposed investment have on the firm's stockholders? Explain.

e. On the basis of your findings in **c** and **d,** who wins and who loses as a result of undertaking the proposed risky investment? Should the firm do it? Why?

Web Exercise

GOTO web site www.smartmoney.com. In the left column Click on BOND INVESTING. Then click on BOND CALCULATOR which is located down the page under the column "UNDERSTANDING BONDS." Read the instructions on how to use the bond calculator. Using the bond calculator:

1. Calculate the yield to maturity (YTM) for a bond whose coupon rate is 7.5 percent with maturity date of July 31, 2090, which you bought for 95.

2. What is the YTM of the above bond if you bought it for 105? For 100?

3. Change the yield % box to 8.5. What would be the price of this bond?

4. Change the yield % box to 6.5. What is this bond's price?

5. Change the maturity date to 2003 and reset yield % to 6.5. What is the price of this bond?

6. Why is the price of the bond in question 5 lower than the price of the bond in question 4?

Now GOTO www.marketguide.com. Click on RESEARCH at the top of the page. Enter LUV, and click on PRICE CHARTS.

7. What was Southwest Airlines' highest price in this 12-month period? What was its lowest price? Has its price been stable or dynamic? Increasing or decreasing?

Click on PERFORMANCE.

8. What has been the price performance YTD for Southwest Airlines? For the S&P 500?

PART 3

LONG-TERM INVESTMENT DECISIONS

CAPITAL BUDGETING AND CASH FLOW PRINCIPLES

LEARNING GOALS

LG1 Understand the key capital expenditure motives and the steps in the capital budgeting process.

LG2 Define the basic terminology used to describe projects, funds availability, decision approaches, and cash flow patterns.

LG3 Discuss the major components of relevant cash flows, expansion versus replacement cash flows, sunk costs and opportunity costs, and international capital budgeting and long-term investments.

LG4 Calculate the initial investment associated with a proposed capital expenditure, given relevant data.

LG5 Determine relevant operating cash inflows using the income statement format.

LG6 Find the terminal cash flow, given relevant data.

ACROSS *the* DISCIPLINES

Before committing resources to expand, replace, or renew fixed assets or to undertake other types of long-term projects, firms carefully estimate and analyze the expected benefits from these expenditures. This evaluation and selection process is called capital budgeting. We address this important topic in finance in two chapters. This chapter outlines the steps in the capital budgeting process and explains how the key cash flows that are inputs to it are developed. Chapter 9 is important to:

- **accounting personnel** who will provide revenue, cost, depreciation, and tax data for use both in monitoring existing projects and developing cash flow projections for proposed projects.
- **information systems analysts** will maintain and facilitate the retrieval of cash flow data on both completed and existing projects.
- **management** because it decides which of the proposed projects that are acceptable will be of greatest value to the company.
- **the marketing department,** which will submit proposals for new products and the expansion of existing product lines.
- **operations,** which will submit proposals for the acquisition of new equipment and plants.

THE CAPITAL BUDGETING DECISION PROCESS

Long-term investments represent sizable outlays of funds that commit a firm to some course of action. Consequently, the firm needs procedures to analyze and properly select its long-term investments. It must be able to measure relevant cash flows and apply appropriate decision techniques. As time passes, fixed assets may become obsolete or may require an overhaul; at these points, too, financial decisions may be required. **Capital budgeting** is the process of evaluating and selecting long-term investments consistent with the firm's goal of owner wealth maximization. Firms typically make a variety of long-term investments, but the most common for the manufacturing firm is in *fixed assets,* which include property (land), plant, and equipment. These assets, often referred to as *earning assets,* generally provide the basis for the firm's earning power and value. Because firms treat capital budgeting (investment) and financing decisions *separately,* both this and the following chapter concentrate on fixed-asset acquisition without regard to the specific method of financing used. We begin by discussing the motives for capital expenditure.

capital budgeting
The process of evaluating and selecting long-term investments that are consistent with the firm's goal of owner wealth maximization.

CAPITAL EXPENDITURE MOTIVES

A **capital expenditure** is an outlay of funds by the firm that is expected to produce benefits over a period of time *greater than* one year. An **operating expenditure** is an outlay resulting in benefits received *within* one year. Fixed asset outlays are capital expenditures, but not all capital expenditures are classified as fixed assets. A $60,000 outlay for a new machine with a usable life of 15 years is a capital expenditure that would appear as a fixed asset on the firm's balance sheet. A $60,000 outlay for advertising that produces benefits over a long period is also a capital expenditure, but would rarely be shown as a fixed asset.

Capital expenditures are made for many reasons. The basic motives for capital expenditures are to expand, replace, or renew fixed assets or to obtain some other less tangible benefit over a long period. Table 9.1 describes the key motives for making capital expenditures.

capital expenditure
An outlay of funds by the firm that is expected to produce benefits over a period of time *greater than* one year.

operating expenditure
An outlay of funds by the firm resulting in benefits received *within* one year.

STEPS IN THE PROCESS

The **capital budgeting process** consists of five distinct but interrelated steps. It begins with *proposal generation,* followed by *review and analysis, decision making, implementation,* and *follow-up.* Table 9.2 on page 271 describes these steps. Each step in the process is important. Review and analysis and decision making—steps 2 and 3—consume the majority of time and effort, however. Follow-up (step 5) is an important, but often ignored, step aimed at allowing the firm to keep improving the accuracy of its cash flow estimates.

Because of their fundamental importance, primary attention in this and the following chapter is given to review and analysis and decision making.

capital budgeting process
Five distinct but interrelated steps: proposal generation, review and analysis, decision making, implementation, and follow-up.

TABLE 9.1	Key Motives for Making Capital Expenditures
Motive	**Description**
Expansion	The most common motive for a capital expenditure is to expand the level of operations—usually through acquisition of fixed assets. A growing firm often needs to acquire new fixed assets rapidly, such as the purchase of property and plant facilities.
Replacement	As a firm's growth slows and it reaches maturity, most capital expenditures will be made to replace or renew obsolete or worn-out assets. Each time a machine requires a major repair, the outlay for the repair should be compared to the outlay to replace the machine and the benefits of replacement.
Renewal	Renewal, an alternative to replacement, may involve rebuilding, overhauling, or retrofitting existing fixed assets. For example, an existing drill press could be renewed by replacing its motor, or a physical facility could be renewed by rewiring or adding air conditioning. To improve efficiency, both replacement and renewal of existing machinery may be suitable solutions.
Other purposes	Some capital expenditures do not result in the acquisition or transformation of tangible fixed assets. Instead, they involve a long-term commitment of funds by the firm in expectation of a future return. These expenditures include outlays for advertising, research and development, management consulting, and new products. Other capital expenditure proposals—such as the installation of pollution-control and safety devices mandated by the government—are difficult to evaluate because they provide intangible returns rather than clearly measurable cash flows.

BASIC TERMINOLOGY

Before we develop the concepts, techniques, and practices related to the capital budgeting process, it will be useful to explain some basic terminology. In addition, we present some key assumptions that are used to simplify the discussion in the remainder of this chapter as well as in Chapter 10.

INDEPENDENT VERSUS MUTUALLY EXCLUSIVE PROJECTS

independent projects
Projects whose cash flows are unrelated or independent of one another; the acceptance of one *does not eliminate* the others from further consideration.

The two most common project types are (1) independent projects and (2) mutually exclusive projects. **Independent projects** are those whose cash flows are unrelated or independent of one another; the acceptance of one *does not eliminate* the others from further consideration. If a firm has unlimited funds to invest, all the independent projects that meet its minimum acceptance criterion can be implemented. For example, a firm with unlimited funds may be faced with three acceptable independent projects—(1) installing air conditioning in the plant, (2) acquiring a small supplier, and (3) purchasing a new computer system. Clearly, the acceptance of any one of these projects does not eliminate the others from further consideration; all three could be undertaken.

mutually exclusive projects
Projects that compete with one another, so that the acceptance of one *eliminates* the others from further consideration.

Mutually exclusive projects are those that have the same function and therefore compete with one another. The acceptance of one *eliminates* from further consideration all other similar-function projects. For example, a firm in need of increased production capacity could obtain it by (1) expanding its plant, (2) acquiring another company, or (3) contracting with another company for production. Clearly, the acceptance of one eliminates the need for either of the others.

| TABLE 9.2 | **Steps in the Capital Budgeting Process** |

Steps (listed in order)	Description
1. Proposal generation	Proposals for capital expenditures are made at all levels within a business organization. To stimulate a flow of ideas, many firms offer cash rewards for proposals that are ultimately adopted. Capital expenditure proposals typically travel from the originator to a reviewer at a higher level in the organization. Clearly, proposals that require large outlays will be much more carefully scrutinized than less costly ones.
2. Review and analysis	Capital expenditure proposals are formally reviewed (1) to assess their appropriateness in light of the firm's overall objectives and plans and, more important, (2) to evaluate their economic validity. The proposed costs and benefits are estimated and then converted into a series of relevant cash flows. Various capital budgeting techniques are applied to these cash flows to measure the investment merit of the potential outlay. In addition, various aspects of the *risk* associated with the proposal are evaluated. Once the economic analysis is completed, a summary report, often with a recommendation, is submitted to the decision maker(s).
3. Decision making	The actual dollar outlay and the importance of a capital expenditure determine the organizational level at which the expenditure decision is made. Firms typically delegate capital expenditure authority on the basis of certain dollar limits. Generally, the board of directors reserves the right to make final decisions on capital expenditures requiring outlays beyond a certain amount. Inexpensive capital expenditures, such as the purchase of a hammer for $15, are treated as operating outlays not requiring formal analysis.[a] Generally, firms operating under critical time constraints with respect to production often give the plant manager the power to make decisions necessary to keep the production line moving.
4. Implementation	Once a proposal has been approved and funding has been made available,[b] the implementation phase begins. For minor outlays, the expenditure is made and payment is rendered. For major expenditures, greater control is required. Often the expenditures for a single proposal may occur in phases, each outlay requiring the signed approval of company officers.
5. Follow-up	Involves monitoring the results during the operating phase of a project. Comparison of actual costs and benefits with those expected and those of previous projects is vital. When actual outcomes deviate from projected outcomes, action may be required to cut the costs, improve benefits, or possibly terminate the project. Analysis of deviations of actual from forecast values provides data that can be used to improve the capital budgeting process, particularly the accuracy of cash flow estimates.

[a]There is a certain dollar limit beyond which outlays are *capitalized* (i.e., treated as a fixed asset) and *depreciated* rather than *expensed*. This dollar limit depends largely on what the U.S. Internal Revenue Service will permit. In accounting, the issue of whether to capitalize or expense an outlay is resolved by using the *principle of materiality*, which suggests that any outlays deemed material (i.e., large) relative to the firm's scale of operations should be capitalized, whereas others should be expensed in the current period.

[b]Capital expenditures are often approved as part of the annual budgeting process, although funding will not be made available until the budget is implemented—frequently as long as 6 months after approval.

unlimited funds
The financial situation in which a firm is able to accept all independent projects that provide an acceptable return.

capital rationing
The financial situation in which a firm has only a fixed number of dollars to allocate among competing capital expenditures.

UNLIMITED FUNDS VERSUS CAPITAL RATIONING

The availability of funds for capital expenditures affects the firm's decisions. If a firm has **unlimited funds** for investment, making capital budgeting decisions is quite simple: All independent projects that will provide returns greater than some predetermined level can be accepted.

Typically, though, firms are not in such a situation; they instead operate under **capital rationing.** This means that they have only a fixed number of dollars available for capital expenditures and that numerous projects will compete for these dollars. Therefore the firm must ration its funds by allocating them to projects that will maximize share value. Procedures for dealing with capital rationing are presented in Chapter 10. The discussions that follow in this chapter assume unlimited funds.

ACCEPT–REJECT VERSUS RANKING APPROACHES

accept–reject approach
The evaluation of capital expenditure proposals to determine whether they meet the firm's minimum acceptance criterion.

ranking approach
The ranking of capital expenditure projects on the basis of some predetermined measure, such as the rate of return.

Two basic approaches to capital budgeting decisions are available. The **accept–reject approach** involves evaluating capital expenditure proposals to determine whether they meet the firm's minimum acceptance criterion. This approach can be used when the firm has unlimited funds, as a preliminary step when evaluating mutually exclusive projects, or in a situation in which capital must be rationed. In these cases, only acceptable projects should be considered.

The second method, the **ranking approach**, involves ranking projects on the basis of some predetermined measure, such as the rate of return. The project with the highest return is ranked first, and the project with the lowest return is ranked last. Only acceptable projects should be ranked. Ranking is useful in selecting the "best" of a group of mutually exclusive projects and in evaluating projects with a view to capital rationing.

CONVENTIONAL VERSUS NONCONVENTIONAL CASH FLOW PATTERNS

conventional cash flow pattern
An initial outflow followed by only a series of inflows.

nonconventional cash flow pattern
A pattern in which an initial outflow is *not* followed by only a series of inflows.

Cash flow patterns associated with capital investment projects can be classified as *conventional* or *nonconventional*. A **conventional cash flow pattern** consists of an initial outflow followed by only a series of inflows. For example, a firm may spend $10,000 today and as a result expect to receive equal annual cash inflows of $2,000 each year for the next 8 years, as depicted on the time line in Figure 9.1.[1]

A **nonconventional cash flow pattern** is one in which an initial outflow is *not* followed by only a series of inflows. For example, the purchase of a machine may

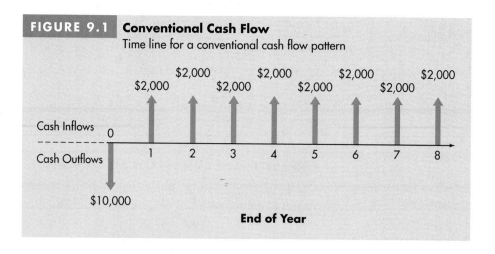

FIGURE 9.1   Conventional Cash Flow
Time line for a conventional cash flow pattern

[1]Arrows rather than plus or minus signs are frequently used on time lines to distinguish between cash inflows and cash outflows. Upward-pointing arrows represent cash inflows (positive cash flows), and downward-pointing arrows represent cash outflows (negative cash flows).

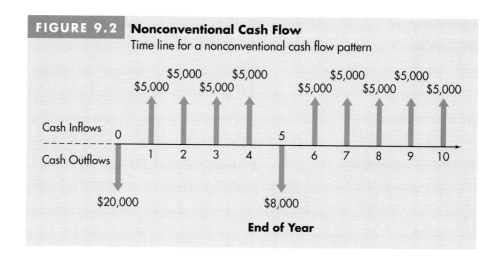

FIGURE 9.2 **Nonconventional Cash Flow**
Time line for a nonconventional cash flow pattern

require an initial cash outflow of $20,000 and may generate cash inflows of $5,000 each year for 4 years. In the fifth year after purchase, an outflow of $8,000 may be required to overhaul the machine, after which it generates inflows of $5,000 each year for 5 more years. This nonconventional pattern is illustrated on the time line in Figure 9.2.

Difficulties often arise in evaluating projects with nonconventional patterns of cash flow. *The discussions in the remainder of this chapter and in the following chapter are therefore limited to the evaluation of conventional patterns.*

ANNUITY VERSUS MIXED STREAM CASH FLOWS

annuity
A stream of equal annual cash flows.

mixed stream
A series of cash flows exhibiting any pattern other than that of an annuity.

As pointed out in Chapter 6, an **annuity** is a stream of equal annual cash flows. A series of cash flows exhibiting any pattern other than that of an annuity is a **mixed stream** of cash flows. The cash inflows of $2,000 per year (for 8 years) in Figure 9.1 are inflows from an annuity, whereas the unequal pattern of inflows in Figure 9.3 (page 274) represents a mixed stream. As you observed in Chapter 6, time value of money techniques are much simpler to apply when the pattern of cash flows is an annuity.

Review Questions

9-1   What is *capital budgeting?* How do capital expenditures relate to the capital budgeting process? Do all capital expenditures involve fixed assets? Explain.

9-2   What are the key motives for making capital expenditures? Discuss, compare, and contrast them.

9-3   Briefly describe each of the five steps involved in the capital budgeting process.

9-4   Define and differentiate between each of the following sets of capital budgeting terms: (a) independent versus mutually exclusive projects; (b) unlimited funds versus capital rationing; (c) accept–reject versus ranking approaches; (d) conventional versus nonconventional cash flow patterns; and (e) annuity versus mixed stream cash flows.

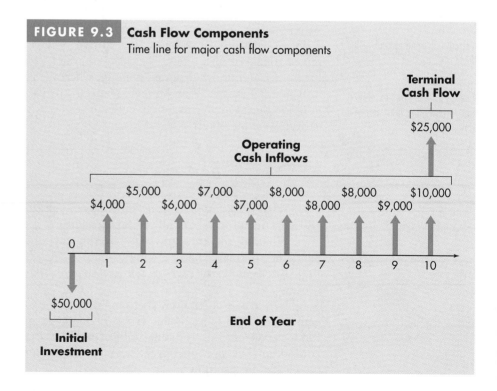

THE RELEVANT CASH FLOWS

relevant cash flows
The incremental after-tax cash outflow (investment) and resulting subsequent inflows associated with a proposed capital expenditure.

incremental cash flows
The *additional* cash flows—outflows or inflows—expected to result from a proposed capital expenditure.

To evaluate capital expenditure alternatives, the firm must determine the **relevant cash flows,** which are the *incremental after-tax cash outflow (investment) and resulting subsequent inflows.* The **incremental cash flows** represent the *additional* cash flows—outflows or inflows—expected to result from a proposed capital expenditure. As noted in Chapter 4, cash flows, rather than accounting figures, are used because cash flows directly affect the firm's ability to pay bills and purchase assets. Furthermore, accounting figures and cash flows are not necessarily the same, due to the presence of certain noncash expenses on the firm's income statement. The remainder of this chapter is devoted to the procedures for measuring the relevant cash flows associated with proposed capital expenditures.

MAJOR CASH FLOW COMPONENTS

initial investment
The relevant cash outflow for a proposed project at time zero.

operating cash inflows
The incremental after-tax cash inflows resulting from use of a project during its life.

The cash flows of any project having the *conventional pattern* can include three basic components: (1) an initial investment, (2) operating cash inflows, and (3) terminal cash flow. All projects—whether for expansion, replacement, or renewal—have the first two components. Some, however, lack the final component, terminal cash flow.

Figure 9.3 depicts on a time line the cash flows for a project. Each of the cash flow components is labeled. The **initial investment** is $50,000 for the proposed project. This is the relevant cash outflow at time zero. The **operating cash inflows,** which are the incremental after-tax cash inflows resulting from use of

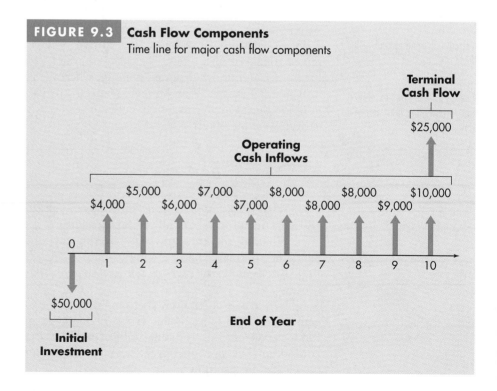

FIGURE 9.3 **Cash Flow Components**
Time line for major cash flow components

terminal cash flow
The after-tax nonoperating cash flow occurring in the final year of a project. It is usually attributable to liquidation of the project.

the project during its life, gradually increase from $4,000 in the first year to $10,000 in its tenth and final year. The **terminal cash flow** of $25,000, received at the end of the project's 10-year life, is the after-tax nonoperating cash flow occurring in the final year of the project. It is usually attributable to liquidation of the project. Note that the terminal cash flow does *not* include the $10,000 operating cash inflow for year 10.

EXPANSION VERSUS REPLACEMENT CASH FLOWS

Developing relevant cash flow estimates is most straightforward in the case of *expansion decisions*. In this case, the initial investment, operating cash inflows, and terminal cash flow are merely the after-tax cash outflow and inflows associated with the proposed outlay. Identifying relevant cash flows for *replacement decisions* is more complicated; the firm must find the *incremental* cash outflow and inflows that would result from the proposed replacement. The initial investment in this case is the difference between the initial investment needed to acquire the new asset and any after-tax cash inflows expected from liquidation today of the old asset (asset being replaced). The operating cash inflows are the difference between the operating cash inflows from the new asset and those from the old asset. The terminal cash flow is the difference between the after-tax cash flows expected upon termination of the new and the old assets. These relationships are shown in Figure 9.4. Later in the chapter we'll calculate these cash flows for a sample replacement decision.

Actually, all capital budgeting decisions can be viewed as replacement decisions. Expansion decisions are merely replacement decisions in which all cash flows from the old asset are zero. In light of this fact, *the following discussions emphasize the more general replacement decisions.*

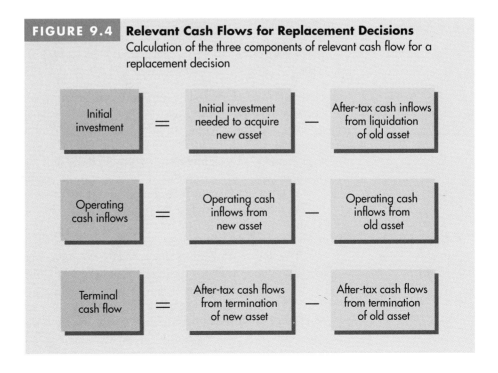

FIGURE 9.4   Relevant Cash Flows for Replacement Decisions
Calculation of the three components of relevant cash flow for a replacement decision

| Initial investment | = | Initial investment needed to acquire new asset | — | After-tax cash inflows from liquidation of old asset |

| Operating cash inflows | = | Operating cash inflows from new asset | — | Operating cash inflows from old asset |

| Terminal cash flow | = | After-tax cash flows from termination of new asset | — | After-tax cash flows from termination of old asset |

SUNK COSTS AND OPPORTUNITY COSTS

sunk costs
Cash outlays that have already been made (i.e., past outlays) and therefore have no effect on the cash flows relevant to a current decision.

opportunity costs
Cash flows that could be realized from the best alternative use of an owned asset.

When estimating the relevant cash flows associated with a proposed capital expenditure, the firm must recognize any *sunk costs* and *opportunity costs*. These costs are easy to mishandle or ignore, particularly when determining incremental cash flows. **Sunk costs** are cash outlays that have already been made (i.e., past outlays) and therefore have no effect on the cash flows relevant to the current decision. As a result, *sunk costs should not be included in a project's incremental cash flows*. **Opportunity costs** are cash flows that could be realized from the best alternative use of an owned asset. They therefore represent cash flows that will *not be realized* as a result of employing that asset in the proposed project. Because of this, any *opportunity costs should be included as cash outflows when determining a project's incremental cash flows*. The following example illustrates sunk costs and opportunity costs.

Example ▼ Jankow Equipment is considering renewing its drill press X12, which it purchased 3 years earlier for $237,000, by retrofitting it with the computerized control system from an obsolete piece of equipment it owns. The obsolete equipment could be sold today for a high bid of $42,000, but without its computerized control system it would be worth nothing. Jankow is in the process of estimating the costs of retrofitting the system to drill press X12 and the benefits expected from the retrofit. The $237,000 cost of drill press X12 is a *sunk cost* because it represents an earlier cash outlay. It *would not be included* as a cash outflow when determining the cash flows relevant to the retrofit decision. Although Jankow owns the obsolete piece of equipment, the proposed use of its computerized control system represents an *opportunity cost* of $42,000—the highest price at which it could be sold today. This opportunity cost *would be included* as a cash ▲ outflow associated with using the computerized control system.

INTERNATIONAL CAPITAL BUDGETING AND LONG-TERM INVESTMENTS

Although the same basic capital budgeting principles are used for domestic and international projects, several additional factors must be addressed in evaluating foreign investment opportunities. International capital budgeting differs from the domestic version because (1) cash inflows and outflows occur in a foreign currency, and (2) foreign investments potentially face significant political risk. Both of these risks can be minimized through careful planning.

Companies face both long- and short-term *currency risks* relating to both the invested capital and the cash flows resulting from it. Long-term currency risk can be minimized by at least partly financing the foreign investment in the local capital markets rather than with dollar-denominated capital from the parent company. This step ensures that the project's revenues, operating costs, and financing costs will be in the local currency. Likewise, the dollar value of short-term, local currency cash flows can be protected by using special securities and strategies such as futures, forwards, and options market instruments.

Political risks can be minimized by using both financial and operating strategies. For example, by structuring the investment as a joint venture and selecting a well-connected local partner, the U.S. company can minimize the risk of its operations being seized or harassed. Companies also can protect themselves from having their investment returns blocked by local governments by structuring the financing of such investments as debt rather than as equity. Debt-service payments are legally enforceable claims, whereas equity returns (such as dividends) are not. Even if local courts do not support the claims of the U.S. company, the company can threaten to pursue its case in U.S. courts.

foreign direct investment

The transfer of capital, managerial, and technical assets to a foreign country.

In spite of the preceding difficulties, **foreign direct investment,** which involves the transfer of capital, managerial, and technical assets to a foreign country, has surged in recent years. This is evident in the growing market values of both foreign assets owned by U.S.-based companies and foreign direct investment in the United States, particularly by British, Canadian, Dutch, German, and Japanese companies. Furthermore, foreign direct investment by U.S. companies seems to be accelerating, particularly in East Asia and Latin America.

PERSONAL FINANCE PERSPECTIVE

Cash Outflows Rule Personal Capital Outlays

Capital spending plans can guide major personal capital outlays such as for a car, house, boat, vacation home, or children's college education. But whereas companies look for projects that earn an acceptable return, the decision to make a personal purchase often focuses on the item's cost and how the purchase will be financed. There is also a tendency to combine the investment and the financing decision, whereby buyers select a particular car or house based on how much they can afford.

Consider a decision on whether to renew or replace personal property. Suppose your car needs major repairs. You'd first evaluate the cost to fix it, how much longer you'd expect the car to last, and other major repairs the older car would require. Then compare those cash outflows to those involved in buying a new car now, analyzing an all-cash purchase, a loan, or a lease— remembering, of course, to consider the time value of money. Finally, you'd consider qualitative factors. The possibility of a job change that requires longer commutes might tip the scales in favor of the new car; if you plan to take an expensive vacation this year, you might postpone the new car purchase until your cash flow improves. ●

Review Questions

9-5   Why is it important to evaluate capital budgeting projects on the basis of *incremental after-tax cash flows?* How can expansion decisions be treated as replacement decisions? Explain.

9-6   What are *sunk costs?* What are *opportunity costs?* What effect do each of these types of costs have on a project's incremental cash flows?

9-7   How can *currency risk* and *political risk* be minimized when making *foreign direct investments?*

FINDING THE INITIAL INVESTMENT

The term *initial investment* as used here refers to the relevant cash outflows to be considered when evaluating a prospective capital expenditure. Because our discussion of capital budgeting is concerned only with investments that exhibit conventional cash flows, the initial investment occurs at *time zero*—the time at which the expenditure is made. The initial investment is calculated by subtracting all cash inflows occurring at time zero from all cash outflows occurring at time zero.

The basic format for determining the initial investment is given in Table 9.3. The cash flows that must be considered when determining the initial investment associated with a capital expenditure are the installed cost of the new asset, the after-tax proceeds (if any) from the sale of an old asset, and the change (if any) in net working capital. Note that if there are no installation costs and the firm is not replacing an existing asset, the purchase price of the asset adjusted for any change in net working capital is equal to the initial investment.

INSTALLED COST OF NEW ASSET

cost of new asset
The net outflow required to acquire a new asset.

installation costs
Any added costs that are necessary to place an asset into operation.

installed cost of new asset
The cost of the asset plus its installation costs; equals the asset's depreciable value.

As shown in Table 9.3, the installed cost of the new asset is found by adding the cost of the new asset to its installation costs. The **cost of new asset** is the net outflow its acquisition requires. Usually, we are concerned with the acquisition of a fixed asset for which a definite purchase price is paid. **Installation costs** are any added costs that are necessary to place an asset into operation. They are considered part of the firm's capital expenditure. The Internal Revenue Service (IRS) requires the firm to add installation costs to the purchase price of an asset to determine its depreciable value, which is expensed over a period of years. The **installed cost of new asset,** calculated by adding the cost of the asset to its installation costs, equals its depreciable value.

AFTER-TAX PROCEEDS FROM SALE OF OLD ASSET

after-tax proceeds from sale of old asset
The difference between the old asset's sale proceeds and any applicable taxes or tax refunds relating to its sale.

Table 9.3 shows that the **after-tax proceeds from sale of old asset** decrease the firm's initial investment in the new asset. These proceeds are the difference between the old asset's sale proceeds and any applicable taxes or tax refunds

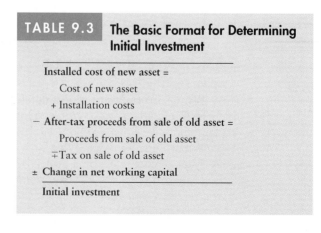

TABLE 9.3   The Basic Format for Determining Initial Investment

Installed cost of new asset =
   Cost of new asset
   + Installation costs
− After-tax proceeds from sale of old asset =
   Proceeds from sale of old asset
   ∓ Tax on sale of old asset
± Change in net working capital

Initial investment

proceeds from sale of old asset
The cash inflows, net of any removal or cleanup costs, resulting from the sale of an existing asset.

relating to its sale. The **proceeds from sale of old asset** are the net cash inflows it provides. This amount is net of any costs incurred in the process of removing the asset. Included in these *removal costs* are *cleanup costs*, such as those related to removal and disposal of chemical and nuclear wastes. These costs may not be trivial.

The proceeds from the sale of an old asset are normally subject to some type of tax.[2] This **tax on sale of old asset** depends on the relationship between its sale price, initial purchase price, and *book value*. The actual tax treatment is dictated by government tax rules, which are periodically revised. An understanding of (1) book value and (2) basic tax rules is necessary to determine the tax on sale of an asset.

tax on sale of old asset
Tax that depends upon the relationship between the old asset's sale price, initial purchase price, and *book value*.

BOOK VALUE

book value
The strict accounting value of an asset, calculated by subtracting its accumulated depreciation from installed cost.

The **book value** of an asset is its strict accounting value. It can be calculated using the following equation:

$$\text{Book value} = \text{installed cost of asset} - \text{accumulated depreciation} \qquad (9.1)$$

E x a m p l e ▼ Kontra Industries, a small electronics company, 2 years ago acquired a machine tool with an installed cost of $100,000. The asset was being depreciated under MACRS using a 5-year recovery period.[3] Table 4.7 (page 91) shows that under MACRS for a 5-year recovery period, 20 and 32 percent of the installed cost would be depreciated in years 1 and 2, respectively. In other words, 52 percent (20% + 32%) of the $100,000 cost, or $52,000 (.52 × $100,000), would represent the accumulated depreciation at the end of year 2. Substituting into Equation 9.1, we get

$$\text{Book value} = \$100,000 - \$52,000 = \underline{\underline{\$48,000}}$$

▲ The book value of Kontra's asset at the end of year 2 is therefore $48,000.

BASIC TAX RULES

Four potential tax situations can occur when selling an asset. These situations depend on the relationship between the asset's sale price, its initial purchase price, and its book value. The three key forms of taxable income and their associated tax treatments are defined and summarized in Table 9.4. The assumed tax rates used throughout this text are noted in the final column. The four possible tax situations, which result in one or more forms of taxable income, are the following: the asset is sold (1) for more than its initial purchase price; (2) for more than its book value but less than its initial purchase price; (3) for its book value; and (4) for less than its book value. An example will illustrate.

---

[2]A brief discussion of the tax treatment of ordinary and capital gains income was presented in Chapter 4.

[3]For a review of MACRS, see Chapter 4. Under current tax law, most manufacturing equipment has a 7-year recovery period, as noted in Table 4.6. Using this recovery period results in 8 years of depreciation, which unnecessarily complicates examples and problems. To simplify, *manufacturing equipment is treated as 5-year assets in this and the following chapters.*

TABLE 9.4	Tax Treatment on Sales of Assets		
Form of taxable income	Definition	Tax treatment	Assumed tax rate
Capital gain	Portion of the sale price that is in excess of the initial purchase price.	Regardless of how long the asset has been held, the total capital gain is taxed as ordinary income.	40%
Recaptured depreciation	Portion of the sale price that is in excess of book value and represents a recovery of previously taken depreciation.	All recaptured depreciation is taxed as ordinary income.	40%
Loss on sale of asset	Amount by which sale price is *less than* book value.	If asset is depreciable and used in business, loss is deducted from ordinary income.	40% of loss is a tax savings
		If asset is *not* depreciable or is *not* used in business, loss is deductible only against capital gains.	40% of loss is a tax savings

Example ▼   The old asset purchased 2 years ago for $100,000 by Kontra Industries has a current book value of $48,000. What will happen if the firm now decides to sell the asset and replace it? The tax consequences depend on the sale price. Figure 9.5 depicts the taxable income resulting from four possible sale prices in light of the asset's initial purchase price of $100,000 and its current book value of $48,000. The taxable consequences of each of these sale prices is described below.

The sale of the asset for more than its initial purchase price   If Kontra sells the old asset for $110,000, it realizes a capital gain of $10,000, which is taxed as ordinary income.[4] The firm also experiences ordinary income in the form of **recaptured depreciation**, which is the portion of the sale price that is above book value and below the initial purchase price. In this case there is recaptured depreciation of $52,000 ($100,000 − $48,000). Both the $10,000 capital gain and the $52,000 recaptured depreciation are shown under the $110,000 sale price in Figure 9.5. The taxes on the total gain of $62,000 are calculated as follows:

recaptured depreciation
The portion of an asset's sale price that is above its book value and below its initial purchase price.

---

[4]Although the current tax law requires corporate capital gains to be treated as ordinary income, the structure for corporate capital gains is retained under the law to facilitate a rate differential in the likely event of future tax revisions. Therefore, this distinction is made throughout the text discussions.

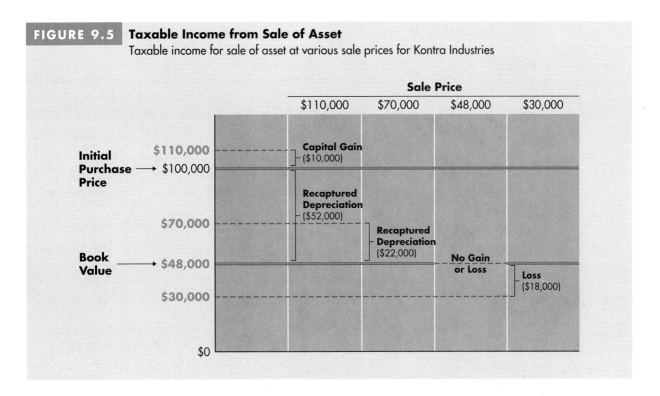

| **FIGURE 9.5** | **Taxable Income from Sale of Asset** |

Taxable income for sale of asset at various sale prices for Kontra Industries

	Amount (1)	Rate (2)	Tax [(1) × (2)] (3)
Capital gain	$10,000	.40	$ 4,000
Recaptured depreciation	52,000	.40	20,800
Totals	$62,000		$24,800

These taxes should be used in calculating the initial investment in the new asset, using the format in Table 9.3. In effect, the taxes raise the amount of the firm's initial investment in the new asset by reducing the proceeds from the sale of the old asset.

The sale of the asset for more than its book value but less than its initial purchase price If Kontra sells the old asset for $70,000, there is no capital gain. However, the firm still experiences a gain in the form of recaptured depreciation of $22,000 ($70,000 − $48,000), as shown under the $70,000 sale price in Figure 9.5. This recaptured depreciation is taxed as ordinary income. Because the firm is assumed to be in the 40 percent tax bracket, the taxes on the $22,000 gain are $8,800. This amount in taxes should be used in calculating the initial investment in the new asset.

The sale of the asset for its book value If the asset is sold for $48,000, its book value, the firm breaks even. There is no gain or loss, as shown under the $48,000

sale price in Figure 9.5. Because *no tax results from selling an asset for its book value,* there is no effect on the initial investment in the new asset.

The sale of the asset for less than its book value If Kontra sells the asset for $30,000, it experiences a loss of $18,000 ($48,000 − $30,000), as shown under the $30,000 sale price in Figure 9.5. If this is a depreciable asset used in the business, the loss may be used to offset ordinary operating income. If the asset is not depreciable or not used in the business, the loss can be used only to offset capital gains. In either case, the loss will save the firm $7,200 ($18,000 × .40) in taxes. And, if current operating earnings or capital gains are not sufficient to offset the loss, the firm may be able to apply these losses to prior or future years' taxes.[5]

CHANGE IN NET WORKING CAPITAL

Net working capital, as noted in Chapter 5, is the amount by which a firm's current assets exceed its current liabilities. This topic is treated in depth in Part 5, especially in Chapter 15, but at this point it is important to note that changes in net working capital often accompany capital expenditure decisions. If a firm acquires new machinery to expand its level of operations, levels of cash, accounts receivable, inventories, accounts payable, and accruals will increase. These increases result from the need for more cash to support expanded operations, more accounts receivable and inventories to support increased sales, and more accounts payable and accruals to support increased purchases made to meet expanded product demand. As noted in Chapter 4, increases in cash, accounts receivable, and inventories are *uses of cash* (cash outflows or investments), whereas increases in accounts payable and accruals are *sources of cash* (cash inflows or financing). As long as the expanded operations continue, the increased investment in current assets (cash, accounts receivable, and inventories) and increased current liability financing (accounts payable and accruals) would be expected to continue.

change in net working capital
The difference between a change in current assets and a change in current liabilities.

The difference between the change in current assets and the change in current liabilities would be the **change in net working capital.** Generally, current assets increase by more than current liabilities, resulting in an increased investment in net working capital, which would be treated as an initial outflow. If the change in net working capital were negative, it would be shown as an initial inflow. The change in net working capital—regardless of whether an increase or a decrease—is *not taxable* because it merely involves a net buildup or reduction of current accounts.

Example ▼ Danson Company, a metal products manufacturer, is contemplating expanding its operations. In addition to Danson's acquiring new capital equipment, financial analysts expect that the changes in current accounts summarized in Table 9.5 will occur and be maintained over the life of the expansion. Current assets are expected to increase by $22,000, and current liabilities are expected to increase

[5]The tax law provides detailed procedures for using *tax loss carrybacks/carryforwards.* Application of such procedures to capital budgeting is beyond the scope of this text, and they are therefore ignored in subsequent discussions.

TABLE 9.5	Calculation of Change in Net Working Capital for Danson Company

Current account	Change in balance	
Cash	+ $ 4,000	
Accounts receivable	+ 10,000	
Inventories	+ 8,000	
(1) Current assets		+ $22,000
Accounts payable	+ $ 7,000	
Accruals	+ 2,000	
(2) Current liabilities		+ 9,000
Change in net working capital [(1) − (2)]		+ $13,000

by $9,000, resulting in a $13,000 increase in net working capital. In this case, the increase would represent an increased net working capital investment and be treated as a cash outflow in calculating the initial investment.

CALCULATING THE INITIAL INVESTMENT

A variety of tax and other considerations enter into the initial investment calculation. The following example illustrates the calculation of the initial investment according to the format in Table 9.3.

Example ▼ Norman Company, a large diversified manufacturer of aircraft components, is trying to determine the initial investment required to replace an old machine with a new, more sophisticated model. The machine's purchase price is $380,000, and an additional $20,000 will be required to install it. It will be depreciated under MACRS using a 5-year recovery period. The present (old) machine was purchased 3 years ago at a cost of $240,000 and was being depreciated under MACRS using a 5-year recovery period. The firm has found a buyer willing to pay $280,000 for the present machine and remove it at the buyer's expense. The firm expects that a $35,000 increase in current assets and an $18,000 increase in current liabilities will accompany the replacement; these changes will result in a $17,000 ($35,000 − $18,000) *increase* in net working capital. Both ordinary income and capital gains are taxed at a rate of 40 percent.

The only component of the initial investment calculation that is difficult to obtain is taxes. Because the firm is planning to sell the present machine for $40,000 more than its initial purchase price, it will realize a *capital gain of $40,000.* The book value of the present machine can be found by using the depreciation percentages from Table 4.7 (page 91) of 20, 32, and 19 percent for years 1, 2, and 3, respectively. The resulting book value is $69,600 ($240,000 − [(.20 + .32 + .19) × $240,000]). An *ordinary gain* of $170,400 ($240,000 − $69,600) in recaptured depreciation is also realized on the sale. The total taxes on the gain are $84,160 [($40,000 + $170,400) × .40]. Substituting these amounts into the format in Table 9.3 results in an initial investment of $221,160, which represents the net cash outflow required at time zero:

Installed cost of proposed machine		
Cost of proposed machine	$380,000	
+ Installation costs	20,000	
Total installed cost—proposed (depreciable value)		$400,000
− After-tax proceeds from sale of present machine		
Proceeds from sale of present machine	$280,000	
− Tax on sale of present machine	84,160	
Total after-tax proceeds—present		195,840
+ Change in net working capital		17,000
Initial investment		$221,160

Review Questions

9-8 Describe each of the following inputs to the initial investment, and use the basic format presented in this chapter to explain how the initial investment is calculated by using them: **(a)** cost of new asset; **(b)** installation costs; **(c)** proceeds from sale of old asset; **(d)** tax on sale of old asset; and **(e)** change in net working capital.

9-9 How is the *book value* of an asset calculated? Describe the three key forms of taxable income and their associated tax treatments.

9-10 What four tax situations may result from the sale of an asset that is being replaced? Describe the tax treatment in each situation.

9-11 Referring to the basic format for calculating initial investment, explain how a firm would determine the *depreciable value* of the new asset.

FINDING THE OPERATING CASH INFLOWS

The benefits expected from a capital expenditure are measured by its *operating cash inflows,* which are *incremental after-tax cash inflows.* In this section we use the income statement format to develop clear definitions of the terms *after-tax, cash inflows,* and *incremental.*

INTERPRETING THE TERM *AFTER-TAX*

Benefits expected to result from proposed capital expenditures must be measured on an *after-tax basis,* because the firm will not have the use of any benefits until it has satisfied the government's tax claims. These claims depend on the firm's taxable income, so the deduction of taxes *prior to* making comparisons between proposed investments is necessary for consistency when evaluating capital expenditure alternatives.

INTERPRETING THE TERM *CASH INFLOWS*

All benefits expected from a proposed project must be measured on a *cash flow basis*. Cash inflows represent dollars that can be spent, not merely "accounting profits." A simple technique for converting after-tax net profits into operating cash inflows was illustrated in Chapter 4. The basic calculation requires adding any *noncash charges* deducted as expenses on the firm's income statement back to net profits after taxes. Probably the most common noncash charge found on income statements is depreciation. It is the only noncash charge that will be considered in this section. The following example calculates after-tax operating cash inflows for a proposed and a present project.

Example ▼ Norman Company's estimates of its revenue and expenses (excluding depreciation), with and without the proposed new machine described in the preceding example, are given in Table 9.6. Note that both the expected usable life of the proposed machine and the remaining usable life of the present machine is 5 years. The amount to be depreciated with the proposed machine is calculated by summing the purchase price of $380,000 and the installation costs of $20,000. The proposed machine is to be depreciated under MACRS using a 5-year recovery period. (See Chapter 4 and Table 4.7 on page 91 for more detail.)[6] The resulting depreciation on this machine for each of the 6 years, as well as the

TABLE 9.6	Norman Company's Revenue and Expenses (Excluding Depreciation) for Proposed and Present Machines	
Year	Revenue (1)	Expenses (excl. depr.) (2)
With proposed machine		
1	$2,520,000	$2,300,000
2	2,520,000	2,300,000
3	2,520,000	2,300,000
4	2,520,000	2,300,000
5	2,520,000	2,300,000
With present machine		
1	$2,200,000	$1,990,000
2	2,300,000	2,110,000
3	2,400,000	2,230,000
4	2,400,000	2,250,000
5	2,250,000	2,120,000

[6]As noted in Chapter 4, it takes *n* + 1 years to depreciate an *n*-year class asset under current tax law. Therefore, MACRS percentages are given for each of 6 years for use in depreciating an asset with a 5-year recovery period.

TABLE 9.7	Depreciation Expense for Proposed and Present Machines for Norman Company

Year	Cost (1)	Applicable MACRS depreciation percentages (from Table 4.7) (2)	Depreciation [(1) × (2)] (3)
With proposed machine			
1	$400,000	20%	$ 80,000
2	400,000	32	128,000
3	400,000	19	76,000
4	400,000	12	48,000
5	400,000	12	48,000
6	400,000	5	20,000
Totals		100%	$400,000
With present machine			
1	$240,000	12% (year-4 depreciation)	$ 28,800
2	240,000	12 (year-5 depreciation)	28,800
3	240,000	5 (year-6 depreciation)	12,000
4	Because the present machine is at the end of the third year of its cost recovery at the time the analysis is performed, it has only the final 3 years of depreciation (as noted above) yet applicable.		0
5			0
6			0
Total			$ 69,600[a]

[a]The total $69,600 represents the book value of the present machine at the end of the third year, as calculated in the preceding example.

remaining 3 years of depreciation (years 4, 5, 6) on the present machine, are calculated in Table 9.7.[7]

The operating cash inflows in each year can be calculated using the income statement format shown in Table 9.8. Substituting the data from Tables 9.6 and 9.7 into this format and assuming a 40 percent tax rate, we get Table 9.9. It demonstrates the calculation of operating cash inflows for each year for both the proposed and the present machine. Because the proposed machine is depreciated over 6 years, the analysis must be performed over the 6-year period to fully capture the tax effect of its year-6 depreciation. The resulting operating cash inflows are shown in the final row of Table 9.9 for each machine. The $8,000 year-6 cash inflow for the proposed machine results solely from the tax benefit of its year-6 depreciation deduction.

---

[7]It is important to recognize that although both machines will provide 5 years of use, the proposed new machine will be depreciated over the 6-year period, whereas the present machine—as noted in the preceding example—has been depreciated over 3 years and therefore has only its final 3 years (years 4, 5, and 6) of depreciation (i.e., 12, 12, and 5 percent, respectively, under MACRS) remaining.

TABLE 9.8	**Calculation of Operating Cash Inflows Using the Income Statement Format**

Revenue
− Expenses (excluding depreciation)
Profits before depreciation and taxes
− Depreciation
Net profits before taxes
− Taxes
Net profits after taxes
+ Depreciation
Operating cash inflows

TABLE 9.9	**Calculation of Operating Cash Inflows for Norman Company's Proposed and Present Machines**

	Year					
	1	2	3	4	5	6
With proposed machine						
Revenue[a]	$2,520,000	$2,520,000	$2,520,000	$2,520,000	$2,520,000	$ 0
− Expenses (excl. depr.)[b]	2,300,000	2,300,000	2,300,000	2,300,000	2,300,000	0
Profits before depr. and taxes	$ 220,000	$ 220,000	$ 220,000	$ 220,000	$ 220,000	$ 0
− Depreciation[c]	80,000	128,000	76,000	48,000	48,000	20,000
Net profits before taxes	$ 140,000	$ 92,000	$ 144,000	$ 172,000	$ 172,000	−$20,000
− Taxes (rate = 40%)	56,000	36,800	57,600	68,800	68,800	− 8,000
Net profits after taxes	$ 84,000	$ 55,200	$ 86,400	$ 103,200	$ 103,200	−$12,000
+ Depreciation[c]	80,000	128,000	76,000	48,000	48,000	20,000
Operating cash inflows	$ 164,000	$ 183,200	$ 162,400	$ 151,200	$ 151,200	$ 8,000
With present machine						
Revenue[a]	$2,200,000	$2,300,000	$2,400,000	$2,400,000	$2,250,000	$ 0
− Expenses (excl. depr.)[b]	1,990,000	2,110,000	2,230,000	2,250,000	2,120,000	0
Profits before depr. and taxes	$ 210,000	$ 190,000	$ 170,000	$ 150,000	$ 130,000	$ 0
− Depreciation[c]	28,800	28,800	12,000	0	0	0
Net profits before taxes	$ 181,200	$ 161,200	$ 158,000	$ 150,000	$ 130,000	$ 0
− Taxes (rate = 40%)	72,480	64,480	63,200	60,000	52,000	0
Net profits after taxes	$ 108,720	$ 96,720	$ 94,800	$ 90,000	$ 78,000	$ 0
+ Depreciation[c]	28,800	28,800	12,000	0	0	0
Operating cash inflows	$ 137,520	$ 125,520	$ 106,800	$ 90,000	$ 78,000	$ 0

[a]From column 1 of Table 9.6.
[b]From column 2 of Table 9.6.
[c]From column 3 of Table 9.7.

TABLE 9.10	Incremental (Relevant) Operating Cash Inflows for Norman Company

	Operating cash inflows		
Year	Proposed machine[a] (1)	Present machine[a] (2)	Incremental (relevant) [(1) − (2)] (3)
1	$164,000	$137,520	$26,480
2	183,200	125,520	57,680
3	162,400	106,800	55,600
4	151,200	90,000	61,200
5	151,200	78,000	73,200
6	8,000	0	8,000

[a]From final row for respective machine in Table 9.9.

INTERPRETING THE TERM *INCREMENTAL*

The final step in estimating the operating cash inflows for a proposed project is to calculate the *incremental (relevant)* cash inflows. Incremental operating cash inflows are needed, because our concern is *only* with the change in operating cash flows as a result of the proposed project.

Example ▼ Table 9.10 demonstrates the calculation of Norman Company's incremental (relevant) operating cash inflows for each year. The estimates of operating cash inflows developed in Table 9.9 are given in columns 1 and 2. Column 2 values represent the amount of operating cash inflows that Norman Company will receive if it does not replace the present machine. If the proposed machine replaces the present machine, the firm's operating cash inflows for each year will be those shown in column 1. Subtracting the present machine's operating cash inflows from the proposed machine's operating cash inflows, we get the incremental operating cash inflows for each year, shown in column 3 of Table 9.10. These cash flows represent the amounts by which each respective year's cash inflows will increase as a result of the replacement. For example, in year 1, Norman Company's cash inflows would increase by $26,480 if the proposed project were undertaken. Clearly, these are the relevant inflows to be considered ▲ when evaluating the benefits of making a capital expenditure.

? Review Questions

9-12   How is the *modified accelerated cost recovery system (MACRS)* used to depreciate an asset? How does depreciation enter into the operating cash inflow calculation?

9-13   Given the revenues, expenses, and depreciation associated with a present asset and a proposed replacement for it, how are the incremental (relevant) operating cash inflows associated with the decision calculated?

FINDING THE TERMINAL CASH FLOW

The cash flow resulting from termination and liquidation of a project at the end of its economic life is its *terminal cash flow*. It represents the after-tax cash flow, exclusive of operating cash inflows, occurring in the final year of the project. When it applies, this flow can significantly affect the capital expenditure decision. Terminal cash flow, which is most often positive, can be calculated for replacement projects by using the basic format presented in Table 9.11.

PROCEEDS FROM SALE OF ASSETS

The proceeds from sale of the new and old asset, often called "salvage value," represent the amount *net of any removal or cleanup costs* expected upon termination of the project. For replacement projects, proceeds from both the new asset and the old asset must be considered. For expansion and renewal types of capital expenditures, the proceeds from the old asset would be zero. Of course, it is not unusual for the values of assets to be zero at termination of a project.

TAXES ON SALE OF ASSETS

Earlier we calculated the tax on sale of old assets (as part of finding the initial investment). Similarly, taxes must be considered on the terminal sale of both the new and the old asset for replacement projects and on only the new asset in other cases. The tax calculations apply whenever an asset is sold for a value different from its book value. If the net proceeds from the sale are expected to exceed book value, a tax payment shown as an *outflow* (deduction from sale proceeds) would occur. When the net proceeds from the sale are less than book value, a tax rebate shown as a cash *inflow* (addition to sale proceeds) would result. For assets sold to net exactly book value, no taxes would be due.

CHANGE IN NET WORKING CAPITAL

When we calculated the initial investment, we took into account any change in net working capital attributable to the new asset. Now, when we calculate the

TABLE 9.11	The Basic Format for Determining Terminal Cash Flow

After-tax proceeds from sale of new asset =
  Proceeds from sale of new asset
  ∓ Tax on sale of new asset
− After-tax proceeds from sale of old asset =
  Proceeds from sale of old asset
  ∓ Tax on sale of old asset
± Change in net working capital

Terminal cash flow

terminal cash flow, the change in net working capital reflects the reversion to its original status of any net working capital investment. Most often this will show up as a cash inflow due to the reduction in net working capital; with termination of the project, the need for the increased net working capital investment is assumed to end. Because the net working capital investment is in no way consumed, the amount recovered at termination will equal the amount shown in the calculation of the initial investment. Tax considerations are not involved. Occasionally net working capital will not be changed by the proposed investment and therefore will not enter into the analysis.

The terminal cash flow calculation involves the same procedures as those used to find the initial investment. The following example calculates the terminal cash flow for a replacement decision.

Example ▼ Continuing with the Norman Company example, assume that the firm expects to be able to liquidate the new machine at the end of its 5-year usable life to net $50,000 after paying removal and cleanup costs. The old machine can be liquidated at the end of the 5 years to net $0 because it will then be completely obsolete. The firm expects to recover its $17,000 net working capital investment upon termination of the project. Both ordinary income and capital gains are taxed at a rate of 40 percent.

From the analysis of the operating cash inflows presented earlier, we can see that while the present (old) machine will be fully depreciated and therefore have a book value of zero at the end of the 5 years, the proposed (new) machine will have a book value of $20,000 (equal to the year-6 depreciation) at the end of 5 years. Because the sale price of $50,000 for the proposed machine is below its initial installed cost of $400,000 but greater than its book value of $20,000, taxes will have to be paid only on the recaptured depreciation of $30,000 ($50,000 sale proceeds − $20,000 book value). Applying the ordinary tax rate of 40 percent to the $30,000 results in a tax of $12,000 (.40 × $30,000) on the sale of the proposed machine. Its after-tax sale proceeds would therefore equal $38,000 ($50,000 sale proceeds − $12,000 taxes). Because the present machine would net $0 at termination and its book value would be $0, no tax would be due on its sale. Its after-tax sale proceeds would therefore equal $0. Substituting the appropriate values into the format in Table 9.11 results in the terminal cash inflow value of $55,000. This represents the after-tax cash flow, exclusive of operating cash inflows, occurring upon termination of the project at the end of year 5.

After-tax proceeds from sale of proposed machine		
Proceeds from sale of proposed machine	$50,000	
− Tax on sale of proposed machine	12,000	
Total after-tax proceeds—proposed		$38,000
− **After-tax proceeds from sale of present machine**		
Proceeds from sale of present machine	$ 0	
∓ Tax on sale of present machine	0	
Total after-tax proceeds—present		0
+ **Change in net working capital**		17,000
Terminal cash flow		$55,000

9-14   What is the *terminal cash flow?* Use the basic format presented to explain how the value of this cash flow is calculated for replacement projects.

LG4 **LG5** **LG6**   SUMMARIZING THE RELEVANT CASH FLOWS

The three cash flow components—the initial investment, operating cash inflows, and terminal cash flow—together represent a project's *relevant cash flows*. These cash flows can be viewed as the incremental after-tax cash flows attributable to the proposed project. They represent, in a cash flow sense, how much better or worse off the firm will be if it chooses to implement the proposal.

Example ▼ The relevant cash flows for Norman Company's proposed replacement expenditure can now be shown graphically, on a time line. Note that because the new asset is assumed to be sold at the end of its 5-year usable life, the year–6 incremental operating cash inflow calculated in Table 9.10 has no relevance; the terminal cash flow effectively replaces this value in the analysis. As the time line shows, the relevant cash flows follow a *conventional cash flow pattern*. Techniques for analyzing this type of pattern to determine whether to undertake a proposed capital investment are discussed in Chapter 10.

Norman Company's relevant cash flows with the proposed machine

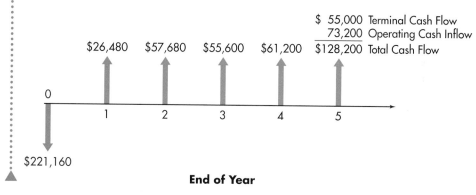

? R e v i e w   Q u e s t i o n

9-15   Diagram and describe the three elements representing the *relevant cash flows* for a capital budgeting project with a *conventional cash flow pattern*.

SUMMARY

LG1 Understand the key capital expenditure motives and the steps in the capital budgeting process. Capital budgeting is the process used to

evaluate and select capital expenditures consistent with the firm's goal of owner wealth maximization. Capital expenditures are long-term investments made to expand, replace, or renew fixed assets or to obtain some other less tangible benefit. The capital budgeting process contains five distinct but interrelated steps: proposal generation, review and analysis, decision making, implementation, and follow-up.

LG2 **Define the basic terminology used to describe projects, funds availability, decision approaches, and cash flow patterns.** Capital expenditure proposals may be independent or mutually exclusive. Typically, firms have only limited funds for capital investments and must ration them among carefully selected projects. To make investment decisions when proposals are mutually exclusive or when capital must be rationed, projects must be ranked; otherwise, accept–reject decisions must be made using minimum acceptance criteria. Conventional cash flow patterns consist of an initial outflow followed by a series of inflows; any other pattern is nonconventional. These patterns can be either annuities or mixed streams.

LG3 **Discuss the major components of relevant cash flows, expansion versus replacement cash flows, sunk costs and opportunity costs, and international capital budgeting and long-term investments.** The relevant cash flows for capital budgeting decisions are the initial investment, the operating cash inflows, and the terminal cash flow for a given project. For replacement decisions, these flows are found by determining the difference between the cash flows of the new asset and the old asset. Expansion decisions are viewed as replacement decisions in which all cash flows from the old asset are zero. When estimating relevant cash flows, sunk costs should be ignored, and opportunity costs should be included as cash outflows. In international capital budgeting, currency risk and political risk can be minimized through careful planning.

LG4 **Calculate the initial investment associated with a proposed capital expenditure, given relevant data.** The initial investment is the initial outflow required, taking into account the installed cost of the new asset, the after-tax proceeds from the sale of the old asset, and any change in net working capital. Finding the after-tax proceeds from sale of the old asset, which reduces the initial investment, involves cost, depreciation, and tax data. The book value of an asset is its accounting value, which is used to determine what taxes are owed as a result of its sale. Any of three forms of taxable income—capital gain, recaptured depreciation, or a loss—can result from sale of an asset. The form of taxable income that applies depends on whether the asset is sold for (1) more than its initial purchase price, (2) more than book value but less than initially paid, (3) book value, or (4) less than book value. The change in net working capital is the difference between the change in current assets (cash outflows or investments) and the change in current liabilities (cash inflows or financing) expected from a given capital expenditure.

LG5 **Determine relevant operating cash inflows using the income statement format.** The operating cash inflows are the incremental after-tax cash inflows expected to result from a project. The income statement format, which involves adding depreciation back to net profits after taxes, gives the operating cash inflows associated with the proposed and present projects. The relevant (incremental) cash inflows, which are used to evaluate the proposed project, are the difference between the operating cash inflows of the proposed project and those of the present project.

LG6 **Find the terminal cash flow, given relevant data.** The terminal cash flow represents the after-tax cash flow, exclusive of operating cash inflows, expected from liquidation of a project. It is found by calculating and then finding the difference between the after-tax proceeds from sale of the new and the old asset at project termination and then adjusting this difference for any change in net working capital. Sale price and depreciation data are used to find the taxes and the after-tax sale proceeds on the new and old assets. The change in net working capital typically represents the recovery of the net working capital investment included in the initial investment.

SELF-TEST PROBLEMS

(Solutions in Appendix B)

ST 9-1 Book value, taxes, and initial investment Irvin Enterprises is considering the purchase of a new piece of equipment to replace the current equipment. The new equipment costs $75,000 and requires $5,000 in installation costs. It will be depreciated under MACRS using a 5-year recovery period. The old piece of equipment was purchased for an installed cost of $50,000 4 years ago; it was being depreciated under MACRS using a 5-year recovery period. The old equipment can be sold today for $55,000 net of any removal and cleanup costs. As a result of the proposed replacement, the firm's investment in net working capital is expected to increase by $15,000. The firm pays taxes at a rate of 40 percent on both ordinary income and capital gains. (Table 4.7 on page 91 contains the applicable MACRS depreciation percentages.)

a. Calculate the book value of the old piece of equipment.

b. Determine the taxes, if any, attributable to the sale of the old equipment.

c. Find the initial investment associated with the proposed equipment replacement.

ST 9-2 Determining relevant cash flows A machine currently in use was originally purchased 2 years ago for $40,000. The machine is being depreciated under MACRS using a 5-year recovery period; it has 3 years of usable life remaining. The current machine can be sold today to net $42,000 after removal and cleanup costs. A new machine, using a 3-year MACRS recovery period, can be purchased at a price of $140,000. It requires $10,000 to install and has a 3-year usable life. If the new machine were acquired, the investment in accounts receivable would be expected to rise by $10,000, the inventory investment will increase by $25,000, and accounts payable will increase by $15,000. *Profits before depreciation and taxes* are expected to be $70,000 for each of the next 3 years with the old machine and $120,000 in the first year and $130,000 in the second and third years with the new machine. At the end of 3 years, the market value of the old machine will equal zero, but the new machine could be sold to net $35,000 before taxes. Both ordinary corporate income and capital gains are subject to a 40 percent tax. (Table 4.7 on page 91 contains the applicable MACRS depreciation percentages.)

a. Determine the initial investment associated with the proposed replacement decision.

b. Calculate the incremental operating cash inflows for years 1 to 4 associated with the proposed replacement. (*Note:* Only depreciation cash flows must be considered in year 4.)

c. Calculate the terminal cash flow associated with the proposed replacement decision. (*Note:* This is at the end of year 3.)

d. Depict on a time line the relevant cash flows found in **a, b,** and **c** associated with the proposed replacement decision assuming that it is terminated at the end of year 3.

PROBLEMS

WARM-UP 9-1 **Classification of expenditures**   Given the following list of outlays, indicate whether each is normally considered a *capital* or an *operating* expenditure. Explain your answers.
  a. An initial lease payment of $5,000 for electronic point-of-sale cash register systems.
  b. An outlay of $20,000 to purchase patent rights from an inventor.
  c. An outlay of $80,000 for a major research and development program.
  d. An $80,000 investment in a portfolio of marketable securities.
  e. A $300 outlay for an office machine.
  f. An outlay of $2,000 for a new machine tool.
  g. An outlay of $240,000 for a new building.
  h. An outlay of $1,000 for a marketing research report.

WARM-UP 9-2 **Basic terminology**   A firm is considering the following three separate situations.

Situation A   Build either a small office building or a convenience store on a parcel of land located in a high-traffic area. Adequate funding is available, and both projects are known to be acceptable. The office building requires an initial investment of $620,000 and is expected to provide operating cash inflows of $40,000 per year for 20 years. The convenience store is expected to cost $500,000 and to provide a growing stream of operating cash inflows over its 20-year life. The initial operating cash inflow is $20,000 and will increase by 5 percent each year.

Situation B   Replace a machine with a new one requiring a $60,000 initial investment and providing operating cash inflows of $10,000 per year for the first 5 years. At the end of year 5, a machine overhaul costing $20,000 is required. After it is completed, expected operating cash inflows are $10,000 in year 6; $7,000 in year 7; $4,000 in year 8; and $1,000 in year 9, at the end of which the machine will be scrapped.

Situation C   Invest in any or all of the four machines whose relevant cash flows are given in the following table. The firm has $500,000 budgeted to fund these machines, all of which are known to be acceptable. Initial investment for each machine is $250,000.

| | Operating cash inflows | | | |
Year	Machine 1	Machine 2	Machine 3	Machine 4
1	$ 50,000	$70,000	$65,000	$90,000
2	70,000	70,000	65,000	80,000
3	90,000	70,000	80,000	70,000
4	−30,000	70,000	80,000	60,000
5	100,000	70,000	−20,000	50,000

For each situation or project, indicate
a. Whether the *situation* is independent or mutually exclusive.
b. Whether the availability of funds is unlimited or if capital rationing exists.
c. Whether accept–reject or ranking decisions are required.
d. Whether each *project's* cash flows are conventional or nonconventional.
e. Whether each *project's* cash flow pattern is an annuity or a mixed stream.

  9-3 Relevant cash flow pattern fundamentals   For each of the following projects, determine the *relevant cash flows,* classify the cash flow pattern, and depict the cash flows on a time line.

a. A project requiring an initial investment of $120,000 that generates annual operating cash inflows of $25,000 for the next 18 years. In each of the 18 years, maintenance of the project will require a $5,000 cash outflow.

b. A new machine having an installed cost of $85,000. Sale of the old machine will yield $30,000 after taxes. Operating cash inflows generated by the replacement will exceed the operating cash inflows of the old machine by $20,000 in each year of a 6-year period. At the end of year 6, liquidation of the new machine will yield $20,000 after taxes, which is $10,000 greater than the after-tax proceeds expected from the old machine had it been retained and liquidated at the end of year 6.

c. An asset requiring an initial investment of $2 million that will yield annual operating cash inflows of $300,000 for each of the next 10 years. Operating cash outlays will be $20,000 for each year except year 6, when an overhaul requiring an additional cash outlay of $500,000 will be required. The asset's liquidation value at the end of year 10 is expected to be $0.

  9-4 Expansion versus replacement cash flows   Nick Stamas, Inc. has estimated the cash flows over the 5-year lives for two projects, A and B. These cash flows are summarized in the following table:

	Project A	Project B
Initial investment	$40,000	$12,000[a]
Year	Operating cash inflows	
1	$10,000	$ 6,000
2	12,000	6,000
3	14,000	6,000
4	16,000	6,000
5	10,000	6,000

[a]After-tax cash inflow expected from liquidation.

a. If project A were actually a *replacement* for project B and if the $12,000 initial investment shown for B were the after-tax cash inflow expected from liquidating it, what would be the relevant cash flow for this replacement decision?

b. How can an *expansion decision* such as project A be viewed as a special form of a replacement decision? Explain.

9-5 Sunk costs and opportunity costs Covol Industries is developing the relevant cash flows associated with the proposed replacement of an existing machine tool with a new technologically advanced one. Given the following costs related to the proposed project, explain whether each would be treated as a *sunk cost* or an *opportunity cost* in developing the relevant cash flows associated with the proposed replacement decision.

a. Covol would be able to use the same tooling, which had a book value of $40,000, on the new machine tool as it had used on the old one.

b. Covol would be able to use its existing computer system to develop programs for operating the new machine tool. The old machine tool did not require these programs. Although the firm's computer has excess capacity available, the capacity could be leased to another firm for an annual fee of $17,000.

c. Covol would have to obtain additional floor space to accommodate the larger new machine tool. The space that would be used is currently being leased to another company for $10,000 per year.

d. Covol would use a small storage facility to store the increased output of the new machine tool. The storage facility was built by Covol at a cost of $120,000 three years earlier. Because of its unique configuration and location, it is currently of no use to either Covol or any other firm.

e. Covol would retain an existing overhead crane, which it had planned to sell for its $180,000 market value. Although the crane was not needed with the old machine tool, it would be used to position raw materials on the new machine tool.

9-6 Book value Find the book value for each of the assets shown in the following table, assuming that MACRS depreciation is being used. (*Note:* See Table 4.7 on page 91 for the applicable depreciation percentages.)

Asset	Installed cost	Recovery period	Elapsed time since purchase
A	$ 950,000	5 years	3 years
B	40,000	3 years	1 year
C	96,000	5 years	4 years
D	350,000	5 years	1 year
E	1,500,000	7 years	5 years

9-7 Book value and taxes on sale of assets Waters Manufacturing purchased a new machine 3 years ago for $80,000. It is being depreciated under MACRS with a 5-year recovery period using the percentages given in Table 4.7 on page 91. Assume 40 percent ordinary and capital gains tax rates.

a. What is the book value of the machine?

b. Calculate the firm's tax liability if it sold the machine for the following amounts: $100,000; $56,000; $23,200; and $15,000.

9-8 Tax calculations For each of the following cases, describe the various taxable components of the funds received through sale of the asset, and determine the total taxes resulting from the transaction. Assume 40 percent ordinary and capital gains tax rates. The asset was purchased for $200,000 two years ago and is being depreciated under MACRS using a 5-year recovery period. (See Table 4.7 on page 91 for the applicable depreciation percentages.)

a. The asset is sold for $220,000.
b. The asset is sold for $150,000.
c. The asset is sold for $96,000.
d. The asset is sold for $80,000.

9-9   Change in net working capital calculation   Samuels Manufacturing is considering the purchase of a new machine to replace one they feel is obsolete. The firm has total current assets of $920,000 and total current liabilities of $640,000. As a result of the proposed replacement, the following *changes* are anticipated in the levels of the current asset and current liability accounts noted.

Account	Change
Accruals	+ $ 40,000
Marketable securities	0
Inventories	− 10,000
Accounts payable	+ 90,000
Notes payable	0
Accounts receivable	+ 150,000
Cash	+ 15,000

a. Using the information given, calculate the change, if any, in net working capital that is expected to result from the proposed replacement action.
b. Explain why a change in these current accounts would be relevant in determining the initial investment for the proposed capital expenditure.
c. Would the change in net working capital enter into any of the other cash flow components comprising the relevant cash flows? Explain.

9-10   Initial investment—Basic calculation   M. Higgins, Inc. is considering the purchase of a new grading machine to replace the existing one. The existing machine was purchased 3 years ago at an installed cost of $20,000; it was being depreciated under MACRS using a 5-year recovery period. (See Table 4.7 on page 91 for the applicable depreciation percentages.) The existing machine is expected to have a usable life of at least 5 more years. The new machine costs $35,000 and requires $5,000 in installation costs; it will be depreciated using a 5-year recovery period under MACRS. The existing machine can currently be sold for $25,000 without incurring any removal or cleanup costs. The firm pays 40 percent taxes on both ordinary income and capital gains. Calculate the *initial investment* associated with the proposed purchase of a new grading machine.

9-11   Initial investment at various sale prices   Bolton Castings Corporation is considering replacing one machine with another. The old machine was purchased 3 years ago for an installed cost of $10,000. The firm is depreciating the machine under MACRS using a 5-year recovery period. (See Table 4.7 on page 91 for the applicable depreciation percentages.) The new machine costs $24,000 and requires $2,000 in installation costs. Assume the firm is subject to a 40 percent tax rate on both ordinary income and capital gains. In each of the following cases, calculate the initial investment for the replacement.

a. Bolton Castings Corporation (BCC) sells the old machine for $11,000.
b. BCC sells the old machine for $7,000.
c. BCC sells the old machine for $2,900.
d. BCC sells the old machine for $1,500.

9-12 Depreciation   A firm is evaluating the acquisition of an asset that costs $64,000 and requires $4,000 in installation costs. If the firm depreciates the asset under MACRS using a 5-year recovery period (see Table 4.7 on page 91 for the applicable depreciation percentages), determine the depreciation charge for each year.

9-13 Incremental operating cash inflows   A firm is considering renewing its equipment to meet increased demand for its product. The cost of equipment modifications is $1.9 million plus $100,000 in installation costs. The firm will depreciate the equipment modifications under MACRS using a 5-year recovery period. (See Table 4.7 on page 91 for the applicable depreciation percentages.) Additional sales revenue from the renewal should amount to $1.2 million per year, and additional operating expenses and other costs (excluding depreciation) will amount to 40 percent of the additional sales. The firm has an ordinary tax rate of 40 percent. (*Note:* Answer the following questions for each of the next 6 years.)

a. What incremental earnings before depreciation and taxes will result from the renewal?
b. What incremental earnings after taxes will result from the renewal?
c. What incremental operating cash inflows will result from the renewal?

9-14 Incremental operating cash inflows—Expense reduction   Tex-Tube Corporation is considering replacing a machine. The replacement will reduce operating expenses (i.e., increase revenues) by $16,000 per year for each of the 5 years the new machine is expected to last. Although the old machine has zero book value, it can be used for five more years. The depreciable value of the new machine is $48,000. The firm will depreciate the machine under MACRS using a 5-year recovery period (see Table 4.7 on page 91 for the applicable depreciation percentages) and is subject to a 40 percent tax rate on ordinary income. Estimate the incremental operating cash inflows generated by the replacement. (*Note:* Be sure to consider the depreciation in year 6.)

9-15 Incremental operating cash inflows   Fenton Tool Company has been considering purchasing a new lathe to replace a fully depreciated lathe that will last 5 more years. The new lathe is expected to have a 5-year life and depreciation charges of $2,000 in year 1; $3,200 in year 2; $1,900 in year 3; $1,200 in both year 4 and year 5; and $500 in year 6. The firm estimates the revenues and expenses (excluding depreciation) for the new and the old lathes as shown in the following table. The firm is subject to a 40 percent tax rate on ordinary income.

	New lathe		Old lathe	
Year	Revenue	Expenses (excl. depr.)	Revenue	Expenses (excl. depr.)
1	$40,000	$30,000	$35,000	$25,000
2	41,000	30,000	35,000	25,000
3	42,000	30,000	35,000	25,000
4	43,000	30,000	35,000	25,000
5	44,000	30,000	35,000	25,000

a. Calculate the operating cash inflows associated with each lathe. (*Note:* Be sure to consider the depreciation in year 6.)
b. Calculate the incremental (relevant) operating cash inflows resulting from the proposed lathe replacement.
c. Depict on a time line the incremental operating cash inflows calculated in **b.**

9-16   **Terminal cash flows—Various lives and sale prices**   Looner Industries is currently analyzing the purchase of a new machine costing $160,000 and requiring $20,000 in installation costs. Purchase of this machine is expected to result in an increase in net working capital of $30,000 to support the expanded level of operations. The firm plans to depreciate the asset under MACRS using a 5-year recovery period (see Table 4.7 on page 91 for the applicable depreciation percentages) and expects to sell the machine to net $10,000 before taxes at the end of its usable life. The firm is subject to a 40 percent tax rate on both ordinary and capital gains income.
a. Calculate the terminal cash flow for a usable life of (1) 3 years, (2) 5 years, and (3) 7 years.
b. Discuss the effect of usable life on terminal cash flows using your findings in **a.**
c. Assuming a 5-year usable life, calculate the terminal cash flow if the machine were sold to net (1) $9,000 or (2) $170,000 (before taxes) at the end of 5 years.
d. Discuss the effect of sale price on terminal cash flows using your findings in **c.**

9-17   **Terminal cash flow—Replacement decision**   Russell Industries is considering replacing a fully depreciated machine having a remaining useful life of 10 years with a newer, more sophisticated machine. The new machine will cost $200,000 and will require $30,000 in installation costs. It will be depreciated under MACRS using a 5-year recovery period (see Table 4.7 on page 91 for the applicable depreciation percentages). A $25,000 increase in net working capital will be required to support the new machine. The firm plans to evaluate the potential replacement over a 4-year period. They estimate that the old machine could be sold at the end of 4 years to net $15,000 before taxes; the new machine at the end of 4 years will be worth $75,000 before taxes. Calculate the terminal cash flow at the end of year 4 that is relevant to the proposed purchase of the new machine. The firm is subject to a 40 percent tax rate on both ordinary and capital gains income.

9-18   Relevant cash flows for a marketing campaign   Maltin Tube, a manufacturer of high-quality aluminum tubing, has maintained stable sales and profits over the past 10 years. Although the market for aluminum tubing has been expanding by 3 percent per year, Maltin has been unsuccessful in sharing this growth. To increase its sales, the firm is considering an aggressive marketing campaign that centers on regularly running ads in all relevant trade journals and exhibiting products at all major regional and national trade shows. The campaign is expected to require an *annual* tax-deductible expenditure of $150,000 over the next 5 years. Sales revenue, as noted in the income statement for 2000 shown in what follows, totaled $20,000,000. If the proposed marketing campaign is not initiated, sales are expected to remain at this level in each of the next 5 years, 2001–2005. With the marketing campaign, sales are expected to rise to the levels shown in the second table for each of the next 5 years; cost of goods sold is expected to remain at 80 percent of sales; general and administrative expense (exclusive of any marketing campaign outlays) is expected to remain at 10 percent of sales; and annual depreciation expense is expected to remain at $500,000. Assuming a 40 percent tax rate, find the relevant cash flows over the next 5 years associated with the proposed marketing campaign.

Income Statement
Maltin Tube
for the year ended December 31, 2000

Sales revenue		$20,000,000
Less: Cost of goods sold (80%)		16,000,000
Gross profits		$ 4,000,000
Less: Operating expenses		
General and administrative expense (10%)	$2,000,000	
Depreciation expense	500,000	
Total operating expense		2,500,000
Net profits before taxes		$ 1,500,000
Less: Taxes (rate = 40%)		600,000
Net profits after taxes		$ 900,000

Sales Forecast
Maltin Tube

Year	Sales revenue
2001	$20,500,000
2002	21,000,000
2003	21,500,000
2004	22,500,000
2005	23,500,000

9-19   Relevant cash flows—No terminal value   Blake Company is considering replacing an existing piece of machinery with a more sophisticated machine. The old machine was purchased 3 years ago at a cost of $50,000, and this amount was being depreciated under MACRS using a 5-year recovery period. The machine has 5 years of usable life remaining. The new machine being considered costs $76,000 and requires $4,000 in installation costs. The new machine would be depreciated under MACRS using a 5-year recovery period. The old machine can currently be sold for $55,000 without incurring any removal or cleanup costs. The firm pays 40 percent taxes on both ordinary income and capital gains. The revenues and expenses (excluding depreciation) associated with the new and the old machine for the next 5 years are given in the table on the following page. (Table 4.7 on page 91 contains the applicable MACRS depreciation percentages.)

a. Calculate the initial investment associated with replacement of the old machine by the new one.

b. Determine the incremental operating cash inflows associated with the proposed replacement. (*Note:* Be sure to consider the depreciation in year 6.)

	New machine		Old machine	
Year	Revenue	Expenses (excl. depr.)	Revenue	Expenses (excl. depr.)
1	$750,000	$720,000	$674,000	$660,000
2	750,000	720,000	676,000	660,000
3	750,000	720,000	680,000	660,000
4	750,000	720,000	678,000	660,000
5	750,000	720,000	674,000	660,000

c. Depict on a time line the relevant cash flows found in **a** and **b** associated with the proposed replacement decision.

9-20   Integrative—Determining relevant cash flows   Sentry Company is contemplating the purchase of a new high-speed widget grinder to replace the existing grinder. The existing grinder was purchased 2 years ago at an installed cost of $60,000; it was being depreciated under MACRS using a 5-year recovery period. The existing grinder is expected to have a usable life of 5 more years. The new grinder costs $105,000 and requires $5,000 in installation costs; it has a 5-year usable life and would be depreciated under MACRS using a 5-year recovery period. The existing grinder can currently be sold for $70,000 without incurring any removal or cleanup costs. To support the increased business resulting from purchase of the new grinder, accounts receivable would increase by $40,000, inventories by $30,000, and accounts payable by $58,000. At the end of 5 years, the existing grinder is expected to have a market value of zero; the new grinder would be sold to net $29,000 after removal and cleanup costs and before taxes. The firm pays 40 percent taxes on both ordinary income and capital gains. The estimated *profits before depreciation and taxes* over the 5 years for both the new and existing grinder are shown in the following table.

(Table 4.7 on page 91 contains the applicable MACRS depreciation percentages.)

	Profits before depreciation and taxes	
Year	New grinder	Existing grinder
1	$43,000	$26,000
2	43,000	24,000
3	43,000	22,000
4	43,000	20,000
5	43,000	18,000

a. Calculate the initial investment associated with the replacement of the existing grinder by the new one.
b. Determine the incremental operating cash inflows associated with the proposed grinder replacement. (*Note:* Be sure to consider the depreciation in year 6.)
c. Determine the terminal cash flow expected at the end of year 5 from the proposed grinder replacement.
d. Depict on a time line the relevant cash flows associated with the proposed grinder replacement decision.

9-21   Integrative—Determining relevant cash flows   East Coast Drydock is considering replacing an existing hoist with one of two newer, more efficient pieces of equipment. The existing hoist is 3 years old, cost $32,000, and is being depreciated under MACRS using a 5-year recovery period. Although the existing hoist has only 3 years (years 4, 5, and 6) of depreciation remaining under MACRS, it has a remaining usable life of 5 years. Hoist A, one of the two possible replacement hoists, costs $40,000 to purchase and $8,000 to install. It has a 5-year usable life and will be depreciated under MACRS using a 5-year recovery period. The other hoist, B, costs $54,000 to purchase and $6,000 to install. It also has a 5-year usable life and will be depreciated under MACRS using a 5-year recovery period.

Increased investments in net working capital will accompany the decision to acquire hoist A or hoist B. Purchase of hoist A would result in a $4,000 increase in net working capital; hoist B would result in a $6,000 increase in net working capital. The projected *profits before depreciation and taxes* with each alternative hoist and the existing hoist are given in the following table.

	Profits before depreciation and taxes		
Year	With hoist A	With hoist B	With existing hoist
1	$21,000	$22,000	$14,000
2	21,000	24,000	14,000
3	21,000	26,000	14,000
4	21,000	26,000	14,000
5	21,000	26,000	14,000

The existing hoist can currently be sold for $18,000 and will not incur any removal or cleanup costs. At the end of 5 years, the existing hoist can be sold to net $1,000 before taxes. Hoists A and B can be sold to net $12,000 and $20,000 before taxes, respectively, at the end of the 5-year period. The firm is subject to a 40 percent tax rate on both ordinary income and capital gains. (Table 4.7 on page 91 contains the applicable MACRS depreciation percentages.)
a. Calculate the initial investment associated with each alternative.
b. Calculate the incremental operating cash inflows associated with each alternative. (*Note:* Be sure to consider the depreciation in year 6.)
c. Calculate the terminal cash flow at the end of year 5 associated with each alternative.
d. Depict on a time line the relevant cash flows associated with each alternative.

 **CASE   Chapter 9**

Developing Relevant Cash Flows for Clark Upholstery Company's Machine Renewal or Replacement Decision

Bo Humphries, chief financial officer of Clark Upholstery Company, expects the firm's *net profits after taxes* for the next 5 years to be as shown in the following table.

Year	Net profits after taxes
1	$100,000
2	150,000
3	200,000
4	250,000
5	320,000

Bo is beginning to develop the relevant cash flows needed to analyze whether to renew or replace Clark's only depreciable asset, a machine that originally cost $30,000, has a current book value of zero, and can now be sold for $20,000.

(*Note:* Because the firm's only depreciable asset is fully depreciated—its book value is zero—its expected net profits after taxes equal its operating cash inflows.) He estimates that at the end of 5 years, the existing machine can be sold to net $2,000 before taxes. Bo plans to use the following information to develop the relevant cash flows for each of the alternatives.

Alternative 1   Renew the existing machine at a total depreciable cost of $90,000. The renewed machine would have a 5-year usable life and be depreciated under MACRS using a 5-year recovery period. Renewing the machine would result in the following projected revenues and expenses (excluding depreciation):

Year	Revenue	Expenses (excluding depreciation)
1	$1,000,000	$801,500
2	1,175,000	884,200
3	1,300,000	918,100
4	1,425,000	943,100
5	1,550,000	968,100

The renewed machine would result in an increased investment of $15,000 in net working capital. At the end of 5 years, the machine could be sold to net $8,000 before taxes.

Alternative 2   Replace the existing machine with a new machine costing $100,000 and requiring installation costs of $10,000. The new machine would have a 5-year usable life and be depreciated under MACRS using a 5-year recovery period. The firm's projected revenues and expenses (excluding depreciation), if it acquires the machine, would be as follows:

Year	Revenue	Expenses (excluding depreciation)
1	$1,000,000	$764,500
2	1,175,000	839,800
3	1,300,000	914,900
4	1,425,000	989,900
5	1,550,000	998,900

The new machine would result in an increased investment of $22,000 in net working capital. At the end of 5 years, the new machine could be sold to net $25,000 before taxes.

The firm is subject to a 40 percent tax on both ordinary income and capital gains. As noted, the company uses MACRS depreciation. (See Table 4.7 on page 91 for the applicable depreciation percentages.)

Required

a. Calculate the initial investment associated with each of Clark Upholstery's alternatives.

b. Calculate the incremental operating cash inflows associated with each of Clark's alternatives. (*Note:* Be sure to consider the depreciation in year 6.)

c. Calculate the terminal cash flow at the end of year 5 associated with each of Clark's alternatives.

d. Use your findings in **a, b,** and **c** to depict on a time line the relevant cash flows associated with each of Clark Upholstery's alternatives.

e. Based solely upon your comparison of their relevant cash flows, which alternative appears to be better? Why?

Web Exercise

GOTO web site www.reportgallery.com. Click ANNUAL REPORT at the top of the page. Scroll down to Alcoa and click on ANNUAL REPORT. In the left column click on Liquidity and Capital Resources. Scroll down to the Investing Activities and click on Capital expenditures.

1. How much did Alcoa spend on capital expenditures for each of the last 5 years?

2. Were their capital expenditures increasing or decreasing?

3. Is their capital spending consistent or erratic?

4. What were their major uses of capital spending for the most recent year?

Click on Consolidated Balance Sheets in the left column.

5. What are the account balances for Properties, Plant, and Equipment for the 2 most recent years?

6. What percent of Properties, Plant, and Equipment does Alcoa replace every year? (*Hint:* For a rough estimate, divide the capital expenditures for a year by that year's balance in Properties, Plant, and Equipment.)

CAPITAL BUDGETING TECHNIQUES: CERTAINTY AND RISK

LEARNING GOALS

LG1 Calculate, interpret, and evaluate the payback period.

LG2 Apply net present value (NPV) and internal rate of return (IRR) to relevant cash flows to choose acceptable capital expenditures.

LG3 Use net present value profiles to compare net present value and internal rate of return techniques in light of conflicting rankings.

LG4 Discuss the two basic approaches—internal rate of return and net present value—for choosing projects under capital rationing.

LG5 Recognize sensitivity and scenario analysis, decision trees, and simulation as behavioral approaches for dealing with project risk, and the unique risks facing multinational companies.

LG6 Understand the calculation, differing approaches, and practical aspects of certainty equivalents (CEs) and risk-adjusted discount rates (RADRs).

ACROSS *the* DISCIPLINES

Firms use the relevant cash flows to make decisions about proposed capital expenditures. These decisions can be expressed in the form of project acceptance or rejection or of project rankings. A number of techniques are used in such decision making, some more sophisticated than others. These techniques are the topic of this chapter, in which we describe the assumptions on which capital budgeting techniques are based, show how they are used in both certain and risky situations, and evaluate their strengths and weaknesses. Chapter 10 is important to:

- **accounting personnel** who will help determine the after-tax cash flows for capital expenditure proposals.

- **information systems analysts** who will design decision modules that help reduce the amount of work required to analyze proposed capital projects.

- **management** because it will determine the decision criteria used to accept, reject, or rank project proposals.

- **the marketing department** because it will provide revenue estimates for the various proposals.

- **operations,** which will help prepare the cost estimates for many project proposals.

CAPITAL BUDGETING TECHNIQUES

When firms have developed relevant cash flows, as demonstrated in Chapter 9, they then analyze them to assess whether a project is acceptable or to rank projects. A number of techniques are available for performing such analyses. The preferred approaches integrate time value procedures (Chapter 6), risk and return considerations (Chapter 7), and valuation concepts (Chapter 8) to select capital expenditures that are consistent with the firm's goal of maximizing owners' wealth. This and the following section focus on the use of these techniques in an environment of certainty. Later in the chapter we will look at capital budgeting under uncertain circumstances.

We will use one basic problem to illustrate all the techniques described in this chapter. The problem concerns Blano Company, a medium-sized metal fabricator that is currently contemplating two projects: Project A requires an initial investment of $42,000, and project B, an initial investment of $45,000. The projected relevant operating cash inflows for the two projects are presented in Table 10.1 and depicted on the time line in Figure 10.1.[1] The projects exhibit *conventional cash flow patterns*, which are assumed throughout the text. In addition, at this point we assume that all projects' cash flows have the same level of risk, that projects being compared have equal usable lives, and that the firm has unlimited funds. Because very few decisions are actually made under such conditions, some of these simplifying assumptions are relaxed in later sections of the chapter. Here

TABLE 10.1	Capital Expenditure Data for Blano Company	
	Project A	Project B
Initial investment	$42,000	$45,000
Year	Operating cash inflows	
1	$14,000	$28,000
2	14,000	12,000
3	14,000	10,000
4	14,000	10,000
5	14,000	10,000
Average	$14,000	$14,000

[1]For simplification, these 5-year-lived projects with 5 years of cash inflows are used throughout this chapter. Projects with usable lives equal to the number of years of cash inflows are also included in the end-of-chapter problems. Recall from Chapter 9 that under current tax law, MACRS depreciation results in $n + 1$ years of depreciation for an n-year class asset. This means that projects will commonly have at least 1 year of cash flow beyond their recovery period. In actual practice, usable lives of projects (and the associated cash inflows) may differ significantly from their depreciable lives. Generally, under MACRS, usable lives are longer than depreciable lives.

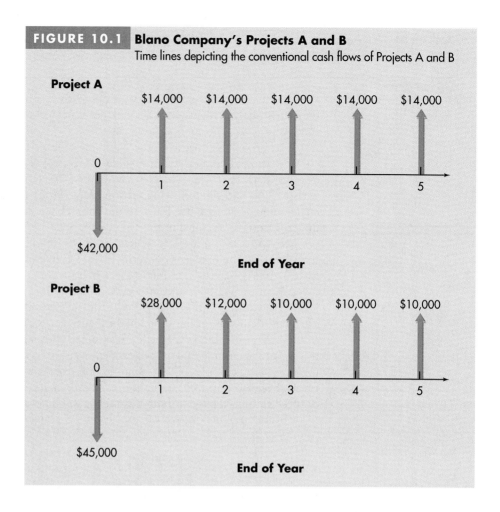

FIGURE 10.1 **Blano Company's Projects A and B**
Time lines depicting the conventional cash flows of Projects A and B

we begin with a look at the three most popular capital budgeting techniques—payback period, net present value, and internal rate of return.[2]

PAYBACK PERIOD

payback period
The exact amount of time required for a firm to recover its initial investment in a project as calculated from *cash inflows*.

Payback periods are commonly used to evaluate proposed investments. The **payback period** is the exact amount of time required for the firm to recover its initial investment in a project as calculated from *cash inflows*. In the case of an *annuity*, the payback period can be found by dividing the initial investment by the annual cash inflow. For a *mixed stream* of cash inflows, the yearly cash inflows must be accumulated until the initial investment is recovered. Although popular, the pay-

[2]Two other closely related techniques that are sometimes used to evaluate capital budgeting projects are the *average (or accounting) rate of return (ARR)* and the *profitability index (PI)*. The ARR is an unsophisticated technique that is calculated by dividing a project's average profits after taxes by its average investment. Because it fails to consider cash flows and the time value of money, it is ignored here. The PI, sometimes called the *benefit-cost ratio*, is calculated by dividing the present value of cash inflows by the initial investment. This technique, which does consider the time value of money, is sometimes used as a starting point in the selection of projects under capital rationing; the more popular NPV and IRR methods are discussed here.

back period is generally viewed as an *unsophisticated capital budgeting technique,* because it does not *explicitly* consider the time value of money.

THE DECISION CRITERIA

When the payback period is used to make accept–reject decisions, the decision criteria are as follows:

- If the payback period is *less than* the maximum acceptable payback period, accept the project.
- If the payback period is *greater than* the maximum acceptable payback period, *reject* the project.

The length of the maximum acceptable payback period is determined by management. This value is set *subjectively,* based upon a number of factors including, but not limited to, the type of project (expansion, replacement, renewal, etc.), the perceived risk of the project, and the perceived relationship between the payback period and share value. It is simply a value that management feels, on average, will result in good—that is, value-creating—investment decisions.

Example ▼ We can calculate the payback period for Blano Company's projects A and B using the data in Table 10.1. For project A, which is an annuity, the payback period is 3.0 years ($42,000 initial investment ÷ $14,000 annual cash inflow). Because project B generates a mixed stream of cash inflows, the calculation of its payback period is not as clear cut. In year 1, the firm will recover $28,000 of its $45,000 initial investment. By the end of year 2, $40,000 ($28,000 from year 1 + $12,000 from year 2) will be recovered. At the end of year 3, $50,000 ($40,000 from years 1 and 2 + $10,000 from year 3) will be recovered. Because the amount received by the end of year 3 is greater than the initial investment of $45,000, the payback period is somewhere between 2 and 3 years. Only 50 percent of the year 3 cash inflow of $10,000 is needed to complete the payback of the initial $45,000. The payback period for project B is therefore 2.5 years (2 years + 50 percent of year 3).

If Blano's maximum acceptable payback period were 2.75 years, project A would be rejected and project B would be accepted. If the maximum payback were 2.25 years, both projects would be rejected. If the projects were being ▲ ranked, B would be preferred over A, because it has a shorter payback period.

PROS AND CONS OF PAYBACK PERIODS

The payback period is widely used by large firms to evaluate small projects and by small firms to evaluate most projects. Its popularity in these instances results from its computational simplicity and intuitive appeal. It is also appealing in that it considers cash flows rather than accounting profits. By measuring how quickly the firm recovers its initial investment, the payback period also gives *implicit* consideration to the timing of cash flows and therefore to the time value of money. Because it can be viewed as a measure of *risk exposure,* many firms use the payback period as a decision criterion or as a supplement to other decision techniques. The longer the firm must wait to recover its invested funds, the greater the possibility of a calamity. Therefore, the shorter the payback period, the lower the firm's exposure to such risk.

The major weakness of the payback period is that the appropriate payback period is merely a subjectively determined number. It does not link the payback period to the wealth maximization goal. A second weakness is that this approach fails to take *fully* into account the time factor in the value of money.[3] A third weakness is the failure to recognize cash flows that occur *after* the payback period. This weakness can be illustrated by an example.

Example ▼ Rashid Company, a software developer, has two investment opportunities—X and Y. Data for X and Y are given in Table 10.2. The payback period for project X is 2 years; for project Y, it is 3 years. Strict adherence to the payback approach suggests that project X is preferable to project Y. However, if we look beyond the payback period, we see that project X returns only an additional $1,200 ($1,000 in year 3 + $100 in year 4 + $100 in year 5), whereas project Y returns an additional $7,000 ($4,000 in year 4 + $3,000 in year 5). On the basis of this information, project Y appears preferable to X. The payback approach ignored ▲ the cash inflows past the end of the payback period.

NET PRESENT VALUE (NPV)

Because *net present value (NPV)* gives explicit consideration to the time value of money, it is considered a *sophisticated capital budgeting technique.* All such techniques in one way or another discount the firm's cash flows at a specified rate. This rate—often called the *discount rate, required return, cost of capital,* or

TABLE 10.2	Calculation of the Payback Period for Rashid Company's Two Alternative Investment Projects	
	Project X	Project Y
Initial investment	$10,000	$10,000
Year	Cash inflows	
1	$5,000	$3,000
2	5,000	4,000
3	1,000	3,000
4	100	4,000
5	100	3,000
Payback period	2 years	3 years

[3]To consider differences in timing *explicitly* in applying the payback method, the *present value payback period* is sometimes used. It is found by first calculating the present value of the cash inflows at the appropriate discount rate and then finding the payback period by using the present value of the cash inflows.

opportunity cost—refers to the minimum return that must be earned on a project to leave the firm's market value unchanged. In this chapter, we take this rate as a "given." In Chapter 11 we will explore how it is calculated.

net present value (NPV)
A sophisticated capital budgeting technique; found by subtracting a project's initial investment from the present value of its cash inflows discounted at a rate equal to the firm's cost of capital.

The **net present value** (**NPV**) is found by subtracting a project's initial investment *(II)* from the present value of its cash inflows *(CF$_t$)* discounted at a rate equal to the firm's cost of capital *(k)*.

$$\text{NPV} = \text{present value of cash inflows} - \text{initial investment}$$

$$\text{NPV} = \sum_{t=1}^{n} \frac{CF_t}{(1+k)^t} - II \tag{10.1}$$

$$= \sum_{t=1}^{n} (CF_t \times PVIF_{k,t}) - II \tag{10.1a}$$

By using NPV, both inflows and outflows are measured in terms of present dollars.[4]

THE DECISION CRITERIA

When NPV is used to make accept–reject decisions, the decision criteria are as follows:

- If the NPV is *greater than* $0, *accept* the project.
- If the NPV is *less than* $0, *reject* the project.

If the NPV is greater than $0, the firm will earn a return greater than its cost of capital. Such action should enhance the market value of the firm and therefore the wealth of its owners.

Example ▼

We can illustrate the net present value (NPV) approach using Blano Company data presented in Table 10.1. If the firm has a 10 percent cost of capital, the net present values for projects A (an annuity) and B (a mixed stream) can be calculated as in Table 10.3. These calculations are based on the techniques presented in Chapter 6 using present value table factors.[5] The results show that the net present values of projects A and B are $11,074 and $10,914, respectively. Both projects are acceptable, because the net present value of each is greater than $0. If the projects were being ranked, project A would be considered superior to B, because it has a higher net present value ($11,074 versus $10,914).

INTERNAL RATE OF RETURN (IRR)

internal rate of return (IRR)
A sophisticated capital budgeting technique; the discount rate that equates the present value of cash inflows with the initial investment associated with a project, thereby causing NPV = $0.

The *internal rate of return (IRR)* is probably the most used *sophisticated capital budgeting technique.* However, it is considerably more difficult than NPV to calculate by hand. The **internal rate of return** (**IRR**) is the discount rate that equates the present value of cash inflows with the initial investment associated with a project. The IRR, in other words, is the discount rate that equates the NPV of an

---

[4]Because we are dealing only with investments that have *conventional cash flow patterns,* the initial investment is automatically stated in terms of today's dollars. If it were not, the present value of a project would be found by subtracting the present value of outflows from the present value of inflows.

[5]Alternatively, an inexpensive financial calculator could have been used to streamline these calculations as described in Chapter 6. Most of the more sophisticated (and expensive) financial calculators are preprogrammed to find NPVs. With these calculators, you merely punch in all cash flows along with the cost of capital or discount rate and depress NPV to find the net present value. Using such a calculator, the resulting values for projects A and B are $11,071 and $10,924, respectively.

TABLE 10.3	The Calculation of NPVs for Blano Company's Capital Expenditure Alternatives

Project A

Annual cash inflow	$14,000
× Present value annuity interest factor, $PVIFA^a$	3.791
Present value of cash inflows	$53,074
− Initial investment	42,000
Net present value (NPV)	$11,074

Project B

Year	Cash inflows (1)	Present value interest factor, $PVIF^b$ (2)	Present value [(1) × (2)] (3)
1	$28,000	.909	$25,452
2	12,000	.826	9,912
3	10,000	.751	7,510
4	10,000	.683	6,830
5	10,000	.621	6,210
		Present value of cash inflows	$55,914
		− Initial investment	45,000
		Net present value (NPV)	$10,914

^{a}From Table A-4, for 5 years and 10 percent.
^{b}From Table A-3, for given year and 10 percent.

investment opportunity with $0 (because the present value of cash inflows equals the initial investment). It is the compound annual rate of return that the firm will earn if it invests in the project and receives the given cash inflows. Mathematically, the IRR is found by solving Equation 10.1 for the value of k that causes NPV to equal $0:

$$\$0 = \sum_{t=1}^{n} \frac{CF_t}{(1 + IRR)^t} - II$$

$$\sum_{t=1}^{n} \frac{CF_t}{(1 + IRR)^t} = II \tag{10.2}$$

As we will show, the actual calculation by hand of the IRR from Equation 10.2 is no easy chore.

THE DECISION CRITERIA

When IRR is used to make accept–reject decisions, the decision criteria are as follows:

- If the IRR is *greater than* the cost of capital, *accept* the project.
- If the IRR is *less than* the cost of capital, *reject* the project.

These criteria guarantee that the firm earns at least its required return. Such an outcome should enhance the market value of the firm and therefore the wealth of its owners.

CALCULATING THE IRR

The IRR can be found either by using trial-and-error techniques or with the aid of a sophisticated financial calculator or a computer.[6] Here we demonstrate the trial-and-error approach. Calculating the IRR for an annuity is considerably easier than calculating it for a mixed stream of operating cash inflows. The steps involved in calculating the IRR in each case are outlined in Table 10.4 and illustrated by the following example.

Example ▼   The two-step procedure given in Table 10.4 for finding the IRR of an *annuity* can be demonstrated by using Blano Company's project A cash flows given in Table 10.1.

Step 1   Dividing the initial investment of $42,000 by the annual cash inflow of $14,000 results in a payback period of 3.000 years ($42,000 ÷ $14,000 = 3.000).

Step 2   In Table A-4, the *PVIFA* factors closest to 3.000 for 5 years are 3.058 (for 19 percent) and 2.991 (for 20 percent). The value closest to 3.000 is 2.991; therefore, the IRR for project A, to the nearest 1 percent, is *20 percent*. The actual value, which is between 19 and 20 percent, could be found by using a calculator[7] or computer or by interpolation; it is 19.86 percent. (*Note:* For our purposes, values rounded to the nearest 1 percent will suffice.) Project A with an IRR of 20 percent is quite acceptable, because this IRR is above the firm's 10 percent cost of capital.

The seven-step procedure given in Table 10.4 for finding the internal rate of return of a *mixed stream* of cash inflows can be illustrated by using Blano Company's project B cash flows given in Table 10.1.

Step 1   Summing the cash inflows for years 1 through 5 results in total cash inflows of $70,000. That amount, when divided by the number of years in the project's life, results in an average annual cash inflow of $14,000 [($28,000 + $12,000 + $10,000 + $10,000 + $10,000) ÷ 5].

Step 2   Dividing the initial outlay of $45,000 by the average annual cash inflow of $14,000 results in an "average payback period" (or present value of an annuity factor, *PVIFA*) of 3.214 years.

---

[6]Nearly all inexpensive financial calculators can be used to find the IRR of an annuity, but they lack a function for finding the IRR of a mixed stream of cash flows. Most more sophisticated financial calculators are preprogrammed to find IRRs. With these calculators, you merely punch in all cash flows and depress IRR to find the internal rate of return. Computer software, like the *PMF BRIEF CD-ROM Software* that accompanies this text, is also available for calculating IRRs.

[7]The procedure for using a financial calculator to find the unknown interest rate on an equal-payment loan described in Chapter 6 can be used to find the IRR for an annuity. When applying this procedure, we treat the life of the annuity the same as the term of the loan, the initial investment the same as the loan principal, and the annual cash inflows the same as the annual loan payments. The resulting solution is the IRR for the annuity rather than the interest rate on the loan.

TABLE 10.4	**Steps for Calculating the Internal Rates of Return (IRRs) of Annuities and Mixed Streams**

FOR AN ANNUITY

Step 1: Calculate the payback period for the project.[a]

Step 2: Find, for the life of the project, the present value interest factor closest to the payback value. (Use Table A-4, which presents *PVIFA*.) The discount rate associated with that factor is the internal rate of return (IRR) to the nearest 1 percent.

FOR A MIXED STREAM[b]

Step 1: Find the average annual cash inflow by dividing the sum of the annual cash inflows by the number of years in the project's life.

Step 2: Divide the average annual cash inflow into the initial investment to get an "average payback period" (or present value interest factor for a $1 annuity, *PVIFA*). The average payback is needed to estimate the IRR for the average annual cash inflow.

Step 3: Find the discount rate associated with the present value interest factor in Table A-4 (*PVIFA*) for the life of the project that is closest to the average payback period (as described in Step 2 for finding the IRR of an annuity). The result will be a *very rough* approximation of the IRR based on the assumption that the mixed stream of cash inflows is an annuity.

Step 4:[c] Adjust subjectively the IRR obtained in Step 3 by comparing the pattern of average annual cash inflows (calculated in Step 1) to the actual mixed stream of cash inflows. If the actual cash flow stream seems to have higher inflows in the earlier years than the average stream, adjust the IRR up. If the actual cash inflows in the earlier years are below the average, adjust the IRR down. The amount of adjustment up or down typically ranges from 1 to 3 percentage points, depending upon how much the actual cash inflow stream's pattern deviates from the average annual cash inflows. For small deviations, an adjustment of around 1 percentage point may be best, whereas for large deviations, adjustments of around 3 percentage points are generally appropriate. If the average cash inflows seem fairly close to the actual pattern, make no adjustment in the IRR.

Step 5: Calculate the net present value of the mixed stream project using the IRR from Step 4. Be sure to use Table A-3 (the present value interest factors for $1, *PVIF*), treating the estimated IRR as the discount rate.

Step 6: If the resulting NPV is greater than zero, subjectively raise the discount rate; if the resulting NPV is less than zero, subjectively lower the discount rate. The greater the deviation of the resulting NPV from zero, the larger the subjective adjustment. Typically, adjustments of 1 to 3 percentage points are used for relatively small deviations, whereas larger adjustments are required for relatively large deviations.

Step 7: Calculate the NPV using the new discount rate. Repeat Step 6. Stop as soon as two *consecutive* discount rates that cause the NPV to be positive and negative, respectively, have been found.[d] Whichever of these rates causes the NPV to be closer to zero is the IRR to the nearest 1 percent.

[a]The payback period calculated actually represents the interest factor for the present value of an annuity (*PVIFA*) for the given life discounted at an unknown rate, which, once determined, represents the IRR for the project.

[b]Note that subjective estimates are suggested in Steps 4 and 6. After working a number of these problems, a "feel" for the appropriate subjective adjustment, or "educated guess," may result.

[c]The purpose of this step is to provide a more accurate first estimate of the IRR. This step can be skipped.

[d]A shortcut method is to find a discount rate that results in a positive NPV and another that results in a negative NPV. Using only these two values, one can interpolate between the two discount rates to find the IRR. This approach, which may be nearly as accurate as that described before, can guarantee an answer after only two NPV calculations. Of course, because interpolation involves a straight-line approximation to an exponential function, the wider the interpolation interval, the less accurate the estimate.

Step 3   In Table A-4, the factor closest to 3.214 for 5 years is 3.199, the factor for a discount rate of 17 percent. The starting estimate of the IRR is therefore 17 percent.

Step 4   Because the actual early-year cash inflows are greater than the average annual cash inflows of $14,000, a *subjective* increase of 2 percent is made in the discount rate. This makes the estimated IRR 19 percent.

Step 5   By using the present value interest factors (*PVIF*) for 19 percent and the correct year from Table A-3, we calculate the net present value of the mixed stream as follows:

Year (t)	Cash inflows (1)	$PVIF_{19\%,t}$ (2)	Present value at 19% [(1) × (2)] (3)
1	$28,000	.840	$23,520
2	12,000	.706	8,472
3	10,000	.593	5,930
4	10,000	.499	4,990
5	10,000	.419	4,190
	Present value of cash inflows		$47,102
	− Initial investment		45,000
	Net present value (NPV)		$ 2,102

Steps 6 and 7   Because the net present value of $2,102, calculated in Step 5, is greater than zero, the discount rate should be subjectively increased. Because the NPV deviates by only about 5 percent from the $45,000 initial investment, let's try a 2 percentage point increase, to 21 percent:

Year (t)	Cash inflows (1)	$PVIF_{21\%,t}$ (2)	Present value at 21% [(1) × (2)] (3)
1	$28,000	.826	$23,128
2	12,000	.683	8,196
3	10,000	.564	5,640
4	10,000	.467	4,670
5	10,000	.386	3,860
	Present value of cash inflows		$45,494
	− Initial investment		45,000
	Net present value (NPV)		$ 494

These calculations indicate that the NPV of $494 for an IRR of 21 percent is reasonably close to, but still greater than, zero. Thus a higher discount rate should be tried. Because we are so close, let's try a 1 percentage point increase, to 22 percent. As the following calculations show, the net present value using a discount rate of 22 percent is −$256.

Year (t)	Cash inflows (1)	$PVIF_{22\%,t}$ (2)	Present value at 22% [(1) × (2)] (3)
1	$28,000	.820	$22,960
2	12,000	.672	8,064
3	10,000	.551	5,510
4	10,000	.451	4,510
5	10,000	.370	3,700
	Present value of cash inflows		$44,744
	− Initial investment		45,000
	Net present value (NPV)		−$ 256

Because 21 and 22 percent are consecutive discount rates that give positive and negative net present values, we can stop the trial-and-error process here. The IRR that we are seeking is the discount rate for which the NPV is closest to $0. For this project, 22 percent causes the NPV to be closer to $0 than 21 percent, so we will use 22 percent as the IRR. If we had used a financial calculator or a computer or interpolation, the exact IRR would be 21.65 percent; as indicated earlier, for our purposes, the IRR rounded to the nearest 1 percent will suffice. Therefore, the IRR of project B is approximately *22 percent*.

Project B is acceptable, because its IRR of approximately 22 percent is greater than Blano Company's 10 percent cost of capital. This is the same conclusion reached by using the NPV criteria.

It is interesting to note in the preceding example that the IRR suggests that project B, which has an IRR of approximately 22 percent, is preferable to project A, which has an IRR of approximately 20 percent. This conflicts with the rankings of the projects obtained in an earlier example by using NPV. Such conflicts are not unusual. *There is no guarantee that these two techniques— NPV and IRR—will rank projects in the same order. However, both methods should reach the same conclusion about the acceptability or nonacceptability of projects.*

? R e v i e w   Q u e s t i o n s

10-1   What is the *payback period?* How is it calculated? What weaknesses are commonly associated with the use of the payback period to evaluate a proposed investment?

10-2   What is the formula for finding the *net present value (NPV)* of a project with a *conventional cash flow pattern?* What are the acceptance criteria for NPV?

10-3   What is the *internal rate of return (IRR)* on an investment? How is it determined? What are its acceptance criteria?

10-4   Do the net present value (NPV) and internal rate of return (IRR) always agree with respect to accept–reject decisions? With respect to ranking decisions? Explain.

LG3

COMPARING NPV AND IRR TECHNIQUES

For conventional projects, *net present value (NPV) and internal rate of return (IRR) will always generate the same accept–reject decision, but differences in their underlying assumptions can cause them to rank projects differently.* To understand the differences and preferences surrounding these techniques, we need to look at net present value profiles, conflicting rankings, and the question of which approach is better.

NET PRESENT VALUE PROFILES

net present value profile
Graph that depicts the net present value of a project for various discount rates.

Projects can be compared graphically by constructing **net present value profiles** that depict their net present values for various discount rates. These profiles are useful in evaluating and comparing projects, especially when conflicting rankings exist. Their development and interpretation are best demonstrated via an example.

E x a m p l e ▼   To prepare net present value profiles for Blano Company's two projects, A and B, the first step is to develop a number of discount-rate–net-present-value coordinates. Three coordinates can be easily obtained for each project; they are at discount rates of 0 percent, 10 percent (the cost of capital, k), and the IRR. The net present value at a 0 percent discount rate is found by merely adding all the cash inflows and subtracting the initial investment. Using the data in Table 10.1 and Figure 10.1, for project A, we get

$$(\$14{,}000 + \$14{,}000 + \$14{,}000 + \$14{,}000 + \$14{,}000) - \$42{,}000 = \$28{,}000$$

For project B, we get

$$(\$28{,}000 + \$12{,}000 + \$10{,}000 + \$10{,}000 + \$10{,}000) - \$45{,}000 = \$25{,}000$$

The net present values for projects A and B at the 10 percent cost of capital are $11,074 and $10,914, respectively (in Table 10.3). Because the IRR is the discount rate for which net present value equals zero, the IRRs of 20 percent for

TABLE 10.5	Discount-Rate–NPV Coordinates for Projects A and B	
	Net present value	
Discount rate	Project A	Project B
0%	$28,000	$25,000
10	11,074	10,914
20	0	—
22	—	0

project A and 22 percent for project B result in $0 NPVs. The three sets of coordinates for each of the projects are summarized in Table 10.5.

Plotting the data from Table 10.5 on a set of discount-rate–NPV axes results in the net present value profiles for projects A and B shown in Figure 10.2. An analysis of Figure 10.2 indicates that for any discount rate less than approximately 10.7 percent, the NPV for project A is greater than the NPV for project B. Beyond this point, the NPV for project B is greater than that for project A. Because the net present value profiles for projects A and B cross at a positive NPV, the IRRs for the projects cause conflicting rankings whenever they are compared to NPVs calculated at discount rates below 10.7 percent.

The NPV profiles for the Blano Company example demonstrate that conflicting rankings of projects by NPV and IRR can occur.

CONFLICTING RANKINGS

Ranking is an important consideration when projects are mutually exclusive or when capital rationing is necessary. When projects are mutually exclusive, ranking enables the firm to determine the best project from a financial viewpoint.

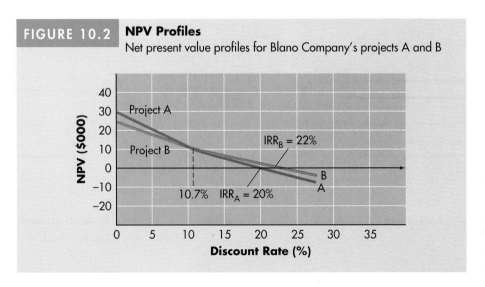

FIGURE 10.2   NPV Profiles
Net present value profiles for Blano Company's projects A and B

conflicting rankings
Conflicts in the ranking given a project by NPV and IRR, resulting from *differences in the magnitude and timing of cash flows.*

intermediate cash inflows
Cash inflows received prior to the termination of a project.

When capital rationing is necessary, ranking projects will provide a logical starting point for determining the group of projects to accept. As we'll see, **conflicting rankings** using NPV and IRR result from *differences in the magnitude and timing of cash flows.*

The underlying cause of conflicting rankings is the implicit assumption concerning the *reinvestment* of **intermediate cash inflows**—cash inflows received prior to the termination of a project. NPV assumes that intermediate cash inflows are reinvested at the cost of capital, whereas IRR assumes that intermediate cash inflows are invested at a rate equal to the project's IRR.

In general, projects with similar-sized investments and lower cash inflows in the early years tend to be preferred at lower discount rates. Projects having higher cash inflows in the early years tend to be preferred at higher discount rates. Why? Because at high discount rates, later year cash inflows tend to be severely penalized in present value terms. For example, at a high discount rate, say 20 percent, the present value of $1 received at the end of 5 years is about 40 cents, whereas for $1 received at the end of 15 years it is less than 7 cents. Clearly, at high discount rates a project's early year cash inflows count most in terms of its NPV. Table 10.6 summarizes the preferences associated with extreme discount rates and dissimilar cash inflow patterns.

Example ▼ In an earlier example, Blano Company's projects A and B were found to have conflicting rankings at the firm's 10 percent cost of capital. This finding is depicted in Figure 10.2. If we review each project's cash inflow pattern as presented in Table 10.1 and Figure 10.1, we see that although the projects require similar initial investments, they have dissimilar cash inflow patterns. Table 10.6 indicates that project B would be preferred over project A at higher discount rates. Figure 10.2 shows that this is in fact the case. At any discount rate in excess of 10.7 percent, project B's NPV is above that of project A. Clearly, the magnitude and ▲ timing of the projects' cash inflows do affect their rankings.

WHICH APPROACH IS BETTER?

It is difficult to choose one approach over the other because the theoretical and practical strengths of the approaches differ. It is therefore wise to view both NPV and IRR techniques in each of those dimensions.

TABLE 10.6	Preferences Associated with Extreme Discount Rates and Dissimilar Cash Inflow Patterns	
	Cash inflow pattern	
Discount rate	Lower early year cash inflows	Higher early year cash inflows
Low	Preferred	Not preferred
High	Not preferred	Preferred

THEORETICAL VIEW

On a purely theoretical basis, NPV is the better approach to capital budgeting. Its theoretical superiority is due to a number of factors. Most important is that the use of NPV implicitly assumes that any intermediate cash inflows generated by an investment are *reinvested at the firm's cost of capital.* The use of IRR assumes *reinvestment at the often high rate specified by the IRR.* Because the cost of capital tends to be a reasonable estimate of the rate at which the firm could *actually reinvest* intermediate cash inflows, the use of NPV with its more conservative and realistic reinvestment rate is in theory preferable.

In addition, certain mathematical properties may cause a project with a non-conventional cash flow pattern to have zero or more than one *real* IRR; this problem does not occur with the NPV approach.

PRACTICAL VIEW

Evidence suggests that in spite of the theoretical superiority of NPV, *financial managers prefer to use IRR.*[8] The preference for IRR is due to the general disposition of businesspeople toward *rates of return* rather than actual *dollar returns.* Because interest rates, profitability, and so on are most often expressed as annual rates of return, the use of IRR makes sense to financial decision makers. They tend to find NPV more difficult to use because it does not measure benefits *relative to the amount invested.* Because a variety of methods and techniques are available for avoiding the pitfalls of the IRR, its widespread use should not be viewed as reflecting a lack of sophistication on the part of financial decision makers.

Review Questions

10-5   How can a *net present value profile* be used to compare projects when conflicting rankings exist? What causes conflicts in the ranking of projects using net present value and internal rate of return?

10-6   Explain how, on a theoretical basis, the assumption concerning the reinvestment of intermediate cash inflows tends to favor the use of NPV over IRR. In practice, which technique is preferred? Why?

CAPITAL RATIONING

In theory, capital rationing should not exist: Firms should accept all projects that have positive NPVs (or IRRs > the cost of capital). If they don't have the funds to do so, firms would raise debt or equity capital to fund all acceptable projects.

---

[8]For example, see Harold Bierman, Jr., "Capital Budgeting in 1992: A Survey," *Financial Management* (Autumn 1993), p. 24, and Lawrence J. Gitman and Charles E. Maxwell, "A Longitudinal Comparison of Capital Budgeting Techniques Used by Major U.S. Firms: 1986 versus 1976," *Journal of Applied Business Research* (Fall 1987), pp. 41–50, for discussions of evidence with respect to capital budgeting decision-making practices in major U.S. firms.

However, *in practice*, most firms operate under *capital rationing*—they have more acceptable independent projects than they can fund. Generally, firms attempt to isolate and select the best acceptable projects subject to a capital expenditure budget set by management. Research has found that management internally imposes capital expenditure constraints to avoid what it deems to be "excessive" levels of new financing, particularly debt. Although failing to fund all acceptable independent projects is theoretically inconsistent with the goal of owner-wealth maximization, here we discuss capital rationing procedures because they are widely used in practice.

The objective of *capital rationing* is to select the group of projects that provides the *highest overall net present value* and does not require more dollars than are budgeted. As a prerequisite to capital rationing, the best of any mutually exclusive projects must be chosen and placed in the group of independent projects. Two basic approaches to project selection under capital rationing are discussed here.

internal rate of return approach
An approach to capital rationing that involves using a graph of project IRRs plotted in descending order against the total dollar investment, to determine the group of acceptable projects.

investment opportunities schedule (IOS)
The graph that plots project IRRs in descending order against the total dollar investment.

INTERNAL RATE OF RETURN APPROACH

The **internal rate of return approach** involves graphing project IRRs in descending order against the total dollar investment. This graph, which is discussed in more detail in Chapter 11, is called the **investment opportunities schedule (IOS)**. By drawing the cost of capital line and then imposing a budget constraint, the financial manager can determine the group of acceptable projects. The problem with this technique is that it does not guarantee the maximum dollar return to the firm. It merely provides a satisfactory solution to capital rationing problems.

Example ▼ Gould Company, a fast-growing plastics company, is confronted with six projects competing for its fixed budget of $250,000. The initial investment and IRR for each project are as follows:

Project	Initial investment	IRR
A	$ 80,000	12%
B	70,000	20
C	100,000	16
D	40,000	8
E	60,000	15
F	110,000	11

The firm has a cost of capital of 10 percent. Figure 10.3 presents the IOS resulting from ranking the six projects in descending order based on IRRs. According to the schedule, only projects B, C, and E should be accepted. Together they will absorb $230,000 of the $250,000 budget. Projects A and F are acceptable but cannot be chosen because of the budget constraint. Project D is not worthy of consideration, because its IRR is less than the firm's 10 percent cost of capital. The drawback of this approach is that there is no guarantee that the acceptance of projects B, C, and E will maximize *total dollar returns* and therefore owners' wealth.

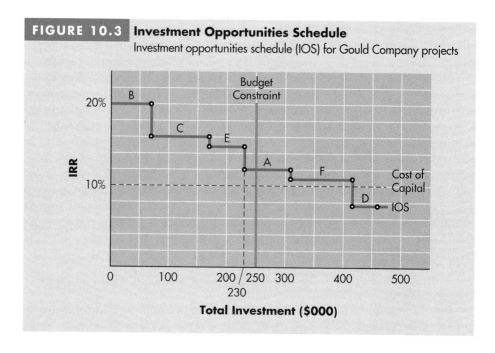

FIGURE 10.3   **Investment Opportunities Schedule**
Investment opportunities schedule (IOS) for Gould Company projects

NET PRESENT VALUE APPROACH

net present value approach
An approach to capital rationing that is based on the use of present values to determine the group of projects that will maximize owners' wealth.

The **net present value approach** uses present values to determine the group of projects that will maximize owners' wealth. It is implemented by ranking projects on the basis of IRRs and then evaluating the present value of the benefits from each project to determine *the combination of projects with the highest overall present value.* This is the same as maximizing net present value, in which the entire budget is viewed as the total initial investment. Any portion of the firm's budget that is not used does not increase the firm's value.

Example ▼ The group of projects described in the preceding example is ranked in Table 10.7 on the basis of IRRs. The present value of the cash inflows associated with the projects is also included in the table. Projects B, C, and E, which together require $230,000, yield a present value of $336,000. However, if projects B, C, and A were implemented, the total budget of $250,000 would be used, and the present

TABLE 10.7   **Rankings for Gould Company Projects**

Project	Initial investment	IRR	Present value of inflows at 10%	
B	$ 70,000	20%	$112,000	
C	100,000	16	145,000	
E	60,000	15	79,000	
A	80,000	12	100,000	
F	110,000	11	126,500	Cutoff point
D	40,000	8	36,000	(IRR < 10%)

value of the cash inflows would be $357,000. This is greater than the return expected from selecting the projects on the basis of the highest IRRs. Implementing B, C, and A is preferable, because they maximize the present value for the given budget. *The firm's objective is to use its budget to generate the highest present value of inflows.* Assuming that any unused portion of the budget does not gain or lose money, the total NPV for projects B, C, and E would be $106,000 ($336,000 − $230,000), whereas for projects B, C, and A the total NPV would be $107,000 ($357,000 − $250,000). Selection of projects B, C, and A will therefore maximize NPV.

❓ R e v i e w   Q u e s t i o n s

10-7   What is *capital rationing?* In theory, should capital rationing exist? Why does it frequently occur in practice?

10-8   Compare and contrast the *internal rate of return approach* and *net present value approach* to capital rationing. Which is better? Why?

BEHAVIORAL APPROACHES FOR DEALING WITH RISK

risk (in capital budgeting)
The chance that a project will prove unacceptable or, more formally, the degree of variability of cash flows.

In the discussion of capital budgeting, **risk** refers to the chance that a project will prove unacceptable—that is, NPV < $0 or IRR < cost of capital. More formally, risk in capital budgeting refers to the degree of variability of cash flows. Projects with a small chance of acceptability and a broad range of expected cash flows are more risky than projects having a high chance of acceptability and a narrow range of expected cash flows.

In the conventional capital budgeting projects assumed here, risk stems almost entirely from *cash inflows,* because the initial investment is generally known with relative certainty. These inflows, of course, derive from a number of variables related to revenues, expenditures, and taxes. Examples would include the level of sales, cost of raw materials, labor rates, utility costs, and tax rates. We will concentrate on the risk in the cash inflows, but remember that this risk actually results from the interaction of these underlying variables. Using the basic risk concepts presented in Chapter 7, here we present a few *behavioral approaches* for dealing with risk in capital budgeting: sensitivity and scenario analysis, decision trees, and simulation. In addition, some international risk considerations are discussed.

SENSITIVITY AND SCENARIO ANALYSIS

sensitivity analysis
A behavioral approach that uses a number of possible values for a given variable to assess its impact on a firm's return.

Two approaches for dealing with project risk to capture the variability of cash inflows and NPVs are sensitivity analysis and scenario analysis. **Sensitivity analysis,** as noted in Chapter 7, is a behavioral approach that uses a number of possible values for a given variable, such as cash inflows, to assess its impact on the firm's return, measured here by NPV. This technique is often useful in getting a feel for the variability of return in response to changes in a key variable. In capital budgeting, one of the most common sensitivity approaches is to estimate the NPVs associated with pessimistic (worst), most likely (expected), and optimistic (best) cash inflow estimates. The *range* can be determined by subtracting the pessimistic-outcome NPV from the optimistic-outcome NPV.

E x a m p l e ▼ Treadwell Tire Company, a tire retailer with a 10 percent cost of capital, is considering investing in either of two mutually exclusive projects, A or B. Each requires a $10,000 initial investment and is expected to provide equal annual cash inflows over their 15-year lives. The firm's financial manager made pessimistic, most likely, and optimistic estimates of the cash inflows for each project. The cash inflow estimates and resulting NPVs in each case are summarized in Table 10.8. Comparing the ranges of cash inflows ($1,000 for project A and $4,000 for B) and, more important, the ranges of NPVs ($7,606 for project A and $30,424 for B) makes it clear that project A is less risky than project B. Given that both projects have the same most likely NPV of $5,212, the assumed risk-averse decision maker will take project A because it has less risk and no possibility of loss.
▲

scenario analysis
A behavioral approach that evaluates the impact on return of simultaneous changes in a number of variables.

   Scenario analysis, which is a behavioral approach similar to sensitivity analysis but broader in scope, is used to evaluate the impact of various circumstances on the firm's return. Rather than isolating the effect of a change in a single variable, scenario analysis evaluates the impact of simultaneous changes in a number

TABLE 10.8	**Sensitivity Analysis of Treadwell's Projects A and B**	
	Project A	Project B
Initial investment	$10,000	$10,000
	Annual cash inflows	
Outcome		
Pessimistic	$ 1,500	$ 0
Most likely	2,000	2,000
Optimistic	2,500	4,000
Range	$ 1,000	$ 4,000
	Net present values[a]	
Outcome		
Pessimistic	$ 1,409	−$10,000
Most likely	5,212	5,212
Optimistic	9,015	20,424
Range	$ 7,606	$30,424

[a]These values were calculated by using the corresponding annual cash inflows. A 10 percent cost of capital and a 15-year life for the annual cash inflows were used.

of variables, such as cash inflows, cash outflows, and the cost of capital. For example, the firm could evaluate the impact of both high inflation (scenario 1) and low inflation (scenario 2) on a project's NPV. Each scenario will affect the firm's cash inflows, cash outflows, and cost of capital, thereby resulting in different levels of NPV. The decision maker can use these NPV estimates to roughly assess the risk involved with respect to the level of inflation. The widespread availability of computer-based spreadsheet programs (such as *Excel* and *Lotus 1-2-3*) has greatly enhanced the use of both scenario and sensitivity analysis.

DECISION TREES

decision trees
A behavioral approach that uses diagrams to map the various investment decision alternatives and payoffs as well as their probabilities of occurrence.

Decision trees are a behavioral approach that uses diagrams to map the various investment decision alternatives and payoffs as well as their probabilities of occurrence. Their name derives from their resemblance to the branches of a tree (see Figure 10.4). Decision trees rely on estimates of the probabilities associated with the outcomes (payoffs) of competing courses of action. The payoffs of each course of action are weighted by the associated probability; the weighted payoffs are summed; and the expected value of each course of action is then determined. The alternative that provides the highest expected value is preferred.

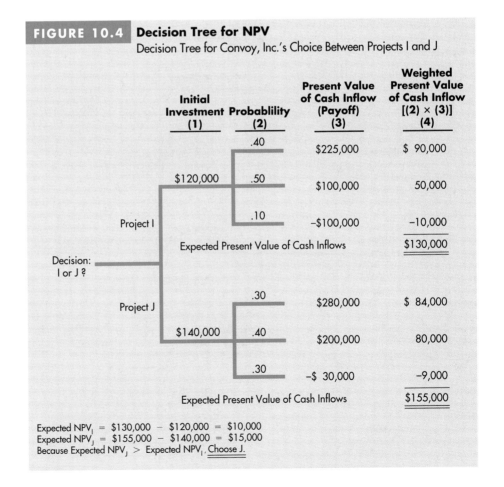

FIGURE 10.4   Decision Tree for NPV
Decision Tree for Convoy, Inc.'s Choice Between Projects I and J

	Initial Investment (1)	Probability (2)	Present Value of Cash Inflow (Payoff) (3)	Weighted Present Value of Cash Inflow [(2) × (3)] (4)
		.40	$225,000	$ 90,000
Project I	$120,000	.50	$100,000	50,000
		.10	−$100,000	−10,000
		Expected Present Value of Cash Inflows		$130,000
		.30	$280,000	$ 84,000
Project J	$140,000	.40	$200,000	80,000
		.30	−$ 30,000	−9,000
		Expected Present Value of Cash Inflows		$155,000

Expected NPV$_I$ = $130,000 − $120,000 = $10,000
Expected NPV$_J$ = $155,000 − $140,000 = $15,000
Because Expected NPV$_J$ > Expected NPV$_I$, Choose J.

Example ▼ Convoy, Inc., a manufacturer of picture frames, wishes to choose between two equally risky projects, I and J. To make this decision, Convoy's management has gathered the necessary data, which are depicted in the decision tree in Figure 10.4. Project I requires an initial investment of $120,000; a resulting expected present value of cash inflows of $130,000 is shown in column 4. Project I's expected net present value, which is calculated below the decision tree, is therefore $10,000. The expected net present value of project J is determined in a similar fashion. Project J is preferred because it offers a higher NPV—$15,000. ▲

SIMULATION

simulation
A statistically based behavioral approach that applies predetermined probability distributions and random numbers to estimate risky outcomes.

Simulation is a statistically based behavioral approach that applies predetermined probability distributions and random numbers to estimate risky outcomes. By tying the various cash flow components together in a mathematical model and repeating the process numerous times, the financial manager can develop a probability distribution of project returns. Figure 10.5 presents a flowchart of the simulation of the net present value of a project.

Although only gross cash inflows and outflows are simulated in Figure 10.5, more sophisticated simulations using individual inflow and outflow components, such as sales volume, sale price, raw material cost, labor cost, maintenance

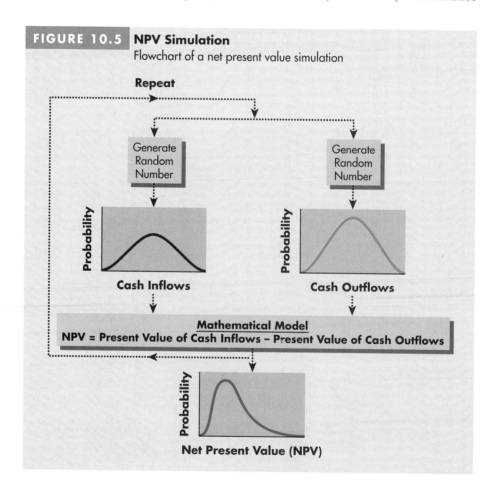

FIGURE 10.5   NPV Simulation
Flowchart of a net present value simulation

expense, and so on, are quite common. From the distribution of returns, the decision maker can determine not only the expected value of the return but also the probability of achieving or surpassing a given return. The use of computers has made the simulation approach feasible. The output of simulation provides an excellent basis for decision making, because it allows the decision maker to view a continuum of risk-return tradeoffs rather than a single-point estimate.

INTERNATIONAL RISK CONSIDERATIONS

Although the basic techniques of capital budgeting are the same for purely domestic firms as for multinational companies (MNCs), firms that operate in several countries face risks that are unique to the international arena. Two types of risk, discussed briefly in earlier chapters, are particularly important: exchange rate risk and political risk.

exchange rate risk
The danger that an unexpected change in the exchange rate between the dollar and the currency in which a project's cash flows are denominated can reduce the market value of that project's cash flow.

Exchange rate risk refers to the danger that an unexpected change in the exchange rate between the dollar and the currency in which a project's cash flows are denominated can reduce the market value of that project's cash flow. Although a project's initial investment can usually be predicted with some certainty, the dollar value of future cash inflows can be dramatically altered if the local currency depreciates against the dollar. In the short term, specific cash flows can be hedged by using financial instruments such as currency futures and options. Long-term exchange rate risk can best be minimized by financing the project, in whole or in part, in local currency.

Political risk is much harder to protect against. The inability to manage political risk after the fact makes it even more important that managers account for political risks before making an investment. They can do so either by adjusting a project's expected cash inflows to account for the probability of political interference or by using risk-adjusted discount rates (discussed later in this chapter) in capital budgeting formulas. In general, it is much better to subjectively adjust individual project cash flows for political risk than to use a blanket adjustment for all projects.

In addition to unique risks that MNCs must face, several other special issues are relevant only for international capital budgeting. These include tax law differences, the importance of *transfer pricing* in evaluating projects, and the need to analyze international projects from a strategic as well as a financial perspective. Because only after-tax cash flows are relevant for capital budgeting, financial managers must carefully account for taxes paid to foreign governments on profits earned within their borders. They must also assess the impact of these tax payments on the parent company's U.S. tax liability, because full or partial credit is generally allowed for foreign tax payments.

transfer prices
Prices that subsidiaries charge each other for the goods and services traded between them.

Much of the international trade involving MNCs is, in reality, simply the shipment of goods and services from one of a parent company's wholly owned subsidiaries to another subsidiary located abroad. The parent company therefore has great discretion in setting **transfer prices**, the prices that subsidiaries charge each other for the goods and services traded between them. The widespread use of transfer pricing in international trade makes capital budgeting in MNCs very difficult unless the transfer prices used accurately reflect actual costs and incremental cash flows.

Finally, MNCs often must approach international capital projects from a strategic point of view, rather than from a strictly financial perspective. For example, an MNC may feel compelled to invest in a country to ensure continued access, even if the project itself may not have a positive net present value. This motivation was important for Japanese automakers who set up assembly plants in the United States in the early 1980s. For much the same reason, U.S. investment in Europe surged during the years before the market integration of the European Community in 1992. MNCs often will invest in production facilities in the home country of major rivals to deny these competitors an uncontested home market. Finally, MNCs may feel compelled to invest in certain industries or countries to achieve a broad corporate objective, such as diversifying raw material sources, even when the project's cash flows may not be sufficiently profitable.

? Review Questions

10-9 Define *risk* in terms of the cash inflows from a capital budgeting project. Briefly describe, compare, and explain how each of the following behavioral approaches can be used to deal with project risk: (**a**) sensitivity analysis; (**b**) scenario analysis; (**c**) decision trees; and (**d**) simulation.

10-10 Briefly define and explain how each of the following items that are unique to multinational companies affect their capital budgeting decisions: (**a**) exchange rate risk; (**b**) political risk; (**c**) tax law differences; (**d**) transfer pricing; and (**e**) strategic rather than financial viewpoint.

LG6 RISK-ADJUSTMENT TECHNIQUES

The approaches for dealing with risk that have been presented so far allow the financial manager to get a "feel" for project risk. Unfortunately, they do not provide a quantitative basis for evaluating risky projects. We will now illustrate the two major risk-adjustment techniques using the net present value (NPV) decision method.[9] The NPV decision rule of accepting only those projects with NPVs > $0 will continue to hold. The basic equation for NPV was presented in Equation 10.1. Close examination of that equation should make it clear that because the initial investment (*II*), which occurs at time zero, is known with certainty, a project's risk is embodied in the present value of its cash inflows:

$$\sum_{t=1}^{n} \frac{CF_t}{(1 + k)^t} \qquad (10.3)$$

Two opportunities to adjust the present value of cash inflows for risk exist: (1) the cash inflows, CF_t, can be adjusted, or (2) the discount rate, k, can be adjusted. Here we describe and compare two techniques—the cash inflow adjustment process, using *certainty equivalents*, and the discount rate adjustment

---

[9]The IRR could just as well have been used, but because NPV is theoretically preferable, it is used instead.

process, using *risk-adjusted discount rates*. In addition, we consider the practical aspects of certainty equivalents and risk-adjusted discount rates.

CERTAINTY EQUIVALENTS (CEs)

certainty equivalents (CEs)

Risk-adjustment factors that represent the percent of estimated cash inflow that investors would be satisfied to receive *for certain* rather than the cash inflows that are *possible* for each year.

One of the most direct and theoretically preferred approaches for risk adjustment is the use of **certainty equivalents (CEs),** which represent the percent of estimated cash inflow that investors would be satisfied to receive *for certain* rather than the cash inflows that are *possible* for each year. Equation 10.4 presents the basic expression for NPV when certainty equivalents are used for risk adjustment:

$$NPV = \sum_{t=1}^{n} \frac{\alpha_t \times CF_t}{(1 + R_F)^t} - II \qquad (10.4)$$

where

α_t = certainty equivalent factor in year t $(0 \leq \alpha_t \leq 1)$
CF_t = relevant cash inflow in year t
R_F = risk-free rate of return

risk-free rate, R_F

The rate of return that one would earn on a virtually riskless investment such as a U.S. Treasury bill.

The equation shows that a project's cash inflows are first adjusted for risk by converting the expected cash inflows to certain amounts, $\alpha_t \times CF_t$. These certain cash inflows are, in effect, equivalent to "cash in hand," but not at time zero. The second part of the calculation adjusts the certain cash inflows for the time value of money by discounting them at the risk-free rate, R_F. The **risk-free rate, R_F,** is the rate of return that one would earn on a virtually riskless investment such as a U.S. Treasury bill. Although the process described here of converting risky cash inflows to certain cash inflows is somewhat subjective, the technique is theoretically sound.

Example ▼ Blano Company wishes to consider risk in the analysis of two projects, A and B. The relevant cash flows for these projects were initially presented in Table 10.1, and the NPVs, assuming that the projects had equivalent risks, were presented in Table 10.3. Ignoring risk differences and using net present value, calculated using the firm's 10 percent cost of capital, we found project A to be preferred over project B, because its NPV of $11,074 was greater than B's NPV of $10,914.

Now let's assume, however, that on further analysis the firm found that project A was actually more risky than project B. To consider the differing risks, the firm estimated the certainty equivalent factors for each project's cash inflows for each year. Columns 2 and 7 of Table 10.9 show the estimated values for projects A and B, respectively. Multiplying the risky cash inflows (in columns 1 and 6) by the corresponding certainty equivalent factors (in columns 2 and 7, respectively) gives the certain cash inflows for projects A and B shown in columns 3 and 8, respectively.

Upon investigation, Blano's management estimated the prevailing risk-free rate of return, R_F, to be 6 percent. Using that rate to discount the certain cash inflows for each of the projects results in the net present values of $4,541 for

TABLE 10.9	Analysis of Blano Company's Projects A and B Using Certainty Equivalents

Project A

Year (t)	Cash inflows (1)	Certainty equivalent factors[a] (2)	Certain cash inflows [(1) × (2)] (3)	$PVIF_{6\%,t}$ (4)	Present value [(3) × (4)] (5)
1	$14,000	.90	$12,600	.943	$11,882
2	14,000	.90	12,600	.890	11,214
3	14,000	.80	11,200	.840	9,408
4	14,000	.70	9,800	.792	7,762
5	14,000	.60	8,400	.747	6,275
			Present value of cash inflows		$46,541
			− Initial investment		42,000
			Net present value (NPV)		$ 4,541

Project B

Year (t)	Cash inflows (6)	Certainty equivalent factors[a] (7)	Certain cash inflows [(6) × (7)] (8)	$PVIF_{6\%,t}$ (9)	Present value [(8) × (9)] (10)
1	$28,000	1.00	$28,000	.943	$26,404
2	12,000	.90	10,800	.890	9,612
3	10,000	.90	9,000	.840	7,560
4	10,000	.80	8,000	.792	6,336
5	10,000	.70	7,000	.747	5,229
			Present value of cash inflows		$55,141
			− Initial investment		45,000
			Net present value (NPV)		$10,141

Note: The relevant cash flows for these projects were presented in Table 10.1, and the analysis of the projects using NPV and assuming equal risk was presented in Table 10.3.

[a]These values were estimated by management; they reflect the risk that managers perceive in the cash inflows.

project A and $10,141 for B, as shown at the bottom of columns 5 and 10, respectively. (The calculated values using a financial calculator are $4,544 and $10,151 for projects A and B, respectively.) Note that as a result of the risk adjustment, project B is now preferred. The usefulness of the certainty equivalent approach for risk adjustment should be quite clear. The only difficulty lies in the need to make subjective estimates of the certainty equivalent factors.

RISK-ADJUSTED DISCOUNT RATES (RADRs)

A more practical approach for risk adjustment involves the use of *risk-adjusted discount rates (RADRs)*. Instead of adjusting the cash inflows for risk, as the certainty equivalent approach does, this approach adjusts the discount rate. Equation 10.5 presents the basic expression for NPV when risk-adjusted discount rates are used:

$$NPV = \sum_{t=1}^{n} \frac{CF_t}{(1 + RADR)^t} - II \tag{10.5}$$

risk-adjusted discount rate (RADR)
The rate of return that must be earned on a given project to compensate the firm's owners adequately—i.e., to maintain or improve the firm's share price.

The **risk-adjusted discount rate (RADR)** is the rate of return that must be earned on a given project to compensate the firm's owners adequately—that is, to maintain or improve the firm's share price. The higher the risk of a project, the higher the RADR and therefore the lower the net present value for a given stream of cash inflows. The logic underlying the use of RADRs is closely linked to the capital asset pricing model (CAPM) developed in Chapter 7. Because the CAPM is based upon an assumed *efficient market*, which does *not* exist for real corporate (nonfinancial) assets such as plant and equipment, the CAPM is not directly applicable in making capital budgeting decisions. Financial managers therefore assess the *total risk* of a project and use it to determine the risk-adjusted discount rate (RADR), which can be used in Equation 10.5 to find the NPV.

In order not to damage its market value, the firm must use the correct discount rate to evaluate a project. If a firm discounts a risky project's cash inflows at too low a rate and accepts the project, the firm's market price may drop as investors recognize that the firm itself has become more risky. On the other hand, if the firm discounts a project's cash inflows at too high a rate, it will reject acceptable projects. Eventually the firm's market price may drop because investors, believing that the firm is being overly conservative, will sell their stock, putting downward pressure on the firm's market value.

Unfortunately there is no formal mechanism for linking total project risk to the level of required return. As a result, most firms subjectively determine the RADR by adjusting their existing required return up or down depending on whether the proposed project is more or less risky, respectively, than the average risk of the firm. Although some firms use a CAPM-type of approach to link project risk and return, such an approach provides merely a "rough estimate" because both (1) the project risk measure and (2) the linkage between risk and return are estimates. The following example will demonstrate a CAPM-type approach that relies on subjectively determined data linking project risk and return.

Example ▼ Blano Company wishes to use the risk-adjusted discount rate approach to determine, according to NPV, whether to implement project A or project B. In addition to the data presented earlier, Blano's management, after much analysis, assigned a "risk index" of 1.6 to project A and 1.0 to B. The risk index is merely a numerical scale used to classify project risk—higher index values are assigned to higher-risk projects, and vice versa. The CAPM-type relationship used by the firm to link risk (measured by the risk index) and the required return (RADR) is shown in the following table:

	Risk index	Required return (RADR)
	0.0	6% (risk-free rate, R_F)
	0.2	7
	0.4	8
	0.6	9
	0.8	10
Project B→	1.0	11
	1.2	12
	1.4	13
Project A→	1.6	14
	1.8	16
	2.0	18

Because project A is riskier than project B (index of 1.6 for A versus 1.0 for B), its RADR of 14 percent is greater than B's 11 percent. The net present value of each project, using its RADR, is calculated in Table 10.10 on the following page. (The calculated values using a financial calculator are $6,063 and $9,798 for projects A and B, respectively.) The results clearly show that project B is preferable, because its risk-adjusted NPV of $9,802 is greater than the $6,062 risk-adjusted NPV for project A. This is the same conclusion reached from using certainty equivalents in the preceding example. As noted by the NPVs in Table 10.3, when the discount rates are not adjusted for risk, project A would be preferred to project B.

The usefulness of risk-adjusted discount rates should now be clear. The real difficulty lies in estimating project risk and linking it to the required return (RADR).

*P*ERSONAL FINANCE PERSPECTIVE

Risk Makes a Difference

The variability of returns on capital budgeting expenditures makes a difference to decision makers as they consider proposed capital expenditures. So, too, does variability of returns—risk—matter in personal investment decisions. You can apply the same techniques to personal investments that financial managers use in capital budgeting. For example, let's say that a friend of yours, an art major with lots of taste but little money, knows of a collectible antique print that he recommends you buy as an investment. The dealer wants $5,000 for the piece, whose value and authenticity have been confirmed. Both your friend and the dealer feel, based on prices of other similar pieces of art, that this print should be worth at least $7,200 after 5 years. Luckily enough, you have enough money to buy the print. You've been earning 6 percent interest on the funds. You discount the

TABLE 10.10	Analysis of Blano Company's Projects A and B Using Risk-Adjusted Discount Rates

Project A

Annual cash inflow	$14,000
$\times PVIFA_{14\%,5yrs}$	3.433
Present value of cash inflows	$48,062
− Initial investment	42,000
Net present value (NPV)	$ 6,062

Project B

Year (t)	Cash inflows (1)	$PVIF_{11\%,t}$ (2)	Present value [(1) × (2)] (3)
1	$28,000	.901	$25,228
2	12,000	.812	9,744
3	10,000	.731	7,310
4	10,000	.659	6,590
5	10,000	.593	5,930
		Present value of cash inflows	$54,802
		− Initial investment	45,000
		Net present value (NPV)	$ 9,802

Note: By using the risk indexes of 1.6 and 1.0 for projects A and B, respectively, along with the table near the top of page 332, a risk-adjusted discount rate (RADR) of 14 percent results for project A and a RADR of 11 percent results for B.

expected $7,200 back at the 6 percent interest rate and find the present value of the print to be about $5,380. Since the investment offers a positive NPV of about $380 ($5,380 − $5,000), you feel inclined to buy the print.

But what if the investment is riskier than you thought? Just to confirm that you're doing a wise thing, you decide you need to do more research. You read up about the recent market in fine art, you consult the curator at the campus art gallery for her opinion, and you look into other investment vehicles for your $5,000. After doing this extra work, you find that you can earn an 8 percent return on investments that have similar risk to the print. So you conclude that you'd better be able to earn a return of at least 8 percent on the print. You again discount the expected $7,200 back to its present value, this time at 8 percent, and find it to be about $4,900. Since the NPV is −$100 ($4,900 − $5,000), you decide against buying the print. Clearly, the revised risk evaluation led to your conclusion that the expenditure would not maximize your wealth. ●

CE VERSUS RADR IN PRACTICE

Certainty equivalents (CEs) are the *theoretically preferred* approach for project risk adjustment because they separately adjust for risk and time; they first eliminate risk from the cash flows and then discount the certain cash flows at a risk-free rate. Risk-adjusted discount rates (RADRs), on the other hand, have a major theoretical problem: They combine the risk and time adjustments in a single discount-rate adjustment. Because of the basic mathematics of compounding and discounting, the RADR approach therefore implicitly assumes that risk is an increasing function of time. Suffice it to say that *CEs are theoretically superior to RADRs*.

However, because of the complexity of developing CEs, *RADRs are more often used in practice*. Their popularity stems from two facts: (1) They are consistent with the general disposition of financial decision makers toward rates of return, and (2) they are easily estimated and applied. The first reason is clearly a matter of personal preference, but the second is based on the computational convenience and well-developed procedures involved in the use of RADRs. In practice, risk is often subjectively categorized rather than related to a continuum of RADRs associated with each level of risk, as was illustrated in the preceding example.

Firms often establish a number of *risk classes,* with an RADR assigned to each. Each project is then subjectively placed in the appropriate risk class, and the corresponding RADR is used to evaluate it. This is sometimes done on a division-by-division basis, each division having its own set of risk classes and associated RADRs similar to those in Table 10.11. The use of *divisional costs of capital* and associated risk classes allows the large multidivisional firm to incorporate differing levels of divisional risk into the capital budgeting process and

TABLE 10.11	Blano Company's Risk Classes and RADRs	
Risk class	Description	Risk-adjusted discount rate, RADR
I	*Below-average risk:* Projects with low risk. Typically involve routine replacement without renewal of existing activities.	8%
II	*Average risk:* Projects similar to those currently implemented. Typically involve replacement or renewal of existing activities.	10%[a]
III	*Above-average risk:* Projects with higher than normal, but not excessive, risk. Typically involve expansion of existing or similar activities.	14%
IV	*Highest risk:* Projects with very high risk. Typically involve expansion into new or unfamiliar activities.	20%

[a]This RADR is actually the firm's cost of capital, which is discussed in detail in Chapter 16. It represents the firm's required return on its existing portfolio of projects, which is assumed unchanged with acceptance of the "average risk" project.

still recognize differences in the levels of individual project risk. An example will illustrate the general use of risk classes and RADRs.

Example ▼ Assume that the management of Blano Company decided to use a more subjective but practical RADR approach to analyze projects. Each project would be placed in one of four risk classes according to its perceived risk. The classes were ranged from I for the lowest-risk projects to IV for the highest-risk projects. Associated with each class was an RADR that was appropriate to the level of risk of projects in the class. A brief description of each class, along with the associated RADR, is given in Table 10.11. It shows that lower-risk projects tend to involve routine replacement or renewal activities, whereas higher-risk projects involve expansion, often into new or unfamiliar activities.

The financial manager of Blano has assigned project A to Class III and project B to Class II. The cash flows for project A would therefore be evaluated by using a 14 percent RADR, and project B's would be evaluated by using a 10 percent RADR.[10] The NPV of project A at 14 percent was calculated in Table 10.10 to be $6,062, and the NPV for project B at a 10 percent RADR was shown in Table 10.3 to be $10,914. Clearly, with RADRs based on the use of risk classes, project B is preferred over project A. As noted earlier, this result is contrary to the preferences shown in Table 10.3, where no attention was given to the differing risk of projects
▲ A and B.

? R e v i e w   Q u e s t i o n s

10-11 Explain the concept of *certainty equivalents (CEs)*. How are they used in the risk-adjustment process?
10-12 Describe the logic involved in using *risk-adjusted discount rates (RADRs)*. How does this approach relate to the *capital asset pricing model (CAPM)?* Explain.
10-13 Compare and contrast CEs and RADRs from both a theoretical and a practical point of view. In practice, how are risk classes often used to apply RADRs? Explain.

S UMMARY

LG1 **Calculate, interpret, and evaluate the payback period.** The payback period measures the exact amount of time required for the firm to recover its initial investment from cash inflows. The formula and decision criterion for the payback period are summarized in Table 10.12. Shorter payback periods are preferred. In addition to its ease of calculation and simple intuitive appeal, the payback period's appeal lies in its consideration of cash

flows, the implicit consideration given to timing, and its ability to measure risk exposure. Its weaknesses include its lack of linkage to the wealth maximization goal, failure to explicitly consider time value, and the fact that it ignores cash flows that occur after the payback period.

 LG2 **Apply net present value (NPV) and internal rate of return (IRR) to relevant cash flows to**

---

[10]Note that the 10 percent RADR for project B using the risk classes in Table 10.11 differs from the 11 percent RADR used in the preceding example for project B. This difference is due to the less precise nature of the use of risk classes.

TABLE 10.12	Summary of Key Formulas/Definitions and Decision Criteria for Capital Budgeting Techniques

Technique	Formula/Definition	Decision criteria
Payback period[a]	*For annuity:* $$\frac{\text{initial investment}}{\text{annual cash inflow}}$$ *For mixed stream:* Calculate cumulative cash inflows on year-to-year basis until the initial investment is recovered.	*Accept* if < maximum acceptable payback period; *reject* if > maximum acceptable payback period.
Net present value (NPV)[b]	Present value of cash inflows − initial investment.	*Accept* if > $0; *reject* if < $0.
Internal rate of return (IRR)[b]	The discount rate that equates the present value of cash inflows with the initial investment, thereby causing NPV = $0.	*Accept* if > the cost of capital; *reject* if < the cost of capital.

[a]Unsophisticated technique, because it does not give explicit consideration to the time value of money.
[b]Sophisticated technique, because it gives explicit consideration to the time value of money.

choose acceptable capital expenditures. Sophisticated capital budgeting techniques use the cost of capital to consider the time factor in the value of money. Two such techniques are net present value (NPV) and internal rate of return (IRR). The key formulas and decision criteria for them are summarized in Table 10.12. Both NPV and IRR provide the same accept–reject decisions but often provide conflicting ranks.

LG3 **Use net present value profiles to compare net present value and internal rate of return techniques in light of conflicting rankings.** Net present value profiles are useful in comparing projects, especially when conflicting rankings exist between NPV and IRR. On a purely theoretical basis, NPV is preferred over IRR, because NPV assumes reinvestment of intermediate cash inflows at the cost of capital and does not exhibit the mathematical problems often occurring when calculating IRRs for nonconventional cash flows. In practice, the IRR is more commonly used because it is consistent with the general preference toward rates of return.

LG4 **Discuss the two basic approaches—internal rate of return and net present value—for choosing projects under capital rationing.** Capital rationing commonly occurs in practice. Its objective is to select from all acceptable projects the group that provides the highest overall net present value but does not require more dollars than are budgeted. Of the two basic approaches for choosing projects under capital rationing, the NPV approach better achieves the objective of using the budget to generate the highest present value of cash inflows.

LG5 **Recognize sensitivity and scenario analysis, decision trees, and simulation as behavioral approaches for dealing with project risk, and the unique risks facing multinational companies.** Risk in capital budgeting is concerned with either the chance that a project will prove unacceptable or, more formally, the degree of variability of cash flows. Sensitivity analysis and scenario analysis are two behavioral approaches for dealing with project risk to capture the variability of cash inflows and NPVs. A decision tree is a behavioral approach for dealing with risk that relies on estimates of probabilities associated with the outcomes of competing courses of action to determine the expected values used to select a preferred action. Simulation is a statistically based behavioral approach that results in a probability distribution of project returns. It usually requires a computer and allows the decision maker to understand the risk-return trade-offs involved in a proposed investment. Although the basic capital budgeting techniques are the same for purely domestic and multinational companies, firms that operate in several countries must also deal with both exchange rate and political risks, tax law differences, transfer pricing, and strategic rather than strict financial issues.

ty equivalents (CEs) and risk-adjusted discount rates (RADRs). Certainty equivalents (CEs) are used to adjust the risky cash inflows to certain amounts, which are discounted at a risk-free rate to find the NPV. The risk-adjusted discount rate (RADR) technique involves a market-based adjustment of the discount rate used to calculate NPV. The RADR is closely linked to the CAPM, but because real corporate assets are generally not traded in an efficient market, the CAPM cannot be applied directly to capital budgeting. CEs are the theoretically superior risk-adjustment technique, but RADRs are more commonly used in practice because decision makers prefer rates of return and find them easier to estimate and apply.

 Understand the calculation, differing approaches, and practical aspects of certain-

SELF-TEST PROBLEMS   (Solutions in Appendix B)

ST 10-1   All techniques with NPV profile—Mutually exclusive projects   Fitch Industries is in the process of choosing the better of two equal-risk, mutually exclusive, capital expenditure projects—M and N. The relevant cash flows for each project are shown in the following table at the top of the following page. The firm's cost of capital is 14 percent.

	Project M	Project N
Initial investment (*II*)	$28,500	$27,000
Year (*t*)	Cash inflows (*CF$_t$*)	
1	$10,000	$11,000
2	10,000	10,000
3	10,000	9,000
4	10,000	8,000

a. Calculate each project's payback period.
b. Calculate the net present value (NPV) for each project.
c. Calculate the internal rate of return (IRR) for each project.
d. Summarize the preferences dictated by each measure calculated above, and indicate which project you would recommend. Explain why.
e. Draw the net present value profiles for each project on the same set of axes, and explain the circumstances under which a conflict in rankings might exist.

ST 10-2 Certainty equivalents and risk-adjusted discount rates The CAPM-type relationship linking a risk index to the required return (RADR) and the certainty equivalent factors applicable to CBA Company's mutually exclusive projects A and B follow:

Risk index	Required return (RADR)
0.0 (risk-free rate, R_F)	7.0%
0.2	8.0
0.4	9.0
0.6	10.0
0.8	11.0
1.0	12.0
1.2	13.0
1.4	14.0
1.6	15.0
1.8	16.0
2.0	17.0

	Certainty equivalent factors (α_t)	
Year *(t)*	Project A	Project B
0	1.00	1.00
1	.95	.90
2	.90	.85
3	.90	.70

The firm is considering two mutually exclusive projects, A and B. Project data are shown in the following table.

	Project A	Project B
Initial investment *(II)*	$15,000	$20,000
Project life	3 years	3 years
Annual cash inflow *(CF)*	$ 7,000	$10,000
Risk index	0.4	1.8

a. Ignoring any differences in risk and assuming that the firm's cost of capital is 10 percent, calculate the net present value (NPV) of each project.
b. Use NPV to evaluate the projects using *certainty equivalents* to account for risk.
c. Use NPV to evaluate the projects using *risk-adjusted discount rates* to account for risk.
d. Compare, contrast, and explain your findings in **a, b,** and **c.**

PROBLEMS

WARM-UP

10-1   Payback period   Lee Corporation is considering a capital expenditure that requires an initial investment of $42,000 and returns after-tax cash inflows of $7,000 per year for 10 years. The firm has a maximum acceptable payback period of 8 years.
a. Determine the payback period for this project.
b. Should the company accept the project? Why or why not?

INTERMEDIATE

10-2   Payback comparisons   Dallas Tool has a 5-year maximum acceptable payback period. The firm is considering the purchase of a new machine and must choose between two alternative ones. The first machine requires an initial investment of $14,000 and generates annual after-tax cash inflows of $3,000 for each of the next 7 years. The second machine requires an initial investment of $21,000 and provides an annual cash inflow after taxes of $4,000 for 20 years.
a. Determine the payback period for each machine.
b. Comment on the acceptability of the machines, assuming they are independent projects.
c. Which machine should the firm accept? Why?
d. Do the machines in this problem illustrate any of the criticisms of using payback? Discuss.

WARM-UP

10-3   NPV   Calculate the net present value (NPV) for the following 20-year projects. Comment on the acceptability of each. Assume that the firm has an opportunity cost of 14 percent.
a. Initial investment is $10,000; cash inflows are $2,000 per year.
b. Initial investment is $25,000; cash inflows are $3,000 per year.
c. Initial investment is $30,000; cash inflows are $5,000 per year.

WARM-UP

10-4   NPV for varying costs of capital   Cheryl's Beauty Aids is evaluating a new fragrance-mixing machine. The machine requires an initial investment of $24,000 and will generate after-tax cash inflows of $5,000 per year for 8 years. For each of the costs of capital listed, (1) calculate the net present value (NPV), (2) indicate whether to accept or reject the machine, and (3) explain your decision.
a. The cost of capital is 10 percent.
b. The cost of capital is 12 percent.
c. The cost of capital is 14 percent.

INTERMEDIATE

10-5   Net present value—Independent projects   Using a 14 percent cost of capital, calculate the net present value for each of the independent projects shown in the following table and indicate whether or not each is acceptable.

	Project A	Project B	Project C	Project D	Project E
Initial investment (*II*)	$26,000	$500,000	$170,000	$950,000	$80,000
Year (*t*)			Cash inflows (*CF$_t$*)		
1	$4,000	$100,000	$20,000	$230,000	$ 0
2	4,000	120,000	19,000	230,000	0
3	4,000	140,000	18,000	230,000	0
4	4,000	160,000	17,000	230,000	20,000
5	4,000	180,000	16,000	230,000	30,000
6	4,000	200,000	15,000	230,000	0
7	4,000		14,000	230,000	50,000
8	4,000		13,000	230,000	60,000
9	4,000		12,000		70,000
10	4,000		11,000		

10-6   **NPV and maximum return**   A firm can purchase a fixed asset for a $13,000 initial investment. If the asset generates an annual after-tax cash inflow of $4,000 for 4 years:

a. Determine the net present value (NPV) of the asset, assuming that the firm has a 10 percent cost of capital. Is the project acceptable?

b. Determine the maximum required rate of return (closest whole-percentage rate) that the firm can have and still accept the asset. Discuss this finding in light of your response in **a.**

10-7   **NPV—Mutually exclusive projects**   Jackson Enterprises is considering the replacement of one of its old drill presses. Three alternative replacement presses are under consideration. The relevant cash flows associated with each are shown in the following table. The firm's cost of capital is 15 percent.

	Press A	Press B	Press C
Initial investment (*II*)	$85,000	$60,000	$130,000
Year (*t*)		Cash inflows (*CF$_t$*)	
1	$18,000	$12,000	$50,000
2	18,000	14,000	30,000
3	18,000	16,000	20,000
4	18,000	18,000	20,000
5	18,000	20,000	20,000
6	18,000	25,000	30,000
7	18,000	—	40,000
8	18,000	—	50,000

a. Calculate the net present value (NPV) of each press.
b. Using NPV, evaluate the acceptability of each press.
c. Rank the presses from best to worst using NPV.

10-8   Payback and NPV   McAllister Products has three projects under consideration. The cash flows for each of them are shown in the following table. The firm has a 16 percent cost of capital.

	Project A	Project B	Project C
Initial investment *(II)*	$40,000	$40,000	$40,000
Year *(t)*		Cash inflows *(CF_t)*	
1	$13,000	$ 7,000	$19,000
2	13,000	10,000	16,000
3	13,000	13,000	13,000
4	13,000	16,000	10,000
5	13,000	19,000	7,000

a. Calculate each project's payback period. Which project is preferred according to this method?
b. Calculate each project's net present value (NPV). Which project is preferred according to this method?
c. Comment on your findings in **a** and **b,** and recommend the best project. Explain your recommendation.

10-9   Internal rate of return   For each of the projects shown in the following table, calculate the internal rate of return (IRR), and indicate for each project the maximum cost of capital that the firm could have and find the IRR acceptable.

	Project A	Project B	Project C	Project D
Initial investment *(II)*	$90,000	$490,000	$20,000	$240,000
Year *(t)*		Cash inflows *(CF_t)*		
1	$20,000	$150,000	$7,500	$120,000
2	25,000	150,000	7,500	100,000
3	30,000	150,000	7,500	80,000
4	35,000	150,000	7,500	60,000
5	40,000	—	7,500	—

10-10   IRR—Mutually exclusive projects   Paulus Corporation is attempting to choose the better of two mutually exclusive projects for expanding the firm's warehouse capacity. The relevant cash flows for the projects are shown in the following table. The firm's cost of capital is 15 percent.

	Project X	Project Y
Initial investment (*II*)	$500,000	$325,000
Year (*t*)	Cash inflows (*CF$_t$*)	
1	$100,000	$140,000
2	120,000	120,000
3	150,000	95,000
4	190,000	70,000
5	250,000	50,000

a. Calculate the IRR to the nearest whole percent for each of the projects.
b. Assess the acceptability of each project based on the IRRs found in **a**.
c. Which project is preferred, based on the IRRs found in **a**?

10-11   IRR, investment life, and cash inflows   Cincinnati Machine Tool (CMT) accepts projects earning more than the firm's 15 percent cost of capital. CMT is currently considering a 10-year project that provides annual cash inflows of $10,000 and requires an initial investment of $61,450. (*Note:* All amounts are after taxes.)
a. Determine the IRR of this project. Is it acceptable?
b. Assuming that the cash inflows continue to be $10,000 per year, how many *additional years* would the flows have to continue to make the project acceptable (i.e., have an IRR of 15 percent)?
c. With the given life, initial investment, and cost of capital, what is the minimum annual cash inflow the firm should accept?

10-12   NPV and IRR   Lilo Manufacturing Enterprises has prepared the following estimates for a long-term project it is considering. The initial investment is $18,250, and the project is expected to yield after-tax cash inflows of $4,000 per year for 7 years. The firm has a 10 percent cost of capital.
a. Determine the net present value (NPV) for the project.
b. Determine the internal rate of return (IRR) for the project.
c. Would you recommend that the firm accept or reject the project? Explain your answer.

10-13   Payback, NPV, and IRR   Bruce Read Enterprises is attempting to evaluate the feasibility of investing $95,000 in a piece of equipment having a 5-year life. The firm has estimated the *cash inflows* associated with the proposal as shown in the following table. The firm has a 12 percent cost of capital.

Year (*t*)	Cash inflows (*CF$_t$*)
1	$20,000
2	25,000
3	30,000
4	35,000
5	40,000

a. Calculate the payback period for the proposed investment.
b. Calculate the net present value (NPV) for the proposed investment.
c. Calculate the internal rate of return (IRR), rounded to the nearest whole percent, for the proposed investment.
d. Evaluate the acceptability of the proposed investment using NPV and IRR. What recommendation would you make relative to implementation of the project? Why?

10-14 **NPV, IRR, and NPV profiles**   Candor Enterprises is considering two mutually exclusive projects. The firm, which has a 12 percent cost of capital, has estimated its cash flows as shown in the following table.

CHALLENGE

	Project A	Project B
Initial investment (II)	$130,000	$85,000
Year (t)	Cash inflows (CF_t)	
1	$ 25,000	$40,000
2	35,000	35,000
3	45,000	30,000
4	50,000	10,000
5	55,000	5,000

a. Calculate the NPV of each project, and assess its acceptability.
b. Calculate the IRR for each project, and assess its acceptability.
c. Draw the NPV profile for each project on the same set of axes.
d. Evaluate and discuss the rankings of the two projects based on your findings in **a, b,** and **c.**
e. Explain your findings in **d** in light of the pattern of cash inflows associated with each project.

10-15 **All techniques—Mutually exclusive investment decision**   Easi Chair Company is attempting to select the best of three mutually exclusive projects. The initial investment and after-tax cash inflows associated with each project are shown in the following table.

CHALLENGE

Cash flows	Project A	Project B	Project C
Initial investment (II)	$60,000	$100,000	$110,000
Cash inflows (CF), years 1–5	$20,000	$ 31,500	$ 32,500

a. Calculate the payback period for each project.
b. Calculate the net present value (NPV) of each project, assuming that the firm has a cost of capital equal to 13 percent.
c. Calculate the internal rate of return (IRR) for each project.
d. Draw the net present value profile for each project on the same set of axes, and discuss any conflict in ranking that may exist between NPV and IRR.

e. Summarize the preferences dictated by each measure, and indicate which project you would recommend. Explain why.

10-16 All techniques with NPV profile—Mutually exclusive projects The following two projects of equal risk are alternatives for expanding the firm's capacity. The firm's cost of capital is 13 percent. The cash flows for each project are shown in the following table.

	Project A	Project B
Initial investment (*II*)	$80,000	$50,000
Year (*t*)	Cash inflows (*CF_t*)	
1	$15,000	$15,000
2	20,000	15,000
3	25,000	15,000
4	30,000	15,000
5	35,000	15,000

a. Calculate each project's payback period.
b. Calculate the net present value (NPV) for each project.
c. Calculate the internal rate of return (IRR) for each project.
d. Draw a net present value profile for each project on the same set of axes, and discuss any conflict in ranking that may exist between NPV and IRR.
e. Summarize the preferences dictated by each measure, and indicate which project you would recommend. Explain why.

10-17 Integrative—Complete investment decision Hot Springs Press is considering the purchase of a new printing press. The total installed cost of the press is $2.2 million. This outlay would be partially offset by the sale of an existing press. The old press has zero book value, cost $1 million 10 years ago, and can be sold currently for $1.2 million before taxes. As a result of the new press, sales in each of the next 5 years are expected to increase by $1.6 million, but product costs (excluding depreciation) will represent 50 percent of sales. The new press will not affect the firm's net working capital requirements. The new press will be depreciated under MACRS using a 5-year recovery period (see Table 4.7 on page 91). The firm is subject to a 40 percent tax rate on both ordinary income and capital gains. Hot Spring Press's cost of capital is 11 percent. (*Note:* Assume that both the old and new press will have terminal values of $0 at the end of year 6.)

a. Determine the initial investment required by the new press.
b. Determine the operating cash inflows attributable to the new press. (*Note:* Be sure to consider the depreciation in year 6.)
c. Determine the payback period.
d. Determine the net present value (NPV) and the internal rate of return (IRR) related to the proposed new press.
e. Make a recommendation to accept or reject the new press, and justify your answer.

10-18 Integrative—Investment decision   Holliday Manufacturing is considering the replacement of an existing machine. The new machine costs $1.2 million and requires installation costs of $150,000. The existing machine can be sold currently for $185,000 before taxes. It is 2 years old, cost $800,000 new, and has a $384,000 book value and a remaining useful life of 5 years. It was being depreciated under MACRS using a 5-year recovery period (see Table 4.7 on page 91) and therefore has the final 4 years of depreciation remaining. If held until the end of 5 years, the machine's market value would be $0. Over its 5-year life, the new machine should reduce operating costs by $350,000 per year. The new machine will be depreciated under MACRS using a 5-year recovery period (see Table 4.7 on page 91). The new machine can be sold for $200,000 net of removal and cleanup costs at the end of 5 years. An increased investment in net working capital of $25,000 will be needed to support operations if the new machine is acquired. Assume that the firm has adequate operating income against which to deduct any loss experienced on the sale of the existing machine. The firm has a 9 percent cost of capital and is subject to a 40 percent tax rate on both ordinary income and capital gains.

a. Develop the relevant cash flows needed to analyze the proposed replacement.
b. Determine the net present value (NPV) of the proposal.
c. Determine the internal rate of return (IRR) of the proposal.
d. Make a recommendation to accept or reject the replacement proposal, and justify your answer.
e. What is the highest cost of capital the firm could have and still accept the proposal? Explain.

10-19 Capital rationing—IRR and NPV approaches   Bromley and Sons is attempting to select the best of a group of independent projects competing for the firm's fixed capital budget of $4.5 million. The firm recognizes that any unused portion of this budget will earn less than its 15 percent cost of capital, thereby resulting in a present value of inflows that is less than the initial investment. The firm has summarized the key data to be used in selecting the best group of projects in the following table.

Project	Initial investment	IRR	Present value of inflows at 15%
A	$5,000,000	17%	$5,400,000
B	800,000	18	1,100,000
C	2,000,000	19	2,300,000
D	1,500,000	16	1,600,000
E	800,000	22	900,000
F	2,500,000	23	3,000,000
G	1,200,000	20	1,300,000

a. Use the *internal rate of return (IRR) approach* to select the best group of projects.
b. Use the *net present value (NPV) approach* to select the best group of projects.
c. Compare, contrast, and discuss your findings in **a** and **b**.
d. Which projects should the firm implement? Why?

10-20   Capital rationing—NPV approach   A firm with a 13 percent cost of capital must select the optimal group of projects from those shown in the following table, given its capital budget of $1 million.

Project	Initial investment	NPV at 13% cost of capital
A	$300,000	$ 84,000
B	200,000	10,000
C	100,000	25,000
D	900,000	90,000
E	500,000	70,000
F	100,000	50,000
G	800,000	160,000

a. Calculate the *present value of cash inflows* associated with each project.
b. Select the optimal group of projects, keeping in mind that unused funds are costly.

10-21   Basic sensitivity analysis   Renaissance Pharmaceutical is in the process of evaluating two mutually exclusive additions to their processing capacity. The firm's financial analysts have developed pessimistic, most likely, and optimistic estimates of the annual cash inflows associated with each project. These estimates are shown in the following table.

	Project A	Project B
Initial investment (*II*)	$8,000	$8,000
Outcome	Annual cash inflows (*CF*)	
Pessimistic	$ 200	$ 900
Most likely	1,000	1,000
Optimistic	1,800	1,100

a. Determine the *range* of annual cash inflows for each of the two projects.
b. Assume that the firm' s cost of capital is 10 percent and that both projects have 20-year lives. Construct a table similar to that above for the NPVs for each project. Include the *range* of NPVs for each project.
c. Do **a** and **b** provide consistent views of the two projects? Explain.
d. Which project do you recommend? Why?

10-22   Sensitivity analysis   James Secretarial Services is considering the purchase of one of two new personal computers, P and Q. Both are expected to provide benefits over a 10-year period, and each has a required investment of $3,000. The firm uses a 10 percent cost of capital. Management has constructed the following table of estimates of probabilities and annual cash inflows for pessimistic, most likely, and optimistic results.

	Computer P	Computer Q
Initial investment (*II*)	$3,000	$3,000
Outcome	Annual cash inflows (*CF*)	
Pessimistic	$ 500	$ 400
Most likely	750	750
Optimistic	1,000	1,200

a. Determine the *range* of annual cash inflows for each of the two computers.
b. Construct a table similar to that above for the NPVs associated with each outcome for both computers.
c. Find the *range* of NPVs, and subjectively compare the risk of each computer.

  10-23 Decision trees The Ouija Board-Games Company can bring out one of two new games this season. The *Signs Away* game has a higher initial cost but also has a higher expected return. *Monopolistic Competition*, the alternative, has a slightly lower initial cost but also a lower expected return. The present values and probabilities associated with each game are listed in the table.

Game	Initial investment	Present value of cash inflows	Probabilities
Signs Away	$140,000		1.00
		$320,000	.30
		220,000	.50
		−80,000	.20
Monopolistic Competition	$120,000		1.00
		$260,000	.20
		200,000	.45
		−50,000	.35

a. Construct a decision tree to analyze the games.
b. Which game do you recommend (following a decision-tree analysis)?
c. Has your analysis captured the differences in project risk? Explain.

 10-24 Simulation Wales Castings has compiled the following information on a capital expenditure proposal:
(1) The projected cash *inflows* are normally distributed with a mean of $36,000 and a standard deviation of $9,000.
(2) The projected cash *outflows* are normally distributed with a mean of $30,000 and a standard deviation of $6,000.
(3) The firm has an 11 percent cost of capital.
(4) The probability distributions of cash inflows and cash outflows are not expected to change over the project's 10-year life.
a. Describe how the preceding data can be used to develop a simulation model for finding the net present value of the project.

b. Discuss the advantages of using a simulation to evaluate the proposed project.

INTERMEDIATE 10-25 **Certainty equivalents—Accept–reject decision**   Pleasantville Ball Valve has constructed a table, shown below, that gives expected cash inflows and certainty equivalent factors for these cash inflows. These measures are for a new machine with a 5-year life that requires an initial investment of $95,000. The firm has a 15 percent cost of capital, and the risk-free rate is 10 percent.

Year (t)	Cash inflows (CF_t)	Certainty equivalent factors (α_t)
1	$35,000	1.0
2	35,000	.8
3	35,000	.6
4	35,000	.6
5	35,000	.2

a. What is the net present value (unadjusted for risk)?
b. What is the certainty equivalent net present value?
c. Should the firm accept the project? Explain.
d. Management has some doubts about the estimate of the certainty equivalent factor for year 5. There is some evidence that it may not be any lower than that for year 4. What impact might this have on the decision you recommended in **c**? Explain.

INTERMEDIATE 10-26 **Certainty equivalents—Mutually exclusive decision**   Jan Ventures, Inc. is considering investing in either of two mutually exclusive projects, C and D. The firm has a 14 percent cost of capital, and the risk-free rate is currently 9 percent. The initial investment, expected cash inflows, and certainty equivalent factors associated with each of the projects are shown in the following table.

	Project C		Project D	
Initial investment (II)	$40,000		$56,000	
Year (t)	Cash inflows (CF_t)	Certainty equivalent factors (α_t)	Cash inflows (CF_t)	Certainty equivalent factors (α_t)
1	$20,000	.90	$20,000	.95
2	16,000	.80	25,000	.90
3	12,000	.60	15,000	.85
4	10,000	.50	20,000	.80
5	10,000	.40	10,000	.80

a. Find the net present value (unadjusted for risk) for each project. Which is preferred using this measure?
b. Find the certainty equivalent net present value for each project. Which is preferred using this risk-adjustment technique?

c. Compare and discuss your findings in **a** and **b.** Which, if either, of the projects do you recommend that the firm accept? Explain.

  10-27 **Risk-adjusted discount rates—Basic**   P. Ladew, Inc., is considering investment in one of three mutually exclusive projects, E, F, and G. The firm's cost of capital, k, is 15 percent, and the risk-free rate, R_F, is 10 percent. The firm has gathered the following basic cash flow and risk index data for each project.

	Project (j)		
	E	F	G
Initial investment (II)	$15,000	$11,000	$19,000
Year (t)	Cash inflows (CF_t)		
1	$ 6,000	$ 6,000	$ 4,000
2	6,000	4,000	6,000
3	6,000	5,000	8,000
4	6,000	2,000	12,000
Risk index (RI_j)	1.80	1.00	0.60

a. Find the net present value (NPV) of each project using the firm's cost of capital. Which project is preferred in this situation?
b. The firm uses the following equation to determine the risk-adjusted discount rate, $RADR_j$, for each project j:

$$RADR_j = R_F + [RI_j \times (k - R_F)]$$

where

$$R_F = \text{risk-free rate}$$
$$RI_j = \text{risk index for project } j$$
$$k = \text{cost of capital cost of capital}$$

Substitute each project's risk index into this equation to determine its RADR.
c. Use the RADR for each project to determine its risk-adjusted NPV. Which project is preferable in this situation?
d. Compare and discuss your findings in **a** and **c.** Which project do you recommend that the firm accept?

  10-28 **Integrative—Certainty equivalents and risk-adjusted discount rates**   After a careful evaluation of investment alternatives and opportunities, Joely Company has developed a CAPM-type relationship linking a risk index to the required return (RADR) as shown in the table at the top of the following page.

Risk index	Required return (RADR)
0.0	7.0% (risk-free rate, R_F)
0.2	8.0
0.4	9.0
0.6	10.0
0.8	11.0
1.0	12.0
1.2	13.0
1.4	14.0
1.6	15.0
1.8	16.0
2.0	17.0

The firm is faced with two mutually exclusive projects, A and B. The following are the data the firm has been able to gather about the projects:

	Project A	Project B
Initial investment (II)	$20,000	$30,000
Project life	5 years	5 years
Annual cash inflow (CF)	$ 7,000	$10,000
Risk index	0.2	1.4

	Certainty equivalent factors (α_t)	
Year (t)	Project A	Project B
0	1.00	1.00
1	.95	.90
2	.90	.80
3	.90	.70
4	.85	.70
Greater than 4	.80	.60

All the firm's cash inflows have already been adjusted for taxes.
a. Evaluate the projects using *certainty equivalents*.
b. Evaluate the projects using *risk-adjusted discount rates*.
c. Discuss your findings in **a** and **b,** and explain why the two approaches are alternative techniques for considering risk in capital budgeting.

WARM-UP   10-29 **Risk classes and RADR**   Attila Industries is attempting to select the best of three mutually exclusive projects, X, Y, and Z. Though all the projects have 5-year lives, they possess differing degrees of risk. Project X is in Class V, the highest-risk class; project Y is in Class II, the below-average-risk class; and project Z is in Class III, the average-risk class. The basic cash flow data for each project and the risk classes and risk-adjusted discount rates (RADRs) used by the firm are shown in the following tables.

	Project X	Project Y	Project Z
Initial investment (*II*)	$180,000	$235,000	$310,000
Year (*t*)	Cash inflows (*CF_t*)		
1	$ 80,000	$ 50,000	$ 90,000
2	70,000	60,000	90,000
3	60,000	70,000	90,000
4	60,000	80,000	90,000
5	60,000	90,000	90,000

Risk Classes and RADRs

Risk Class	Description	Risk-adjusted discount rate (RADR)
I	Lowest risk	10%
II	Below-average risk	13
III	Average risk	15
IV	Above-average risk	19
V	Highest risk	22

a. Find the risk-adjusted NPV for each project.
b. Which, if any, project would you recommend that the firm undertake?

CASE   Chapter 10   **Making Norwich Tool's Lathe Investment Decision**

Norwich Tool, a large machine shop, is considering replacing one of its lathes with either of two new lathes—lathe A or lathe B. Lathe A is a highly automated, computer-controlled lathe; lathe B is a less expensive lathe that uses standard technology. To analyze these alternatives, Mario Jackson, a financial analyst, prepared estimates of the initial investment and incremental (relevant) cash inflows associated with each lathe. These are shown in the following table.

	Lathe A	Lathe B
Initial investment (*II*)	$660,000	$360,000
Year (*t*)	Cash inflows (*CF_t*)	
1	$128,000	$ 88,000
2	182,000	120,000
3	166,000	96,000
4	168,000	86,000
5	450,000	207,000

Note that Mario plans to analyze both lathes over a 5-year period. At the end of that time, the lathes would be sold, thus accounting for the large fifth-year cash inflows.

One of Mario's major dilemmas centered on the risk of the two lathes. He feels that although the two lathes have similar risk, lathe A has a much higher chance of breakdown and repair due to its sophisticated and not fully proven solid-state electronic technology. Because he is unable to effectively quantify this possibility, Mario decides to apply the firm's 13 percent cost of capital when analyzing the lathes. Norwich Tool requires all projects to have a maximum payback period of 4.0 years.

Required

a. Use the payback period to assess the acceptability and relative ranking of each lathe.
b. Assuming equal risk, use the following sophisticated capital budgeting techniques to assess the acceptability and relative ranking of each lathe:
   (1) Net present value (NPV).
   (2) Internal rate of return (IRR).
c. Summarize the preferences indicated by the techniques used in **a** and **b,** and indicate which lathe you recommend, if either, if the firm has (1) unlimited funds or (2) capital rationing.
d. Repeat part **b** assuming that Mario decides that, due to its greater risk, lathe A's cash inflows should be evaluated by using a 15 percent cost of capital.
e. What effect, if any, does recognition of lathe A's greater risk in **d** have on your recommendation in **c?**

Web Exercise

GOTO web site www.arachnoid.com/lutusp/finance_old.html. Page down to the portions of this screen that contains the financial calculator.

1. To determine the internal rate of return (IRR) of a project whose initial investment was $5,000 and its cash flows are $1,000/year for the next 10 years, perform the steps outlined below. By entering various interest rates you will eventually get a present value of $5,000. When this happens you have determined the IRR of the project.
   To get started, into PV, enter 0; into FV, enter 0; into np, enter 1000; into pmt, enter 10; and to start, into ir, enter 8. Click Calculate PV. This gives you a number much greater than $5,000. Now change ir to 20 and then click Calculate PV. Keeping changing the ir until PV = $5,000, the same as the initial investment.
2. Try another problem. The initial investment is $10,000. The time of the cash flows is 6 years, and the cash flow per year is $2,500. What is its IRR?
3. To calculate the IRR of an investment of $3,000 with a single cash flow of $4,800 in 3 years from the investment, do the following: Into FV, enter 4800; into np, enter 3; into pmt, enter 0; and then into ir, enter 8. Then click Calculate PV. As above, keep changing ir until the PV is equal to the initial investment of $3,000. What is this investment's IRR?

PART 4

LONG-TERM FINANCIAL DECISIONS

CHAPTERS IN THIS PART

11 THE COST OF CAPITAL

ACROSS *the* DISCIPLINES

The cost of capital is used to select capital investments that increase shareholder value. In applying the net present value and internal rate of return techniques in Chapter 10, we simply assumed a reasonable cost of capital. Now we will demonstrate how the cost of capital is calculated. This chapter considers the costs of long-term debt, preferred stock, common stock, and retained earnings, and shows how to combine them to determine two important cost of capital measures the firm will use in making long-term financing and investment decisions. Chapter 11 is important to:

- **accounting personnel** who will provide data used to determine the firm's capital costs.

- **information systems analysts** who will develop systems for estimating the cost of the various sources of capital.

- **management** because it will use the cost of capital when assessing the acceptability and relative ranking of capital expenditure projects.

- **the marketing department** because it will face the rejection of proposals for new projects that earn a return below the firm's cost of capital.

- **operations,** which must realize that the more profit it can produce, the lower the firm's future cost of capital will be.

AN OVERVIEW OF THE COST OF CAPITAL

The cost of capital is an extremely important financial concept. It acts as a major link between the firm's long-term investment decisions (discussed in Part 3) and the wealth of the owners as determined by investors in the marketplace. It is in effect the "magic number" that is used to decide whether a proposed corporate investment will increase or decrease the firm's stock price. Clearly, only those investments that are expected to increase stock price [NPV > $0, or IRR > cost of capital] would be recommended. Due to its key role in financial decision making, the importance of the cost of capital cannot be overemphasized.

cost of capital
The rate of return that a firm must earn on its project investments to maintain its market value and attract funds.

The **cost of capital** is the rate of return that a firm must earn on its project investments to maintain the market value of its stock. It can also be thought of as the rate of return required by the market suppliers of capital to attract their funds to the firm. If risk is held constant, projects with a rate of return above the cost of capital will increase the value of the firm, and projects with a rate of return below the cost of capital will decrease the value of the firm.

THE BASIC CONCEPT

The cost of capital is estimated at a given point in time. It reflects the expected average future cost of funds over the long run, based on the best information available. Although firms typically raise money in lumps, the cost of capital should reflect the interrelatedness of financing activities. For example, if a firm raises funds with debt (borrowing) today, it is likely that some form of equity, such as common stock, will have to be used next time. Most firms maintain a deliberate, optimal mix of debt and equity financing. This mix is commonly called a **target capital structure**—a topic that will be addressed in Chapter 12. It is sufficient here to say that although firms raise money in lumps, they tend toward some desired *mix of financing*.

target capital structure
The desired optimal mix of debt and equity financing that most firms attempt to maintain.

To capture the interrelatedness of financing assuming the presence of a target capital structure, we need to look at the *overall cost of capital* rather than the cost of the specific source of funds used to finance a given expenditure. A simple example will illustrate.

E x a m p l e ▼ A firm is *currently* faced with an investment opportunity. Assume the following:

Best project available today

Cost = $100,000
Life = 20 years
IRR = 7 percent

Cost of least-cost financing source available

Debt = 6 percent

Because it can earn 7 percent on the investment of funds costing only 6 percent, the firm undertakes the opportunity. Imagine that *1 week later* a new investment opportunity is available:

Best project available 1 week later

> Cost = $100,000
> Life = 20 years
> IRR = 12 percent

Cost of least-cost financing source available

> Equity = 14 percent

In this instance, the firm rejects the opportunity, because the 14 percent financing cost is greater than the 12 percent expected return.

Were the firm's actions in the best interests of its owners? No—it accepted a project yielding a 7 percent return and rejected one with a 12 percent return. Clearly, there should be a better way, and there is: The firm can use a combined cost, which over the long run would provide for better decisions. By weighting the cost of each source of financing by its target proportion in the firm's capital structure, the firm can obtain a *weighted average cost* that reflects the interrelationship of financing decisions. Assuming that a 50–50 mix of debt and equity is targeted, the weighted average cost above would be 10 percent [(.50 × 6% debt) + (.50 × 14% equity)]. With this cost, the first opportunity would have been rejected (7% IRR < 10% weighted average cost), and the second one would have been accepted (12% IRR > 10% weighted average cost). Such an outcome would clearly be more desirable.

THE COST OF SPECIFIC SOURCES OF CAPITAL

This chapter focuses on finding the costs of specific sources of capital and combining them to determine the weighted average cost of capital. Our concern is only with the *long-term* sources of funds available to a business firm, because these sources supply the permanent financing. Long-term financing supports the firm's fixed-asset investments.[1] We assume throughout the chapter that such investments are selected using appropriate capital budgeting techniques.

There are four basic sources of long-term funds for the business firm: long-term debt, preferred stock, common stock, and retained earnings. The right-hand side of a balance sheet can be used to illustrate these sources:

---

[1]The role of both long-term and short-term financing in supporting both fixed and current asset investments is addressed in Chapter 15. Suffice it to say that long-term funds are at minimum used to finance fixed assets.

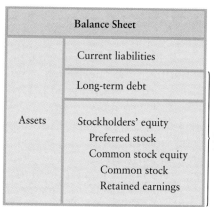

Although not all firms will use each of these methods of financing, each firm is expected to have funds from some of these sources in its capital structure. The *specific cost* of each source of financing is the *after-tax* cost of obtaining the financing *today,* not the historically based cost reflected by the existing financing on the firm's books. Techniques for determining the specific cost of each source of long-term funds are presented on the following pages. Although these techniques tend to develop precisely calculated values, the resulting values are at best *rough approximations* because of the numerous assumptions and forecasts that underlie them. Although we round calculated costs to the nearest .1 percent throughout this chapter, it is not unusual for practicing financial managers to use costs rounded to the nearest 1 percent because these values are merely estimates.

R e v i e w   Q u e s t i o n s

11-1   What is the *cost of capital?* What role does it play in making long-term investment decisions? Why is use of a weighted average cost rather than the specific cost recommended?

11-2   You have just been told, "Because we are going to finance this project with debt, its required rate of return must exceed the cost of debt." Do you agree or disagree? Explain.

11-3   Why is the cost of capital most appropriately measured on an after-tax basis?

THE COST OF LONG-TERM DEBT

cost of long-term debt, k_i
The after-tax cost today of raising long-term funds through borrowing.

The **cost of long-term debt, k_i,** is the after-tax cost today of raising long-term funds through borrowing. For convenience, we typically assume that the funds are raised through the sale of bonds. In addition, consistent with Chapter 8, we assume that the bonds pay *annual*—rather than *semiannual*—interest.

net proceeds
Funds actually received from the sale of a security.

flotation costs
The total costs of issuing and selling a security.

NET PROCEEDS

Most corporate long-term debts are incurred through the sale of bonds. The **net proceeds** from the sale of a bond, or any security, are the funds that are actually received from the sale. **Flotation costs**—the total costs of issuing and selling a security—reduce the net proceeds from the sale.

E x a m p l e ▼ Debbo Company, a major hardware manufacturer, is contemplating selling $10 million worth of 20-year, 9 percent coupon (stated *annual* interest rate) bonds, each with a par value of $1,000. Because similar-risk bonds earn returns greater than 9 percent, the firm must sell the bonds for $980 to compensate for the lower coupon interest rate. The flotation costs are 2 percent of the par value of the bond (2% × $1,000), or $20.[2] The net proceeds to the firm from the sale of each ▲ bond are therefore $960 ($980 − $20).

BEFORE-TAX COST OF DEBT

The before-tax cost of debt, k_d, for a bond can be obtained in any of three ways—quotation, calculation, or approximation.

USING COST QUOTATIONS

When the net proceeds from sale of a bond equal its par value, the before-tax cost would just equal the coupon interest rate. For example, a 10 percent coupon interest rate bond that nets proceeds equal to the bond's $1,000 par value would have a before-tax cost, k_d, of 10 percent.

A second quotation that is sometimes used is the *yield to maturity (YTM)* (see Chapter 8) on a similar-risk bond.[3] For example, if a similar-risk bond has a YTM of 9.7 percent, this value can be used as the before-tax cost of debt, k_d.

CALCULATING THE COST

This approach finds the before-tax cost of debt by calculating the *internal rate of return (IRR)* on the bond cash flows. From the issuer's point of view, this value can be referred to as the *cost to maturity* of the cash flows associated with the debt. The cost to maturity can be calculated by using either the trial-and-error techniques for finding IRR demonstrated in Chapter 10 or a financial calculator. It represents the annual before-tax percentage cost of the debt.

E x a m p l e ▼ In the preceding example, the net proceeds of a $1,000, 9 percent coupon interest rate, 20-year bond were found to be $960. The calculation of the annual cost is quite simple. The cash flow pattern is exactly the opposite of a conventional pat-

---

[2]Firms often hire investment bankers to find buyers for new security issues, regardless of whether they are privately placed or sold through a public offering. The flotation cost includes compensation to the investment banker for marketing the issue. Detailed discussion of the functions, organization, and cost of investment banking is included in Chapter 2.

[3]Generally, the yield to maturity of bonds with a similar "rating" is used. Bond ratings, which are published by independent agencies, are discussed in Chapter 3.

tern; it consists of an initial inflow (the net proceeds) followed by a series of annual outlays (the interest payments). In the final year, when the debt is retired, an outlay representing the repayment of the principal also occurs. The cash flows associated with Debbo Company's bond issue are as follows:

End of year(s)	Cash flow
0	$ 960
1–20	–$ 90
20	–$1,000

The initial $960 inflow is followed by annual interest outflows of $90 (9% coupon interest rate × $1,000 par value) over the 20-year life of the bond. In year 20, an outflow of $1,000 (the repayment of the principal) occurs. The before-tax cost of debt can be determined by finding the IRR—the discount rate that equates the present value of the outflows with the initial inflow.

Trial and Error   We know from the discussions in Chapter 8 that discounting a bond's future cash flows at its coupon interest rate will result in its $1,000 par value. Therefore the discount rate necessary to cause Debbo Company's bond value to equal $960 must be greater than its 9 percent coupon interest rate. (Remember that the higher the discount rate, the lower the present value, and the lower the discount rate, the higher the present value.) Applying a 10 percent discount rate to the bond's future cash flows, we get

$$\$90 \times (PVIFA_{10\%,20yrs}) + \$1,000 \times (PVIF_{10\%,20yrs})$$
$$= \$90 \times (8.514) + \$1,000 \times (.149)$$
$$= \$766.26 + \$149.00 = \$915.26$$

Because the bond's value of $1,000 at its 9 percent coupon interest rate is higher than $960 and the $915.26 value at the 10 percent discount rate is lower than $960, the bond's before-tax cost must be between 9 and 10 percent. Because the $1,000 value is closer to $960, the before-tax cost of the bond rounded to the nearest whole percent would be 9 percent. By using *interpolation* (as defined in footnote 13 in Chapter 6) the more precise value for the bond's before-tax cost is 9.47 percent.

Calculator Use   [*Note:* Most calculators require either the present (net proceeds) or future (annual interest payments and repayment of principal) values to be input as a negative number to calculate cost to maturity. That approach is used here.] Using the calculator and the inputs shown below, the before-tax cost (cost to maturity) of 9.452 percent should appear on the calculator display. Note that this number is the precise value of the bond's cost to maturity, which is closely approximated by the interpolated value of 9.47 percent resulting before from application of the trial-and-error approach.

Inputs: | 20 | -960 | 90 | 1000 |

Functions: | N | PV | PMT | FV | CPT | I |

Outputs: 9.452

PERSONAL FINANCE PERSPECTIVE

Lowering Your Personal Debt Costs

Your bills are mounting, and your raise didn't come through, so you need cash in a hurry. Although your credit card is a convenient source, you'll pay as much as 18 percent on unpaid balances. With excellent credit, you could transfer your balances to a new card and qualify for a temporary "teaser" rate as low as 5.9 percent. However, after 6 months, the rate reverts to the higher level. Lower-cost alternatives are available, especially if you own a house or have a 401(k) plan at work.

With a home equity (second-mortgage) loan, your loan is based on the additional equity in your home and costs much less than most other loans. Unlike other consumer loans, interest on up to $100,000 is tax deductible. Rates and terms vary, so shop around. One caution, however: If you run into problems repaying this loan, you risk losing your house.

Alternatively, many employers will allow you to borrow against your 401(k) retirement investment plan. But remember that anything you borrow is not available to grow for your retirement. And if you should leave the company or lose your job before age 59½, you must repay the loan immediately or be faced with tax penalties. ●

APPROXIMATING THE COST

The before-tax cost of debt, k_d, for a bond with a $1,000 par value can be approximated by using the following equation:

$$k_d = \frac{I + \dfrac{\$1,000 - N_d}{n}}{\dfrac{N_d + \$1,000}{2}}$$

(11.1)

where

$$I = \text{annual interest in dollars}$$
$$N_d = \text{net proceeds from the sale of debt (bond)}$$
$$n = \text{number of years to the bond's maturity}$$

Example ▼ Substituting the appropriate values from the Debbo Company example into the approximation formula given in Equation 11.1, we get

$$k_d = \frac{\$90 + \dfrac{\$1{,}000 - \$960}{20}}{\dfrac{\$960 + \$1{,}000}{2}} = \frac{\$90 + \$2}{\$980}$$

$$= \frac{\$92}{\$980} = \underline{\underline{9.4\%}}$$

This approximate before-tax cost of debt is close to the 9.452 percent value calculated precisely in the preceding example. ▲

AFTER-TAX COST OF DEBT

As indicated earlier, the *specific cost* of financing must be stated on an after-tax basis. Because interest on debt is tax deductible, it reduces the firm's taxable income. The interest deduction therefore reduces taxes by an amount equal to the product of the deductible interest and the firm's tax rate. In light of this, the after-tax cost of debt, k_i, can be found by multiplying the before-tax cost, k_d, by 1 minus the tax rate, T, as stated in the following equation:

$$k_i = k_d \times (1 - T) \tag{11.2}$$

Example ▼ We can demonstrate the after-tax debt cost calculation using the 9.4 percent before-tax debt cost approximation for Debbo Company, which has a 40 percent tax rate. Applying Equation 11.2 results in an after-tax cost of debt of 5.6 percent [9.4% × (1 − .40)]. Typically, the explicit cost of long-term debt is less than the explicit cost of any of the alternative forms of long-term financing, primarily because of the tax deductibility of interest. ▲

? Review Questions

11-4   What is meant by the *net proceeds* from the sale of a bond?

11-5   Describe the trial-and-error approach used to calculate the before-tax cost of debt. How does this calculation relate to a bond's *cost to maturity* and IRR? How can this value be found more efficiently and accurately?

11-6   What sort of general approximation can be used to find the before-tax cost of debt? How is the before-tax cost of debt converted into the after-tax cost?

LG2   THE COST OF PREFERRED STOCK

Preferred stock represents a special type of ownership interest in the firm. It gives preferred stockholders the right to receive their *stated* dividends before any earnings can be distributed to common stockholders. Because preferred stock is a form of ownership, the proceeds from its sale are expected to be held for an infinite period of time. The key characteristics of preferred stock were described in Chapter 3. However, the one aspect of preferred stock that requires review is dividends.

PREFERRED STOCK DIVIDENDS

Most preferred stock dividends are stated as a *dollar amount*—"x dollars per year." When dividends are stated this way, the stock is often referred to as "x-dollar preferred stock." Thus, a "$4 preferred stock" is expected to pay preferred stockholders $4 in dividends each year on each share of preferred stock owned.

Sometimes preferred stock dividends are stated as an *annual percentage rate*. This rate represents the percentage of the stock's par, or face, value that equals the annual dividend. For instance, an 8 percent preferred stock with a $50 par value would be expected to pay an annual dividend of $4 a share (.08 × $50 par = $4). Before the cost of preferred stock is calculated, any dividends stated as percentages should be converted to annual dollar dividends.

CALCULATING THE COST OF PREFERRED STOCK

cost of preferred stock, k_p
The relationship between the cost of the preferred stock and the amount of funds provided by the preferred stock issue; found by dividing the annual dividend, D_p, by the net proceeds from the sale of the preferred stock, N_p.

The **cost of preferred stock, k_p**, is the ratio of the preferred stock dividend to the firm's net proceeds from the sale of the preferred stock—that is, the relationship between the "cost" of the preferred stock, in the form of its annual dividend, and the amount of funds provided by the preferred stock issue. The net proceeds represent the amount of money to be received minus any flotation costs. Equation 11.3 gives the cost of preferred stock, k_p, in terms of the annual dollar dividend, D_p, and the net proceeds from the sale of the stock, N_p:

$$k_p = \frac{D_p}{N_p} \qquad (11.3)$$

Because preferred stock dividends are paid out of the firm's *after-tax* cash flows, a tax adjustment is not required.

Example ▼ Debbo Company is contemplating issuance of a 10 percent preferred stock that is expected to sell for its $87 per share par value. The cost of issuing and selling the stock is expected to be $5 per share. The first step in finding the cost of the stock is to calculate the dollar amount of the annual preferred dividend, which is $8.70 (.10 × $87). The net proceeds from the proposed sale of stock can be found by subtracting the flotation costs from the sale price. This gives a value of $82 per share ($87 − $5). Substituting the annual dividend, D_p, of $8.70 and the net proceeds, N_p, of $82 into Equation 11.3 gives the cost of preferred stock, 10.6 percent ($8.70 ÷ $82).
▲

The cost of Debbo's preferred stock (10.6 percent) is more expensive than its cost of the long-term debt (5.6 percent). This difference results primarily because the cost of long-term debt—interest—is tax deductible.

? R e v i e w   Q u e s t i o n

11-7   How would you calculate the cost of preferred stock? Why do we concern ourselves with the net proceeds from the sale of the stock instead of its sale price?

THE COST OF COMMON STOCK

The *cost of common stock* is the return required on the stock by investors in the marketplace. There are two forms of common stock financing: (1) retained earnings and (2) new issues of common stock. As a first step in finding each of these costs, we must estimate the cost of common stock equity.

FINDING THE COST OF COMMON STOCK EQUITY

cost of common stock equity, k_s
The rate at which investors discount the expected dividends of the firm to determine its share value.

The **cost of common stock equity, k_s,** is the rate at which investors discount the expected dividends of the firm to determine its share value. Two techniques measure the cost of common stock equity. One uses the constant-growth valuation model; the other relies on the capital asset pricing model (CAPM).

USING THE CONSTANT-GROWTH VALUATION (GORDON) MODEL

constant-growth valuation (Gordon) model
Assumes that the value of a share of stock is equal to the present value of all future dividends (assumed to grow at a constant rate) over an infinite time horizon.

The **constant-growth valuation model**—the **Gordon model**—was presented in Chapter 8. It is based on the widely accepted premise that the value of a share of stock is equal to the present value of all future dividends (assumed to grow at a constant rate) over an infinite time horizon. The key expression derived in Chapter 8 and presented as Equation 8.8 is restated in Equation 11.4:

$$P_0 = \frac{D_1}{k_s - g} \qquad (11.4)$$

where

P_0 = value of common stock

D_1 = per-share dividend expected at the end of year 1

k_s = required return on common stock

g = constant rate of growth in dividends

Solving Equation 11.4 for k_s results in the following expression for the *cost of common stock equity:*

$$k_s = \frac{D_1}{P_0} + g \qquad (11.5)$$

Equation 11.5 indicates that the cost of common stock equity can be found by dividing the dividend expected at the end of year 1 by the current price of the stock and adding the expected growth rate. Because common stock dividends are paid from *after-tax* income, no tax adjustment is required.

Example ▼ Debbo Company wishes to determine its cost of common stock equity, k_s. The market price, P_0, of its common stock is $50 per share. The firm expects to pay a dividend, D_1, of $4 at the end of the coming year, 2001. The dividends paid on the outstanding stock over the past 6 years (1995–2000) were as follows:

Year	Dividend
2000	$3.80
1999	3.62
1998	3.47
1997	3.33
1996	3.12
1995	2.97

Using the table for the present value interest factors, *PVIF* (Table A-3), or a financial calculator in conjunction with the technique described for finding growth rates in Chapter 6, we can calculate the annual growth rate of dividends, *g*. It turns out to be approximately 5 percent (more precisely, 5.05 percent). Substituting $D_1 = \$4$, $P_0 = \$50$, and $g = 5$ percent into Equation 11.5 results in the cost of common stock equity:

$$k_s = \frac{\$4}{\$50} + 5.0\% = 8.0\% + 5.0\% = \underline{\underline{13.0\%}}$$

The 13.0 percent cost of common stock equity represents the return required by *existing* shareholders on their investment to leave the market price of the firm's ▲ outstanding shares unchanged.

Using The Capital Asset Pricing Model (CAPM)

capital asset pricing model (CAPM)
Describes the relationship between the required return, or cost of common stock equity, k_s, and the nondiversifiable risk of the firm as measured by the beta coefficient, b.

The **capital asset pricing model (CAPM)** was developed and discussed in Chapter 7. It describes the relationship between the required return, or cost of common stock equity, k_s, and the nondiversifiable risk of the firm as measured by the beta coefficient, b. The basic CAPM is given in Equation 11.6:

$$k_s = R_F + [b \times (k_m - R_F)] \tag{11.6}$$

where

R_F = risk-free rate of return
k_m = market return; return on the market portfolio of assets

By using CAPM, the cost of common stock equity is the return required by investors as compensation for the firm's nondiversifiable risk, measured by beta.

Example ▼ Debbo Company now wishes to calculate its cost of common stock equity, k_s, by using the capital asset pricing model. The firm's investment advisers and its own analyses indicate that the risk-free rate, R_F, equals 7 percent; the firm's beta, b, equals 1.5; and the market return, k_m, equals 11 percent. Substituting these values into Equation 11.6, the company estimates the cost of common stock equity, k_s, as follows:

$$k_s = 7.0\% + [1.5 \times (11.0\% - 7.0\%)] = 7.0\% + 6.0\% = \underline{\underline{13.0\%}}$$

The 13.0 percent cost of common stock equity, which is the same as that found by using the constant growth valuation model in the preceding example, represents the required return of investors in Debbo Company common stock.

THE COST OF RETAINED EARNINGS

cost of retained earnings, k_r
The same as the cost of an *equivalent fully subscribed issue of additional common stock*, which is equal to the cost of common stock equity, k_s.

As you know, dividends are paid out of a firm's earnings. Their payment, made in cash to common stockholders, reduces the firm's retained earnings. Let's say a firm needs common stock equity financing of a certain amount; it has two choices that relate to retained earnings: It could issue additional common in that amount and still pay dividends to stockholders out of retained earnings. Or it could increase common stock equity by retaining the earnings (not paying the cash dividends) in the needed amount. In a strict accounting sense, the retention of earnings increases common stock equity in the same way that the sale of additional shares of common stock does. Thus, the **cost of retained earnings, k_r,** to the firm is the same as the cost of an *equivalent fully subscribed issue of additional common stock*. Stockholders find the firm's retention of earnings acceptable only if they expect that it will earn at least their required return on the reinvested funds.

Viewing retained earnings as a fully subscribed issue of additional common stock, we can set the firm's cost of retained earnings, k_r, equal to the cost of common stock equity as given by Equations 11.5 and 11.6.[4]

$$k_r = k_s \tag{11.7}$$

It is not necessary to adjust the cost of retained earnings for flotation costs because by retaining earnings, the firm "raises" equity capital without incurring these costs.

E x a m p l e ▼ The cost of retained earnings for Debbo Company was actually calculated in the preceding example: It is equal to the cost of common stock equity. Thus, k_r equals 13.0 percent. As we will show in the next section, the cost of retained earnings is always lower than the cost of a new issue of common stock, due to the absence of flotation costs when financing projects with retained earnings.

cost of a new issue of common stock, k_n
The cost of common stock, net of underpricing and associated flotation costs.

THE COST OF NEW ISSUES OF COMMON STOCK

Our purpose in finding the firm's overall cost of capital is to determine the after-tax cost of *new* funds required for financing projects. Attention must therefore be given to the **cost of a new issue of common stock, k_n.** As will be explained

---

[4]Technically, if a stockholder received dividends and wished to invest them in additional shares of the firm's stock, he or she would have to first pay personal taxes on the dividends and then pay brokerage fees before acquiring additional shares. By using pt as the average stockholder's personal tax rate and bf as the average brokerage fees stated as a percentage, the cost of retained earnings, k_r, can be specified as: $k_r = k_s \times (1 - pt) \times (1 - bf)$. Due to the difficulty in estimating pt and bf, only the simpler definition of k_r given in Equation 11.7 is used here.

underpriced
Stock sold at a price below its current market price, P_0.

later, this cost is important only when sufficient retained earnings are unavailable. The cost of a new issue of common stock is determined by calculating the cost of common stock, net of underpricing and associated flotation costs. Normally, to sell a new issue, it will have to be **underpriced**—sold at a price below its current market price, P_0. In addition, flotation costs paid for issuing and selling the new issue will further reduce proceeds.

The cost of new issues can be calculated using the constant-growth valuation model expression for the cost of existing common stock, k_s, as a starting point. If we let N_n represent the net proceeds from the sale of new common stock after subtracting underpricing and flotation costs, the cost of the new issue, k_n, can be expressed as follows:

$$k_n = \frac{D_1}{N_n} + g \qquad (11.8)$$

The net proceeds from sale of new common stock, N_n, will be less than the current market price, P_0. Therefore the cost of new issues, k_n, will always be greater than the cost of existing issues, k_s, which is equal to the cost of retained earnings, k_r. *The cost of new common stock is normally greater than any other long-term financing cost.* Because common stock dividends are paid from after-tax cash flows, no tax adjustment is required.

Example ▼ In the constant-growth valuation example, we found Debbo Company's cost of common stock equity, k_s, to be 13 percent, using the following values: an expected dividend, D_1, of $4; a current market price, P_0, of $50; and an expected growth rate of dividends, g, of 5 percent.

To determine its cost of *new* common stock, k_n, Debbo Company has estimated that, on average, new shares can be sold for $47. The $3 per share underpricing is due to the competitive nature of the market. A second cost associated with a new issue is flotation costs of $2.50 per share that would be paid to issue and sell the new shares. The total underpricing and flotation costs per share are therefore expected to be $5.50.

Subtracting the $5.50 per share underpricing and flotation cost from the current $50 share price, P_0, results in expected net proceeds, N_n, of $44.50 per share ($50.00 − $5.50). Substituting $D_1 = 4, $N_n = 44.50, and $g = 5$ percent into Equation 11.8 results in a cost of new common stock, k_n, as follows:

$$k_n = \frac{\$4.00}{\$44.50} + 5.0\% = 9.0\% + 5.0\% = \underline{14.0\%}$$

Debbo Company's cost of new common stock, k_n, is therefore 14.0 percent. This is the value to be used in subsequent calculations of the firm's overall cost of capital. ▲

? R e v i e w   Q u e s t i o n s

11-8 What premise about share value underlies the constant-growth valuation (Gordon) model that is used to measure the cost of common stock equity, k_s? What does each component of the equation represent?

11-9   If retained earnings are viewed as an *equivalent fully subscribed issue of additional common stock*, why is the cost of financing a project with retained earnings less than the cost of using a new issue of common stock?

THE WEIGHTED AVERAGE COST OF CAPITAL (WACC)

weighted average cost of capital (WACC), k_a
Reflects the expected average future cost of funds over the long run; found by weighting the cost of each specific type of capital by its proportion in the firm's capital structure.

Now that we have reviewed methods for calculating the cost of specific sources of financing, we can present techniques for determining the overall cost of capital. As noted earlier, the **weighted average cost of capital** (WACC), k_a, reflects the expected average future cost of funds over the long run. It is found by weighting the cost of each specific type of capital by its proportion in the firm's capital structure.

CALCULATING THE WACC

The calculation of the weighted average cost of capital (WACC) is performed by multiplying the specific cost of each form of financing by its proportion in the firm's capital structure and summing the weighted values. As an equation, the weighted average cost of capital, k_a, can be specified as follows:

$$k_a = (w_i \times k_i) + (w_p \times k_p) + (w_s \times k_{r \, or \, n}) \tag{11.9}$$

where

$$w_i = \text{proportion of long-term debt in capital structure}$$
$$w_p = \text{proportion of preferred stock in capital structure}$$
$$w_s = \text{proportion of common stock equity in capital structure}$$
$$w_i + w_p + w_s = 1.0$$

Three important points should be noted in Equation 11.9:

1. For computational convenience, it is best to convert the weights to decimal form and leave the specific costs in percentage terms.
2. *The sum of weights must equal 1.0.* Simply stated, all capital structure components must be accounted for.
3. The firm's common stock equity weight, w_s, is multiplied by either the cost of retained earnings, k_r, or the cost of new common stock, k_n. Which cost is used depends on whether the firm's common stock equity will be financed using retained earnings, k_r, or new common stock, k_n.

Example ▼   In earlier examples, we found the costs of the various types of capital for Debbo Company to be as follows:

Cost of debt, k_i = 5.6 percent
Cost of preferred stock, k_p = 10.6 percent
Cost of retained earnings, k_r = 13.0 percent
Cost of new common stock, k_n = 14.0 percent

TABLE 11.1	Calculation of the Weighted Average Cost of Capital for Debbo Company

Source of capital	Weight (1)	Cost (2)	Weighted cost [(1) × (2)] (3)
Long-term debt	.40	5.6%	2.2%
Preferred stock	.10	10.6	1.1
Common stock equity	.50	13.0	6.5
Totals	1.00		9.8%
	Weighted average cost of capital = 9.8%		

The company uses the following weights in calculating its weighted average cost of capital:

Source of capital	Weight
Long-term debt	40%
Preferred stock	10
Common stock equity	50
Total	100%

Because the firm expects to have a sizable amount of retained earnings available ($300,000), it plans to use its cost of retained earnings, k_r, as the cost of common stock equity. Debbo Company's weighted average cost of capital is calculated in Table 11.1. The resulting weighted average cost of capital for Debbo is 9.8 percent. Assuming an unchanged risk level, the firm should accept all projects that will earn a return greater than 9.8 percent.

WEIGHTING SCHEMES

Weights can be calculated based on *book value* or on *market value* and using *historic* or *target* proportions.

book value weights
Weights that use accounting values to measure the proportion of each type of capital in the firm's financial structure.

market value weights
Weights that use market values to measure the proportion of each type of capital in the firm's financial structure.

BOOK VALUE VERSUS MARKET VALUE

Book value weights use accounting values to measure the proportion of each type of capital in the firm's financial structure. **Market value weights** measure the proportion of each type of capital at its market value. Market value weights are appealing, because the market values of securities closely approximate the actual dollars to be received from their sale. Moreover, because the costs of the various types of capital are calculated using prevailing market prices, it seems reasonable to use market value weights. In addition, the long-term investment cash flows to which the cost of capital is applied are estimated in terms of current as well as future market values. *Market value weights are clearly preferred over book value weights.*

HISTORIC VERSUS TARGET

historic weights
Either book or market value weights based on *actual* capital structure proportions.

Historic weights can be either book or market value weights, based on *actual* capital structure proportions. For example, past or current book value proportions would constitute a form of historic weighting, as would past or current market value proportions. Such a weighting scheme would therefore be based on real—rather than desired—proportions.

target weights
Either book or market value weights based on *desired* capital structure proportions.

Target weights, which can also be based on either book or market values, reflect the firm's *desired* capital structure proportions. Firms using target weights establish such proportions on the basis of the "optimal" capital structure they wish to achieve. (The development of these proportions and the optimal structure are discussed in Chapter 12.)

When one considers the approximate nature of the weighted average cost of capital calculation, the choice of weights may not be critical. However, from a strictly theoretical point of view, the *preferred weighting scheme is target market value proportions*, and these are assumed throughout this chapter.

? R e v i e w   Q u e s t i o n

11-10   What is the *weighted average cost of capital (WACC),* and how is it calculated? Describe the logic underlying the use of *target capital structure weights,* and compare and contrast this approach with the use of *historic weights.*

THE MARGINAL COST AND INVESTMENT DECISIONS

The firm's weighted average cost of capital is a key input to the investment decision-making process. As demonstrated earlier in the chapter, the firm should make only those investments for which the expected return is greater than the weighted average cost of capital. Of course, at any given time, the firm's financing costs and investment returns will be affected by the volume of financing and investment undertaken. The concepts of a *weighted marginal cost of capital* and an *investment opportunities schedule* provide the mechanisms whereby financing and investment decisions can be made simultaneously.

THE WEIGHTED MARGINAL COST OF CAPITAL (WMCC)

The weighted average cost of capital may vary over time depending on the volume of financing the firm plans to raise. *As the volume of financing increases, the costs of the various types of financing will increase, raising the firm's weighted average*

weighted marginal cost of capital (WMCC)
The firm's weighted average cost of capital (WACC) associated with its *next dollar* of total new financing.

cost of capital. Therefore, it is useful to calculate the **weighted marginal cost of capital (WMCC),** which is simply the firm's weighted average cost of capital associated with its *next dollar* of total new financing. This marginal cost is relevant to current decisions.

Because the costs of the financing components—debt, preferred stock, and common stock—rise as larger amounts are raised, the WMCC is an increasing function of the level of total new financing. Increases in the component financing costs occur because the larger the amount of new financing, the greater the risk to the funds supplier. In other words, funds suppliers require greater returns in the form of interest, dividends, or growth as compensation for the increased risk introduced by larger volumes of *new* financing.

Another factor that causes the weighted average cost of capital to increase is the use of common stock equity financing. New financing provided by common stock equity will be taken from available retained earnings until exhausted and then will be obtained through new common stock financing. Because retained earnings are a less expensive form of common stock equity financing than the sale of new common stock, once retained earnings have been exhausted, the weighted average cost of capital will rise with the addition of more expensive new common stock.

FINDING BREAKING POINTS

breaking point
The level of *total* new financing at which the cost of one of the financing components rises, thereby causing an upward shift in the *weighted marginal cost of capital (WMCC).*

To calculate the WMCC, we must calculate the **breaking points,** which reflect the level of *total* new financing at which the cost of one of the financing components rises. The following general equation can be used to find breaking points:

$$BP_j = \frac{AF_j}{w_j} \tag{11.10}$$

where

BP_j = breaking point for financing source j
AF_j = amount of funds available from financing source j at a given cost
w_j = capital structure weight (historic or target, stated in decimal form) for financing source j

Example ▼ When Debbo Company exhausts its $300,000 of available retained earnings (k_r = 13.0%), it must use the more expensive new common stock financing (k_n = 14.0%) to meet its common stock equity needs. In addition, the firm expects that it can borrow only $400,000 of debt at the 5.6 percent cost; additional debt will have an after-tax cost (k_i) of 8.4 percent. Two breaking points therefore exist— (1) when the $300,000 of retained earnings costing 13.0 percent is exhausted and (2) when the $400,000 of long-term debt costing 5.6 percent is exhausted.

The breaking points can be found by substituting these values and the corresponding capital structure weights given earlier into Equation 11.10. We get

$$BP_{\text{common equity}} = \frac{\$300,000}{.50} = \$600,000$$

$$BP_{\text{long-term debt}} = \frac{\$400,000}{.40} = \$1,000,000$$

CALCULATING THE WMCC

Once the breaking points have been determined, the next step is to calculate the weighted average cost of capital over the range of total new financing between breaking points. First, we find the WACC for a level of total new financing between zero and the first breaking point. Next, we find the WACC for a level of total new financing between the first and second breaking points, and so on. By definition, for each of the ranges of total new financing between breaking points, certain component capital costs will increase, causing the weighted average cost of capital to increase to a higher level than that over the preceding range.

weighted marginal cost of capital (WMCC) schedule
Graph that relates the firm's weighted average cost of capital (WACC) to the level of total new financing.

Together, these data can be used to prepare the **weighted marginal cost of capital (WMCC) schedule,** which is a graph that relates the firm's weighted average cost of capital to the level of total new financing.

E x a m p l e ▼ Table 11.2 summarizes the calculation of the WACC for Debbo Company over the three total new financing ranges created by the two breaking points—$600,000 and $1,000,000. Comparing the costs in column 3 of the table for each of the three ranges, we can see that the costs in the first range ($0 to $600,000) are those calculated in earlier examples and used in Table 11.1. The second range ($600,000 to $1,000,000) reflects the increase in the common stock equity cost to 14.0 percent. In the final range, the increase in the long-term debt cost to 8.4 percent is introduced.

The weighted average costs of capital for the three ranges created by the two breaking points are summarized in the table shown at the bottom of Figure 11.1 on the following page. These data describe the weighted marginal cost of capital,

TABLE 11.2 **Weighted Average Cost of Capital for Ranges of Total New Financing for Debbo Company**

Range of total new financing	Source of capital (1)	Weight (2)	Cost (3)	Weighted cost [(2) × (3)] (4)
$0 to $600,000	Debt	.40	5.6%	2.2%
	Preferred	.10	10.6	1.1
	Common	.50	13.0	6.5
			Weighted average cost of capital	9.8%
$600,000 to $1,000,000	Debt	.40	5.6%	2.2%
	Preferred	.10	10.6	1.1
	Common	.50	14.0	7.0
			Weighted average cost of capital	10.3%
$1,000,000 and above	Debt	.40	8.4%	3.4%
	Preferred	.10	10.6	1.1
	Common	.50	14.0	7.0
			Weighted average cost of capital	11.5%

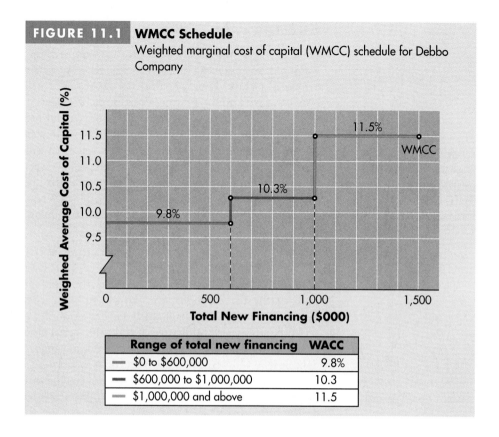

FIGURE 11.1 **WMCC Schedule**
Weighted marginal cost of capital (WMCC) schedule for Debbo Company

Range of total new financing	WACC
— $0 to $600,000	9.8%
— $600,000 to $1,000,000	10.3
— $1,000,000 and above	11.5

which increases as levels of total new financing increase. Figure 11.1 presents the WMCC schedule. Again, it is clear that the WMCC is an increasing function of the amount of total new financing raised.

THE INVESTMENT OPPORTUNITIES SCHEDULE (IOS)

investment opportunities schedule (IOS)
A ranking of investment possibilities from best (highest return) to worst (lowest return).

At any given time, a firm has certain investment opportunities available to it. These opportunities differ with respect to the size of investment, risk, and return.[5] The firm's **investment opportunities schedule (IOS)** is a ranking of investment possibilities from best (highest return) to worst (lowest return). As the cumulative amount of money invested in a firm's capital projects increases, its return (IRR) on the projects will decrease; generally, the first project selected will have the highest return, the next project the second highest, and so on. In other words, the return on investments will *decrease* as the firm accepts additional projects.

Example ▼ Debbo Company's current investment opportunities schedule (IOS) lists the best (highest return) to the worst (lowest return) investment possibilities in column 1 of Table 11.3. Column 2 of the table shows the initial investment required by each project. Column 3 shows the cumulative total invested funds required to

[5]Because the calculated weighted average cost of capital does not apply to risk-changing investments, we assume that all opportunities have equal risk similar to the firm's risk.

| TABLE 11.3 | Investment Opportunities Schedule (IOS) for Debbo Company | | |

Investment opportunity	Internal rate of return (IRR) (1)	Initial investment (2)	Cumulative investment[a] (3)
A	15.0%	$100,000	$ 100,000
B	14.5	200,000	300,000
C	14.0	400,000	700,000
D	13.0	100,000	800,000
E	12.0	300,000	1,100,000
F	11.0	200,000	1,300,000
G	10.0	100,000	1,400,000

[a]The cumulative investment represents the total amount invested in projects with higher returns plus the investment required for the given investment opportunity.

finance all projects better than and including the corresponding investment opportunity. Plotting the project returns against the cumulative investment (column 1 against column 3 in Table 11.3) on a set of total new financing or investment–weighted average cost of capital and IRR axes results in the firm's investment opportunities schedule (IOS). A graph of the IOS for Debbo Company is given in Figure 11.2 on the following page.

USING THE WMCC AND IOS TO MAKE FINANCING/ INVESTMENT DECISIONS

As long as a project's internal rate of return is greater than the weighted marginal cost of new financing, the firm should accept the project.[6] The return will decrease with the acceptance of more projects, and the weighted marginal cost of capital will increase because greater amounts of financing will be required. The firm would therefore *accept projects up to the point at which the marginal return on its investment equals its weighted marginal cost of capital.* Beyond that point, its investment return will be less than its capital cost.

This approach is consistent with the maximization of net present value (NPV), because for conventional projects (1) the NPV is positive as long as the IRR exceeds the weighted average cost of capital, k_a, and (2) the larger the difference between the IRR and k_a, the larger the resulting NPV. Therefore, the acceptance of projects beginning with those having the greatest positive difference between IRR and k_a down to the point at which IRR just equals k_a should result

---

[6]Although net present value could be used to make these decisions, the internal rate of return is used here because of the ease of comparison it offers.

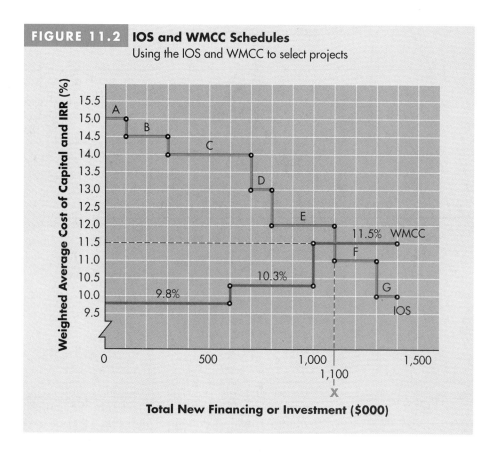

FIGURE 11.2 **IOS and WMCC Schedules**
Using the IOS and WMCC to select projects

in the maximum total NPV for all independent projects accepted. Such an outcome is completely consistent with the firm's goal of owner wealth maximization. Returning to the Debbo Company example, we can demonstrate the application of this procedure.

Example ▼ Figure 11.2 shows the Debbo Company's WMCC schedule and IOS on the same set of axes. By using these two functions in combination, the firm's optimal capital budget ("X" in the figure) is determined. By raising $1.1 million of new financing and investing these funds in projects A, B, C, D, and E, the firm should maximize the wealth of its owners, because these projects result in the maximum total net present value. Note that the 12.0 percent return on the last dollar invested (in project E) *exceeds* its 11.5 percent weighted average cost; investment in project F is not feasible because its 11.0 percent return is *less than* the 11.5 ▲ percent cost of funds available for investment.

Note that at the point at which the IRR equals the weighted average cost of capital, k_a—the optimal capital budget of $1,100,000 at point X in Figure 11.2—the firm's size as well as its shareholder value will be optimized. In a sense, the size of the firm is determined by the market—the availability of and returns on investment opportunities, and the availability and cost of financing.

Of course, as noted in Chapter 10, most firms operate under *capital rationing* because management imposes a capital expenditure budget constraint that is below the optimum capital budget (where IRR = k_a). Suffice it to say that due to capital rationing, a gap frequently exists between the theoretically optimal capital budget and the firm's actual level of financing/investment.

? Review Questions

11-11   What is the *weighted marginal cost of capital (WMCC)?* What does the WMCC *schedule* represent? Why does this schedule increase?

11-12   What is the *investment opportunities schedule (IOS)?* Is it typically depicted as an increasing or decreasing function of the level of investment at a given point in time? Why?

11-13   Use a graph to show how the weighted marginal cost of capital (WMCC) schedule and the investment opportunities schedule (IOS) can be used to find the level of financing/investment that maximizes owner wealth. Why, on a practical basis, do many firms finance/invest at a level below this optimum?

SUMMARY

LG1 **Understand the basic cost of capital concept and the specific sources of capital it includes.** The cost of capital is the rate of return that a firm must earn on its investments to maintain its market value and attract needed funds. To capture the inter-relatedness of financing, a weighted average cost of capital should be used. By combining the costs of long-term financing sources, this approach results in an expected average future cost of funds over the long run. The specific costs of the basic sources of capital (long-term debt, preferred stock, retained earnings, and common stock) can be calculated individually.

LG2 **Determine the cost of long-term debt using an approximation technique, and the cost of preferred stock.** The cost of long-term debt is the after-tax cost today of raising long-term funds through borrowing. Cost quotations, calculation using trial-and-error techniques, a financial calculator, or an approximation can be used to find the before-tax cost of debt, which must then be tax-adjusted. The cost of preferred stock is the stated annual dividend expressed as a percentage of the net proceeds from the sale of preferred shares. The key variable definitions and formulas for the

before- and after-tax cost of debt and the cost of preferred stock are given in Table 11.4.

LG3 **Calculate the cost of common stock equity and convert it into the cost of retained earnings and the cost of new issues of common stock.** The cost of common stock equity can be calculated by using the constant growth valuation model or the capital asset pricing model (CAPM). The cost of retained earnings is equal to the cost of common stock equity. An adjustment in the cost of common stock equity to reflect underpricing and flotation cost is required to find the cost of new issues of common stock. The key variable definitions and formulas for the cost of common stock equity, the cost of retained earnings, and the cost of new issues of common stock are given in Table 11.4.

LG4 **Find the weighted average cost of capital (WACC) and discuss the alternative weighting schemes.** The firm's WACC reflects the expected average future cost of funds over the long run. It can be determined by combining the costs of specific types of capital after weighting each cost using historical book or market value weights, and target book or market value weights. The theoretically

TABLE 11.4	Summary of Key Definitions and Formulas for Cost of Capital

Variable definitions

AF_j = amount of funds available from financing source j at a given cost

b = beta coefficient or measure of nondiversifiable risk

BP_j = breaking point for financing source j

D_1 = per-share dividend expected at the end of year 1

D_p = annual preferred stock dividend (in dollars)

g = constant rate of growth in dividends

I = annual interest in dollars

k_a = weighted average cost of capital

k_d = before-tax cost of debt

k_i = after-tax cost of debt

k_m = required return on the market portfolio

k_n = cost of a new issue of common stock

k_p = cost of preferred stock

k_r = cost of retained earnings

k_s = required return on common stock

n = number of years to the bond's maturity

N_d = net proceeds from the sale of debt (bond)

N_n = net proceeds from the sale of new common stock

N_p = net proceeds from the sale of preferred stock

P_0 = value of common stock

R_F = risk-free rate of return

T = firm's tax rate

w_i = proportion of long-term debt in capital structure

w_j = capital structure proportion (historic or target, stated in decimal form) for financing source j

w_p = proportion of preferred stock in capital structure

w_s = proportion of common stock equity in capital structure

Cost of capital formulas

Before-tax cost of debt:

$$k_d = \frac{I + \dfrac{\$1{,}000 - N_d}{n}}{\dfrac{N_d + \$1{,}000}{2}} \qquad \text{[Eq. 11.1]}$$

After-tax cost of debt:

$$k_i = k_d \times (1 - T) \qquad \text{[Eq. 11.2]}$$

Cost of preferred stock:

$$k_p = \frac{D_p}{N_p} \qquad \text{[Eq. 11.3]}$$

Cost of common stock equity:

   Using constant-growth valuation model:

$$k_s = \frac{D_1}{P_0} + g \qquad \text{[Eq. 11.5]}$$

   Using CAPM:

$$k_s = R_F + [b \times (k_m - R_F)] \qquad \text{[Eq. 11.6]}$$

Cost of retained earnings:

$$k_r = k_s \qquad \text{[Eq. 11.7]}$$

Cost of new issues of common stock:

$$k_n = \frac{D_1}{N_n} + g \qquad \text{[Eq. 11.8]}$$

Weighted average cost of capital (WACC):

$$k_a = (w_i \times k_i) + (w_p \times k_p) + (w_s \times k_{r \text{ or } n}) \qquad \text{[Eq. 11.9]}$$

Breaking point:

$$BP_j = \frac{AF_j}{w_j} \qquad \text{[Eq. 11.10]}$$

preferred approach uses target weights based on market values. The key variable definitions and formula for WACC are given in Table 11.4.

next dollar of total new financing. The WMCC schedule relates the WACC to each level of total new financing.

LG5 **Describe the rationale for and procedures used to determine breaking points and the weighted marginal cost of capital (WMCC).** A firm's weighted marginal cost of capital (WMCC) reflects the fact that as the volume of total new financing increases, the costs of the various types of financing will increase, raising the firm's WACC. Breaking points represent the level of total new financing at which the cost of one of the financing components rises, causing an upward shift in the WMCC. The key variable definitions and general formula for breaking points are given in Table 11.4. The WMCC is the firm's WACC associated with its

LG6 **Explain how the weighted marginal cost of capital (WMCC) can be used with the investment opportunities schedule (IOS) to make the firm's financing/investment decisions.** The IOS presents a ranking of currently available investments from those with the highest returns to those with the lowest returns. It is used in combination with the WMCC to find the level of financing/investment that maximizes owner wealth. With this approach, the firm accepts projects up to the point at which the marginal return on its investment equals its weighted marginal cost of capital.

SELF-TEST PROBLEM   (Solution in Appendix B)

ST 11–1   Specific costs, WACC, WMCC, and IOS   Humble Manufacturing is interested in measuring its overall cost of capital. Current investigation has gathered the following data. The firm is in the 40 percent tax bracket.

Debt   The firm can raise an unlimited amount of debt by selling $1,000 par value, 10 percent coupon interest rate, 10-year bonds on which *annual interest* payments will be made. To sell the issue, an average discount of $30 per bond must be given. The firm must also pay flotation costs of $20 per bond.

Preferred stock   The firm can sell 11 percent (annual dividend) preferred stock at its $100-per-share par value. The cost of issuing and selling the preferred stock is expected to be $4 per share. An unlimited amount of preferred stock can be sold under these terms.

Common stock   The firm's common stock is currently selling for $80 per share. The firm expects to pay cash dividends of $6 per share next year. The firm's dividends have been growing at an annual rate of 6 percent, and this rate is expected to continue in the future. The stock will have to be underpriced by $4 per share, and flotation costs are expected to amount to $4 per share. The firm can sell an unlimited amount of new common stock under these terms.

Retained earnings   The firm expects to have $225,000 of retained earnings available in the coming year. Once these retained earnings are exhausted, the firm will use new common stock as the form of common stock equity financing.

a. Calculate the specific cost of each source of financing. (Round to the nearest .1 percent.)

b. The firm uses the weights shown in the following table, which are based on target capital structure proportions, to calculate its weighted average cost of capital. (Round to the nearest .1 percent.)

Source of capital	Weight
Long-term debt	40%
Preferred stock	15
Common stock equity	45
Total	100%

(1) Calculate the single breaking point associated with the firm's financial situation. *(Hint: This point results from the exhaustion of the firm's retained earnings.)*

(2) Calculate the weighted average cost of capital associated with total new financing below the breaking point calculated in (1).

(3) Calculate the weighted average cost of capital associated with total new financing above the breaking point calculated in (1).

c. Using the results of **b** along with the information shown in the following table on the available investment opportunities, draw the firm's weighted marginal cost of capital (WMCC) schedule and investment opportunities schedule (IOS) on the same set of total new financing or investment (x axis)–weighted average cost of capital and IRR (y axis) axes.

Investment opportunity	Internal rate of return (IRR)	Initial investment
A	11.2%	$100,000
B	9.7	500,000
C	12.9	150,000
D	16.5	200,000
E	11.8	450,000
F	10.1	600,000
G	10.5	300,000

d. Which, if any, of the available investments do you recommend that the firm accept? Explain your answer. How much total new financing is required?

PROBLEMS

  11–1 Concept of cost of capital Ren Manufacturing is in the process of analyzing its investment decision-making procedures. The two projects evaluated by the firm during the past month were projects 263 and 264. The basic variables surrounding each project analysis using the IRR decision technique and the resulting decision actions are summarized in the following table.

Basic variables	Project 263	Project 264
Cost	$64,000	$58,000
Life	15 years	15 years
IRR	8%	15%
Least-cost financing		
Source	Debt	Equity
Cost (after-tax)	7%	16%
Decision		
Action	Accept	Reject
Reason	8% IRR > 7% cost	15% IRR < 16% cost

a. Evaluate the firm's decision-making procedures, and explain why the acceptance of project 263 and rejection of project 264 may not be in the owners' best interest.
b. If the firm maintains a capital structure containing 40 percent debt and 60 percent equity, find its weighted average cost using the data in the table.
c. Had the firm used the weighted average cost calculated in **b**, what actions would have been taken relative to projects 263 and 264?
d. Compare and contrast the firm's actions with your findings in **c**. Which decision method seems more appropriate? Explain why.

11-2 **Cost of debt using both methods**   Currently, Krick and Company can sell 15-year, $1,000 par-value bonds paying *annual interest* at a 12 percent coupon rate. As a result of current interest rates, the bonds can be sold for $1,010 each; flotation costs of $30 per bond will be incurred in this process. The firm is in the 40 percent tax bracket.

a. Find the net proceeds from sale of the bond, N_d.
b. Show the cash flows from the firm's point of view over the maturity of the bond.
c. Use the *IRR approach* to calculate the before-tax and after-tax cost of debt.
d. Use the *approximation formula* to estimate the before-tax and after-tax cost of debt.
e. Compare and contrast the cost of debt calculated in **c** and **d**. Which approach do you prefer? Why?

11-3 **Cost of debt using the approximation formula**   For each of the $1,000 par-value bonds shown in the table at the top of the following page, assuming *annual interest* payment and a 40 percent tax rate, calculate the *after-tax* cost to maturity using the *approximation formula*.

Bond	Life	Flotation cost	Discount (−) or premium (+)	Coupon interest rate
A	20 years	$25	−$20	9%
B	16	40	+ 10	10
C	15	30	− 15	12
D	25	15	Par	9
E	22	20	− 60	11

11-4 **Cost of preferred stock**   Tread Systems has just issued preferred stock. The stock has a 12 percent annual dividend and a $100 par value and was sold at $97.50 per share. In addition, flotation costs of $2.50 per share must be paid.
a. Calculate the cost of the preferred stock.
b. If the firm sells the preferred stock with a 10 percent annual dividend and nets $90.00 after flotation costs, what is its cost?

11-5 **Cost of preferred stock**   Determine the cost for each of the following preferred stocks.

Preferred stock	Par value	Sale price	Flotation cost	Annual dividend
A	$100	$101	$9.00	11%
B	40	38	$3.50	8%
C	35	37	$4.00	$5.00
D	30	26	5% of par	$3.00
E	20	20	$2.50	9%

11-6 **Cost of common stock equity—CAPM**   JAM Corporation common stock has a beta, b, of 1.2. The risk-free rate is 6 percent, and the market return is 11 percent.
a. Determine the risk premium on JAM common stock.
b. Determine the required return that JAM common stock should provide.
c. Determine JAM's cost of common stock equity using the CAPM.

11-7 **Cost of common stock equity**   Delico Meat Packing wishes to measure its cost of common stock equity. The firm's stock is currently selling for $57.50. The firm expects to pay a $3.40 dividend at the end of the year (2001). The dividends for the past 5 years are shown in the following table.

Year	Dividend
2000	$3.10
1999	2.92
1998	2.60
1997	2.30
1996	2.12

After underpricing and flotation costs, the firm expects to net $52 per share on a new issue.

a. Determine the growth rate of dividends.
b. Determine the net proceeds, N_n, that the firm actually receives.
c. Using the constant growth valuation model, determine the cost of retained earnings, k_r.
d. Using the constant growth valuation model, determine the cost of new common stock, k_n.

11-8   Retained earnings versus new common stock   Using the data for each firm shown in the following table, calculate the cost of retained earnings and the cost of new common stock using the constant-growth valuation model.

Firm	Current market price per share	Dividend growth rate	Projected dividend per share next year	Underpricing per share	Flotation cost per share
A	$50.00	8%	$2.25	$2.00	$1.00
B	20.00	4	1.00	.50	1.50
C	42.50	6	2.00	1.00	2.00
D	19.00	2	2.10	1.30	1.70

11-9   WACC—Book weights   Atlanta Tire has on its books the amounts and specific (after-tax) costs shown in the following table for each source of capital.

Source of capital	Book value	Specific cost
Long-term debt	$700,000	5.3%
Preferred stock	50,000	12.0
Common stock equity	650,000	16.0

a. Calculate the firm's weighted average cost of capital using book value weights.
b. Explain how the firm can use this cost in the investment decision-making process.

11-10   WACC—Book weights and market weights   Pure Air Company has compiled the information shown in the following table.

Source of capital	Book value	Market value	After-tax cost
Long-term debt	$4,000,000	$3,840,000	6.0%
Preferred stock	40,000	60,000	13.0
Common stock equity	1,060,000	3,000,000	17.0
Totals	$5,100,000	$6,900,000	

a. Calculate the weighted average cost of capital using book value weights.
b. Calculate the weighted average cost of capital using market value weights.
c. Compare the answers obtained in **a** and **b**. Explain the differences.

11-11   **WACC and target weights**   After careful analysis, Ellwood Company has determined that its optimal capital structure is composed of the sources and target market value weights shown in the following table.

Source of capital	Target market value weight
Long-term debt	30%
Preferred stock	15
Common stock equity	55
Total	100%

The cost of debt is estimated to be 7.2 percent; the cost of preferred stock is estimated to be 13.5 percent; the cost of retained earnings is estimated to be 16.0 percent; and the cost of new common stock is estimated to be 18.0 percent. All of these are after-tax rates. Currently, the company's debt represents 25 percent, the preferred stock represents 10 percent, and the common stock equity represents 65 percent of total capital based on the market values of the three components. The company expects to have a significant amount of retained earnings available and does not expect to sell any new common stock.

a. Calculate the weighted average cost of capital based on historic market value weights.
b. Calculate the weighted average cost of capital based on target market value weights.

11-12   **Calculation of specific costs, WACC, and WMCC**   Keystone Pump has asked its financial manager to measure the cost of each specific type of capital as well as the weighted average cost of capital. The weighted average cost is to be measured by using the following weights: 40 percent long-term debt, 10 percent preferred stock, and 50 percent common stock equity (retained earnings, new common stock, or both). The firm's tax rate is 40 percent.

Debt   The firm can sell for $980 a 10-year, $1,000-par-value bond paying *annual interest* at a 10 percent coupon rate. A flotation cost of 3 percent of the par value is required in addition to the discount of $20 per bond.

Preferred stock   Eight percent (annual dividend) preferred stock having a par value of $100 can be sold for $65. An additional fee of $2 per share must be paid to the underwriters.

Common stock   The firm's common stock is currently selling for $50 per share. The dividend expected to be paid at the end of the coming year (2001) is $4. Its dividend payments, which have been approximately 60 percent of earnings per share in each of the past 5 years, were as shown in the following table.

Year	Dividend
2000	$3.75
1999	3.50
1998	3.30
1997	3.15
1996	2.85

It is expected that, to sell, new common stock must be underpriced $5 per share and the firm must also pay $3 per share in flotation costs. Dividend payments are expected to continue at 60 percent of earnings.

a. Calculate the specific cost of each source of financing. (Assume that $k_r = k_s$.)

b. If earnings available to common shareholders are expected to be $7 million, what is the breaking point associated with the exhaustion of retained earnings?

c. Determine the weighted average cost of capital between zero and the breaking point calculated in **b**.

d. Determine the weighted average cost of capital just beyond the breaking point calculated in **b**.

11-13   Calculation of specific costs, WACC, and WMCC   Cloak, Inc. is interested in measuring its overall cost of capital. Current investigation has gathered the following data. The firm is in the 40 percent tax bracket.

Debt   The firm can raise an unlimited amount of debt by selling $1,000 par-value, 8 percent coupon interest rate, 20-year bonds on which *annual interest* payments will be made. To sell the issue, an average discount of $30 per bond would have to be given. The firm also must pay flotation costs of $30 per bond.

Preferred stock   The firm can sell 8 percent preferred stock at its $95-per-share par value. The cost of issuing and selling the preferred stock is expected to be $5 per share. An unlimited amount of preferred stock can be sold under these terms.

Common stock   The firm's common stock is currently selling for $90 per share. The firm expects to pay cash dividends of $7 per share next year. The firm's dividends have been growing at an annual rate of 6 percent, and this is expected to continue into the future. The stock must be underpriced by $7 per share, and flotation costs are expected to amount to $5 per share. The firm can sell an unlimited amount of new common stock under these terms.

Retained earnings   When measuring this cost, the firm does not concern itself with the tax bracket or brokerage fees of owners. It expects to have available $100,000 of retained earnings in the coming year; once these retained earnings are exhausted, the firm will use new common stock as the form of common stock equity financing.

a. Calculate the specific cost of each source of financing. (Round answers to the nearest .1 percent.)

b. The firm's capital structure weights used in calculating its weighted average cost of capital are shown in the following table. (Round answer to the nearest .1 percent.)

Source of capital	Weight
Long-term debt	30%
Preferred stock	20
Common stock equity	50
Total	100%

(1) Calculate the single breaking point associated with the firm's financial situation. (*Hint:* This point results from exhaustion of the firm's retained earnings.)
(2) Calculate the weighted average cost of capital associated with total new financing below the breaking point calculated in (1).
(3) Calculate the weighted average cost of capital associated with total new financing above the breaking point calculated in (1).

11-14   Integrative—WACC, WMCC, and IOS   H. Grimmer Company has compiled the data shown in the table at the top of the following page for the current costs of its three basic sources of capital—long-term debt, preferred stock, and common stock equity—for various ranges of new financing.

Source of capital	Range of new financing	After-tax cost
Long-term debt	$0 to $320,000	6%
	$320,000 and above	8
Preferred stock	$0 and above	17%
Common stock equity	$0 to $200,000	20%
	$200,000 and above	24

The company's capital structure weights used in calculating its weighted average cost of capital are shown in the following table.

Source of capital	Weight
Long-term debt	40%
Preferred stock	20
Common stock equity	40
Total	100%

a. Determine the breaking points and ranges of *total* new financing associated with each source of capital.
b. Using the data developed in **a,** determine the breaking points (levels of *total* new financing) at which the firm's weighted average cost of capital will change.
c. Calculate the weighted average cost of capital for each range of total new financing found in **b.** (*Hint:* There are three ranges.)
d. Using the results of **c** along with the following information on the available investment opportunities, draw the firm's weighted marginal cost of capital (WMCC) schedule and investment opportunities schedule (IOS) on the same set of total new financing or investment (*x* axis)–weighted average cost of capital and IRR (*y* axis) axes.

Investment opportunity	Internal rate of return (IRR)	Initial investment
A	19%	$200,000
B	15	300,000
C	22	100,000
D	14	600,000
E	23	200,000
F	13	100,000
G	21	300,000
H	17	100,000
I	16	400,000

e. Which, if any, of the available investments do you recommend that the firm accept? Explain your answer.

CASE   Chapter 11   **Making Dude Surfwear's Financing/Investment Decision**

Dude Surfwear Company is a growing manufacturer of casual clothing whose stock is actively traded on the over-the-counter exchange. During 2000, the Los Angeles–based company experienced sharp increases in both sales and earnings. Because of this recent growth, Melissa Jen, the company's treasurer, wants to make sure that available funds are being used to their fullest. Management policy is to maintain the current capital structure proportions of 30 percent long-term debt, 10 percent preferred stock, and 60 percent common stock equity for at least the next 3 years. The firm is in the 40 percent tax bracket.

Dude's division and product managers have presented several competing investment opportunities to Ms. Jen. However, because funds are limited, choices of which projects to accept must be made. The investment opportunities schedule (IOS) is shown in the following table.

Investment Opportunities Schedule (IOS) for Dude Surfwear Company

Investment opportunity	Internal rate of return (IRR)	Initial investment
A	15%	$400,000
B	22	200,000
C	25	700,000
D	23	400,000
E	17	500,000
F	19	600,000
G	14	500,000

To estimate the firm's weighted average cost of capital (WACC), Ms. Jen contacted a leading investment banking firm, which provided the financing cost data shown in the following table.

Financing Cost Data Dude Surfwear Company

Long-term debt: The firm can raise $450,000 of additional debt by selling 15-year, $1,000 par-value, 9 percent coupon interest rate bonds that pay *annual interest*. It expects to net $960 per bond after flotation costs. Any debt in excess of $450,000 will have a before-tax cost, k_d, of 13 percent.

Preferred stock: Preferred stock, regardless of the amount sold, can be issued with a $70 par-value, 14 percent annual dividend rate, and will net $65 per share after flotation costs.

Common stock equity: The firm expects dividends and earnings per share to be $.96 and $3.20, respectively, in 2001 and to continue to grow at a constant rate of 11 percent per year. The firm's stock currently sells for $12 per share. Dude expects to have $1,500,000 of retained earnings available in the coming year. Once the retained earnings have been exhausted, the firm can raise additional funds by selling new common stock, netting $9 per share after underpricing and flotation costs.

Required

a. Calculate the cost of each source of financing, as specified:
   (1) Long-term debt, first $450,000.
   (2) Long-term debt, greater than $450,000.
   (3) Preferred stock, all amounts.
   (4) Common stock equity, first $1,500,000.
   (5) Common stock equity, greater than $1,500,000.

b. Find the breaking points associated with each source of capital, and use them to specify each of the ranges of total new financing over which the firm's weighted average cost of capital (WACC) remains constant.

c. Calculate the weighted average cost of capital (WACC) over each of the ranges of total new financing specified in **b**.

d. Using your findings in **c** along with the investment opportunities schedule (IOS), draw the firm's weighted marginal cost of capital (WMCC) and IOS on the same set of total new financing or investment (*x* axis)–weighted average cost of capital and IRR (*y* axis) axes.

e. Which, if any, of the available investments would you recommend that the firm accept? Explain your answer.

Web Exercise

GOTO web site www.stls.frb.org. Click on ECONOMIC RESEARCH; click on FRED; click on MONTHLY INTEREST RATES; and then click on BANK PRIME LOAN RATE CHANGES—HISTORIC DATES OF CHANGES AND RATES—1929.

1. What was the prime interest rate in 1934?
2. What was the highest the prime interest rate has been? When was that?
3. What was the highest prime interest rate since you've been born?
4. What is the present prime interest rate?
5. Between the years of 1987 and the present, what was the lowest prime interest rate? The highest prime interest rate?

Now GOTO web site www.stern.nyu.edu/~adamodar/New_Home_Page/datafile/histret.html.

6. What was the arithmetic average for stock returns during the same time period as in question 5? How does this return compare to your answers to question 5?

12 LEVERAGE AND CAPITAL STRUCTURE

LEARNING GOALS

LG1 Discuss the role of breakeven analysis, how to determine the operating breakeven point, and the effect of changing costs on the breakeven point.

LG2 Understand operating, financial, and total leverage and the relationships among them.

LG3 Describe the basic types of capital, external assessment of capital structure, capital structure of non-U.S. firms, and capital structure theory.

LG4 Explain the optimal capital structure using a graphic view of the firm's cost of capital functions and a modified form of the zero-growth valuation model.

LG5 Discuss the graphic presentation, risk considerations, and basic shortcomings of the EBIT–EPS approach to capital structure.

LG6 Review the return and risk of alternative capital structures and their linkage to market value, and other important capital structure considerations.

ACROSS the DISCIPLINES

Leverage involves the use of fixed costs to magnify returns. Its use in the capital structure of the firm has the potential to increase its return and risk. Leverage and capital structure are closely related concepts that are linked to capital budgeting decisions through the cost of capital. These concepts can be used to minimize the firm's cost of capital and maximize its owners' wealth. This chapter discusses leverage and capital structure concepts and techniques, and how the firm can use them to create the best capital structure. Chapter 12 is important to:

- **accounting personnel** who will be involved in the calculation and analysis of operating and financial leverage.

- **information systems analysts** who will provide much of the information needed in management's determination of the best capital structure.

- **management** because it will make decisions about the firm's desired operating and financial leverage and its target capital structure.

- **the marketing department** because it will use breakeven analysis in pricing and product feasibility decisions.

- **operations,** because what it does and spends will have major impact on the firm's operating leverage.

LEVERAGE

leverage
Results from the use of fixed-cost assets or funds to magnify returns to the firm's owners.

capital structure
The mix of long-term debt and equity maintained by the firm.

Leverage results from the use of fixed-cost assets or funds to magnify returns to the firm's owners. Generally, increases in leverage result in increased return and risk, whereas decreases in leverage result in decreased return and risk. The amount of leverage in the firm's **capital structure**—the mix of long-term debt and equity maintained by the firm—can significantly affect its value by affecting return and risk. Unlike some causes of risk, management has almost complete control over the risk introduced through the use of leverage.

The three basic types of leverage can best be defined with reference to the firm's income statement, as shown in the general income statement format in Table 12.1:

- *Operating leverage* is concerned with the relationship between the firm's sales revenue and its earnings before interest and taxes, or EBIT. (EBIT is a descriptive label for *operating profits*.)
- *Financial leverage* is concerned with the relationship between the firm's EBIT and its common stock earnings per share (EPS).
- *Total leverage* is concerned with the relationship between the firm's sales revenue and EPS.

We will examine the three types of leverage concepts in detail in sections that follow. First, though, we will look at breakeven analysis, which lays the foundation for leverage concepts by demonstrating the effects of fixed costs on the firm's operations.

breakeven analysis
Indicates the level of operations necessary to cover all operating costs and the profitability associated with various levels of sales.

BREAKEVEN ANALYSIS

Breakeven analysis, sometimes called **cost-volume-profit analysis,** is used by the firm (1) to determine the level of operations necessary to cover all operating costs and (2) to evaluate the profitability associated with various levels of sales. The

TABLE 12.1   General Income Statement Format and Types of Leverage

Operating leverage	Sales revenue Less: Cost of goods sold Gross profits Less: Operating expenses Earnings before interest and taxes (EBIT)
Financial leverage	Less: Interest Net profits before taxes Less: Taxes Net profits after taxes Less: Preferred stock dividends Earnings available for common stockholders Earnings per share (EPS)

Total leverage spans the full statement from Sales revenue to EPS.

operating breakeven point
The level of sales necessary to cover all *operating costs*; the point at which EBIT = $0.

firm's **operating breakeven point** is the level of sales necessary to cover all *operating costs*. At that point, earnings before interest and taxes equals $0.[1]

The first step in finding the operating breakeven point is to divide the cost of goods sold and operating expenses into fixed and variable operating costs. *Fixed costs* are a function of time, not sales volume, and are typically contractual; rent, for example, is a fixed cost. *Variable costs* vary directly with sales and are a function of volume, not time; shipping costs, for example, are a variable cost.[2]

THE ALGEBRAIC APPROACH

Using the following variables, we can recast the operating portion of the firm's income statement given in Table 12.1 into the algebraic representation shown in Table 12.2.

$$P = \text{sale price per unit}$$
$$Q = \text{sales quantity in units}$$
$$FC = \text{fixed operating cost per period}$$
$$VC = \text{variable operating cost per unit}$$

Rewriting the algebraic calculations in Table 12.2 as a formula for earnings before interest and taxes yields Equation 12.1:

$$\text{EBIT} = (P \times Q) - FC - (VC \times Q) \tag{12.1}$$

Simplifying Equation 12.1 yields

$$\text{EBIT} = Q \times (P - VC) - FC \tag{12.2}$$

As noted above, the operating breakeven point is the level of sales at which all fixed and variable *operating costs* are covered—the level at which EBIT equals $0. Setting EBIT equal to $0 and solving Equation 12.2 for Q yields

$$Q = \frac{FC}{P - VC} \tag{12.3}$$

Q is the firm's operating breakeven point. Let us look at an example.

TABLE 12.2	**Operating Leverage, Costs, and Breakeven Analysis**	
	Item	Algebraic representation
	Sales revenue	$(P \times Q)$
Operating leverage	Less: Fixed operating costs	$- \quad FC$
	Less: Variable operating costs	$-(VC \times Q)$
	Earnings before interest and taxes	EBIT

[1]Quite often, the breakeven point is calculated so that it represents the point at which all operating and financial costs are covered. Our concern in this chapter is not with this overall breakeven point.

[2]Some costs, commonly called *semifixed* or *semivariable*, are partly fixed and partly variable. One example would be sales commissions that are fixed for a certain volume of sales and then increase to higher levels for higher volumes. For convenience and clarity, we assume that all costs can be classified as either fixed or variable.

E x a m p l e ▼ Assume that Omnibus Posters, a small poster retailer, has fixed operating costs of $2,500, its sale price per unit (poster) is $10, and its variable operating cost per unit is $5. Applying Equation 12.3 to these data yields

$$Q = \frac{\$2,500}{\$10 - \$5} = \frac{\$2,500}{\$5} = 500 \text{ units}$$

At sales of 500 units, the firm's EBIT should just equal $0. The firm will have positive EBIT for sales greater than 500 units and negative EBIT, or a loss, for sales less than 500 units. We can confirm this by substituting values above and below 500 units, along with the other values given, into Equation 12.1. ▲

THE GRAPHIC APPROACH

Figure 12.1 presents in graph form the breakeven analysis of the data in the preceding example. The firm's operating breakeven point is the point at which its *total operating cost*—the sum of its fixed and variable operating costs—equals sales revenue. At this point, EBIT equals $0. The figure shows that for sales *below* the operating breakeven point of 500 units, total operating cost exceeds sales revenue, and EBIT is less than $0 (a loss). For sales *above* the breakeven point of 500 units, sales revenue exceeds total operating cost, and EBIT is greater than $0.

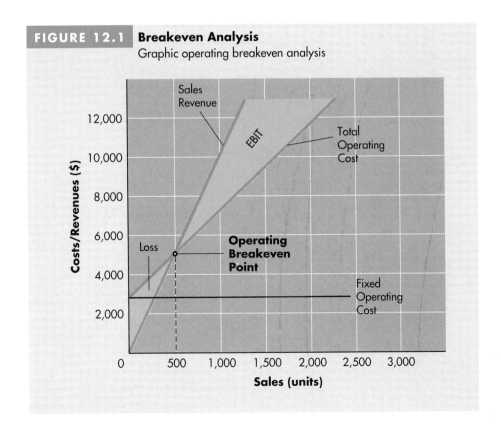

FIGURE 12.1   Breakeven Analysis
Graphic operating breakeven analysis

TABLE 12.3	Sensitivity of Operating Breakeven Point to Increases in Key Breakeven Variables

Increase in variable	Effect on operating breakeven point
Fixed operating cost *(FC)*	Increase
Sale price per unit *(P)*	Decrease
Variable operating cost per unit *(VC)*	Increase

Note: Decreases in each of the variables shown would have the opposite effect from that indicated on the breakeven point.

CHANGING COSTS AND THE OPERATING BREAKEVEN POINT

A firm's operating breakeven point is sensitive to a number of variables: fixed operating cost *(FC)*, the sale price per unit *(P)*, and the variable operating cost per unit *(VC)*. The effects of increases or decreases in these variables can be readily seen by referring to Equation 12.3. The sensitivity of the breakeven sales volume *(Q)* to an *increase* in each of these variables is summarized in Table 12.3. As might be expected, an increase in cost *(FC* or *VC)* tends to increase the operating breakeven point, whereas an increase in the sale price per unit *(P)* will decrease the operating breakeven point.

Example ▼ Assume that Omnibus Posters wishes to evaluate the impact of several options: (1) increasing fixed operating costs to $3,000, (2) increasing the sale price per unit to $12.50, (3) increasing the variable operating cost per unit to $7.50, and (4) simultaneously implementing all three of these changes. Substituting the appropriate data into Equation 12.3 yields the following results:

$$(1)\ \text{Operating breakeven point} = \frac{\$3,000}{\$10 - \$5} = 600 \text{ units}$$

$$(2)\ \text{Operating breakeven point} = \frac{\$2,500}{\$12.50 - \$5} = 333\tfrac{1}{3} \text{ units}$$

$$(3)\ \text{Operating breakeven point} = \frac{\$2,500}{\$10 - \$7.50} = 1,000 \text{ units}$$

$$(4)\ \text{Operating breakeven point} = \frac{\$3,000}{\$12.50 - \$7.50} = 600 \text{ units}$$

Comparing the resulting operating breakeven points to the initial value of 500 units, we can see that the cost increases (actions 1 and 3) raise the breakeven point, whereas the revenue increase (action 2) lowers the breakeven point. The combined effect of increasing all three variables (action 4) also results in an ▲ increased operating breakeven point.

We now turn our attention to the three types of leverage. It is important to recognize that the demonstrations of leverage that follow are conceptual in nature and that the measures presented are *not* routinely used by financial managers for decision-making purposes.

OPERATING LEVERAGE

operating leverage
The potential use of *fixed operating costs* to magnify the effects of changes in sales on the firm's earnings before interest and taxes.

Operating leverage results from the existence of *fixed operating costs* in the firm's income stream. Using the structure presented in Table 12.2, we can define **operating leverage** as the potential use of *fixed operating costs* to magnify the effects of changes in sales on the firm's earnings before interest and taxes. The following example illustrates how operating leverage works.

E x a m p l e ▼ Using the data presented earlier for Omnibus Posters (sale price, P = $10 per unit; variable operating cost, VC = $5 per unit; fixed operating cost, FC = $2,500), Figure 12.2 presents the operating breakeven graph originally shown in Figure 12.1. The additional notations on the graph indicate that as the firm's sales increase from 1,000 to 1,500 units (Q_1 to Q_2), its EBIT increases from $2,500 to $5,000 (EBIT$_1$ to EBIT$_2$). In other words, a 50 percent increase in sales (1,000 to 1,500 units) results in a 100 percent increase in EBIT. Table 12.4 includes the

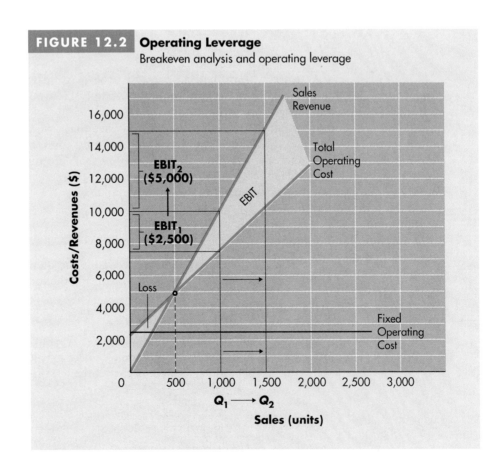

FIGURE 12.2   **Operating Leverage**
Breakeven analysis and operating leverage

TABLE 12.4	The EBIT for Various Sales Levels		
		Case 2	Case 1
		−50%	+50%
Sales (in units)		500	1,000	1,500
Sales revenue[a]	$5,000	$10,000	$15,000
Less: Variable operating costs[b]	2,500	5,000	7,500
Less: Fixed operating costs	2,500	2,500	2,500
Earnings before interest and taxes (EBIT)	$ 0	$ 2,500	$ 5,000
		−100%	+100%

[a]Sales revenue = $10/unit × sales in units.
[b]Variable operating costs = $5/unit × sales in units.

data for Figure 12.2 as well as relevant data for a 500-unit sales level. We can illustrate two cases using the 1,000-unit sales level as a reference point:

Case 1   A 50 percent *increase* in sales (from 1,000 to 1,500 units) results in a 100 percent *increase* in EBIT (from $2,500 to $5,000).

Case 2   A 50 percent *decrease* in sales (from 1,000 to 500 units) results in a 100 percent *decrease* in EBIT (from $2,500 to $0).

From the preceding example, we see that operating leverage works *in both directions*. When a firm has fixed operating costs, operating leverage is present. An increase in sales results in a more-than-proportional increase in earnings before interest and taxes; a decrease in sales results in a more-than-proportional decrease in earnings before interest and taxes.

MEASURING THE DEGREE OF OPERATING LEVERAGE (DOL)

degree of operating leverage (DOL)
The numerical measure of the firm's operating leverage.

The **degree of operating leverage (DOL)** is the numerical measure of the firm's operating leverage. It can be derived by using the following equation:[3]

$$DOL = \frac{\text{percentage change in EBIT}}{\text{percentage change in sales}} \qquad (12.4)$$

Whenever the percentage change in EBIT resulting from a given percentage change in sales is greater than the percentage change in sales, operating leverage exists. This means that as long as DOL is greater than 1, there is operating leverage.

---

[3]The degree of operating leverage also depends on the base level of sales used as a point of reference. The closer the base sales level used is to the operating breakeven point, the greater the operating leverage. *Comparison of the degree of operating leverage of two firms is valid only when the base level of sales used for each firm is the same.*

Example ▼ Applying Equation 12.4 to cases 1 and 2 in Table 12.4 yields the following results:[4]

$$\text{Case 1:} \quad \frac{+100\%}{+50\%} = 2.0$$

$$\text{Case 2:} \quad \frac{-100\%}{-50\%} = 2.0$$

Because the result is greater than 1, operating leverage exists. For a given base level of sales, the higher the value resulting from applying Equation 12.4, the greater the degree of operating leverage. ▲

A more direct formula for calculating the degree of operating leverage at a base sales level, Q, is shown in Equation 12.5.

$$\text{DOL at base sales level } Q = \frac{Q \times (P - VC)}{Q \times (P - VC) - FC} \tag{12.5}$$

Example ▼ Substituting $Q = 1,000$, $P = \$10$, $VC = \$5$, and $FC = \$2,500$ into Equation 12.5 yields the following result:

$$\text{DOL at 1,000 units} = \frac{1,000 \times (\$10 - \$5)}{1,000 \times (\$10 - \$5) - \$2,500} = \frac{\$5,000}{\$2,500} = 2.0$$

The use of the formula results in the same value for DOL (2.0) as that found by using Table 12.4 and Equation 12.4.[5] ▲

FIXED COSTS AND OPERATING LEVERAGE

Changes in fixed operating costs affect operating leverage significantly. Firms can sometimes incur fixed operating costs rather than variable operating costs. For example, a firm could make fixed-dollar lease payments rather than payments equal to a specified percentage of sales. Or it could compensate sales representatives with a fixed salary and bonus rather than on a pure percent-of-sales commission basis. Let's see the effects of changes in fixed operating costs on operating leverage.

Example ▼ Assume that Omnibus Posters exchanges a portion of its variable operating costs for fixed operating costs by eliminating sales commissions and increasing sales

---

[4]Because the concept of leverage is linear, positive and negative changes of equal magnitude will always result in equal degrees of leverage when the same base sales level is used as a point of reference. This relationship holds for all types of leverage discussed in this chapter.

[5]When total sales in dollars—instead of unit sales—are available, the following equation in which TR = dollar level of base sales and TVC = total variable operating costs in dollars can be used:

$$\text{DOL at base dollar sales } TR = \frac{TR - TVC}{TR - TVC - FC}$$

This formula is especially useful for finding the DOL for multiproduct firms. It should be clear that because in the case of a single-product firm, $TR = P \times Q$ and $TVC = VC \times Q$, substitution of these values into Equation 12.5 results in the equation given here.

TABLE 12.5	Operating Leverage and Increased Fixed Costs		
		Case 2	Case 1
		−50%	+50%
Sales (in units)	500	1,000	1,500
Sales revenue[a]	$5,000	$10,000	$15,000
Less: Variable operating costs[b]	2,250	4,500	6,750
Less: Fixed operating costs	3,000	3,000	3,000
Earnings before interest and taxes (EBIT)	−$ 250	$ 2,500	$ 5,250
		−110%	+110%

[a]Sales revenue was calculated as indicated in Table 12.4.
[b]Variable operating costs = $4.50/unit × sales in units.

salaries. This exchange results in a reduction in the variable operating cost per unit from $5 to $4.50 and an increase in the fixed operating costs from $2,500 to $3,000. Table 12.5 presents an analysis like that in Table 12.4, but using these new costs. Although the EBIT of $2,500 at the 1,000-unit sales level is the same as before the shift in cost structure, Table 12.5 shows that the firm has increased its operating leverage by shifting to greater fixed operating costs.

With the substitution of the appropriate values into Equation 12.5, the degree of operating leverage at the 1,000-unit base level of sales becomes

$$\text{DOL at 1,000 units} = \frac{1,000 \times (\$10 - \$4.50)}{1,000 \times (\$10 - \$4.50) - \$3,000} = \frac{\$5,500}{\$2,500} = 2.2$$

By comparing this value to the DOL of 2.0 before the shift to more fixed costs, it is clear that the higher the firm's fixed operating costs relative to variable operating costs, the greater the degree of operating leverage.

FINANCIAL LEVERAGE

financial leverage
The potential use of *fixed financial costs* to magnify the effects of changes in earning before interest and taxes on the firm's earnings per share.

Financial leverage results from the presence of *fixed financial costs* in the firm's income stream. Using the framework in Table 12.1, we can define **financial leverage** as the potential use of *fixed financial costs* to magnify the effects of changes in earnings before interest and taxes on the firm's earnings per share. The two fixed financial costs that may be found on the firm's income statement are (1) interest on debt and (2) preferred stock dividends.[6] The following example illustrates how financial leverage works.

---

[6]As noted in Chapter 3, although preferred stock dividends can be "passed" (not paid) at the option of the firm's directors, it is generally believed that the payment of such dividends is necessary. *This text therefore treats the preferred stock dividend as if it were a contractual obligation, not only to be paid as a fixed amount, but also to be paid as scheduled.* Although failure to pay preferred dividends cannot force the firm into bankruptcy, it increases the common stockholders' risk because they cannot be paid dividends until the claims of preferred stockholders are satisfied.

TABLE 12.6	The EPS for Various EBIT Levels		
		Case 2		Case 1
		−40%		+40%
EBIT	$6,000	$10,000	$14,000
Less: Interest (I)	2,000	2,000	2,000
Net profits before taxes	$4,000	$ 8,000	$12,000
Less: Taxes ($T = .40$)	1,600	3,200	4,800
Net profits after taxes	$2,400	$ 4,800	$ 7,200
Less: Preferred stock dividends (PD)	2,400	2,400	2,400
Earnings available for common (EAC)	$ 0	$ 2,400	$ 4,800
Earnings per share (EPS)	$\dfrac{\$0}{1{,}000} = \$0$	$\dfrac{\$2{,}400}{1{,}000} = \$2.40$	$\dfrac{\$4{,}800}{1{,}000} = \$4.80$
		−100%		+100%

Example ▼ Pedros, a small Mexican food company, expects EBIT of $10,000 in the current year. It has a $20,000 bond with a 10 percent (annual) coupon rate of interest and an issue of 600 shares of $4 (annual dividend per share) preferred stock outstanding. It also has 1,000 shares of common stock outstanding. The annual interest on the bond issue is $2,000 (.10 × $20,000). The annual dividends on the preferred stock are $2,400 ($4.00/share × 600 shares). Table 12.6 presents the earnings per share corresponding to levels of EBIT of $6,000, $10,000, and $14,000, assuming that the firm is in the 40 percent tax bracket. Two situations are illustrated in the table.

Case 1 A 40 percent *increase* in EBIT (from $10,000 to $14,000) results in a 100 percent *increase* in earnings per share (from $2.40 to $4.80).

Case 2 A 40 percent *decrease* in EBIT (from $10,000 to $6,000) results in a 100 percent *decrease* in earnings per share (from $2.40 to $0).

The effect of financial leverage is such that an increase in the firm's EBIT results in a more-than-proportional increase in the firm's earnings per share, whereas a decrease in the firm's EBIT results in a more-than-proportional decrease in EPS.

MEASURING THE DEGREE OF FINANCIAL LEVERAGE (DFL)

degree of financial leverage (DFL)
The numerical measure of the firm's financial leverage.

The **degree of financial leverage (DFL)** is the numerical measure of the firm's financial leverage. It can be computed much like the degree of operating leverage. The following equation presents one approach for obtaining the DFL.[7]

---

[7]This approach is valid only when the base level of EBIT used to calculate and compare these values is the same. In other words, *the base level of EBIT must be held constant to compare the financial leverage associated with different levels of fixed financial costs.*

$$DFL = \frac{\text{percentage change in EPS}}{\text{percentage change in EBIT}} \tag{12.6}$$

Whenever the percentage change in EPS resulting from a given percentage change in EBIT is greater than the percentage change in EBIT, financial leverage exists. This means that whenever DFL is greater than 1, there is financial leverage.

Example ▼ Applying Equation 12.6 to cases 1 and 2 in Table 12.6 yields

$$\text{Case 1:} \quad \frac{+100\%}{+40\%} = 2.5$$

$$\text{Case 2:} \quad \frac{-100\%}{-40\%} = 2.5$$

In both cases, the quotient is greater than 1, so financial leverage exists. The higher this value, the greater the degree of financial leverage. ▲

A more direct formula for calculating the degree of financial leverage at a base level of EBIT is given by Equation 12.7, using the notation from Table 12.6. Note that in the denominator, the term $1/(1 - T)$ converts the after-tax preferred stock dividend to a before-tax amount for consistency with the other terms in the equation.

$$\text{DFL at base level EBIT} = \frac{\text{EBIT}}{\text{EBIT} - I - \left(PD \times \dfrac{1}{1-T}\right)} \tag{12.7}$$

Example ▼ Substituting EBIT = \$10,000, I = \$2,000, PD = \$2,400, and the tax rate (T = .40) into Equation 12.7 yields the following result:

$$\text{DFL at \$10,000 EBIT} = \frac{\$10,000}{\$10,000 - \$2,000 - \left(\$2,400 \times \dfrac{1}{1 - .40}\right)}$$

$$= \frac{\$10,000}{\$4,000} = 2.5$$

Notice that the formula given in Equation 12.7 provides a more direct method for calculating the degree of financial leverage than the approach illustrated using Table 12.6 and Equation 12.6. ▲

ⓟERSONAL FINANCE PERSPECTIVE

Leveraging Your Securities Portfolio

You can apply the principles of financial leverage to your own investment portfolio. You can magnify your investment returns with margin trading. By borrowing funds from your broker (up to 50 percent of the value of common stocks, mutual funds, and bonds), you can reduce the amount of capital that you invest.

Let's look at a simple example of margin trading. This example ignores brokerage commissions and interest costs. Assume that you buy 100 shares of a stock *priced at $50 a share, for a total of $5,000. If the price rises to $80 per share, your capital gain is $3,000 (100 shares at $80 = $8,000 − $5,000 investment cost) and your return is 60 percent ($3,000 gain ÷ $5,000 equity). Buy the same stock on 50 percent margin, however, and your equity in the investment is $2,500. At a price of $80, the capital gain is still $3,000, but your return jumps to 120 percent ($3,000 gain ÷ $2,500 equity). But leverage works both ways; should the stock price drop to $20 a share, your losses would be magnified as well.* ●

TOTAL LEVERAGE

total leverage
The potential use of *fixed costs, both operating and financial,* to magnify the effect of changes in sales on the firm's earnings per share.

We can also assess the combined effect of operating and financial leverage on the firm's risk. This combined effect, or **total leverage,** can be defined as the potential use of *fixed costs, both operating and financial,* to magnify the effect of changes in sales on the firm's earnings per share. Total leverage can therefore be viewed as the *total impact of the fixed costs* in the firm's operating and financial structure.

E x a m p l e ▼

Health Cereal, a small cereal company, expects sales of 20,000 units at $5 per unit in the coming year and must meet the following: variable operating costs of $2 per unit, fixed operating costs of $10,000, interest of $20,000, and preferred stock dividends of $12,000. The firm is in the 40 percent tax bracket and has 5,000 shares of common stock outstanding. Table 12.7, on page 400, presents the levels of earnings per share associated with two levels of expected sales: 20,000 units and 30,000 units.

The table illustrates that as a result of a 50 percent increase in sales (from 20,000 to 30,000 units), the firm would experience a 300 percent increase in earnings per share (from $1.20 to $4.80). Although not shown in the table, a 50 percent decrease in sales would, conversely, result in a 300 percent decrease in earnings per share. The linear nature of the leverage relationship accounts for the fact that sales changes of equal magnitude in opposite directions result in EPS changes of equal magnitude in the corresponding direction. At this point, it should be clear that whenever a firm has fixed costs—operating or financial—in its structure, total leverage will exist.

▲

MEASURING THE DEGREE OF TOTAL LEVERAGE (DTL)

degree of total leverage (DTL)
The numerical measure of the firm's total leverage.

The **degree of total leverage (DTL)** is the numerical measure of the firm's total leverage. It can be computed much like operating and financial leverage. The following equation presents one approach for measuring DTL.[8]

$$DTL = \frac{\text{percentage change in EPS}}{\text{percentage change in sales}} \qquad (12.8)$$

Whenever the percentage change in EPS resulting from a given percentage change in sales is greater than the percentage change in sales, total leverage exists. When the DTL is greater than 1, there is total leverage.

---

[8]This approach is valid only when the base level of sales used to calculate and compare these values is the same. In other words, *the base level of sales must be held constant to compare the total leverage associated with different levels of fixed costs.*

TABLE 12.7	The Total Leverage Effect			

		+50%	
Sales (in units)	20,000	30,000	
Sales revenue*a*	$100,000	$150,000	DOL =
Less: Variable operating costs*b*	40,000	60,000	
Less: Fixed operating costs	10,000	10,000	$\dfrac{+60\%}{+50\%} = 1.2$
Earnings before interest and taxes (EBIT)	$ 50,000	$ 80,000	
		+60%	
Less: Interest	20,000	20,000	DFL =
Net profits before taxes	$ 30,000	$ 60,000	
Less: Taxes (*T* = .40)	12,000	24,000	$\dfrac{+300\%}{+60\%} = 5.0$
Net profits after taxes	$ 18,000	$ 36,000	
Less: Preferred stock dividends	12,000	12,000	
Earnings available for common	$ 6,000	$ 24,000	
Earnings per share (EPS)	$\dfrac{\$6,000}{5,000} = \$1.20$	$\dfrac{\$24,000}{5,000} = \$4.80$	
		+300%	

DTL =

$\dfrac{+300\%}{+50\%} = 6.0$

*a*Sales revenue = $5/unit × sales in units.
*b*Variable operating costs = $2/unit × sales in units.

Example ▼ Applying Equation 12.8 to the data in Table 12.7 yields

$$\text{DTL} = \frac{+300\%}{+50\%} = 6.0$$

Because this result is greater than 1, total leverage exists. The higher the value, the greater the degree of total leverage. ▲

A more direct formula for calculating the degree of total leverage at a given base level of sales, *Q*, is given by Equation 12.9, which uses the same notation presented earlier:

$$\text{DTL at base sales level } Q = \frac{Q \times (P - VC)}{Q \times (P - VC) - FC - I - \left(PD \times \dfrac{1}{1-T}\right)} \tag{12.9}$$

Example ▼ Substituting *Q* = 20,000, *P* = $5, *VC* = $2, *FC* = $10,000, *I* = $20,000, *PD* = $12,000, and the tax rate (*T* = .40) into Equation 12.9 yields the following result:

$$\text{DTL at 20,000 units} = \frac{20,000 \times (\$5 - \$2)}{20,000 \times (\$5 - \$2) - \$10,000 - \$20,000 - \left(\$12,000 \times \dfrac{1}{1-.40}\right)}$$

$$= \frac{\$60,000}{\$10,000} = 6.0$$

Clearly, the formula used in Equation 12.9 provides a more direct method for calculating the degree of total leverage than the approach illustrated using Table 12.7 and Equation 12.8.

THE RELATIONSHIP OF OPERATING, FINANCIAL, AND TOTAL LEVERAGE

Total leverage reflects the *combined impact* of operating and financial leverage on the firm. High operating leverage and high financial leverage will cause total leverage to be high. The opposite will also be true. The relationship between operating leverage and financial leverage is *multiplicative* rather than *additive*. The relationship between the degree of total leverage (DTL) and the degrees of operating leverage (DOL) and financial leverage (DFL) is given by Equation 12.10.

$$DTL = DOL \times DFL \qquad (12.10)$$

Example ▼ Substituting the values calculated for DOL and DFL, shown on the right-hand side of Table 12.7, into Equation 12.10 yields

$$DTL = 1.2 \times 5.0 = 6.0$$

The resulting degree of total leverage is the same value as calculated directly in the preceding examples. ▲

? Review Questions

12-1   What is meant by the term *leverage?* How do operating leverage, financial leverage, and total leverage relate to the income statement?

12-2   What is the *operating breakeven point?* How do changes in fixed operating costs, the sale price per unit, and the variable operating cost per unit affect it?

12-3   What is *operating leverage?* What causes it? How is the *degree of operating leverage (DOL)* measured?

12-4   What is *financial leverage?* What causes it? How is the *degree of financial leverage (DFL)* measured?

12-5   What is the general relationship among operating leverage, financial leverage, and the total leverage of the firm? Do these types of leverage complement each other? Why or why not?

THE FIRM'S CAPITAL STRUCTURE

Capital structure is one of the most complex areas of financial decision making due to its interrelationship with other financial decision variables.[9] Poor capital structure decisions can result in a high cost of capital, thereby lowering project NPVs and making more of them unacceptable. Effective decisions can lower the

---

[9]Of course, although capital structure is financially important, it, like many business decisions, is generally not as important as the firm's products or services. In a practical sense, a firm can probably more readily increase its value by improving quality and reducing costs than by fine-tuning its capital structure.

cost of capital, resulting in higher NPVs and more acceptable projects, thereby increasing the value of the firm. This section links together the concepts presented in Chapters 6, 7, 8, and 11 and the discussion of leverage in this chapter.

TYPES OF CAPITAL

All of the items on the right-hand side of the firm's balance sheet, excluding current liabilities, are sources of *capital*. The following simplified balance sheet illustrates the basic breakdown of total capital into its two components—*debt capital* and *equity capital*.

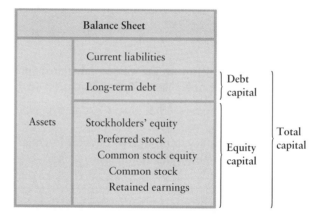

The various types and characteristics of *corporate bonds*, a major source of *debt capital*, were discussed in detail in Chapter 3. In Chapter 11, the cost of debt was found to be less than the cost of other forms of financing. Lenders demand relatively lower returns because they take the least risk of any long-term contributors of capital: (1) They have a higher priority of claim against any earnings or assets available for payment. (2) They have a far stronger legal pressure against the company to make payment than do preferred or common stockholders. And (3) the tax deductibility of interest payments lowers the debt cost to the firm substantially.

Unlike borrowed funds that must be repaid at a specified future date, *equity capital* is expected to remain in the firm for an indefinite period of time. The two basic sources of equity capital are (1) preferred stock and (2) common stock equity, which includes common stock and retained earnings. As was demonstrated in Chapter 11, common stock is typically the most expensive form of equity, followed by retained earnings and preferred stock, respectively. Our concern here is the relationship between debt and equity capital: Due to its secondary position relative to debt, suppliers of equity capital take greater risk and therefore must be compensated with higher expected returns than suppliers of debt capital.

EXTERNAL ASSESSMENT OF CAPITAL STRUCTURE

Earlier it was shown that *financial leverage* results from the use of fixed-payment financing, such as debt and preferred stock, to magnify return and risk. A direct measure of the degree of indebtedness is the *debt ratio*. The higher this ratio, the greater the firm's financial leverage.[10] A measure of the firm's ability to meet fixed payments associated with debt is the *times interest earned ratio*. This ratio provides indirect information on financial leverage. The smaller it is, the greater the firm's financial leverage and the less able it is to meet payments as they come due. The more risk a firm is willing to take, the greater its financial leverage. In theory, the firm should maintain financial leverage consistent with a capital structure that maximizes owners' wealth.

An acceptable degree of financial leverage for one industry or line of business can be highly risky in another, due to differing operating characteristics between industries or lines of business. Table 12.8 presents the debt and times interest earned ratios for selected industries and lines of business. Significant industry differences can be seen in these data. For example, the debt ratio for electronic computer manufacturers is 52.6 percent, whereas for auto retailers it is 78.4 percent. Differences in debt positions are also likely to exist *within* an industry or line of business.

CAPITAL STRUCTURE OF NON-U.S. FIRMS

Modern capital structure theory has developed largely within the framework of the U.S. financial system, and most studies of these theories have employed data from U.S. companies. In recent years, however, both corporate executives and academic researchers have focused greater attention on financing patterns of European, Japanese, Canadian, and other non-U.S. companies. They have found important differences as well as striking similarities between U.S. and non-U.S. companies.

In general, non-U.S. companies have much higher degrees of indebtedness than their U.S. counterparts. Most of the reasons for this are related to the fact that U.S. capital markets are much more developed than those elsewhere and have played a greater role in corporate financing than has been the case in other countries. In most European countries and especially in Japan and other Pacific Rim nations, large commercial banks are more actively involved in the financing of corporate activity than has been true in the United States. Furthermore, in many of these countries, banks are allowed to make large equity investments in nonfinancial corporations—a practice that is prohibited for U.S. banks. Finally, share ownership tends to be more tightly controlled among founding family, institutional, and even public investors in Europe and Asia than it is for most large U.S. corporations, many of which have up to a million individual shareholders. The tight ownership structure of non-U.S. firms enables them to tolerate a higher degree of indebtedness.

On the other hand, similarities do exist between U.S. corporations and corporations in other countries. First, the same industry patterns of capital structure tend to be found around the world. For example, in almost all countries, pharmaceutical and other high-growth industrial firms tend to have lower debt ratios than do steel companies, airlines, and electric utility companies. Second, the capital structures of the largest U.S.-based multinational companies, which have access to many different capital markets around the world, typically resemble the

---

[10]Debt ratios, which measure, directly and indirectly, the firm's degree of financial leverage, were presented in Chapter 5.

TABLE 12.8	Debt Ratios for Selected Industries and Lines of Business (1997–1998)	

Industry or line of business	Debt ratio	Times interest earned ratio
Manufacturing industries		
Books	63.9%	3.6
Electronic computers	52.6	5.1
Fertilizers	61.0	2.7
Iron and steel foundries	62.1	4.1
Jewelry and precious metals	61.1	2.0
Women's dresses	55.1	4.0
Wholesaling industries		
Furniture	66.1	3.2
General groceries	66.5	2.5
Hardware and paints	58.1	3.1
Men's and boys' clothing	60.4	2.5
Petroleum products	66.1	2.4
Retailing industries		
Autos, new and used	78.4	2.0
Department stores	54.9	2.8
Radios, TV, consumer electronics	64.8	1.9
Restaurants	71.1	2.8
Shoes	58.1	2.2
Service industries		
Accounting, auditing, bookkeeping	53.4	5.7
Advertising agencies	72.9	6.0
Auto repair—general	65.8	2.7
Insurance agents and brokers	73.6	3.6
Physicians	72.7	2.7
Travel agencies	70.5	3.2

(*Source: RMA Annual Statement Studies, 1998* (fiscal years ended 4/1/97 through 3/31/98) (Philadelphia: Robert Morris Associates, 1998). Copyright © 1998 by Robert Morris Associates.)

Note: Robert Morris Associates recommends that these ratios be regarded only as general guidelines and not as absolute industry norms. No claim is made as to the representativeness of their figures.

capital structures of multinational companies from other countries more than they resemble those of smaller U.S. companies. Finally, the worldwide trend is away from reliance on banks for corporate financing and toward greater reliance on security issuance. Over time the differences in the capital structures of U.S. and non-U.S. firms will probably lessen.

CAPITAL STRUCTURE THEORY

Scholarly research suggests that there is an optimal capital structure range. However, *the understanding of capital structure at this point does not provide financial managers with a specified methodology for use in determining a firm's optimal capital structure.* Nevertheless, financial theory does provide help in understanding how a firm's chosen financing mix affects the firm's value.

In 1958, Franco Modigliani and Merton H. Miller[11] (commonly known as "M and M") demonstrated algebraically that assuming perfect markets,[12] the capital structure that a firm chooses does not affect its value. Many researchers, including M and M, have examined the effects of less restrictive market assumptions on the relationship between capital structure and the firm's value. The result is a *theoretical* optimal capital structure based on balancing the benefits and costs of debt financing. The major benefit of debt financing is the tax shield, which allows interest payments to be deducted in calculating taxable income. The cost of debt financing results from (1) the increased probability of bankruptcy caused by debt obligations, (2) the *agency costs* of the lender's monitoring the firm's actions, and (3) the costs associated with managers having more information about the firm's prospects than do investors.

TAX BENEFITS

Allowing firms to deduct interest payments on debt when calculating taxable income reduces the amount of the firm's earnings paid in taxes, thereby making more earnings available for investors (bondholders and stockholders). The deductibility of interest means the cost of debt, k_i, to the firm is subsidized by the government. Letting k_d equal the before-tax cost of debt and T equal the tax rate, from Chapter 11 (Equation 11.2), we have $k_i = k_d \times (1 - T)$.

PROBABILITY OF BANKRUPTCY

The chance that a firm will become bankrupt due to an inability to meet its obligations as they come due depends largely on its level of both business risk and financial risk.

business risk
The risk to the firm of being unable to cover operating costs.

Business Risk   **Business risk** is the risk to the firm of being unable to cover operating costs. In general, the greater the firm's *operating leverage*—the use of fixed operating costs—the higher its business risk. Although operating leverage is an important factor affecting business risk, two other factors—revenue stability and cost stability—also affect it. *Revenue stability* refers to the relative variability of the firm's sales revenues. Firms with reasonably stable levels of demand and with products that have stable prices have stable revenues. The result is low levels of business risk. Firms with highly volatile product demand and prices have unstable revenues that result in high levels of business risk. *Cost stability* refers to the relative predictability of input prices such as those for labor and materials. The more predictable and stable these input prices are, the lower the business risk; the less predictable and stable they are, the higher the business risk.

Business risk varies among firms, regardless of their lines of business, and is not affected by capital structure decisions. The level of business risk must be taken as a "given." The higher a firm's business risk, the more cautious the firm

---

[11]Franco Modigliani and Merton H. Miller, "The Cost of Capital, Corporation Finance, and the Theory of Investment," *American Economic Review* (June 1958), pp. 261–297.

[12]Perfect market assumptions include (1) no taxes, (2) no brokerage or flotation costs for securities, (3) symmetrical information—investors and managers have the same information about the firm's investment prospects, and (4) investors can borrow at the same rate as corporations.

must be in establishing its capital structure. Firms with high business risk therefore tend toward less highly leveraged capital structures, and firms with low business risk tend toward more highly leveraged capital structures. We will hold business risk constant throughout the discussions that follow.

financial risk
The risk to the firm of being unable to cover required financial obligations.

Financial Risk   The firm's capital structure directly affects its **financial risk**, which is the risk to the firm of being unable to cover required financial obligations. The penalty for not meeting financial obligations is bankruptcy. The more fixed-cost financing—debt and preferred stock—a firm has in its capital structure, the greater its financial leverage and risk. Financial risk depends on the capital structure decision made by management, and that decision is affected by the *business risk* the firm faces. The *total risk* of a firm—business and financial risk combined—determines its probability of bankruptcy.

AGENCY COSTS IMPOSED BY LENDERS

As noted in Chapter 1, the managers of firms typically act as *agents* of the owners (stockholders). The owners give the managers the authority to manage the firm for the owners' benefit. The *agency problem* created by this relationship extends not only to the relationship between owners and managers, but also to the relationship between owners and lenders. This latter problem is due to the fact that lenders provide funds to the firm on the basis of their expectations for the firm's current and future capital expenditures and capital structure.

When a lender provides funds to a firm, the interest rate charged is based on the lender's assessment of the firm's risk. The lender-borrower relationship, therefore, depends on the lender's expectations for the firm's subsequent behavior. The borrowing rates are, in effect, locked in when the loans are negotiated. After obtaining a loan at a certain rate, the firm could increase its risk by investing in risky projects or by incurring additional debt. Such action could weaken the lender's position in terms of its claim on the cash flow of the firm. From another point of view, if these risky investment strategies paid off, only the stockholders would benefit. Because payment obligations to the lender remain unchanged, the excess cash flows generated by a positive outcome from the riskier action would enhance the value of the firm to its owners. In other words, if the risky investments pay off, the owners receive all the benefits; but if the risky investments do not pay off, the lenders share in the costs.

Clearly, an incentive exists for the managers acting on behalf of the stockholders to "take advantage" of lenders. To avoid this situation, lenders impose certain monitoring techniques on borrowers, who as a result incur *agency costs*. The most obvious strategy is to deny subsequent loan requests or to increase the cost of future loans to the firm. Because this strategy is an after-the-fact approach, other controls must be included in the loan agreement. Lenders typically protect themselves by including provisions that limit the firm's ability to significantly alter its business and financial risk. These loan provisions tend to center on issues such as the minimum level of liquidity, asset acquisitions, executive salaries, and dividend payments.[13]

By including appropriate provisions in the loan agreement, the lender can control the firm's risk and thus protect itself against the adverse consequences of

---

[13]Typical loan provisions are discussed in Chapter 3.

this agency problem. Of course, in exchange for incurring agency costs by agreeing to the operating and financial constraints placed on it by the loan provisions, the firm should benefit by obtaining funds at a lower cost.

ASYMMETRIC INFORMATION

pecking order
A hierarchy of financing beginning with retained earnings followed by debt financing and finally external equity financing.

Two relatively recent surveys examined capital structure decisions.[14] Financial executives were asked which of two major criteria determined their financing decisions: (1) maintaining a *target capital structure* or (2) following a hierarchy of financing. This hierarchy, called a **pecking order,** begins with retained earnings followed by debt financing and finally external equity financing. Respondents from 31 percent of Fortune 500 firms and from 11 percent of the (smaller) 500 largest over-the-counter firms answered target capital structure. Respondents from 69 percent of the Fortune 500 firms and from 89 percent of the 500 largest OTC firms chose the pecking order.

asymmetric information
The situation in which managers of a firm have more information about operations and future prospects than do investors.

At first glance, on the basis of financial theory, this choice appears inconsistent with wealth maximizing goals. However, Stewart Myers explained how "asymmetric information" could account for the pecking order financing preferences of financial managers.[15] **Asymmetric information** results when managers of a firm have more information about operations and future prospects than do investors. Assuming that managers make decisions with the goal of maximizing the wealth of existing stockholders, then asymmetric information can affect the capital structure decisions that managers make.

Suppose, for example, that management has found a valuable investment that will require additional financing. Management believes that the prospects for the firm's future are very good and that the market does not fully appreciate the firm's value, as indicated by its current stock price, which is low given management's knowledge of the firm's prospects. In this case it would be more advantageous to current stockholders if management raised the required funds using debt rather than issuing new stock. Using debt to raise funds is frequently viewed as a **signal** that reflects management's view of the firm's stock value. Debt financing is a *positive signal* suggesting that management believes that the stock is "undervalued" and therefore a bargain. When the firm's future outlook becomes known to the market, the increased value would be fully captured by existing owners, rather than having to be shared with new stockholders.

signal
A financing action by management that is believed to reflect its view with respect to the firm's stock value; generally, debt financing is viewed as a *positive signal* that management believes that the stock is "undervalued," and a stock issue is viewed as a *negative signal* that management believes that the stock is "overvalued."

If, however, the outlook for the firm is poor, management may believe that the firm's stock is "overvalued." In that case, it would be in the best interest of existing stockholders for the firm to issue new stock. Therefore investors often interpret the announcement of a stock issue as a *negative signal*—bad news concerning the firm's prospects—and the stock price declines. This decrease in stock value, along with high underwriting costs for stock issues (compared to debt issues), make new stock financing very expensive. When the negative future outlook becomes known to the market, the decreased value would be shared with new stockholders, rather than fully experienced by existing owners.

---

[14]The results of the survey of Fortune 500 firms are reported in J. Michael Pinegar and Lisa Wilbricht, "What Managers Think of Capital Structure Theory: A Survey," *Financial Management* (Winter 1989), pp. 82–91, and the results of a similar survey of the 500 largest OTC firms are reported in Linda C. Hittle, Kamal Haddad, and Lawrence J. Gitman, "Over-the-Counter Firms, Asymmetric Information, and Financing Preferences," *Review of Financial Economics* (Fall 1992), pp. 81–92.

[15]Stewart C. Myers, "The Capital Structure Puzzle," *Journal of Finance* (July 1984), pp. 575–592.

Because asymmetric information conditions exist from time to time, firms should maintain some reserve borrowing capacity, by keeping debt levels low. This reserve allows the firm to take advantage of good investment opportunities without having to sell stock at a low price or send signals that unduly influence the stock price.

THE OPTIMAL CAPITAL STRUCTURE

So, what *is* an optimal capital structure, even if it exists (so far) only in theory? To provide some insight into an answer, we will examine some basic financial relationships. It is generally believed that *the value of the firm is maximized when the cost of capital is minimized.* By using a modification of the simple zero-growth valuation model (see Equation 8.6 in Chapter 8), we can define the value of the firm, *V*, by Equation 12.11, where EBIT equals earnings before interest and taxes, *T* is the tax rate, EBIT $\times$ (1 − *T*) represents the after-tax operating earnings available to the debt and equity holders, and k_a is the weighted average cost of capital:

$$V = \frac{\text{EBIT} \times (1 - T)}{k_a} \tag{12.11}$$

Clearly, if we assume that EBIT is constant, the value of the firm, *V*, is maximized by minimizing the weighted average cost of capital, k_a.

COST FUNCTIONS

Figure 12.3(a) plots three cost functions—the after-tax cost of debt, k_i; the cost of equity, k_s; and the weighted average cost of capital, k_a—as a function of financial leverage measured by the debt ratio (debt to total assets). The *cost of debt, k_i,* remains low due to the tax shield but slowly increases with increasing leverage to compensate lenders for increasing risk. The *cost of equity, k_s,* is above the cost of debt and increases with increasing financial leverage, but generally increases more rapidly than the cost of debt. The increase in the cost of equity occurs because the stockholders require a higher return as leverage increases, to compensate for the higher degree of financial risk.

The *weighted average cost of capital, k_a,* results from a weighted average of the firm's debt and equity capital costs. At a debt ratio of zero, the firm is 100 percent equity financed. As debt is substituted for equity and as the debt ratio increases, the weighted average cost of capital declines because the debt cost is less than the equity cost ($k_i < k_s$). As the debt ratio continues to increase, the increased debt and equity costs eventually cause the weighted average cost of capital to rise (after point *M* in Figure 12.3(*a*)). This behavior results in a U-shaped, or saucer-shaped, weighted average cost of capital function, k_a.

A GRAPHIC VIEW OF THE OPTIMAL STRUCTURE

optimal capital structure
The capital structure at which the weighted average cost of capital is minimized, thereby maximizing the firm's value.

Because the maximization of value, *V*, is achieved when the overall cost of capital, k_a, is at a minimum (see Equation 12.11), the **optimal capital structure** is therefore that at which the weighted average cost of capital, k_a, is minimized. In Figure 12.3(a), point *M* represents the *minimum weighted average cost of capital*—the point of optimal financial leverage and hence of optimal capital struc-

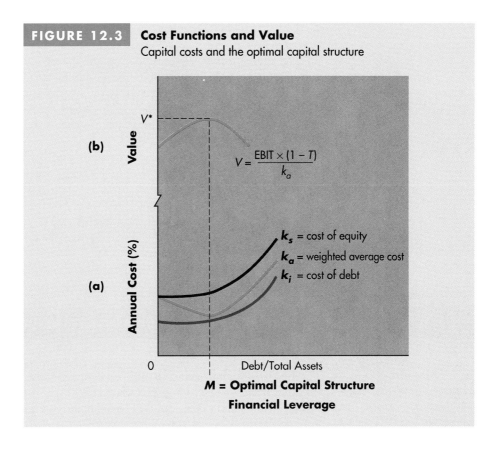

FIGURE 12.3   **Cost Functions and Value**
Capital costs and the optimal capital structure

ture for the firm. Figure 12.3(b) plots the value of the firm resulting from substitution of k_a in Figure 12.3(a) for various levels of financial leverage into the zero-growth valuation model in Equation 12.11. As shown in Figure 12.3(b), at the optimal capital structure, point M, the value of the firm is maximized at V^*.

Generally, the lower the firm's weighted average cost of capital, the greater the difference between the return on a project and this cost, and therefore the greater the owners' return. Simply stated, minimizing the weighted average cost of capital allows management to undertake a larger number of profitable projects, thereby further increasing the value of the firm.

As a practical matter, there is no way to calculate the optimal capital structure implied by Figure 12.3. Because it is impossible to either know or remain at the precise optimal capital structure, firms generally try to operate in a range that places them near what they believe to be the optimal capital structure. The fact that retained earnings and other new financings will cause the firm's actual capital structure to change further justifies the focus on a capital structure range rather than a single optimum point.

? R e v i e w   Q u e s t i o n s

12-6   What is a firm's *capital structure?* What ratios assess the degree of financial leverage in a firm's capital structure?

12-7   Discuss the differences in the capital structures of U.S. and non-U.S. companies. In what ways are the capital structures of U.S. and non-U.S. firms similar?

12-8   What is the major benefit of debt financing? How does it affect the firm's cost of debt?

12-9   Define *business risk*, and discuss the three factors that affect it. What influence does business risk have on the firm's capital structure decisions? Define *financial risk*, and explain its relationship to the firm's capital structure.

12-10   Briefly describe the *agency problem* that exists between owners and lenders. Explain how the firm must incur *agency costs* for the lender to resolve this problem.

12-11   How does *asymmetric information* affect the firm's capital structure decisions? Explain how and why investors may view the firm's financing actions as *signals*.

12-12   Describe the generally accepted theory concerning the behavior of the cost of debt, the cost of equity, and the weighted average cost of capital as the firm's financial leverage increases from zero. Where is the *optimal capital structure* under this theory? What is its relationship to the firm's value at that point?

LG5   THE EBIT–EPS APPROACH TO CAPITAL STRUCTURE

EBIT–EPS approach
An approach for selecting the capital structure that maximizes earnings per share (EPS) over the expected range of earnings before interest and taxes (EBIT).

The **EBIT–EPS approach** to capital structure involves selecting the capital structure that maximizes earnings per share (EPS) over the expected range of earnings before interest and taxes (EBIT). Here the main emphasis is on the effects of various capital structures on *owners' returns*. Because one of the key variables affecting the market value of the firm's shares is its earnings, EPS can be conveniently used to analyze alternative capital structures.

PRESENTING A FINANCING PLAN GRAPHICALLY

To analyze the effects of a firm's capital structure on the owners' returns, we consider the relationship between earnings before interest and taxes and earnings per share. A constant level of EBIT—constant *business risk*—is assumed, to isolate the effect on returns of the financing costs associated with alternative capital structures. EPS is used to measure the owners' returns, which are expected to be closely related to share price.

THE DATA REQUIRED

To graph a financing plan, we need to know at least two EBIT–EPS coordinates. The approach for obtaining coordinates can be illustrated by the following example.

Example ▼   The current capital structure of JSG Company, a soft-drink manufacturer, is as shown in the following table. Note that JSG's capital structure currently contains only common stock equity; the firm has no debt or preferred stock. If for convenience we assume the firm has no current liabilities, its debt ratio (total liabilities ÷ total assets) is currently 0 percent ($0 ÷ $500,000); it therefore has *zero* financial leverage. Assume the firm is in the 40 percent tax bracket.

Current capital structure	
Long-term debt	$ 0
Common stock equity (25,000 shares @ $20)	500,000
Total capital (assets)	$500,000

EBIT–EPS coordinates for JSG's current capital structure can be found by assuming two EBIT values and calculating the EPS associated with them.[16] Because the EBIT–EPS graph is a straight line, any two EBIT values can be used to find coordinates. Here we arbitrarily use values of $100,000 and $200,000.

EBIT (assumed)	$100,000	$200,000
− Interest (rate × $0 debt)	0	0
Net profits before taxes	$100,000	$200,000
− Taxes (T = .40)	40,000	80,000
Net profits after taxes	$ 60,000	$120,000
EPS	$\dfrac{\$60{,}000}{25{,}000 \text{ sh.}} = \$2.40$	$\dfrac{\$120{,}000}{25{,}000 \text{ sh.}} = \$4.80$

The two EBIT–EPS coordinates resulting from these calculations are (1) $100,000 EBIT and $2.40 EPS and (2) $200,000 EBIT and $4.80 EPS.

PLOTTING THE DATA

financial breakeven point
The level of EBIT necessary just to cover all *fixed financial costs;* the level of EBIT for which EPS = $0.

The two EBIT–EPS coordinates developed for JSG Company's current zero-leverage (debt ratio = 0 percent) situation can be plotted on a set of EBIT–EPS axes, as shown in Figure 12.4 on the following page. The figure shows the level of EPS expected for each level of EBIT. For levels of EBIT below the *x*-axis intercept, a loss (negative EPS) results. Each of the *x*-axis intercepts is a **financial breakeven point,** where EBIT just covers all *fixed financial costs* (EPS = $0).

COMPARING ALTERNATIVE CAPITAL STRUCTURES

We can compare alternative capital structures by graphing financing plans, as shown in Figure 12.4. The following example illustrates this procedure.

Example ▼ JSG Company, whose current zero-leverage capital structure was described in the preceding example, is contemplating shifting its capital structure to either of two leveraged positions. To maintain its $500,000 of total capital, JSG's capital

---

[16]A convenient method for finding one EBIT–EPS coordinate is to calculate the *financial breakeven point,* the level of EBIT for which the firm's EPS just equals $0. It is the level of EBIT needed just to cover all *fixed financial costs*—annual interest (*I*) and preferred stock dividends (*PD*). The equation for the financial breakeven point is

$$\text{Financial breakeven point} = I + \frac{PD}{1 - T}$$

where *T* is the tax rate. It can be seen that when *PD* = $0, the financial breakeven point is equal to *I*, the annual interest payment.

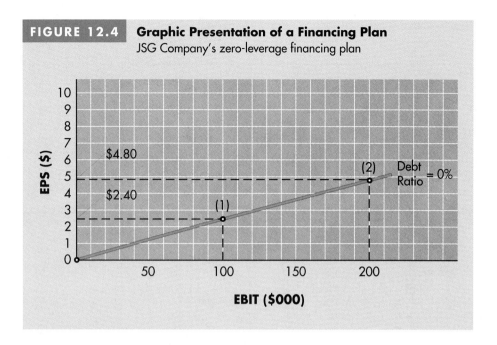

FIGURE 12.4 **Graphic Presentation of a Financing Plan**
JSG Company's zero-leverage financing plan

structure will be shifted to greater leverage by issuing debt and using the proceeds to retire an equivalent amount of common stock. The two alternative capital structures result in debt ratios of 30 percent and 60 percent, respectively. The basic information on the current and two alternative capital structures is summarized in Table 12.9.

Using the data in Table 12.9, we can calculate the coordinates needed to plot the 30 percent and 60 percent debt capital structures. For convenience, using the

TABLE 12.9 **Basic Information on JSG Company's Current and Alternative Capital Structures**

Capital structure debt ratio (1)	Total assets[a] (2)	Debt [(1) × (2)] (3)	Equity [(2) − (3)] (4)	Interest rate on debt[b] (5)	Annual interest [(3) × (5)] (6)	Shares of common stock outstanding [(4) ÷ $20][c] (7)
0% (current)	$500,000	$ 0	$500,000	0 %	$ 0	25,000
30	500,000	150,000	350,000	10	15,000	17,500
60	500,000	300,000	200,000	16.5	49,500	10,000

[a]Because for convenience the firm is assumed to have no current liabilities, total assets equals total capital of $500,000.
[b]The interest rate on all debt increases with increases in the debt ratio due to the greater leverage and risk associated with higher debt ratios.
[c]The $20 value represents the book value of common stock equity.

same $100,000 and $200,000 EBIT values used earlier to plot the current capital structure, we get the information in the following table.

	Capital structure			
	30% Debt ratio		60% Debt ratio	
EBIT (assumed)	$100,000	$200,000	$100,000	$200,000
− Interest (Table 12.9)	15,000	15,000	49,500	49,500
Net profits before taxes	$ 85,000	$185,000	$ 50,500	$150,500
− Taxes ($T = .40$)	34,000	74,000	20,200	60,200
Net profits after taxes	$ 51,000	$111,000	$ 30,300	$ 90,300
EPS	$\dfrac{\$51,000}{17,500\ \text{sh.}} = \underline{\underline{\$2.91}}$	$\dfrac{\$111,000}{17,500\ \text{sh.}} = \underline{\underline{\$6.34}}$	$\dfrac{\$30,300}{10,000\ \text{sh.}} = \underline{\underline{\$3.03}}$	$\dfrac{\$90,300}{10,000\ \text{sh.}} = \underline{\underline{\$9.03}}$

The two sets of EBIT–EPS coordinates developed in the preceding table, along with those developed for the current zero-leverage capital structure, are summarized and plotted on the EBIT–EPS axes in Figure 12.5. We see in this figure that *each* capital structure is superior to the others in terms of maximizing EPS over certain ranges of EBIT: The zero-leverage capital structure (debt ratio = 0 percent) is superior to either of the other capital structures for levels of EBIT between $0 and $50,000. Between $50,000 and $95,500 of EBIT, the capital structure associated with a debt ratio of 30 percent is preferred. At a level of EBIT in excess of $95,500, the capital structure associated with a debt ratio of 60 percent provides the highest earnings per share.[17]

CONSIDERING RISK IN EBIT–EPS ANALYSIS

When interpreting EBIT–EPS analysis, it is important to consider the risk of each capital structure alternative. Graphically, the risk of each capital structure can be viewed in light of the *financial breakeven point* (EBIT-axis intercept) and the *degree of financial leverage* reflected in the slope of the capital structure line: The higher the financial breakeven point and the steeper the slope of the capital structure line, the greater the financial risk.

Further assessment of risk can be performed by using ratios. With increased financial leverage, as measured by using the debt ratio, we expect a corresponding decline in the firm's ability to make scheduled interest payments, as measured by the times interest earned ratio.

Example ▼ Reviewing the three capital structures plotted for JSG Company in Figure 12.5, we can see that as the debt ratio increases, so does the financial risk of each alternative. Both the financial breakeven point and the slope of the capital structure lines increase with increasing debt ratios. If we use the $100,000 EBIT value, the times interest earned ratio (EBIT ÷ interest) for the zero-leverage capital structure

---

[17]An algebraic technique can be used to find the *indifference points* between the capital structure alternatives. Due to its relative complexity, this technique is not presented. Instead, emphasis is given here to the visual estimation of these points from the graph.

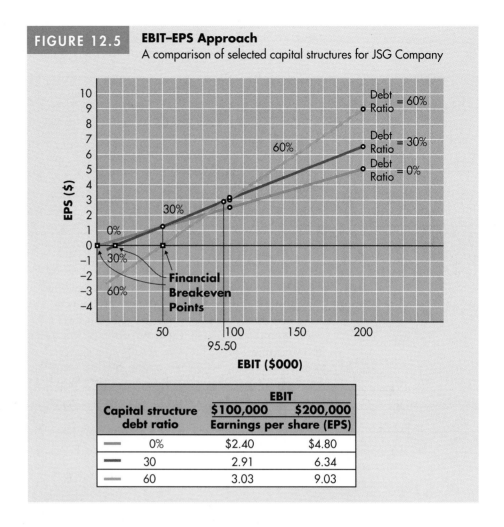

FIGURE 12.5

EBIT–EPS Approach
A comparison of selected capital structures for JSG Company

Capital structure debt ratio	EBIT	
	$100,000	**$200,000**
	Earnings per share (EPS)	
0%	$2.40	$4.80
30	2.91	6.34
60	3.03	9.03

is infinity ($100,000 ÷ $0); for the 30 percent debt case, it is 6.67 ($100,000 ÷ $15,000); and for the 60 percent debt case, it is 2.02 ($100,000 ÷ $49,500). Because lower times interest earned ratios reflect higher risk, these ratios support the earlier conclusion that the risk of the capital structures increases with increasing financial leverage. The capital structure for a debt ratio of 60 percent is riskier than that for a debt ratio of 30 percent, which in turn is riskier than the capital structure for a debt ratio of 0 percent.

BASIC SHORTCOMING OF EBIT–EPS ANALYSIS

The most important point to recognize when using EBIT–EPS analysis is that this technique tends to concentrate on *maximizing earnings* rather than maximizing owner wealth. The use of an EPS-maximizing approach generally ignores risk. If investors did not require risk premiums (additional returns) as the firm increased the proportion of debt in its capital structure, a strategy involving maximizing EPS would also maximize owner wealth. Because risk premiums increase with increases in financial leverage, the maximization of EPS *does not* ensure owner wealth maximization. To select the best capital structure, both return (EPS) and risk (via the required return, k_s) must be integrated into a valuation framework consistent with the capital structure theory presented earlier.

? R e v i e w   Q u e s t i o n

12-13 Explain the *EBIT–EPS approach* to capital structure. Include in your explanation a graph indicating the *financial breakeven point;* label the axes. Is this approach consistent with maximization of value? Explain.

CHOOSING THE OPTIMAL CAPITAL STRUCTURE

Creating a wealth maximization framework for use in making capital structure decisions is not easy. Although the two key factors—return and risk—can be used separately to make capital structure decisions, integrating them into a market value context provides the best results. This section describes the procedures for linking the return and risk associated with alternative capital structures to market value to select the best capital structure.

LINKAGE

To determine its value under alternative capital structures, the firm must find the level of return that must be earned to compensate owners for the risk being incurred. Such a framework is consistent with the overall valuation framework developed in Chapter 8 and applied to capital budgeting decisions in Chapter 10.

The required return associated with a given level of financial risk can be estimated in a number of ways. Theoretically, the preferred approach would be to first estimate the beta associated with each alternative capital structure and then use the CAPM framework presented in Equation 7.7 to calculate the required return, k_s. A more operational approach involves linking the financial risk associated with each capital structure alternative directly to the required return. Such an approach is similar to the CAPM-type approach demonstrated in Chapter 10 for linking project risk and required return (RADR). Here it involves estimating the required return associated with each level of financial risk, as measured by a statistic such as the coefficient of variation of EPS. Regardless of the approach used, one would expect that the required return would increase as the financial risk increases. An example will illustrate.

E x a m p l e ▼ Expanding the JSG Company example presented earlier, we assume that the firm is attempting to choose the best of seven alternative capital structures—debt ratios of 0, 10, 20, 30, 40, 50, and 60 percent. For each of these structures the firm estimated the (1) EPS, (2) coefficient of variation of EPS, and (3) required return, k_s. These values are shown in columns 1 through 3 of Table 12.10. Note that EPS (in column 1) is maximized at a 50 percent debt ratio whereas the risk of EPS measured by its coefficient of variation (in column 2) is constantly increasing. As expected, the estimated required return of owners, k_s (in column 3) increases with increasing risk, as measured by the coefficient of variation of EPS (in column 2). Simply stated, for higher degrees of financial leverage—debt ratios—owners require higher rates of return.

ESTIMATING VALUE

The value of the firm associated with alternative capital structures can be estimated by using one of the standard valuation models. If, for simplicity, we assume that all earnings are paid out as dividends, we can use a zero growth valuation model such as that developed in Chapter 8. The model, originally stated in Equation 8.6, is restated here with EPS substituted for dividends, because in each year the dividends would equal EPS:

$$P_0 = \frac{\text{EPS}}{k_s} \tag{12.12}$$

By substituting the estimated level of EPS and the associated required return, k_s, into Equation 12.12, we can estimate the per-share value of the firm, P_0.

Example ▼ Returning again to JSG Company, we can now estimate the value of its stock under each of the alternative capital structures. Substituting the expected EPS (from column 1 of Table 12.10) and the required returns, k_s (from column 3 of Table 12.10), into Equation 12.12 for each of the alternative capital structures, we obtain the share values given in column 4 of Table 12.10. Plotting the resulting share values against the associated debt ratios, as shown in Figure 12.6, clearly illustrates that the maximum share value occurs at the capital structure associated with a debt ratio of 30 percent. ▲

MAXIMIZING VALUE VERSUS MAXIMIZING EPS

Throughout this text, the goal of the financial manager has been specified as maximizing owner wealth, not profit. Although there is some relationship between the level of expected profit and value, there is no reason to believe that

| TABLE 12.10 | Calculation of Share Value Estimates Associated with Alternative Capital Structures for JSG Company |

Capital structure debt ratio	Expected EPS (1)	Estimated coefficient of variation of EPS (2)	Estimated required return, k_s (3)	Estimated share value [(1) ÷ (3)] (4)
0%	$2.40	0.71	.115	$20.87
10	2.55	0.74	.117	21.79
20	2.72	0.78	.121	22.48
30	2.91	0.83	.125	23.28
40	3.12	0.91	.140	22.29
50	3.18	1.07	.165	19.27
60	3.03	1.40	.190	15.95

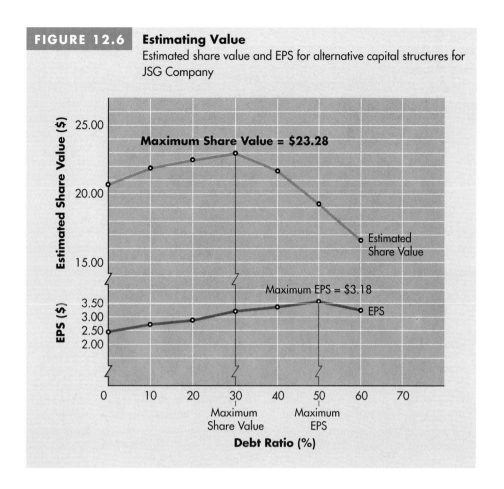

FIGURE 12.6 **Estimating Value**
Estimated share value and EPS for alternative capital structures for JSG Company

profit-maximizing strategies necessarily result in wealth maximization. It is therefore the wealth of the owners as reflected in the estimated share value that should serve as the criterion for selecting the best capital structure. A final look at JSG Company will help to highlight this point.

Example ▼ Further analysis of Figure 12.6 clearly shows that although the firm's profits (EPS) are maximized at a debt ratio of 50 percent, share value is maximized at a 30 percent debt ratio. In this case, the preferred capital structure would be the 30 percent debt ratio. The EPS-maximization approach does not provide a similar conclusion because it does not consider risk. Therefore, to maximize owner wealth, JSG Company should employ the capital structure that results in a 30 ▲ percent debt ratio.

SOME OTHER IMPORTANT CONSIDERATIONS

Because there is really no practical way to calculate the optimal capital structure, any quantitative analysis of capital structure must be tempered with other important considerations. Numerous additional factors relative to capital structure decisions could be listed; some of the more important factors, categorized by broad area of concern, are summarized in Table 12.11.

TABLE 12.11	Important Factors to Consider in Making Capital Structure Decisions	
Concern	Factor	Description
Business risk	Revenue stability	Firms having stable and predictable revenues can more safely undertake highly levered capital structures than can firms with volatile patterns of sales revenue. Firms with growing sales tend to benefit from added debt because they can reap the positive benefits of leverage, which magnifies the effect of these increases.
	Cash flow	When considering a new capital structure, the firm must focus on its ability to generate the necessary cash flows to meet obligations. Cash forecasts reflecting an ability to service debts (and preferred stock) must support any capital structure shift.
Agency costs	Contractual obligations	A firm may be contractually constrained with respect to the type of funds that it can raise. For example, a firm might be prohibited from selling additional debt except when the claims of holders of such debt are made subordinate to the existing debt. Contractual constraints on the sale of additional stock as well as the ability to distribute dividends on stock might also exist.
	Management preferences	Occasionally, a firm will impose an internal constraint on the use of debt to limit its risk exposure to a level deemed acceptable to management. In other words, due to risk aversion, the firm's management constrains the firm's capital structure at a level that may or may not be the true optimum.
	Control	A management concerned about control may prefer to issue debt rather than (voting) common stock. Under favorable market conditions, a firm that wanted to sell equity could make a *preemptive offering* or issue *nonvoting shares* (see Chapter 3), allowing each shareholder to maintain proportionate ownership. Generally, only in closely held firms or firms threatened by takeover does control become a major concern in the capital structure decision.
Asymmetric information	External risk assessment	The firm's ability to raise funds quickly and at favorable rates depends on the external risk assessments of lenders and bond raters. The firm must therefore consider the impact of capital structure decisions both on share value and on published financial statements from which lenders and raters assess the firm's risk.
	Timing	At times when the general level of interest rates is low, debt financing might be more attractive; when interest rates are high, the sale of stock may be more appealing. Sometimes both debt and equity capital become unavailable at what would be viewed as reasonable terms. General economic conditions—especially those of the capital market—can thus significantly affect capital structure decisions.

? Review Questions

12-14 Do *maximizing value* and *maximizing EPS* lead to the same conclusion about the optimal capital structure? If not, what is the cause?

12-15 How might a firm go about determining its optimal capital structure? What important factors in addition to quantitative considerations should a firm consider when it is making a capital structure decision?

Summary

LG1 **Discuss the role of breakeven analysis, how to determine the operating breakeven point, and the effect of changing costs on the breakeven**

point. Breakeven analysis measures the level of sales necessary to cover total operating costs and to evaluate profitability. The operating breakeven point may be calculated algebraically, by dividing fixed operating costs by the difference between the sale price per unit and variable operating cost per unit, or it may be determined graphically. The operating breakeven point increases with increased fixed and variable operating costs and decreases with an increase in sale price, and vice versa.

LG2 **Understand operating, financial, and total leverage and the relationships among them.** Operating leverage is the use of fixed operating costs by the firm to magnify the effects of changes in sales on earnings before interest and taxes. The higher the fixed operating costs, the greater the operating leverage. Financial leverage is the use of fixed financial costs by the firm to magnify the effects of changes in earnings before interest and taxes on earnings per share. The higher the fixed financial costs—typically, interest on debt and pre-ferred stock dividends—the greater the financial leverage. The total leverage of the firm is the use of fixed costs—both operating and financial—to mag-nify the effects of changes in sales on earnings per share. Total leverage reflects the combined effect of operating and financial leverage.

LG3 **Describe the basic types of capital, external assessment of capital structure, capital struc-ture of non-U.S. firms, and capital structure theory.** Two basic types of capital—debt capital and equity capital—make up a firm's capital structure. Capital structure can be externally assessed by using the debt ratio and the times interest earned ratio. Non-U.S. companies tend to have much higher leverage ratios than do their U.S. counterparts, primarily because U.S. capital markets are much better devel-oped. Similarities between U.S. corporations and those of other countries include industry patterns of capital structure, large multinational company capi-tal structures, and the trend toward greater reliance on securities issuance and less reliance on banks for financing.

Research suggests that there is an optimal capi-tal structure that balances the firm's benefits and costs of debt financing. The major benefit of debt financing is the tax shield. The costs of debt financ-ing include the probability of bankruptcy, caused by business and financial risk; agency costs imposed by lenders; and asymmetric information, which typical-ly causes firms to raise funds in a pecking order of retained earnings, then debt, and finally external equity financing, in order to send positive signals to the market and thereby enhance the wealth of shareholders.

LG4 **Explain the optimal capital structure using a graphic view of the firm's cost of capital func-tions and a modified form of the zero-growth valua-tion model.** The zero-growth valuation model can be used to define the firm's value as its after-tax EBIT divided by its weighted average cost of capital. Assuming that EBIT is constant, the value of the firm is maximized by minimizing its weighted aver-age cost of capital (WACC). The optimal capital structure is the one that minimizes the WACC. Graphically, although both debt and equity costs rise with increasing financial leverage, the lower cost of debt causes the WACC to decline and then rise with increasing financial leverage. As a result, the firm's WACC exhibits a U-shape having a minimum value, which defines the optimum capital structure—the one that maximizes owner wealth.

LG5 **Discuss the graphic presentation, risk consider-ations, and basic shortcomings of the EBIT–EPS approach to capital structure.** The EBIT–EPS approach evaluates capital structures in light of the returns they provide the firm's owners and their degree of financial risk. Under the EBIT–EPS approach, the preferred capital structure is the one that is expected to provide maximum EPS over the firm's expected range of EBIT. Graphically, this approach reflects risk in terms of the financial breakeven point and the slope of the capital structure line. The major shortcoming of EBIT–EPS analysis is that by ignoring risk, it concentrates on maximizing earnings rather than owners' wealth.

LG6 **Review the return and risk of alternative cap-ital structures and their linkage to market value, and other important capital structure consid-erations.** The best capital structure can be selected by using a valuation model to link return and risk factors. The preferred capital structure would be the one that results in the highest estimated share value—not the highest EPS. Other important non-quantitative factors, such as revenue stability, cash flow, contractual obligations, management preferences, control, external risk assessment, and timing, must also be considered when making capital structure decisions.

ST 12-1 Breakeven point and all forms of leverage   Cirque Plastics most recently sold 100,000 units at $7.50 each; its variable operating costs are $3.00 per unit, and its fixed operating costs are $250,000. Annual interest charges total $80,000, and the firm has 8,000 shares of $5 (annual dividend) preferred stock outstanding. It currently has 20,000 shares of common stock outstanding. Assume that the firm has a 40 percent tax rate.

a. At what level of sales (in units) would the firm break even on operations (i.e., EBIT = $0)?

b. Calculate the firm's earnings per share (EPS) in tabular form at (1) the current level of sales and (2) a 120,000-unit sales level.

c. Using the current *$750,000 level of sales as a base,* calculate the firm's degree of operating leverage (DOL).

d. Using the EBIT *associated with the $750,000 level of sales as a base,* calculate the firm's degree of financial leverage (DFL).

e. Use the degree of total leverage (DTL) concept to determine the effect (in percentage terms) of a 50 percent increase in Cirque's sales *from the $750,000 base level* on its earnings per share.

ST 12-2 EBIT–EPS analysis   Newlin Electronics is considering additional financing of $10,000. It currently has $50,000 of 12 percent (annual interest) bonds and 10,000 shares of common stock outstanding. The firm can obtain the financing through a 12 percent (annual interest) bond issue or the sale of 1,000 shares of common stock. The firm has a 40 percent tax rate.

a. Calculate two EBIT–EPS coordinates for each plan by selecting any two EBIT values and finding their associated EPS.

b. Plot the two financing plans on a set of EBIT–EPS axes.

c. On the basis of your graph in **b,** at what level of EBIT does the bond plan become superior to the stock plan?

ST 12-3 Optimal capital structure   Hawaiian Macadamia Nut Company has collected the following data with respect to its capital structure, expected earnings per share, and required return.

Capital structure debt ratio	Expected earnings per share	Required return, k_s
0%	$3.12	13%
10	3.90	15
20	4.80	16
30	5.44	17
40	5.51	19
50	5.00	20
60	4.40	22

a. Compute the estimated share value associated with each of the capital structures using the simplified method described in this chapter (see Equation 12.12).
b. Determine the optimal capital structure based on (1) maximization of expected earnings per share and (2) maximization of share value.
c. Which capital structure do you recommend? Why?

PROBLEMS

  12-1 Breakeven point—Algebraic   Marilyn Cosgrove wishes to estimate the number of pairs of shoes her firm must sell at $24.95 per pair to break even. She has estimated fixed operating costs of $12,350 per year and variable operating costs of $15.45 per pair. How many pairs of shoes must Marilyn sell to break even on operating costs?

 12-2 Breakeven comparisons—Algebraic   Given the price and cost data shown in the following table for each of the three firms, M, N, and O, answer the following questions.

Firm	M	N	O
Sale price per unit	$ 18.00	$ 21.00	$ 30.00
Variable operating cost per unit	6.75	13.50	12.00
Fixed operating cost	45,000	30,000	90,000

a. What is the operating breakeven point in units for each firm?
b. How would you rank these firms in terms of their risk?

  12-3 Breakeven point—Algebraic and graphic   Sting Industries sells its single product for $129.00 per unit. The firm's fixed operating costs are $473,000 annually, and its variable operating costs are $86.00 per unit.
a. Find the firm's operating breakeven point in units.
b. Label the x axis "Sales (units)" and the y axis "Costs/Revenues ($)," and then graph the firm's sales revenue, total operating cost, and fixed operating cost functions on these axes. In addition, label the operating breakeven point and the areas of loss and profit (EBIT).

 12-4 Breakeven analysis   Doug Mills is considering opening a record store. He wants to estimate the number of CDs he must sell to break even. The CDs will be sold for $13.98 each, variable operating costs are $10.48 per CD, and annual fixed operating costs are $73,500.
a. Find the operating breakeven point in CDs.
b. Calculate the total operating costs at the breakeven volume found in **a**.
c. If Doug estimates that at a minimum he can sell 2,000 CDs *per month*, should he go into the record business?
d. How much EBIT would Doug realize if he sells the minimum 2,000 CDs per month noted in **c**?

12-5 **Breakeven point—Changing costs/revenues** Hi-Tek Press publishes the *Video Yearbook*. Last year the book sold for $10 with variable operating cost per book of $8 and fixed operating costs of $40,000. How many books must be sold this year to achieve the breakeven point for the stated operating costs, given the following different circumstances?
a. All figures remain the same as last year.
b. Fixed operating costs increase to $44,000; all other figures remain the same as last year.
c. The selling price increases to $10.50; all costs remain the same as last year.
d. Variable operating cost per book increases to $8.50; all other figures remain the same.
e. What conclusions about the operating breakeven point can be drawn from your answers?

12-6 **EBIT sensitivity** Harlow Company sells its finished product for $9 per unit. Its fixed operating costs are $20,000, and the variable operating cost per unit is $5.
a. Calculate the firm's EBIT for sales of 10,000 units.
b. Calculate the firm's EBIT for sales of 8,000 and 12,000 units, respectively.
c. Calculate the percentage changes in sales (from the 10,000-unit base level) and associated percentage changes in EBIT for the shifts in sales indicated in **b**.
d. On the basis of your findings in **c**, comment on the sensitivity of changes in EBIT in response to changes in sales.

12-7 **Degree of operating leverage** Winters Design Group has fixed operating costs of $380,000, variable operating costs per unit of $16, and a selling price of $63.50 per unit.
a. Calculate the operating breakeven point in units.
b. Calculate the firm's EBIT at 9,000, 10,000, and 11,000 units, respectively.
c. By using 10,000 units as a base, what are the percentage changes in units sold and EBIT as sales move from the base to the other sales levels used in **b**?
d. Use the percentages computed in **c** to determine the degree of operating leverage (DOL).
e. Use the formula for degree of operating leverage to determine the DOL at 10,000 units.

12-8 **Degree of operating leverage—Graphic** Zandy, Inc. has fixed operating costs of $72,000, variable operating costs of $6.75 per unit, and a selling price of $9.75 per unit.
a. Calculate the operating breakeven point in units.
b. Compute the DOL for the following unit sales levels: 25,000, 30,000, 40,000. Use the formula given in the chapter.
c. Graph the DOL figures that you computed in **b** (on the *y* axis) against sales levels (on the *x* axis).
d. Compute the degree of operating leverage at 24,000 units; add this point to your graph.
e. What principle is illustrated by your graph and figures?

12-9 **EPS calculations** Fleet Corporation has $60,000 of 16 percent (annual interest) bonds outstanding, 1,500 shares of preferred stock paying an annual dividend of $5 per share, and 4,000 shares of common stock outstanding. Assuming that the firm has a 40 percent tax rate, compute earnings per share (EPS) for the following levels of EBIT:

a. $24,600
b. $30,600
c. $35,000

  12-10   Degree of financial leverage   Western Oil Corporation has a current capital structure consisting of $250,000 of 16 percent (annual interest) debt and 2,000 shares of common stock. The firm pays taxes at the rate of 40 percent.

a. Using EBIT values of $80,000 and $120,000, determine the associated EPS.
b. Using $80,000 of EBIT as a base, calculate the degree of financial leverage (DFL).
c. Rework parts **a** and **b** assuming that the firm has $100,000 of 16 percent (annual interest) debt and 3,000 shares of common stock.

  12-11   DFL and graphic display of financing plans   Central Canning Company has EBIT of $67,500. Interest costs are $22,500, and the firm has 15,000 shares of common stock outstanding. Assume a 40 percent tax rate.

a. Use the degree of financial leverage (DFL) formula to calculate the DFL for the firm.
b. Using a set of EBIT–EPS axes, plot Central Canning's financing plan.
c. Assuming that the firm also has 1,000 shares of preferred stock paying a $6.00 annual dividend per share, what is the DFL?
d. Plot the financing plan including the 1,000 shares of $6.00 preferred stock on the axes used in **b**.
e. Briefly discuss the graph of the two financing plans.

  12-12   Integrative—Multiple leverage measures   Musk Oil Cosmetics produces skin-care products, selling 400,000 bottles a year. Each bottle produced has a variable operating cost of $.84 and sells for $1.00. Fixed operating costs are $28,000. The firm has annual interest charges of $6,000, preferred dividends of $2,000, and a 40 percent tax rate.

a. Calculate the operating breakeven point in units.
b. Use the DOL formula to calculate DOL.
c. Use the DFL formula to calculate DFL.
d. Use the degree of total leverage (DTL) formula to calculate DTL. Compare this to the product of DOL and DFL calculated in **b** and **c**.

 12-13   Integrative—Leverage and risk   Firm J has sales of 100,000 units at $2.00 per unit, variable operating costs of $1.70 per unit, and fixed operating costs of $6,000. Interest is $10,000 per year. Firm R has sales of 100,000 units at $2.50 per unit, variable operating costs of $1.00 per unit, and fixed operating costs of $62,500. Interest is $17,500 per year. Assume that both firms are in the 40 percent tax bracket.

a. Compute the degree of operating, financial, and total leverage for firm J.
b. Compute the degree of operating, financial, and total leverage for firm R.
c. Compare the relative risks of the two firms.
d. Discuss the principles of leverage illustrated in your answers.

WARM-UP **LG3** 12-14 **Various capital structures** Zachary Corporation currently has $1 million in total assets and is totally equity financed. It is contemplating a change in capital structure. Compute the amount of debt and equity that would be outstanding if the firm were to shift to one of the following debt ratios: 10, 20, 30, 40, 50, 60, and 90 percent. (*Note:* The amount of total assets would not change.) Is there a limit to the debt ratio's value?

INTERMEDIATE **LG5** 12-15 **EBIT–EPS and capital structure** Parker Petroleum is considering two capital structures. The key information is shown in the following table. Assume a 40 percent tax rate.

Source of capital	Structure A	Structure B
Long-term debt	$100,000 at 16% coupon rate	$200,000 at 17% coupon rate
Common stock	4,000 shares	2,000 shares

a. Calculate two EBIT–EPS coordinates for each of the structures by selecting any two EBIT values and finding their associated EPS.
b. Plot the two capital structures on a set of EBIT–EPS axes.
c. Indicate over what EBIT range, if any, each structure is preferred.
d. Discuss the leverage and risk aspects of each structure.
e. If the firm is fairly certain that its EBIT will exceed $75,000, which structure would you recommend? Why?

INTERMEDIATE **LG5** 12-16 **EBIT–EPS and preferred stock** Wonder Diaper is considering two possible capital structures, A and B, shown in the following table. Assume a 40 percent tax rate.

Source of capital	Structure A	Structure B
Long-term debt	$75,000 at 16% coupon rate	$50,000 at 15% coupon rate
Preferred stock	$10,000 with an 18% annual dividend	$15,000 with an 18% annual dividend
Common stock	8,000 shares	10,000 shares

a. Calculate two EBIT–EPS coordinates for each of the structures by selecting any two EBIT values and finding their associated EPS.
b. Graph the two capital structures on the same set of EBIT–EPS axes.
c. Discuss the leverage and risk associated with each of the structures.
d. Over what range of EBIT is each structure preferred?

e. Which structure do you recommend if the firm expects its EBIT to be $35,000? Explain.

  12-17 Optimal capital structure   Nelson Corporation has collected the following data associated with four possible capital structures.

Capital structure debt ratio	Expected EPS	Estimated coefficient of variation of EPS
0%	$1.92	.4743
20	2.25	.5060
40	2.72	.5581
60	3.54	.6432

The firm's research indicates that the marketplace assigns the following required returns to risky earnings per share.

Coefficient of variation of EPS	Estimated required return, k_s
.43	15%
.47	16
.51	17
.56	18
.60	22
.64	24

a. Find the required return associated with each of the four capital structures.
b. Compute the estimated share value associated with each of the four capital structures using the simplified method described in this chapter (see Equation 12.12).
c. Determine the optimal capital structure based on (1) maximization of expected EPS and (2) maximization of share value.
d. Construct a graph (similar to Figure 12.6) showing the relationships in c.
e. Which capital structure do you recommend? Why?

  12-18 Integrative—Optimal capital structure   Triple D Corporation wishes to analyze five possible capital structures—0, 15, 30, 45, and 60 percent debt ratios. The firm's total assets of $1 million are assumed to be constant. Its common stock has a book value of $25 per share, and the firm is in the 40 percent tax bracket.

The following additional data have been gathered for use in analyzing the five capital structures under consideration.

Capital structure debt ratio	Interest rate on debt, k_d	Expected EPS	Required return, k_s
0%	0.0%	$3.60	10.0%
15	8.0	4.03	10.5
30	10.0	4.50	11.6
45	13.0	4.95	14.0
60	17.0	5.18	20.0

a. Calculate the amount of debt, the amount of equity, and the number of shares of common stock outstanding for each of the capital structures being considered.

b. Calculate the annual interest on the debt under each of the capital structures being considered. (*Note:* The interest rate given is applicable to *all* debt associated with the corresponding debt ratio.)

c. Calculate the EPS associated with $150,000 and $250,000 of EBIT for each of the five capital structures being considered.

d. Using the EBIT–EPS data developed in c, plot the capital structures on the same set of EBIT–EPS axes, and discuss the ranges over which each is preferred. What is the major problem with the use of this approach?

e. Using the valuation model given in Equation 12.12 and the appropriate data, estimate the share value for each of the capital structures being considered.

f. Construct a graph similar to Figure 12.6 showing the relationships between the debt ratio (*x* axis) and expected EPS (*y* axis) and share value (*y* axis).

g. Referring to the graph in f: Which structure is preferred if the goal is to maximize EPS? Which structure is preferred if the goal is to maximize share value? Which capital structure do you recommend? Explain.

CASE   Chapter 12   **Evaluating McGraw Industries' Capital Structure**

McGraw Industries, an established producer of printing equipment, expects its sales to remain flat for the next 3 to 5 years due to both a weak economic outlook and an expectation of little new printing technology development over that period. On the basis of this scenario, the firm's management has been instructed by its board to institute programs that will allow it to operate more efficiently, earn higher profits, and, most important, maximize share value. In this regard, the firm's chief financial officer, Ron Lewis, has been charged with evaluating the firm's capital structure. Lewis believes that the current capital structure, which contains 10 percent debt and 90 percent equity, may lack adequate financial leverage. To evaluate the firm's capital structure, Lewis has gathered the data summarized in the following table on the current capital structure (10 percent debt ratio) and two alternative capital structures—A (30 percent debt ratio) and B (50 percent debt ratio)—that he would like to consider.

	Capital structure[a]		
Source of capital	Current (10% debt)	A (30% debt)	B (50% debt)
Long-term debt	$1,000,000	$3,000,000	$5,000,000
Coupon interest rate[b]	9%	10%	12%
Common stock	100,000 shares	70,000 shares	40,000 shares
Required return on equity, k_s[c]	12%	13%	18%

[a]These structures are based on maintaining the firm's current level of $10,000,000 of total financing.
[b]Interest rate applicable to *all* debt.
[c]Market-based return for the given level of risk.

Lewis expects the firm's EBIT to remain at its current level of $1,200,000. The firm has a 40 percent tax rate.

Required

a. Use the current level of EBIT to calculate the times interest earned ratio for each capital structure. Evaluate the current and two alternative capital structures using the times interest earned and debt ratios.
b. Prepare a single EBIT–EPS graph showing the current and two alternative capital structures.
c. On the basis of the graph in **b,** which capital structure will maximize McGraw's EPS at its expected level of EBIT of $1,200,000? Why might this *not* be the best capital structure?
d. Using the zero-growth valuation model given in Equation 12.12, find the market value of McGraw's equity under each of the three capital structures at the $1,200,000 level of expected EBIT.
e. On the basis of the findings in **c** and **d,** which capital structure should Ron Lewis recommend? Why?

Web Exercise

GOTO web site www.smartmoney.com. In the column on the right under Quotes & Research enter the symbol DIS; click Stock Snapshot; and then click GO.

1. What is the name of the company?

Click on Financials.

2. What is the 5-year high and the 5-year low for the company's debt/equity ratio (the ratio of long term debt to stockholders' equity)?

At the bottom of this page under Stock Search enter the next stock symbol from the list below and then click Submit. Enter the name of the company in the matrix below and then click Financials. Enter the 5-year high and low for the debt/equity ratios in the matrix for each of the stock symbols.

SYMBOL	COMPANY NAME	DEBT/EQUITY RATIO	
		5-yr. low	5-yr. high
DIS			
AIT			
MRK			
LG			
LUV			
IBM			
GE			
BUD			
PFE			
INTC			

3. Which of the companies have high debt/equity ratios?
4. Which of the companies have low debt/equity ratios?
5. Why do the companies that have a low debt/equity ratio use more equity even though it is more expensive than debt?

DIVIDEND POLICY

13

LEARNING GOALS

LG1 Understand cash dividend payment procedures and the role of dividend reinvestment plans.

LG2 Describe the residual theory of dividends and the key arguments with regard to dividend irrelevance and relevance.

LG3 Discuss the key factors involved in formulating a dividend policy.

LG4 Review and evaluate the three basic types of dividend policies.

LG5 Evaluate stock dividends from accounting, shareholder, and company points of view.

LG6 Explain stock splits and stock repurchases and the firm's motivation for undertaking each of them.

ACROSS the DISCIPLINES

Dividends represent a source of cash flow to stockholders and provide them with information about the firm's current and future performance. Some stockholders want and expect to receive dividends, whereas others are content to see an increase in stock price without receiving dividends. The firm's dividend policy depends on a variety of factors. This chapter addresses the issue of whether dividends matter to stockholders, discusses the key factors in formulating a dividend policy, explains basic types of dividend policies, and describes alternative forms of dividends. Chapter 13 is important to:

- **accounting personnel** who will provide the financial data needed by management to make dividend decisions.
- **information systems analysts** who will establish financial information systems that will be used when making and implementing dividend decisions.
- **management** because it determines and implements the firm's dividend policy.
- **the marketing department** because paying dividends may reduce the amount of money available for marketing research and new product development.
- **operations,** which may find that the firm's dividend policy imposes limitations on expansion.

DIVIDEND FUNDAMENTALS

Expected cash dividends are the key return variable from which owners and investors determine share value. They represent a source of cash flow to stockholders and provide information about the firm's current and future performance. Because **retained earnings**—earnings not distributed as dividends—are a form of *internal* financing, the dividend decision can significantly affect the firm's *external* financing requirements. In other words, if the firm needs financing, the larger the cash dividend paid, the greater the amount of financing that must be raised externally through borrowing or through the sale of common or preferred stock. (Remember that although dividends are charged to retained earnings, they are actually paid out of cash.) To understand the fundamentals of dividend policy, you first need to understand the procedures for paying cash dividends and how dividend reinvestment plans work.

retained earnings
Earnings not distributed as dividends; a form of *internal* financing.

CASH DIVIDEND PAYMENT PROCEDURES

The payment of cash dividends to corporate stockholders is decided by the firm's board of directors. The directors normally meet quarterly or semiannually to determine whether and in what amount dividends should be paid. The past period's financial performance and future outlook, as well as recent dividends paid, are key inputs to the dividend decision. The payment date of the cash dividend, if one is declared, must also be established.

AMOUNT OF DIVIDENDS

Whether dividends should be paid and, if so, how large they should be are important decisions that depend primarily on the firm's dividend policy. Many firms pay some cash dividends each period. Most firms have a set policy with respect to the amount of the periodic dividend, but the firm's directors can change this amount at the dividend meeting, based largely on significant increases or decreases in earnings.

RELEVANT DATES

If the directors of the firm declare a dividend, they also indicate the record and payment dates associated with the dividend. Typically, they issue a statement indicating the dividend decision, the record date, and the payment date. This statement is generally quoted in the *Wall Street Journal* and other financial news media.

Record Date   All persons whose names are recorded as stockholders on the **date of record,** which is set by the directors, receive a declared dividend at a specified future time. These stockholders are often referred to as *holders of record.*

Due to the time needed to make bookkeeping entries when a stock is traded, the stock begins selling **ex dividend** 4 *business days* prior to the date of record. Purchasers of a stock selling ex dividend do not receive the current dividend. A simple way to determine the first day on which the stock sells ex dividend is to

date of record (dividends)
Set by the firm's directors, the date on which all persons whose names are recorded as stockholders receive a declared dividend at a specified future time.

ex dividend
Period beginning 4 *business days* prior to the date of record during which a stock is sold without the right to receive the current dividend.

subtract 4 days from the date of record; if a weekend intervenes, subtract 6 days. Ignoring general market fluctuations, the stock's price is expected to drop by the amount of the declared dividend on the ex dividend date.

payment date
The actual date on which the firm mails the dividend payment to the holders of record.

Payment Date   The payment date is also set by the directors and is generally a few weeks after the record date. The **payment date** is the actual date on which the firm mails the dividend payment to the holders of record. An example will clarify the various dates and the accounting effects.

E x a m p l e ▼   At the quarterly dividend meeting of Junot Company, a distributor of office products, held June 10, the directors declared an $.80-per-share cash dividend for holders of record on Monday, July 1. The firm had 100,000 shares of common stock outstanding. The payment date for the dividend was August 1. Before the dividend was declared, the key accounts of the firm were as follows:

Cash	$200,000	Dividends payable	$ 0
		Retained earnings	1,000,000

When the dividend was announced by the directors, $80,000 of the retained earnings ($.80 per share × 100,000 shares) was transferred to the dividends payable account. The key accounts thus became:

Cash	$200,000	Dividends payable	$ 80,000
		Retained earnings	920,000

Junot Company's stock began selling ex dividend 4 *business days* prior to the date of record, which was June 25. This date was found by subtracting 6 days (because a weekend intervened) from the July 1 date of record. Purchasers of Junot's stock on June 24 or earlier received the rights to the dividends; those purchasing the stock on or after June 25 did not. Assuming a stable market, Junot's stock price was expected to drop by approximately $.80 per share when it began selling ex dividend on June 25. When the August 1 payment date arrived, the firm mailed dividend checks to the holders of record as of July 1. This produced the following balances in the key accounts of the firm:

Cash	$120,000	Dividends payable	$ 0
		Retained earnings	920,000

The net effect of declaring and paying the dividend was to reduce the firm's total ▲ assets (and stockholders' equity) by $80,000.

DIVIDEND REINVESTMENT PLANS

dividend reinvestment plans (DRPs)
Plans that enable stockholders to use dividends received on the firm's stock to acquire additional full or fractional shares at little or no transaction (brokerage) cost.

Today many firms offer **dividend reinvestment plans** (DRPs), which enable stockholders to use dividends received on the firm's stock to acquire additional shares—even fractional shares—at little or no transaction (brokerage) cost. A small number of these companies, such as Exxon, Texaco, and W.R. Grace, even allow investors to make their *initial purchases* of the firm's stock directly from the company without going through a broker. Under current tax law, cash dividends from all plans (or the value of the stocks received through a DRP) are taxed as ordinary income. In addition, when the acquired shares are sold, if the proceeds are in excess of the original purchase price, the capital gain is taxed at the applicable capital gains tax rate.

Dividend reinvestment plans can be handled by a company in either of two ways. Both allow the stockholder to elect to have dividends reinvested in the firm's shares. In one approach, a third-party trustee is paid a fee to buy the firm's *outstanding shares* in the open market on behalf of the shareholders who wish to reinvest their dividends. This type of plan benefits participating shareholders by allowing them to use their dividends to purchase shares generally at a lower transaction cost than they would otherwise pay. The second approach involves buying *newly issued shares* directly from the firm without paying any transaction costs. This approach allows the firm to raise new capital while permitting owners to reinvest their dividends, frequently at about 5 percent below the current market price. The firm can justify the below-market sale price economically because it saves the underpricing and flotation costs that would accompany the public sale of new shares. Clearly, the existence of a DRP may enhance the appeal of a firm's shares.

? R e v i e w   Q u e s t i o n s

13-1 How do the *date of record* and the *holders of record* relate to the payment of cash dividends? What does the term *ex dividend* mean?

13-2 What is a *dividend reinvestment plan?* What benefit is available to plan participants? Describe the two ways in which companies can handle such plans.

LG2   THE RELEVANCE OF DIVIDEND POLICY

Numerous theories and empirical findings concerning dividend policy have been reported in the financial literature. Although this research provides some interesting insights about dividend policy, capital budgeting and capital structure decisions are generally considered far more important than dividend decisions. In other words, good investment and financing decisions should not be sacrificed for a dividend policy of questionable importance.

A number of key questions have yet to be resolved: Does dividend policy matter? What effect does dividend policy have on share price? Is there a model that can be used to evaluate alternative dividend policies in view of share value? Here we begin by describing the residual theory of dividends, which is used as a backdrop for discussion of the key arguments in support of dividend irrelevance and then those in support of dividend relevance.

residual theory of dividends
A theory that the dividend paid by a firm should be the amount left over after all acceptable investment opportunities have been undertaken.

THE RESIDUAL THEORY OF DIVIDENDS

One school of thought—the **residual theory of dividends**—suggests that the dividend paid by a firm should be viewed as a *residual*—the amount left over after all acceptable investment opportunities have been undertaken. Using this approach, the firm would treat the dividend decision in three steps as follows:

Step 1   Determine its optimum level of capital expenditures, which would be the level generated by the point of intersection of the investment opportunities schedule (IOS) and weighted marginal cost of capital (WMCC) schedule (see Chapter 11).

Step 2   Using the optimal capital structure proportions (see Chapter 12), estimate the total amount of equity financing needed to support the expenditures generated in Step 1.

Step 3   Because the cost of retained earnings, k_r, is less than the cost of new common stock, k_n, use retained earnings to meet the equity requirement determined in Step 2. If retained earnings are inadequate to meet this need, sell new common stock. If the available retained earnings are in excess of this need, distribute the surplus amount—the residual—as dividends.

In this approach, no cash dividend is paid as long as the firm's equity need is in excess of the amount of retained earnings. The argument supporting this approach is that it is sound management to be certain that the company has the money it needs to compete effectively and therefore increase share price. This view of dividends tends to suggest that the required return of investors, k_s, is *not* influenced by the firm's dividend policy—a premise that in turn suggests that dividend policy is irrelevant. Let us look at an example.

Example ▼ Overbrook Industries, a manufacturer of canoes and other small watercraft, has available from the current period's operations $1.8 million that can be retained or paid out in dividends. The firm's optimal capital structure is at a debt ratio of 30 percent, which represents 30 percent debt and 70 percent equity. Figure 13.1 depicts the firm's weighted marginal cost of capital (WMCC) schedule along with three investment opportunities schedules. For each IOS, the level of total new financing or investment determined by the point of intersection of the IOS and the WMCC has been noted. For IOS_1, it is $1.5 million; for IOS_2, $2.4 million; and for IOS_3, $3.2 million. Although only one IOS will exist in practice, it is useful to look at the possible dividend decisions generated by applying the residual theory in each of the three cases. Table 13.1 summarizes this analysis.

Table 13.1 shows that if IOS_1 exists, the firm will pay out $750,000 in dividends, because only $1,050,000 of the $1,800,000 of available earnings is needed. A 41.7 percent payout ratio results. For IOS_2, dividends of $120,000 (a payout ratio of 6.7 percent) result. Should IOS_3 exist, the firm would pay no dividends (a zero percent payout ratio), because its retained earnings of $1,800,000 would be less than the $2,240,000 of equity needed. In this case, the firm would have to obtain additional new common stock financing to meet the new requirements generated by the intersection of the IOS_3 and WMCC. Depending on which IOS exists, the firm's dividend would in effect be the residual, if any, remaining after financing all acceptable investments. ▲

DIVIDEND IRRELEVANCE ARGUMENTS

The residual theory of dividends implies that if the firm cannot earn a return (IRR) from investment of its earnings that is in excess of cost (WMCC), it should distribute the earnings by paying dividends to stockholders. This approach suggests that

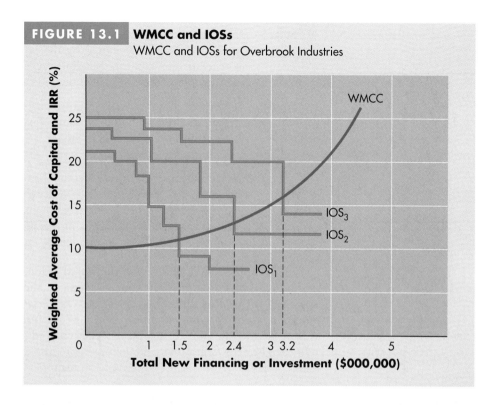

FIGURE 13.1 **WMCC and IOSs**
WMCC and IOSs for Overbrook Industries

TABLE 13.1 **Applying the Residual Theory of Dividends to Overbrook Industries for Each of Three IOSs (Shown in Figure 13.1)**

| Item | Investment opportunities schedules | | |
	IOS_1	IOS_2	IOS_3
(1) New financing or investment (Fig. 13.1)	$1,500,000	$2,400,000	$3,200,000
(2) Retained earnings available (given)	$1,800,000	$1,800,000	$1,800,000
(3) Equity needed [70% × (1)]	1,050,000	1,680,000	2,240,000
(4) Dividends [(2) − (3)]	$ 750,000	$ 120,000	$ 0[a]
(5) Dividend payout ratio [(4) ÷ (2)]	41.7%	6.7%	0%

[a]In this case, additional new common stock in the amount of $440,000 ($2,240,000 needed − $1,800,000 available) would have to be sold; no dividends would be paid.

dividends are irrelevant—that they represent an earnings residual rather than an active decision variable that affects the firm's value. Such a view is consistent with the **dividend irrelevance theory** put forth by Merton H. Miller and Franco

dividend irrelevance theory
A theory put forth by Miller and Modigliani that, in a perfect world, the value of a firm is unaffected by the distribution of dividends and is determined solely by the earning power and risk of its assets.

informational content
The information provided by the dividends of a firm with respect to future earnings, which causes owners to bid up or down the price of the firm's stock.

clientele effect
The argument that a firm attracts shareholders whose preferences with respect to the payment and stability of dividends correspond to the payment pattern and stability of the firm itself.

Modigliani.[1] M and M's theory shows that in a perfect world (certainty, no taxes, no transactions costs, and no other market imperfections), the value of the firm is unaffected by the distribution of dividends. They argue that the firm's value is determined solely by the earning power and risk of its assets (investments) and that the manner in which it splits its earnings stream between dividends and internally retained (and reinvested) funds does not affect this value.

However, studies have shown that large dividend changes affect share price in the same direction—increases in dividends result in increased share price, and decreases in dividends result in decreased share price. In response, M and M argue that these effects are attributable not to the dividend itself but rather to the **informational content** of dividends with respect to future earnings. In other words, it is not the preference of shareholders for current dividends (rather than future capital gains) that is responsible for this behavior. Instead, a change in dividends, up or down, is viewed as a *signal* that management expects future earnings to change in the same direction. An increase in dividends is viewed as a *positive signal* that causes investors to bid up the share price; a decrease in dividends is a *negative signal* that causes a decrease in share price.

M and M further argue that a **clientele effect** exists: A firm attracts shareholders whose preferences with respect to the payment and stability of dividends correspond to the payment pattern and stability of the firm itself. Investors desiring stable dividends as a source of income hold the stock of firms that pay about the same dividend amount each period. Investors preferring to earn capital gains are more attracted to growing firms that reinvest a large portion of their earnings, resulting in a fairly unstable pattern of dividends. Because the shareholders get what they expect, M and M argue that the value of their firm's stock is unaffected by dividend policy.

In summary, M and M and other dividend irrelevance proponents argue that, all else being equal, an investor's required return—and therefore the value of the firm—is unaffected by dividend policy for three reasons:

1. The firm's value is determined solely by the earning power and risk of its assets.
2. If dividends do affect value, they do so solely because of their informational content, which signals management's earnings expectations.
3. A clientele effect exists that causes a firm's shareholders to receive the dividends they expect.

These views of M and M with respect to dividend irrelevance are consistent with the residual theory, which focuses on making the best investment decisions to maximize share value. The proponents of dividend irrelevance conclude that because dividends are irrelevant to a firm's value, the firm does not need to have a dividend policy. Although many research studies have been performed to validate or refute the dividend irrelevance theory, none has been successful in providing irrefutable evidence.

---

[1]Merton H. Miller and Franco Modigliani, "Dividend Policy, Growth and the Valuation of Shares," *Journal of Business* 34 (October 1961), pp. 411–433.

DIVIDEND RELEVANCE ARGUMENTS

dividend relevance theory
The theory, attributed to Gordon and Lintner, that there is a direct relationship between a firm's dividend policy and its market value.

bird-in-the-hand argument
The belief, in support of *dividend relevance theory*, that current dividend payments ("a bird in the hand") reduce investor uncertainty and result in a higher value for the firm's stock.

The key argument in support of **dividend relevance theory** is attributed to Myron J. Gordon and John Lintner,[2] who suggest that there is, in fact, a direct relationship between the firm's dividend policy and its market value. Fundamental to this proposition is their **bird-in-the-hand argument,** which suggests that investors are generally risk-averse and attach less risk to current dividends than to future dividends or capital gains. Simply stated, "a bird in the hand is worth two in the bush." Current dividend payments are therefore believed to reduce investor uncertainty, causing investors to discount the firm's earnings at a lower rate and, all else being equal, to place a higher value on the firm's stock. Conversely, if dividends are reduced or not paid, investor uncertainty will increase, raising the required return and lowering the stock's value.

Although many other arguments relating to dividend relevance have been put forward, *numerous empirical studies fail to provide conclusive evidence in support of the intuitively appealing dividend relevance argument.* In practice, however, the actions of financial managers and stockholders alike tend to support the belief that dividend policy does affect stock value.[3] Because our concern centers on the day-to-day behavior of business firms, the remainder of this chapter is consistent with the belief that *dividends are relevant*—that each firm must develop a dividend policy that fulfills the goals of its owners and maximizes their wealth as reflected in the firm's share price.

⁈ R e v i e w   Q u e s t i o n s

13-3 Describe the *residual theory of dividends.* Does following this approach lead to a stable dividend? Is this approach consistent with dividend relevance? Explain.

13-4 Describe, compare, and contrast the basic arguments relative to the irrelevance or relevance of dividend policy given by: **(a)** Miller and Modigliani (M and M), and **(b)** Gordon and Lintner.

FACTORS AFFECTING DIVIDEND POLICY

Before discussing the basic types of dividend policies, we should consider the factors involved in formulating dividend policy. These include legal constraints, contractual constraints, internal constraints, the firm's growth prospects, owner considerations, and market considerations.

---

[2]Myron J. Gordon, "Optimal Investment and Financing Policy," *Journal of Finance* 18 (May 1963), pp. 264–272, and John Lintner, "Dividends, Earnings, Leverage, Stock Prices, and the Supply of Capital to Corporations," *Review of Economics and Statistics* 44 (August 1962), pp. 243–269.

[3]A common exception is small firms, because they frequently treat dividends as a residual remaining after all acceptable investments have been initiated. This course of action occurs because small firms usually do not have ready access to capital markets. The use of retained earnings therefore acts as a key source of financing for growth, which is generally an important goal of a small firm.

LEGAL CONSTRAINTS

Most states prohibit corporations from paying out as cash dividends any portion of the firm's "legal capital," which is measured by the par value of common stock. Other states define legal capital to include not only the par value of the common stock, but also any paid-in capital in excess of par. These *capital impairment restrictions* are generally established to provide a sufficient equity base to protect creditors' claims. An example will clarify the differing definitions of capital.

Example ▼ The stockholders' equity account of Moeller Flour Company, a large grain processor, is presented in the following table.

Moeller Flour Company Stockholders' Equity	
Common stock at par	$100,000
Paid-in capital in excess of par	200,000
Retained earnings	140,000
Total stockholders' equity	$440,000

In states where the firm's legal capital is defined as the par value of its common stock, the firm could pay out $340,000 ($200,000 + $140,000) in cash dividends without impairing its capital. In states where the firm's legal capital includes all paid-in capital, the firm could pay out only $140,000 in cash dividends. ▲

An earnings requirement limiting the amount of dividends to the sum of the firm's present and past earnings is sometimes imposed. In other words, the firm cannot pay more in cash dividends than the sum of its most recent and past retained earnings. However, *the firm is not prohibited from paying more in dividends than its current earnings.*[4]

Example ▼ Assume Moeller Flour Company, from the preceding example, in the year just ended has $30,000 in earnings available for common stock dividends. As the preceding table indicates, the firm has past retained earnings of $140,000. Thus, it can legally pay dividends of up to $170,000. ▲

If a firm has overdue liabilities or is legally insolvent or bankrupt (if the fair market value of its assets is less than its liabilities), most states prohibit its payment of cash dividends. In addition, the Internal Revenue Service prohibits firms from accumulating earnings to reduce the owners' taxes. A firm's owners must pay income taxes on dividends when received, but the owners are not taxed on

---

[4]A firm having an operating loss in the current period can still pay cash dividends as long as sufficient retained earnings against which to charge the dividend are available and, of course, as long as it has the cash with which to make the payments.

**excess earnings accu-
mulation tax**
The tax levied by the IRS on
retained earnings above
$250,000, when it has deter-
mined that the firm has accumulated an excess of earnings to
allow owners to delay paying
ordinary income taxes.

capital gains in market value until the stock is sold. If the IRS can determine that a firm has accumulated an excess of earnings to allow owners to delay paying ordinary income taxes, it may levy an **excess earnings accumulation tax** on any retained earnings above $250,000—the amount that is currently exempt from this tax for all firms except personal service corporations.

CONTRACTUAL CONSTRAINTS

Often the firm's ability to pay cash dividends is constrained by restrictive provisions in a loan agreement. Generally, these constraints prohibit the payment of cash dividends until a certain level of earnings has been achieved, or they may limit dividends to a certain dollar amount or percentage of earnings. Constraints on dividends help to protect creditors from losses due to the firm's insolvency. The violation of a contractual constraint is generally grounds for a demand of immediate payment by the funds supplier.

INTERNAL CONSTRAINTS

The firm's ability to pay cash dividends is generally constrained by the amount of excess cash available rather than the level of retained earnings against which to charge them. Although it is possible for a firm to borrow funds to pay dividends, lenders are generally reluctant to make such loans because they produce no tangible or operating benefits that will help the firm repay the loan. Although a firm may have high earnings, its ability to pay dividends may be constrained by a low level of liquid assets (cash and marketable securities).

Example ▼ Moeller Flour Company's stockholders' equity account presented earlier indicates that if the firm's legal capital is defined as all paid-in capital, the firm can pay $140,000 in dividends. If the firm has total liquid assets of $50,000 ($20,000 in cash plus marketable securities worth $30,000) and $35,000 of this is needed for operations, the maximum cash dividend the firm can pay is ▲ $15,000 ($50,000 − $35,000).

GROWTH PROSPECTS

The firm's financial requirements are directly related to the anticipated degree of asset expansion. If the firm is in a growth stage, it may need all its funds to finance capital expenditures. Firms exhibiting little or no growth may nevertheless periodically need funds to replace or renew assets.

A firm must evaluate its financial position from the standpoint of profitability and risk to develop insight into its ability to raise capital externally. It must determine not only its ability to raise funds, but also the cost and speed with which financing can be obtained. Generally, a large, mature firm has adequate access to new capital, whereas a rapidly growing firm may not have sufficient funds available to support its numerous acceptable projects. A growth firm is likely to have to depend heavily on internal financing through retained earnings; it is likely to pay out only a very small percentage of its earnings as dividends. A more stable firm that needs long-term funds only for planned outlays is in a better position to pay out a large proportion of its earnings, particularly if it has ready sources of financing.

OWNER CONSIDERATIONS

In establishing a dividend policy, the firm's primary concern should be to maximize owner wealth. Although it is impossible to establish a policy that maximizes each owner's wealth, the firm must establish a policy that has a favorable effect on the wealth of the *majority* of owners.

One consideration is the *tax status of a firm's owners*. If a firm has a large percentage of wealthy stockholders who are in a high tax bracket, it may decide to pay out a *lower* percentage of its earnings to allow the owners to delay the payment of taxes until they sell the stock. Of course, when the stock is sold, if the proceeds are in excess of the original purchase price, the capital gain will be taxed, possibly at a more favorable rate than the one applied to ordinary income. Lower-income shareholders, however, who need dividend income, will prefer a *higher* payout of earnings.

A second consideration is the *owners' investment opportunities*. A firm should not retain funds for investment in projects yielding lower returns than the owners could obtain from external investments of equal risk. The firm should evaluate the returns that are expected on its own investment opportunities and, using present value techniques, determine whether greater returns are obtainable from external investments such as government securities or other corporate stocks. If it appears that the owners have better opportunities externally, the firm should pay out a higher percentage of its earnings. If the firm's investment opportunities are at least as good as similar-risk external investments, a lower payout would be justifiable.

A final consideration is the *potential dilution of ownership*. If a firm pays out a higher percentage of earnings, new equity capital will have to be raised with common stock, which may result in the dilution of both control and earnings for the existing owners. By paying out a low percentage of its earnings, the firm can minimize such possibility of dilution.

MARKET CONSIDERATIONS

An awareness of the market's probable response to certain types of policies is helpful in formulating a suitable dividend policy. Stockholders are believed to value a *fixed or increasing level of dividends* as opposed to a fluctuating pattern of dividends. In addition, stockholders are believed to value a policy of *continuous dividend payment*. Because regularly paying a fixed or increasing dividend eliminates uncertainty about the frequency and magnitude of dividends, the earnings of the firm are likely to be discounted at a lower rate. This should result in an increase in the market value of the stock and therefore increased owners' wealth.

A final market consideration is the *informational content* of dividends. As indicated earlier, shareholders often view the firm's dividend payment as a *signal* of its future success. A stable and continuous dividend is a *positive signal* that conveys that the firm is in good health. If the firm skips a dividend payment in a given period due to a loss or to very low earnings, shareholders are likely to interpret this as a *negative signal*. The nonpayment of the dividend creates uncertainty about the future, and this uncertainty is likely to result in lower stock value. Owners and investors generally construe a dividend payment during a period of losses as an indication that the loss is merely temporary.

? R e v i e w Q u e s t i o n

13-5 Briefly describe each of the following factors affecting dividend policy: (**a**) legal constraints; (**b**) contractual constraints; (**c**) internal constraints; (**d**) growth prospects; (**e**) owner considerations; and (**f**) market considerations.

TYPES OF DIVIDEND POLICIES

dividend policy
The firm's plan of action to be followed whenever a dividend decision must be made.

The firm's **dividend policy** represents a plan of action to be followed whenever the dividend decision must be made. The dividend policy must be formulated with two basic objectives in mind: maximizing the wealth of the firm's owners and providing for sufficient financing. These two interrelated objectives must be fulfilled in light of a number of factors—legal, contractual, internal, growth, owner-related, and market-related—that limit the policy alternatives. Three of the more commonly used dividend policies are described in the following sections. A particular firm's cash dividend policy may incorporate elements of each.

dividend payout ratio
Indicates the percentage of each dollar earned that is distributed to the owners in the form of cash; calculated by dividing the firm's cash dividend per share by its earnings per share.

CONSTANT-PAYOUT-RATIO DIVIDEND POLICY

One type of dividend policy occasionally adopted by firms is the use of a constant payout ratio. The **dividend payout ratio,** calculated by dividing the firm's cash dividend per share by its earnings per share, indicates the percentage of each dollar earned that is distributed to the owners in the form of cash. With a **constant-payout-ratio dividend policy,** the firm establishes that a certain percentage of earnings is paid to owners in each dividend period.

constant-payout-ratio dividend policy
A dividend policy based on the payment of a certain percentage of earnings to owners in each dividend period.

The problem with this policy is that if the firm's earnings drop or if a loss occurs in a given period, the dividends may be low or even nonexistent. Because dividends are often considered an indicator of the firm's future condition and status, the firm's stock price may thus be adversely affected. An example clarifies the problems stemming from a constant-payout-ratio dividend policy.

Example ▼ Nader Industries, a miner of potassium, has a policy of paying out 40 percent of earnings in cash dividends. In periods when a loss occurs, the firm's policy is to pay no cash dividends. Nader's earnings per share, dividends per share, and average price per share for the past 6 years are shown in the following table.

Year	Earnings/share	Dividends/share	Average price/share
2000	−$ .50	$ .00	$42.00
1999	3.00	1.20	52.00
1998	1.75	.70	48.00
1997	− 1.50	.00	38.00
1996	2.00	.80	46.00
1995	4.50	1.80	50.00

Dividends increased in 1997–1998 and in 1998–1999 and decreased in the other years. The data show that in years of decreasing dividends, the firm's stock price dropped; when dividends increased, the price of the stock increased. Nader's sporadic dividend payments appear to make its owners uncertain about the returns they can expect from their investment in the firm and therefore tend to generally depress the stock's price.

Although a constant-payout-ratio dividend policy is used by some firms, it is *not* recommended.

REGULAR DIVIDEND POLICY

regular dividend policy
A dividend policy based on the payment of a fixed-dollar dividend in each period.

Another type of dividend policy, the **regular dividend policy,** is based on the payment of a fixed-dollar dividend in each period. The regular dividend policy provides the owners with generally positive information, indicating that the firm is okay and thereby minimizing their uncertainty. Often, firms using this policy increase the regular dividend once a *proven* increase in earnings has occurred. Under this policy, dividends are almost never decreased.

E x a m p l e ▼ The dividend policy of Holly Laboratories, a producer of a popular artificial sweetener, is to pay annual dividends of $1.00 per share until per-share earnings have exceeded $4.00 for three consecutive years, at which time the annual dividend is raised to $1.50 per share and a new earnings plateau is established. The firm does not anticipate decreasing its dividend unless its liquidity is in jeopardy. Holly's earnings per share, dividends per share, and average price per share for the past 12 years are shown in the following table.

Year	Earnings/share	Dividends/share	Average price/share
2000	$4.50	$1.50	$47.50
1999	3.90	1.50	46.50
1998	4.60	1.50	45.00
1997	4.20	1.00	43.00
1996	5.00	1.00	42.00
1995	2.00	1.00	38.50
1994	6.00	1.00	38.00
1993	3.00	1.00	36.00
1992	.75	1.00	33.00
1991	.50	1.00	33.00
1990	2.70	1.00	33.50
1989	2.85	1.00	35.00

Whatever the level of earnings, Holly Laboratories paid dividends of $1.00 per share through 1997. In 1998, the dividend was raised to $1.50 per share because earnings in excess of $4.00 per share had been achieved for 3 years. In 1998, the firm also had to establish a new earnings plateau for further dividend increases. Holly Laboratories' average price per share exhibited a stable, increasing behavior in spite of a somewhat volatile pattern of earnings. ▲

target dividend-payout ratio
A policy under which the firm attempts to pay out a certain percentage of earnings as a stated dollar dividend, which it adjusts toward a target payout as proven earnings increases occur.

Often, a regular dividend policy is built around a **target dividend-payout ratio.** Under this policy, the firm attempts to pay out a certain percentage of earnings, but rather than let dividends fluctuate, it pays a stated dollar dividend and adjusts it toward the target payout as proven earnings increases occur. For instance, Holly Laboratories appears to have a target payout ratio of around 35 percent. The payout was about 35 percent ($1.00 ÷ $2.85) when the dividend policy was set in 1989, and when the dividend was raised to $1.50 in 1998, the payout ratio was about 33 percent ($1.50 ÷ $4.60).

LOW-REGULAR-AND-EXTRA DIVIDEND POLICY

low-regular-and-extra dividend policy
A dividend policy based on paying a low regular dividend, supplemented by an additional dividend when earnings warrant it.

extra dividend
An additional dividend optionally paid by the firm if earnings are higher than normal in a given period.

Some firms establish a **low-regular-and-extra dividend policy,** paying a low regular dividend, supplemented by an additional dividend when earnings warrant it. When earnings are higher than normal in a given period, the firm may pay this additional dividend, which is designated an **extra dividend.** By calling the additional dividend an extra dividend, the firm avoids giving shareholders false hopes. The use of the "extra" designation is especially common among companies that experience cyclical shifts in earnings.

By establishing a low regular dividend that is paid each period, the firm gives investors the stable income necessary to build confidence in the firm, and the extra dividend permits them to share in the earnings from an especially good period. Firms using this policy must raise the level of the regular dividend once proven increases in earnings have been achieved. The extra dividend should not be a regular event, or it becomes meaningless. The use of a target dividend-payout ratio in establishing the regular dividend level is advisable.

? R e v i e w   Q u e s t i o n

13-6   What are (**a**) a constant-payout-ratio dividend policy; (**b**) a regular dividend policy; and (**c**) a low-regular-and-extra dividend policy? What are the effects of these policies?

LG5   LG6   OTHER FORMS OF DIVIDENDS

A number of other forms of dividends are available to the firm. In this section, we discuss two other methods of paying dividends—stock dividends and stock repurchases—as well as a closely related topic, stock splits.

STOCK DIVIDENDS

stock dividend
The payment to existing owners of a dividend in the form of stock.

A **stock dividend** is the payment to existing owners of a dividend in the form of stock. Often, firms pay stock dividends as a replacement for or a supplement to cash dividends. Although stock dividends do not have a real value, stockholders may perceive them to represent something they did not have before and therefore to have value.

ACCOUNTING ASPECTS

small (ordinary) stock dividend
A stock dividend that represents less than 20 to 25 percent of the common stock outstanding at the time the dividend is declared.

In an accounting sense, the payment of a stock dividend is a shifting of funds between capital accounts rather than a use of funds. When a firm declares a stock dividend, the procedures for announcement and distribution are the same as those described earlier for a cash dividend. The accounting entries associated with the payment of stock dividends vary depending on whether it is a **small (ordinary) stock dividend,** which is generally a stock dividend representing less than 20 to 25 percent of the common stock outstanding at the time the dividend is declared. Because small stock dividends are most common, the accounting entries associated with them are illustrated in the following example.

Example ▼ The current stockholders' equity on the balance sheet of Barry Corporation, a distributor of prefabricated cabinets, is as shown in the following accounts.

Preferred stock	$ 300,000
Common stock (100,000 shares at $4 par)	400,000
Paid-in capital in excess of par	600,000
Retained earnings	700,000
Total stockholders' equity	$2,000,000

If Barry declares a 10 percent stock dividend and the market price of its stock is $15 per share, $150,000 of retained earnings (10% × 100,000 shares × $15 per share) will be capitalized. The $150,000 will be distributed between common stock and paid-in capital in excess of par accounts based on the par value of the common stock. The resulting account balances are as follows:

Preferred stock	$ 300,000
Common stock (110,000 shares at $4 par)	440,000
Paid-in capital in excess of par	710,000
Retained earnings	550,000
Total stockholders' equity	$2,000,000

Because 10,000 new shares (10% of 100,000) have been issued and the prevailing market price is $15 per share, $150,000 ($15 per share × 10,000 shares) is shifted from retained earnings to the common stock and paid-in capital accounts. A total of $40,000 ($4 par × 10,000 shares) is added to common stock, and the remaining $110,000 [($15 − $4) × 10,000 shares] is added to the paid-in capital in excess of par. The firm's total stockholders' equity has not changed; funds have only been *redistributed* among stockholders' equity
▲ accounts.

THE SHAREHOLDER'S VIEWPOINT

The shareholder receiving a stock dividend typically receives nothing of value. After the dividend is paid, the per-share value of the shareholder's stock decreases in proportion to the dividend in such a way that the market value of his or her total holdings in the firm remains unchanged. The shareholder's proportion of ownership in the firm also remains the same, and *as long as the firm's earnings remain unchanged,* so does his or her share of total earnings. (Clearly, if the firm's earnings and cash dividends increase at the time the stock dividend is issued, an increase in share value is likely to result.) A continuation of the preceding example will clarify this point.

Example ▼ Ms. X owned 10,000 shares of Barry Corporation's stock. The company's most recent earnings were $220,000, and earnings are not expected to change in the near future. Before the stock dividend, Ms. X owned 10 percent (10,000 shares ÷ 100,000 shares) of the firm's stock, which was selling for $15 per share. Earnings per share were $2.20 ($220,000 ÷ 100,000 shares). Because Ms. X owned 10,000 shares, her earnings were $22,000 ($2.20 per share × 10,000 shares). After receiving the 10 percent stock dividend, Ms. X has 11,000 shares, which again is 10 percent (11,000 shares ÷ 110,000 shares) of the ownership. The market price of the stock can be expected to drop to $13.64 per share [$15 × (1.00 ÷ 1.10)], which means that the market value of Ms. X's holdings is about $150,000 (11,000 shares × $13.64 per share). This is the same as the initial value of her holdings (10,000 shares × $15 per share). The future earnings per share drops to $2 ($220,000 ÷ 110,000 shares) because the same $220,000 in earnings must now be divided among 110,000 shares. Because Ms. X still owns 10 percent of the stock, her share of total earnings is still $22,000 ($2 per **▲** share × 11,000 shares).

In summary, if the firm's earnings remain constant and total cash dividends do not increase, a stock dividend results in a lower per-share market value for the firm's stock.

THE COMPANY'S VIEWPOINT

Although stock dividends are more costly to issue than cash dividends, certain advantages may outweigh these costs. Firms find the stock dividend a way to give owners something without having to use cash. Generally, when a firm needs to preserve cash to finance rapid growth, a stock dividend is used. As long as the stockholders recognize that the firm is reinvesting the cash flow generated from earnings so as to maximize future earnings, the market value of the firm should at least remain unchanged. However, if the stock dividend is paid so that cash can be retained to satisfy past-due bills, a decline in market value may result.

STOCK SPLITS

stock split
A method commonly used to lower the market price of a firm's stock by increasing the number of shares belonging to each shareholder.

Although not a type of dividend, *stock splits* have an effect on a firm's share price similar to that of stock dividends. A **stock split** is a method commonly used to lower the market price of a firm's stock by increasing the number of shares belonging to each shareholder. Quite often, a firm believes that its stock is priced too high and that lowering the market price will enhance trading activity. Stock splits are often made prior to issuing additional stock to enhance its marketability and stimulate market activity.

A stock split has no effect on the firm's capital structure. It commonly increases the number of shares outstanding and reduces the stock's per-share par value. In a 2-for-1 split, for example, two new shares are exchanged for each old share, with each new share worth half the value of each old share.

Example ▼ Brandt Company, a forest products concern, had 200,000 shares of $2 par-value common stock and no preferred stock outstanding. Because the stock is selling at a high market price, the firm has declared a 2-for-1 stock split. The total before- and after-split stockholders' equity is shown in the following table.

Before split	
Common stock (200,000 shares at $2 par)	$ 400,000
Paid-in capital in excess of par	4,000,000
Retained earnings	2,000,000
Total stockholders' equity	$6,400,000

After 2-for-1 split	
Common stock (400,000 shares at $1 par)	$ 400,000
Paid-in capital in excess of par	4,000,000
Retained earnings	2,000,000
Total stockholders' equity	$6,400,000

▲ The insignificant effect of the stock split on the firm's books is obvious.

reverse stock split
A method used to raise the market price of a firm's stock by exchanging a certain number of outstanding shares for one new share of stock.

Stock can be split in any way desired. Sometimes a **reverse stock split** is made: A certain number of outstanding shares are exchanged for one new share. For example, in a 2-for-3 split, two new shares are exchanged for three old shares; and so on. Reverse stock splits are initiated when a stock is selling at too low a price to appear respectable.[5]

It is not unusual for a stock split to cause a slight increase in the market value of the stock. This is attributable to the informational content of stock splits and the fact that *total* dividends paid commonly increase slightly after a split.

ⓟERSONAL FINANCE PERSPECTIVE

Investors Head to Splitsville

Typically, companies announce stock splits when their shares reach a point—often $50 or $100—where investors consider the stock expensive. Dividing a high-priced stock into two or three lower-priced shares can increase its marketability by attracting more investors.

---

[5]If a firm's stock is selling at a low price—possibly less than a few dollars—many investors are hesitant to purchase it because they believe it is "cheap." These somewhat unsophisticated investors correlate cheapness and quality, and they feel that a low-priced stock is a low-quality investment. A reverse stock split raises the stock price and increases per-share earnings.

"Splits are very important to individual investors, even though you're essentially getting two fives for a 10," explains Zach Wagner, an analyst at Edward Jones in St. Louis. Generally, stocks that split have performed very well in the past, so that many investors believe splits indicate that good performance may continue. There is some evidence that this is indeed true. One study showed that over 15 years, a portfolio of 1,275 stocks that split yielded an average return of 8 percent more in the first year after the split and 12 percent more over 3 years than did a similar group of stocks that did not split. And, in the short term, stock prices tend to rise between the time the split is announced and the date of the split. However, some analysts point out that stocks that split have already risen in price, so that the above-average performance simply reflects an increase in the company's growth and earnings. Splits also signal management's confidence that the upward trend will continue.

Financial advisers remind investors that a stock split, by itself, is not a reason to buy a stock. As with any stock purchase, you should evaluate the fundamentals of the company, including key ratios, its price/earnings multiple, profit outlook, and industry factors. In terms of a company's underlying value, a stock split is essentially a nonevent. ●

STOCK REPURCHASES

stock repurchase
The repurchasing by the firm of outstanding shares of its common stock in the marketplace; desired effects of stock repurchases are that they either enhance shareholder value or help to discourage unfriendly takeovers.

Over the past 15 or so years, firms have increased their repurchasing of outstanding common stock in the marketplace. The practical motives for **stock repurchases** include obtaining shares to be used in acquisitions, having shares available for employee stock option plans, or retiring shares. The recent increase in frequency and importance of stock repurchases is due to the fact that they either enhance shareholder value or help to discourage an unfriendly takeover. Stock repurchases enhance shareholder value by (1) reducing the number of shares outstanding and thereby raising earnings per share, (2) sending a *positive signal* to investors in the marketplace that management believes that the stock is undervalued, and (3) providing a temporary floor for the stock price, which may have been declining. The use of repurchases to discourage unfriendly takeovers is predicated on the belief that a corporate raider is less likely to gain control of the firm if there are fewer publicly traded shares available. Here we focus on retiring shares through repurchase, because this motive for repurchase is similar to the payment of cash dividends.

STOCK REPURCHASES VIEWED AS A CASH DIVIDEND

When common stock is repurchased for retirement, the underlying motive is to distribute excess cash to the owners. As a result of any repurchase, the owners receive cash for their shares. Generally, as long as earnings remain constant, the repurchase reduces the number of outstanding shares, raising the earnings per share and therefore the market price per share. In addition, certain owner tax benefits may result. The repurchase of common stock results in a type of *reverse dilution*, because the earnings per share and the market price of stock are increased by reducing the number of shares outstanding. The net effect of the repurchase is similar to the payment of a cash dividend. A simple example clarifies this point.

E x a m p l e ▼ Farrell Company, a national sportswear chain, has released the following financial data:

Earnings available for common stockholders	$1,000,000
Number of shares of common stock outstanding	400,000
Earnings per share ($1,000,000 ÷ 400,000)	$2.50
Market price per share	$50
Price/earnings (P/E) ratio ($50 ÷ $2.50)	20

The firm is contemplating using $800,000 of its earnings either to pay cash dividends or to repurchase shares. If the firm pays cash dividends, the amount of the dividend would be $2 per share ($800,000 ÷ 400,000 shares). If the firm pays $52 per share to repurchase stock, it could repurchase approximately 15,385 shares ($800,000 ÷ $52 per share). As a result of this repurchase, 384,615 shares (400,000 shares − 15,385 shares) of common stock remain outstanding. Earnings per share (EPS) rise to $2.60 ($1,000,000 ÷ 384,615). If the stock still sold at 20 times earnings (P/E = 20), applying the *price/earnings (P/E) multiple approach* presented in Chapter 8, its market price would rise to $52 per share ($2.60 × 20). In both cases, the stockholders would receive $2 per share—a $2 cash dividend in the dividend case or a $2 increase in share price ($50 per share ▲ to $52 per share) in the repurchase case.

The advantages of stock repurchases are an increase in per-share earnings and certain owner tax benefits. The tax advantage occurs because if the cash dividend were paid, the owners would have to pay ordinary income taxes on it, whereas the $2 increase in the market value of the stock due to the repurchase would not be taxed until the owner sells the stock. Of course, when the stock is sold, and the proceeds are in excess of the original purchase price, the capital gain is taxed, possibly at a more favorable rate than the one applied to ordinary income. The IRS allegedly watches firms that regularly repurchase stock and levies a penalty if it believes repurchases have been made to delay the payment of taxes by the stockholders.

ACCOUNTING ENTRIES

The accounting entries that result when common stock is repurchased are a reduction in cash and the establishment of a contra capital account called "treasury stock," which is shown as a deduction from stockholders' equity. The label *treasury stock* is used on the balance sheet to indicate the presence of repurchased shares.

THE REPURCHASE PROCESS

When a company intends to repurchase a block of outstanding shares, it should make shareholders aware of its intentions. Specifically, it should advise them of the purpose of the repurchase (acquisition, stock options, retirement) and the disposition (if any) planned for the repurchased shares (traded for shares of another firm, distribution to executives, or held in the treasury).

Three basic methods of repurchase are commonly used. One is to purchase shares on the *open market*. This places upward pressure on the price of shares if the number of shares being repurchased is reasonably large in comparison with the total number outstanding. The second method is through tender offers. A **tender offer** is a formal offer to purchase a given number of shares of a firm's stock at a specified price. The price at which a tender offer is made is set above the current market price to attract sellers. If the number of shares desired cannot be repurchased through the tender offer, open-market purchases can be used to obtain the additional shares. Tender offers are preferred when large numbers of shares are repurchased, because the company's intentions are clearly stated and each stockholder has an opportunity to sell shares at the tendered price. A third method that is sometimes used involves the purchase on a *negotiated basis* of a large block of shares from one or more major stockholders. Again, in this case, the firm would have to state its intentions and make certain that the purchase price is fair and equitable in view of the interests and opportunities of the remaining shareholders.

tender offer
A formal offer to purchase a given number of shares of a firm's stock at a specified price.

? Review Questions

13-7 What is a *stock dividend?* Why do firms issue stock dividends? Comment on the following statement: "I have a stock that promises to pay a 20 percent stock dividend every year, and therefore it guarantees that I will break even in 5 years."

13-8 What is a *stock split?* What is a *reverse stock split?* Compare a stock split with a stock dividend.

13-9 What is the logic behind *repurchasing shares* of common stock to distribute excess cash to the firm's owners? How might this raise the per-share earnings and market price of outstanding shares?

S UMMARY

LG1 **Understand cash dividend payment procedures and the role of dividend reinvestment plans.** The cash dividend decision is normally a quarterly decision made by the board of directors that establishes the record date and payment date. Generally, the larger the dividend charged to retained earnings and paid in cash, the greater the amount of financing that must be raised externally. Some firms offer dividend reinvestment plans that allow stockholders to acquire shares in lieu of cash dividends, often at an attractive price. A company offering such a plan can either have a trustee buy outstanding shares on behalf of participating shareholders, or it can issue new shares to participants.

LG2 **Describe the residual theory of dividends and the key arguments with regard to dividend**

irrelevance and relevance. The residual theory suggests that dividends should be viewed as the earnings left after all acceptable investment opportunities have been undertaken. Dividend irrelevance, which is implied by the residual theory, is argued by Miller and Modigliani using a perfect world wherein information content and clientele effects exist. Gordon and Lintner argue dividend relevance based on the uncertainty-reducing effect of dividends, supported by their bird-in-the-hand argument. Although intuitively appealing, empirical studies fail to provide clear support of dividend relevance. The actions of financial managers and stockholders alike, however, tend to support the belief that dividend policy does affect stock value.

LG3 **Discuss the key factors involved in formulating a dividend policy.** A firm's dividend policy should maximize the wealth of its owners while providing for sufficient financing. Dividend policy is affected by certain legal, contractual, and internal constraints as well as growth prospects, owner considerations, and market considerations. Legal constraints prohibit corporations from paying out as cash dividends any portion of the firm's "legal capital"; they also constrain firms with over-due liabilities or legally insolvent or bankrupt firms from paying cash dividends. Contractual con-straints result from restrictive provisions in the firm's loan agreements. Internal constraints tend to result from a firm's limited excess cash availability. Growth prospects affect the relative importance of retaining earnings rather than paying them out in dividends. The tax status of owners, the owners' investment opportunities, and the potential dilution of ownership are important owner considerations. Finally, market considerations relate to stock-holders' preference for the continuous payment of fixed or increasing streams of dividends and the perceived informational content of dividends.

LG4 **Review and evaluate the three basic types of dividend policies.** With a constant-payout ratio dividend policy, the firm pays a fixed percent-age of earnings out to the owners each period. With this policy, dividends move up and down with earn-ings, and no dividend is paid when a loss occurs. Under a regular dividend policy, the firm pays a fixed-dollar dividend each period; it increases the amount of dividends only after a proven increase in earnings has occurred. The low-regular-and-extra dividend policy is similar to the regular dividend policy, except that it pays an "extra dividend" in periods when the firm's earnings are higher than normal. The regular and the low-regular-and-extra

dividend policies are generally preferred over the constant-payout-ratio dividend policy because their stable patterns of dividends reduce uncertainty.

LG5 **Evaluate stock dividends from accounting, shareholder, and company points of view.** Occasionally, firms pay stock dividends as a replacement for or supplement to cash dividends. The payment of stock dividends involves a shifting of funds between capital accounts rather than a use of funds. Shareholders receiving stock dividends typically receive nothing of value—the market value of their holdings, their proportion of ownership, and their share of total earnings remain unchanged. Although more costly than cash dividends to issue, the firm may be able to use stock dividends to satis-fy owners and therefore retain its market value without having to use cash.

LG6 **Explain stock splits and stock repurchases and the firm's motivation for undertaking each of them.** Stock splits are sometimes used to enhance trading activity of a firm's shares by lower-ing or raising the market price of its stock. A stock split merely involves accounting adjustments—it has no effect on either the firm's cash or its capital structure. Stock repurchases can be made in lieu of cash dividend payments to retire outstanding shares and delay the payment of taxes. They involve the actual outflow of cash to reduce the number of out-standing shares and thereby increase earnings per share and the market price per share. Whereas stock repurchases can be viewed as dividend alter-natives, stock splits are used to deliberately adjust the market price of shares.

SELF-TEST PROBLEM   (Solution in Appendix B)

 ST 13-1 **Stock repurchase**   The Off-Shore Steel Company has earnings available for common stockholders of $2 million and 500,000 shares of common stock out-standing at $60 per share. The firm is currently contemplating the payment of $2 per share in cash dividends.
a. Calculate the firm's current earnings per share (EPS) and price/earnings (P/E) ratio.
b. If the firm can repurchase stock at $62 per share, how many shares can be purchased in lieu of making the proposed cash dividend payment?
c. How much will the EPS be after the proposed repurchase? Why?

   d. If the stock sells at the old P/E ratio, what will the market price be after repurchase?

   e. Compare and contrast the earnings per share before and after the proposed repurchase.

   f. Compare and contrast the stockholders' position under the dividend and repurchase alternatives.

PROBLEMS

  13-1 **Dividend payment procedures**   Dayton Widget, at the quarterly dividend meeting, declared a cash dividend of $1.10 per share for holders of record on Monday, July 10. The firm has 300,000 shares of common stock outstanding and has set a payment date of July 31. Prior to the dividend declaration, the firm's key accounts were as follows:

Cash	$500,000	Dividends payable	$ 0
		Retained earnings	2,500,000

   a. Show the entries after the meeting adjourned.

   b. When is the *ex dividend* date?

   c. After the July 31 payment date, what values would the key accounts have?

   d. What effect, if any, will the dividend have on the firm's total assets?

   e. Ignoring general market fluctuations, what effect, if any, will the dividend have on the firm's stock price on the ex dividend date?

  13-2 **Residual dividend policy**   As president of Young's of California, a large clothing chain, you have just received a letter from a major stockholder. The stockholder asks about the company's dividend policy. In fact, the stockholder has asked you to estimate the amount of the dividend that you are likely to pay next year. You have not yet collected all the information about the expected dividend payment, but you do know the following:

   (1) The company follows a residual dividend policy.

   (2) The total capital budget for next year is likely to be one of three amounts, depending on the results of capital budgeting studies that are currently under way. The capital expenditure amounts are $2 million, $3 million, and $4 million.

   (3) The forecasted level of potential retained earnings next year is $2 million.

   (4) The target or optimal capital structure is a debt ratio of 40 percent.

   You have decided to respond by sending the stockholder the best information available to you.

   a. Describe a *residual dividend policy.*

   b. Compute the amount of the dividend (or the amount of new common stock needed) and the dividend payout ratio for each of the three capital expenditure amounts.

   c. Compare, contrast, and discuss the amount of dividends (calculated in **b**) associated with each of the three capital expenditure amounts.

13-3 Dividend constraints   The Boulder Company's stockholders' equity account is as follows:

Common stock (400,000 shares at $4 par)	$1,600,000
Paid-in capital in excess of par	1,000,000
Retained earnings	1,900,000
Total stockholders' equity	$4,500,000

The earnings available for common stockholders from this period's operations are $100,000, which have been included as part of the $1.9 million retained earnings.

a. What is the maximum dividend per share that the firm can pay? (Assume that legal capital includes *all* paid-in capital.)

b. If the firm has $160,000 in cash, what is the largest per-share dividend it can pay without borrowing?

c. Indicate the accounts and changes, if any, that will result if the firm pays the dividends indicated in **a** and **b**.

d. Indicate the effects of an $80,000 cash dividend on stockholders' equity.

13-4 Dividend constraints   A firm has $800,000 in paid-in capital, retained earnings of $40,000 (including the current year's earnings), and 25,000 shares of common stock outstanding. In the current year, it has $29,000 of earnings available for the common stockholders.

a. What is the most the firm can pay in cash dividends to each common stockholder? (Assume that legal capital includes *all* paid-in capital.)

b. What effect would a cash dividend of $.80 per share have on the firm's balance sheet entries?

c. If the firm cannot raise any new funds from external sources, what do you consider the key constraint with respect to the magnitude of the firm's dividend payments? Why?

13-5 Alternative dividend policies   A firm has had the earnings per share over the last 10 years shown in the following table.

Year	Earnings per share
2000	$4.00
1999	3.80
1998	3.20
1997	2.80
1996	3.20
1995	2.40
1994	1.20
1993	1.80
1992	− .50
1991	.25

a. If the firm's dividend policy were based on a constant payout ratio of 40 percent for all years with positive earnings and 0 percent otherwise, what would be the annual dividend for each year?

b. If the firm had a dividend payout of $1.00 per share, increasing by $.10 per share whenever the dividend payout fell below 50 percent for two consecutive years, what annual dividend would the firm pay each year?

c. If the firm's policy were to pay $.50 per share each period except when earnings per share exceed $3.00, when an extra dividend equal to 80 percent of earnings beyond $3.00 would be paid, what annual dividend would the firm pay each year?

d. Discuss the pros and cons of each dividend policy described in **a** through **c**.

 CHALLENGE   **LG4**   13-6   Alternative dividend policies   Given the earnings per share over the period 1993–2000 shown in the following table, determine the annual dividend per share under each of the policies set forth in **a** through **d**.

Year	Earnings per share
2000	$1.40
1999	1.56
1998	1.20
1997	– .85
1996	1.05
1995	.60
1994	1.00
1993	.44

a. Pay out 50 percent of earnings in all years with positive earnings.

b. Pay $.50 per share and increase to $.60 per share whenever earnings per share rise above $.90 per share for two consecutive years.

c. Pay $.50 per share except when earnings exceed $1.00 per share, in which case an extra dividend of 60 percent of earnings above $1.00 per share is paid.

d. Combine policies in **b** and **c**. When the dividend is raised (in **b**), raise the excess dividend base (in **c**) from $1.00 to $1.10 per share.

e. Compare and contrast each of the dividend policies described in **a** through **d**.

 INTERMEDIATE   **LG5**   13-7   Stock dividend—Firm   TFS has the stockholders' equity account given below. The firm's common stock has a current market price of $30 per share.

Preferred stock	$100,000
Common stock (10,000 shares at $2 par)	20,000
Paid-in capital in excess of par	280,000
Retained earnings	100,000
Total stockholders' equity	$500,000

a. Show the effects on TFS of a 5 percent stock dividend.

b. Show the effects of (1) a 10 percent and (2) a 20 percent stock dividend.

c. In light of your answers to **a** and **b**, discuss the effects of stock dividends on stockholders' equity.

  13-8   Cash versus stock dividend   Nimms Steel has the stockholders' equity account given below. The firm's common stock currently sells for $4 per share.

Preferred stock	$ 100,000
Common stock (400,000 shares at $1 par)	400,000
Paid-in capital in excess of par	200,000
Retained earnings	320,000
Total stockholders' equity	$1,020,000

a. Show the effects on the firm of a $.01, $.05, $.10, and $.20 per-share *cash* dividend.
b. Show the effects on the firm of a 1, 5, 10, and 20 percent *stock* dividend.
c. Compare the effects in **a** and **b**. What are the significant differences in the two methods of paying dividends?

  13-9   Stock dividend—Investor   Dana Bond currently holds 400 shares of Mountain Grown Coffee. The firm has 40,000 shares outstanding. The firm most recently had earnings available for common stockholders of $80,000, and its stock has been selling for $22 per share. The firm intends to retain its earnings and pay a 10 percent stock dividend.
a. How much does the firm currently earn per share?
b. What proportion of the firm does Dana Bond currently own?
c. What proportion of the firm will Ms. Bond own after the stock dividend? Explain your answer.
d. At what market price would you expect the stock to sell after the stock dividend?
e. Discuss what effect, if any, the payment of stock dividends will have on Ms. Bond's share of the ownership and earnings of Mountain Grown Coffee.

  13-10   Stock dividend—Investor   Mission Company has outstanding 50,000 shares of common stock currently selling at $40 per share. The firm most recently had earnings available for common stockholders of $120,000, but it has decided to retain these funds and is considering either a 5 or 10 percent stock dividend in lieu of a cash dividend.
a. Determine the firm's current earnings per share.
b. If Jack Frost currently owns 500 shares of the firm's stock, determine his proportion of ownership currently and under each of the proposed stock dividend plans. Explain your findings.
c. Calculate and explain the market price per share under each of the stock dividend plans.
d. For each of the proposed stock dividends, calculate the earnings per share after payment of the stock dividend.
e. What is the value of Jack Frost's holdings under each of the plans? Explain.
f. Should Mr. Frost have any preference with respect to the proposed stock dividends? Why or why not?

13-11 **Stock split—Firm**   U.S. Oil Company's current stockholders' equity account is as follows:

Preferred stock	$ 400,000
Common stock (600,000 shares at $3 par)	1,800,000
Paid-in capital in excess of par	200,000
Retained earnings	800,000
Total stockholders' equity	$3,200,000

a. Indicate the change, if any, expected if the firm declares a 2-for-1 stock split.
b. Indicate the change, if any, expected if the firm declares a 1-for-1½ *reverse* stock split.
c. Indicate the change, if any, expected if the firm declares a 3-for-1 stock split.
d. Indicate the change, if any, expected if the firm declares a 6-for-1 stock split.
e. Indicate the change, if any, expected if the firm declares a 1-for-4 *reverse* stock split.

  13-12 **Stock split versus stock dividend—Firm**   Grande Company is considering a 3-for-2 stock split. It currently has the stockholders' equity position shown. The current stock price is $120 per share. The most recent period's earnings available for common stock is included in retained earnings.

Preferred stock	$ 1,000,000
Common stock (100,000 shares at $3 par)	300,000
Paid-in capital in excess of par	1,700,000
Retained earnings	10,000,000
Total stockholders' equity	$13,000,000

a. What effects on Grande Company would result from the stock split?
b. What change in stock price would you expect to result from the stock split?
c. What is the maximum cash dividend per share that the firm could pay on common stock before and after the stock split? (Assume that legal capital includes *all* paid-in capital.)
d. Contrast your answers to a through c with the circumstances surrounding a 50 percent stock dividend.
e. Explain the differences between stock splits and stock dividends.

 13-13 **Stock repurchase**   The following financial data on the Victor Stock Company are available:

Earnings available for common stockholders	$800,000
Number of shares of common stock outstanding	400,000
Earnings per share ($800,000 ÷ 400,000)	$2
Market price per share	$20
Price/earnings (P/E) ratio ($20 ÷ $2)	10

The firm is currently contemplating using $400,000 of its earnings to pay cash dividends of $1 per share or repurchasing stock at $21 per share.

a. Approximately how many shares of stock can the firm repurchase at the $21-per-share price using the funds that would have gone to pay the cash dividend?

b. Calculate EPS after the repurchase. Explain your calculations.

c. If the stock still sells at 10 times earnings, how much will the market price be after the repurchase?

d. Compare and contrast the pre- and post-repurchase earnings per share.

e. Compare and contrast the stockholders' position under the dividend and repurchase alternatives. What are the tax implications under each alternative?

CASE   Chapter 13   **Establishing General Access Company's Dividend Policy and Initial Dividend**

General Access Company (GAC) is a fast-growing Internet access provider that initially went public in early 1994. Its revenue growth and profitability have steadily risen since the firm's inception in late 1992. GAC's growth has been financed through the initial common stock offering, the sale of bonds in 1997, and the retention of all earnings. Because of its rapid growth in revenue and profits, with only short-term earnings declines, GAC's common stockholders have been content to let the firm reinvest earnings to expand capacity to meet the growing demand for its services. This strategy has benefitted most stockholders in terms of stock splits and capital gains. Since the company's initial public offering in 1994, GAC's stock twice has been split 2-for-1. In terms of total growth, the market price of GAC's stock, after adjustment for stock splits, has increased by 800 percent during the six-year period, 1994–2000.

Because GAC's rapid growth is beginning to slow, the firm's CEO, Marilyn McNeely, believes that its shares are becoming less attractive to investors. Ms. McNeely has had discussions with her CFO, Bobby Joe Rook, who believes that the firm must begin to pay cash dividends. He argues that many investors value regular dividends, and that by beginning to pay them, GAC would increase the demand—and therefore price—for its shares. Ms. McNeely decided that at the next board meeting she would propose that the firm begin to pay dividends on a regular basis.

Ms. McNeely realized that if the board approved her recommendation, it would have to (1) establish a dividend policy and (2) set the amount of the initial annual dividend. She had Mr. Rook prepare the summary of the firm's annual EPS given in the following table.

Year	EPS	Year	EPS
2000	$3.70	1996	$2.20
1999	4.10	1995	.83
1998	3.90	1994	.55
1997	3.30		

Mr. Rook indicated that he expects EPS to remain within 10 percent (plus or minus) of the most recent (2000) value during the next three years. His most likely estimate is an annual increase of about 5 percent.

After much discussion, Ms. McNeely and Mr. Rook agreed that she would recommend to the board one of the following types of dividend policies:

1. Constant-payout-ratio dividend policy
2. Regular dividend policy
3. Low-regular-and-extra dividend policy

Ms. McNeely realizes that her dividend proposal would significantly affect the firm's share price and future financing opportunities and costs. She also knows that she must be sure her proposal is complete and that it fully educates the board with regard to the long-run implications of each policy.

Required

a. Analyze each of the three dividend policies in light of GAC's financial position.
b. Which dividend policy would you recommend? Justify your recommendation.
c. What are the key factors to consider when setting the amount of a firm's initial annual dividend.
d. How should Ms. McNeely go about setting the initial annual dividend she will recommend to the board?
e. In view of your dividend policy recommendation in **b,** how large an initial dividend would you recommend? Justify your recommendation.

Web Exercise

GOTO web site www.smartmoney.com. In the column on the right under Quotes & Research enter the symbol DIS; click Stock Snapshot; and then click GO.

1. What is the name of the company?
2. What is its dividend amount? Its dividend frequency? Its dividend yield?

Enter that data into the matrix that follows. Enter the next stock symbol into the box on the bottom of the page under Stock Search and then click Submit. Complete the following matrix in that manner.

SYMBOL	COMPANY NAME	DIVIDEND		
		$ Amount	Frequency	Yield %
DIS				
AIT				
MRK				
LG				
LUV				
IBM				
GE				
BUD				
PFE				
INTC				

3. Which of the companies have the lowest dividend yields?
4. Which of the companies have the highest dividend yields?

PART 5

SHORT-TERM FINANCIAL DECISIONS

14 FINANCIAL PLANNING

LEARNING GOALS

LG1 Understand the financial planning process, including long-term (strategic) financial plans and short-term (operating) plans.

LG2 Discuss the cash planning process, the role of sales forecasts, and the procedures for preparing the cash budget.

LG3 Describe the cash budget evaluation process and the procedures for coping with uncertainty in the cash budget.

LG4 Prepare a pro forma income statement using both the percent-of-sales method and a breakdown of costs and expenses into their fixed and variable components.

LG5 Explain the procedures used to develop a pro forma balance sheet using the judgmental approach and the use of the plug figure—external financing required—in this process.

LG6 Describe the weaknesses of the simplified approaches to pro forma preparation and the common uses of pro forma financial statements.

ACROSS *the* DISCIPLINES

We now turn our attention to short-term financial decisions. Central to such decisions is short-term financial planning, by which the firm specifies its intended near-term financial actions and their expected results. Short-term financial planning focuses on the firm's cash and profits—both of which are key elements of continued financial success, and even survival. This chapter outlines the short-term financial planning process and examines both cash planning using the cash budget and profit planning using pro forma financial statements. Chapter 14 is important to:

- **accounting personnel** who will prepare pro forma financial statements and provide other departments with historical data for use in the financial planning process.

- **information systems analysts** who will design financial planning and budgeting modules within the financial information system.

- **management** because it will adopt a strategic plan that forms the basis for both long-term and short-term financial plans.

- **the marketing department** because it must provide a sales forecast which is the key input to the financial planning process.

- **operations,** which will prepare the operating plans and budgets to support the forecast sales levels.

THE FINANCIAL PLANNING PROCESS

Financial planning is an important aspect of the firm's operations, because it provides road maps for guiding, coordinating, and controlling the firm's actions to achieve its objectives. Two key aspects of the financial planning process are *cash planning* and *profit planning*. Cash planning involves the preparation of the firm's cash budget; profit planning involves the preparation of pro forma financial statements. These statements not only are useful for internal financial planning, but also are routinely required by existing and prospective lenders.

financial planning process
Planning that begins with long-term (strategic) financial plans that in turn guide the formulation of short-term (operating) plans and budgets.

The **financial planning process** begins with long-term, or strategic, financial plans that in turn guide the formulation of short-term, or operating, plans and budgets. Generally, the short-term plans and budgets implement the firm's long-term strategic objectives. The major emphasis in this chapter is on preparing short-term financial plans and budgets; the following three chapters focus on the implementation of those short-term plans. First, though, we begin with a few comments on long-term financial plans.

LONG-TERM (STRATEGIC) FINANCIAL PLANS

long-term (strategic) financial plans
Planned financial actions and the anticipated impact of those actions over periods ranging from 2 to 10 years.

Long-term (strategic) financial plans lay out a company's planned financial actions and the anticipated impact of those actions over periods ranging from 2 to 10 years. The use of 5-year strategic plans, which are revised as significant new information becomes available, is common. Generally, firms that are subject to high degrees of operating uncertainty, relatively short production cycles, or both, tend to use shorter planning horizons.

Long-term financial plans are part of an integrated strategy that, along with production and marketing plans, guides the firm toward achievement of its strategic goals. These long-term plans consider proposed fixed asset outlays, research and development activities, marketing and product development actions, capital structure, and major sources of financing. Also included would be termination of existing projects, product lines, or lines of business; repayment or retirement of outstanding debts; and any planned acquisitions. Such plans tend to be supported by a series of annual budgets and profit plans.

SHORT-TERM (OPERATING) FINANCIAL PLANS

short-term (operating) financial plans
Specify short-term financial actions and the anticipated impact of those actions.

Short-term (operating) financial plans specify short-term financial actions and the anticipated impact of those actions. These plans most often cover a 1- to 2-year period. Key inputs include the sales forecast and various forms of operating and financial data. Key outputs include a number of operating budgets, the cash budget, and pro forma financial statements. The entire short-term financial planning process is outlined in the flow diagram of Figure 14.1.

Short-term financial planning begins with the sales forecast. From it, production plans are developed that take into account lead (preparation) times and include estimates of the required types and quantities of raw materials. Using the production plans, the firm can estimate direct labor requirements, factory overhead outlays, and operating expenses. Once these estimates have been made, the

FIGURE 14.1 **Short-Term Financial Planning**
The short-term (operating) financial planning process

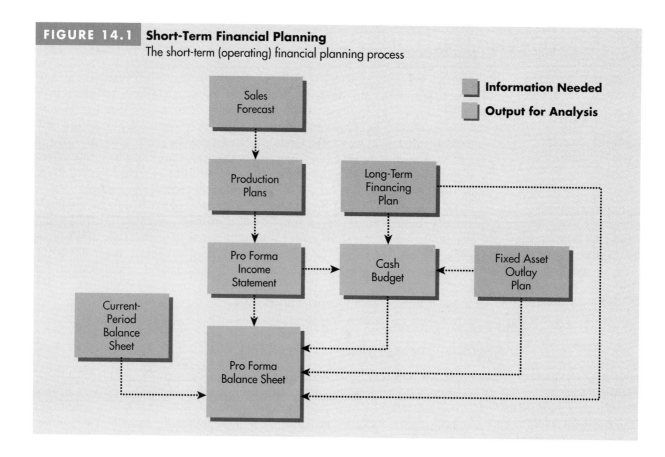

firm's pro forma income statement and cash budget can be prepared. With the basic inputs—pro forma income statement, cash budget, fixed asset outlay plan, long-term financing plan, and current-period balance sheet—the pro forma balance sheet can finally be developed. Throughout the remainder of this chapter, we will concentrate on the key outputs of the short-term financial planning process: the cash budget, the pro forma income statement, and the pro forma balance sheet. Although they are not specifically discussed in this chapter, electronic spreadsheets such as Excel, Lotus 1-2-3, and QuattroPro are widely used to streamline the process of preparing and evaluating these short-term financial planning statements.

PERSONAL FINANCE PERSPECTIVE

When Earnings Are Erratic

Standard financial planning strategies don't apply when your earnings are erratic. Personal financial planning is more complicated if you're self-employed, or a salesperson earning commissions, or if your company has adopted performance-oriented pay incentives. It would be financially risky to set up automatic monthly savings plans, and your budgeting should be done at intervals shorter than annually. It's critical to monitor income and expenses monthly and first pay essential expenses—rent/mortgage payment, utilities, food. Set up a tax account in which to regularly accumulate money for quarterly estimated taxes. Then, use any remaining funds each month to build a large cash reserve account to get through lean times.

A common mistake is to upgrade your lifestyle at the first sign of increased earnings. Some rewards are fine, but don't saddle yourself with higher car or mortgage payments. There's no guarantee you'll continue to earn at the same level. Your income will rise and fall during the year, so postpone long-term investments for retirement or children's education until year-end. Your cash budget will show how much you need for at least 3 months' living expenses; then you can invest any surplus. ●

? Review Questions

14-1   What is the *financial planning process?* Define and contrast *long-term (strategic) financial plans* and *short-term (operating) financial plans.*

14-2   Which three statements result as part of the short-term (operating) financial planning process?

CASH PLANNING: CASH BUDGETS

cash budget (cash forecast)
A statement of the firm's planned inflows and outflows of cash that is used to estimate its short-term cash requirements.

The **cash budget,** or **cash forecast,** is a statement of the firm's planned inflows and outflows of cash. It is used by the firm to estimate its short-term cash requirements, with particular attention to planning for surplus cash and for cash shortages. A firm expecting a cash surplus can plan short-term investments (marketable securities), whereas a firm expecting shortages in cash must arrange for short-term financing (notes payable). The cash budget gives the financial manager a clear view of the timing of the firm's expected cash inflows and outflows over a given period.

Typically, the cash budget is designed to cover a 1-year period, divided into smaller time intervals. The number and type of intervals depend on the nature of the business. The more seasonal and uncertain a firm's cash flows, the greater the number of intervals. Because many firms are confronted with a seasonal cash flow pattern, the cash budget is quite often presented on a monthly basis. Firms with stable patterns of cash flow may use quarterly or annual time intervals.

THE SALES FORECAST

sales forecast
The prediction of the firm's sales over a given period, based on external and/or internal data, and used as the key input to the short-term financial planning process.

The key input to the short-term financial planning process, and therefore the cash budget, is the **sales forecast.** This prediction of the firm's sales over a given period is ordinarily furnished to the financial manager by the marketing department. On the basis of this forecast, the financial manager estimates the monthly cash flows that will result from projected sales receipts and from outlays related to production, inventory, and sales. The manager also determines the level of fixed assets required and the amount of financing, if any, needed to support the forecast level of production and sales. In practice, obtaining good data is the most difficult aspect of forecasting. The sales forecast may be based on an analysis of external or internal data or on a combination of the two.

EXTERNAL FORECASTS

external forecast
A sales forecast based on the relationships observed between the firm's sales and certain key external economic indicators.

An **external forecast** is based on the relationships observed between the firm's sales and certain key external economic indicators such as the gross domestic product (GDP), new housing starts, and disposable personal income. Forecasts containing these indicators are readily available. The rationale for this approach is that because the firm's sales are often closely related to some aspect of overall national economic activity, a forecast of economic activity should provide insight into future sales.

INTERNAL FORECASTS

internal forecast
A sales forecast based on a buildup, or consensus, of forecasts through the firm's own sales channels.

Internal forecasts are based on a buildup, or consensus, of sales forecasts through the firm's own sales channels. Typically, the firm's salespeople in the field are asked to estimate the number of units of each type of product that they expect to sell in the coming year. These forecasts are collected and totaled by the sales manager, who may adjust the figures using knowledge of specific markets or of the salesperson's forecasting ability. Finally, adjustments may be made for additional internal factors, such as production capabilities.

COMBINED FORECASTS

Firms generally use a combination of external and internal forecast data to make the final sales forecast. The internal data provide insight into sales expectations, and the external data provide a means of adjusting these expectations to take into account general economic factors. The nature of the firm's product also often affects the mix and types of forecasting methods used.

PREPARING THE CASH BUDGET

The general format of the cash budget is presented in Table 14.1. We will discuss each of its components individually.

TABLE 14.1 **The General Format of the Cash Budget**

	Jan.	Feb.	. . .	Nov.	Dec.
Cash receipts	$XXX	$XXG		$XXM	$XXT
Less: Cash disbursements	XXA	XXH	. . .	XXN	XXU
Net cash flow	XXB	XXI		XXO	XXV
Add: Beginning cash	XXC	XXD	XXJ	XXP	XXQ
Ending cash	XXD	XXJ		XXQ	XXW
Less: Minimum cash balance	XXE	XXK	. . .	XXR	XXY
Required total financing		$XXL		$XXS	
Excess cash balance	$XXF				$XXZ

CASH RECEIPTS

Cash receipts include all of a firm's inflows of cash in a given financial period. The most common components of cash receipts are cash sales, collections of accounts receivable, and other cash receipts.

E x a m p l e ▼   Halley Company, a defense contractor, is developing a cash budget for October, November, and December. Halley's sales in August and September were $100,000 and $200,000, respectively. Sales of $400,000, $300,000, and $200,000 have been forecast for October, November, and December, respectively. Historically, 20 percent of the firm's sales have been for cash, 50 percent have generated accounts receivable collected after 1 month, and the remaining 30 percent have generated accounts receivable collected after 2 months. Bad debt expenses (uncollectible accounts) have been negligible.[1] In December, the firm will receive a $30,000 dividend from stock in a subsidiary. The schedule of expected cash receipts for the company is presented in Table 14.2. It contains the following items.

Forecast sales   This initial entry is *merely informational*. It is provided as an aid in calculating other sales-related items.

Cash sales   The cash sales shown for each month represent 20 percent of the total sales forecast for that month.

Collections of A/R   These entries represent the collection of accounts receivable (A/R) resulting from sales in earlier months.

Lagged 1 month   These figures represent sales made in the preceding month that generated accounts receivable collected in the current month. Because 50 percent of the current month's sales are collected 1 month later, the collections of

TABLE 14.2	A Schedule of Projected Cash Receipts for Halley Company ($000)				
	Aug.	Sept.	Oct.	Nov.	Dec.
Forecast sales	$100	$200	$400	$300	$200
Cash sales (.20)	$ 20	$ 40	$ 80	$ 60	$ 40
Collections of A/R:					
Lagged 1 month (.50)		50	100	200	150
Lagged 2 months (.30)			30	60	120
Other cash receipts					30
Total cash receipts			$210	$320	$340

---

[1]Normally, it would be expected that the collection percentages would total slightly less than 100 percent, because some of the accounts receivable would be uncollectible. In this example, the sum of the collection percentages is 100 percent (20% + 50% + 30%), which reflects the fact that all sales are assumed to be collected.

A/R with a 1-month lag shown for September represent 50 percent of the sales in August, 50 percent of September sales, and so on.

Lagged 2 months   These figures represent sales made 2 months earlier that generated accounts receivable collected in the current month. Because 30 percent of sales are collected 2 months later, the collections with a 2-month lag shown for October represent 30 percent of the sales in August, and so on.

Other cash receipts   These are cash receipts expected from sources other than sales. Interest received, dividends received, proceeds from the sale of equipment, stock and bond sale proceeds, and lease receipts may show up here. For Halley Company, the only other cash receipt is the $30,000 dividend due in December.

Total cash receipts   This figure represents the total of all the cash receipts listed for each month. For Halley Company, we are concerned only with October, November, and December, as shown in Table 14.2.

CASH DISBURSEMENTS

cash disbursements
All outlays of cash by the firm during a given financial period.

Cash disbursements include all outlays of cash by the firm during a given financial period. The most common cash disbursements are

> Cash purchases
> Payments of accounts payable
> Rent (and lease) payments
> Wages and salaries
> Tax payments
> Fixed asset outlays
> Interest payments
> Cash dividend payments
> Principal payments (loans)
> Repurchases or retirements of stock

It is important to recognize that *depreciation and other noncash charges are NOT included in the cash budget,* because they merely represent a scheduled write-off of an earlier cash outflow. The impact of depreciation, as noted in Chapter 4, is reflected in the cash outflow for tax payments.

Example ▼ Halley Company has gathered the following data needed for the preparation of a cash disbursements schedule for October, November, and December.

Purchases   The firm's purchases represent 70 percent of sales. Of this amount, 10 percent is paid in cash, 70 percent is paid in the month immediately following the month of purchase, and the remaining 20 percent is paid 2 months following the month of purchase.[2]

---

[2]Unlike the collection percentages for sales, the total of the payment percentages should equal 100 percent, because it is expected that the firm will pay off all of its accounts payable.

Rent payments   Rent of $5,000 will be paid each month.

Wages and salaries   Fixed salary cost for the year is $96,000, or $8,000 per month. In addition, wages are estimated as 10 percent of monthly sales.

Tax payments   Taxes of $25,000 must be paid in December.

Fixed asset outlays   New machinery costing $130,000 will be purchased and paid for in November.

Interest payments   An interest payment of $10,000 is due in December.

Cash dividend payments   Cash dividends of $20,000 will be paid in October.

Principal payments (loans)   A $20,000 principal payment is due in December.

Repurchases or retirements of stock   No repurchase or retirement of stock is expected during the October–December period.

The firm's cash disbursements schedule, using the preceding data, is shown in Table 14.3. Some items in the table are explained in greater detail below.

Purchases   This entry is *merely informational.* The figures represent 70 percent of the forecast sales for each month. They have been included to facilitate the calculation of the cash purchases and related payments.

Cash purchases   The cash purchases for each month represent 10 percent of the month's purchases.

TABLE 14.3	**A Schedule of Projected Cash Disbursements for Halley Company ($000)**				
Purchases (.70 × sales)	Aug. $70	Sept. $140	Oct. $280	Nov. $210	Dec. $140
Cash purchases (.10)	$ 7	$ 14	$ 28	$ 21	$ 14
Payments of A/P:					
Lagged 1 month (.70)		49	98	196	147
Lagged 2 months (.20)			14	28	56
Rent payments			5	5	5
Wages and salaries			48	38	28
Tax payments					25
Fixed asset outlays				130	
Interest payments					10
Cash dividend payments			20		
Principal payments					20
Total cash disbursements			$213	$418	$305

Payments of A/P   These entries represent the payment of accounts payable (A/P) resulting from purchases in earlier months.

Lagged 1 month   These figures represent purchases made in the preceding month that are paid for in the current month. Because 70 percent of the firm's purchases are paid for 1 month later, the payments with a 1-month lag shown for September, October, November, and December represent 70 percent of the August purchases, payments for October represent 70 percent of September purchases, and so on.

Lagged 2 months   These figures represent purchases made 2 months earlier that are paid for in the current month. Because 20 percent of the firm's purchases are paid for 2 months later, the payments with a 2-month lag for October represent 20 percent of the August purchases, and so on.

Wages and salaries   These amounts were obtained by adding $8,000 to 10 percent of the sales in each month. The $8,000 represents the fixed salary component; the rest represents wages.

▲ The remaining items on the cash disbursements schedule are self-explanatory.

net cash flow
The mathematical difference between the firm's cash receipts and its cash disbursements in each period.

ending cash
The sum of the firm's beginning cash and its net cash flow for the period.

required total financing
Amount of funds needed by the firm if the ending cash for the period is less than the desired minimum cash balance; typically represented by notes payable.

excess cash balance
The (excess) amount available for investment by the firm if the period's ending cash is greater than the desired minimum cash balance; assumed to be invested in marketable securities.

Net Cash Flow, Ending Cash, Financing, and Excess Cash

Now look back at the general-format cash budget in Table 14.1. We have inputs for the first two entries and now continue calculating the firm's cash needs. The firm's **net cash flow** is found by subtracting the cash disbursements from cash receipts in each period. Then, by adding beginning cash to the firm's net cash flow, the **ending cash** for each period can be found. Finally, subtracting the desired minimum cash balance from ending cash yields the **required total financing** or the **excess cash balance**. If the ending cash is less than the minimum cash balance, *financing* is required. Such financing is typically viewed as short-term and therefore represented by notes payable. If the ending cash is greater than the minimum cash balance, *excess cash* exists. Any excess cash is assumed to be invested in a liquid, short-term, interest-paying vehicle—that is, in marketable securities.

Example ▼ Table 14.4 presents Halley Company's cash budget, based on the cash receipt and cash disbursement data already developed. At the end of September, Halley's cash balance was $50,000 and its notes payable and marketable securities equaled $0. The company wishes to maintain as a reserve for unexpected needs a minimum cash balance of $25,000.

For Halley Company to maintain its required $25,000 ending cash balance, it will need total borrowing of $76,000 in November and $41,000 in December. In the month of October, the firm will have an excess cash balance of $22,000, which can be held in an interest-earning marketable security. The required total financing figures in the cash budget refer to *how much will be owed at the end of the month*; they do *not* represent the monthly changes in borrowing.

The monthly changes in borrowing and in excess cash can be found by further analyzing the cash budget. In October, the $50,000 beginning cash, which

TABLE 14.4	A Cash Budget for Halley Company ($000)		
	Oct.	Nov.	Dec.
Total cash receipts[a]	$210	$320	$340
Less: Total cash disbursements[b]	213	418	305
Net cash flow	$ (3)	$ (98)	$ 35
Add: Beginning cash	50	47	(51)
Ending cash	$ 47	$ (51)	$ (16)
Less: Minimum cash balance	25	25	25
Required total financing (notes payable)[c]	—	$ 76	$ 41
Excess cash balance (marketable securities)[d]	$ 22	—	—

[a]From Table 14.2.

[b]From Table 14.3.

[c]Values are placed in this line when the ending cash is less than the desired minimum cash balance. These amounts are typically financed short-term and therefore are represented by notes payable.

[d]Values are placed in this line when the ending cash is greater than the desired minimum cash balance. These amounts are typically assumed to be invested short-term and therefore are represented by marketable securities.

becomes $47,000 after the $3,000 net cash outflow, results in a $22,000 excess cash balance once the $25,000 minimum cash is deducted. In November, the $76,000 of required total financing resulted from the $98,000 net cash outflow less the $22,000 of excess cash from October. The $41,000 of required total financing in December resulted from reducing November's $76,000 of required total financing by the $35,000 of net cash inflow during December. Summarizing, the financial activities for each month would be as follows:

October: Invest the $22,000 excess cash balance in marketable securities.
November: Liquidate the $22,000 of marketable securities and borrow $76,000 (notes payable).
December: Repay $35,000 of notes payable, to leave $41,000 of outstanding required total financing.

EVALUATING THE CASH BUDGET

The cash budget provides the firm with figures indicating whether a cash shortage or surplus is expected in each of the months covered by the forecast. Each month's figure is based on the internally imposed requirement of a minimum cash balance and *represents the total balance at the end of the month.*

At the end of each of the 3 months, Halley Company expects the following balances in cash, marketable securities, and notes payable:

	End-of-month balance ($000)		
Account	Oct.	Nov.	Dec.
Cash	$25	$25	$25
Marketable securities	22	0	0
Notes payable	0	76	41

The excess cash balance of $22,000 in October can be invested in marketable securities. The deficits in November and December will have to be financed, typically, by short-term borrowing (notes payable). Note that the firm is assumed to first liquidate its marketable securities to meet deficits and then borrow with notes payable if additional financing is needed. As a result, it will not have marketable securities and notes payable on its books at the same time.

Because it may be necessary for the firm to borrow up to $76,000 for the 3-month period, the financial manager should be sure that a line of credit is established or some other arrangement made to ensure the availability of these funds. The manager will usually request to borrow more than the maximum financing indicated in the cash budget, because of the uncertainty of the ending cash values, which are derived from various forecasts.

COPING WITH UNCERTAINTY IN THE CASH BUDGET

Aside from careful estimating of the inputs to the cash budget, there are two ways of coping with the uncertainty of the cash budget. One way is to prepare several cash budgets—based on pessimistic, most likely, and optimistic forecasts. From this range of cash flows, the financial manager can determine the amount of financing necessary to cover the most adverse situation. The use of several cash budgets, each based on differing assumptions, also should give the financial manager a sense of the riskiness of alternatives so that he or she can make more intelligent short-term financial decisions. This sensitivity analysis, or "what if" approach, is often used to analyze cash flows under a variety of possible circumstances. Computers and electronic spreadsheets are commonly used to simplify the process of performing sensitivity analysis.

Example ▼ Table 14.5 presents the summary of Halley Company's cash budget prepared for each month of concern using pessimistic, most likely, and optimistic estimates of cash receipts and disbursements. The most likely estimate is based on the expected outcomes presented earlier in Tables 14.2 through 14.4.

During the month of October, Halley will, at worst, need a maximum of $15,000 of financing, and at best will have a $62,000 excess cash balance available for short-term investment. During November, its financing requirement will be between $0 and $185,000, or it could experience an excess cash balance of $5,000. The December projections show maximum borrowing of $190,000 with a possible excess cash balance of $107,000. By considering the extreme values reflected in the pessimistic and optimistic outcomes, Halley Company should be better able to plan cash requirements. For the 3-month period, the peak borrowing requirement under the worst circumstances would be $190,000, which happens to be considerably greater than the most likely estimate of $76,000 for this period. **▲**

A second and much more sophisticated way of coping with uncertainty in the cash budget is *simulation*.[3] By simulating the occurrence of sales and other uncertain events, the firm can develop a probability distribution of its ending

---

[3]A more detailed discussion of the use of simulation is included among the approaches for dealing with risk in capital budgeting in Chapter 10.

| TABLE 14.5 | A Sensitivity Analysis of Halley Company's Cash Budget ($000) | | | | | | | | |

	October			November			December		
	Pessi-mistic	Most likely	Opti-mistic	Pessi-mistic	Most likely	Opti-mistic	Pessi-mistic	Most likely	Opti-mistic
Total cash receipts	$160	$210	$285	$ 210	$320	$ 410	$ 275	$340	$422
Less: Total cash disbursements	200	213	248	380	418	467	280	305	320
Net cash flow	$(40)	$ (3)	$ 37	$(170)	$ (98)	$ (57)	$ (5)	$ 35	$102
Add: Beginning cash	50	50	50	10	47	87	(160)	(51)	30
Ending cash	$ 10	$ 47	$ 87	$(160)	$ (51)	$ 30	$(165)	$(16)	$132
Less: Minimum cash balance	25	25	25	25	25	25	25	25	25
Required total financing	$ 15	—	—	$ 185	$ 76	—	$ 190	$ 41	—
Excess cash balance	—	$ 22	$ 62	—	—	$ 5	—	—	$107

cash flows for each month. The financial decision maker can then use the probability distribution to determine the amount of financing necessary to provide a desired degree of protection against a cash shortage.

? R e v i e w Q u e s t i o n s

14-3 What is the purpose of the *cash budget?* The key input to the cash budget is the sales forecast. What is the difference between *external* and *internal* forecast data?

14-4 Briefly describe the basic format of the cash budget, beginning with forecast sales and ending with *required total financing* or *excess cash balance.*

14-5 How can the two "bottom lines" of the cash budget be used to determine the firm's short-term borrowing and investment requirements?

14-6 What is the cause of uncertainty in the cash budget? What two techniques can be used to cope with this uncertainty?

LG4   PROFIT PLANNING: PRO FORMA STATEMENT FUNDAMENTALS

pro forma statements
Projected, or forecast, financial statements—income statements and balance sheets.

Whereas cash planning focuses on forecasting cash flows, the profit-planning process centers on the preparation of **pro forma statements,** which are projected, or forecast, financial statements—income statements and balance sheets. The preparation of these statements requires a careful blending of a number of procedures to account for the revenues, costs, expenses, assets, liabilities, and equity resulting from the firm's anticipated level of operations. The basic steps in this process were shown in Figure 14.1. The financial manager frequently uses one of a number of simplified approaches to estimate the pro forma statements. The most popular approaches are based on the belief that the financial relationships reflected in the firm's past financial statements will not change in the coming period. The commonly used approaches are presented in subsequent discussions.

Two inputs are required for preparing pro forma statements using the simplified approaches: (1) financial statements for the preceding year and (2) the sales forecast for the coming year. A variety of assumptions must also be made. The company that we will use to illustrate the simplified approaches to pro forma preparation is Metcalfe Manufacturing Company, which manufactures and sells one product. It has two basic models—X and Y—which are produced by the same process but require different amounts of raw material and labor.

PRECEDING YEAR'S FINANCIAL STATEMENTS

The income statement for the firm's 2000 operations is given in Table 14.6. It indicates that Metcalfe had sales of $100,000, total cost of goods sold of $80,000, net profits before taxes of $9,000, and net profits after taxes of $7,650. The firm paid $4,000 in cash dividends, leaving $3,650 to be transferred to retained earnings. The firm's balance sheet for 2000 is given in Table 14.7.

TABLE 14.6	An Income Statement for Metcalfe Manufacturing Company for the Year Ended December 31, 2000	
Sales revenue		
Model X (1,000 units at $20/unit)	$20,000	
Model Y (2,000 units at $40/unit)	80,000	
Total sales		$100,000
Less: Cost of goods sold		
Labor	$28,500	
Material A	8,000	
Material B	5,500	
Overhead	38,000	
Total cost of goods sold		80,000
Gross profits		$ 20,000
Less: Operating expenses		10,000
Operating profits		$ 10,000
Less: Interest expense		1,000
Net profits before taxes		$ 9,000
Less: Taxes (.15 × $9,000)		1,350
Net profits after taxes		$ 7,650
Less: Common stock dividends		4,000
To retained earnings		$ 3,650

TABLE 14.7	A Balance Sheet for Metcalfe Manufacturing Company (December 31, 2000)		
Assets		**Liabilities and equities**	
Cash	$ 6,000	Accounts payable	$ 7,000
Marketable securities	4,000	Taxes payable	300
Accounts receivable	13,000	Notes payable	8,300
Inventories	16,000	Other current liabilities	3,400
Total current assets	$39,000	Total current liabilities	$19,000
Net fixed assets	$51,000	Long-term debt	$18,000
Total assets	$90,000	Stockholders' equity	
		Common stock	$30,000
		Retained earnings	$23,000
		Total liabilities and stockholders' equity	$90,000

TABLE 14.8	2001 Sales Forecast for Metcalfe Manufacturing Company	
Unit sales		
Model X		1,500
Model Y		1,950
Dollar sales		
Model X ($25/unit)		$ 37,500
Model Y ($50/unit)		97,500
Total		$135,000

SALES FORECAST

Like the cash budget, the key input for pro forma statements is the sales forecast. The sales forecast for the coming year, 2001, for Metcalfe Manufacturing Company is presented in Table 14.8. This forecast is based on both external and internal data. The unit sale prices of the products reflect an increase from $20 to $25 for model X and from $40 to $50 for model Y. These increases are required to cover anticipated increases in the costs of labor, material, overhead, and operating expenses.

? R e v i e w   Q u e s t i o n

14-7   What are the two key inputs required for preparing *pro forma statements* using the simplified approaches?

PREPARING THE PRO FORMA INCOME STATEMENT

percent-of-sales method
A simple method for developing the pro forma income statement that expresses the cost of goods sold, operating expenses, and interest expense as percentages of projected sales.

A simple method for developing a pro forma income statement is the **percent-of-sales method.** It forecasts sales and then expresses the cost of goods sold, operating expenses, and interest expense as percentages of projected sales. The percentages used are likely to be the percentage of sales for these items in the previous year. For Metcalfe Manufacturing Company, these percentages are:

$$\frac{\text{Cost of goods sold}}{\text{Sales}} = \frac{\$80,000}{\$100,000} = 80.0\%$$

$$\frac{\text{Operating expenses}}{\text{Sales}} = \frac{\$10,000}{\$100,000} = 10.0\%$$

$$\frac{\text{Interest expense}}{\text{Sales}} = \frac{\$1,000}{\$100,000} = 1.0\%$$

The dollar values used are taken from the 2000 income statement (Table 14.6).

Applying these percentages to the firm's forecast sales of $135,000, developed in Table 14.8, and assuming that the firm will pay $4,000 in common stock dividends in 2001, results in the pro forma income statement in Table 14.9. The expected contribution to retained earnings is $6,327, which represents a considerable increase over $3,650 in the preceding year (Table 14.6).

CONSIDERING TYPES OF COSTS AND EXPENSES

The technique that is used to prepare the pro forma income statement in Table 14.9 assumes that all the firm's costs and expenses are variable. This means that the use of the historical (2000) ratios of cost of goods sold, operating expenses,

TABLE 14.9	**Pro Forma Income Statement, Using the Percent-of-Sales Method, for Metcalfe Manufacturing Company for the Year Ended December 31, 2001**
Sales revenue	$135,000
Less: Cost of goods sold (.80)	108,000
Gross profits	$ 27,000
Less: Operating expenses (.10)	13,500
Operating profits	$ 13,500
Less: Interest expense (.01)	1,350
Net profits before taxes	$ 12,150
Less: Taxes (.15 × $12,150)	1,823
Net profits after taxes	$ 10,327
Less: Common stock dividends	4,000
To retained earnings	$ 6,327

and interest expense to sales assumes that for a given percentage increase in sales, the same percentage increase in each of these components results. For example, as Metcalfe's sales increased by 35 percent (from $100,000 in 2000 to $135,000 projected for 2001), its cost of goods sold also increased by 35 percent (from $80,000 in 2000 to $108,000 projected for 2001). On the basis of this assumption, the firm's net profits before taxes also increased by 35 percent (from $9,000 in 2000 to $12,150 projected for 2001).

A broad implication of this approach is that because the firm has no fixed costs, it will not receive the benefits that often result from them.[4] Therefore, the use of past cost and expense ratios generally *tends to understate profits when sales are increasing* and *overstate profits when sales are decreasing.* Clearly, if the firm has fixed costs, these costs do not change when sales increase; the result is increased profits. By remaining unchanged when sales decline, these costs tend to lower profits. The best way to adjust for the presence of fixed costs in pro forma income statement preparation is to break the firm's historical costs and expenses into *fixed* and *variable components.*

Example ▼ Metcalfe Manufacturing Company's 2000 actual and 2001 pro forma income statements, which are broken into fixed and variable cost components, follow:

Income Statements Metcalfe Manufacturing Company	2000 Actual	2001 Pro forma
Sales revenue	$100,000	$135,000
Less: Cost of good sold		
Fixed cost	40,000	40,000
Variable cost (.40 × sales)	40,000	54,000
Gross profits	$ 20,000	$ 41,000
Less: Operating expenses		
Fixed expense	5,000	5,000
Variable expense (.05 × sales)	5,000	6,750
Operating profits	$ 10,000	$ 29,250
Less: Interest expense (all fixed)	1,000	1,000
Net profits before taxes	$ 9,000	$ 28,250
Less: Taxes (.15 × net profits before taxes)	1,350	4,238
Net profits after taxes	$ 7,650	$ 24,012

Breaking Metcalfe's costs and expenses into fixed and variable components provides a more accurate projection of its pro forma profit. Had the firm treated all costs as variable, its pro forma (2001) net profits before taxes would equal 9 percent of sales, as was the case in 2000 ($9,000 net profits before taxes ÷ $100,000 sales). As shown in Table 14.9, by assuming that *all* costs are variable, projected

---

[4]The potential returns as well as risks resulting from use of fixed costs to create "leverage" are discussed in Chapter 12. The key point to recognize here is that when the firm's revenue is *increasing*, fixed costs can magnify returns.

net profits before taxes would have been $12,150 (.09 × $135,000 projected sales) instead of the $28,250 of net profits before taxes obtained by using the firm's fixed cost–variable cost breakdown.

This example should make it clear that ignoring fixed costs in the pro forma income statement preparation process typically results in misstatement of the firm's forecast profit. Therefore, when using a simplified approach to pro forma income statement preparation, it is advisable to consider first breaking down costs and expenses into fixed and variable components.

Review Questions

14-8   Briefly describe the pro forma income statement preparation process using the *percent-of-sales method*. What are the strengths and weaknesses of this simplified approach?

14-9   Comment on the following statement: "Because nearly all firms have fixed costs, ignoring them in the pro forma income statement preparation process typically results in misstatement of the firm's forecast profit." How can such a "misstatement" be avoided?

PREPARING THE PRO FORMA BALANCE SHEET

judgmental approach
A simplified method for developing the pro forma balance sheet in which the values of certain balance sheet accounts are estimated, and others are calculated, using the firm's external financing as a balancing, or "plug," figure.

A number of simplified approaches are available for preparing the pro forma balance sheet. Probably the best and most popular is the judgmental approach.[5] Under the **judgmental approach,** the values of certain balance sheet accounts are estimated and others are calculated. The firm's external financing is used as a balancing, or "plug," figure. To apply the judgmental approach to prepare Metcalfe Manufacturing Company's 2001 pro forma balance sheet, a number of assumptions must be made:

1. A minimum cash balance of $6,000 is desired.
2. Marketable securities are assumed to remain unchanged from their current level of $4,000.
3. Accounts receivable on average represents 45 days of sales. Because Metcalfe's annual sales are projected to be $135,000, accounts receivable should average $16,875 ($\frac{1}{8}$ × $135,000). (Forty-five days expressed fractionally is one-eighth of a year: 45/360 = $\frac{1}{8}$.)
4. The ending inventory should remain at a level of about $16,000, of which 25 percent (approximately $4,000) should be raw materials and the remaining 75 percent (approximately $12,000) should consist of finished goods.

---

[5]The judgmental approach represents an improved version of the often discussed *percent-of-sales approach* to pro forma balance sheet preparation. Because the judgmental approach requires only slightly more information and should yield better estimates than the somewhat naive percent-of-sales approach, it is presented here.

5. A new machine costing $20,000 will be purchased. Total depreciation for the year is $8,000. Adding the $20,000 acquisition to the existing net fixed assets of $51,000 and subtracting the depreciation of $8,000 yields net fixed assets of $63,000.

6. Purchases are expected to represent approximately 30 percent of annual sales, which in this case is approximately $40,500 (.30 × $135,000). The firm estimates that it can take 72 days on average to satisfy its accounts payable. Thus, accounts payable should equal one-fifth (72 days ÷ 360 days) of the firm's purchases, or $8,100 (⅕ × $40,500).

7. Taxes payable are expected to equal one-fourth of the current year's tax liability, which equals $455 (one-fourth of the tax liability of $1,823 shown in the pro forma income statement presented in Table 14.9).

8. Notes payable are assumed to remain unchanged from their current level of $8,300.

9. No change in other current liabilities is expected. They remain at the level of the previous year: $3,400.

10. The firm's long-term debt and its common stock are expected to remain unchanged at $18,000 and $30,000, respectively; no issues, retirements, or repurchases of bonds or stocks are planned.

11. Retained earnings will increase from the beginning level of $23,000 (from the balance sheet dated December 31, 2000, in Table 14.7) to $29,327. The increase of $6,327 represents the amount of retained earnings calculated in the year-end 2001 pro forma income statement in Table 14.9.

A 2001 pro forma balance sheet for Metcalfe Manufacturing Company based on these assumptions is presented in Table 14.10. A **"plug" figure**—called

TABLE 14.10   **A Pro Forma Balance Sheet, Using the Judgmental Approach, for Metcalfe Manufacturing Company (December 31, 2001)**

Assets			Liabilities and equities	
Cash		$ 6,000	Accounts payable	$ 8,100
Marketable securities		4,000	Taxes payable	455
Accounts receivable		16,875	Notes payable	8,300
Inventories			Other current liabilities	3,400
Raw materials	$ 4,000		Total current liabilities	$ 20,255
Finished goods	12,000		Long-term debt	$ 18,000
Total inventory		16,000	Stockholders' equity	
Total current assets		$ 42,875	Common stock	$ 30,000
Net fixed assets		$ 63,000	Retained earnings	$ 29,327
Total assets		$105,875	Total	$ 97,582
			External financing required[a]	$ 8,293
			Total liabilities and stockholders'	
			equity	$105,875

[a]The amount of external financing needed to force the firm's balance sheet to balance. Due to the nature of the judgmental approach, the balance sheet is not expected to balance without some type of adjustment.

external financing required ("plug" figure) Under the judgmental approach for developing a pro forma balance sheet, the amount of external financing needed to bring the statement into balance.

the **external financing required**—of $8,293 is needed to bring the statement into balance. This means that the firm will have to obtain about $8,293 of additional external financing to support the increased sales level of $135,000 for 2001.

A *positive* value for "external financing required," like that shown in Table 14.10, means that to support the forecast level of operation, the firm must raise funds externally using debt and/or equity financing. Once the form of financing is determined, the pro forma balance sheet is modified to replace "external financing required" with the planned increases in the debt and/or equity accounts.

A *negative* value for external financing required indicates that the firm's forecast financing is in excess of its needs. In this case, funds would be available for use in repaying debt, repurchasing stock, or increasing dividends. Once the specific actions are determined, "external financing required" is replaced in the pro forma balance sheet with the planned reductions in the debt and/or equity accounts. Obviously, besides being used to prepare the pro forma balance sheet, the judgmental approach is also frequently used specifically to estimate the firm's financing requirements.

? Review Questions

14-10 Describe the *judgmental approach* for simplified preparation of the pro forma balance sheet. Contrast this with the more detailed approach shown in Figure 14.1.

14-11 What is the significance of the "plug" figure, *external financing required*, used with the judgmental approach for preparing the pro forma balance sheet? Differentiate between the interpretation and strategy associated with positive and negative values for *external financing required*.

LG6 EVALUATION OF PRO FORMA STATEMENTS

It is difficult to forecast the many variables involved in pro forma statement preparation. As a result, analysts—including investors, lenders, and managers—frequently use the techniques presented here to make rough estimates of pro forma financial statements. Simplified approaches to pro forma preparation are expected to remain popular despite the growing use of computers to streamline financial planning. An understanding of the basic weaknesses of these simplified approaches is therefore important. Equally important is the ability to effectively use pro forma statements to make financial decisions.

WEAKNESSES OF SIMPLIFIED APPROACHES

The basic weaknesses of the simplified pro forma approaches shown in the chapter lie in two assumptions: (1) that the firm's past financial condition is an accurate indicator of its future, and (2) that certain variables, such as cash, accounts receivable, and inventories, can be forced to take on certain "desired" values. These assumptions cannot be justified solely on the basis of their ability to simplify the calculations involved. Good financial analysts do not generally assume that simplification of the forecasting model enhances insight into what's going to happen. Because the quality of pro forma statements depends on the quality of the forecasting model, practicing analysts seek out the models and assumptions that best suit their particular situation.

USING PRO FORMA STATEMENTS

In addition to estimating the amount of external financing that is required to support a given level of sales, pro forma statements also provide a basis for analyzing in advance the level of profitability and overall financial performance of the firm in the coming year. Using pro forma statements, both financial managers and lenders can analyze the firm's sources and uses of cash as well as its liquidity, activity, debt, and profitability. Sources and uses can be evaluated by preparing a pro forma statement of cash flows. Various ratios can be calculated from the pro forma income statement and balance sheet to evaluate performance.

After analyzing the pro forma statements, the financial manager can take steps to adjust planned operations to achieve short-term financial goals. For example, if projected profits on the pro forma income statement are too low, a variety of pricing or cost-cutting actions, or both, might be initiated. If the projected level of accounts receivable on the pro forma balance sheet is too high, changes in credit or collection policy may be called for. Pro forma statements are therefore of key importance in solidifying the firm's financial plans for the coming year.

? Review Questions

14-12   What are the two key weaknesses of the simplified approaches to pro forma statement preparation?

14-13   What is the financial manager's objective in evaluating pro forma statements?

SUMMARY

LG1 **Understand the financial planning process, including long-term (strategic) financial plans and short-term (operating) plans.** The two key aspects of the financial planning process are cash planning and profit planning. Cash planning involves the cash budget or cash forecast. Profit planning relies on the pro forma income statement and balance sheet. Long-term (strategic) financial plans act as a guide for preparing short-term (operating) financial plans. Long-term plans tend to cover periods ranging from 2 to 10 years and are

updated periodically. Short-term plans most often cover a 1- to 2-year period.

LG2 **Discuss the cash planning process, the role of sales forecasts, and the procedures for preparing the cash budget.** The cash planning process uses the cash budget, which is based on a sales forecast, to estimate short-term cash surpluses and shortages. The sales forecast may be based on external or internal data or on a combination of the two. The cash budget is typically prepared for a 1-year period divided into months. It nets cash receipts and disbursements for each period to calculate net cash flow. Ending cash is estimated by adding beginning cash to the net cash flow. By subtracting the desired minimum cash balance from the ending cash, the financial manager can determine required total financing (typically notes payable) or the excess cash balance (typically held as marketable securities).

LG3 **Describe the cash budget evaluation process and the procedures for coping with uncertainty in the cash budget.** The cash budget allows the firm to plan investment of cash surpluses and to arrange for adequate borrowing to meet forecast cash shortages. To cope with uncertainty in the cash budget, sensitivity analysis (preparation of several cash budgets) or computer simulation can be used.

LG4 **Prepare a pro forma income statement using both the percent-of-sales method and a breakdown of costs and expenses into their fixed and variable components.** A pro forma income statement can be developed by calculating past percentage relationships between certain cost and expense items and the firm's sales and then applying these percentages to forecasts. Because this approach implies that all costs and expenses are variable, it tends to understate profits when sales are increasing and overstate profits when sales are decreasing. This problem can be avoided by breaking down costs and expenses into fixed and variable components. In this case, the fixed components remain unchanged from the most recent year, and the variable costs and expenses are forecast on a percent-of-sales basis.

LG5 **Explain the procedures used to develop a pro forma balance sheet using the judgmental approach and the use of the plug figure—external financing required—in this process.** Under the judgmental approach, the values of certain balance sheet accounts are estimated and others are calculated, frequently on the basis of their relationship to sales. The firm's external financing is used as a balancing, or "plug," figure. A positive value for "external financing required" means that the firm must raise funds externally; a negative value indicates that funds are available for use in repaying debt, repurchasing stock, or increasing dividends.

LG6 **Describe the weaknesses of the simplified approaches to pro forma preparation and the common uses of pro forma financial statements.** Simplified approaches for pro forma statement preparation, although popular, can be criticized for assuming that the firm's past condition is an accurate predictor of the future and that certain variables can be forced to take on desired values. Pro forma statements are commonly used to analyze the firm's level of profitability and overall financial performance so that adjustments can be made to planned operations in order to achieve short-term financial goals.

SELF-TEST PROBLEMS   (Solutions in Appendix B)

ST 14-1   Cash budget and pro forma balance sheet inputs   Jane McDonald, a financial analyst for Carroll Company, has prepared the following sales and cash disbursement estimates for the period February–June of the current year.

Month	Sales	Cash disbursements
February	$500	$400
March	600	300
April	400	600
May	200	500
June	200	200

Ms. McDonald notes that historically, 30 percent of sales have been for cash. Of *credit sales,* 70 percent are collected 1 month after the sale, and the remaining 30 percent are collected 2 months after the sale. The firm wishes to maintain a minimum ending balance in its cash account of $25. Balances above this amount would be invested in short-term government securities (marketable securities), whereas any deficits would be financed through short-term bank borrowing (notes payable). The beginning cash balance at April 1 is $115.
a. Prepare a cash budget for April, May, and June.
b. How much financing, if any, at a maximum would Carroll Company need to meet its obligations during this 3-month period?
c. If a pro forma balance sheet dated at the end of June were prepared from the information presented, give the size of each of the following: cash, notes payable, marketable securities, and accounts receivable.

 ST 14-2   Pro forma income statement   Euro Designs, Inc., expects sales during 2001 to rise from the 2000 level of $3.5 million to $3.9 million. Due to a scheduled large loan payment, the interest expense in 2001 is expected to drop to $325,000. The firm plans to increase its cash dividend payments during 2001 to $320,000. The company's year-end 2000 income statement follows.

Income Statement Euro Designs, Inc. for the year ended December 31, 2000	
Sales revenue	$3,500,000
Less: Cost of goods sold	1,925,000
Gross profits	$1,575,000
Less: Operating expenses	420,000
Operating profits	$1,155,000
Less: Interest expense	400,000
Net profits before taxes	$ 755,000
Less: Taxes (rate = 40%)	302,000
Net profits after taxes	$ 453,000
Less: Cash dividends	250,000
To retained earnings	$ 203,000

a. Use the *percent-of-sales method* to prepare a 2001 pro forma income statement for Euro Designs, Inc.
b. Explain why the statement may underestimate the company's actual 2001 pro forma income.

PROBLEMS

  14-1   Cash receipts   A firm has actual sales of $65,000 in April and $60,000 in May. It expects sales of $70,000 in June and $100,000 in July and in August. Assuming that sales are the only source of cash inflows and that half of these are for cash and the remainder are collected evenly over the following 2 months, what are the firm's expected cash receipts for June, July, and August?

14-2   **Cash budget—Basic**   Quick Digital Company had sales of $50,000 in March and $60,000 in April. Forecast sales for May, June, and July are $70,000, $80,000, and $100,000, respectively. The firm has a cash balance of $5,000 on May 1 and wishes to maintain a minimum cash balance of $5,000. Given the following data, prepare and interpret a cash budget for the months of May, June, and July.

(1) The firm makes 20 percent of its sales for cash, 60 percent are collected in the next month, and the remaining 20 percent are collected in the second month following sale.

(2) The firm receives other income of $2,000 per month.

(3) The firm's actual or expected purchases, all made for cash, are $50,000, $70,000, and $80,000 for the months of May through July, respectively.

(4) Rent is $3,000 per month.

(5) Wages and salaries are 10 percent of the previous month's sales.

(6) Cash dividends of $3,000 will be paid in June.

(7) Payment of principal and interest of $4,000 is due in June.

(8) A cash purchase of equipment costing $6,000 is scheduled in July.

(9) Taxes of $6,000 are due in June.

14-3   **Cash budget—Advanced**   The actual sales and purchases for Advanced Appliance Company, for September and October 2000, along with its forecast sales and purchases for the period November 2000 through April 2001, follow.

Year	Month	Sales	Purchases
2000	September	$210,000	$120,000
2000	October	250,000	150,000
2000	November	170,000	140,000
2000	December	160,000	100,000
2001	January	140,000	80,000
2001	February	180,000	110,000
2001	March	200,000	100,000
2001	April	250,000	90,000

The firm makes 20 percent of all sales for cash and collects on 40 percent of its sales in each of the 2 months following the sale. Other cash inflows are expected to be $12,000 in September and April, $15,000 in January and March, and $27,000 in February. The firm pays cash for 10 percent of its purchases. It pays for 50 percent of its purchases in the following month and for 40 percent of its purchases 2 months later.

Wages and salaries amount to 20 percent of the preceding month's sales. Rent of $20,000 per month must be paid. Interest payments of $10,000 are due in January and April. A principal payment of $30,000 is also due in April. The firm expects to pay cash dividends of $20,000 in January and April. Taxes of $80,000 are due in April. The firm also intends to make a $25,000 cash purchase of fixed assets in December.

a. Assuming that the firm has a cash balance of $22,000 at the beginning of November, determine the end-of-month cash balances for each month, November through April.

b. Assuming that the firm wishes to maintain a $15,000 minimum cash balance, determine the required total financing or excess cash balance for each month, November through April.

c. If the firm were requesting a line of credit to cover needed financing for the period November to April, how large would this line have to be? Explain your answer.

 WARM-UP   **14-4**   Cash flow concepts   The following represent financial transactions that Ballou Company will be undertaking in the next planning period. For each transaction, check the statement or statements that will be affected immediately.

| | Statement | | |
Transaction	Cash budget	Pro forma income statement	Pro forma balance sheet
Cash sale			
Credit sale			
Accounts receivable are collected			
Asset with 5-year life is purchased			
Depreciation is taken			
Amortization of goodwill is taken			
Sale of common stock			
Retirement of outstanding bonds			
Fire insurance premium is paid for the next 3 years			

 INTERMEDIATE   **14-5**   Multiple cash budgets—Sensitivity analysis   Patterson's Parts Store expects sales of $100,000 during each of the next 3 months. It will make monthly purchases of $60,000 during this time. Wages and salaries are $10,000 per month plus 5 percent of sales. Patterson's expects to make a tax payment of $20,000 in the next month and a $15,000 purchase of fixed assets in the second month and to receive $8,000 in cash from the sale of an asset in the third month. All sales and purchases are for cash. Beginning cash and the minimum cash balance are assumed to be zero.

a. Construct a cash budget for the next 3 months.

b. Patterson's is unsure of the sales levels, but all other figures are certain. If the most pessimistic sales figure is $80,000 per month and the most optimistic is $120,000 per month, what are the monthly minimum and maximum ending cash balances that the firm can expect for each of the 1-month periods?

c. Briefly discuss how the financial manager can use the data in a and b to plan for Patterson's financing needs.

 INTERMEDIATE   **14-6**   Pro forma income statement   The marketing department of Hartman Manufacturing estimates that its sales in 2001 will be $1.5 million. Interest expense is expected to remain unchanged at $35,000, and the firm plans to pay $70,000 in cash dividends during 2001. Hartman Manufacturing's income statement for the year ended December 31, 2000, is given below, followed by a breakdown of the firm's cost of goods sold and operating expenses into their fixed and variable cost components.

Income Statement Hartman Manufacturing for the year ended December 31, 2000	
Sales revenue	$1,400,000
Less: Cost of goods sold	910,000
Gross profits	$ 490,000
Less: Operating expenses	120,000
Operating profits	$ 370,000
Less: Interest expense	35,000
Net profits before taxes	$ 335,000
Less: Taxes (rate = 40%)	134,000
Net profits after taxes	$ 201,000
Less: Cash dividends	66,000
To retained earnings	$ 135,000

Fixed and Variable Cost Breakdown Hartman Manufacturing for the year ended December 31, 2000	
Cost of goods sold	
Fixed cost	$210,000
Variable cost	700,000
Total cost	$910,000
Operating expenses	
Fixed expenses	$ 36,000
Variable expenses	84,000
Total expenses	$120,000

a. Use the *percent-of-sales method* to prepare a pro forma income statement for the year ended December 31, 2001.
b. Use *fixed and variable cost data* to develop a pro forma income statement for the year ended December 31, 2001.
c. Compare and contrast the statements developed in **a** and **b**. Which statement will likely provide the better estimates of 2001 income? Explain why.

  14-7 Pro forma balance sheet—Basic   Nezi Cosmetics wishes to prepare a pro forma balance sheet for December 31, 2001. The firm expects 2001 sales to total $3,000,000. The following information has been gathered.
(1) A minimum cash balance of $50,000 is desired.
(2) Marketable securities are expected to remain unchanged.

(3) Accounts receivable represent 10 percent of sales.
(4) Inventories represent 12 percent of sales.
(5) A new machine costing $90,000 will be acquired during 2001. Total depreciation for the year will be $32,000.
(6) Accounts payable represent 14 percent of sales.
(7) Accruals, other current liabilities, long-term debt, and common stock are expected to remain unchanged.
(8) The firm's net profit margin is 4 percent, and it expects to pay out $70,000 in cash dividends during 2001.
(9) The December 31, 2000, balance sheet follows.

		Balance Sheet Nezi Cosmetics December 31, 2000	
Assets		**Liabilities and equities**	
Cash	$ 45,000	Accounts payable	$ 395,000
Marketable securities	15,000	Accruals	60,000
Accounts receivable	255,000	Other current liabilities	30,000
Inventories	340,000	Total current liabilities	$ 485,000
Total current assets	$ 655,000	Long-term debt	$ 350,000
Net fixed assets	$ 600,000	Common stock	$ 200,000
Total assets	$1,255,000	Retained earnings	$ 220,000
		Total liabilities and stockholders' equity	$1,255,000

a. Use the *judgmental approach* to prepare a pro forma balance sheet dated December 31, 2001, for Nezi Cosmetics.
b. How much, if any, additional financing will Nezi Cosmetics require in 2001? Discuss.
c. Could Nezi Cosmetics adjust its planned 2001 dividend to avoid the situation described in **b**? Explain how.

14-8   Pro forma balance sheet   Widget Tool has 2000 sales of $10 million. It wishes to analyze expected performance and financing needs for 2002—2 years ahead. Given the following information, answer questions **a** and **b**.
(1) The percent of sales for items that vary directly with sales are as follows:
Accounts receivable, 12 percent
Inventory, 18 percent
Accounts payable, 14 percent
Net profit margin, 3 percent
(2) Marketable securities and other current liabilities are expected to remain unchanged.
(3) A minimum cash balance of $480,000 is desired.
(4) A new machine costing $650,000 will be acquired in 2001, and equipment costing $850,000 will be purchased in 2002. Total depreciation in 2001 is forecast as $290,000, and in 2002, $390,000 of depreciation will be taken.
(5) Accruals are expected to rise to $500,000 by the end of 2002.

(6) No sale or retirement of long-term debt is expected.
(7) No sale or repurchase of common stock is expected.
(8) The dividend payout of 50 percent of net profits is expected to continue.
(9) Sales are expected to be $11 million in 2001 and $12 million in 2002.
(10) The December 31, 2000, balance sheet follows.

Balance Sheet			
Widget Tool			
December 31, 2000			
($000)			
Assets		**Liabilities and equities**	
Cash	$ 400	Accounts payable	$1,400
Marketable securities	200	Accruals	400
Accounts receivable	1,200	Other current liabilities	80
Inventories	1,800	Total current liabilities	$1,880
Total current assets	$3,600	Long-term debt	$2,000
Net fixed assets	$4,000	Common equity	$3,720
Total assets	$7,600	Total liabilities and stockholders' equity	$7,600

a. Prepare a pro forma balance sheet dated December 31, 2002.
b. Discuss the financing changes suggested by the statement prepared in a.

CHALLENGE

14-9 Integrative—Pro forma statements   Clancey Daughters Corporation wishes to prepare financial plans. Use the financial statements and the other information provided in what follows and on page 487 to prepare the financial plans.

Income Statement	
Clancey Daughters Corporation	
for the year ended December 31, 2000	
Sales revenue	$800,000
Less: Cost of goods sold	600,000
Gross profits	$200,000
Less: Operating expenses	100,000
Net profits before taxes	$100,000
Less: Taxes (rate = 40%)	40,000
Net profits after taxes	$ 60,000
Less: Cash dividends	20,000
To retained earnings	$ 40,000

Balance Sheet
Clancey Daughters Corporation
December 31, 2000

Assets		Liabilities and equities	
Cash	$ 32,000	Accounts payable	$100,000
Marketable securities	18,000	Taxes payable	20,000
Accounts receivable	150,000	Other current liabilities	5,000
Inventories	100,000	Total current liabilities	$125,000
Total current assets	$300,000	Long-term debt	$200,000
Net fixed assets	$350,000	Common stock	$150,000
Total assets	$650,000	Retained earnings	$175,000
		Total liabilities and stockholders' equity	$650,000

The following financial data are also available:
(1) The firm has estimated that its sales for 2001 will be $900,000.
(2) The firm expects to pay $35,000 in cash dividends in 2001.
(3) The firm wishes to maintain a minimum cash balance of $30,000.
(4) Accounts receivable represent approximately 18 percent of annual sales.
(5) The firm's ending inventory will change directly with changes in sales in 2001.
(6) A new machine costing $42,000 will be purchased in 2001. Total depreciation for 2001 will be $17,000.
(7) Accounts payable will change directly in response to changes in sales in 2001.
(8) Taxes payable will equal one-fourth of the tax liability on the pro forma income statement.
(9) Marketable securities, other current liabilities, long-term debt, and common stock will remain unchanged.

a. Prepare a pro forma income statement for the year ended December 31, 2001, using the *percent-of-sales method.*
b. Prepare a pro forma balance sheet dated December 31, 2001, using the *judgmental approach.*
c. Analyze these statements, and discuss the resulting *external financing required.*

CASE   Chapter 14

Preparing Martin Manufacturing's 2001 Pro Forma Financial Statements

To improve its competitive position, Martin Manufacturing is planning to implement a major plant-modernization program. Included will be construction of a state-of-the-art manufacturing facility that will cost $400 million in 2001 and is expected to lower the variable cost per ton of steel. Terry Spiro, an experienced budget analyst, has been charged with preparing a forecast of the firm's 2001 financial position assuming construction of the proposed new facility. She plans to use the 2000 financial statements presented on page 146 and 147, along with the key projected financial data summarized in the following table.

Key Projected Financial Data (2001) Martin Manufacturing Company ($000)	
Data item	Value
Sales revenue	$6,500,000
Minimum cash balance	$25,000
Inventory turnover (times)	7.0
Average collection period	50 days
Fixed asset purchases	$400,000
Dividend payments	$20,000
Depreciation expense	$185,000
Interest expense	$97,000
Accounts payable increase	20%
Accruals and long-term debt	Unchanged
Notes payable, preferred and common stock	Unchanged

Required

a. As a member of Terry Spiro's staff, use the historic and projected financial data provided to prepare a pro forma income statement for the year ended December 31, 2001. (*Hint:* Use the *percent-of-sales method* to estimate all values *except* for depreciation expense and interest expense, which have been estimated by management and included in the table.)
b. Use the projected financial data along with relevant data from the pro forma income statement prepared in **a** to prepare the pro forma balance sheet at December 31, 2001. (*Hint:* Use the *judgmental approach.*)
c. What should Terry tell the management of Martin Manufacturing Company about the need to obtain *external financing* to fund construction of the proposed facility? Explain.

Web Exercise

GOTO web site metalab.unc.edu/reference/moss/usbus. Under INDUSTRY RESEARCH click on Key Industry Overviews.

1. What are the printed sources of Multi-Industry Overviews?
2. What are the Related Internet Links listed on this screen?

GOTO web site www.edgeonline.com.

3. What tools are available in the INTERACTIVE TOOLBOX?

Select Profit and Loss Statement from the menu in the INTERACTIVE TOOLBOX.

4. Enter the following account balances into the Profit and Loss Statement.

Net sales	$5,000,000
Salaries and wages	2,000,000
Rent	1,000,000
Light, heat, and power	500,000
Other expenses	100,000
Provision for income tax	100,000
In all other blanks, enter a	0

Click CALCULATE. What is the net profit after income tax?

To gather information useful for sales forecasting, financial managers need data that relate to the market for their products. To see some data sources that could be useful for sales forecasting, GOTO web site www.census.gov.

5. What is the U.S. population?

Select the state in which you live or go to school. Click GET STATE PROFILE. Double click on the county in which your home or school is located. Click on the 19xx Economic Census. (Choose the latest available year.)

6. In the country data, how many manufacturing establishments are there?
7. In the state data, how many manufacturing establishments are there?
8. In the United States data, how many manufacturing establishments are there?
9. Which is the largest city in your county? What is its population?

15 WORKING CAPITAL AND SHORT-TERM FINANCING

LEARNING GOALS

LG1 Understand the two definitions of net working capital and the tradeoff between profitability and risk as it relates to changing levels of current assets and current liabilities.

LG2 Discuss, in terms of profitability and risk, the aggressive financing strategy and the conservative financing strategy for meeting the firm's total financing requirement.

LG3 Review the key characteristics of the two major sources of spontaneous short-term financing.

LG4 Analyze credit terms offered by suppliers to determine whether to take or give up cash discounts and whether to stretch accounts payable.

LG5 Describe the interest rates and basic types of unsecured short-term bank loans, commercial paper, and short-term international loans.

LG6 Explain the characteristics of secured short-term loans and the use of accounts receivable and inventory as short-term loan collateral.

ACROSS *the* DISCIPLINES

An important consideration for all firms is the ability to finance recurring operations—the transition from cash, to inventories, to receivables, and eventually back to cash. Various strategies exist for managing the financing of this cycle, depending on the extent to which the firm matches its need for funds with short-term or long-term financing. This chapter explains the key short-term financing strategies in light of their risk and return behaviors and describes the various sources of short-term financing. Chapter 15 is important to:

- **accounting personnel** who will analyze credit terms from suppliers and decide whether to take or give up cash discounts offered for early payment.

- **information systems analysts** who will design financial information systems to enhance the effectiveness of short-term financial management.

- **management** because it will decide whether to aggressively or conservatively finance the firm's funds requirements.

- **the marketing department** because sales will be affected by the availability of credit to purchasers which depends on the firm's short-term financing.

- **operations,** because inventory levels will be affected by management's financing decisions.

NET WORKING CAPITAL FUNDAMENTALS

The firm's balance sheet provides information about the structure of the firm's investments on the one hand and the structure of its financing sources on the other. The structures chosen should consistently lead to maximization of the value of the owners' investment in the firm.

Important components of the firm's structure include the level of investment in current assets and the extent of current liability financing. In U.S. manufacturing firms, current assets currently account for about 40 percent of total assets; current liabilities represent about 26 percent of total financing. Therefore, it should not be surprising to learn that **short-term financial management**—managing current assets and current liabilities—is one of the financial manager's most important and time-consuming activities. The goal of short-term financial management is to manage each of the firm's current assets (cash, marketable securities, accounts receivable, and inventory) and current liabilities (accounts payable, notes payable, and accruals) to achieve a balance between profitability and risk that contributes positively to the firm's value.

This chapter does not discuss the optimal level of current assets and current liabilities that a firm should have. That issue is unresolved in the financial literature. Here we first consider the basic relationship between current assets and current liabilities, and then look at the key features of the major sources of short-term (current liability) financing. Subsequent chapters address the management of current assets.

NET WORKING CAPITAL

short-term financial management
Management of current assets and current liabilities.

Current assets, commonly called **working capital,** represent the portion of investment that circulates from one form to another in the ordinary conduct of business. This idea embraces the recurring transition from cash to inventories to receivables and back to cash that forms the **operating cycle** of the firm. As cash substitutes, *marketable securities* are considered part of working capital.

working capital
Current assets, which represent the portion of investment that circulates from one form to another in the ordinary conduct of business.

Current liabilities represent the firm's short-term financing, because they include all debts of the firm that come due (must be paid) in 1 year or less. These debts usually include amounts owed to suppliers (accounts payable), banks (notes payable), and employees and governments (accruals), among others.

operating cycle
The recurring transition of a firm's working capital from cash to inventories to receivables and back to cash.

As noted in Chapter 5, **net working capital** is commonly defined as the difference between the firm's current assets and its current liabilities. When the current assets exceed the current liabilities, the firm has *positive net working capital.* In this most common case, net working capital is alternatively defined as *the portion of the firm's current assets financed with long-term funds* (the sum of long-term debt and stockholders' equity). Because current liabilities represent the firm's sources of short-term funds, the amount by which current assets exceed current liabilities must be financed with long-term funds. When current assets are less than current liabilities, the firm has *negative net working capital.* In this less common case, net working capital is the portion of the firm's fixed assets financed with current liabilities. This conclusion follows from the balance sheet equation: assets equal liabilities plus equity.

net working capital
The difference between the firm's current assets and its current liabilities, or, alternatively, the portion of current assets financed with long-term funds; can be *positive* or *negative.*

The conversion of current assets from inventory to receivables to cash provides the source of cash used to pay the current liabilities. The cash outlays for current liabilities are relatively predictable. When an obligation is incurred, the firm generally knows when the corresponding payment will be due. What is difficult to predict are the cash inflows—the conversion of the current assets to more liquid forms. The more predictable its cash inflows, the less net working capital a firm needs. Because most firms are unable to match cash inflows to outflows with certainty, current assets that more than cover outflows for current liabilities are usually necessary. In general, the greater the margin by which a firm's current assets cover its current liabilities, the better able it will be to pay its bills as they come due.

Example ▼ Berenson Company, a packager of pork sausage, has the current position given in Table 15.1. All $600 of the firm's accounts payable, plus $200 of its notes payable and $100 of accruals, are due at the end of the current period. The $900 in outflows is certain; how the firm will cover these outflows is not certain. The firm can be sure that $700 will be available, because it has $500 in cash and $200 in marketable securities, which can be easily converted into cash. The remaining $200 must come from the collection of accounts receivable, the sale of inventory for cash, or both.[1] However, the firm cannot be sure when either the collection of an account receivable or a cash sale will occur. Generally, the more accounts receivable and inventories that are on hand, the greater the probability that some of these items will be converted into cash.[2] Thus, a certain level of net working capital is often recommended to ensure the firm's ability to pay bills. Berenson Company has $1,100 of net working capital (current assets minus current liabilities, or $2,700 − $1,600), which will most likely be sufficient to cover its bills. Its current ratio of 1.69 (current assets divided by current liabilities, or $2,700 ÷ $1,600) should provide sufficient liquidity as long as its accounts
▲ receivable and inventories remain relatively active.

TABLE 15.1   **The Current Position of Berenson Company**

Current assets		Current liabilities	
Cash	$ 500	Accounts payable	$ 600
Marketable securities	200	Notes payable	800
Accounts receivable	800	Accruals	200
Inventories	1,200	Total	$1,600
Total	$2,700		

---

[1] A sale of inventory for credit would show up as a new account receivable, which could not be easily converted into cash. Only a *cash sale* will guarantee the firm that its bill-paying ability during the period of the sale has been enhanced.

[2] Note that levels of accounts receivable or inventory can be high, reflecting certain management inefficiencies. Reductions in these accounts create a *source of cash* that provides financing to the firm. Acceptable levels of accounts receivable and inventory can be calculated. The efficient management of these accounts is discussed in Chapter 17.

THE TRADEOFF BETWEEN PROFITABILITY AND RISK

profitability
The relationship between revenues and costs generated by using the firm's assets—both current and fixed—in productive activities.

risk (of technical insolvency)
The probability that a firm will be unable to pay its bills as they come due.

technically insolvent
Describes a firm that is unable to pay its bills as they come due.

A tradeoff exists between a firm's profitability and its risk. **Profitability,** in this context, is the relationship between revenues and costs generated by using the firm's assets—both current and fixed—in productive activities. A firm's profits can be increased by (1) increasing revenues or (2) decreasing costs. **Risk,** in the context of short-term financial management, is the probability that a firm will be unable to pay its bills as they come due. A firm that cannot pay its bills as they come due is said to be **technically insolvent.** It is generally assumed that the greater the firm's net working capital, the lower its risk. In other words, the more net working capital, the more liquid the firm and therefore the lower its risk of becoming technically insolvent. Using these definitions of profitability and risk, we can demonstrate the tradeoff between them by separately considering changes in current assets and current liabilities.

CHANGES IN CURRENT ASSETS

The effects of changing the level of the firm's current assets on its profitability-risk tradeoff can be demonstrated by using the ratio of current assets to total assets. This ratio indicates the *percentage of total assets* that is current. For purposes of illustration, we will assume that the level of total assets remains unchanged.[3] The effects on both profitability and risk of an increase or decrease in this ratio are summarized in the upper portion of Table 15.2. When the ratio increases (that is, when current assets increase), profitability decreases. Why? Because current assets are less profitable than fixed assets. Fixed assets are more profitable because they add more value to the product than that provided by current assets. Without fixed assets, the firm could not produce the product. The risk effect, however, decreases as the ratio of current assets to total assets increases. The increase in current assets increases net working capital, thereby reducing the risk of technical insolvency. The opposite effects on profit and risk result from a decrease in the ratio of current assets to total assets.

| TABLE 15.2 | Effects of Changing Ratios on Profits and Risk |

Ratio	Change in ratio	Effect on profit	Effect on risk
Current assets / Total assets	Increase Decrease	Decrease Increase	Decrease Increase
Current liabilities / Total assets	Increase Decrease	Increase Decrease	Increase Decrease

---

[3]The level of total assets is assumed to be *constant* in this and the following discussion to isolate the effect of changing asset and financing mixes on the firm's profitability and risk.

CHANGES IN CURRENT LIABILITIES

The effects of changing the level of the firm's current liabilities on its profitability-risk tradeoff can be demonstrated by using the ratio of current liabilities to total assets. This ratio indicates the percentage of total assets that has been financed with current liabilities. Again assuming that total assets remain unchanged, the effects on both profitability and risk of an increase or decrease in the ratio are summarized in the lower portion of Table 15.2. When the ratio increases, profitability increases. Why? Because the firm uses more of the less expensive current-liability financing and less long-term financing. Current liabilities are less expensive because only notes payable, which represent about 20 percent of the typical manufacturer's current liabilities, have a cost. The other current liabilities are basically debts on which the firm pays no charge or interest. However, when the ratio increases, the risk of technical insolvency also increases, because the increase in current liabilities in turn decreases net working capital. The opposite effects on profit and risk result from a decrease in the ratio of current liabilities to total assets.

? Review Questions

15-1 Why is *short-term financial management* one of the most important activities of the financial manager? What are the two most common definitions of *net working capital?*

15-2 What relationship would you expect between the predictability of a firm's cash inflows and its required level of net working capital? How are net working capital, liquidity, and *risk of technical insolvency* related?

15-3 Why does an increase in the ratio of current to total assets decrease both profits and risk as measured by net working capital? How do changes in the ratio of current liabilities to total assets affect profitability and risk?

NET WORKING CAPITAL STRATEGIES

LG2

One of the most important decisions that must be made with respect to current assets and liabilities is how current liabilities will be used to finance current assets. The amount of current liabilities that is available is limited by the dollar amount of purchases in the case of accounts payable, by the dollar amount of accrued liabilities in the case of accruals, and by the amount of seasonal borrowing considered acceptable by lenders in the case of notes payable. Lenders make short-term loans to allow a firm to finance seasonal buildups of accounts receivable or inventory. *They generally do not lend short-term money for long-term uses.*[4]

---

[4]The rationale for, techniques of, and parties to short-term business loans are discussed in detail later in this chapter. The primary source of short-term loans to businesses—commercial banks—make these loans *only for seasonal or self-liquidating purposes* such as temporary buildups of accounts receivable or inventory.

There are two basic strategies for determining an appropriate mix of short-term (current liability) and long-term financing—the aggressive strategy and the conservative strategy. Before discussing the cost and risk considerations of each of these strategies, we will consider the permanent and seasonal components of the firm's financing need. In these discussions, we use the alternative definition that defines net working capital as *the portion of current assets financed with long-term funds.*

permanent need
Financing requirements for the firm's fixed assets plus the permanent portion of the firm's current assets; these requirements remain unchanged over the year.

seasonal need
Financing requirements for the firm's temporary portion of current assets, which vary over the year.

THE FIRM'S FINANCING NEED

The firm's financing requirements can be separated into a permanent and a seasonal need. The **permanent need,** which consists of fixed assets plus the permanent portion of the firm's current assets, remains unchanged over the year. The **seasonal need,** which consists of the temporary portion of current assets, varies over the year. The relationship between current and fixed assets and permanent and seasonal funds requirements can be illustrated with a simple example.

E x a m p l e ▼ Berenson Company's estimate of current, fixed, and total asset requirements on a monthly basis for the coming year is given in columns 1, 2, and 3 of Table 15.3. Note that the relatively stable level of total assets over the year reflects, for convenience, an absence of growth by the firm. Columns 4 and 5 break down the total requirement into permanent and seasonal components. The permanent

TABLE 15.3	Estimated Funds Requirements for Berenson Company				
Month	Current assets (1)	Fixed assets (2)	Total assets[a] [(1) + (2)] (3)	Permanent funds requirement[b] (4)	Seasonal funds requirement [(3) − (4)] (5)
January	$4,000	$13,000	$17,000	$13,800	$3,200
February	3,000	13,000	16,000	13,800	2,200
March	2,000	13,000	15,000	13,800	1,200
April	1,000	13,000	14,000	13,800	200
May	800	13,000	13,800	13,800	0
June	1,500	13,000	14,500	13,800	700
July	3,000	13,000	16,000	13,800	2,200
August	3,700	13,000	16,700	13,800	2,900
September	4,000	13,000	17,000	13,800	3,200
October	5,000	13,000	18,000	13,800	4,200
November	3,000	13,000	16,000	13,800	2,200
December	2,000	13,000	15,000	13,800	1,200
Monthly average[c]				$13,800	$1,950

[a]This represents the firm's total funds requirement.
[b]This represents the minimum total asset requirement.
[c]Found by summing the monthly amounts for the 12 months and dividing the resulting totals by 12.

component (column 4) is the lowest level of total assets during the period; the seasonal portion is the difference between the total funds requirement for each month and the permanent funds requirement.

By comparing the firm's fixed assets (column 2) to its permanent funds requirement (column 4), we see that the permanent funds requirement exceeds the firm's level of fixed assets. That is, *a portion of the firm's current assets is permanent,* because they are apparently always being replaced. The size of Berenson's permanent component of current assets is $800. This value represents the base level of current assets that remains on the firm's books throughout the entire year. This value can also be found by subtracting the level of fixed assets from the permanent funds requirement ($13,800 − $13,000 = $800). The relationships presented in Table 15.3 are depicted graphically in Figure 15.1.

aggressive financing strategy
Strategy by which the firm finances at least its seasonal requirements, and possibly some of its permanent requirements, with short-term funds and the balance of its permanent requirements with long-term funds.

AN AGGRESSIVE FINANCING STRATEGY

An **aggressive financing strategy** is one by which the firm finances at least its seasonal requirements, and possibly some of its permanent requirements, with short-term funds. The balance is financed with long-term funds. This strategy can be illustrated graphically.

Example ▼ Berenson Company's estimate of its total funds requirement and its permanent and seasonal requirements were shown in Table 15.3. An aggressive strategy would finance the permanent portion of the firm's funds requirement ($13,800) with long-term funds and the seasonal portion (ranging from $0 in May to $4,200 in October) with short-term funds. Much of the short-term financing

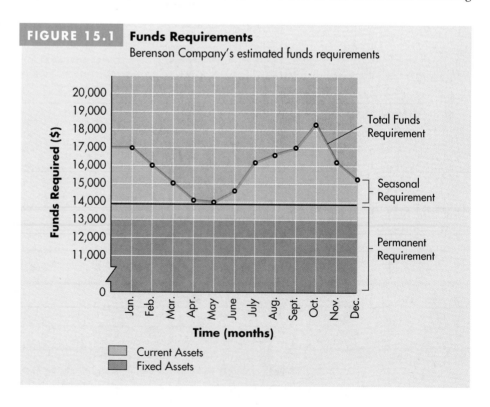

FIGURE 15.1   **Funds Requirements**
Berenson Company's estimated funds requirements

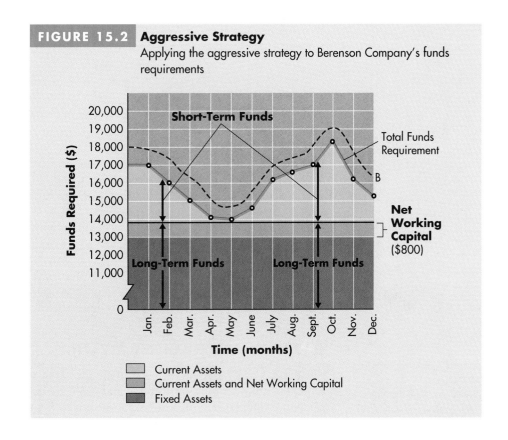

FIGURE 15.2 **Aggressive Strategy**
Applying the aggressive strategy to Berenson Company's funds requirements

would likely be in the form of *trade credit* (i.e., accounts payable). The application of this financing strategy to the firm's total funds requirement is illustrated graphically in Figure 15.2.

COST CONSIDERATIONS

Under the aggressive strategy, Berenson's average short-term borrowing (seasonal funds requirement) is $1,950, and average long-term borrowing (permanent funds requirement) is $13,800 (see columns 4 and 5 of Table 15.3). If the annual cost of short-term funds needed by Berenson is 3 percent and the annual cost of long-term financing is 11 percent, the total cost of the financing strategy is estimated as follows:

$$\text{Cost of short-term financing} = 3\% \times \$\ 1,950 = \$\quad 58.50$$
$$\text{Cost of long-term financing} = 11\% \times\quad 13,800 = \underline{\quad 1,518.00}$$
$$\text{Total cost} \qquad\qquad\qquad\qquad\qquad \underline{\underline{\$1,576.50}}$$

The total annual cost of $1,576.50 will become more meaningful when compared to the cost of the conservative financing strategy. The relatively low cost of short-term financing (3%) results from using a high amount of free trade credit (a topic discussed later in the chapter).

RISK CONSIDERATIONS

The aggressive strategy operates with minimum net working capital, because only the permanent portion of the firm's current assets is financed with long-term funds. For Berenson Company, as shown in Figure 15.2, the level of net working capital is $800, which is the amount of permanent current assets ($13,800 permanent funds requirement − $13,000 fixed assets = $800).

In addition to the risk of low net working capital, the aggressive financing strategy also forces the firm to draw heavily on its short-term sources of funds to meet seasonal fluctuations. If the total requirement turns out to be, say, the level represented by dashed line B in Figure 15.2, the firm may find it difficult to obtain longer-term funds quickly enough to satisfy short-term needs. This risk associated with the aggressive strategy results because a firm has only a limited amount of short-term borrowing capacity. If it draws too heavily on this capacity, unexpected needs for funds may become difficult to satisfy.

A CONSERVATIVE FINANCING STRATEGY

conservative financing strategy
Strategy by which the firm finances all projected funds requirements with long-term funds and uses short-term financing only for emergencies or unexpected outflows.

The most **conservative financing strategy** should be to finance all projected funds requirements with long-term funds and use short-term financing only for emergencies or unexpected outflows of funds. It is difficult to imagine how this strategy could actually be implemented, because the use of short-term financing tools, such as accounts payable and accruals, is virtually unavoidable. In illustrating this strategy, the spontaneous short-term financing provided by payables and accruals is ignored.

Example ▼

Figure 15.3 shows the application of the conservative strategy to the total funds requirement for Berenson Company. Long-term financing of $18,000, which equals the firm's peak need (during October), is used under this strategy. Therefore, all the funds required over the 1-year period, including the entire $18,000 forecast for October, are financed with long-term funds.

▲

COST CONSIDERATIONS

Here, as in the preceding example, we use 11 percent per year as the annual cost of long-term funds. Because the average long-term financing balance under the conservative financing strategy is $18,000, the total cost of this strategy is $1,980 (11% × $18,000). Compared to the total cost of $1,576.50 for the aggressive strategy, the conservative strategy is more expensive. The reason for this higher expense is apparent in Figure 15.3. The area above the total funds requirement curve and below the long-term funds, or borrowing, line represents the level of funds that are not actually needed but for which the firm is paying interest. Although the financial manager invests these excess available funds in marketable securities so as partially to offset their borrowing cost, it is unlikely that the firm can earn a large enough return on these funds to cause the cost of this strategy to fall below the cost of the aggressive strategy.

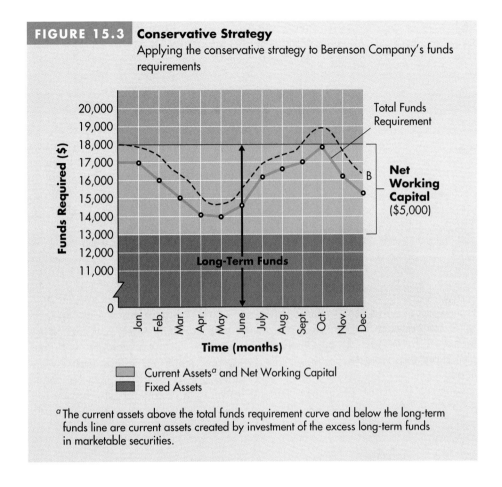

FIGURE 15.3 **Conservative Strategy**
Applying the conservative strategy to Berenson Company's funds requirements

a The current assets above the total funds requirement curve and below the long-term funds line are current assets created by investment of the excess long-term funds in marketable securities.

RISK CONSIDERATIONS

The $5,000 of net working capital ($18,000 long-term financing − $13,000 fixed assets) associated with the conservative strategy should mean a very low level of risk for the firm.[5] The firm's risk should also be lowered because the strategy does not require the firm to use any of its limited short-term borrowing capacity. In other words, if total required financing actually turns out to be the level represented by the dashed line B in Figure 15.3, sufficient short-term borrowing capacity should be available to cover the unexpected needs and avoid technical insolvency.

CONSERVATIVE VERSUS AGGRESSIVE STRATEGY

Unlike the aggressive strategy, the conservative strategy requires the firm to pay interest on unneeded funds. The lower cost of the aggressive strategy therefore makes it more profitable than the conservative strategy. However, the aggressive

---

[5] The level of net working capital is constant throughout the year, because the firm has $5,000 in current assets that are fully financed with long-term funds. Because the portion of the $5,000 in excess of the scheduled level of current assets is assumed to be held as marketable securities, the firm's current asset balance increases to this level.

strategy involves much more risk. For most firms, a tradeoff between the extremes represented by these two strategies should result in an acceptable financing strategy.

? Review Question

15-4 Describe both the *aggressive financing strategy* and the *conservative financing strategy* for meeting a firm's funds requirements. Compare and contrast the effects of each of these strategies on the firm's profitability and risk.

SPONTANEOUS SOURCES OF SHORT-TERM FINANCING

spontaneous financing
Financing that arises from the normal operations of the firm, the two major short-term sources of which are accounts payable and accruals.

Spontaneous financing arises from the normal operations of the firm. The two major spontaneous sources of short-term financing are accounts payable and accruals. As the firm's sales increase, accounts payable increase in response to the increased purchases required to produce at higher levels. Also in response to increasing sales, the firm's accruals increase as wages and taxes rise due to greater labor requirements and the increased taxes on the firm's increased earnings. There is normally no explicit cost attached to either of these current liabilities, although they do have certain implicit costs. In addition, both are forms of **unsecured short-term financing**—short-term financing obtained without pledging specific assets as collateral. The firm should take advantage of these "interest-free" sources of unsecured short-term financing whenever possible.

unsecured short-term financing
Short-term financing obtained without pledging specific assets as collateral.

ACCOUNTS PAYABLE

Accounts payable are the major source of unsecured short-term financing for business firms. They result from transactions in which merchandise is purchased but no formal note is signed to show the purchaser's liability to the seller. The purchaser, by accepting merchandise, agrees to pay the supplier the amount required in accordance with credit terms normally stated on the supplier's invoice. The discussion of accounts payable here is presented from the viewpoint of the purchaser.[6]

CREDIT TERMS

The supplier's credit terms state the credit period, the size of the cash discount offered (if any), the cash discount period, and the date the credit period begins. Each of these aspects of a firm's credit terms is concisely stated in such expressions as "2/10 net 30 EOM." These expressions are a shorthand containing the

---

[6]An account payable of a purchaser is an account receivable on the supplier's books. Chapter 17 highlights the key strategies and considerations involved in extending "trade credit" to customers.

key information about the length of the credit period (30 days), the cash discount (2 percent), the cash discount period (10 days), and the date the credit period begins, which is the end of each month (EOM).

credit period
The number of days until full payment of an account payable is required.

Credit Period   The **credit period** of an account payable is the number of days until full payment is required. Regardless of whether a cash discount is offered, the credit period associated with any transaction must always be indicated. Credit periods usually range from zero to 120 days. Most credit terms refer to the credit period as the "net period." The word net indicates that the full amount of the purchase must be paid within the number of days indicated from the beginning of the credit period. For example, "net 30 days" means that the firm must make *full payment* within 30 days of the beginning of the credit period.

cash discount
A percentage deduction from the purchase price if the buyer pays within a specified time.

Cash Discount   A **cash discount,** if offered as part of the credit terms, is a percentage deduction from the purchase price if the buyer pays within a specified time. Cash discounts normally range from between 1 and 5 percent. A 2 percent cash discount indicates that the purchaser of $100 of merchandise need pay only $98 if payment is made within the specified shorter interval. Techniques for analyzing the benefits of taking a cash discount or paying at the end of the full credit period are discussed later.

cash discount period
The number of days after the beginning of the credit period during which the cash discount is available.

Cash Discount Period   The **cash discount period** is the number of days after the beginning of the credit period during which the cash discount is available. Typically, the cash discount period is between 5 and 20 days. Often, large customers of smaller firms use their position as key customers as a form of leverage, enabling them to take cash discounts far beyond the end of the cash discount period. This strategy, although ethically questionable, is not uncommon.

date of invoice
Indicates that the beginning of the credit period is the date on the invoice for the purchase.

end of month (EOM)
Indicates that the credit period for all purchases made within a given month begins on the first day of the month immediately following.

Beginning of the Credit Period   The beginning of the credit period is stated as part of the supplier's credit terms. One of the most common designations for the beginning of the credit period is the **date of invoice.** Both the cash discount period and the net period are then measured from the invoice date. **End of month (EOM)** indicates that the credit period for all purchases made within a given month begins on the first day of the month immediately following. These terms simplify record keeping on the part of the firm extending credit. The following example may help to clarify the differences between credit period beginnings.

E x a m p l e ▼   McKinley Company, a producer of computer graphics software, made two purchases from a certain supplier offering credit terms of 2/10 net 30. One purchase was made on September 10 and the other on September 20. The payment dates for each purchase, based on date of invoice and end of month (EOM) credit period beginnings, are given in Table 15.4. The payment dates if the firm takes the cash discount and if it pays the net amount are shown. From the point of view of the credit recipient, a credit period beginning at the end of the month is preferable in both cases, because purchases can be paid for without penalty at a
▲   later date than otherwise would have been possible.

To maintain their competitive position, firms within an industry generally offer the same terms. In many cases, stated credit terms are not the terms that are

TABLE 15.4	**Payment Dates for McKinley Company Given Various Assumptions**			
	September 10 purchase		September 20 purchase	
Beginning of credit period	Discount taken	Net amount paid	Discount taken	Net amount paid
Date of invoice	Sept. 20	Oct. 10	Sept. 30	Oct. 20
End of month (EOM)	Oct. 10	Oct. 30	Oct. 10	Oct. 30

actually given to a customer. Special arrangements, or "deals," are made to provide certain customers with more favorable terms. The prospective purchaser is wise to look closely at the credit terms of suppliers when making a purchase decision. In many instances, concessions may be available.

ANALYZING CREDIT TERMS

The credit terms that a firm is offered by its suppliers allow it to delay payments for its purchases. Because the supplier's cost of having its money tied up in merchandise after it is sold is probably reflected in the purchase price, the purchaser is already indirectly paying for this benefit. The purchaser should therefore carefully analyze credit terms to determine the best trade credit strategy. If a firm is extended credit terms that include a cash discount, it has two options—to take the cash discount or to give it up.

Taking the Cash Discount   If a firm intends to take a cash discount, it should pay on the last day of the discount period. There is no cost associated with taking a cash discount.

Example ▼   Presti Corporation, operator of a small chain of video stores, purchased $1,000 worth of merchandise on February 27 from a supplier extending terms of 2/10 net 30 EOM. If the firm takes the cash discount, it must pay $980 [$1,000 − (.02 × $1,000)] by March 10, thereby saving $20. **▲**

cost of giving up a cash discount
The implied rate of interest paid to delay payment of an account payable for an additional number of days.

Giving Up the Cash Discount   If the firm chooses to give up the cash discount, it should pay on the final day of the credit period. There is an implicit cost associated with giving up a cash discount. The **cost of giving up a cash discount** is the implied rate of interest paid to delay payment of an account payable for an additional number of days. In other words, the amount is the interest being paid by the firm to delay payment. This cost can be illustrated by a simple example. The example assumes that if the firm takes a cash discount, payment will be made on the final day of the cash discount period, or if the cash discount is given up, payment will be made on the final day of the credit period.

Example ▼   In the preceding example, we saw that Presti Corporation has been extended credit terms of 2/10 net 30 EOM on $1,000 worth of merchandise. It could take

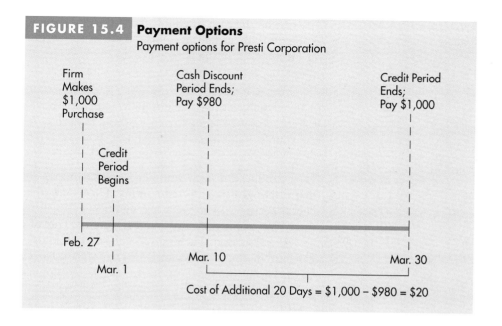

FIGURE 15.4 **Payment Options**
Payment options for Presti Corporation

Firm
Makes
$1,000
Purchase

Cash Discount
Period Ends;
Pay $980

Credit Period
Ends;
Pay $1,000

Credit
Period
Begins

Feb. 27

Mar. 1

Mar. 10

Mar. 30

Cost of Additional 20 Days = $1,000 − $980 = $20

the cash discount on its February 27 purchase by paying $980 on March 10. If Presti gives up the cash discount, payment can be made on March 30. To keep its money for an extra 20 days (from March 10 to March 30), the firm must give up an opportunity to pay $980 for its $1,000 purchase. In other words, it will cost the firm $20 to delay payment for 20 days. Figure 15.4 shows the payment options that are open to the company.

To calculate the cost of giving up the cash discount, the *true purchase price* must be viewed as the *discounted cost of the merchandise*, which is $980 for Presti Corporation. The annual percentage cost of giving up the cash discount can be calculated using Equation 15.1:

$$\text{Cost of giving up cash discount} = \frac{CD}{100\% - CD} \times \frac{360}{N} \qquad (15.1)$$

where

CD = stated cash discount in percentage terms
N = number of days payment can be delayed by giving up the cash discount

Substituting the values for CD (2%) and N (20 days) into Equation 15.1 results in an annualized cost of giving up the cash discount of 36.73 percent [(2% ÷ 98%) × (360 ÷ 20)]. A 360-day year is assumed.

A simple way to *approximate* the cost of giving up a cash discount is to use the stated cash discount percentage, CD, in place of the first term of Equation 15.1:

$$\text{Approximate cost of giving up cash discount} = CD \times \frac{360}{N} \qquad (15.2)$$

The smaller the cash discount, the closer the approximation to the actual cost of giving it up. By using this approximation, the cost of giving up the cash discount for Presti Corporation is 36 percent [2% × (360 ÷ 20)].

Using the Cost of Giving Up a Cash Discount in Decision Making The financial manager must determine whether it is advisable to take a cash discount. It is important to recognize that taking cash discounts may represent an important source of additional profitability.

Example ▼ Omst Products, a large building supply company, has four possible suppliers, each offering different credit terms. Except for the differences in credit terms, their products and services are identical. Table 15.5 presents the credit terms offered by suppliers A, B, C, and D, and the cost of giving up the cash discounts in each transaction. The approximation method of calculating the cost of giving up a cash discount (Equation 15.2) has been used. The cost of giving up the cash discount from supplier A is 36 percent; from supplier B, 8 percent; from supplier C, 21.6 percent; and from supplier D, 28.8 percent.

If the firm needs short-term funds, which it can borrow from its bank at an interest rate of 13 percent, and if each of the suppliers is viewed *separately*, which (if any) of the suppliers' cash discounts will the firm give up? In dealing with supplier A, the firm takes the cash discount, because the cost of giving it up is 36 percent, and then borrows the funds it requires from its bank at 13 percent interest. With supplier B, the firm would do better to give up the cash discount because the cost of this action is less than the cost of borrowing money from the bank (8 percent versus 13 percent). With supplier C and supplier D, the firm should take the cash discount because in both cases the cost of giving up the discount is greater than the 13 percent cost of borrowing from the bank. ▲

The example shows that the cost of giving up a cash discount is relevant when evaluating a single supplier's credit terms in light of certain *bank borrowing costs*. It is important to note that some firms, particularly small firms and poorly managed firms, routinely give up *all* discounts because either they lack alternative sources of unsecured short-term financing or they fail to recognize the high implicit costs of their actions.

TABLE 15.5	Cash Discounts and Associated Costs for Omst Products	
Supplier	Credit terms	Approximate cost of giving up a cash discount
A	2/10 net 30 EOM	36.0%
B	1/10 net 55 EOM	8.0
C	3/20 net 70 EOM	21.6
D	4/10 net 60 EOM	28.8

stretching accounts payable
Paying bills as late as possible without damaging the firm's credit rating.

EFFECTS OF STRETCHING ACCOUNTS PAYABLE

A strategy that is often employed by a firm is **stretching accounts payable**—that is, paying bills as late as possible without damaging its credit rating. Such a strategy can reduce the cost of giving up a cash discount.

Example ▼ Presti Corporation was extended credit terms of 2/10 net 30 EOM. The cost of giving up the cash discount, assuming payment on the last day of the credit period, was found to be approximately 36 percent [2% × (360 ÷ 20)]. If the firm were able to stretch its account payable to 70 days without damaging its credit rating, the cost of giving up the cash discount would be only 12 percent [2% × (360 ÷ 60)].
▲ Stretching accounts payable reduces the implicit cost of giving up a cash discount.

Although stretching accounts payable is financially attractive, this strategy raises an important ethical issue: It may cause the firm to violate the agreement it entered into with its supplier when it purchased merchandise. Clearly, a supplier would not look kindly on a customer who regularly and purposely postponed paying for purchases.

ACCRUALS

accruals
Liabilities for services received for which payment has yet to be made.

The second spontaneous source of short-term business financing is accruals. **Accruals** are liabilities for services received for which payment has yet to be made. The most common items accrued by a firm are wages and taxes. Because taxes are payments to the government, their accrual cannot be manipulated by the firm. However, the accrual of wages can be manipulated to some extent. This is accomplished by delaying payment of wages, thereby receiving an interest-free loan from employees who are paid sometime after they have performed the work. The pay period for employees who earn an hourly rate is often governed by union regulations or by state or federal law. However, in other cases, the frequency of payment is at the discretion of the company's management.

Example ▼ Chan Company, a large janitorial service company, currently pays its employees at the end of each work week. The weekly payroll totals $400,000. If the firm were to extend the pay period so as to pay its employees 1 week later throughout an entire year, the employees would in effect be loaning the firm $400,000 for a year. If the firm could earn 10 percent annually on invested funds, such a strategy would be worth $40,000 per year (.10 × $400,000). By delaying payment of
▲ accruals in this way, the firm could save this amount of money.

❓ R e v i e w   Q u e s t i o n s

15-5   What are the two key spontaneous sources of short-term financing for a firm? Why are these sources considered *spontaneous,* and how are they related to the firm's sales? Do they normally have a stated cost?
15-6   Is there a cost associated with *taking a cash discount?* Is there any cost associated with *giving up a cash discount?* How is the decision to take a cash discount affected by the firm's cost of borrowing short-term funds?

UNSECURED SOURCES OF SHORT-TERM LOANS

Businesses obtain unsecured short-term loans from two major sources—banks and commercial paper. Unlike the spontaneous sources of unsecured short-term financing, bank loans and commercial paper are negotiated and result from actions taken by the financial manager. Bank loans are more popular because they are available to firms of all sizes; commercial paper tends to be available only to large firms. In addition, international loans can be used to finance international transactions.

BANK LOANS

short-term, self-liquidating loan
An unsecured short-term loan in which the use to which the borrowed money is put provides the mechanism through which the loan is repaid.

Banks are a major source of unsecured short-term loans to businesses. The major type of loan made by banks to businesses is the **short-term, self-liquidating loan.** Self-liquidating loans are intended merely to carry the firm through seasonal peaks in financing needs that are due primarily to buildups of accounts receivable and inventory. As receivables and inventories are converted into cash, the funds needed to retire these loans are generated. In other words, the use to which the borrowed money is put provides the mechanism through which the loan is repaid—hence the term *self-liquidating.* Banks lend unsecured, short-term funds in three basic ways: through single-payment notes, lines of credit, and revolving credit agreements. Before we look at these types of loans, we need to lay some groundwork about loan interest rates.

LOAN INTEREST RATES

The interest rate on a bank loan is typically based on the *prime rate of interest* and can be a fixed or a floating rate. It should be evaluated by using one of two calculations of the effective interest rate. Each of these aspects of loan interest rates is discussed below.

prime rate of interest (prime rate)
The lowest rate of interest charged by the nation's leading banks on business loans to their most important and reliable business borrowers.

Prime Rate of Interest   The **prime rate of interest (prime rate)** is the lowest rate of interest charged by the nation's leading banks on business loans to their most important and reliable business borrowers. The prime rate fluctuates with changing supply-and-demand relationships for short-term funds.[7] Banks generally determine the rate to be charged to various borrowers by adding a premium to the prime rate to adjust it for the borrower's "riskiness." The premium may amount to 4 percent or more, although most unsecured short-term loans carry premiums of less than 2 percent.

fixed-rate loan
A loan with a rate of interest determined at a set increment above the prime rate at which it remains fixed until maturity.

Fixed- and Floating-Rate Loans   Loans can have either fixed or floating interest rates. On a **fixed-rate loan,** the rate of interest is determined at a set increment above the prime rate on the date of the loan and remains unvarying at

---

[7]During the past 25 years the prime rate has varied from a record high of 21.5 percent (December 1980) to a low of 6.0 percent (mid-1992 through early 1994). Since 1995 it has fluctuated in the range of 8 to 9 percent, and in April 1999 was 7.75 percent.

floating-rate loan
A loan with a rate of interest initially set at an increment above the prime rate and allowed to "float," or vary, above prime *as the prime rate varies* until maturity.

that fixed rate until maturity. On a **floating-rate loan,** the increment above the prime rate is initially established, and the rate of interest is allowed to "float," or vary, above prime *as the prime rate varies* until maturity. Generally, the increment above the prime rate on a floating-rate loan will be *lower* than on a fixed-rate loan of equivalent risk because the lender bears less risk with a floating-rate loan. The sometimes volatile nature of the prime rate, coupled with the widespread use of computers by banks to monitor and calculate loan interest, has been responsible for the popularity of floating-rate loans.

Method of Computing Interest   Once the *nominal (or stated) annual rate* is established, the method of computing interest is determined. Interest can be paid either when a loan matures or in advance. If interest is paid at *maturity*, the *effective (or true) annual rate*—the actual rate of interest paid—for an assumed 1-year period[8] is equal to

$$\frac{\text{Interest}}{\text{Amount borrowed}} \qquad (15.3)$$

Most bank loans to businesses require the interest payment at maturity.

When interest is paid *in advance*, it is deducted from the loan so that the borrower actually receives less money than is requested. Loans on which interest is paid in advance are called **discount loans.** The *effective annual rate for a discount loan*, assuming a 1-year period, is calculated as

discount loans
Loans on which interest is paid in advance by deducting it from the amount borrowed.

$$\frac{\text{Interest}}{\text{Amount borrowed} - \text{interest}} \qquad (15.4)$$

Paying interest in advance raises the effective annual rate above the stated annual rate. Let us look at an example.

Example ▼   Booster Company, a manufacturer of athletic apparel, wants to borrow $10,000 at a stated annual rate of 10 percent interest for 1 year. If the interest on the loan is paid at maturity, the firm will pay $1,000 (.10 × $10,000) for the use of the $10,000 for the year. Substituting into Equation 15.3, the effective annual rate is therefore

$$\frac{\$1,000}{\$10,000} = 10.0 \text{ percent}$$

If the money is borrowed at the same *stated* annual rate for 1 year but interest is paid in advance, the firm still pays $1,000 in interest, but it receives only $9,000 ($10,000 − $1,000). Thus, the effective annual rate in this case is

$$\frac{\$1,000}{\$10,000 - \$1,000} = \frac{\$1,000}{\$9,000} = 11.1 \text{ percent}$$

Paying interest in advance thus makes the effective annual rate (11.1 percent) ▲ greater than the stated annual rate (10.0 percent).

---

[8]Effective annual rates (EARs) for loans with maturities of less than 1 year can be found by using the technique presented in Chapter 6 for finding EARs when interest is compounded more frequently than annually. See Equation 6.10 on page 163.

SINGLE-PAYMENT NOTES

A **single-payment note** can be obtained from a commercial bank by a creditworthy business borrower. This type of loan is usually a "one-shot" deal made when a borrower needs funds for a short period. The resulting instrument is a *note*, which must be signed by the borrower. The note states the terms of the loan, which include the length of the loan and the interest rate. This type of short-term note generally has a maturity of 30 days to 9 months or more. The interest charged is generally tied in some way to the prime rate of interest, and may be either a fixed or a floating rate. Let us look at an example.

Example ▼ Golden Manufacturing, a producer of rotary mower blades, recently borrowed $100,000 from each of two banks—bank A and bank B. The loans were incurred on the same day, when the prime rate of interest was 9 percent. Each loan involved a 90-day note with interest to be paid at the end of 90 days. The interest rate was set at 1½ percent above the prime rate on bank A's fixed-rate note. Over the 90-day period, the rate of interest on this note will remain at 10½ percent (9% prime rate + 1½% increment) regardless of fluctuations in the prime rate. The total interest cost on this loan is $2,625 [$100,000 × (10½% × 90/360)]. The effective annual rate on this 90-day loan is 2.625 percent ($2,625/$100,000).

Assuming that the loan from bank A is rolled over each 90 days throughout the year under the same terms and circumstances, its effective *annual* rate is found by using Equation 6.10. Because the loan costs 2.625 percent for 90 days, it is necessary to compound (1 + 0.02625) for four periods in the year (i.e., 360/90) and then subtract 1:

$$\text{Effective annual rate} = (1 + 0.02625)^4 - 1$$
$$= 1.1092 - 1 = 0.1092 = \underline{\underline{10.92\%}}$$

The effective annual rate of interest on the fixed-rate, 90-day note is 10.92 percent.

Bank B set the interest rate at 1 percent above the prime rate on its floating-rate note. The rate charged over the 90 days will vary directly *with* the prime rate. Initially, the rate will be 10 percent (9% + 1%), but when the prime rate changes, so will the rate of interest on the note. For instance, if after 30 days, the prime rate rises to 9.5 percent, and after another 30 days, it drops to 9.25 percent, the firm would be paying .833 percent for the first 30 days (10% × 30/360), .875 percent for the next 30 days (10.5% × 30/360), and .854 percent for the last 30 days (10.25% × 30/360). Its total interest cost would be $2,562 [$100,000 × (.833% + .875% + .854%)] resulting in an effective 90-day rate of 2.562 percent ($2,562/$100,000). Again assuming the loan is rolled over each 90 days throughout the year under the same terms and circumstances, its effective annual rate is:

$$\text{Effective annual rate} = (1 + 0.02562)^4 - 1$$
$$= 1.1065 - 1 = 0.1065 = \underline{\underline{10.65\%}}$$

Clearly, in this case the floating-rate loan would have been less expensive (10.65 percent) than the fixed-rate loan (10.92 percent) due to its generally lower effective interest rate. ▲

LINES OF CREDIT

line of credit
An agreement between a commercial bank and a business specifying the amount of unsecured short-term borrowing the bank will make available to the firm over a given period of time.

A **line of credit** is an agreement between a commercial bank and a business specifying the amount of unsecured short-term borrowing the bank will make available to the firm over a given period of time. It is similar to the agreement under which issuers of bank credit cards, such as MasterCard, Visa, and Discover, extend preapproved credit to cardholders. A line of credit agreement is typically made for a period of 1 year and often places certain constraints on the borrower. It is *not a guaranteed loan* but indicates that if the bank has sufficient funds available, it will allow the borrower to owe it *up to* a certain amount of money. The amount of a line of credit is *the maximum amount the firm can owe the bank* at any point in time.

When applying for a line of credit, the borrower may be required to submit such documents as its cash budget, its pro forma income statement, its pro forma balance sheet, and its recent financial statements. If the bank finds the customer acceptable, the line of credit will be extended. The major attraction of a line of credit from the bank's point of view is that it eliminates the need to examine the creditworthiness of a customer each time it borrows money.

Interest Rates   The interest rate on a line of credit is normally stated as a floating rate—the *prime rate plus a percentage.* If the prime rate changes, the interest rate charged on new as well as outstanding borrowing automatically changes. The amount a borrower is charged in excess of the prime rate depends on its creditworthiness. The more creditworthy the borrower, the lower the interest increment above prime, and vice versa.

operating change restrictions
Contractual restrictions that a bank may impose on a firm's financial condition or operations as part of a line of credit agreement.

Operating Change Restrictions   In a line of credit agreement, a bank may impose **operating change restrictions,** which give it the right to revoke the line if any major changes occur in the firm's financial condition or operations. The firm is usually required to submit for periodic review up-to-date and, preferably, audited financial statements. In addition, the bank typically needs to be informed of shifts in key managerial personnel or in the firm's operations prior to changes taking place. Such changes may affect the future success and debt-paying ability of the firm and thus could alter its credit status. If the bank does not agree with the proposed changes and the firm makes them anyway, the bank has the right to revoke the line of credit.

compensating balance
A required checking account balance equal to a certain percentage of the amount borrowed from a bank under a line of credit or revolving credit agreement.

Compensating Balances   To ensure that the borrower will be a good customer, many short-term unsecured bank loans—lines of credit and revolving credit agreements—often require the borrower to maintain a **compensating balance** in a checking account equal to a certain percentage of the amount borrowed. Compensating balances of 10 to 20 percent are frequently required. A compensating balance not only forces the borrower to be a good customer of the bank, but may also raise the interest cost to the borrower. An example illustrates this arrangement.

Example ▼   Exact Graphics, a graphic design firm, has borrowed $1 million under a line of credit agreement. It must pay a stated interest rate of 10 percent and maintain in its checking account a compensating balance equal to 20 percent of the amount borrowed, or $200,000. Thus, it actually receives the use of only $800,000. To use that amount for a year, the firm pays interest of $100,000 (.10 × $1,000,000). The effective annual rate on the funds is therefore 12.5 percent ($100,000 ÷ $800,000), 2.5 percent more than the stated rate of 10 percent.

If the firm normally maintains a balance of $200,000 or more in its checking account, the effective annual rate equals the stated annual rate of 10 percent because none of the $1 million borrowed is needed to satisfy the compensating balance requirement. If the firm normally maintains a $100,000 balance in its checking account, only an additional $100,000 will have to be tied up, leaving it with $900,000 ($1,000,000 − $100,000) of usable funds. The effective annual rate in this case would be 11.1 percent ($100,000 ÷ $900,000). Thus, a compensating balance raises the cost of borrowing *only if* it is larger than the firm's normal cash balance.

Annual Cleanups To ensure that money lent under a line of credit agreement is actually being used to finance seasonal needs, many banks require an **annual cleanup.** This means that the borrower must have a loan balance of zero—that is, owe the bank nothing—for a certain number of days during the year. Forcing the borrower to carry a zero loan balance for a certain period ensures that short-term loans do not turn into long-term loans.

annual cleanup
The requirement that for a certain number of days during the year borrowers under a line of credit carry a zero loan balance (i.e., owe the bank nothing).

All the characteristics of a line of credit agreement are negotiable to some extent. Today, banks bid competitively to attract large, well-known firms. A prospective borrower should attempt to negotiate a line of credit with the most favorable interest rate, for an optimal amount of funds, and with a minimum of restrictions. Borrowers today frequently pay fees to lenders instead of maintaining deposit balances as compensation for loans and other services. The lender attempts to get a good return with maximum safety. These negotiations should produce a line of credit that is suitable to both borrower and lender.

REVOLVING CREDIT AGREEMENTS

revolving credit agreement
A line of credit *guaranteed* to a borrower by a bank for a stated period regardless of the scarcity of money.

A **revolving credit agreement** is nothing more than a *guaranteed line of credit*. It is guaranteed in the sense that the commercial bank assures the borrower that a specified amount of funds will be made available regardless of the scarcity of money. The interest rate and other requirements are similar to those for a line of credit. It is not uncommon for a revolving credit agreement to be for a period greater than 1 year. Because the bank guarantees the availability of funds, a **commitment fee** is normally charged on a revolving credit agreement. This fee often applies to the average unused balance of the credit line. It is normally about .5 percent of the *average unused portion* of the funds. An example will clarify the nature of the commitment fees.

commitment fee
The fee that is normally charged on a *revolving credit agreement;* it often applies to the average unused balance of the borrower's credit line.

Example ▼ Blount Company, a major real estate developer, has a $2 million revolving credit agreement with its bank. Its average borrowing under the agreement for the past year was $1.5 million. The bank charges a commitment fee of .5 percent. Because the average unused portion of the committed funds was $500,000 ($2 million − $1.5 million), the commitment fee for the year was $2,500 (.005 × $500,000). Of course, Blount also had to pay interest on the actual $1.5 million borrowed under the agreement. Assuming that $160,000 interest was paid on the $1.5 million borrowed, the effective cost of the agreement is 10.83 percent [($160,000 + $2,500)/$1,500,000]. Although more expensive than a line of credit, a revolving credit agreement can be less risky from the borrower's viewpoint, because the availability of funds is guaranteed by the bank.

ⓟERSONAL FINANCE PERSPECTIVE
Choosing the Best Credit Card Pays Off

A personal line of credit comes in handy for emergencies or large purchases when you don't have enough cash on hand. A bank credit card like MasterCard or Visa provides an easy way to get your own credit line. Before you choose a card, consider the card's fees and interest rate in light of your spending habits and financial requirements. The right card can save you money. If you never carry a balance, your best bet is a no-fee card; the interest rate doesn't matter much. When you carry balances, a card with an annual fee may have a lower interest rate than those without such a fee. Watch out for penalty rates for late payments. And although rebate or airline mileage cards sound great, you need to charge a lot before you get any benefits. If you carry large balances, interest charges will wipe out any gains.

Finally, don't be tempted to accumulate too many cards, no matter how great the rates; it's easy to overspend. Instead, transfer balances to the new lower-rate card and then cancel the old ones. ●

COMMERCIAL PAPER

commercial paper
A form of financing consisting of short-term, unsecured promissory notes issued by firms with a high credit standing.

Commercial paper is a form of financing that consists of short-term, unsecured promissory notes issued by firms with a high credit standing. Generally, only quite large firms of unquestionable financial soundness are able to issue commercial paper. Most commercial paper has maturities ranging from 3 to 270 days. Although there is no set denomination, it is generally issued in multiples of $100,000 or more. A large portion of the commercial paper today is issued by finance companies; manufacturing firms account for a smaller portion of this type of financing. Businesses often purchase commercial paper, which they hold as marketable securities, to provide an interest-earning reserve of liquidity.

INTEREST ON COMMERCIAL PAPER

Commercial paper is sold at a discount from its *par*, or *face, value*. The interest paid by the issuer of commercial paper is determined by the size of the discount and the length of time to maturity. The actual interest earned by the purchaser is determined by certain calculations, as illustrated by the following example.

Example ▼ Deems Corporation, a large shipbuilder, has just issued $1 million worth of commercial paper that has a 90-day maturity and sells for $980,000. At the end of 90 days, the purchaser of this paper will receive $1 million for its $980,000 investment. The interest paid on the financing is therefore $20,000 on a principal of $980,000. The effective 90-day rate on the paper is 2.04 percent ($20,000/$980,000).

Assuming the paper is rolled over each 90 days throughout the year, the effective annual rate for Deems Corporation's commercial paper, found by using Equation 6.10, is 8.41 percent $[(1 + 0.0204)^4 - 1]$.

An interesting characteristic of commercial paper is that it *normally* has a yield of 2 to 4 percent below the prime rate. In other words, firms are able to raise funds more cheaply through the sale of commercial paper than by borrowing from a commercial bank. The reason is that many suppliers of short-term funds do not have the option, as banks do, of making low-risk business loans at the prime rate. They can invest only in marketable securities such as Treasury bills and commercial paper. The yields on these marketable securities on January 22, 1999, when the prime rate of interest was 7.75 percent, were about 4.3 percent for 3-month Treasury bills and about 4.9 percent for 3-month commercial paper.

Although the stated interest cost of borrowing through the sale of commercial paper is normally lower than the prime rate, the *overall cost* of commercial paper may not be cheaper than a bank loan. Additional costs include the fees paid by most issuers to obtain the bank line of credit used to back the paper, fees paid to obtain third-party ratings used to make the paper more salable, and flotation costs. In addition, even if it is slightly more expensive to borrow from a commercial bank, it may at times be advisable to do so to establish a good working relationship with the bank. This strategy ensures that when money is tight, funds can be obtained promptly and at a reasonable interest rate.

SALE OF COMMERCIAL PAPER

Commercial paper is *directly placed with investors* by the issuer or is *sold by commercial paper dealers*. Regardless of the method of sale, most commercial paper is purchased by other businesses, banks, life insurance companies, pension funds, and money market mutual funds.

INTERNATIONAL LOANS

In some ways, arranging short-term financing for international trade is no different from financing purely domestic operations. In both cases, producers must finance the production and storage of goods for sale and then continue to finance accounts receivable before collecting any cash payments from sales. In other ways, however, the short-term financing of international sales and purchases is fundamentally different from strictly domestic trade.

INTERNATIONAL TRANSACTIONS

The important difference between international and domestic transactions is that payments are often made or received in a foreign currency. Not only must a U.S. company pay the costs of doing business in the foreign exchange market, but it also is exposed to *exchange rate risk*. A U.S.-based company that exports goods and has accounts receivable denominated in a foreign currency faces the risk that the U.S. dollar will appreciate in value relative to the foreign currency. The risk to a U.S. importer with foreign-currency-denominated accounts payable is that the dollar will depreciate. Typical international transactions are large in size and have long maturity dates. Therefore, companies that are involved in international trade generally have to finance larger dollar amounts for longer time periods than companies who operate domestically.

FINANCING INTERNATIONAL TRADE

letter of credit
A letter written by a company's bank to the company's foreign supplier, stating that the bank guarantees payment of an invoiced amount if all the underlying agreements are met.

Several specialized techniques have evolved for financing international trade. Perhaps the most important financing vehicle is the **letter of credit,** a letter written by a company's bank to the company's foreign supplier, stating that the bank guarantees payment of an invoiced amount if all the underlying agreements are met. The letter of credit essentially substitutes the bank's reputation and creditworthiness for that of its commercial customer, increasing the likelihood that foreign suppliers will sell to a U.S. importer. Likewise, a U.S. exporter is more willing to sell goods to a foreign buyer if the transaction is covered by a letter of credit issued by a well-known bank in the buyer's home country.

Firms that do business in foreign countries on an ongoing basis often finance their operations, at least in part, in the local market. A company that has an assembly plant in Mexico, for example, might choose to finance its purchases of Mexican goods and services with peso funds borrowed from a Mexican bank. This not only minimizes exchange rate risk, but also improves the company's business ties to the host community. Multinational companies, however, sometimes finance their international transactions through dollar-denominated loans from international banks. The *Eurocurrency loan markets* allow creditworthy borrowers to obtain financing on very attractive terms.

TRANSACTIONS BETWEEN SUBSIDIARIES

Much international trade involves transactions between corporate subsidiaries. A U.S. company might, for example, manufacture one part in an Asian plant and another part in the United States, assemble the product in Brazil, and sell it in Europe. The shipment of goods back and forth between subsidiaries creates accounts receivable and accounts payable, but the parent company has considerable discretion about how and when payments are made. In particular, the parent can minimize foreign exchange fees and other transaction costs by "netting" what affiliates owe each other and paying only the net amount due, rather than having both subsidiaries pay each other the gross amounts due.

? R e v i e w   Q u e s t i o n s

15-7   What is the *prime rate of interest,* and how is it relevant to the cost of short-term bank borrowing? What is a *floating-rate loan?* How does the *effective annual rate* differ between a loan requiring interest payments *at maturity* and another similar loan requiring interest *in advance?*

15-8   What are the basic terms and characteristics of a *single-payment note?* How is the *effective annual rate* on such a note found?

15-9   What is a *line of credit?* Describe each of the following features that are often included in these agreements: (**a**) operating change restrictions; (**b**) compensating balance; and (**c**) annual cleanup.

15-10   What is a *revolving credit agreement?* How does this arrangement differ from the line of credit agreement? What is a *commitment fee?*

15-11   How is *commercial paper* used to raise short-term funds? Who can issue commercial paper? Who buys commercial paper?

15-12   What is the important difference between international and domestic transactions? How is a *letter of credit* used in financing international trade transactions? How is "netting" used in transactions between subsidiaries?

SECURED SOURCES OF SHORT-TERM LOANS

secured short-term financing
Short-term financing (loans) obtained by pledging specific assets as collateral.

security agreement
The agreement between the borrower and the lender that specifies the collateral held against a secured loan.

When a firm has exhausted its unsecured sources of short-term financing, it may be able to obtain additional short-term loans on a secured basis. **Secured short-term financing** has specific assets pledged as collateral. The *collateral* commonly takes the form of an asset, such as accounts receivable or inventory. The lender obtains a security interest in the collateral through the execution of a **security agreement** with the borrower that specifies the collateral held against the loan. In addition, the terms of the loan against which the security is held form part of the security agreement. They specify the conditions required for the security interest to be removed, along with the interest rate on the loan, repayment dates, and other loan provisions. A copy of the security agreement is filed in a public office within the state—typically, a county or state court. Filing provides subsequent lenders with information about which assets of a prospective borrower are unavailable for use as collateral. The filing requirement protects the lender by legally establishing the lender's security interest.

CHARACTERISTICS OF SECURED SHORT-TERM LOANS

Although many people believe that holding collateral as security reduces the risk of a loan, lenders do not usually view loans in this way. Lenders recognize that holding collateral can reduce losses if the borrower defaults, but *the presence of collateral has no impact on the risk of default.* A lender requires collateral to ensure recovery of some portion of the loan in the event of default. What the lender wants above all, however, is to be repaid as scheduled. In general, lenders prefer to make less risky loans at lower rates of interest than to be in a position in which they must liquidate collateral.

COLLATERAL AND TERMS

Lenders of secured short-term funds prefer collateral that has a life, or duration, that is closely matched to the term of the loan. Current assets—accounts receivable and inventories—are the most desirable short-term loan collateral, because they normally convert into cash much sooner than do fixed assets. Thus, the short-term lender of secured funds generally accepts only liquid current assets as collateral.

percentage advance
The percent of the book value of the collateral that constitutes the principal of a secured loan.

Typically, the lender determines the desirable **percentage advance** to make against the collateral. This percentage advance constitutes the principal of the secured loan and is normally between 30 and 100 percent of the book value of the collateral. It varies according to the type and liquidity of collateral.

The interest rate that is charged on secured short-term loans is typically *higher* than the rate on unsecured short-term loans. Commercial banks and other institutions do not normally consider secured loans less risky than unsecured loans. In addition, negotiating and administering secured loans is more troublesome for the lender than negotiating and administering unsecured loans. The lender therefore normally requires added compensation in the form of a service charge, a higher interest rate, or both. (Remember that firms typically borrow on a secured basis only after exhausting less costly unsecured sources of short-term funds.)

INSTITUTIONS EXTENDING SECURED SHORT-TERM LOANS

The primary sources of secured short-term loans to businesses are commercial banks and commercial finance companies. Both institutions deal in short-term loans secured primarily by accounts receivable and inventory. The operations of commercial banks have already been described. **Commercial finance companies** are lending institutions that make *only* secured loans—both short-term and long-term—to businesses. Unlike banks, finance companies are not permitted to hold deposits.

Only when its unsecured and secured short-term borrowing power from the commercial bank is exhausted will a borrower turn to a commercial finance company for additional secured borrowing. Because the finance company generally ends up with higher-risk borrowers, its interest charges on secured short-term loans are usually higher than those of commercial banks. The leading U.S. commercial finance companies include the CIT Group and GE Capital.

commercial finance companies
Lending institutions that make *only* secured loans—both short-term and long-term—to businesses.

THE USE OF ACCOUNTS RECEIVABLE AS COLLATERAL

Two commonly used means of obtaining short-term financing with accounts receivable are pledging accounts receivable and factoring accounts receivable. Actually, only a pledge of accounts receivable creates a secured short-term loan; factoring really entails the *sale* of accounts receivable at a discount. Although factoring is not actually a form of secured short-term borrowing, it does involve the use of accounts receivable to obtain needed short-term funds.

PLEDGING ACCOUNTS RECEIVABLE

A **pledge of accounts receivable** is often used to secure a short-term loan. Because accounts receivable are normally quite liquid, they are an attractive form of short-term loan collateral. Both commercial banks and commercial finance companies extend loans against pledges of accounts receivable.

When a firm requests a loan against accounts receivable, the lender first evaluates the firm's accounts receivable to determine their desirability as collateral. Next, the dollar value of the acceptable accounts is adjusted by the lender for expected returns on sales and other allowances. Then, the percentage to be advanced against the adjusted collateral is determined by the lender, based on its evaluation of the quality of the acceptable receivables and the expected cost of their liquidation. This percentage represents the principal of the loan. It typically

pledge of accounts receivable
The use of a firm's accounts receivable as security, or collateral, to obtain a short-term loan.

lien
A publicly disclosed legal claim on collateral.

nonnotification basis
The basis on which a borrower, having pledged an account receivable, continues to collect the account payments without notifying the account customer.

notification basis
The basis on which an account customer whose account has been pledged (or factored) is notified to remit payment directly to the lender (or factor).

factoring accounts receivable
The outright sale of accounts receivable at a discount to a *factor* or other financial institution.

factor
A financial institution that specializes in purchasing accounts receivable from businesses.

nonrecourse basis
The basis on which accounts receivable are sold to a factor with the understanding that the factor accepts all credit risks on the purchased account.

ranges between 50 and 90 percent of the face value of acceptable accounts receivable. Finally, to protect its interest in the collateral the lender files a **lien,** which is a publicly disclosed legal claim on the collateral.

Pledges of accounts receivable are normally made on a **nonnotification basis.** This means that a customer whose account has been pledged as collateral is not notified of this action. Under the nonnotification arrangement, the borrower still collects the pledged account receivable and the lender trusts the borrower to remit these payments as they are received. If a pledge of accounts receivable is made on a **notification basis,** the customer is notified to remit payment directly to the lender (or factor).

The stated cost of a pledge of accounts receivable is normally 2 to 5 percent above the prime rate. In addition to the stated interest rate, a service charge of up to 3 percent may be levied by the lender to cover its administrative costs. Clearly, pledges of accounts receivable are typically a high-cost source of short-term financing.

FACTORING ACCOUNTS RECEIVABLE

Factoring accounts receivable involves their outright sale at a discount to a financial institution. A **factor** is a financial institution that specializes in purchasing accounts receivable from businesses. Some commercial banks and commercial finance companies also factor accounts receivable. Although not the same as obtaining a short-term loan, factoring accounts receivable is similar to borrowing with accounts receivable as collateral.

A factoring agreement normally states the exact conditions and procedures for the purchase of an account. The factor, like a lender against a pledge of accounts receivable, chooses accounts for purchase, selecting only those that appear to be acceptable credit risks. Factoring is normally done on a *notification basis*, and the factor receives payment of the account directly from the customer. In addition, most sales of accounts receivable to a factor are made on a **nonrecourse basis.** This means that the factor agrees to accept all credit risks. Thus if a purchased account turns out to be uncollectible, the factor must absorb the loss.

Typically, the factor is not required to pay the firm until the account is collected or until the last day of the credit period, whichever occurs first. As payment is received or as due dates arrive, the factor deposits money into the seller's account, from which the seller can make withdrawals as needed. In many cases, if the firm leaves the money in the account, a *surplus* exists on which the factor pays interest. In other instances, the factor may make *advances* to the firm against uncollected accounts that are not yet due. These advances represent a negative balance in the firm's account, on which interest is charged.

Factoring costs include commissions, interest levied on advances, and interest earned on surpluses. The factor deposits in the firm's account the book value of the collected or due accounts purchased by the factor, less the commissions. The commissions are typically stated as a 1 to 3 percent discount from the book value of factored accounts receivable. The *interest levied on advances* is generally 2 to 4 percent above the prime rate. It is levied on the actual amount advanced. The *interest paid on surpluses* is generally around .5 percent per month. Although its cost may seem high, factoring has certain advantages that make it attractive. One is the ability it gives the firm to *turn accounts receivable immediately into cash* without having to worry about repayment. Another advantage is that it ensures a *known pattern of cash inflows*. In addition, if factoring is undertaken on a continuing basis, the firm *can eliminate its credit and collection departments*.

THE USE OF INVENTORY AS COLLATERAL

Inventory is generally second to accounts receivable in desirability as short-term loan collateral. Inventory normally has a market value greater than its book value, which is used to establish its value as collateral. A lender securing a loan with inventory will probably be able to sell it for at least book value if the borrower defaults on its obligations.

The most important characteristic of inventory being evaluated as loan collateral is *marketability*, which must be considered in light of its physical properties. A warehouse of *perishable* items, such as fresh peaches, may be quite marketable, but if the cost of storing and selling the peaches is high, they may not be desirable collateral. *Specialized items*, such as moon-roving vehicles, are not desirable collateral either, because finding a buyer for them could be difficult. When evaluating inventory as possible loan collateral, the lender looks for items with very stable market prices that have ready markets and that lack undesirable physical properties.

FLOATING INVENTORY LIENS

floating inventory lien
A lender's claim on the borrower's general inventory as collateral for a secured loan.

A lender may be willing to secure a loan under a **floating inventory lien,** which is a claim on inventory in general. This arrangement is most attractive when the firm has a stable level of inventory that consists of a diversified group of relatively inexpensive merchandise. Inventories of items such as auto tires, screws and bolts, and shoes are candidates for floating-lien loans. Because it is difficult for a lender to verify the presence of the inventory, the lender will generally advance less than 50 percent of the book value of the average inventory. The interest charge on a floating lien is 3 to 5 percent above the prime rate. Commercial banks often require floating liens as extra security on what would otherwise be an unsecured loan.

TRUST RECEIPT INVENTORY LOANS

trust receipt inventory loan
An agreement under which the lender advances 80 to 100 percent of the cost of the borrower's relatively expensive inventory items in exchange for the borrower's promise to immediately repay the loan, with accrued interest, on the sale of each item.

A **trust receipt inventory loan** often can be made against relatively expensive automotive, consumer durable, and industrial goods that can be identified by serial number. Under this agreement, the borrower keeps the inventory and the lender may advance 80 to 100 percent of its cost. The lender files a *lien* on all the items financed. The borrower is free to sell the merchandise but is trusted to remit the amount lent, along with accrued interest, to the lender immediately after the sale. The lender then releases the lien on the item. The lender makes periodic checks of the borrower's inventory to make sure that the required amount of collateral remains in the hands of the borrower. The interest charge to the borrower is normally 2 percent or more above the prime rate. Trust receipt loans are often made by manufacturers' wholly owned financing subsidiaries, known as *captive finance companies,* to their customers. Trust receipt loans are also available through commercial banks and commercial finance companies.

WAREHOUSE RECEIPT LOANS

warehouse receipt loan
An arrangement in which the lender receives control of the pledged inventory collateral, which is stored by a designated warehousing company on the lender's behalf.

A **warehouse receipt loan** is an arrangement whereby the lender, who may be a commercial bank or commercial finance company, receives control of the pledged inventory collateral, which is stored by a designated agent on the lender's behalf. After selecting acceptable collateral, the lender hires a warehousing company to act as its agent and take possession of the inventory.

Two types of warehousing arrangements are possible: terminal warehouses and field warehouses. A *terminal warehouse* is a central warehouse that is used to store the merchandise of various customers. The lender normally uses such a warehouse when the inventory is easily transported and can be delivered to the warehouse relatively inexpensively. Under a *field warehouse* arrangement, the lender hires a field warehousing company to set up a warehouse on the borrower's premises or to lease part of the borrower's warehouse to store the pledged collateral. Regardless of which type of warehouse is used, the warehousing company places a guard over the inventory. Only on written approval of the lender can any portion of the secured inventory be released.

The actual lending agreement specifically states the requirements for the release of inventory. As in the case of other secured loans, the lender accepts only collateral that is believed to be readily marketable and advances only a portion—generally 75 to 90 percent—of the collateral's value. The specific costs of warehouse receipt loans are generally higher than those of any other secured lending arrangements due to the need to hire and pay a third party (the warehousing company) to guard and supervise the collateral. The basic interest charged on warehouse receipt loans is higher than that charged on unsecured loans, generally ranging from 3 to 5 percent above the prime rate. In addition to the interest charge, the borrower must absorb the costs of warehousing by paying the warehouse fee, which is generally between 1 and 3 percent of the amount of the loan. The borrower is normally also required to pay the insurance costs on the warehoused merchandise.

? Review Questions

15-13 In general, what interest rates and fees are levied on secured short-term loans? Why are these rates generally *higher* than the rates on unsecured short-term loans?

15-14 Describe and compare the basic features of the following methods of using accounts receivable to obtain short-term financing: (a) pledging accounts receivable and (b) factoring accounts receivable. Be sure to mention the institutions offering each of them.

15-15 Describe the basic features and compare each of the following methods of using *inventory* as short-term loan collateral: (a) floating lien; (b) trust receipt loan; and (c) warehouse receipt loan.

SUMMARY

LG1 Understand the two definitions of net working capital and the tradeoff between profitability and risk as it relates to changing levels of current assets and current liabilities. Net working capital is the difference between current assets and current liabilities or, alternatively, the portion of a firm's current assets financed with long-term funds. Profitability is the relationship between revenues and costs. Risk, in the context of short-term financial decisions, is the probability that a firm will become technically insolvent—unable to pay its bills as they come due. By assuming a constant level of total assets, the higher a firm's ratio of current assets to total assets, the less profitable the firm, and the less risky it is. The converse is also true. With constant total assets, the higher a firm's ratio of current liabilities to total assets, the more profitable and more risky the firm is. The converse of this statement is also true.

LG2 **Discuss, in terms of profitability and risk, the aggressive financing strategy and the conservative financing strategy for meeting the firm's total financing requirement.** The aggressive strategy for determining the appropriate financing mix is a high-profit, high-risk strategy under which the firm finances at least its seasonal needs, and possibly some of its permanent needs, with short-term funds and the majority of its permanent needs with long-term funds. The conservative strategy is a low-profit, low-risk strategy under which all funds requirements—both permanent and seasonal—are financed with long-term funds. Short-term funds are saved for emergencies or unexpected outflows.

LG3 **Review the key characteristics of the two major sources of spontaneous short-term financing.** Spontaneous sources of short-term financing include accounts payable, which are the primary source of short-term funds, and accruals. Accounts payable result from credit purchases of merchandise, and accruals result primarily from wage and tax obligations. The key features of these forms of financing are summarized in part I of Table 15.6.

LG4 **Analyze credit terms offered by suppliers to determine whether to take or give up cash discounts and whether to stretch accounts payable.** Credit terms may differ with respect to the credit period, cash discount, cash discount period, and beginning of the credit period. The cost of giving up cash discounts is a factor in deciding whether to take or give up a cash discount. Cash discounts should be given up only when a firm in need of short-term funds must pay an interest rate on borrowing that is greater than the cost of giving up the cash discount.

Stretching accounts payable can lower the cost of giving up a cash discount.

LG5 **Describe the interest rates and basic types of unsecured short-term bank loans, commercial paper, and short-term international loans.** Banks are the major source of unsecured short-term loans to businesses. The interest rate on these loans is tied to the prime rate of interest by a risk premium and may be fixed or floating. It should be evaluated by using the effective annual rate. This rate is calculated differently depending on whether interest is paid when the loan matures or in advance. Bank loans may take the form of a single-payment note, a line of credit, or a revolving credit agreement. Commercial paper is an unsecured IOU issued by firms with high credit standing. The key features of the various types of bank loans as well as commercial paper are summarized in part II of Table 15.6.

International sales and purchases expose firms to exchange rate risk. They are larger and of longer maturity than typical transactions, and can be financed using a letter of credit, by borrowing in the local market, or through dollar-denominated loans from international banks. On transactions between subsidiaries "netting" can be used to minimize foreign exchange fees and other transaction costs.

LG6 **Explain the characteristics of secured short-term loans and the use of accounts receivable and inventory as short-term loan collateral.** Secured short-term loans are those for which the lender requires collateral—typically, current assets such as accounts receivable or inventory. Only a percentage of the book value of acceptable collateral is advanced by the lender. These loans are more expensive than unsecured loans; collateral does not lower the risk of default, and increased administrative costs result. Both commercial banks and commercial finance companies make secured short-term loans. Both pledging, the use of accounts receivable as loan collateral, and factoring, the outright sale of accounts receivable at a discount, involve the use of accounts receivable to obtain needed short-term funds. Inventory can be used as short-term loan collateral under a floating lien, a trust receipt loan, or a warehouse receipt loan. The key features of the popular forms of these loans are summarized in part III of Table 15.6.

TABLE 15.6 Summary of Key Features of Common Sources of Short-Term Financing

Type of short-term financing	Source	Cost or conditions	Characteristics
I. Spontaneous sources of short-term financing			
Accounts payable	Suppliers of merchandise	No stated cost except when a cash discount is offered for early payment.	Credit extended on open account for 0 to 120 days. The largest source of short-term financing.
Accruals	Employees and government	Free.	Result because wages (employees) and taxes (government) are paid at discrete points in time after the service has been rendered. Hard to manipulate this source of financing.
II. Unsecured sources of short-term loans			
Bank sources			
(1) Single-payment notes	Commercial banks	Prime plus 0% to 4% risk premium—fixed or floating rate.	A single-payment loan used to meet a funds shortage expected to last only a short period of time.
(2) Lines of credit	Commercial banks	Prime plus 0% to 4% risk premium—fixed or floating rate. Often must maintain 10% to 20% compensating balance and clean up the line.	A prearranged borrowing limit under which funds, if available, will be lent to allow the borrower to meet seasonal needs.
(3) Revolving credit agreements	Commercial banks	Prime plus 0% to 4% risk premium—fixed or floating rate. Often must maintain 10% to 20% compensating balance and pay a commitment fee of approximately .5% of the average unused balance.	A line of credit agreement under which the availability of funds is guaranteed. Often for a period greater than 1 year.
Commercial paper	Other businesses, banks, life insurance companies, pension funds, and money market mutual funds	Generally 2% to 4% below the prime rate of interest.	An unsecured short-term promissory note issued by the most financially sound firms. May be placed directly or sold through commercial paper dealers.

(continued)

TABLE 15.6 *(continued)*

Type of short-term financing	Source	Cost or conditions	Characteristics
III. Secured sources of short-term loans			
Accounts receivable collateral			
(1) Pledging	Commercial banks and commercial finance companies	2% to 5% above prime plus up to 3% in fees. Advance 50% to 90% of collateral value.	Selected accounts receivable are used as collateral. The borrower is trusted to remit to the lender on collection of pledged accounts. Done on a non-notification basis.
(2) Factoring	Factors, commercial banks, and commercial finance companies	1% to 3% discount from face value of factored accounts. Interest levied on advances of 2% to 4% above prime. Interest earned on surplus balances left with factor of about .5% per month.	Selected accounts are sold—generally without recourse—at a discount. All credit risks go with the accounts. Factor will also pay loan (make advances) against uncollected accounts that are not yet due. Factor will also pay interest on surplus balances. Typically done on a notification basis.
Inventory collateral			
(1) Floating liens	Commercial banks and commercial finance companies	3% to 5% above prime. Advance less than 50% of collateral value.	A loan against inventory in general. Made when firm has stable inventory of a variety of inexpensive items.
(2) Trust receipts	Manufacturers' captive financing subsidiaries, commercial banks, and commercial finance companies	2% or more above prime. Advance 80% to 100% of cost of collateral.	Loan against large and relatively expensive goods that can be identified by serial number. Collateral remains in possession of borrower, who is trusted to remit proceeds to lender upon its sale.
(3) Warehouse receipts	Commercial banks and commercial finance companies	3% to 5% above prime plus a 1% to 3% warehouse fee. Advance 75% to 90% of collateral value.	Inventory used as collateral is placed under control of the lender by putting it in a terminal warehouse or through a field warehouse. A third party—a warehousing company—guards the inventory for the lender. Inventory is released only on written approval of the lender.

SELF-TEST PROBLEMS (Solutions in Appendix B)

 ST 15-1 **Aggressive versus conservative financing strategy** Santo Gas has forecast its total funds requirements for the coming year as shown in the following table.

Month	Amount	Month	Amount
January	$7,400,000	July	$5,800,000
February	5,500,000	August	5,400,000
March	5,000,000	September	5,000,000
April	5,300,000	October	5,300,000
May	6,200,000	November	6,000,000
June	6,000,000	December	6,800,000

a. Divide the firm's monthly funds requirement into a *permanent* and a *seasonal* component, and find the monthly average for each of these components.
b. Describe the amount of long-term and short-term financing that is used to meet the total funds requirement under (1) an *aggressive financing strategy* and (2) a *conservative financing strategy*. Assume that under the aggressive strategy, long-term funds finance permanent needs and short-term funds are used to finance seasonal needs.
c. Assuming short-term funds cost 10 percent annually and long-term funds cost 16 percent annually, use the averages in **a** to calculate the total cost of each of the strategies described in **b**.
d. Discuss the profitability–risk tradeoffs associated with the aggressive strategy and the conservative strategy.

 ST 15-2 **Cash discount decisions** The credit terms for each of three suppliers are shown in the following table.

Supplier	Credit terms
X	1/10 net 55 EOM
Y	2/10 net 30 EOM
Z	2/20 net 60 EOM

a. Determine the *approximate* cost of giving up the cash discount from each supplier.
b. Assuming that the firm needs short-term financing, recommend whether it would be better to give up the cash discount or take the discount and borrow from a bank at 15 percent annual interest. Evaluate each supplier separately using your findings in **a**.
c. What impact, if any, would the fact that the firm could stretch its accounts payable (net period only) by 20 days from supplier Z have on your answer in **b** relative to this supplier?

PROBLEMS

 15-1 **Permanent versus seasonal funds requirements**   Mintex Corporation's current, fixed, and total assets for each month of the coming year are summarized in the following table.

Month	Current assets (1)	Fixed assets (2)	Total assets [(1) + (2)] (3)
January	$15,000	$30,000	$45,000
February	22,000	30,000	52,000
March	30,000	30,000	60,000
April	18,000	30,000	48,000
May	10,000	30,000	40,000
June	6,000	30,000	36,000
July	9,000	30,000	39,000
August	9,000	30,000	39,000
September	15,000	30,000	45,000
October	20,000	30,000	50,000
November	22,000	30,000	52,000
December	20,000	30,000	50,000

a. Divide the firm's monthly total funds requirement (total assets) into a *permanent* and a *seasonal* component.
b. Find the monthly average (1) permanent and (2) seasonal funds requirements using your findings in **a.**

 15-2 **Annual loan cost**   What are the average loan balance and the annual loan cost, given an annual interest rate on loans of 15 percent, for a firm with the total monthly borrowings shown in the following table?

Month	Amount	Month	Amount
January	$12,000	July	$6,000
February	13,000	August	5,000
March	9,000	September	6,000
April	8,000	October	5,000
May	9,000	November	7,000
June	7,000	December	9,000

 15-3 **Aggressive versus conservative financing strategy**   Dynabase Tool has forecast its total funds requirements for the coming year as shown in the following table.

Month	Amount	Month	Amount
January	$2,000,000	July	$12,000,000
February	2,000,000	August	14,000,000
March	2,000,000	September	9,000,000
April	4,000,000	October	5,000,000
May	6,000,000	November	4,000,000
June	9,000,000	December	3,000,000

a. Divide the firm's monthly funds requirement into (1) a *permanent* and (2) a *seasonal* component, and find the monthly average for each of these components.

b. Describe the amount of long-term and short-term financing used to meet the total funds requirement under (1) an *aggressive financing strategy* and (2) a *conservative financing strategy*. Assume that under the aggressive strategy, long-term funds finance permanent needs and short-term funds are used to finance seasonal needs.

c. Assuming that short-term funds cost 12 percent annually and the cost of long-term funds is 17 percent annually, use the averages found in **a** to calculate the total cost of each of the strategies described in **b**.

d. Discuss the profitability–risk tradeoffs associated with the aggressive strategy and the conservative strategy.

INTERMEDIATE   **LG2**   15-4   Aggressive versus conservative financing strategy   Marbell International has forecast its seasonal financing needs for the next year as shown in the table below. Assuming that the firm's permanent funds requirement is $4 million, calculate the total annual financing costs using an *aggressive financing strategy* and a *conservative financing strategy*. Recommend one of the strategies under each of the following conditions:

a. Short-term funds cost 9 percent annually, and long-term funds cost 15 percent annually.

b. Short-term funds cost 10 percent annually, and long-term funds cost 13 percent annually.

c. Both short-term and long-term funds cost 11 percent annually.

Month	Seasonal requirement	Month	Seasonal requirement
January	$ 0	July	$700,000
February	300,000	August	400,000
March	500,000	September	0
April	900,000	October	200,000
May	1,200,000	November	700,000
June	1,000,000	December	300,000

WARM-UP   **LG3**   15-5   Payment dates   Determine when a firm must make payment for purchases made and invoices dated on November 25 under each of the following credit terms.

a. net 30 date of invoice

b. net 30 EOM
c. net 45 date of invoice
d. net 60 EOM

WARM-UP **15-6   Cost of giving up cash discounts**   Determine the cost of giving up cash discounts under each of the following terms of sale.
  a. 2/10 net 30
  b. 1/10 net 30
  c. 2/10 net 45
  d. 3/10 net 45
  e. 1/10 net 60
  f. 3/10 net 30
  g. 4/10 net 180

WARM-UP **15-7   Cash discount versus loan**   Ann Daniels works in an accounts payable department. She has attempted to convince her boss to take the discount on the 3/10 net 45 credit terms most suppliers offer, but her boss argues that giving up the 3 percent discount is less costly than a short-term loan at 14 percent. Prove that either Ann or her boss is incorrect.

INTERMEDIATE **15-8   Cash discount decisions**   Lenly Manufacturing has four possible suppliers, each offering different credit terms. Except for the differences in credit terms, their products and services are virtually identical. The credit terms offered by each supplier are shown in the following table.

Supplier	Credit terms
Q	1/10 net 30 EOM
R	2/20 net 80 EOM
S	1/20 net 60 EOM
T	3/10 net 55 EOM

  a. Calculate the *approximate* cost of giving up the cash discount from each supplier.
  b. If the firm needs short-term funds, which are currently available from its commercial bank at 16 percent, and if each of the suppliers is viewed *separately*, which, if any, of the suppliers' cash discounts should the firm give up? Explain why.
  c. What impact, if any, would the fact that the firm could stretch its accounts payable (net period only) by 30 days from supplier T have on your answer in b relative to this supplier?

WARM-UP **15-9   Changing payment cycle**   Upon accepting the position of chief executive officer and chairman of Reeves Cash Register, David Stanley changed the firm's weekly payday from Monday afternoon to the following Friday afternoon. The firm's weekly payroll was $10 million, and the cost of short-term funds was 13 percent. If the effect of this change was to delay check clearing by 1 week, what *annual* savings, if any, were realized?

15-10 Cost of bank loan Quick Enterprises has obtained a $10,000, 90-day bank loan at an annual interest rate of 15 percent, payable at maturity. (*Note:* Assume a 360-day year.)

INTERMEDIATE

a. How much interest (in dollars) will the firm pay on the 90-day loan?
b. Find the effective 90-day rate on the loan.
c. Annualize your finding in **b** to find the effective annual rate for this loan, assuming that it is rolled over each 90 days throughout the year under the same terms and circumstances.

WARM-UP

15-11 Effective annual rate A financial institution made a $10,000, 1-year discount loan at 10 percent interest, requiring a compensating balance equal to 20 percent of the face value of the loan. Determine the effective annual rate associated with this loan.

INTERMEDIATE

15-12 Compensating balances and effective annual rates LH has a line of credit at First Bank that requires it to pay 11 percent interest on its borrowing and maintain a compensating balance equal to 15 percent of the amount borrowed. The firm has borrowed $800,000 during the year under the agreement. Calculate the effective annual rate on the firm's borrowing in each of the following circumstances:

a. The firm normally maintains no deposit balances at First Bank.
b. The firm normally maintains $70,000 in deposit balances at First Bank.
c. The firm normally maintains $150,000 in deposit balances at First Bank.
d. Compare, contrast, and discuss your findings in **a**, **b**, and **c**.

CHALLENGE

15-13 Integrative—Comparison of loan terms Cumberland Furniture wishes to establish a prearranged borrowing agreement with its local commercial bank. The bank's terms for a line of credit are 3.30 percent over the prime rate, and the borrowing must be reduced to zero for a 30-day period. For an equivalent revolving credit agreement, the rate is 2.80 percent over prime with a commitment fee of .50 percent on the average unused balance. With both loans, the required compensating balance is equal to 20 percent of the amount borrowed. The prime rate is currently 8 percent. Both agreements have $4 million borrowing limits. The firm expects on average to borrow $2 million during the year no matter which loan agreement it decides to use.

a. What is the effective annual rate under the line of credit?
b. What is the effective annual rate under the revolving credit agreement? (*Hint:* Compute the ratio of the dollars that the firm will pay in interest and commitment fees to the dollars that the firm will effectively have use of.)
c. If the firm does expect to borrow an average of half the amount available, which arrangement would you recommend for the borrower? Explain why.

INTERMEDIATE

15-14 Cost of commercial paper Commercial paper is usually sold at a discount. PULP has just sold an issue of 90-day commercial paper with a face value of $1 million. The firm has received initial proceeds of $978,000.

a. What effective annual rate will the firm pay for financing with commercial paper assuming it is rolled over each 90 days throughout the year?
b. If a brokerage fee of $9,612 was paid from the initial proceeds to an investment banker for selling the issue, what effective annual rate will the firm pay assuming the paper is rolled over each 90 days throughout the year?

15-15   Accounts receivable as collateral   Vosburgh Plate and Glass wishes to borrow $80,000 from a local bank using its accounts receivable to secure the loan. The bank's policy is to accept as collateral any accounts that are normally paid within 30 days of the end of the credit period as long as the average age of the account is not greater than the customer's average payment period. Vosburgh Plate's accounts receivable, their average ages, and the average payment period for each customer are shown in the following table. The company extends terms of net 30 days.

Customer	Account receivable	Average age of account	Average payment period of customer
A	$20,000	10 days	40 days
B	6,000	40	35
C	22,000	62	50
D	11,000	68	65
E	2,000	14	30
F	12,000	38	50
G	27,000	55	60
H	19,000	20	35

a. Calculate the dollar amount of acceptable accounts receivable collateral held by Vosburgh Plate and Glass.
b. The bank reduces collateral by 10 percent for returns and allowances. What is the level of acceptable collateral under this condition?
c. The bank will advance 75 percent against the firm's acceptable collateral (after adjusting for returns and allowances). What amount can Vosburgh Plate and Glass borrow against these accounts?

 15-16   Factoring   Freedom Finance factors the accounts of the Mooring Company. All eight factored accounts are shown in the table at the top of page 529, with the amount factored, the date due, and the status on May 30. Indicate the amounts Freedom should have remitted to Mooring as of May 30 and the dates of those remittances. Assume that the factor's commission of 2 percent is deducted as part of determining the amount of the remittance.

Account	Amount	Date due	Status on May 30
A	$200,000	May 30	Collected May 15
B	90,000	May 30	Uncollected
C	110,000	May 30	Uncollected
D	85,000	June 15	Collected May 30
E	120,000	May 30	Collected May 27
F	180,000	June 15	Collected May 30
G	90,000	May 15	Uncollected
H	30,000	June 30	Collected May 30

CHALLENGE **15-17 Inventory financing** Lake Turbine Company faces a liquidity crisis—it needs a loan of $100,000 for 30 days. Having no source of additional unsecured borrowing, the firm must find a secured short-term lender. The firm's accounts receivable are quite low, but its inventory is considered liquid and reasonably good collateral. The book value of the inventory is $300,000, of which $120,000 is finished goods.

(1) Center City Bank will make a $100,000 trust receipt loan against the finished goods inventory. The annual interest rate on the loan is 12 percent on the outstanding loan balance plus a .25 percent administration fee levied against the $100,000 initial loan amount. Because it will be liquidated as inventory is sold, the average amount owed over the month is expected to be $75,000.

(2) First Local Bank is willing to lend $100,000 against a floating lien on the book value of inventory for the 30-day period at an annual interest rate of 13 percent.

(3) North Mall Bank and Trust will loan $100,000 against a warehouse receipt on the finished goods inventory and charge 15 percent annual interest on the outstanding loan balance. A .5 percent warehousing fee will be levied against the average amount borrowed. Because the loan will be liquidated as inventory is sold, the average loan balance is expected to be $60,000.

a. Calculate the dollar cost of each of the proposed plans for obtaining an initial loan amount of $100,000.

b. Which plan do you recommend? Why?

c. If the firm had made a purchase of $100,000 for which it had been given terms of 2/10 net 30, would it increase the firm's profitability to give up the discount and not borrow as recommended in **b**? Why or why not?

CASE Chapter 15

Selecting Kent Company's Financing Strategy and Unsecured Short-Term Borrowing Arrangement

Miriam Hirt, the CFO of Kent Company, carefully developed the estimates of the firm's total funds requirements for the coming year shown in the following table.

Month	Total Funds	Month	Total Funds
January	$1,000,000	July	$6,000,000
February	1,000,000	August	5,000,000
March	2,000,000	September	5,000,000
April	3,000,000	October	4,000,000
May	5,000,000	November	2,000,000
June	7,000,000	December	1,000,000

In addition, Miriam expects short-term financing costs of about 10 percent and long-term financing costs of about 14 percent during that period. She developed the three possible financing strategies that follow:

Strategy 1—Aggressive: Finance seasonal needs with short-term funds and permanent needs with long-term funds.

Strategy 2—Conservative: Finance an amount equal to the peak need with long-term funds and use short-term funds only in an emergency.

Strategy 3—Tradeoff: Finance $3,000,000 with long-term funds and finance the remaining funds requirements with short-term funds.

To ensure that, along with spontaneous financing from accounts payable and accruals, adequate short-term financing will be available, Miriam plans to establish an unsecured short-term borrowing arrangement with its local bank, Third National. The bank has offered either a line of credit or a revolving credit agreement. Third National's terms for a line of credit are an interest rate of 2.50 percent above the prime rate, and the borrowing must be reduced to zero for a 30-day period during the year. On an equivalent revolving credit agreement, the interest rate would be 3.00 percent above prime with a commitment fee of .50 percent on the average unused balance. Under both loans, a compensating balance equal to 20 percent of the amount borrowed would be required. The prime rate is currently 7 percent. Both the line of credit and the revolving credit agreement would have borrowing limits of $1,000,000. For purposes of her analysis, Miriam estimates that Kent will borrow $600,000 on the average during the year, regardless of the financing strategy and loan arrangement it chooses.

Required

a. Divide Kent's monthly funds requirements into (1) a *permanent* component and (2) a *seasonal* component, and find the monthly average for each.
b. For each of the three possible financing strategies, determine (1) the amount of long-term and short-term financing required and (2) the total annual cost of each strategy.
c. Assuming that the firm expects its current assets to total $4 million throughout the year, determine the average amount of net working capital under each financing strategy. (*Hint:* Current liabilities equal average short-term financing.)
d. Discuss the profitability–risk tradeoff associated with each financing strategy. Which strategy would you recommend to Miriam Hirt for Kent Company? Why?
e. Find the effective annual rate under:
   (1) The line of credit agreement.
   (2) The revolving credit agreement. (*Hint:* Compare the ratio of the dollars that the firm will pay in interest and commitment fees to the dollars that the firm will effectively have use of.)
f. If the firm does expect to borrow an average of $600,000, which borrowing arrangement would you recommend to Kent? Explain why.

Web Exercise

GOTO web site citgroup.com.

1. On the menu at the lower left of the screen under BUSINESS FINANCING SOLUTIONS, scroll down to "I want to know more info about." What options are available?

On that same menu select FACTORING SERVICES. Then click GO.

2. What is the complete financial package of factoring?

At the end of that screen, click "Why do companies use factoring?"

3. Why use factoring?

At the end of that screen, click "How does factoring work?"

4. What are the four steps in factoring?

On the BUSINESS FINANCING SOLUTIONS menu select RECEIVABLES OUTSOURCING SERVICE. Then click GO.

5. What are the commercial services options available?

Click on BULK PURCHASE OF ACCOUNTS RECEIVABLE. Then click GO.

6. When do companies take advantage of bulk purchases of accounts receivable?

CASH AND MARKETABLE SECURITIES

16

ACROSS *the* DISCIPLINES

Firms need to hold enough cash to maintain solvency but not so much that it sits idly in the bank, earning little. An attractive place to warehouse "idle" cash is in marketable securities. In previous chapters we saw how cash and profit planning and various financing strategies impact the levels of cash and marketable securities. In this chapter we turn our attention specifically to techniques and strategies for managing cash, particularly by speeding up collections and slowing down disbursements. We also look briefly at the characteristics of commonly held marketable securities. Chapter 16 is important to:

■ **accounting personnel** who will assist in determining the appropriate cash balances needed for the firm's transactions.

■ **information systems analysts** who will design a financial information system that will interface with the firm's banks.

■ **management** because it will decide on the appropriate mix of cash and marketable securities and will determine which marketable securities to acquire.

■ **the marketing department** because it will be involved in activities aimed at accelerating the collection of accounts receivable.

■ **operations,** which will be required to reduce the operating cycle by more efficiently managing inventory and production.

CASH AND MARKETABLE SECURITY BALANCES

cash
The ready currency to which all liquid assets can be reduced.

marketable securities
Short-term, interest-earning, money market instruments that are used by the firm to obtain a return on temporarily idle funds.

Cash and marketable securities are the most liquid of the firm's assets. **Cash** is the ready currency to which all liquid assets can be reduced. **Marketable securities** are short-term, interest-earning, money market instruments that are used by the firm to obtain a return on temporarily idle funds. Together, cash and marketable securities serve as a pool of funds that can be used to pay bills as they come due and to meet any unexpected outlays. Because the rate of interest applied by banks to checking accounts is relatively low, firms tend to use excess bank balances to purchase marketable securities. The firm must therefore determine the appropriate balances for both cash and marketable securities, by carefully considering the motives for holding them. The higher these balances are, the lower the risk of technical insolvency, and the lower the balances are, the higher the risk of technical insolvency.

MOTIVES FOR HOLDING CASH AND NEAR-CASH BALANCES

near-cash
Marketable securities viewed the same as cash because of their high liquidity.

There are three motives for holding cash and **near-cash** (marketable securities) balances. Each motive is based on two underlying questions: (1) What is the appropriate degree of liquidity to maintain? (2) What is the appropriate distribution of liquidity between cash and marketable securities?

TRANSACTIONS MOTIVE

transactions motive
A motive for holding cash or near-cash—to make planned payments for items such as materials and wages.

A firm maintains cash balances to satisfy the **transactions motive,** which is to make planned payments for items such as materials and wages. If cash inflows and cash outflows are closely matched, transactional cash balances can be minimized. Although firms *must* achieve this motive, they typically *try* to achieve the following two motives as well.

SAFETY MOTIVE

safety motive
A motive for holding cash or near-cash—to protect the firm against being unable to satisfy unexpected demands for cash.

Balances held to satisfy the **safety motive** are invested in highly liquid marketable securities that can be immediately transferred from securities to cash. Such securities protect the firm against being unable to satisfy unexpected demands for cash.

SPECULATIVE MOTIVE

speculative motive
A motive for holding cash or near-cash—to put unneeded funds to work or to be able to quickly take advantage of opportunities that may arise.

When they have satisfied the safety motive, firms may invest excess funds in marketable securities, as well as in long-term instruments. A firm may do so because it currently has no other use for certain funds or because it wants to be able to quickly take advantage of opportunities that may arise. These funds satisfy the **speculative motive,** which is the least common of the three motives.

ESTIMATING DESIRABLE CASH BALANCES

Management's goal should be to *maintain levels of transactional cash balances and marketable securities investments that contribute to improving the value of the firm.* If levels of cash or marketable securities are too high, the profitability of the firm will be lower than if more optimal balances were maintained. (This concept was examined in the preceding chapter in the profitability-risk tradeoff discussion.) Firms can use either *quantitative models* or *subjective approaches* to determine appropriate transactional cash balances. Quantitative cash balance models are beyond the scope of this text. A subjective approach might be to maintain a transactional balance equal to 10 percent of the following month's forecast sales. For example, if the forecast amount of sales for the following month is $500,000, the firm would maintain a $50,000 transactional cash balance (i.e., .10 × $500,000).

THE LEVEL OF MARKETABLE SECURITIES INVESTMENT

In addition to earning a positive return on temporarily idle funds, the marketable securities portfolio serves as a *safety stock* of cash that can be used to satisfy unexpected demands for funds. The level of the safety stock is the difference between management's desired liquidity level and the level of transactional cash balances determined by the firm. For example, if management wishes to maintain $70,000 of liquid funds and a transactional cash balance of $50,000, a $20,000 safety stock of cash ($70,000 − $50,000) would be held as marketable securities. The firm may use a *line of credit* (as discussed in Chapter 15) instead of a portfolio of marketable securities, or a combination of line of credit reserves and marketable securities, as safety stocks.

Review Questions

16-1   List and describe the three motives for holding cash and near-cash balances. Which are the most common motives?
16-2   What is management's goal with respect to the management of cash and marketable securities? How is the level of the *safety stock* of cash determined? In what forms would it be held?

THE EFFICIENT MANAGEMENT OF CASH

Cash balances and safety stocks of cash are significantly influenced by the firm's production and sales techniques and by its procedures for collecting sales receipts and paying for purchases. These influences can be better understood by analyzing the firm's operating and cash conversion cycles.[1] By efficiently managing these cycles, the financial manager can maintain a low level of cash investment and thereby contribute toward maximization of share value.

---

[1]The conceptual model that is used in this part to demonstrate basic cash management strategies was developed by Lawrence J. Gitman in "Estimating Corporate Liquidity Requirements: A Simplified Approach," *The Financial Review* (1974), pp. 79–88, and refined and operationalized by Lawrence J. Gitman and Kanwal S. Sachdeva in "A Framework for Estimating and Analyzing the Required Working Capital Investment," *Review of Business and Economic Research* (Spring 1982), pp. 35–44.

THE OPERATING CYCLE

operating cycle (OC)
The amount of time that elapses from the point when the firm inputs material and labor into the production process to the point when cash is collected from the sale of the resulting finished product.

The **operating cycle (OC)** of a firm is defined as the amount of time that elapses from the point when the firm inputs material and labor into the production process (i.e., begins to build inventory) to the point when cash is collected from the sale of the finished product that contains these production inputs. The cycle is made up of two components: the average age of inventory and the average collection period of sales. The firm's operating cycle (OC) is simply the sum of the *average age of inventory (AAI)* and the *average collection period (ACP)*:

$$OC = AAI + ACP \qquad (16.1)$$

A simple example illustrates the operating cycle.

Example ▼ RIF Company, a producer of paper dinnerware, sells all its merchandise on credit. The credit terms require customers to pay within 60 days of a sale. On average, it takes the firm 85 days to manufacture, warehouse, and ultimately sell a finished good. In other words, the firm's average age of inventory (AAI) is 85 days. It is taking the firm, on average, 70 days to collect its accounts receivable. Substituting AAI = 85 days and ACP = 70 days into Equation 16.1, we find RIF's operating cycle ▲ to be 155 days (85 days + 70 days), as shown above the time line in Figure 16.1.

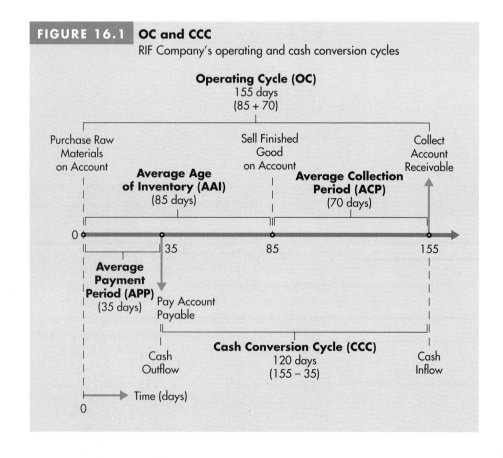

FIGURE 16.1 **OC and CCC**
RIF Company's operating and cash conversion cycles

THE CASH CONVERSION CYCLE

A company is usually able to purchase many of its production inputs (i.e., raw materials and labor) on credit. The time it takes the firm to pay for these inputs is called the *average payment period (APP)*. These production inputs therefore generate sources of spontaneous short-term financing. As was noted in Chapter 15, spontaneous financing represents free financing as long as the firm takes any cash discounts offered. The ability to purchase production inputs on credit allows the firm to partially (or maybe even totally) offset the length of time resources are tied up in the operating cycle. The total number of days in the operating cycle less the average payment period for inputs to production represents the **cash conversion cycle (CCC)**:

cash conversion cycle (CCC)
The amount of time the firm's cash is tied up between payment for production inputs and receipt of payment from the sale of the resulting finished product.

$$\text{CCC} = \text{OC} - \text{APP} = \text{AAI} + \text{ACP} - \text{APP} \qquad (16.2)$$

A continuation of the RIF Company example illustrates this concept.

Example ▼   The credit terms for the firm's raw material purchases currently require payment within 40 days, and employees are paid every 15 days. The firm's calculated weighted average payment period for raw materials and labor is 35 days, which represents the average payment period (APP). Substituting RIF Company's 155-day operating cycle (OC), found in the preceding example, and its 35-day average payment period (APP) into Equation 16.2 results in its cash conversion cycle (CCC):

$$\begin{aligned}\text{CCC} &= \text{OC} - \text{APP} \\ &= 155 - 35 = 120 \text{ days}\end{aligned}$$

RIF Company's cash conversion cycle is shown below the time line in Figure 16.1. There are 120 days between the cash *outflow* to pay the accounts payable (on day 35) and the cash *inflow* from the collection of the account receivable (on day 155). During this period—the cash conversion cycle—the firm's money is ▲ tied up.

MANAGING THE CASH CONVERSION CYCLE

A *positive* cash conversion cycle, like that of RIF Company, means that the firm must use negotiated forms of financing, such as unsecured short-term loans or secured sources of financing, to support the cash conversion cycle.

Ideally, a firm would like to have a *negative* cash conversion cycle. A negative CCC means the average payment period (APP) exceeds the operating cycle (OC) (see Equation 16.2). Manufacturing firms usually will *not* have negative cash conversion cycles unless they extend their average payment periods an unreasonable length of time. Nonmanufacturing firms are more likely to have negative cash conversion cycles because they generally carry smaller, faster-moving inventories and often sell their products or services for cash. As a result, these firms have shorter operating cycles, which may be exceeded in length by the firm's average payment periods, thereby resulting in negative cash conversion cycles. When a firm's cash conversion cycle is negative, the firm should benefit by being able to use spontaneous financing to help support aspects of the business other than just the operating cycle.

In the more common case of a positive cash conversion cycle, the firm needs to pursue strategies to minimize the CCC without losing sales or damaging its credit rating. Basic strategies for managing the cash conversion cycle are as follows:

1. Turn over inventory as quickly as possible, avoiding stockouts (depletions of stock) that might result in a loss of sales.
2. Collect accounts receivable as quickly as possible without losing future sales due to high-pressure collection techniques. Cash discounts, if they are economically justifiable, may be used to accomplish this objective.
3. Pay accounts payable as late as possible without damaging the firm's credit rating, but take advantage of any favorable cash discounts.[2]

The effects of implementing these strategies are described in the following paragraphs using RIF Company data. We ignore the costs of implementing each proposed strategy; in practice, these costs would be measured against the calculated savings in order to make the appropriate strategic decision.

EFFICIENT INVENTORY–PRODUCTION MANAGEMENT

One strategy available to RIF is to increase inventory turnover. To do so, the firm can increase raw materials turnover, shorten the production cycle, or increase finished goods turnover. Each of these approaches will result in a reduction in the amount of negotiated financing required—that is, the cash conversion cycle will be shortened.

Example ▼ If RIF Company increases inventory turnover by reducing the average age of inventory from the current level of 85 days to 70 days, it will reduce its cash conversion cycle by 15 days, to 105 days (CCC = 120 days − 15 days). The effect of this change on the firm can be estimated as follows: Suppose RIF currently spends $12 million annually on operating cycle investments. The daily expenditure is $33,333 ($12 million ÷ 360 days). Because the cash conversion cycle is reduced 15 days, $500,000 of financing ($33,333 × 15) can be repaid. If RIF pays 10 percent for its negotiated financing, the firm will reduce financing costs and thereby increase profit by $50,000 (.10 × $500,000) as a result of managing ▲ inventory more efficiently.

ACCELERATING THE COLLECTION OF ACCOUNTS RECEIVABLE

Another means of reducing the cash conversion cycle is to speed up—accelerate—the collection of accounts receivable. Accounts receivable, like inventory, tie up dollars that could otherwise be used to reduce financing or be invested in earning assets. Consider the following example.

Example ▼ If RIF Company, by changing its credit terms, is able to reduce the average collection period from the current level of 70 days to 50 days, it will reduce its cash

---

[2]A discussion of the variables to consider when determining whether to take cash discounts appears in Chapter 15. A cash discount is often an enticement to pay accounts payable early.

conversion cycle by 20 days, to 100 days (CCC = 120 days − 20 days = 100 days). Again, assume that $12 million is spent annually—$33,333 daily—to support the operating cycle. By improving the management of accounts receivable by 20 days, the firm will require $666,666 less in negotiated financing ($33,333 × 20). With an interest rate of 10 percent, the firm is able to reduce financing costs and thereby increase profits by $66,666 (.10 × $666,666).

STRETCHING ACCOUNTS PAYABLE

A third strategy is to *stretch accounts payable*—that is, to pay bills as late as possible without damaging the firm's credit rating. Although this approach is financially attractive, it involves an important ethical issue. Clearly, a supplier would not favor a customer that purposely postponed payment.[3]

Example ▼ If RIF Company can stretch the payment period from the current average of 35 days to an average of 45 days, its cash conversion cycle will be reduced by 10 days to 110 days (CCC = 120 days − 10 days = 110 days). Once more, if operating cycle expenditures total $12 million annually, stretching accounts payable 10 additional days will reduce the firm's negotiated financing need by $333,333 [($12 million ÷ 360) × 10 days]. With an interest rate of 10 percent, the firm can reduce its financing costs and thereby increase profits by $33,333 (.10 × $333,333).

COMBINING CASH MANAGEMENT STRATEGIES

Firms typically do not attempt to implement just one cash management strategy; rather, they attempt to use them all to reduce their reliance on negotiated financing. Of course, when implementing these strategies, firms should take care to avoid repeated inventory stockouts, to avoid losing sales due to the use of high-pressure collection techniques, and not to damage the firm's credit rating by overstretching accounts payable. A combination of these strategies would have the following effects on RIF Company.

Example ▼ If RIF simultaneously decreased the average age of inventory by 15 days, sped the collection of accounts receivable by 20 days, and increased the average payment period by 10 days, its cash conversion cycle would be reduced to 75 days, as shown at the top of the following page. The 45-day reduction in the cash conversion cycle means that RIF Company can reduce its reliance on negotiated financing. If annual expenditures for operations are $12 million, then interest-bearing financing can be reduced by $1.5 million [($12 million ÷ 360 days) × 45 days]. If the company pays 10 percent interest on its financing, then it can save $150,000 (i.e., .10 × $1,500,000) through improved management of the cash conversion cycle.

---

[3]The resolution of this ethical issue is not further addressed in this text. Suffice it to say that although the use of various techniques to slow down payments is widespread due to its financial appeal, it may not be justifiable on ethical grounds.

Initial cash conversion cycle	120 days
Reduction due to:	
1. Decreased inventory age	
85 days to 70 days = 15 days	
2. Decreased collection period	
70 days to 50 days = 20 days	
3. Increased payment period	
35 days to 45 days = 10 days	
Less: Total reduction in cash conversion cycle	45 days
New cash conversion cycle	75 days

? Review Questions

16-3   Compare and contrast the firm's *operating cycle* and its *cash conversion cycle*. What is the firm's objective with respect to each of them?

16-4   What are the *key strategies* with respect to inventory, accounts receivable, and accounts payable for the firm that wants to manage its cash conversion cycle efficiently?

16-5   If a firm reduces the average age of its inventory, what effect might this action have on the cash conversion cycle? On the firm's total sales? Is there a trade-off between average inventory and sales? Give reasons for your answers.

LG3   **LG4**

CASH MANAGEMENT TECHNIQUES

Financial managers have available a variety of cash management techniques that are aimed at minimizing the firm's negotiated financing requirements. Assuming that the firm has done all that it can to stimulate customers to pay promptly and to select vendors offering the most attractive and flexible credit terms, the firm can further speed collections and slow disbursements by taking advantage of the "float" existing in the collection and payment systems.

FLOAT

float
Funds that have been dispatched by a payer but are not yet in a form that can be spent by the payee.

In the broadest sense, **float** refers to funds that have been dispatched by a payer (the firm or individual *making* payment) but are not yet in a form that can be spent by the payee (the firm or individual *receiving* payment). Float also exists when a payee has received funds in a spendable form but these funds have not been withdrawn from the account of the payer. Delays in the collection–payment system resulting from the transportation and processing of checks are responsible for float. However, with electronic payment systems, as well as changes being put into place by the Federal Reserve System, in the foreseeable future float will virtually disappear. Until that time, financial managers will continue to take advantage of float.

TYPES OF FLOAT

collection float
The delay between the time when a payer deducts a payment from its checking account ledger and the time when the payee actually receives these funds in a spendable form.

Currently, business firms and individuals can experience both collection and disbursement float in the process of making financial transactions. **Collection float** results from the delay between the time when a payer deducts a payment from its checking account ledger and the time when the payee actually receives the funds in a spendable form. Thus, collection float is experienced by the payee and is a delay in the receipt of funds.

disbursement float
The lapse between the time when a payer deducts a payment from its checking account ledger (disburses it) and the time when funds are actually withdrawn from its account.

Disbursement float results from the lapse between the time when a payer deducts a payment from its checking account ledger (disburses it) and the time when funds are actually withdrawn from its account. Disbursement float is experienced by the payer and is a delay in the actual withdrawal of funds.

COMPONENTS OF FLOAT

mail float
The delay between the time when a payer mails a payment and the time when the payee receives it.

Both collection float and disbursement float have the same three basic components:

1. **Mail float:** The delay between the time when a payer places payment in the mail and the time when it is received by the payee.

processing float
The delay between the receipt of a check by the payee and its deposit in the firm's account.

2. **Processing float:** The delay between the receipt of a check by the payee and the deposit of it in the firm's account.
3. **Clearing float:** The delay between the deposit of a check by the payee and the actual availability of the funds. This component of float is attributable to the time required for a check to clear the banking system. The use of new electronic methods to process checks within the banking system continues to reduce clearing float.

clearing float
The delay between the deposit of a check by the payee and the actual availability of the funds.

Figure 16.2 illustrates the key components of float resulting from the issuance and mailing of a check by the payer company to the payee company on day zero. The entire process required a total of 9 days: 3 days' mail float, 2 days' processing float, and 4 days' clearing float. To the payer company, the delay is disbursement float; to the payee company, the delay is collection float.

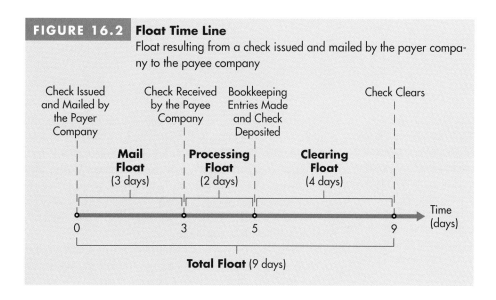

FIGURE 16.2   Float Time Line
Float resulting from a check issued and mailed by the payer company to the payee company

SPEEDING UP COLLECTIONS

Firms want not only to stimulate customers to pay accounts as promptly as possible but also to convert their payments into a spendable form as quickly as possible—in other words, to *minimize collection float.* A variety of techniques are aimed at *speeding up collections,* and thereby reducing collection float.

CONCENTRATION BANKING

Firms with numerous sales outlets throughout the country often designate certain offices as collection centers for given geographic areas. Customers in these areas remit their payments to these offices, which in turn deposit the receipts in local banks. At certain times, or when needed, funds are transferred by wire from these regional banks to a concentration, or disbursing, bank, from which bill payments are dispatched.

concentration banking
A collection procedure in which payments are made to regional collection centers, then deposited in local banks for quick clearing. Shortens mail and clearing float.

    Concentration banking is used to reduce collection float by shortening the mail and clearing float components. Mail float is reduced because regional collection centers are closer to the point from which the check is sent. Clearing float may also be reduced, because the payee's regional bank is likely to be in the same Federal Reserve district or the same city as the bank on which the check is drawn; it may even be the same bank. A reduction in clearing float will, of course, make funds available to the firm more quickly.

Example ▼   Suppose Style, Inc., a hair products manufacturer, could change to concentration banking and reduce its collection period by 3 days. If the company normally carried $10 million in receivables and that level represented 30 days of sales, cutting 3 days from the collection process would result in a $1 million decline in receivables [(3 ÷ 30) × $10,000,000]. Given a 10 percent opportunity cost, the gross annual benefits of concentration banking would amount to $100,000 (.10 × $1,000,000). Clearly, assuming no change in risk, as long as total annual costs—*incremental* administrative costs and bank service fees and the opportunity cost of holding specified minimum bank balances—are less than the expected annual benefits of $100,000, Style, Inc.'s proposed program of concentration banking
▲   should be implemented.

LOCKBOXES

lockbox system
A collection procedure in which payers send their payments to a nearby post office box that is emptied by the firm's bank several times daily; the bank deposits the payment checks in the firm's account. Reduces collection float by shortening processing float as well as mail and clearing float.

Another method used to reduce collection float is the **lockbox system,** which differs from concentration banking in several important ways. Instead of mailing payment to a collection center, the payer sends it to a nearby post office box that is emptied by the firm's bank several times daily. The bank deposits the checks in the firm's account and sends to the collecting firm a deposit slip (or a computer file) indicating the payments received. Lockboxes normally are geographically dispersed, and the funds, when collected, are wired from each lockbox bank to the firm's disbursing bank.

    The lockbox system is superior to concentration banking because it reduces processing float as well as mail and clearing float. The bank immediately deposits the receipts in the firm's account, so that processing occurs *after* funds are deposited. This allows the firm to use the funds almost immediately. Additional reductions in mail float may also result, because payments do not have to be delivered but are picked up by the bank at the post office.

Example ▼ Davidson Products, a manufacturer of disposable razors, has annual credit sales of $6 million, which are billed at a constant rate each day. It takes about 4 days to receive customers' payments at corporate headquarters. It takes another day for the credit department to process receipts and deposit them in the bank. A cash management consultant has told Davidson that a lockbox system would shorten the mail float from 4 days to 1½ days and completely eliminate the processing float. The lockbox system would cost the firm $8,000 per year. Davidson currently earns 12 percent on investments of comparable risk. The lockbox system would free $58,333 of cash [($6 million ÷ 360 days) × (4 days mail float + 1 day processing float − 1½ days mail float)] that is currently tied up in mail and processing float. The gross annual benefit would be $7,000 (.12 × $58,333). Because the $7,000 gross annual benefit is less than the $8,000 annual cost,
▲ Davidson should *not* use the lockbox.

DIRECT SENDS

To reduce clearing float, firms that have received large checks drawn on distant banks or a large number of checks drawn on banks in a given city may arrange to present these checks directly for payment to the bank on which they are drawn. Such a procedure is called a **direct send.** Rather than depositing these checks in its collection account, the firm arranges to present the checks to the bank on which they are drawn and receive immediate payment. The firm can use Express Mail or private express services to get the checks into a bank in the same city or to a sales office where an employee can take the checks to the bank and present them for payment. In most cases, the funds will be transferred via wire into the firm's disbursement account.

direct send
A collection procedure in which the payee presents checks for payment directly to the banks on which they are drawn, reducing clearing float.

Deciding whether to use direct sends is relatively straightforward. If the benefits from the reduced clearing time are greater than the cost, the checks should be sent directly for payment rather than cleared through normal banking channels.

Example ▼ If a firm with an opportunity to earn 10 percent on its idle balances can, through a direct send, make available $1.2 million 3 days earlier than would otherwise be the case, the benefit of this direct send would be $1,000 [.10 × (3 days ÷ 360 days) × $1,200,000]. If the cost of achieving this 3-day reduction in float is less
▲ than $1,000, the direct send would be recommended.

preauthorized check (PAC)
A check written by the payee against a customer's checking account for a previously agreed-upon amount.

OTHER TECHNIQUES

A number of other techniques can be used to reduce collection float. One method commonly used by firms that collect a fixed amount from customers on a regular basis is the preauthorized check. A **preauthorized check (PAC)** is written against a customer's checking account for a previously agreed-upon amount by the firm to which it is payable. Because the check has been legally authorized by the customer, it does not require the customer's signature. The payee merely issues and then deposits the PAC in its account. The check then clears through the banking system in the usual way.

depository transfer check (DTC)
An unsigned check drawn on one of the firm's bank accounts and deposited into its account at a concentration or major disbursing bank.

Firms with multiple collection points use depository transfer checks to speed up the transfer of funds. A **depository transfer check (DTC)** is an unsigned check

wire transfers
Telegraphic communications that, via bookkeeping entries, remove funds from the payer's bank and deposit them into the payee's bank, thereby reducing collection float.

ACH (automated clearinghouse) debits
Preauthorized electronic withdrawals from the payer's account that are transferred to the payee's account via a settlement among banks by the automated clearinghouse.

drawn on one of the firm's bank accounts and deposited into its account at another bank—typically, a concentration or major disbursing bank. Once the DTC has cleared the bank on which it is drawn, the actual transfer of funds is completed. Most firms currently transmit deposit information via telephone rather than by mail to their concentration banks, which then prepare and deposit DTCs into the firm's accounts.

Firms also frequently use wire transfers to reduce collection float. **Wire transfers** are telegraphic communications that, via bookkeeping entries, remove funds from the payer's bank and deposit them into the payee's bank. Wire transfers can eliminate mail and clearing float and may reduce processing float as well. They are sometimes used instead of DTCs to move funds into key disbursing accounts, although a wire transfer is more expensive than a DTC.

Another popular method of accelerating cash inflows is the use of **ACH (automated clearinghouse) debits.** These are preauthorized electronic withdrawals from the payer's account. A computerized clearing facility (called an automated clearinghouse, or ACH) makes a paperless transfer of funds between the payer and payee banks, and settles accounts among participating banks. Individual depositor accounts are settled by respective bank balance adjustments. ACH transfers clear in 1 day, in most cases reducing mail, processing, and clearing float.

SLOWING DOWN DISBURSEMENTS

Relative to accounts payable, the firm wants not only to pay its accounts as late as possible but also to slow down the availability of funds to suppliers and employees once the payment has been dispatched—in other words, to *maximize disbursement float.* A variety of techniques aimed at *slowing down disbursements,* and thereby increasing disbursement float, are available.

CONTROLLED DISBURSING

controlled disbursing
The strategic use of mailing points and bank accounts to lengthen mail float and clearing float, respectively.

Controlled disbursing involves the strategic use of mailing points and bank accounts to lengthen mail float and clearing float, respectively. When the date of postmark is considered the effective date of payment by the supplier, the firm may be able to lengthen the mail time associated with disbursements. It can place payments in the mail at locations from which they will take considerable time to reach the supplier. Typically, small towns that are not close to major highways or cities provide opportunities to increase mail float. Of course, the benefits of using selected mailing points may not justify the costs of this strategy, particularly because the U.S. Postal Service gives rate reductions on mail that is presorted by ZIP Code and sent from designated major post offices.

Availability of data on check clearing times allows firms to develop disbursement schemes that maximize clearing float on their payments. These methods involve assigning payments to vendors in certain geographic areas to be drawn on specific banks from which maximum clearing float will result.

playing the float
A method of consciously anticipating the resulting float, or delay, associated with the payment process and using it to keep funds in an interest-earning form for as long as possible.

PLAYING THE FLOAT

Playing the float is a method of consciously anticipating the resulting float, or delay, associated with the payment process. Firms often play the float by writing checks against funds that are not currently in their checking accounts. They can do this because they know that a delay will occur between the receipt and the deposit of checks by suppliers and the actual withdrawal of funds from their checking accounts. Although the ineffective use of this practice could result in problems associated with "bounced checks," many firms use float to stretch out their accounts payable.

Firms play the float in a variety of ways—all of which are aimed at keeping funds in an interest-earning form for as long as possible. For example, one way of playing the float is to deposit a certain proportion of a payroll into the firm's checking account on several successive days *following* the issuance of a group of checks. This technique is commonly referred to as **staggered funding.** If the firm can determine from historic data that only 25 percent of its payroll checks are cashed on the day immediately following the issuance of the checks, then only 25 percent of the value of the payroll needs to be in its checking account 1 day later. The amount of checks cashed on each of several succeeding days can also be estimated until the entire payroll is accounted for. Normally, however, to protect itself against any irregularities, a firm will place slightly more money in its account than is needed to cover the expected withdrawals.

staggered funding
A way to *play the float* by depositing a certain proportion of a payroll or payment into the firm's checking account on several successive days *following* the actual issuance of a group of checks.

PERSONAL FINANCE PERSPECTIVE

The Bank Branch in Your PC

It's 10 p.m. and you are worried. Did the big check you wrote yesterday clear today and overdraw your checking account? There's no need to spend a sleepless night until the bank opens. With online banking, you can check your account status right away from your computer, via the Internet or through direct phone lines that work with personal finance software. If necessary, you can transfer funds from your savings account. While you are at it, you may as well pay some bills electronically. It's easy: no need to write checks or spend money on postage.

Online banking is finally catching on with consumers. Mercer Management, a national consulting firm, estimates that about 20 percent of U.S. households will bank via computer by 2003. Banks typically charge customers monthly fees for online bill-paying services, plus the cost of the Internet service. But monthly charges aren't the only thing to consider before switching to online banking. With electronic payments, you may lose your ability to play the float because the bank withdraws funds on the payment date. When you pay a bill by writing a check and mailing it, 4 to 6 days may pass before the money is actually withdrawn from your account, so you keep the float. If you opt for electronic banking, you'd be wise to monitor your account balances closely—an easy enough task from your in-home bank branch! ●

OVERDRAFT SYSTEMS, ZERO-BALANCE ACCOUNTS, AND ACH CREDITS

overdraft system
Automatic coverage by the bank of all checks presented against the firm's account, regardless of the account balance.

Firms that aggressively manage cash disbursements often arrange for some type of overdraft system or a zero-balance account. In an **overdraft system,** if the firm's checking account balance is insufficient to cover all checks presented against the account, the bank will automatically lend the firm enough money to cover the amount of the overdraft. The bank, of course, will charge the firm interest on the funds lent and will limit the amount of overdraft coverage. Such an arrangement is important for a business that actively plays the float.

zero-balance account
A checking account in which a zero balance is maintained and the firm is required to deposit funds to cover checks drawn on the account only as they are presented for payment.

ACH (automated clearinghouse) credits
Deposits of payroll directly into the payees' (employees') accounts. Sacrifices disbursement float but may generate goodwill for the employer.

Firms can also establish **zero-balance accounts**—checking accounts in which zero balances are maintained. Under this arrangement, each day the bank will notify the firm of the total amount of checks presented against the account. The firm then transfers only that amount—typically, from a master account or through liquidation of a portion of its marketable securities—into the account. Once the corresponding checks have been paid, the account balance reverts to zero. The bank, of course, must be compensated for this service.

ACH (automated clearinghouse) credits are frequently used by corporations for making direct bank deposits of payroll into the payees' (employees') accounts. Disbursement float is sacrificed with this technique because ACH transactions immediately draw down the company's payroll account on payday, whereas in check-based payroll systems, not all employees cash their checks on payday, thus allowing the firm to use *staggered funding* as discussed earlier. The benefit of ACH credits is that employees enjoy convenience, which may generate enough goodwill to justify the firm's loss of float.

THE ROLE OF BANKING RELATIONSHIPS

Maintaining strong banking relations is one of the most important elements in an effective cash management system. Banks have become keenly aware of the profitability of corporate accounts and in recent years have developed a number of innovative services to attract businesses. No longer are banks simply places to establish checking accounts and to obtain loans; instead, they have become the source of a variety of cash management services. For example, banks now sell sophisticated information-processing packages to commercial clients. These packages deal with everything from basic accounting and budgeting to complex multinational disbursement and centralized cash control. All are designed to help financial managers maximize day-to-day cash availability and facilitate short-term investing. Of course, bank services should be used only when the benefits derived from them are greater than their costs.

INTERNATIONAL CASH MANAGEMENT

Although the motivations for holding cash and the basic concepts underlying cash management are the same worldwide, there are dramatic differences in practical cash management techniques for international versus strictly domestic business transactions. In fact, the differences between U.S. and international banking and payment systems are so great that only an elementary comparison is made here. More detailed information about payments and cash management systems abroad can be found in textbooks on international finance or short-term financial (working capital) management.

DIFFERENCES IN BANKING SYSTEMS

Giro system
Payment system through which retail transactions are handled in association with a foreign country's national postal system.

Banking systems outside the United States differ fundamentally from the U.S. model in several key aspects. First, foreign banks are generally far less restricted either geographically or in the services they are allowed to offer. Second, retail transactions are typically routed through a **Giro system** that is usually operated by, or in association with, the national postal system. Because of this direct payment system, checks are used much less frequently than in the United States. Third, banks in other countries are allowed to pay interest on corporate demand deposits, and they also routinely provide overdraft protection.

To recoup the cost of these services, however, non-U.S. banks generally charge more and higher fees for services and also engage in the practice of **value dating.** This involves delaying, often for days or even weeks, the availability of funds deposited with the bank. This lag between the date funds are deposited and when they are usable obviously complicates cash management procedures.

CASH MANAGEMENT PRACTICES

The cash management practices of multinational corporations are complicated by the need both to maintain local currency deposit balances in banks in every country in which the firm operates and to retain centralized control over cash balances and cash flows that, in total, can be quite large. The largest multinational corporations have honed their treasury operations to such an extent that they can balance these conflicting objectives efficiently and even profitably. To do so, they rely on the cash collection, disbursement, and foreign exchange trading expertise of large international banks, all of which operate very sophisticated computerized treasury services.

Multinational firms can also minimize their cash requirements by using **intracompany netting technique.** For example, when two subsidiaries in different countries trade with each other—thereby generating payment obligations to each other—only the net amount of payment owed will be transferred across national boundaries. In fact, it may be possible to handle many of these transactions strictly internally—on the books of the parent company—without having to resort to the international payment system at all.

Large international cash payments are almost invariably handled by one of the wire transfer services operated by international banking consortia. The most important of these networks is the **Clearing House Interbank Payment System,** called **CHIPS.** Hundreds of billions of dollars worth of payments are settled *every day* using wire transfer and settlement services. Although the bulk of these transactions result from foreign exchange trading, many are also due to settlement of international payment obligations.

Multinational companies with excess funds to invest benefit from having access to a wide variety of government and corporate investment vehicles. Companies naturally have access to all of the marketable securities offered to U.S. investors (described in the following section). Multinational companies can also invest funds in foreign government securities, or they can invest directly in the *Eurocurrency market* either in dollars or in other convertible currencies. This financial flexibility often provides multinational corporations with a key competitive advantage, particularly if they need to transfer funds into or out of countries experiencing political or financial difficulties.

value dating
A procedure used by non-U.S. banks to delay, often for days or even weeks, the availability of funds deposited with them.

intracompany netting technique
A technique used by subsidiaries of multinational firms to minimize their cash requirements by transferring across national boundaries only the net amount of payments owed between them.

Clearing House Interbank Payment System (CHIPS)
The most important international wire transfer service; operated by international banking consortia.

? R e v i e w   Q u e s t i o n s

16-6   Define *float* and describe its three basic components. Compare and contrast collection and disbursement float, and state the financial manager's goal with respect to each of these types of float.

16-7 Briefly describe the key features of each of the following techniques for *speeding up collections:* (**a**) concentration banking; (**b**) lockboxes; (**c**) direct sends; (**d**) preauthorized checks (PACs); (**e**) depository transfer checks (DTCs); (**f**) wire transfers; and (**g**) ACH (automated clearinghouse) debits.

16-8 Briefly describe the key features of each of the following techniques for *slowing down disbursements:* (**a**) controlled disbursing; (**b**) playing the float; (**c**) overdraft systems; (**d**) zero-balance accounts; and (**e**) ACH (automated clearinghouse) credits.

16-9 How should available bank services used in the cash management process be evaluated?

16-10 Describe the key differences between banking systems outside the United States and the U.S. model. What is *value dating* and how does it affect international cash management?

16-11 What is *intracompany netting* and what is its purpose? What is *CHIPS* and what role does it play in the international payment system?

MARKETABLE SECURITIES

Marketable securities are short-term, interest-earning, money market instruments that can easily be converted into cash.[4] Marketable securities are classified as part of the firm's liquid assets. The securities that are most commonly held as part of the firm's marketable securities portfolio are divided into two groups: (1) government issues and (2) nongovernment issues. Before describing both of these types of marketable securities, we discuss the basic characteristics of marketable securities and making purchase decisions. Table 16.1 summarizes the key features and recent (April 7, 1999) yields for the marketable securities described in the sections that follow.

CHARACTERISTICS OF MARKETABLE SECURITIES

The basic characteristics of marketable securities affect the degree of their salability. To be truly marketable, a security must have two basic characteristics: (1) a ready market and (2) safety of principal (no likelihood of loss in value).

breadth of a market
A characteristic of a ready market, determined by the number of participants (buyers) in the market.

depth of a market
A characteristic of a ready market, determined by its ability to absorb the purchase or sale of a large dollar amount of a particular security.

A READY MARKET

The market for a security should have both breadth and depth to minimize the amount of time required to convert it into cash. The **breadth of a market** is determined by the number of participants (buyers). A broad market is one that has many participants. The **depth of a market** is determined by its ability to absorb the purchase or sale of a large dollar amount of a particular security. It is therefore possible to have a broad market that has no depth. Thus, 100,000 partici-

---

[4]As explained in Chapter 2, the *money market* results from a financial relationship between the suppliers and demanders of short-term funds, that is, marketable securities.

TABLE 16.1	Features and Recent Yields on Popular Marketable Securities[a]

Security	Issuer	Description	Initial maturity	Risk and return	Yield on April 7, 1999[b]
Government Issues					
Treasury bills	U.S. Treasury	Issued weekly at auction; sold at a discount; strong secondary market	91 and 182 days, occasionally 1 year	Lowest, virtually risk-free	4.38%
Treasury notes	U.S. Treasury	Stated interest rate; interest paid semiannually; strong secondary market	1 to 10 years	Low, but slightly higher than U.S. Treasury bills	4.49%
Federal agency issues	Agencies of federal government	Not an obligation of U.S. Treasury; strong secondary market	9 months to 30 years	Slightly higher than U.S. Treasury issues	4.64%[c]
Nongovernment Issues					
Negotiable certificates of deposit (CDs)	Commercial banks	Represent specific cash deposits in commercial banks; amounts and maturities tailored to investor needs; large denominations; good secondary market	1 month to 3 years	Higher than U.S. Treasury issues and comparable to commercial paper	4.90%
Commercial paper	Corporation with a high credit standing	Unsecured note of issuer; large denominations	3 to 270 days	Higher than U.S. Treasury issues and comparable to negotiable CDs	4.83%
Banker's acceptances	Banks	Results from a bank guarantee of a business transaction; sold at discount from maturity value	30 to 180 days	Slightly lower than negotiable CDs and commercial paper but higher than U.S. Treasury issues	4.76%
Eurodollar deposits	Foreign banks	Deposits of currency not native to the country in which the bank is located; large denominations; active secondary market	1 day to 3 years	Highest, due to less regulation of depository banks and some foreign exchange risk	4.93%
Money market mutual funds	Professional portfolio management companies	Professionally managed portfolios of marketable securities; provide instant liquidity	None— depends on wishes of investor	Vary, but generally higher than U.S. Treasury issues and comparable to negotiable CDs and commercial paper	4.27%[d]
Repurchase agreements	Bank or security dealer	Bank or security dealer sells specific securities to firm and agrees to repurchase them at a specific price and time	Customized to purchaser's needs	Generally slightly below that associated with the outright purchase of the security	—

[a]The prime rate of interest at this time was 7.75%.

[b]Yields obtained for 3-month maturities of each security.

[c]A Federal National Mortgage Association (FNMA) issue maturing in July 1999 is used here in the absence of any average-yield data.

[d]The Schwab Money Market Fund with an average maturity of 71 days is used here in the absence of any average-yield data.

Source: Wall Street Journal, April 8, 1999, pp. C13, C18, C20.

pants each willing to purchase one share of a security is less desirable than 1,000 participants each willing to purchase 2,000 shares. Although both breadth and depth are needed to make a security salable, it is much more important for a market to have depth.

SAFETY OF PRINCIPAL

safety of principal
The ease of salability of a security for close to the amount initially invested.

There should be little or no loss in the value of a marketable security over time. Consider a security that was recently purchased for $1,000. If it can be sold quickly for $500, does that make it marketable? No. According to the definition of marketability, the security not only must be salable quickly, but also must be salable for close to the amount initially invested. This aspect of marketability is referred to as **safety of principal.** Only securities that can be easily converted into cash without experiencing any appreciable reduction in principal are candidates for short-term investment.

MAKING PURCHASE DECISIONS

A major decision confronting the business firm is when to purchase marketable securities. This decision is difficult because it involves a tradeoff between the opportunity to earn a return on idle funds during the holding period and the brokerage costs associated with the purchase and sale of marketable securities.

Example ▼ Assume that a firm must pay $35 in brokerage costs to purchase and sell $4,500 worth of marketable securities yielding an annual return of 8 percent that will be held for one month. Because the securities are to be held for $1/12$ of a year, the firm earns interest of .67 percent ($1/12 \times 8\%$) or $30 (.0067 \times $4,500). Because the interest return is less than the $35 cost of the transaction, the firm should *not* make the investment. This tradeoff between interest returns and brokerage costs is a key factor in determining when and whether to purchase marketable
▲ securities.

GOVERNMENT ISSUES

The short-term obligations issued by the federal government and available as marketable security investments are Treasury bills, Treasury notes, and federal agency issues. These securities have relatively low yields due to their low risk and because the interest income on all Treasury issues and most federal agency issues, although taxable at the federal level, is exempt from state and local taxes.

TREASURY BILLS

Treasury bills
U.S. Treasury obligations issued weekly on an auction basis, having varying maturities, generally under 1 year, and considered virtually risk-free.

Treasury bills are obligations of the U.S. Treasury that are issued weekly on an auction basis. The most common maturities are 91 and 182 days, although bills with 1-year maturities are occasionally sold. Treasury bills are sold by competitive bidding. Because they are issued in bearer form, there is a strong *secondary (resale) market.* The bills are sold at a discount from their face value, the face value being received at maturity. The smallest denomination of a Treasury bill currently available is $1,000. Because Treasury bills are issues of the United States government, they are considered to be virtually risk-free. For this reason, and because of the strong secondary market for them, Treasury bills are one of the most popular marketable securities. The yields on Treasury bills are generally lower than those on any other marketable securities due to their virtually risk-free nature and favorable tax status.

TREASURY NOTES

Treasury notes
U.S. Treasury obligations with initial maturities of between 1 and 10 years, paying interest at a stated rate semiannually, and considered virtually risk-free.

Treasury notes have initial maturities of between 1 and 10 years; due to the existence of a strong secondary market, they are attractive marketable security investments. They are generally issued in minimum denominations of either $1,000 or $5,000, carry a coupon interest rate, and pay interest semiannually. Because of their virtually risk-free nature and favorable tax status, Treasury notes generally have a low yield relative to other, nongovernment securities with similar maturities.

FEDERAL AGENCY ISSUES

federal agency issues
Low-risk securities issued by government agencies but not guaranteed by the U.S. Treasury, having generally short maturities, and offering slightly higher yields than comparable U.S. Treasury issues.

Certain agencies of the federal government issue their own debt. These **federal agency issues** are not part of the public debt, are not a legal obligation of the U.S. Treasury, and are not guaranteed by the U.S. Treasury. Regardless of their lack of direct government backing, the issues of government agencies are readily accepted as low-risk securities, because most purchasers feel that they are implicitly guaranteed by the federal government. Agency issues generally have minimum denominations of $1,000 or more and are issued either with a stated interest rate or at a discount. Agencies commonly issuing short-term instruments include the Federal Farm Credit Bank (FFCB), the Federal Home Loan Bank (FHLB), and the Federal National Mortgage Association (FNMA). Of course, instead of agency issues with short initial maturities, other longer-term agency issues with less than 1 year to maturity could be purchased. Most agency issues offer slightly higher yields than U.S. Treasury issues having similar maturities. Agency issues have a strong secondary market, which is most easily reached through government securities dealers.

NONGOVERNMENT ISSUES

negotiable certificates of deposit (CDs)
Legally transferable instruments that represent specific cash deposits in commercial banks and have varying maturities and yields based on size, maturity, and prevailing money market conditions. Yields are generally above those on U.S. Treasury issues and comparable to those on commercial paper with similar maturities.

Additional marketable securities are issued by banks or businesses. These nongovernment issues typically have slightly higher yields than government issues with similar maturities due to the slightly higher risks associated with them and the fact that their interest income is taxable at all levels—federal, state, and local. The principal nongovernment marketable securities are described below.

NEGOTIABLE CERTIFICATES OF DEPOSIT (CDs)

Negotiable certificates of deposit (CDs) are legally transferable (negotiable) instruments that represent the deposit of a certain number of dollars in a commercial bank. The amounts and maturities are normally tailored to the investor's needs. Average maturities of 30 days are common. A good secondary market for CDs exists. Normally, the smallest denomination for a negotiable CD is $100,000. The yields on CDs are initially set on the basis of size, maturity, and prevailing money market conditions. They are typically above those on U.S. Treasury issues and comparable to the yields on commercial paper with similar maturities.

COMMERCIAL PAPER

commercial paper
A short-term, unsecured promissory note issued by a corporation that has a very high credit standing, having a yield above that paid on U.S. Treasury issues and comparable to that available on negotiable CDs with similar maturities

Commercial paper is a short-term, unsecured promissory note issued by a corporation that has a very high credit standing.[5] These notes are generally issued in multiples of $100,000 and have initial maturities of anywhere from 3 to 270 days.[6] They can be sold directly by the issuer or through dealers. The yield on commercial paper typically is above that paid on U.S. Treasury issues and comparable to that on negotiable CDs with similar maturities.

BANKER'S ACCEPTANCES

banker's acceptances
Short-term, low-risk marketable securities arising from bank guarantees of business transactions; are sold by banks at a discount from their maturity value and provide yields slightly below those on negotiable CDs and commercial paper, but higher than those on U.S. Treasury issues.

Banker's acceptances arise from a short-term credit arrangement used by businesses to finance transactions, especially those involving firms in foreign countries or firms with unknown credit capacities. The purchaser requests its bank to issue a *letter of credit* on its behalf, authorizing the seller to draw a *time draft*—an order to pay a specified amount at a specified time—in payment for the goods. Once the goods are shipped, the seller presents the time draft along with proof of shipment to its bank. The seller's bank then forwards the draft to the buyer's bank for acceptance and receives payment. The buyer's bank may either hold the acceptance to maturity or sell it at a discount in the money market. If it is sold, the size of the discount from the acceptance's maturity value and the amount of time until the acceptance is paid determine the purchaser's yield.

As a result of its sale, the banker's acceptance becomes a marketable security that can be traded in the marketplace. The initial maturities of banker's acceptances are typically between 30 and 180 days, 90 days being most common. A banker's acceptance is a low-risk security because at least two, and sometimes three, parties may be liable for its payment at maturity. The yields on banker's acceptances are generally slightly below those on negotiable CDs and commercial paper, but higher than those on U.S. Treasury issues.

EURODOLLAR DEPOSITS

Eurodollar deposits
Deposits of currency not native to the country in which the bank is located; legally transferable, usually pay interest at maturity, and typically denominated in units of $1 million. Provide yields above nearly all other marketable securities with similar maturities.

Eurodollar deposits are deposits of currency that are not native to the country in which the bank is located. London is the center of the Eurodollar market. Other important centers are Paris, Frankfurt, Zurich, Nassau (Bahamas), Singapore, and Hong Kong. Nearly 75 percent of these deposits are in the form of U.S. dol-

---

[5]The role of commercial paper from the point of view of the issuer is included in the discussion of sources of short-term financing available to business in Chapter 15.

[6]The maximum maturity is 270 days because the Securities and Exchange Commission (SEC) requires formal registration of corporate issues having maturities greater than 270 days.

lars. The deposits are legally transferable, usually pay interest at maturity, and are typically denominated in units of $1 million. Maturities range from overnight to several years, with most being in the 1-week to 6-month maturity range.

Eurodollar deposits tend to provide yields above nearly all other marketable securities, government or nongovernment, with similar maturities. These higher yields are attributable to (1) the fact that the depository banks are generally less closely regulated than U.S. banks and are therefore more risky, and (2) some foreign exchange risk may be present. An active secondary market allows Eurodollar deposits to be used to meet all three motives for holding cash and near-cash balances.

MONEY MARKET MUTUAL FUNDS

money market mutual funds
Professionally managed portfolios of marketable securities, having instant liquidity, competitive yields, and often-low transactions costs.

Money market mutual funds, often called *money funds*, are professionally managed portfolios of marketable securities. Shares in these funds can be easily acquired. A minimum initial investment of as low as $500, but generally $1,000 or more, is required. Money funds provide instant liquidity in much the same way as a checking or savings account. By investing in these funds, investors often earn returns that are comparable to or higher than those from negotiable CDs and commercial paper—especially during periods of high interest rates. In recent years, generally low interest rates have caused money fund returns to fall below those on most other marketable securities. Nevertheless, due to the high liquidity, competitive yields, and often-low transactions costs, these funds have achieved significant growth in size and popularity.

REPURCHASE AGREEMENTS

repurchase agreement
An arrangement whereby a bank or securities dealer sells specific marketable securities to a firm and agrees to buy them back at a specific price and time.

A **repurchase agreement** is not a specific security. It is an arrangement whereby a bank or securities dealer sells specific marketable securities to a firm and agrees to buy them back at a specific price at a specified point in time. In exchange for the tailor-made maturity date provided by this arrangement, the seller provides the purchaser with a return slightly below that obtainable through outright purchase of similar marketable securities. The benefit to the purchaser is the guaranteed repurchase, and the tailor-made maturity date ensures that the purchaser will have cash at a specified point in time. The actual securities involved may be government or nongovernment issues. Repurchase agreements are ideal for marketable securities investments made to satisfy the transactions motive.

Review Questions

16-12   What two characteristics make a security marketable? Which aspect of a market for a security is more important—breadth or depth? Why?
16-13   Discuss the two reasons why government issues of marketable securities have generally lower yields than nongovernment issues with similar maturities.
16-14   For each of the following government-based marketable securities, give a brief description emphasizing issuer, initial maturity, liquidity, risk, and return: (a) Treasury bill; (b) Treasury note; and (c) federal agency issue.

16-15 Describe the basic features—including issuer, initial maturity, liquidity, risk, and return—of each of the following nongovernment marketable securities: (a) negotiable certificate of deposit (CD); (b) commercial paper; (c) banker's acceptance; and (d) Eurodollar deposit.

16-16 Briefly describe the basic features of the following marketable securities, and explain how they both involve other marketable securities: (a) money market mutual fund and (b) repurchase agreement

SUMMARY

LG1 **Discuss why firms hold cash and marketable securities, and how the levels they hold of each relate to those motives.** The three motives for holding cash and near-cash (marketable securities) are (1) the transactions motive, (2) the safety motive, and (3) the speculative motive. Management's goal should be to maintain levels of cash balances and marketable securities that contribute to improving the value of the firm. Cash balances satisfy transactional needs; marketable securities provide a safety stock of liquid resources and, possibly, the ability to profit from unexpected events that may arise.

LG2 **Demonstrate the three basic strategies for the efficient management of cash using the firm's operating and cash conversion cycles.** The efficient management of cash is affected by the firm's operating and cash conversion cycles. Management wants to minimize the length of these cycles without jeopardizing profitability. Three basic strategies for managing the cash conversion cycle are (1) turning over inventory as quickly as possible, (2) collecting accounts receivable as quickly as possible, and (3) paying accounts payable as late as possible without damaging the firm's credit rating. These strategies should reduce the firm's cash conversion cycle and negotiated financing need, thereby improving its profitability.

LG3 **Explain *float*, including its three basic components, and the firm's major objectives with respect to collection float and disbursement float.** Float refers to funds that have been dispatched by a payer but are not yet in a form that can be spent by the payee. Both collection and disbursement float have the same three components: (1) mail float, (2) processing float, and (3) clearing float. The firm's major objective with respect to float is to minimize collection float and maximize disbursement float within reasonable limits.

LG4 **Review popular techniques for speeding up collections and slowing down disbursements, the role of banking relationships, and international cash management.** Popular techniques for speeding up collections include concentration banking, lockboxes, direct sends, preauthorized checks (PACs), depository transfer checks (DTCs), wire transfers, and ACH (automated clearinghouse) debits. Techniques for slowing down disbursements include controlled disbursing, playing the float, overdraft systems, zero-balance accounts, and ACH (automated clearinghouse) credits. Banks now offer many cash management services, and strong banking relationships are crucial for effective cash management. Dramatic differences between foreign and domestic banking systems result in more complex cash management practices for international firms.

LG5 **Understand the basic characteristics of marketable securities and the key government issues.** Marketable securities allow the firm to earn a return on temporarily idle funds. To be considered marketable, a security must have a ready market with both breadth and depth. Furthermore, the risk associated with the safety of the principal must be quite low. The decision to purchase marketable securities depends on the tradeoff between the return earned during the holding period and the brokerage costs associated with purchasing and selling the securities. The key features and recent yields for each of the three key government issues were summarized in the upper portion of Table 16.1. These securities have relatively low yields due to their low risk and because interest income on all

Treasury issues and most federal agency issues is exempt from state and local taxes.

 Describe the popular nongovernment marketable securities and their key features. Nongovernment issues include negotiable certificates of deposit (CDs), commercial paper, banker's acceptances, Eurodollar deposits, money market mutual funds, and repurchase agreements. The key features and recent yields for each of these marketable securities were summarized in the lower portion of Table 16.1. These securities have slightly higher yields than government issues with similar maturities due to the slightly higher risks associated with them and because their interest income is taxable at all levels—federal, state, and local.

SELF-TEST PROBLEMS   (Solutions in Appendix B)

 ST 16-1   Cash conversion cycle   Hurkin Manufacturing Company pays accounts payable on the tenth day after purchase. The average collection period is 30 days, and the average age of inventory is 40 days. The firm currently spends about $18 million on operating cycle investments. The firm is considering a plan that would stretch its accounts payable by 20 days. If the firm pays 12 percent per year for its financing, what annual savings can it realize by this plan? Assume no discount for early payment of trade credit and a 360-day year.

ST 16-2   Lockbox decision   A firm that has an annual opportunity cost of 9 percent is contemplating installation of a lockbox system at an annual cost of $90,000. The system is expected to reduce mailing time by 1½ days, reducing processing time by 1½ days, and reduce check clearing time by 1 day. If the firm collects $300,000 per day, would you recommend the system? Explain.

PROBLEMS

  16-1   Cash conversion cycle   Wilderness Products is concerned about managing cash efficiently. On the average, inventories have an average age of 90 days, and accounts receivable are collected in 60 days. Accounts payable are paid approximately 30 days after they arise. The firm spends $30 million on operating cycle investments each year, at a constant rate. Assuming a 360-day year:
a. Calculate the firm's operating cycle.
b. Calculate the firm's cash conversion cycle.
c. Calculate the amount of negotiated financing required to support the firm's cash conversion cycle.
d. Discuss how management might be able to reduce the cash conversion cycle.

 16-2   Cash conversion cycle   Gerald & Company has an inventory turnover of 12 times each year, an average collection period of 45 days, and an average payment period of 40 days. The firm spends $1 million on operating cycle investments each year. Assuming a 360-day year:
a. Calculate the firm's operating cycle.
b. Calculate the firm's cash conversion cycle.

c. Calculate the amount of negotiated financing required to support the firm's cash conversion cycle.

d. If the firm's operating cycle were lengthened, without any change in its average payment period (APP), how would this affect its cash conversion cycle and negotiated financing need?

 16-3 Comparison of cash conversion cycles A firm turns its inventory, on average, every 105 days. Its accounts receivable are collected, on the average, after 75 days, and accounts payable are paid an average of 60 days after they arise. Assuming a 360-day year, what changes will occur in the cash conversion cycle under each of the following circumstances?

a. The average age of inventory changes to 90 days.
b. The average collection period changes to 60 days.
c. The average payment period changes to 105 days.
d. The circumstances in **a, b,** and **c** occur simultaneously.

 16-4 Changes in cash conversion cycles A firm is considering several plans that affect its current accounts. Given the five plans and their probable results shown in the following table, which one would you favor? Explain.

| | Change | | |
Plan	Average age of inventory	Average collection period	Average payment period
A	+30 days	+20 days	+5 days
B	+20 days	−10 days	+15 days
C	−10 days	0 days	−5 days
D	−15 days	+15 days	+10 days
E	+5 days	−10 days	+15 days

 16-5 Changing cash conversion cycle Barnstead Industries turns its inventory 8 times each year, has an average payment period of 35 days, and has an average collection period of 60 days. The firm's total annual outlays for operating cycle investments are $3.5 million. Assuming a 360-day year:

a. Calculate the firm's operating and cash conversion cycles.
b. Calculate the firm's daily cash operating expenditure. How much negotiated financing is required to support its cash conversion cycle?
c. Assuming the firm pays 14 percent for its financing, by how much would it increase its annual profits by *favorably* changing its current cash conversion cycle by 20 days?

 16-6 Multiple changes in cash conversion cycle Hubbard Corporation turns its inventory six times each year; it has an average collection period of 45 days and an average payment period of 30 days. The firm's annual operating cycle investment is $3 million. Assuming a 360-day year:

a. Calculate the firm's cash conversion cycle, its daily cash operating expenditure, and the amount of negotiated financing required to support its cash conversion cycle.

    b. Find the firm's cash conversion cycle and negotiated financing requirement if it makes the following changes simultaneously.

      (1) Shortens the average age of inventory by 5 days.

      (2) Speeds the collection of accounts receivable by an average of 10 days.

      (3) Extends the average payment period by 10 days.

    c. If the firm pays 13 percent for its negotiated financing, by how much, if anything, could it increase its annual profit as a result of the changes in **b**?

    d. If the annual cost of achieving the profit in **c** is $35,000, what action would you recommend to the firm? Why?

16-7 **Float** Breeland Industries has daily cash receipts of $65,000. A recent analysis of its collections indicated that customers' payments were in the mail an average of 2½ days. Once received, the payments are processed in 1½ days. After payments are deposited, it takes an average of 3 days for these receipts to clear the banking system.

    a. How much collection float (in days) does the firm currently have?

    b. If the firm's opportunity cost is 11 percent, would it be economically advisable for the firm to pay an annual fee of $16,500 to reduce collection float by 3 days? Explain why or why not.

16-8 **Concentration banking** Tal-Off Corporation sells to a national market and bills all credit customers from the New York City office. Using a continuous billing system, the firm has collections of $1.2 million per day. Under consideration is a concentration banking system that would require customers to mail payments to the nearest regional office to be deposited in local banks.

    Tal-Off estimates that the collection period for accounts will be shortened an average of 2½ days under this system. The firm also estimates that *annual* service charges and administrative costs of $300,000 will result from the proposed system. The firm can earn 14 percent on equal-risk investments.

    a. How much cash will be made available for other uses if the firm accepts the proposed concentration banking system?

    b. What savings will the firm realize on the 2½-day reduction in the collection period?

    c. Would you recommend the change? Explain your answer.

16-9 **Concentration banking—Range of outcomes** Pet-Care Company markets its products through widely dispersed distributors in the United States. It currently takes between 6 and 9 days for cash-receipt checks to become available to the firm once they are mailed. Through use of a concentration banking system, the firm estimates that the collection float can be reduced to between 2 and 4 days. Daily cash receipts currently average $10,000. The firm's minimum opportunity cost is 5.5 percent.

    a. Use the data given to determine the minimum and maximum annual savings from implementing the proposed system.

    b. If the annual cost of the concentration banking system is $7,500, what recommendation would you make?

    c. What impact, if any, would the fact that the firm's opportunity cost is 12 percent have on your analysis? Explain.

16-10 Lockbox system   Orient Oil feels that a lockbox system can shorten its accounts receivable collection period by 3 days. Credit sales are $3,240,000 per year, billed on a continuous basis. The firm has other equally risky investments with a return of 15 percent. The cost of the lockbox system is $9,000 per year.

a. What amount of cash will be made available for other uses under the lockbox system?

b. What net benefit (cost) will the firm receive if it adopts the lockbox system? Should it adopt the proposed lockbox system?

16-11 Direct send—Single   Lorca Industries of San Diego, California, just received a check in the amount of $800,000 from a customer in Bangor, Maine. If the firm processes the check in the normal manner, the funds will become available in 6 days. To speed up this process, the firm could send an employee to the bank in Bangor on which the check is drawn to present it for payment. Such action will cause the funds to become available after 2 days. If the cost of the direct send is $650 and the firm can earn 11 percent on these funds, what recommendation would you make? Explain.

16-12 Direct sends—Multiple   Ricor Enterprises just received four sizable checks drawn on various distant banks throughout the United States. The data on these checks are summarized in the table shown below. The firm, which has a 12 percent opportunity cost, can lease a small business jet with pilot to fly the checks to the cities of the banks on which they are drawn and present them for immediate payment. This task can be accomplished in a single day—thereby reducing to 1 day the funds availability from each of the four checks. The total cost of leasing the jet with pilot and other incidental expenditures is $4,500. Analyze the proposed action and make a recommendation.

Check	Amount	Number of days until funds are available
1	$ 600,000	7 days
2	2,000,000	5
3	1,300,000	4
4	400,000	6

16-13 Controlled disbursing   A large midwestern firm has annual cash disbursements of $360 million made continuously over the year. Although annual service and administrative costs would increase by $100,000, the firm is considering writing all disbursement checks on a small bank in Oregon. The firm estimates that this will allow an additional 1½ days of cash usage. If the firm earns a return on other equally risky investments of 12 percent, should it change to the distant bank? Why or why not?

16-14 Playing the float   Tollfree Enterprises routinely funds its checking account to cover all checks when written. A thorough analysis of its checking account discloses that the firm could maintain an average account balance that is 25 percent below the current level and adequately cover all checks presented. The average account balance is currently $900,000. If the firm can earn 10 percent on short-term investments, what, if any, annual savings would result from maintaining the lower average account balance?

16-15 Payroll account management   Clearview Window has a weekly payroll of $250,000. The payroll checks are issued on Friday afternoon each week. In examining the check-cashing behavior of its employees, it has found the pattern shown in the following table.

Number of business days[a] since issue of check	Percentage of checks cleared
1	20%
2	40
3	30
4	10

[a]Excludes Saturday and Sunday.

Given the information above, what recommendation would you make to the firm with respect to managing its payroll account? Explain.

16-16 Zero-balance account   Danzig Industries is considering establishment of a zero-balance account. The firm currently maintains an average balance of $420,000 in its disbursement account. As compensation to the bank for maintaining the zero-balance account, the firm will have to pay a monthly fee of $1,000 and maintain a $300,000 noninterest-earning deposit in the bank. The firm currently has no other deposits in the bank. Evaluate the proposed zero-balance account, and make a recommendation to the firm assuming that it has a 12 percent opportunity cost.

16-17 Marketable securities purchase decisions   To purchase and sell $25,000 in marketable securities, a firm must pay $800. If the marketable securities have a yield of 12 percent annually, recommend purchasing or not if:
a. The securities are held for 1 month.
b. The securities are held for 3 months.
c. The securities are held for 6 months.
d. The securities are held for 1 year.

CASE   Chapter 16   **Assessing Mexicali Furniture's Cash Management Efficiency**

Marie Chen, vice president of finance at Mexicali Furniture, a manufacturer of contemporary Spanish furniture, is concerned about the firm's high level of short-term negotiated financing. She feels that the firm can improve the management of its cash and, as a result, reduce its heavy reliance on negotiated financing. In this regard, she charged David Bunten, the treasurer, with assessing the firm's cash management efficiency. David decided to begin his investigation by studying the firm's operating and cash conversion cycles.

David found that Mexicali's average payment period was 25 days. He consulted industry data, which showed that the average payment period for the industry was 40 days. Investigation of three similar furniture manufacturers revealed that their average payment period was also 40 days.

Next, David studied the production cycle and inventory policies. The average age of inventory was 120 days. He determined that the industry standard as reported in a survey done by *Furniture Age,* the trade association journal, was 85 days.

Further analysis showed David that the firm's average collection period was 60 days. The industry average, derived from the trade association data and information on three similar furniture manufacturers, was found to be 42 days—30 percent lower than Mexicali's.

Mexicali Furniture was spending an estimated $14,400,000 per year on its operating cycle investments. David considered this expenditure level to be the minimum that he could expect the firm to disburse during the coming year. His concern was whether the firm's cash management was as efficient as it could be. He estimated that the firm could achieve the industry standards in managing its payables, inventory, and receivables by incurring an annual cost of $120,000. David knew that the company paid 15 percent annual interest for its negotiated financing. For this reason, he was concerned about the financing cost resulting from any inefficiencies in the management of Mexicali's cash conversion cycle.

Required

a. Assuming a constant rate for purchases, production, and sales throughout the year, what are Mexicali's existing operating cycle (OC), cash conversion cycle (CCC), and negotiated financing need?

b. If Mexicali can optimize operations according to industry standards, what would its operating cycle (OC), cash conversion cycle (CCC), and negotiated financing need be under these more efficient conditions?

c. In terms of negotiated financing requirements, what is the annual cost of Mexicali Furniture's operational inefficiency?

d. Should the firm incur the $120,000 annual cost to achieve the industry level of operational efficiency? Explain why or why not.

Web Exercise

GOTO web site www.mercantile.com. Click BUSINESS BANKING in the left column.

1. What are the business services offered in the left column?

Click CASH MANAGEMENT.

2. What are the services offered in the cash management area?

Click RECEIPTS.

3. What are the areas of service involving receipts?
4. What are the three types of lockbox services?

Next GOTO web site www.national-city.com. Click BUSINESS BANKING.

5. Under the MORE INFO menu, what are the services available for small businesses?
6. Under the MORE INFO menu, what are the services available for Treasury Management?
7. Under the MORE INFO menu, what are the services available for International Services?

Now GOTO web site www.firstmerchants.com. Click on COMMERCIAL BANKING SERVICES.

8. What are the services available to businesses?

17 ACCOUNTS RECEIVABLE AND INVENTORY

LEARNING GOALS

LG1 Discuss credit selection, including the five C's of credit, obtaining and analyzing credit information, credit scoring, and managing international credit.

LG2 Use the key variables to evaluate quantitatively the effects of either relaxing or tightening a firm's credit standards.

LG3 Review the effects of changes in each of the three components of credit terms on the key financial variables and on profits, and the procedure for quantitatively evaluating cash discount changes.

LG4 Explain the key features of collection policy, including aging accounts receivable, the effects of changes in collection efforts, and the popular collection techniques.

LG5 Understand inventory fundamentals, the relationship between inventory and accounts receivable, and international inventory management.

LG6 Describe the common techniques for managing inventory, including the ABC system, the basic economic order quantity model, the reorder point, the materials requirement planning system, and the just-in-time system.

ACROSS the DISCIPLINES

In addition to managing cash and marketable securities, firms also must manage their accounts receivable and inventories. These two accounts typically represent the largest investment in the firm's current assets, so their wise management can affect the firm's costs in a big way, as well as impact the firm's competitive position. This chapter demonstrates the effects that credit and collection policies can have on the firm's investment in accounts receivable, and it presents basic information on inventory management. Chapter 17 is important to:

- **accounting personnel** who will help estimate and manage accounts receivable and inventory costs.

- **information systems analysts** who will design and manage information systems that monitor the collection process and track all types of inventory.

- **management** because it will set the firm's credit and collection policies and will establish appropriate levels of inventory.

- **the marketing department** because sales volume will be affected by the firm's credit policy and order fulfillment will be affected by the levels of inventory that management has established.

- **operations,** which will design and implement the inventory management and control systems.

CREDIT SELECTION

LG 1

credit policy
The determination of credit selection, credit standards, and credit terms.

Accounts receivable represent the firm's extension of credit to its customers. For the average manufacturer, accounts receivable make up about 37 percent of *current assets* and about 16 percent of *total assets*. For most manufacturers, extending credit to customers is a cost of doing business. By keeping its money tied up in accounts receivable, the firm loses the time value of the money and runs the risk of not being paid the amounts owed. In return for incurring these costs, the firm can be competitive, attract and retain customers, and maintain and improve sales and profits.

Generally, the firm's financial manager controls accounts receivable through the establishment and management of (1) **credit policy,** which includes determining credit selection, credit standards, and credit terms, and (2) *collection policy.* The firm's approach to managing these two aspects of accounts receivable is heavily influenced by competitive conditions—typically, greater leniency enhances competition, and less leniency hinders competition. Here we discuss credit selection; in later sections, we look at credit standards, credit terms, and collection policy.

credit selection
The decision whether to extend credit to a customer and how much credit to extend.

A firm's **credit selection** involves deciding whether to extend credit to a customer and how much credit to extend. First, we look at the five C's of credit, which are the traditional focus of credit investigation.

THE FIVE C'S OF CREDIT

five C's of credit
The five key dimensions—character, capacity, capital, collateral, and conditions—used by credit analysts to focus their analysis of an applicant's creditworthiness.

Credit analysts often use the **five C's of credit** to focus their analysis on the key dimensions of an applicant's creditworthiness—character, capacity, capital, collateral, and conditions. Each is described below:

1. *Character:* The applicant's record of meeting past obligations—financial, contractual, and moral. Past payment history as well as any pending or resolved legal judgments against the applicant would be used.
2. *Capacity:* The applicant's ability to repay the requested credit. Financial statement analysis (see Chapter 5), with particular emphasis on liquidity and debt ratios, is typically used to assess the applicant's capacity.
3. *Capital:* The financial strength of the applicant as reflected by its ownership position. Analysis of the applicant's debt relative to equity and its profitability ratios are frequently used to assess its capital.
4. *Collateral:* The amount of assets the applicant has available for use in securing the credit. The larger the amount of available assets, the greater the chance that a firm will recover its funds if the applicant defaults. A review of the applicant's balance sheet, asset-value appraisals, and any legal claims filed against the applicant's assets can be used to evaluate its collateral.
5. *Conditions:* The current economic and business climate as well as any unique circumstances affecting either party to the credit transaction. For example, if the firm has excess inventory of the items the applicant wishes to purchase on credit, the firm may be willing to sell on more favorable terms or to less creditworthy applicants. General economic and business conditions, as well as special circumstances, are considered in assessing conditions.

The credit analyst typically gives primary attention to the first two C's—character and capacity—because they represent the most basic requirements for extending credit. The last three C's—capital, collateral, and conditions—are important in structuring the credit arrangement and making the final credit decision, which is also affected by the credit analyst's experience and judgment.

OBTAINING CREDIT INFORMATION

When a business is approached by a customer desiring credit terms, the credit department typically begins the evaluation process by requiring the applicant to fill out forms that request financial and credit information and references. Working from the application, the firm obtains additional information from other sources. If the firm has previously extended credit to the applicant, it will have its own information on the applicant's payment history. The major external sources of credit information are as follows:

1. **Financial Statements.** By requiring the credit applicant to provide financial statements for the past few years, the firm can analyze the applicant firm's liquidity, activity, debt, and profitability positions.

Dun & Bradstreet (D&B)
The largest mercantile credit-reporting agency in the United States.

2. **Dun & Bradstreet.** Dun & Bradstreet (D&B) is the largest mercantile credit-reporting agency in the United States. It provides subscribers with a copy of its *Reference Book,* which contains credit ratings and keyed estimates of overall financial strength for virtually millions of U.S. and international companies. The key to the D&B ratings is shown in Figure 17.1. For example, a

---

FIGURE 17.1 Key to Ratings
The key to Dun & Bradstreet's ratings

Key to Ratings

Estimated Financial Strength			High	Good	Fair	Limited
5A	$50,000,000	and over	1	2	3	4
4A	$10,000,000 to	49,999,999	1	2	3	4
3A	1,000,000 to	9,999,999	1	2	3	4
2A	750,000 to	999,999	1	2	3	4
1A	500,000 to	749,999	1	2	3	4
BA	300,000 to	499,999	1	2	3	4
BB	200,000 to	299,999	1	2	3	4
CB	125,000 to	199,999	1	2	3	4
CC	75,000 to	124,999	1	2	3	4
DC	50,000 to	74,999	1	2	3	4
DD	35,000 to	49,999	1	2	3	4
EE	20,000 to	34,999	1	2	3	4
FF	10,000 to	19,999	1	2	3	4
GG	5,000 to	9,999	1	2	3	4
HH	Up to	4,999	1	2	3	4

Composite Credit Appraisal

DUN & BRADSTREET
Information Services
DB a company of
The Dun & Bradstreet Corporation

firm rated 2A3 would have estimated financial strength (net worth) in the range of $750,000 to $999,999 and would have a *fair* credit appraisal. D&B subscribers can also purchase detailed reports on specific companies and electronic access to D&B's database of business information through its *Electronic Access Systems.*

3. **Credit Interchange Bureaus.** The National Credit Interchange System is a national network of local credit bureaus that exchange information. The reports obtained through these exchanges contain factual data rather than analyses. A fee is usually levied for each inquiry.

4. **Direct Credit Information Exchanges.** Often, local, regional, or national trade associations serve as clearinghouses for credit information that is supplied by and made available to their member companies. Another approach is to contact other suppliers selling to the applicant and request information on the applicant's payment history.

5. **Bank Checking.** It may be possible for the firm's bank to obtain credit information from the applicant's bank. However, the type of information obtained will most likely be vague unless the applicant helps the firm obtain it. Typically, an estimate of the firm's cash balance is provided. For instance, the bank may indicate that the applicant normally maintains a "high-five-figure" balance in its checking account.

ANALYZING CREDIT INFORMATION

credit analysis
The evaluation of credit applicants.

line of credit
The maximum amount a credit customer can owe the selling firm at any one time.

Firms typically establish procedures for use in **credit analysis**—the evaluation of credit applicants. Often the firm not only must determine the creditworthiness of a customer, but also must estimate the maximum amount of credit the customer is capable of supporting. Once this is done, the firm can establish a **line of credit,** the maximum amount the customer can owe the firm at any one time. The line of credit is similar to a line of credit extended by a bank to a short-term borrower, as described in Chapter 15. Lines of credit eliminate the necessity of checking a major customer's credit each time a large purchase is made.

We now consider procedures for analyzing credit information, the economic considerations involved in such analyses, and the small business problem.

PROCEDURES

A credit applicant's financial statements and accounts payable ledger can be used to calculate its "average payment period." This value can be compared to the credit terms currently extended to the applicant by others. For customers requesting large amounts of credit, a thorough ratio analysis of the firm's liquidity, activity, debt, and profitability should be performed by using the financial statements. A time-series comparison (discussed in Chapter 5) of similar ratios for various years should uncover any developing trends. The *Dun & Bradstreet Reference Book* can be used for estimating the maximum line of credit to extend. Dun & Bradstreet suggests no more than 10 percent of the amount it assigns as a customer's "estimated financial strength" (see Figure 17.1).

One of the key inputs to the final credit decision is the credit analyst's *subjective judgment* of a firm's creditworthiness. Experience provides a "feel" for the nonquantifiable aspects of the quality of a firm's operations. The analyst will add his or her knowledge of the character of the applicant's management, references from other suppliers, and the firm's historic payment patterns to any quantitative figures developed, to determine creditworthiness. The analyst will then make the final decision as to whether to extend credit to the applicant and in what amount. Often these decisions are made by a credit review committee.

ECONOMIC CONSIDERATIONS

Regardless of whether the firm's credit department is evaluating the creditworthiness of a customer desiring credit for a specific transaction or that of a regular customer to establish a line of credit, the basic procedures are the same. The only difference is the depth of the analysis. A firm would be unwise to spend $100 to investigate the creditworthiness of a customer making a one-time $40 purchase, but $100 for a credit investigation may be a good investment in the case of a customer expected to make credit purchases of $60,000 annually. Clearly, the firm's credit selection procedures must consider the benefits and costs of obtaining and analyzing credit information.

THE SMALL BUSINESS PROBLEM

Managing accounts receivable is one of the biggest financial problems facing small businesses. Small firms typically lack the personnel and processes needed to make informed credit decisions. In addition, they are eager to increase sales volumes through the extension of credit, sometimes incurring bad debts in the process. Frequently, the credit customers of small firms are local businesses managed by personal friends, which makes denying credit particularly difficult. However, the credit decision must be made on the basis of sound financial and business principles. Clearly, it is better to have a potential credit customer get upset than for excessive uncollectible receivables to jeopardize the firm.

CREDIT SCORING

credit scoring
A procedure resulting in a score that measures an applicant's overall credit strength; the credit score is derived as a weighted average of the scores obtained on key financial and credit characteristics.

Consumer credit decisions involve a large group of similar applicants, each representing a small part of the firm's total business. These can be handled by using impersonal, computer-based, credit decision techniques. One popular technique is **credit scoring**—a procedure resulting in a score that measures an applicant's overall credit strength. The credit score is derived as a weighted average of scores obtained on key financial and credit characteristics. Credit scoring is often used by large credit card operations such as oil companies and department stores. This technique can best be illustrated by an example.

Example ▼ Paula's Stores, a major regional department store chain, uses a credit scoring model to make its consumer credit decisions. Each credit applicant fills out a credit application. The application is reviewed and scored by one of the company's credit analysts, and the relevant information is entered into a computer program. The rest of the process, including making the credit decision, generating a letter of acceptance or rejection, and mailing a credit card, is automated.

Table 17.1 demonstrates the calculation of Herb Conseca's credit score, and the firm's predetermined credit standards are summarized in Table 17.2. In

TABLE 17.1	Credit Scoring of Herb Conseca by Paula's Stores		
Financial and credit characteristics	Score (0 to 100) (1)	Predetermined weight (2)	Weighted score [(1) × (2)] (3)
Credit references	80	.15	12.00
Home ownership	100	.15	15.00
Income range	70	.25	17.50
Payment history	75	.25	18.75
Years at address	90	.10	9.00
Years on job	80	.10	8.00
Total		1.00	Credit score 80.25

Key: Column 1: Scores assigned by analyst or computer using company guidelines on the basis of data presented in credit application. Scores range from 0 (lowest) to 100 (highest). Column 2: Weights based on the company's analysis of the relative importance of each financial and credit characteristic in predicting whether or not a customer will pay its account. The sum of these weights must equal 1.00.

TABLE 17.2	Credit Standards for Paula's Stores
Credit score	Action
Greater than 75	Extend standard credit terms.
65 to 75	Extend limited credit; if account is properly maintained, convert to standard credit terms after 1 year.
Less than 65	Reject application.

evaluating Herb Conseca's credit score of 80.25 in light of the firm's credit standards, Paula's Stores would decide to *extend standard credit terms* to him (because 80.25 > 75).

The attractiveness of credit scoring should be clear from the preceding example. Unfortunately, most manufacturers sell to a diversified group of different-sized businesses, not to individuals. The statistical characteristics necessary for applying credit scoring to decisions regarding *mercantile credit*—credit extended by business firms to other business firms—rarely exist. In the following discussions, we concentrate on the basic concepts of mercantile credit decisions, which cannot be expressed easily in quantifiable terms.

*P*ERSONAL FINANCE PERSPECTIVE

Learning Credit Lessons the Hard Way

For college students, getting a first credit card is easy. Card issuers run promotions on campuses, offering gifts just for applying. After the first card, students get inundated with other offers; before long, you may have several cards—and large unpaid balances. If you skip payments, the card issuer will report you to credit agencies. The result is a poor credit history, which can affect your ability to rent an apartment, get a job, or get credit in the future.

If your credit history leaves something to be desired, you might be tempted to use a credit repair service that claims it can improve a poor credit record. In most cases, these services are scams that can cost you $1,000 or more in fees but do nothing to change your record. Although there are legitimate, not-for-profit credit counseling services, the Federal Trade Commission (FTC) has never seen a legitimate credit repair company, warns Jodie Bernstein, the FTC's director of consumer protection.

The best defense against a poor credit history is to limit your use of credit cards in the first place. But if you do run into credit problems, look for a non-profit counseling service like the National Foundation for Consumer Credit (www.nfcc.org), Debt Counselors of America (www.getoutofdebt.org), or Genus (www.genus.org). These services provide budget counseling and help you develop a repayment plan. Budget help should be free or cost very little. There is a monthly charge for debt repayment plans, often only a few dollars per creditor. If the fees seem high, look for another counselor. ●

MANAGING INTERNATIONAL CREDIT

Whereas credit management is difficult enough for managers of purely domestic companies, these tasks become much more complex for companies that operate internationally. This is partly because (as we have seen before) international operations typically expose a firm to *exchange rate risk*. It is also due to the dangers and delays involved in shipping goods long distances and having to cross at least two international borders.

Exports of finished goods are usually denominated in the currency of the importer's local market; most commodities, on the other hand, are denominated in dollars. Therefore, a U.S. company that sells a product in France, for example, would have to price that product in French francs and extend credit to a French wholesaler in the local currency (francs). If the franc *depreciates* against the dollar before the U.S. exporter collects on its account receivable, the U.S. company experiences an exchange rate loss; the francs collected are worth fewer dollars than expected at the time the sale was made. Of course, the dollar could just as easily depreciate against the franc, yielding an exchange rate gain to the U.S. exporter. Most companies fear the loss more than they welcome the gain.

For a major currency like the French franc, the exporter can *hedge* against this risk by using the currency futures, forward, or options markets, but it is costly to do so, particularly for relatively small amounts. If the exporter is selling to a customer in a developing country—where 40 percent of U.S. exports are now sold—there will probably be no effective instrument available for protecting against exchange rate risk at any price. This risk may be further magnified because credit standards (and acceptable collection techniques) may be much lower in developing countries than in the United States. Although it may seem tempting to just "not bother" with exporting, U.S. companies no longer can concede foreign markets to international rivals. These export sales, if carefully monitored and, where possible, effectively hedged against exchange rate risk, often prove to be very profitable. Novice or infrequent exporters may choose to rely on *factors* (see Chapter 15) to manage their international export (credit) sales.

Although expensive, these firms are typically much better at evaluating the creditworthiness of foreign customers and are better able to bear credit risk than are most small exporters.

? Review Questions

17-1   What do a firm's *accounts receivable* represent? What is meant by a firm's *credit policy*?

17-2   Briefly list the *five C's of credit* and discuss their role in the *credit selection* activity.

17-3   Summarize the basic sources of credit information.

17-4   How do economic considerations affect the depth of credit analysis performed by a firm? Explain why managing accounts receivable is one of the biggest financial problems facing small businesses.

17-5   Describe *credit scoring* and explain why this technique is typically applied to consumer credit decisions rather than to mercantile credit decisions.

17-6   Why are the risks involved in international credit management more complex than those associated with purely domestic credit sales?

 ## CHANGING CREDIT STANDARDS

credit standards
The minimum requirements for extending credit to a customer.

The firm's **credit standards** are the minimum requirements for extending credit to a customer. Understanding the key variables that must be considered when a firm is contemplating relaxing or tightening its credit standards will give a general idea of the kinds of decisions involved.

KEY VARIABLES

The major variables to be considered when evaluating proposed changes in credit standards are (1) sales volume, (2) the investment in accounts receivable, and (3) bad debt expenses. Let us examine each in more detail.

SALES VOLUME

Changing credit standards can be expected to change the volume of sales. If credit standards are relaxed, sales are expected to increase; if credit standards are tightened, sales are expected to decrease. Generally, increases in sales affect profits positively, whereas decreases in sales affect profits negatively.

INVESTMENT IN ACCOUNTS RECEIVABLE

Accounts receivable involve a cost to the firm, attributable to the forgone earnings opportunities from the funds tied up in accounts receivable. The higher the firm's investment in accounts receivable, the greater the carrying cost; and the lower the firm's investment in accounts receivable, the lower the carrying cost. If the firm relaxes its credit standards, the volume of accounts receivable increases, and so does the firm's carrying cost. This change results from increased sales and longer collection periods due to slower payment. The opposite occurs if credit standards are tightened. Thus, a relaxation of credit standards is expected to affect profits negatively because of higher carrying costs, whereas tightening credit standards would affect profits positively as a result of lower carrying costs.

BAD DEBT EXPENSES

The probability, or risk, of acquiring a bad debt increases as credit standards are relaxed. The increase in bad debts associated with relaxation of credit standards raises bad debt expenses and affects profits negatively. The opposite effects on bad debt expenses and profits result from a tightening of credit standards.

The basic changes and effects on profits expected to result from the *relaxation* of credit standards are summarized as follows:

Effects of Relaxation of Credit Standards		
Variable	Direction of change	Effect on profits
Sales volume	Increase	Positive
Investment in accounts receivable	Increase	Negative
Bad debt expenses	Increase	Negative

If credit standards were tightened, the opposite effects would be expected.

DETERMINING VALUES OF KEY VARIABLES

Determining the key credit standard variables can be illustrated by an example.

Example ▼ Binz Tool, a manufacturer of lathe tools, is currently selling a product for $10 per unit. Sales (all on credit) for last year were 60,000 units. The variable cost per unit is $6. The firm's total fixed costs are $120,000.

The firm is currently contemplating a *relaxation of credit standards* that is expected to result in a 5 percent increase in unit sales to 63,000 units, an increase in the average collection period from its current level of 30 days to 45 days, and an increase in bad debt expenses from the current level of 1 percent of sales to 2 percent. The firm's required return on equal-risk investments, which is the opportunity cost of tying up funds in accounts receivable, is 15 percent.

To determine whether to implement the proposed relaxation of credit standards, Binz Tool must calculate the effect on the firm's additional profit contribution from sales, the cost of the marginal investment in accounts receivable, and the cost of marginal bad debts.

Additional Profit Contribution from Sales   Because fixed costs are "sunk" and thereby unaffected by a change in the sales level, the only cost relevant to a change in sales would be out-of-pocket or variable costs. Sales are expected to increase by 5 percent, or 3,000 units. The profit contribution per unit will equal the difference between the sale price per unit ($10) and the variable cost per unit ($6). The profit contribution per unit therefore will be $4. The total additional profit contribution from sales will be $12,000 (3,000 units × $4 per unit).

Cost of the Marginal Investment in Accounts Receivable   The cost of the marginal investment in accounts receivable can be calculated by finding the difference between the cost of carrying receivables before and after the introduction of the relaxed credit standards. Because our concern is only with the out-of-pocket costs, *the relevant cost in this analysis is the variable cost.* The average investment in accounts receivable can be calculated by using the following formula:

Average investment in accounts receivable

$$= \frac{\text{total variable cost of annual sales}}{\text{turnover of accounts receivable}} \tag{17.1}$$

where

$$\text{Turnover of accounts receivable}^1 = \frac{360}{\text{average collection period}}$$

The total variable cost of annual sales under the proposed and present plans can be found as follows, using the variable cost per unit of $6.

Total variable cost of annual sales:

Under proposed plan: ($6 × 63,000 units) = $378,000
Under present plan: ($6 × 60,000 units) = $360,000

Implementation of the proposed plan will cause the total variable cost of annual sales to increase from $360,000 to $378,000.

The turnover of accounts receivable refers to the number of times each year the firm's accounts receivable are actually turned into cash. In each case, it is found by dividing the average collection period into 360—the number of days assumed in a year.

Turnover of accounts receivable:

$$\text{Under proposed plan: } \frac{360}{45} = 8$$

$$\text{Under present plan: } \frac{360}{30} = 12$$

With implementation of the proposed plan, the accounts receivable turnover would slow from 12 to 8 times per year.

---

[1]The turnover of accounts receivable can also be calculated by *dividing annual sales by accounts receivable.* For the purposes of this chapter, only the formula transforming the average collection period to a turnover of accounts receivable is emphasized.

By substituting the cost and turnover data just calculated into Equation 17.1 for each case, we get the following average investments in accounts receivable:

Average investment in accounts receivable:

$$\text{Under proposed plan: } \frac{\$378,000}{8} = \$47,250$$

$$\text{Under present plan: } \frac{\$360,000}{12} = \$30,000$$

The marginal investment in accounts receivable as well as its cost are calculated as follows:

Cost of marginal investment in accounts receivable:

Average investment under proposed plan	$47,250
− Average investment under present plan	30,000
Marginal investment in accounts receivable	$17,250
× Required return on investment	.15
Cost of marginal investment in A/R[2]	$ 2,588

The resulting value of $2,588 is considered a cost because it represents the maximum amount that could have been earned on the $17,250 had it been placed in the best equal-risk investment alternative available at the firm's required return on investment of 15 percent.

Cost of Marginal Bad Debts   The cost of marginal bad debts is found by taking the difference between the level of bad debts before and after the proposed relaxation of credit standards.

Cost of marginal bad debts:

Under proposed plan: (.02 × $10/unit × 63,000 units) =	$12,600
Under present plan: (.01 × $10/unit × 60,000 units) =	6,000
Cost of marginal bad debts	$ 6,600

Note that the bad debt costs are calculated by using the sale price per unit ($10) to back out not just the true loss of variable cost ($6) that results when a customer fails to pay its account, but also the profit contribution per unit—in this case $4—that is included in the "additional profit contribution from sales." Thus, the resulting cost of marginal bad debts is $6,600.

MAKING THE CREDIT STANDARD DECISION

To decide whether to relax its credit standards, the firm must compare the additional profit contribution from sales to the added costs of the marginal investment in accounts receivable and marginal bad debts. If the additional profit contribution is

---

[2]Throughout this chapter, *A/R* will frequently be used interchangeably with *accounts receivable*.

TABLE 17.3   **The Effects on Binz Tool of a Relaxation of Credit Standards**

Additional profit contribution from sales		
[3,000 units × ($10 − $6)]		$12,000
Cost of marginal investment in A/R[a]		
Average investment under proposed plan:		
$\dfrac{\$6 \times 63,000}{8} = \dfrac{\$378,000}{8}$	$47,250	
Average investment under present plan:		
$\dfrac{\$6 \times 60,000}{12} = \dfrac{\$360,000}{12}$	30,000	
Marginal investment in A/R	$17,250	
Cost of marginal investment in A/R (.15 × $17,250)		($ 2,588)
Cost of marginal bad debts		
Bad debts under proposed plan (.02 × $10 × 63,000)	$12,600	
Bad debts under present plan (.01 × $10 × 60,000)	6,000	
Cost of marginal bad debts		($ 6,600)
Net profit from implementation of proposed plan		$ 2,812

[a]The denominators 8 and 12 in the calculation of the average investment in accounts receivable under the proposed and present plans are the accounts receivable turnovers for each of these plans (360/45 = 8 and 360/30 = 12).

greater than marginal costs, credit standards should be relaxed; otherwise, present standards should remain unchanged. Let us look at an example.

Example ▼ The results and key calculations relating to Binz Tool's decision to relax its credit standards are summarized in Table 17.3. The additional profit contribution from the increased sales would be $12,000, which exceeds the sum of the costs of the marginal investment in accounts receivable and bad debts. Therefore, the firm *should* relax its credits standards as proposed. The net addition to total profits ▲ resulting from such an action will be $2,812 per year.

The procedure described here for making a credit standard decision is also commonly used for evaluating other changes in the management of accounts receivable. If Binz Tool had been contemplating tightening its credit standards, for example, the cost would have been a reduction in the profit contribution from sales, and the return would have been from reductions in the cost of the investment in accounts receivable and in the cost of bad debts. Another application of this procedure is demonstrated later in the chapter.

? Review Question

17-7   What key variables should be considered when evaluating possible changes in a firm's *credit standards?* What are the basic tradeoffs in a *tightening* of credit standards?

CHANGING CREDIT TERMS

credit terms
Specify the repayment terms required of a firm's credit customers.

A firm's **credit terms** specify the repayment terms required of all its credit customers.[3] A type of shorthand is used to indicate the terms. For example, credit terms stated as *2/10 net 30* mean that the purchaser receives a 2 percent cash discount if the bill is paid within 10 days after the beginning of the credit period; if the customer does not take the cash discount, the full amount must be paid within 30 days after the beginning of the credit period. Credit terms cover three things: (1) the cash discount, if any (in this case, 2 percent); (2) the cash discount period (in this case, 10 days); and (3) the credit period (in this case, 30 days). Changes in any aspect of the firm's credit terms may have an effect on its overall profitability. This section discusses the positive and negative factors associated with such changes and quantitative procedures for evaluating them.

CASH DISCOUNT

When a firm initiates or *increases* a cash discount, the changes and effects on profits shown in the following table can be expected.

Effects of Increase in Cash Discount		
Variable	Direction of change	Effect on profits
Sales volume	Increase	Positive
Investment in accounts receivable due to nondiscount takers paying earlier	Decrease	Positive
Investment in accounts receivable due to new customers	Increase	Negative
Bad debt expenses	Decrease	Positive
Profit per unit	Decrease	Negative

The sales volume should increase because if the buyer is willing to pay by day 10, the unit price decreases, making the product more competitive. The net effect on accounts receivable is difficult to determine: the nondiscount takers paying earlier will reduce the accounts receivable, but new customers attracted by the change in terms will increase accounts receivable. The bad debt expenses should decline: as customers on the average will pay earlier, the probability of their not paying at all will decrease.[4] Both the assumed net decrease in the receivables investment and the decrease in bad debt expenses should result in increased

---

[3] An in-depth discussion of credit terms as viewed by the customer—that is, *accounts payable*—is presented in Chapter 15. In this chapter, our concern is with *accounts receivable*—credit terms from the point of view of the *seller*.

[4] This contention is based on the fact that the longer a person has to pay, the less likely it is that the person will pay. The more time that elapses, the more opportunities there are for a customer to become technically insolvent or fail. Therefore, the probability of a bad debt is expected to increase directly with increases in the credit period.

profits. The negative aspect of an increased cash discount is a decreased profit per unit as more customers take the discount and pay the reduced price.

Decreasing or eliminating a cash discount would have opposite effects. The quantitative effects of changes in cash discounts can be evaluated by a procedure similar to that used earlier to evaluate changes in credit standards.

Example ▼

Assume that Binz Tool is considering initiating a cash discount of 2 percent for payment within 10 days after a purchase. The firm's current average collection period is 30 days (turnover = 360/30 = 12), credit sales of 60,000 units are made at $10 per unit, and the variable cost per unit is $6. The firm expects that if the cash discount is initiated, 60 percent of its sales will be on discount, and sales will increase by 5 percent to 63,000 units. The average collection period is expected to drop to 15 days (turnover = 360/15 = 24). Bad debt expenses are expected to drop from the current level of 1 percent of sales to .5 percent of sales. The firm's required return on equal-risk investments remains at 15 percent.

The analysis of this decision is presented in Table 17.4 at the bottom of this page. The calculations are similar to those presented for Binz's credit standard decision in Table 17.3 except for the final entry, "Cost of cash discount." This cost of $7,560 reflects the fact that *profits will be reduced* as a result of a 2 percent cash discount being taken on 60 percent of the new level of sales. Even with that cost of the cash discount, Binz Tool can increase profit by $9,428 by initiating the proposed cash discount. Such an action therefore seems advisable. This type of analysis can also be applied to decisions concerning the elimination or reduction of cash discounts.

TABLE 17.4	**The Effects on Binz Tool of Initiating a Cash Discount**		
Additional profit contribution from sales			
[3,000 units × ($10 − $6)]			$12,000
Cost of marginal investment in A/R			
Average investment under proposed plan:			
$\frac{\$6 \times 63,000}{24} = \frac{\$378,000}{24}$		$15,750	
Average investment under present plan:			
$\frac{\$6 \times 60,000}{12} = \frac{\$360,000}{12}$		30,000	
Marginal investment in A/R		($14,250)	
Cost of marginal investment in A/R (.15 × $14,250)			$ 2,138[a]
Cost of marginal bad debts			
Bad debts under proposed plan (.005 × $10 × 63,000)	$ 3,150		
Bad debts under present plan (.01 × $10 × 60,000)	6,000		
Cost of marginal bad debts			$ 2,850[a]
Cost of cash discount[b] (.02 × .60 × $10 × 63,000)			($ 7,560)
Net profit from implementation of proposed plan			$ 9,428

[a]This value is positive, because it represents a savings rather than a cost.

[b]This calculation reflects the fact that a 2 percent cash discount will be taken on 60 percent of the new level of sales—63,000 units at $10 each.

CASH DISCOUNT PERIOD

The net effect of changes in the cash discount period is difficult to analyze because of the nature of the forces involved. For example, if the cash discount period were increased, the changes noted in the following table could be expected.

Effects of Increase in Cash Discount Period		
Variable	Direction of change	Effect on profits
Sales volume	Increase	Positive
Investment in accounts receivable due to nondiscount takers paying earlier	Decrease	Positive
Investment in accounts receivable due to discount takers still getting cash discount but paying later	Increase	Negative
Investment in accounts receivable due to new customers	Increase	Negative
Bad debt expenses	Decrease	Positive
Profit per unit	Decrease	Negative

The problems in determining the exact results of changes in the cash discount period are directly attributable to the three forces affecting the firm's *investment in accounts receivable*. If the firm were to shorten the cash discount period, the effects would be the opposite of those just described.

CREDIT PERIOD

Changes in the credit period also affect the firm's profitability. The following effects on profits can be expected from an *increase* in the length of the credit period:

Effects of Increase in Length of Credit Period		
Variable	Direction of change	Effect on profits
Sales volume	Increase	Positive
Investment in accounts receivable	Increase	Negative
Bad debt expenses	Increase	Negative

Increasing the length of the credit period should increase sales, but both accounts receivable and bad debt expenses are likely to increase as well. Thus, the sales increase will have a positive net effect on profits, whereas the increases in accounts receivable investment and bad debt expenses will negatively affect profits. A decrease in the length of the credit period is likely to have the opposite effect. The credit period decision is analyzed in the same ways as the credit standard decision illustrated in Table 17.3.

R e v i e w   Q u e s t i o n s

17-8   What is meant by *credit terms?* What are the three components of credit terms? How do credit terms affect the firm's accounts receivable?

17-9   What are the expected effects of a *decrease* in the firm's cash discount? In such a case, what is likely to happen to sales volume, accounts receivable, bad debt expenses, and per-unit profits?

17-10   What are the expected effects of a *decrease* in the firm's credit period? In such a case, what is likely to happen to sales volume, accounts receivable, and bad debt expenses?

LG4

COLLECTION POLICY

collection policy
The procedures for collecting a firm's accounts receivable when they are due.

The firm's **collection policy** is its procedures for collecting accounts receivable when they are due. The effectiveness of this policy can be partly evaluated by looking at the level of bad debt expenses. This level depends not only on collection policy, but also on the firm's credit policy. If the level of bad debts attributable to credit policy is relatively constant, increasing collection expenditures can be expected to reduce bad debts. This relationship is depicted in Figure 17.2. As the figure indicates, up to point A, additional collection expenditures will reduce bad debt losses. Beyond that point, additional collection expenditures will not reduce bad debt losses sufficiently to justify the outlay of funds. Popular

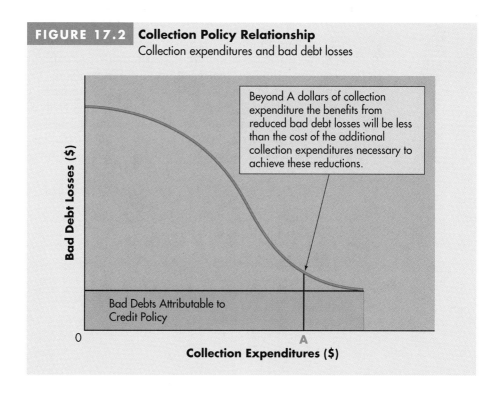

FIGURE 17.2   **Collection Policy Relationship**
Collection expenditures and bad debt losses

Beyond A dollars of collection expenditure the benefits from reduced bad debt losses will be less than the cost of the additional collection expenditures necessary to achieve these reductions.

Bad Debts Attributable to Credit Policy

approaches used to evaluate credit and collection policies include the *average collection period ratio* (presented in Chapter 5) and *aging accounts receivable.*

aging
A technique used to evaluate credit or collection policies by indicating the proportion of the accounts receivable balance that has been outstanding for a specified period of time.

AGING ACCOUNTS RECEIVABLE

Aging is a technique that indicates the proportion of the accounts receivable balance that has been outstanding for a specified period of time. It requires that the firm's accounts receivable be broken down into groups based on the time of origin. This breakdown is typically made on a month-by-month basis, going back 3 or 4 months. Let us look at an example.

Example ▼ Assume that Binz Tool extends 30-day EOM credit terms to its customers. The firm's December 31, 2000, balance sheet shows $200,000 of accounts receivable. An evaluation of those accounts receivable results in the following breakdown:

Days	Current	0–30	31–60	61–90	Over 90	
Month	December	November	October	September	August	Total
Accounts receivable	$60,000	$40,000	$66,000	$26,000	$8,000	$200,000
Percentage of total	30	20	33	13	4	100

Because it is assumed that Binz Tool gives its customers 30 days after the end of the month in which the sale is made to pay off their accounts, any December receivables that are still on the firm's books are considered current. November receivables are between zero and 30 days overdue, October receivables still unpaid are 31 to 60 days overdue, and so on.

The table shows that 30 percent of the firm's receivables are current, 20 percent are 1 month late, 33 percent are 2 months late, 13 percent are 3 months late, and 4 percent are more than 3 months late. Although payment seems generally slow, a noticeable irregularity in these data is the high percentage represented by October receivables. This indicates that some problem may have occurred in October. Investigation may find that the problem can be attributed to the hiring of a new credit manager, the acceptance of a new account that has made a large credit purchase it has not yet paid for, or ineffective collection policy. When such ▲ a discrepancy is found, the analyst should determine its cause.

EFFECTS OF CHANGES IN COLLECTION EFFORTS

The changes and effects on profits that are expected to result from an *increase* in collection efforts are as follows:

Effects of Increase in Collection Efforts		
Variable	Direction of change	Effect on profits
Sales volume	None or decrease	None or negative
Investment in accounts receivable	Decrease	Positive
Bad debt expenses	Decrease	Positive
Collection expenditures	Increase	Negative

Increased collection efforts should reduce accounts receivable and bad debt expenses, thus increasing profits. If the level of collection effort is too intense, the cost of this strategy may include lost sales in addition to increased collection expenditures. In other words, if the firm pushes its customers too hard to pay their accounts, they may take their business elsewhere. The firm should therefore be careful not to be overly aggressive. The quantitative effects of changes in collection policy can be evaluated in a way similar to that used to evaluate changes in credit standards and cash discounts.

POPULAR COLLECTION TECHNIQUES

A number of collection techniques, ranging from letters to legal action, are employed. As an account becomes more and more overdue, the collection effort becomes more personal and more intense. The popular collection techniques are briefly described in Table 17.5, listed in the order typically followed in the collection process.

TABLE 17.5	Popular Collection Techniques
Technique[a]	**Brief description**
Letters	After a certain number of days, the firm sends a polite letter reminding the customer of its overdue account. If the account is not paid within a certain period after the letter has been sent, a second, more demanding letter is sent. This letter may be followed by yet another letter, if necessary.
Telephone calls	If letters prove unsuccessful, a telephone call may be made to the customer to personally request immediate payment. Such a call is typically directed to the customer's accounts payable department. If the customer has a reasonable excuse, arrangements may be made to extend the payment period. A call from the seller's attorney may be used if all other discussions seem to fail.
Personal visits	This technique is much more common at the consumer credit level, but it may also be effectively employed by industrial suppliers. Sending a local salesperson or a collection person to confront the customer can be very effective. Payment may be made on the spot.
Collection agencies	A firm can turn uncollectible accounts over to a collection agency or an attorney for collection. The fees for this service are typically quite high; the firm may receive less than 50 cents on the dollar from accounts collected in this way.
Legal action	Legal action is the most stringent step in the collection process. It is an alternative to the use of a collection agency. Not only is direct legal action expensive, but it may force the debtor into bankruptcy, thereby reducing the possibility of future business without guaranteeing the ultimate receipt of the overdue amount.

[a]Techniques are listed in the order typically followed in the collection process.

17-11 What is meant by a firm's *collection policy?* Explain how *aging* accounts receivable can be used to evaluate the effectiveness of both the credit policy and the collection policy.

17-12 What effects on profits are expected to result from a *decrease* in collection efforts? Describe the popular collection techniques.

LG5

INVENTORY MANAGEMENT

Inventory is a necessary current asset that permits the production–sale process to operate with a minimum of disturbance. Like accounts receivable, inventory represents a significant investment for most firms. For the average manufacturer, it accounts for about 42 percent of *current assets* and about 18 percent of *total assets.* Chapter 16 illustrated the importance of turning over inventory quickly to reduce financing costs. The financial manager may act as a "watchdog" and adviser in matters concerning inventory; he or she does not have direct control over inventory, but does provide input into the inventory management process.

INVENTORY FUNDAMENTALS

Two aspects of inventory require some explanation. One is the *types of inventory;* the other concerns differing viewpoints as to the *appropriate level of inventory.*

TYPES OF INVENTORY

raw materials inventory
Items purchased by the firm for use in the manufacture of a finished product.

The three basic types of inventory are raw materials, work in process, and finished goods. **Raw materials inventory** consists of items purchased by the firm—usually, basic materials such as screws, plastic, raw steel, or rivets—for use in the manufacture of a finished product. If a firm manufactures complex products with numerous parts, its raw materials inventory may consist of manufactured items that have been purchased from another company or from another division of the same firm. **Work-in-process inventory** consists of all items that are currently in production. These are normally partially finished goods at some intermediate stage of completion. **Finished goods inventory** consists of items that have been produced but not yet sold.

work-in-process inventory
All items that are currently in production.

finished goods inventory
Items that have been produced but not yet sold.

DIFFERING VIEWPOINTS ABOUT INVENTORY LEVEL

Differing viewpoints about appropriate inventory levels commonly exist among a firm's finance, marketing, manufacturing, and purchasing managers. Each views inventory levels in light of his or her own objectives. The *financial manager's* general disposition toward inventory levels is to keep them low, to ensure that the firm's money is not being unwisely invested in excess resources. The *marketing manager,* on the other hand, would like to have large inventories of the firm's finished products. This would ensure that all orders could be filled quickly, eliminating the need for backorders due to stockouts.

The *manufacturing manager's* major responsibility is to correctly implement the production plan, so that it results in the desired amount of finished goods of acceptable quality at a low cost. In fulfilling this role, the manufacturing manager would keep raw materials inventories high to avoid production delays and would favor high finished goods inventories by making large production runs for the sake of lower unit production costs. The *purchasing manager* is concerned solely with the raw materials inventories. He or she is responsible for seeing that whatever raw materials are required by production are available in the correct quantities at the desired times and at a favorable price. Without proper control, the purchasing manager may purchase larger quantities of resources than are actually needed to get quantity discounts or in anticipation of rising prices or a shortage of certain materials.

INVENTORY AS AN INVESTMENT

Inventory is an investment in the sense that it requires that the firm tie up its money, thereby giving up certain other earning opportunities. In general, the higher a firm's average inventories, the larger the dollar investment and cost required; the lower its average inventories, the smaller the dollar investment and cost required. When evaluating planned changes in inventory levels, the financial manager should consider such changes from a benefit-versus-cost standpoint.

Example ▼ Excellent Manufacturing is contemplating making larger production runs to reduce the high setup costs associated with the production of its only product, industrial hoists. The total *annual* reduction in setup costs that can be obtained has been estimated to be $10,000. As a result of the larger production runs, the average inventory investment is expected to increase from $200,000 to $300,000. If the firm can earn 15 percent per year on equal-risk investments, the *annual* cost of the additional $100,000 ($300,000 − $200,000) inventory investment will be $15,000 (.15 × $100,000). Comparing the annual $15,000 cost of the system with the annual savings of $10,000 shows that the *proposal should be* ▲ *rejected* because it results in a net annual *loss* of $5,000.

THE RELATIONSHIP BETWEEN INVENTORY AND ACCOUNTS RECEIVABLE

The level and the management of inventory and accounts receivable are closely related. Generally, in manufacturing firms, when an item is sold, it moves from inventory to accounts receivable and ultimately to cash. Because of the close relationship between inventory and accounts receivable, their management should not be viewed independently. For example, the decision to extend credit to a customer can result in an increased level of sales, which can be supported only by higher levels of inventory and accounts receivable. The credit terms extended will also affect the investment in inventory and receivables, because longer credit terms may allow a firm to move items from inventory to accounts receivable. Generally, such a strategy is advantageous because *the cost of carrying an item in inventory is greater than the cost of carrying an account receivable.* The cost of carrying inventory includes, in addition to the required return on the invested funds, the costs of storing, insuring, and otherwise maintaining the physical inventory. This relationship can be shown using a simple example.

Example ▼ Most Industries, a producer of PVC pipe, estimates that the annual cost of carrying $1 of merchandise in inventory for a 1-year period is 25 cents, whereas the annual cost of carrying $1 of receivables is 15 cents. The firm currently maintains average inventories of $300,000 and an average *investment* in accounts receivable of $200,000. The firm believes that by altering its credit terms, it can cause its customers to purchase in larger quantities, thereby reducing its average inventories to $150,000 and increasing the average investment in accounts receivable to $350,000. The altered credit terms are not expected to generate new business but merely to result in a shift in purchasing and payment patterns. The costs of the present and proposed inventory–accounts receivable systems are calculated in Table 17.6.

Table 17.6 shows that by shifting $150,000 of inventory to accounts receivable, Most Industries is able to lower the cost of carrying inventory and accounts receivable from $105,000 to $90,000—a $15,000 addition to profits. This profit is achieved without changing the level of average inventory and accounts receivable investment from its $500,000 total. Rather, the profit is attributed to a shift in the mix of these current assets so that a larger portion of them is held in the less costly form of accounts receivable. ▲

The inventory–accounts receivable relationship is affected by decisions made in all areas of the firm—finance, marketing, manufacturing, and purchasing. The financial manager should consider the interaction between inventory and accounts receivable when developing strategies and making decisions related to the production-sale process. This interaction is especially important when making credit decisions, because the required as well as actual levels of inventory will be directly affected.

TABLE 17.6   **Analysis of Inventory–Accounts Receivable Systems for Most Industries**

		Present		Proposed	
Variable	Cost/return (1)	Average investment (2)	Cost [(1) × (2)] (3)	Average investment (4)	Cost [(1) × (4)] (5)
Average inventory	25%	$300,000	$ 75,000	$150,000	$37,500
Average receivables	15	200,000	30,000	350,000	52,500
Totals		$500,000	$105,000	$500,000	$90,000

INTERNATIONAL INVENTORY MANAGEMENT

International inventory management is typically much more complicated for exporters in general, and for multinational companies in particular, than for purely domestic companies. The production and manufacturing economies of scale that might be expected from selling products globally may prove elusive if products must be tailored for individual local markets, as very frequently happens, or if actual production takes place in factories around the world. When raw materials, intermediate goods, or finished products must be transported long distances—particularly by ocean shipping—there will inevitably be more delays, confusion, damage, theft, and other difficulties than occur in a one-country operation. The international inventory manager therefore puts a premium on flexibility, and he or she is usually less concerned about ordering the economically optimal quantity of inventory than about making sure that sufficient quantities of inventory are delivered where they are needed, when they are needed, and in a condition to be used as planned.

Review Questions

17-13   What is the financial manager's role with respect to the management of inventory? What are likely to be the viewpoints of each of the following managers about the levels of the various types of inventory: **a.** finance; **b.** marketing; **c.** manufacturing; and **d.** purchasing?

17-14   Explain the relationship between inventory and accounts receivable. Assuming that the total investment in inventory and accounts receivable remains constant, what impact would lengthening the credit terms have on the firm's profits? Why?

17-15   What factors make managing inventory more difficult for exporters and multinational companies?

TECHNIQUES FOR MANAGING INVENTORY

LG6

Although the techniques that are commonly used in managing inventory are not strictly financial, it is helpful for the financial manager to understand them. In this section we will examine five common inventory management techniques.

THE ABC SYSTEM

ABC system
Inventory management technique that divides inventory into three groups of descending importance based on the dollar investment in each.

A firm using the **ABC system** divides its inventory into three groups, A, B, and C. The *A group* includes those items that require the largest dollar investment. In the typical distribution of inventory items, this group consists of the 20 percent of inventory items that account for 80 percent of the firm's dollar investment. The *B group* consists of the items accounting for the next largest investment. The *C group* typically consists of a large number of items accounting for a relatively small dollar investment.

Dividing inventory into A, B, and C items allows the firm to determine the level and types of inventory control procedures needed. Control of the A items should be most intensive because of the high dollar investment involved. The use of *perpetual inventory record keeping* that allows daily monitoring of these inventory levels is appropriate. B items are frequently controlled through *periodic checking*—possibly weekly—of their levels. C items could be controlled by using unsophisticated procedures such as a **red-line method,** in which a reorder is placed when enough inventory has been removed from a bin containing the inventory item to expose a red line drawn around the inside of the bin. The economic order quantity (EOQ) model, discussed next, is appropriate for use in monitoring A and B items.

THE BASIC ECONOMIC ORDER QUANTITY (EOQ) MODEL

One of the most commonly used sophisticated tools for determining the optimal order quantity for an item of inventory is the **economic order quantity (EOQ) model.** It takes into account various operating and financial costs and determines the order quantity that minimizes total inventory cost.

BASIC COSTS

Excluding the actual cost of the merchandise, the costs associated with inventory can be divided into three broad groups: order costs, carrying costs, and total cost. Each has certain key components and characteristics.

Order Costs   **Order costs** include the fixed clerical costs of placing and receiving an order—the cost of writing a purchase order, of processing the resulting paperwork, and of receiving an order and checking it against the invoice. Order costs are normally stated as dollars per order.

Carrying Costs   **Carrying costs** are the variable costs per unit of holding an item in inventory for a specified time period. These costs are typically stated as dollars per unit per period. Carrying costs include costs for storage, insurance, deterioration and obsolescence, and most important, the opportunity cost of tying up funds in inventory. A commonly cited rule of thumb suggests that the cost of carrying an item in inventory for 1 year is between 20 and 30 percent of the cost (value) of the item.

Total Cost   The **total cost (of inventory)** is defined as the sum of the order and carrying costs. Total cost is important in the EOQ model, because the model's objective is to determine the order quantity that minimizes it.

A GRAPHIC APPROACH

The stated objective of the EOQ model is to find the order quantity that minimizes the firm's total inventory cost. The economic order quantity can be found graphically by plotting order quantities on the *x*, or horizontal, axis and costs on the *y*, or vertical, axis. Figure 17.3 shows the general behavior of these costs. The total cost line represents the sum of the order costs and carrying costs for each

red-line method
Unsophisticated inventory management technique in which a reorder is placed when enough inventory has been removed from a bin containing the inventory item to expose a red line drawn around the inside of the bin.

economic order quantity (EOQ) model
Inventory management technique for determining an item's optimal order quantity, which is the one that minimizes the total of its order and carrying costs.

order costs
The fixed clerical costs of placing and receiving an inventory order.

carrying costs
The variable costs per unit of holding an item in inventory for a specified time period.

total cost (of inventory)
The sum of the *order costs* and *carrying costs* of inventory.

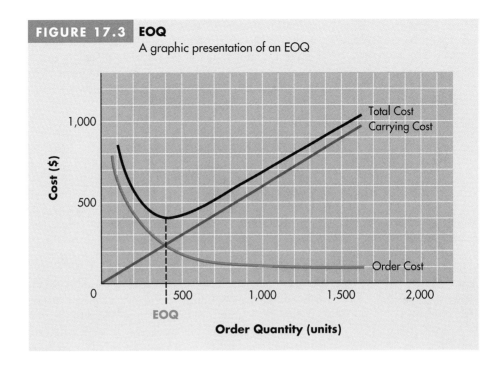

FIGURE 17.3 **EOQ**

A graphic presentation of an EOQ

order quantity. The minimum total cost occurs at the point labeled EOQ, where the order cost line and the carrying cost line intersect.

A MATHEMATICAL APPROACH

The formula given in Equation 17.2 can be used to determine the firm's EOQ for a given inventory item:

$$EOQ = \sqrt{\frac{2 \times S \times O}{C}} \qquad (17.2)$$

where

S = usage in units per period
O = order cost per order
C = carrying cost per unit per period

Example ▼ Assume that RLB, Inc., a manufacturer of electronic test equipment, uses 1,600 units of an item annually. Its order cost is $50 per order, and the carrying cost is $1 per unit per year. Substituting S = 1,600, O = $50, and C = $1 into Equation 17.2 yields an EOQ of 400 units:

$$EOQ = \sqrt{\frac{2 \times 1,600 \times \$50}{\$1}} = \sqrt{160,000} = \underline{\underline{400 \text{ units}}}$$

If the firm orders in quantities of 400 units, it will minimize its total inventory
▲ cost. This solution is depicted in Figure 17.3.

Although even the simple EOQ model has weaknesses, it certainly provides decision makers with better grounds for a decision than subjective observations. Despite the fact that the financial manager is normally not directly associated with the use of the EOQ model, he or she must be aware of its utility, and must also provide certain financial inputs, specifically with respect to inventory carrying costs.

THE REORDER POINT

reorder point
The point at which to reorder inventory, expressed equationally as: lead time in days × daily usage.

Once the firm has calculated its economic order quantity, it must determine *when* to place orders. A reorder point is required that considers the lead time needed to place and receive orders. Assuming a constant usage rate for inventory, the **reorder point** can be determined by the following equation:

$$\text{Reorder point} = \text{lead time in days} \times \text{daily usage} \qquad (17.3)$$

For example, if a firm knows that it requires 10 days to place and receive an order, and if it uses 5 units of inventory daily, the reorder point would be 50 units (10 days × 5 units per day). Thus, when the firm's inventory level reaches 50 units, an order will be placed for an amount equal to the economic order quantity. If the estimates of lead time and daily usage are correct, the order will be received exactly when the inventory level reaches zero. Because of the difficulty in precisely predicting lead times and daily usage rates, many firms typically maintain **safety stocks**, which are extra inventories that can be drawn down if needed.

safety stocks
Extra inventories that can be drawn down if needed.

MATERIALS REQUIREMENT PLANNING (MRP) SYSTEM

materials requirement planning (MRP) system
Inventory management system that uses EOQ concepts and a computer to compare production needs to available inventory balances and determine when orders should be placed for various items on a product's *bill of materials.*

Many companies use a **materials requirement planning (MRP) system** to determine what to order, when to order, and what priorities to assign to ordering materials. MRP uses EOQ concepts to determine how much to order. Using a computer, it simulates each product's bill of materials structure, inventory status, and manufacturing process. The *bill of materials* structure simply refers to every part or material that goes into making the finished product. For a given production plan, the computer simulates needed materials requirements by comparing production needs to available inventory balances. On the basis of the time it takes for a product that is in process to move through the various production stages and the lead time required to get materials, the MRP system determines when orders should be placed for the various items on the bill of materials.

The advantage of the MRP system is that it forces the firm to more thoughtfully consider its inventory needs and plan accordingly. The objective is to lower the firm's inventory investment without impairing production. If the firm's opportunity cost of capital for investments of equal risk is 15 percent, every $1.00 of investment released from inventory increases before-tax profits by $.15.

JUST-IN-TIME (JIT) SYSTEM

just-in-time (JIT) system
Inventory management system that minimizes inventory investment by having material inputs arrive at exactly the time they are needed for production.

The **just-in-time (JIT) system** is used to minimize inventory investment. The philosophy is that materials should arrive at exactly the time they are needed for production. Ideally, the firm would have only work-in-process inventory.

Because its objective is to minimize inventory investment, a JIT system uses no, or very little, safety stocks. Extensive coordination must exist between the firm, its suppliers, and shipping companies to ensure that material inputs arrive on time. Failure of materials to arrive on time results in a shutdown of the production line until the materials arrive. Likewise, a JIT system requires high-quality parts from suppliers. When quality problems arise, production must be stopped until the problems are resolved.

The goal of the JIT system is manufacturing efficiency. It uses inventory as a tool for attaining efficiency by emphasizing quality in terms of both the materials used and their timely delivery. When JIT is working properly, it forces process inefficiencies to surface and be resolved. A JIT system requires cooperation among all parties involved in the process—suppliers, shipping companies, and the firm's employees.

? R e v i e w   Q u e s t i o n s

17-16   Briefly describe each of the following techniques for managing inventory: (a) ABC system; (b) reorder point; (c) materials requirement planning (MRP) system; and (d) just-in-time (JIT) system.

17-17   What is the *EOQ model*? To which group of inventory items is it most applicable? What costs does it consider? What financial cost is involved?

S UMMARY

LG1 **Discuss credit selection, including the five C's of credit, obtaining and analyzing credit information, credit scoring, and managing international credit.** Credit selection includes deciding whether to extend credit to a customer and how much credit to extend. The five C's of credit—character, capacity, capital, collateral, and conditions—guide credit investigation. Credit information can be obtained from a variety of external sources and analyzed in a number of ways. An analyst's subjective judgment is an important input to the final decision. Impersonal credit decision techniques, such as credit scoring, are often used at the consumer level. Credit management is difficult for companies that operate internationally due to the presence of exchange rate risk, difficulties in shipping across international borders, and the need to assess and bear the credit risks of foreign customers.

LG2 **Use the key variables to evaluate quantitatively the effects of either relaxing or tightening a firm's credit standards.** At the mercantile level, credit standards must be set by considering the tradeoffs between the key variables—the profit contribution from sales, the cost of investment in accounts receivable, and the cost of bad debts. Generally, when credit standards are relaxed, the profit contribution from sales increases, as do the costs of investment in accounts receivable and bad debts. If the increased profit contribution exceeds the increased costs, the credit standards should be relaxed. A tightening of credit standards would result in decreases in each of the key variables; if the cost reductions exceed the reduced profit contribution, credit standards should be tightened.

LG3 **Review the effects of changes in each of the three components of credit terms on the key financial variables and on profits, and the procedure for quantitatively evaluating cash discount changes.** Credit terms have three components: (1) the cash discount, (2) the cash discount period, and (3) the credit period. Changes in these variables affect the firm's sales, investment in accounts receivable, bad debt expenses, and profit per unit.

Quantitatively, a proposed increase of a cash discount is evaluated by comparing the profit increases attributable to the added sales, the assumed net reduction in accounts receivable investment, and the reduction in bad debts to the cost of the cash discount. If the profit increases exceed the cost, the discount increase should be undertaken. The proposed decrease of a cash discount would be analyzed similarly, except that the profit and cost factors would be reversed.

LG4 **Explain the key features of collection policy, including aging accounts receivable, the effects of changes in collection efforts, and the popular collection techniques.** Collection policy determines the type and degree of effort exercised to collect overdue accounts. Firms look at the average collection period ratio and also often age accounts receivable to evaluate the effectiveness of the firm's credit and collection policies. The procedures used to evaluate changes in collection efforts are similar to those for credit standards and credit terms. Generally, increased collection expenditures will have little effect on sales volume and will reduce the investment in accounts receivable and bad debt expenses. The popular collection techniques include letters, telephone calls, personal visits, collection agencies, and legal action.

LG5 **Understand inventory fundamentals, the relationship between inventory and accounts receivable, and international inventory management.** The viewpoints held by marketing, manufacturing, and purchasing managers as to the appropriate levels of inventory (raw materials, work in process, and finished goods) tend to conflict with that of the financial manager. The financial manager views inventory as an investment that consumes dollars and should be kept at a low level. Because it is more expensive to carry an item in inventory than to carry an account receivable, the financial manager must consider the relationship between inventory and accounts receivable when making related decisions. International inventory managers place greater emphasis on making sure that sufficient quantities of inventory are delivered where they are needed, when they are needed, and in the right condition than on ordering the economically optimal quantities.

LG6 **Describe the common techniques for managing inventory, including the ABC system, the basic economic order quantity model, the reorder point, the materials requirement planning system, and the just-in-time system.** The ABC system determines which inventories require the most attention according to dollar investment. The economic order quantity (EOQ) model determines the optimal order quantity, which is placed when the level of inventory reaches the reorder point. A materials requirement planning (MRP) system can be used to determine when orders should be placed for various items on a firm's bill of materials. Just-in-time (JIT) systems are used to minimize inventory investment by having materials arrive at exactly the time they are needed for production.

SELF-TEST PROBLEMS (Solutions in Appendix B)

  ST 17-1 **Easing collection efforts** Regency Rug Repair Company is attempting to evaluate whether it should ease collection efforts. The firm repairs 72,000 rugs per year at an average price of $32 each. Bad debt expenses are 1 percent of sales, and collection expenditures are $60,000. The average collection period is 40 days, and the variable cost per unit is $28. By easing the collection efforts, Regency expects to save $40,000 per year in collection expense. Bad debts will increase to 2 percent of sales, and the average collection period will increase to 58 days. Sales will increase by 1,000 repairs per year. If the firm has a required rate of return on equal-risk investments of 24 percent, what recommendation would you give the firm? Use your analysis to justify your answer.

ST 17-2   EOQ analysis   Thompson Paint Company uses 60,000 gallons of pigment per year. The cost of ordering pigment is $200 per order, and the cost of carrying the pigment in inventory is $1 per gallon per year. The firm uses pigment at a constant rate every day throughout the year.
a. Calculate the EOQ.
b. Assuming that it takes 20 days to receive an order once it has been placed, determine the reorder point in terms of gallons of pigment. (*Note:* Use a 360-day year.)

PROBLEMS

17-1   Credit scoring   Dooley Department Store uses credit scoring to evaluate retail credit applications. The financial and credit characteristics considered and weights indicating their relative importance in the credit decision are given in the table below. The firm's credit standards are to accept all applicants with credit scores of 80 or more, to extend limited credit on a probationary basis to applicants with scores of greater than 70 and less than 80, and to reject all applicants with scores below 70.

Financial and credit characteristics	Predetermined weight
Credit references	.25
Education	.15
Home ownership	.10
Income range	.10
Payment history	.30
Years on job	.10

The firm currently needs to process three applications that were recently received and scored by one of its credit analysts. The scores for each of the applicants on each of the financial and credit characteristics are summarized in the following table:

	Applicant		
Financial and credit characteristics	A	B	C
	Score (0 to 100)		
Credit references	60	90	80
Education	70	70	80
Home ownership	100	90	60
Income range	75	80	80
Payment history	60	85	70
Years on job	50	60	90

a. Use the data presented to find the credit score for each of the applicants.
b. Recommend the appropriate action for each of the three applicants.

17-2 **Accounts receivable and costs**   Wicklow Products currently has an average collection period of 45 days and annual credit sales of $1 million. Assume a 360-day year.
a. What is the firm's average accounts receivable balance?
b. If the variable cost of each product is 60 percent of sales, what is the average *investment* in accounts receivable?
c. If the equal-risk opportunity cost of the investment in accounts receivable is 12 percent, what is the total opportunity cost of the investment in accounts receivable?

17-3 **Accounts receivable changes without bad debts**   Small Appliance currently has credit sales of $360 million per year and an average collection period of 60 days. Assume that the price of Small's products is $60 per unit and the variable costs are $55 per unit. The firm is considering an account receivable change that will result in a 20 percent increase in sales and an equal 20 percent increase in the average collection period. No change in bad debts is expected. The firm's equal-risk opportunity cost on its investment in accounts receivable is 14 percent.
a. Calculate the additional profit contribution from new sales that the firm will realize if it makes the proposed change.
b. What marginal investment in accounts receivable will result?
c. Calculate the cost of the marginal investment in accounts receivable.
d. Should the firm implement the proposed change? What other information would be helpful in your analysis?

17-4 **Accounts receivable changes and bad debts**   A firm is evaluating an account receivable change that would increase bad debts from 2 to 4 percent of sales. Sales are currently 50,000 units, the selling price is $20 per unit, and the variable cost per unit is $15. As a result of the proposed change, sales are forecast to increase to 60,000 units.
a. What are bad debts in dollars currently and under the proposed change?
b. Calculate the cost of the marginal bad debts to the firm.
c. Ignoring the additional profit contribution from increased sales, if the proposed change saves $3,500 and causes no change in the average investment in accounts receivable, would you recommend it? Explain.
d. Considering *all* changes in costs and benefits, would you recommend the proposed change? Explain.
e. Compare and discuss your answers in c and d.

17-5 **Tightening credit standards—Sales and bad debt effects only**   Cheryl's Menswear feels that its credit costs are too high. By tightening its credit standards, bad debts will fall from 5 percent of sales to 2 percent. However, sales will fall from $100,000 to $90,000 per year. The variable cost per unit is 50 percent of the sale price, and the average investment in receivables is expected to remain unchanged.

a. What cost will the firm face in a reduced contribution to profits from sales?

b. Should the firm tighten its credit standards? Explain your answer.

17-6   Relaxation of credit standards   Adair Industries is considering relaxing its credit standards to increase its currently sagging sales. As a result of the proposed relaxation, sales are expected to increase by 10 percent from 10,000 to 11,000 units during the coming year, the average collection period is expected to increase from 45 to 60 days, and bad debts are expected to increase from 1 to 3 percent of sales. The sale price per unit is $40, and the variable cost per unit is $31. If the firm's required return on equal-risk investments is 25 percent, evaluate the proposed relaxation, and make a recommendation to the firm.

17-7   Initiating a cash discount   Prichard Products currently makes all sales on credit and offers no cash discount. The firm is considering a 2 percent cash discount for payment within 15 days. The firm's current average collection period is 60 days, sales are 40,000 units, selling price is $45 per unit, and variable cost per unit is $36. The firm expects that the change in credit terms will result in an increase in sales to 42,000 units, that 70 percent of the sales will take the discount, and that the average collection period will fall to 30 days. If the firm's required rate of return on equal-risk investments is 25 percent, should the proposed discount be offered?

17-8   Shortening the credit period   Spectradyne, Inc., is contemplating *shortening* its credit period from 40 to 30 days and believes that as a result of this change, its average collection period will decline from 45 to 36 days. Bad debt expenses are expected to decrease from 1.5 to 1 percent of sales. The firm is currently selling 12,000 units but believes that as a result of the proposed change, sales will decline to 10,000 units. The sale price per unit is $56, and its variable cost per unit is $45. The firm has a required return on equal-risk investments of 25 percent. Evaluate this decision, and make a recommendation to the firm.

17-9   Lengthening the credit period   Heaton Equipment Company is considering lengthening its credit period from 30 to 60 days. All customers will continue to pay on the net date. The firm currently bills $450,000 for sales and has $345,000 in variable costs. The change in credit terms is expected to increase sales to $510,000. Bad debt expense will increase from 1 to 1.5 percent of sales. The firm has a required rate of return on equal-risk investments of 20 percent.

a. What additional profit contribution from sales will be realized from the proposed change?

b. What is the cost of the marginal investment in accounts receivable?

c. What is the cost of the marginal bad debts?

d. Do you recommend this change in credit terms? Why or why not?

17-10   Aging accounts receivable   Cellular Corporation's accounts receivable totaled $874,000 on August 31, 2000. A breakdown of these outstanding accounts on the basis of the month in which the credit sale was initially made follows. The firm extends 30-day EOM credit terms to its credit customers.

Month of credit sale	Accounts receivable
August 2000	$320,000
July 2000	250,000
June 2000	81,000
May 2000	195,000
April 2000 or before	28,000
Total (August 31, 2000)	$874,000

a. Prepare an aging schedule for Cellular Corporation's August 31, 2000, accounts receivable balance.
b. Using your findings in a, evaluate the firm's credit and collection activities.
c. What are some probable causes of the situation discussed in b?

WARM-UP

17-11 Inventory investment   Winblad, Inc., is considering leasing a computerized inventory control system to reduce its average inventories. The annual cost of the system is $46,000. It is expected that with the system the firm's average inventory will decline by 50 percent from its current level of $980,000. The level of stockouts is expected to be unaffected by this system. The firm can earn 20 percent per year on equal-risk investments.
a. How much of a reduction in average inventory will result from the proposed installation of the computerized inventory control system?
b. How much, if any, annual savings will the firm realize on the reduced level of average inventory?
c. Should the firm lease the computerized inventory control system? Explain why or why not.

 INTERMEDIATE   **17-12 Inventory versus accounts receivable costs**   Harbor Manufacturing estimates the annual cost of carrying a dollar of inventory is $.27, and the annual carrying cost of an equal investment in accounts receivable is $.17. The firm's current balance sheet reflects its average inventory of $400,000 and average investment in accounts receivable of $100,000. If the firm can convince its customers to purchase in large quantities, the average level of inventory can be reduced by $200,000, and the average investment in receivables can be increased by the same amount. Assuming no change in annual sales, what addition to profits will be generated from this shift? Explain your answer.

 INTERMEDIATE   **17-13 Inventory—The ABC system**   Zap Supply has 16 different items in its inventory. The average number of units held in inventory and the average unit cost for each item are listed in the following table. The firm wishes to introduce the ABC system of inventory management. Suggest a breakdown of the items into classifications of A, B, and C. Justify your selection and point out items that could be considered borderline cases.

Item	Average number of units in inventory	Average cost per unit
1	1,800	$ 0.54
2	1,000	8.20
3	100	6.00
4	250	1.20
5	8	94.50
6	400	3.00
7	80	45.00
8	1,600	1.45
9	600	0.95
10	3,000	0.18
11	900	15.00
12	65	1.35
13	2,200	4.75
14	1,800	1.30
15	60	18.00
16	200	17.50

INTERMEDIATE   **17-14 EOQ analysis**   Lyons Electronics purchases 1,200,000 units per year of one component. The fixed cost per order is $25. The annual carrying cost of the item is 27 percent of its $2 cost.
  a. Determine the EOQ under the following conditions: (1) no changes, (2) order cost of zero, and (3) carrying cost of zero.
  b. What do your answers illustrate about the EOQ model? Explain.

WARM-UP   **17-15 Reorder point**   Ticho Gas and Electric (TG&E) is required to carry a minimum of 20 days' average coal usage, which is 100 tons of coal. It takes 10 days between order and delivery. At what level of coal would TG&E reorder?

INTERMEDIATE   **17-16 EOQ, reorder point, and safety stock**   Sabra Company uses 800 units of a product per year on a continuous basis. The product has a fixed cost of $50 per order, and its carrying cost is $2 per unit per year. It takes 5 days to receive a shipment after an order is placed, and the firm wishes to hold in inventory 10 days' usage as a safety stock.
  a. Calculate the EOQ.
  b. Determine the average level of inventory. (*Note:* Use a 360-day year to calculate daily usage.)
  c. Determine the reorder point.
  d. Which of the following variables change if the firm does not hold the safety stock: (1) order cost, (2) carrying cost, (3) total inventory cost, (4) reorder point, (5) economic order quantity? Explain.

CASE   Chapter 17   **Evaluating Global Textiles' Proposed Change in Credit Terms**

Ken Steinbacher, a financial analyst for Global Textiles, has been asked to investigate a proposed change in the firm's credit terms. The company's founder and president believes that by increasing the credit period from 30 to 65 days, two important benefits will result: (1) sales will increase as a result of attracting *new customers,* and (2) some *existing customers* will purchase merchandise sooner to ensure its availability, given the unpredictable timing of the selling seasons. Annual sales are estimated to increase from the current level of $4,000,000 to $4,800,000. Eighty percent of this increase is expected to be attributable to new customers, and the other 20 percent is expected to result from existing customers. Because some existing customers will be making their purchases earlier than in the past, their actions will merely result in a shifting of inventory to accounts receivable. Ken estimated that the decline in inventory investment attributable to the actions of existing customers would just equal the additional accounts receivable investment associated with their actions.

Ken's investigation indicates that with the extended credit period, the firm's average collection period will increase from 45 to 90 days. In addition, bad debts will increase from 1 to 2½ percent of sales. The firm's variable costs are expected to continue to amount to 80 percent of each $1 of sales. Global currently requires a 16 percent rate of return on equal-risk accounts receivable investments and its cost of carrying $1 of inventory for 1 year is 26 cents.

Required

a. Find the additional annual profit contribution expected from the increased credit period.
b. Determine the increase in Global's average investment in accounts receivable and the resulting annual cost attributable to the proposed increase in the credit period.
c. Calculate the annual savings resulting from the reduced inventory investment attributable to the existing customers' earlier purchases.
d. Calculate the annual cost expected to result from the increase in bad debt expenses attributable to the proposed lengthening of the credit period.
e. Use your findings in **a** through **d** to advise Ken on whether or not the proposed increase in the credit period can be financially justified. Explain your recommendation.
f. What impact, if any, would ignoring the effect of the proposed increase in the credit period on the level of inventory investment found in **c** have on your recommendation in **e**? Explain.

W eb Exercise

1. What does the Z-score indicate?
2. What are the five ratios that are used in calculating the Altman's Z-score? Which ratio is the most significant in determining the Z-score?
3. What is the score for a healthy company? For a company in fiscal danger?
4. Using the Z-score worksheet, enter the following account balances and determine these two companies' Z-scores:

	(in millions)	
	Company A	Company B
Earnings before interest and taxes	−$ 251	$ 1,602
Total assets	761	13,071
Net sales	1,389	13,319
Market value of equity	18	6,440
Total liabilities	621	7,212
Working capital	341	3,964
Retained earnings	41	8,717

After entering these account balances, click CALCULATE Z-SCORE.

5. Would you give credit to either of these two companies? Why or why not?

Appendixes

Appendix A

Financial Tables

TABLE A-1   Future Value Interest Factors for One Dollar Compounded at k Percent for n Periods:

$$FVIF_{k,n} = (1 + k)^n$$

TABLE A-2   Future Value Interest Factors for a One-Dollar Annuity Compounded at k Percent for n Periods:

$$FVIFA_{k,n} = \sum_{t=1}^{n} (1 + k)^{t-1}$$

TABLE A-3   Present Value Interest Factors for One Dollar Discounted at k Percent for n Periods:

$$PVIF_{k,n} = \frac{1}{(1 + k)^n}$$

TABLE A-4   Present Value Interest Factors for a One-Dollar Annuity Discounted at k Percent for n Periods:

$$PVIFA_{k,n} = \sum_{t=1}^{n} \frac{1}{(1 + k)^t}$$

TABLE A-1 Future Value Interest Factors for One Dollar Compounded at k Percent for n Periods: $FVIF_{k,n} = (1 + k)^n$

Period	1%	2%	3%	4%	5%	6%	7%	8%	9%	10%	11%	12%	13%	14%	15%	16%	17%	18%	19%	20%
1	1.010	1.020	1.030	1.040	1.050	1.060	1.070	1.080	1.090	1.100	1.110	1.120	1.130	1.140	1.150	1.160	1.170	1.180	1.190	1.200
2	1.020	1.040	1.061	1.082	1.102	1.124	1.145	1.166	1.188	1.210	1.232	1.254	1.277	1.300	1.322	1.346	1.369	1.392	1.416	1.440
3	1.030	1.061	1.093	1.125	1.158	1.191	1.225	1.260	1.295	1.331	1.368	1.405	1.443	1.482	1.521	1.561	1.602	1.643	1.685	1.728
4	1.041	1.082	1.126	1.170	1.216	1.262	1.311	1.360	1.412	1.464	1.518	1.574	1.630	1.689	1.749	1.811	1.874	1.939	2.005	2.074
5	1.051	1.104	1.159	1.217	1.276	1.338	1.403	1.469	1.539	1.611	1.685	1.762	1.842	1.925	2.011	2.100	2.192	2.288	2.386	2.488
6	1.062	1.126	1.194	1.265	1.340	1.419	1.501	1.587	1.677	1.772	1.870	1.974	2.082	2.195	2.313	2.436	2.565	2.700	2.840	2.986
7	1.072	1.149	1.230	1.316	1.407	1.504	1.606	1.714	1.828	1.949	2.076	2.211	2.353	2.502	2.660	2.826	3.001	3.185	3.379	3.583
8	1.083	1.172	1.267	1.369	1.477	1.594	1.718	1.851	1.993	2.144	2.305	2.476	2.658	2.853	3.059	3.278	3.511	3.759	4.021	4.300
9	1.094	1.195	1.305	1.423	1.551	1.689	1.838	1.999	2.172	2.358	2.558	2.773	3.004	3.252	3.518	3.803	4.108	4.435	4.785	5.160
10	1.105	1.219	1.344	1.480	1.629	1.791	1.967	2.159	2.367	2.594	2.839	3.106	3.395	3.707	4.046	4.411	4.807	5.234	5.695	6.192
11	1.116	1.243	1.384	1.539	1.710	1.898	2.105	2.332	2.580	2.853	3.152	3.479	3.836	4.226	4.652	5.117	5.624	6.176	6.777	7.430
12	1.127	1.268	1.426	1.601	1.796	2.012	2.252	2.518	2.813	3.138	3.498	3.896	4.334	4.818	5.350	5.936	6.580	7.288	8.064	8.916
13	1.138	1.294	1.469	1.665	1.886	2.133	2.410	2.720	3.066	3.452	3.883	4.363	4.898	5.492	6.153	6.886	7.699	8.599	9.596	10.699
14	1.149	1.319	1.513	1.732	1.980	2.261	2.579	2.937	3.342	3.797	4.310	4.887	5.535	6.261	7.076	7.987	9.007	10.147	11.420	12.839
15	1.161	1.346	1.558	1.801	2.079	2.397	2.759	3.172	3.642	4.177	4.785	5.474	6.254	7.138	8.137	9.265	10.539	11.974	13.589	15.407
16	1.173	1.373	1.605	1.873	2.183	2.540	2.952	3.426	3.970	4.595	5.311	6.130	7.067	8.137	9.358	10.748	12.330	14.129	16.171	18.488
17	1.184	1.400	1.653	1.948	2.292	2.693	3.159	3.700	4.328	5.054	5.895	6.866	7.986	9.276	10.761	12.468	14.426	16.672	19.244	22.186
18	1.196	1.428	1.702	2.026	2.407	2.854	3.380	3.996	4.717	5.560	6.543	7.690	9.024	10.575	12.375	14.462	16.879	19.673	22.900	26.623
19	1.208	1.457	1.753	2.107	2.527	3.026	3.616	4.316	5.142	6.116	7.263	8.613	10.197	12.055	14.232	16.776	19.748	23.214	27.251	31.948
20	1.220	1.486	1.806	2.191	2.653	3.207	3.870	4.661	5.604	6.727	8.062	9.646	11.523	13.743	16.366	19.461	23.105	27.393	32.429	38.337
21	1.232	1.516	1.860	2.279	2.786	3.399	4.140	5.034	6.109	7.400	8.949	10.804	13.021	15.667	18.821	22.574	27.033	32.323	38.591	46.005
22	1.245	1.546	1.916	2.370	2.925	3.603	4.430	5.436	6.658	8.140	9.933	12.100	14.713	17.861	21.644	26.186	31.629	38.141	45.923	55.205
23	1.257	1.577	1.974	2.465	3.071	3.820	4.740	5.871	7.258	8.954	11.026	13.552	16.626	20.361	24.891	30.376	37.005	45.007	54.648	66.247
24	1.270	1.608	2.033	2.563	3.225	4.049	5.072	6.341	7.911	9.850	12.239	15.178	18.788	23.212	28.625	35.236	43.296	53.108	65.031	79.496
25	1.282	1.641	2.094	2.666	3.386	4.292	5.427	6.848	8.623	10.834	13.585	17.000	21.230	26.461	32.918	40.874	50.656	62.667	77.387	95.395
30	1.348	1.811	2.427	3.243	4.322	5.743	7.612	10.062	13.267	17.449	22.892	29.960	39.115	50.949	66.210	85.849	111.061	143.367	184.672	237.373
35	1.417	2.000	2.814	3.946	5.516	7.686	10.676	14.785	20.413	28.102	38.574	52.799	72.066	98.097	133.172	180.311	243.495	327.988	440.691	590.657
40	1.489	2.208	3.262	4.801	7.040	10.285	14.974	21.724	31.408	45.258	64.999	93.049	132.776	188.876	267.856	378.715	533.846	750.353	1051.642	1469.740
45	1.565	2.438	3.781	5.841	8.985	13.764	21.002	31.920	48.325	72.888	109.527	163.985	244.629	363.662	538.752	795.429	1170.425	1716.619	2509.583	3657.176
50	1.645	2.691	4.384	7.106	11.467	18.419	29.456	46.900	74.354	117.386	184.559	288.996	450.711	700.197	1083.619	1670.669	2566.080	3927.189	5988.730	9100.191

USING THE CALCULATOR TO COMPUTE THE FUTURE VALUE OF A SINGLE AMOUNT

Before you begin, make sure to clear the memory, ensure that you are in the *end mode* and your calculator is set for *one payment per year,* and set the number of decimal places that you want (usually two for dollar-related accuracy).

SAMPLE PROBLEM

You place $800 in a savings account at 6 percent compounded annually. What is your account balance at the end of 5 years?

Hewlett-Packard HP 12C, 17 BII, and 19 BII[a]

Inputs:	800	5	6
Functions:	PV	N	I%YR	FV
Outputs:				1070.58[b]

[a]For the 12C, you would use the n key instead of the N key, and the i key instead of the I%YR key.
[b]The minus sign that precedes the output should be ignored.

TABLE A-1   (Continued)

Period	21%	22%	23%	24%	25%	26%	27%	28%	29%	30%	31%	32%	33%	34%	35%	40%	45%	50%
1	1.210	1.220	1.230	1.240	1.250	1.260	1.270	1.280	1.290	1.300	1.310	1.320	1.330	1.340	1.350	1.400	1.450	1.500
2	1.464	1.488	1.513	1.538	1.562	1.588	1.613	1.638	1.664	1.690	1.716	1.742	1.769	1.796	1.822	1.960	2.102	2.250
3	1.772	1.816	1.861	1.907	1.953	2.000	2.048	2.097	2.147	2.197	2.248	2.300	2.353	2.406	2.460	2.744	3.049	3.375
4	2.144	2.215	2.289	2.364	2.441	2.520	2.601	2.684	2.769	2.856	2.945	3.036	3.129	3.224	3.321	3.842	4.421	5.063
5	2.594	2.703	2.815	2.932	3.052	3.176	3.304	3.436	3.572	3.713	3.858	4.007	4.162	4.320	4.484	5.378	6.410	7.594
6	3.138	3.297	3.463	3.635	3.815	4.001	4.196	4.398	4.608	4.827	5.054	5.290	5.535	5.789	6.053	7.530	9.294	11.391
7	3.797	4.023	4.259	4.508	4.768	5.042	5.329	5.629	5.945	6.275	6.621	6.983	7.361	7.758	8.172	10.541	13.476	17.086
8	4.595	4.908	5.239	5.589	5.960	6.353	6.767	7.206	7.669	8.157	8.673	9.217	9.791	10.395	11.032	14.758	19.541	25.629
9	5.560	5.987	6.444	6.931	7.451	8.004	8.595	9.223	9.893	10.604	11.362	12.166	13.022	13.930	14.894	20.661	28.334	38.443
10	6.727	7.305	7.926	8.594	9.313	10.086	10.915	11.806	12.761	13.786	14.884	16.060	17.319	18.666	20.106	28.925	41.085	57.665
11	8.140	8.912	9.749	10.657	11.642	12.708	13.862	15.112	16.462	17.921	19.498	21.199	23.034	25.012	27.144	40.495	59.573	86.498
12	9.850	10.872	11.991	13.215	14.552	16.012	17.605	19.343	21.236	23.298	25.542	27.982	30.635	33.516	36.644	56.694	86.380	129.746
13	11.918	13.264	14.749	16.386	18.190	20.175	22.359	24.759	27.395	30.287	33.460	36.937	40.745	44.912	49.469	79.371	125.251	194.620
14	14.421	16.182	18.141	20.319	22.737	25.420	28.395	31.691	35.339	39.373	43.832	48.756	54.190	60.181	66.784	111.119	181.614	291.929
15	17.449	19.742	22.314	25.195	28.422	32.030	36.062	40.565	45.587	51.185	57.420	64.358	72.073	80.643	90.158	155.567	263.341	437.894
16	21.113	24.085	27.446	31.242	35.527	40.357	45.799	51.923	58.808	66.541	75.220	84.953	95.857	108.061	121.713	217.793	381.844	656.841
17	25.547	29.384	33.758	38.740	44.409	50.850	58.165	66.461	75.862	86.503	98.539	112.138	127.490	144.802	164.312	304.911	553.674	985.261
18	30.912	35.848	41.523	48.038	55.511	64.071	73.869	85.070	97.862	112.454	129.086	148.022	169.561	194.035	221.822	426.875	802.826	1477.892
19	37.404	43.735	51.073	59.567	69.389	80.730	93.813	108.890	126.242	146.190	169.102	195.389	225.517	260.006	299.459	597.625	1164.098	2216.838
20	45.258	53.357	62.820	73.863	86.736	101.720	119.143	139.379	162.852	190.047	221.523	257.913	299.937	348.408	404.270	836.674	1687.942	3325.257
21	54.762	65.095	77.268	91.591	108.420	128.167	151.312	178.405	210.079	247.061	290.196	340.446	398.916	466.867	545.764	1171.343	2447.515	4987.883
22	66.262	79.416	95.040	113.572	135.525	161.490	192.165	228.358	271.002	321.178	380.156	449.388	530.558	625.601	736.781	1639.878	3548.896	7481.824
23	80.178	96.887	116.899	140.829	169.407	203.477	244.050	292.298	349.592	417.531	498.004	593.192	705.642	838.305	994.653	2295.829	5145.898	11222.738
24	97.015	118.203	143.786	174.628	211.758	256.381	309.943	374.141	450.974	542.791	652.385	783.013	938.504	1123.328	1342.781	3214.158	7461.547	16834.109
25	117.388	144.207	176.857	216.539	264.698	323.040	393.628	478.901	581.756	705.627	854.623	1033.577	1248.210	1505.258	1812.754	4499.816	10819.242	25251.164
30	304.471	389.748	497.904	634.810	807.793	1025.904	1300.477	1645.488	2078.208	2619.936	3297.081	4142.008	5194.516	6503.285	8128.426	24201.043	69348.375	191751.000
35	789.716	1053.370	1401.749	1861.020	2465.189	3258.053	4296.547	5653.840	7423.988	9727.598	12719.918	16598.906	21617.363	28096.695	36448.051	130158.687	*	*
40	2048.309	2846.941	3946.340	5455.797	7523.156	10346.879	14195.051	19426.418	26520.723	36117.754	49072.621	66519.313	89962.188	121388.437	163433.875	700022.688	*	*
45	5312.758	7694.418	11110.121	15994.316	22958.844	32859.457	46897.973	66748.500	94739.937	134102.187	*	*	*	*	*	*	*	*
50	13779.844	20795.680	31278.301	46889.207	70064.812	104354.562	154942.687	229345.875	338440.000	497910.125	*	*	*	*	*	*	*	*

*Not shown due to space limitations.

Texas Instruments BA-35, BAII, BAII Plus[c]

Inputs:	800	5	6		
Functions:	PV	N	%i	CPT	FV
Outputs:					1070.58 [d]

[c]For the Texas Instruments BAII, you would use the 2nd key instead of the CPT key; for the Texas Instruments BAII Plus, you would use the I/Y key instead of the %i key.

[d]If a minus sign precedes the output, it should be ignored.

TABLE A-2 Future Value Interest Factors for a One-Dollar Annuity Compounded at k Percent for n Periods: $FVIFA_{k,n} = \sum_{t=1}^{n}(1+k)^{t-1}$

Period	1%	2%	3%	4%	5%	6%	7%	8%	9%	10%	11%	12%	13%	14%	15%	16%	17%	18%	19%	20%
1	1.000	1.000	1.000	1.000	1.000	1.000	1.000	1.000	1.000	1.000	1.000	1.000	1.000	1.000	1.000	1.000	1.000	1.000	1.000	1.000
2	2.010	2.020	2.030	2.040	2.050	2.060	2.070	2.080	2.090	2.100	2.110	2.120	2.130	2.140	2.150	2.160	2.170	2.180	2.190	2.200
3	3.030	3.060	3.091	3.122	3.152	3.184	3.215	3.246	3.278	3.310	3.342	3.374	3.407	3.440	3.472	3.506	3.539	3.572	3.606	3.640
4	4.060	4.122	4.184	4.246	4.310	4.375	4.440	4.506	4.573	4.641	4.710	4.779	4.850	4.921	4.993	5.066	5.141	5.215	5.291	5.368
5	5.101	5.204	5.309	5.416	5.526	5.637	5.751	5.867	5.985	6.105	6.228	6.353	6.480	6.610	6.742	6.877	7.014	7.154	7.297	7.442
6	6.152	6.308	6.468	6.633	6.802	6.975	7.153	7.336	7.523	7.716	7.913	8.115	8.323	8.535	8.754	8.977	9.207	9.442	9.683	9.930
7	7.214	7.434	7.662	7.898	8.142	8.394	8.654	8.923	9.200	9.487	9.783	10.089	10.405	10.730	11.067	11.414	11.772	12.141	12.523	12.916
8	8.286	8.583	8.892	9.214	9.549	9.897	10.260	10.637	11.028	11.436	11.859	12.300	12.757	13.233	13.727	14.240	14.773	15.327	15.902	16.499
9	9.368	9.755	10.159	10.583	11.027	11.491	11.978	12.488	13.021	13.579	14.164	14.776	15.416	16.085	16.786	17.518	18.285	19.086	19.923	20.799
10	10.462	10.950	11.464	12.006	12.578	13.181	13.816	14.487	15.193	15.937	16.722	17.549	18.420	19.337	20.304	21.321	22.393	23.521	24.709	25.959
11	11.567	12.169	12.808	13.486	14.207	14.972	15.784	16.645	17.560	18.531	19.561	20.655	21.814	23.044	24.349	25.733	27.200	28.755	30.403	32.150
12	12.682	13.412	14.192	15.026	15.917	16.870	17.888	18.977	20.141	21.384	22.713	24.133	25.650	27.271	29.001	30.850	32.824	34.931	37.180	39.580
13	13.809	14.680	15.618	16.627	17.713	18.882	20.141	21.495	22.953	24.523	26.211	28.029	29.984	32.088	34.352	36.786	39.404	42.218	45.244	48.496
14	14.947	15.974	17.086	18.292	19.598	21.015	22.550	24.215	26.019	27.975	30.095	32.392	34.882	37.581	40.504	43.672	47.102	50.818	54.841	59.196
15	16.097	17.293	18.599	20.023	21.578	23.276	25.129	27.152	29.361	31.772	34.405	37.280	40.417	43.842	47.580	51.659	56.109	60.965	66.260	72.035
16	17.258	18.639	20.157	21.824	23.657	25.672	27.888	30.324	33.003	35.949	39.190	42.753	46.671	50.980	55.717	60.925	66.648	72.938	79.850	87.442
17	18.430	20.012	21.761	23.697	25.840	28.213	30.840	33.750	36.973	40.544	44.500	48.883	53.738	59.117	65.075	71.673	78.978	87.067	96.021	105.930
18	19.614	21.412	23.414	25.645	28.132	30.905	33.999	37.450	41.301	45.599	50.396	55.749	61.724	68.393	75.836	84.140	93.404	103.739	115.265	128.116
19	20.811	22.840	25.117	27.671	30.539	33.760	37.379	41.446	46.018	51.158	56.939	63.439	70.748	78.968	88.211	98.603	110.283	123.412	138.165	154.739
20	22.019	24.297	26.870	29.778	33.066	36.785	40.995	45.762	51.159	57.274	64.202	72.052	80.946	91.024	102.443	115.379	130.031	146.626	165.417	186.687
21	23.239	25.783	28.676	31.969	35.719	39.992	44.865	50.422	56.764	64.002	72.264	81.698	92.468	104.767	118.809	134.840	153.136	174.019	197.846	225.024
22	24.471	27.299	30.536	34.248	38.505	43.392	49.005	55.456	62.872	71.402	81.213	92.502	105.489	120.434	137.630	157.414	180.169	206.342	236.436	271.028
23	25.716	28.845	32.452	36.618	41.430	46.995	53.435	60.893	69.531	79.542	91.147	104.602	120.203	138.295	159.274	183.600	211.798	244.483	282.359	326.234
24	26.973	30.421	34.426	39.082	44.501	50.815	58.176	66.764	76.789	88.496	102.173	118.154	136.829	158.656	184.166	213.976	248.803	289.490	337.007	392.480
25	28.243	32.030	36.459	41.645	47.726	54.864	63.248	73.105	84.699	98.346	114.412	133.333	155.616	181.867	212.790	249.212	292.099	342.598	402.038	471.976
30	34.784	40.567	47.575	56.084	66.438	79.057	94.459	113.282	136.305	164.491	199.018	241.330	293.192	356.778	434.738	530.306	647.423	790.932	966.698	1181.865
35	41.659	49.994	60.461	73.651	90.318	111.432	138.234	172.314	215.705	271.018	341.583	431.658	546.663	693.552	881.152	1120.699	1426.448	1816.607	2314.173	2948.294
40	48.885	60.401	75.400	95.024	120.797	154.758	199.630	259.052	337.872	442.580	581.812	767.080	1013.667	1341.979	1779.048	2360.724	3134.412	4163.094	5529.711	7343.715
45	56.479	71.891	92.718	121.027	159.695	212.737	285.741	386.497	525.840	718.881	986.613	1358.208	1874.086	2590.464	3585.031	4965.191	6879.008	9531.258	13203.105	18280.914
50	64.461	84.577	112.794	152.664	209.341	290.325	406.516	573.756	815.051	1163.865	1668.723	2399.975	3459.344	4994.301	7217.488	10435.449	15088.805	21812.273	31514.492	45496.094

USING THE CALCULATOR TO COMPUTE THE FUTURE VALUE OF AN ANNUITY

Before you begin, make sure to clear the memory, ensure that you are in the *end mode* and your calculator is set for *one payment per year,* and set the number of decimal places that you want (usually two for dollar-related accuracy).

SAMPLE PROBLEM

You want to know what the future value will be at the end of 5 years if you place five end-of-year deposits of $1,000 in an account paying 7 percent annually. What is your account balance at the end of 5 years?

Hewlett-Packard HP 12C, 17 BII, and 19 BII[a]

Inputs: | 1000 | 5 | 7 |

Functions: | PMT | N | I%YR | FV |

Outputs: | 5750.74 |[b]

---

[a]For the 12C, you would use the [n] key instead of the [N] key, and the [i] key instead of the [I%YR] key.
[b]The minus sign that precedes the output should be ignored.

TABLE A-2   (Continued)

Period	21%	22%	23%	24%	25%	26%	27%	28%	29%	30%	31%	32%	33%	34%	35%	40%	45%	50%
1	1.000	1.000	1.000	1.000	1.000	1.000	1.000	1.000	1.000	1.000	1.000	1.000	1.000	1.000	1.000	1.000	1.000	1.000
2	2.210	2.220	2.230	2.240	2.250	2.260	2.270	2.280	2.290	2.300	2.310	2.320	2.330	2.340	2.350	2.400	2.450	2.500
3	3.674	3.708	3.743	3.778	3.813	3.848	3.883	3.918	3.954	3.990	4.026	4.062	4.099	4.136	4.172	4.360	4.552	4.750
4	5.446	5.524	5.604	5.684	5.766	5.848	5.931	6.016	6.101	6.187	6.274	6.362	6.452	6.542	6.633	7.104	7.601	8.125
5	7.589	7.740	7.893	8.048	8.207	8.368	8.533	8.700	8.870	9.043	9.219	9.398	9.581	9.766	9.954	10.946	12.022	13.188
6	10.183	10.442	10.708	10.980	11.259	11.544	11.837	12.136	12.442	12.756	13.077	13.406	13.742	14.086	14.438	16.324	18.431	20.781
7	13.321	13.740	14.171	14.615	15.073	15.546	16.032	16.534	17.051	17.583	18.131	18.696	19.277	19.876	20.492	23.853	27.725	32.172
8	17.119	17.762	18.430	19.123	19.842	20.588	21.361	22.163	22.995	23.858	24.752	25.678	26.638	27.633	28.664	34.395	41.202	49.258
9	21.714	22.670	23.669	24.712	25.802	26.940	28.129	29.369	30.664	32.015	33.425	34.895	36.429	38.028	39.696	49.152	60.743	74.887
10	27.274	28.657	30.113	31.643	33.253	34.945	36.723	38.592	40.556	42.619	44.786	47.062	49.451	51.958	54.590	69.813	89.077	113.330
11	34.001	35.962	38.039	40.238	42.566	45.030	47.639	50.398	53.318	56.405	59.670	63.121	66.769	70.624	74.696	98.739	130.161	170.995
12	42.141	44.873	47.787	50.895	54.208	57.738	61.501	65.510	69.780	74.326	79.167	84.320	89.803	95.636	101.840	139.234	189.734	257.493
13	51.991	55.745	59.778	64.109	68.760	73.750	79.106	84.853	91.016	97.624	104.709	112.302	120.438	129.152	138.484	195.928	276.114	387.239
14	63.909	69.009	74.528	80.496	86.949	93.925	101.465	109.611	118.411	127.912	138.169	149.239	161.183	174.063	187.953	275.299	401.365	581.858
15	78.330	85.191	92.669	100.815	109.687	119.346	129.860	141.302	153.750	167.285	182.001	197.996	215.373	234.245	254.737	386.418	582.980	873.788
16	95.779	104.933	114.983	126.010	138.109	151.375	165.922	181.867	199.337	218.470	239.421	262.354	287.446	314.888	344.895	541.985	846.321	1311.681
17	116.892	129.019	142.428	157.252	173.636	191.733	211.721	233.790	258.145	285.011	314.642	347.307	383.303	422.949	466.608	759.778	1228.165	1968.522
18	142.439	158.403	176.187	195.993	218.045	242.583	269.885	300.250	334.006	371.514	413.180	459.445	510.792	567.751	630.920	1064.689	1781.838	2953.783
19	173.351	194.251	217.710	244.031	273.556	306.654	343.754	385.321	431.868	483.968	542.266	607.467	680.354	761.786	852.741	1491.563	2584.665	4431.672
20	210.755	237.986	268.783	303.598	342.945	387.384	437.568	494.210	558.110	630.157	711.368	802.856	905.870	1021.792	1152.200	2089.188	3748.763	6648.508
21	256.013	291.343	331.603	377.461	429.681	489.104	556.710	633.589	720.962	820.204	932.891	1060.769	1205.807	1370.201	1556.470	2925.862	5436.703	9973.762
22	310.775	356.438	408.871	469.052	538.101	617.270	708.022	811.993	931.040	1067.265	1223.087	1401.215	1604.724	1837.068	2102.234	4097.203	7884.215	14961.645
23	377.038	435.854	503.911	582.624	673.626	778.760	900.187	1040.351	1202.042	1388.443	1603.243	1850.603	2135.282	2462.669	2839.014	5737.078	11433.109	22443.469
24	457.215	532.741	620.810	723.453	843.032	982.237	1144.237	1332.649	1551.634	1805.975	2101.247	2443.795	2840.924	3300.974	3833.667	8032.906	16579.008	33666.207
25	554.230	650.944	764.596	898.082	1054.791	1238.617	1454.180	1706.790	2002.608	2348.765	2753.631	3226.808	3779.428	4424.301	5176.445	11247.062	24040.555	50500.316
30	1445.111	1767.044	2160.459	2640.881	3227.172	3941.953	4812.891	5873.172	7162.785	8729.805	10632.543	12940.672	15737.945	19124.434	23221.258	60500.207	154105.313	383500.000
35	3755.814	4783.520	6090.227	7750.094	9856.746	12527.160	15909.480	20188.742	25596.512	32422.090	41028.887	51868.563	65504.199	82634.625	104134.500	325394.688	*	*
40	9749.141	12936.141	17153.691	22728.367	30088.621	39791.957	52570.707	69376.562	91447.375	120389.375	*	*	*	*	*	*	*	*
45	25294.223	34970.230	48300.660	66638.937	91831.312	126378.937	173692.875	238384.312	326686.375	447005.062	*	*	*	*	*	*	*	*

*Not shown due to space limitations.

Texas Instruments BA-35, BAII, BAII Plus[c]

Inputs:	1000	5	7		
Functions:	PMT	N	%i	CPT	FV
Outputs:				5750.74 [d]	

[c]For the Texas Instruments BAII, you would use the 2nd key instead of the CPT key; for the Texas Instruments BAII Plus, you would use the I/Y key instead of the %i key.

[d]If a minus sign precedes the output, it should be ignored.

TABLE A-3 **Present Value Interest Factors for One Dollar Discounted at k Percent for n Periods:**

$$PVIF_{k,n} = \frac{1}{(1+k)^n}$$

Period	1%	2%	3%	4%	5%	6%	7%	8%	9%	10%	11%	12%	13%	14%	15%	16%	17%	18%	19%	20%
1	.990	.980	.971	.962	.952	.943	.935	.926	.917	.909	.901	.893	.885	.877	.870	.862	.855	.847	.840	.833
2	.980	.961	.943	.925	.907	.890	.873	.857	.842	.826	.812	.797	.783	.769	.756	.743	.731	.718	.706	.694
3	.971	.942	.915	.889	.864	.840	.816	.794	.772	.751	.731	.712	.693	.675	.658	.641	.624	.609	.593	.579
4	.961	.924	.888	.855	.823	.792	.763	.735	.708	.683	.659	.636	.613	.592	.572	.552	.534	.516	.499	.482
5	.951	.906	.863	.822	.784	.747	.713	.681	.650	.621	.593	.567	.543	.519	.497	.476	.456	.437	.419	.402
6	.942	.888	.837	.790	.746	.705	.666	.630	.596	.564	.535	.507	.480	.456	.432	.410	.390	.370	.352	.335
7	.933	.871	.813	.760	.711	.665	.623	.583	.547	.513	.482	.452	.425	.400	.376	.354	.333	.314	.296	.279
8	.923	.853	.789	.731	.677	.627	.582	.540	.502	.467	.434	.404	.376	.351	.327	.305	.285	.266	.249	.233
9	.914	.837	.766	.703	.645	.592	.544	.500	.460	.424	.391	.361	.333	.308	.284	.263	.243	.225	.209	.194
10	.905	.820	.744	.676	.614	.558	.508	.463	.422	.386	.352	.322	.295	.270	.247	.227	.208	.191	.176	.162
11	.896	.804	.722	.650	.585	.527	.475	.429	.388	.350	.317	.287	.261	.237	.215	.195	.178	.162	.148	.135
12	.887	.789	.701	.625	.557	.497	.444	.397	.356	.319	.286	.257	.231	.208	.187	.168	.152	.137	.124	.112
13	.879	.773	.681	.601	.530	.469	.415	.368	.326	.290	.258	.229	.204	.182	.163	.145	.130	.116	.104	.093
14	.870	.758	.661	.577	.505	.442	.388	.340	.299	.263	.232	.205	.181	.160	.141	.125	.111	.099	.088	.078
15	.861	.743	.642	.555	.481	.417	.362	.315	.275	.239	.209	.183	.160	.140	.123	.108	.095	.084	.074	.065
16	.853	.728	.623	.534	.458	.394	.339	.292	.252	.218	.188	.163	.141	.123	.107	.093	.081	.071	.062	.054
17	.844	.714	.605	.513	.436	.371	.317	.270	.231	.198	.170	.146	.125	.108	.093	.080	.069	.060	.052	.045
18	.836	.700	.587	.494	.416	.350	.296	.250	.212	.180	.153	.130	.111	.095	.081	.069	.059	.051	.044	.038
19	.828	.686	.570	.475	.396	.331	.277	.232	.194	.164	.138	.116	.098	.083	.070	.060	.051	.043	.037	.031
20	.820	.673	.554	.456	.377	.312	.258	.215	.178	.149	.124	.104	.087	.073	.061	.051	.043	.037	.031	.026
21	.811	.660	.538	.439	.359	.294	.242	.199	.164	.135	.112	.093	.077	.064	.053	.044	.037	.031	.026	.022
22	.803	.647	.522	.422	.342	.278	.226	.184	.150	.123	.101	.083	.068	.056	.046	.038	.032	.026	.022	.018
23	.795	.634	.507	.406	.326	.262	.211	.170	.138	.112	.091	.074	.060	.049	.040	.033	.027	.022	.018	.015
24	.788	.622	.492	.390	.310	.247	.197	.158	.126	.102	.082	.066	.053	.043	.035	.028	.023	.019	.015	.013
25	.780	.610	.478	.375	.295	.233	.184	.146	.116	.092	.074	.059	.047	.038	.030	.024	.020	.016	.013	.010
30	.742	.552	.412	.308	.231	.174	.131	.099	.075	.057	.044	.033	.026	.020	.015	.012	.009	.007	.005	.004
35	.706	.500	.355	.253	.181	.130	.094	.068	.049	.036	.026	.019	.014	.010	.008	.006	.004	.003	.002	.002
40	.672	.453	.307	.208	.142	.097	.067	.046	.032	.022	.015	.011	.008	.005	.004	.003	.002	.001	.001	.001
45	.639	.410	.264	.171	.111	.073	.048	.031	.021	.014	.009	.006	.004	.003	.002	.001	.001	.001	*	*
50	.608	.372	.228	.141	.087	.054	.034	.021	.013	.009	.005	.003	.002	.001	.001	.001	*	*	*	*

*PVIF is zero to three decimal places.

USING THE CALCULATOR TO COMPUTE THE PRESENT VALUE OF A SINGLE AMOUNT

Before you begin, make sure to clear the memory, ensure that you are in the *end mode* and your calculator is set for *one payment per year,* and set the number of decimal places that you want (usually two for dollar-related accuracy).

SAMPLE PROBLEM

You want to know the present value of $1,700 to be received at the end of 8 years, assuming an 8 percent discount rate.

Hewlett-Packard HP 12C, 17 BII, and 19 BII[a]

Inputs:	1700	8	8	
Functions:	FV	N	I%YR	PV
Outputs:				918.46 [b]

[a] For the 12C, you would use the `n` key instead of the `N` key, and the `i` key instead of the `I%YR` key.
[b] The minus sign that precedes the output should be ignored.

TABLE A-3 (Continued)

Period	21%	22%	23%	24%	25%	26%	27%	28%	29%	30%	31%	32%	33%	34%	35%	40%	45%	50%
1	.826	.820	.813	.806	.800	.794	.787	.781	.775	.769	.763	.758	.752	.746	.741	.714	.690	.667
2	.683	.672	.661	.650	.640	.630	.620	.610	.601	.592	.583	.574	.565	.557	.549	.510	.476	.444
3	.564	.551	.537	.524	.512	.500	.488	.477	.466	.455	.445	.435	.425	.416	.406	.364	.328	.296
4	.467	.451	.437	.423	.410	.397	.384	.373	.361	.350	.340	.329	.320	.310	.301	.260	.226	.198
5	.386	.370	.355	.341	.328	.315	.303	.291	.280	.269	.259	.250	.240	.231	.223	.186	.156	.132
6	.319	.303	.289	.275	.262	.250	.238	.227	.217	.207	.198	.189	.181	.173	.165	.133	.108	.088
7	.263	.249	.235	.222	.210	.198	.188	.178	.168	.159	.151	.143	.136	.129	.122	.095	.074	.059
8	.218	.204	.191	.179	.168	.157	.148	.139	.130	.123	.115	.108	.102	.096	.091	.068	.051	.039
9	.180	.167	.155	.144	.134	.125	.116	.108	.101	.094	.088	.082	.077	.072	.067	.048	.035	.026
10	.149	.137	.126	.116	.107	.099	.092	.085	.078	.073	.067	.062	.058	.054	.050	.035	.024	.017
11	.123	.112	.103	.094	.086	.079	.072	.066	.061	.056	.051	.047	.043	.040	.037	.025	.017	.012
12	.102	.092	.083	.076	.069	.062	.057	.052	.047	.043	.039	.036	.033	.030	.027	.018	.012	.008
13	.084	.075	.068	.061	.055	.050	.045	.040	.037	.033	.030	.027	.025	.022	.020	.013	.008	.005
14	.069	.062	.055	.049	.044	.039	.035	.032	.028	.025	.023	.021	.018	.017	.015	.009	.006	.003
15	.057	.051	.045	.040	.035	.031	.028	.025	.022	.020	.017	.016	.014	.012	.011	.006	.004	.002
16	.047	.042	.036	.032	.028	.025	.022	.019	.017	.015	.013	.012	.010	.009	.008	.005	.003	.002
17	.039	.034	.030	.026	.023	.020	.017	.015	.013	.012	.010	.009	.008	.007	.006	.003	.002	.001
18	.032	.028	.024	.021	.018	.016	.014	.012	.010	.009	.008	.007	.006	.005	.005	.002	.001	.001
19	.027	.023	.020	.017	.014	.012	.011	.009	.008	.007	.006	.005	.004	.004	.003	.002	.001	*
20	.022	.019	.016	.014	.012	.010	.008	.007	.006	.005	.005	.004	.003	.003	.002	.001	.001	*
21	.018	.015	.013	.011	.009	.008	.007	.006	.005	.004	.003	.003	.003	.002	.002	.001	*	*
22	.015	.013	.011	.009	.007	.006	.005	.004	.004	.003	.003	.002	.002	.002	.001	.001	*	*
23	.012	.010	.009	.007	.006	.005	.004	.003	.003	.002	.002	.002	.001	.001	.001	*	*	*
24	.010	.008	.007	.006	.005	.004	.003	.003	.002	.002	.002	.001	.001	.001	.001	*	*	*
25	.009	.007	.006	.005	.004	.003	.003	.002	.002	.001	.001	.001	.001	.001	.001	*	*	*
30	.003	.003	.002	.002	.001	.001	.001	.001	*	*	*	*	*	*	*	*	*	*
35	.001	.001	.001	.001	*	*	*	*	*	*	*	*	*	*	*	*	*	*
40	*	*	*	*	*	*	*	*	*	*	*	*	*	*	*	*	*	*
45	*	*	*	*	*	*	*	*	*	*	*	*	*	*	*	*	*	*
50	*	*	*	*	*	*	*	*	*	*	*	*	*	*	*	*	*	*

*$PVIF$ is zero to three decimal places.

Texas Instruments BA-35, BAII, BAII Plus[c]

Inputs:	1700	8	8		
Functions:	FV	N	%i	CPT	PV
Outputs:					918.46 [d]

---

[c]For the Texas Instruments BAII, you would use the 2nd key instead of the CPT key; for the Texas Instruments BAII Plus, you would use the I/Y key instead of the %i key.
[d]If a minus sign precedes the output, it should be ignored.

TABLE A-4   Present Value Interest Factors for a One-Dollar Annuity Discounted at k Percent for n Periods: $PVIFA_{k,n} = \sum\limits_{t=1}^{n} \dfrac{1}{(1+k)^t}$

Period	1%	2%	3%	4%	5%	6%	7%	8%	9%	10%	11%	12%	13%	14%	15%	16%	17%	18%	19%	20%
1	.990	.980	.971	.962	.952	.943	.935	.926	.917	.909	.901	.893	.885	.877	.870	.862	.855	.847	.840	.833
2	1.970	1.942	1.913	1.886	1.859	1.833	1.808	1.783	1.759	1.736	1.713	1.690	1.668	1.647	1.626	1.605	1.585	1.566	1.547	1.528
3	2.941	2.884	2.829	2.775	2.723	2.673	2.624	2.577	2.531	2.487	2.444	2.402	2.361	2.322	2.283	2.246	2.210	2.174	2.140	2.106
4	3.902	3.808	3.717	3.630	3.546	3.465	3.387	3.312	3.240	3.170	3.102	3.037	2.974	2.914	2.855	2.798	2.743	2.690	2.639	2.589
5	4.853	4.713	4.580	4.452	4.329	4.212	4.100	3.993	3.890	3.791	3.696	3.605	3.517	3.433	3.352	3.274	3.199	3.127	3.058	2.991
6	5.795	5.601	5.417	5.242	5.076	4.917	4.767	4.623	4.486	4.355	4.231	4.111	3.998	3.889	3.784	3.685	3.589	3.498	3.410	3.326
7	6.728	6.472	6.230	6.002	5.786	5.582	5.389	5.206	5.033	4.868	4.712	4.564	4.423	4.288	4.160	4.039	3.922	3.812	3.706	3.605
8	7.652	7.326	7.020	6.733	6.463	6.210	5.971	5.747	5.535	5.335	5.146	4.968	4.799	4.639	4.487	4.344	4.207	4.078	3.954	3.837
9	8.566	8.162	7.786	7.435	7.108	6.802	6.515	6.247	5.995	5.759	5.537	5.328	5.132	4.946	4.772	4.607	4.451	4.303	4.163	4.031
10	9.471	8.983	8.530	8.111	7.722	7.360	7.024	6.710	6.418	6.145	5.889	5.650	5.426	5.216	5.019	4.833	4.659	4.494	4.339	4.192
11	10.368	9.787	9.253	8.760	8.306	7.887	7.499	7.139	6.805	6.495	6.207	5.938	5.687	5.453	5.234	5.029	4.836	4.656	4.486	4.327
12	11.255	10.575	9.954	9.385	8.863	8.384	7.943	7.536	7.161	6.814	6.492	6.194	5.918	5.660	5.421	5.197	4.988	4.793	4.611	4.439
13	12.134	11.348	10.635	9.986	9.394	8.853	8.358	7.904	7.487	7.013	6.750	6.424	6.122	5.842	5.583	5.342	5.118	4.910	4.715	4.533
14	13.004	12.106	11.296	10.563	9.899	9.295	8.745	8.244	7.786	7.367	6.982	6.628	6.302	6.002	5.724	5.468	5.229	5.008	4.802	4.611
15	13.865	12.849	11.938	11.118	10.380	9.712	9.108	8.560	8.061	7.606	7.191	6.811	6.462	6.142	5.847	5.575	5.324	5.092	4.876	4.675
16	14.718	13.578	12.561	11.652	10.838	10.106	9.447	8.851	8.313	7.824	7.379	6.974	6.604	6.265	5.954	5.668	5.405	5.162	4.938	4.730
17	15.562	14.292	13.166	12.166	11.274	10.477	9.763	9.122	8.544	8.022	7.549	7.120	6.729	6.373	6.047	5.749	5.475	5.222	4.990	4.775
18	16.398	14.992	13.754	12.659	11.690	10.828	10.059	9.372	8.756	8.201	7.702	7.250	6.840	6.467	6.128	5.818	5.534	5.273	5.033	4.812
19	17.226	15.679	14.324	13.134	12.085	11.158	10.336	9.604	8.950	8.365	7.839	7.366	6.938	6.550	6.198	5.877	5.584	5.316	5.070	4.843
20	18.046	16.352	14.878	13.590	12.462	11.470	10.594	9.818	9.129	8.514	7.963	7.469	7.025	6.623	6.259	5.929	5.628	5.353	5.101	4.870
21	18.857	17.011	15.415	14.029	12.821	11.764	10.836	10.017	9.292	8.649	8.075	7.562	7.102	6.687	6.312	5.973	5.665	5.384	5.127	4.891
22	19.661	17.658	15.937	14.451	13.163	12.042	11.061	10.201	9.442	8.772	8.176	7.645	7.170	6.743	6.359	6.011	5.696	5.410	5.149	4.909
23	20.456	18.292	16.444	14.857	13.489	12.303	11.272	10.371	9.580	8.883	8.266	7.718	7.230	6.792	6.399	6.044	5.723	5.432	5.167	4.925
24	21.244	18.914	16.936	15.247	13.799	12.550	11.469	10.529	9.707	8.985	8.348	7.784	7.283	6.835	6.434	6.073	5.746	5.451	5.182	4.937
25	22.023	19.524	17.413	15.622	14.094	12.783	11.654	10.675	9.823	9.077	8.422	7.843	7.330	6.873	6.464	6.097	5.766	5.467	5.195	4.948
30	25.808	22.396	19.601	17.292	15.373	13.765	12.409	11.258	10.274	9.427	8.694	8.055	7.496	7.003	6.566	6.177	5.829	5.517	5.235	4.979
35	29.409	24.999	21.487	18.665	16.374	14.498	12.948	11.655	10.567	9.644	8.855	8.176	7.586	7.070	6.617	6.215	5.858	5.539	5.251	4.992
40	32.835	27.356	23.115	19.793	17.159	15.046	13.332	11.925	10.757	9.779	8.951	8.244	7.634	7.105	6.642	6.233	5.871	5.548	5.258	4.997
45	36.095	29.490	24.519	20.720	17.774	15.456	13.606	12.108	10.881	9.863	9.008	8.283	7.661	7.123	6.654	6.242	5.877	5.552	5.261	4.999
50	39.196	31.424	25.730	21.482	18.256	15.762	13.801	12.233	10.962	9.915	9.042	8.304	7.675	7.133	6.661	6.246	5.880	5.554	5.262	4.999

USING THE CALCULATOR TO COMPUTE THE PRESENT VALUE OF AN ANNUITY

Before you begin, make sure to clear the memory, ensure that you are in the *end mode* and your calculator is set for *one payment per year,* and set the number of decimal places that you want (usually two for dollar-related accuracy).

SAMPLE PROBLEM

You want to know what the present value will be of an annuity of $700 per year at the end of each year for 5 years, given a discount rate of 8 percent.

Hewlett-Packard HP 12C, 17 BII, and 19 BII[a]

Inputs:	700	5	8
Functions:	PMT	N	I%YR PV
Outputs:			2794.90 [b]

---

[a]For the 12C, you would use the n key instead of the N key, and the i key instead of the I%YR key.
[b]The minus sign that precedes the output should be ignored.

TABLE A-4 (Continued)

Period	21%	22%	23%	24%	25%	26%	27%	28%	29%	30%	31%	32%	33%	34%	35%	40%	45%	50%
1	.826	.820	.813	.806	.800	.794	.787	.781	.775	.769	.763	.758	.752	.746	.741	.714	.690	.667
2	1.509	1.492	1.474	1.457	1.440	1.424	1.407	1.392	1.376	1.361	1.346	1.331	1.317	1.303	1.289	1.224	1.165	1.111
3	2.074	2.042	2.011	1.981	1.952	1.923	1.896	1.868	1.842	1.816	1.791	1.766	1.742	1.719	1.696	1.589	1.493	1.407
4	2.540	2.494	2.448	2.404	2.362	2.320	2.280	2.241	2.203	2.166	2.130	2.096	2.062	2.029	1.997	1.849	1.720	1.605
5	2.926	2.864	2.803	2.745	2.689	2.635	2.583	2.532	2.483	2.436	2.390	2.345	2.302	2.260	2.220	2.035	1.876	1.737
6	3.245	3.167	3.092	3.020	2.951	2.885	2.821	2.759	2.700	2.643	2.588	2.534	2.483	2.433	2.385	2.168	1.983	1.824
7	3.508	3.416	3.327	3.242	3.161	3.083	3.009	2.937	2.868	2.802	2.739	2.677	2.619	2.562	2.508	2.263	2.057	1.883
8	3.726	3.619	3.518	3.421	3.329	3.241	3.156	3.076	2.999	2.925	2.854	2.786	2.721	2.658	2.598	2.331	2.109	1.922
9	3.905	3.786	3.673	3.566	3.463	3.366	3.273	3.184	3.100	3.019	2.942	2.868	2.798	2.730	2.665	2.379	2.144	1.948
10	4.054	3.923	3.799	3.682	3.570	3.465	3.364	3.269	3.178	3.092	3.009	2.930	2.855	2.784	2.715	2.414	2.168	1.965
11	4.177	4.035	3.902	3.776	3.656	3.544	3.437	3.335	3.239	3.147	3.060	2.978	2.899	2.824	2.752	2.438	2.185	1.977
12	4.278	4.127	3.985	3.851	3.725	3.606	3.493	3.387	3.286	3.190	3.100	3.013	2.931	2.853	2.779	2.456	2.196	1.985
13	4.362	4.203	4.053	3.912	3.780	3.656	3.538	3.427	3.322	3.223	3.129	3.040	2.956	2.876	2.799	2.469	2.204	1.990
14	4.432	4.265	4.108	3.962	3.824	3.695	3.573	3.459	3.351	3.249	3.152	3.061	2.974	2.892	2.814	2.478	2.210	1.993
15	4.489	4.315	4.153	4.001	3.859	3.726	3.601	3.483	3.373	3.268	3.170	3.076	2.988	2.905	2.825	2.484	2.214	1.995
16	4.536	4.357	4.189	4.033	3.887	3.751	3.623	3.503	3.390	3.283	3.183	3.088	2.999	2.914	2.834	2.489	2.216	1.997
17	4.576	4.391	4.219	4.059	3.910	3.771	3.640	3.518	3.403	3.295	3.193	3.097	3.007	2.921	2.840	2.492	2.218	1.998
18	4.608	4.419	4.243	4.080	3.928	3.786	3.654	3.529	3.413	3.304	3.201	3.104	3.012	2.926	2.844	2.494	2.219	1.999
19	4.635	4.442	4.263	4.097	3.942	3.799	3.664	3.539	3.421	3.311	3.207	3.109	3.017	2.930	2.848	2.496	2.220	1.999
20	4.657	4.460	4.279	4.110	3.954	3.808	3.673	3.546	3.427	3.316	3.211	3.113	3.020	2.933	2.850	2.497	2.221	1.999
21	4.675	4.476	4.292	4.121	3.963	3.816	3.679	3.551	3.432	3.320	3.215	3.116	3.023	2.935	2.852	2.498	2.221	2.000
22	4.690	4.488	4.302	4.130	3.970	3.822	3.684	3.556	3.436	3.323	3.217	3.118	3.025	2.936	2.853	2.498	2.222	2.000
23	4.703	4.499	4.311	4.137	3.976	3.827	3.689	3.559	3.438	3.325	3.219	3.120	3.026	2.938	2.854	2.499	2.222	2.000
24	4.713	4.507	4.318	4.143	3.981	3.831	3.692	3.562	3.441	3.327	3.221	3.121	3.027	2.939	2.855	2.499	2.222	2.000
25	4.721	4.514	4.323	4.147	3.985	3.834	3.694	3.564	3.442	3.329	3.222	3.122	3.028	2.939	2.856	2.499	2.222	2.000
30	4.746	4.534	4.339	4.160	3.995	3.842	3.701	3.569	3.447	3.332	3.225	3.124	3.030	2.941	2.857	2.500	2.222	2.000
35	4.756	4.541	4.345	4.164	3.998	3.845	3.703	3.571	3.448	3.333	3.226	3.125	3.030	2.941	2.857	2.500	2.222	2.000
40	4.760	4.544	4.347	4.166	3.999	3.846	3.703	3.571	3.448	3.333	3.226	3.125	3.030	2.941	2.857	2.500	2.222	2.000
45	4.761	4.545	4.347	4.166	4.000	3.846	3.704	3.571	3.448	3.333	3.226	3.125	3.030	2.941	2.857	2.500	2.222	2.000
50	4.762	4.545	4.348	4.167	4.000	3.846	3.704	3.571	3.448	3.333	3.226	3.125	3.030	2.941	2.857	2.500	2.222	2.000

Texas Instruments BA-35, BAII, BAII Plus[c]

Inputs:	700	5	8		
Functions:	PMT	N	%i	CPT	FV
Outputs:				2794.90 [d]	

---

[c]For the Texas Instruments BAII, you would use the 2nd key instead of the CPT key; for the Texas Instruments BAII Plus, you would use the I/Y key instead of the %i key.

[d]If a minus sign precedes the output, it should be ignored.

Appendix **B**

Solutions to Self-Test Problems

CHAPTER 2

ST 2-1

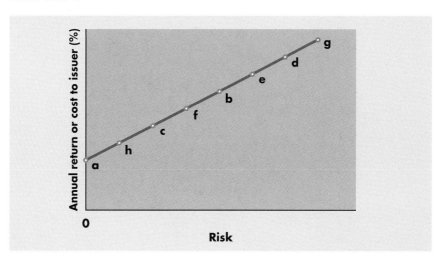

Key:

a. A 3-month U.S. Treasury bill paying 5.24%

b. A 30-year $30 million bond issue offered by Ford Motor Company

c. A 10-year U.S. Treasury bond

d. Coca-Cola common stock

e. Citicorp preferred stock

f. A $100,000 IOU from Mobil Oil (commercial paper), to be repaid in 90 days.

g. An initial public offering of common stock in Night Flyer, a new high-tech company

h. A 12-month U.S. Treasury note

The three U.S. Treasury issues have the least risk. The 3-month Treasury bill (a) is considered the risk-free asset. The 12-month Treasury note (h) would be next lowest in risk, because it has a shorter maturity than the 10-year Treasury bond (c). The remainder of the securities follow the general sequence shown in Figure 2.6. The Night Flyer IPO has the greatest risk because it is a speculative common stock.

CHAPTER 4

ST 4-1   **a.** Capital gains = $180,000 sale price − $150,000 original purchase price = <u>$30,000</u>

b. Total taxable income = $280,000 operating earnings + $30,000 capital gain = <u>$310,000</u>

c. Firm's tax liability:

Using Table 2.3:

$$\text{Total taxes due} = \$22,250 + [.39 \times (\$310,000 - \$100,000)]$$
$$= \$22,250 + (.39 \times \$210,000) = \$22,250 + \$81,900$$
$$= \underline{\$104,150}$$

d. Average tax rate = $\dfrac{\$104,150}{\$310,000}$ = <u>33.6%</u>

Marginal tax rate = <u>39%</u>

ST 4-2   **a.** Depreciation Schedule

Year	Cost^a (1)	Percentages (from Table 4.7) (2)	Depreciation [(1) × (2)] (3)
1	$150,000	20%	$ 30,000
2	150,000	32	48,000
3	150,000	19	28,500
4	150,000	12	18,000
5	150,000	12	18,000
6	150,000	5	7,500
	Totals	100%	$150,000

^{a}$140,000 asset cost + $10,000 installation cost.

b. Cash flow schedule

Year	EBDT (1)	Deprec. (2)	Net profits before taxes [(1) − (2)] (3)	Taxes [.4 × (3)] (4)	Net profits after taxes [(3) − (4)] (5)	Operating cash flows [(2) + (5)] (6)
1	$160,000	$30,000	$130,000	$52,000	$78,000	$108,000
2	160,000	48,000	112,000	44,800	67,200	115,200
3	160,000	28,500	131,500	52,600	78,900	107,400
4	160,000	18,000	142,000	56,800	85,200	103,200
5	160,000	18,000	142,000	56,800	85,200	103,200
6	160,000	7,500	152,500	61,000	91,500	99,000

c. The purchase of the asset allows the firm to deduct depreciation—a noncash charge—for tax purposes. This results in lower taxable income and therefore lower tax payments. As a result, the firm's operating cash flows (in column 6 of the preceding table) exceed its net profits after taxes (in column 5 of the table).

CHAPTER 5

ST 5-1

Ratio	Too high	Too low
Current ratio = current assets/current liabilities	May indicate that the firm is holding excessive cash, accounts receivable, or inventory.	May indicate poor ability to satisfy short-term obligations.
Inventory turnover = CGS/inventory	May indicate lower level of inventory, which may cause stockouts and lost sales.	May indicate poor inventory management, excessive inventory, or obsolete inventory.
Times interest earned = earnings before interest and taxes/interest		May indicate poor ability to pay contractual interest payments.
Gross profit margin = gross profits/sales	Indicates the low cost of merchandise sold relative to the sales price; may indicate noncompetitive pricing and potential lost sales.	Indicates the high cost of the merchandise sold relative to the sales price; may indicate either a low sales price or a high cost of goods sold.
Return on total assets = net profits after taxes/total assets		Indicates ineffective management in generating profits with the available assets.

ST 5-2

Balance Sheet
O'Keefe Industries
December 31, 2000

Cash	$ 30,000	Accounts payable	$ 120,000
Marketable securities	25,000	Notes payable	160,000^e
Accounts receivable	200,000^a	Accruals	20,000
Inventories	225,000^b	Total current	
Total current assets	$ 480,000	liabilities	$ 300,000^d
Net fixed assets	$1,020,000^c	Long-term debt	$ 600,000^f
Total assets	$1,500,000	Stockholders' equity	$ 600,000
		Total liabilities and	
		stockholders' equity	$1,500,000

^{a}Average collection period (ACP) = 40 days
ACP = accounts receivable/average sales per day
40 = accounts receivable/($1,800,000/360)
40 = accounts receivable/$5,000
$200,000 = accounts receivable

^{b}Inventory turnover = 6.0
Inventory turnover = cost of goods sold/inventory
6.0 = [sales × (1 − gross profit margin)]/inventory
6.0 = [$1,800,000 × (1 − .25)]/inventory
$225,000 = inventory

^{c}Total asset turnover = 1.20
Total asset turnover = sales/total assets
1.20 = $1,800,000/total assets
$1,500,000 = total assets
Total assets = current assets + net fixed assets
$1,500,000 = $480,000 + net fixed assets
$1,020,000 = net fixed assets

^{d}Current ratio = 1.60
Current ratio = current assets/current liabilities
1.60 = $480,000/current liabilities
$300,000 = current liabilities

^{e}Notes payable $=$ total current liabilities $-$ accounts payable $-$ accruals

$\quad$ = $300,000 − $120,000 − $20,000
$\quad$ = $160,000

^{f}Debt ratio = .60
Debt ratio = total liabilities/total assets
.60 = total liabilities/$1,500,000
$900,000 = total liabilities

Total liabilities $=$ current liabilities $+$ long-term debt

$900,000 = $300,000 + long-term debt
$600,000 = long-term debt

CHAPTER 6

ST 6-1   **a.** *Bank A:*

$$FV_3 = \$10,000 \times FVIF_{4\%/3\text{yrs}} = \$10,000 \times 1.125 = \underline{\$11,250}$$
$$(\text{Calculator solution} = \$11,248.64)$$

Bank B:

$$FV_3 = \$10,000 \times FVIF_{4\%/2,2 \times 3\text{yrs}} = \$10,000 \times FVIF_{2\%,6\text{yrs}}$$
$$= \$10,000 \times 1.126 = \underline{\$11,260}$$
$$(\text{Calculator solution} = \$11,261.62)$$

Bank C:

$$FV_3 = \$10,000 \times FVIF_{4\%/4,4 \times 3\text{yrs}} = \$10,000 \times FVIF_{1\%,12\text{yrs}}$$
$$= \$10,000 \times 1.127 = \underline{\$11,270}$$
$$(\text{Calculator solution} = \$11,268.25)$$

b. Bank A: $k_{EAR} = (1 + 4\%/1)^1 - 1 = (1 + .04)^1 - 1 = 1.04 - 1 = .04 = \underline{4\%}$

Bank B: $k_{EAR} = (1 + 4\%/2)^2 - 1 = (1 + .02)^2 - 1 = 1.0404 - 1 = .0404 = \underline{4.04\%}$

Bank C: $k_{EAR} = (1 + 4\%/4)^4 - 1 = (1 + .01)^4 - 1 = 1.0406 - 1 = .0406 = \underline{4.06\%}$

c. Ms. Martin should deal with Bank C: The quarterly compounding of interest at the given 4 percent rate results in the highest future value as a result of the corresponding highest effective annual rate.

d. *Bank D:*

$$FV_3 = \$10,000 \times FVIF_{4\%,3yrs} \text{ (continuous compounding)}$$
$$= \$10,000 \times e^{.04 \times 3} = \$10,000 \times e^{.12}$$
$$= \$10,000 \times 1.127497$$
$$= \underline{\$11,274.97}$$

This alternative is better than Bank C, because it results in a higher future value because of the use of continuous compounding, which with otherwise identical cash flows always results in the highest future value of any compounding period.

ST 6-2   **a.** On a purely subjective basis, annuity Y looks more attractive than annuity X because it provides $1,000 more each year than does annuity X. Of course its lower earnings rate of 11 percent versus 15 percent for annuity X may favor annuity X.

b. *Annuity X:*

$$FVA_6 = \$9,000 \times FVIFA_{15\%,6yrs}$$
$$= \$9,000 \times 8.754 = \underline{\$78,786.00}$$

(Calculator solution = $78,783.65)

Annuity Y:

$$FVA_6 = \$10,000 \times FVIFA_{11\%,6yrs}$$
$$= \$10,000 \times 7.913 = \underline{\$79,130.00}$$

(Calculator solution = $79,128.60)

c. Annuity Y is more attractive, because its future value at the end of year 6, FVA_6, of $79,130.00 is greater than annuity X's end-of-year-6 future value, FVA_6, of $78,786.00. The subjective assessment in **a** was correct. The benefit of receiving annuity Y's larger annual cash flows more than offset the fact that it only earned 11 percent annually whereas annuity X earned 15 percent annually.

ST 6-3   *Alternative A:*

Cash flow stream:

$$PVA_5 = \$700 \times PVIFA_{9\%,5yrs}$$
$$= \$700 \times 3.890 = \underline{\$2,723}$$
$$\text{(Calculator solution} = \$2,722.76)$$

Lump sum: $\underline{\$2,825}$

Alternative B:

Cash flow stream:

Year (n)	Cash flow (1)	$FVIF_{9\%,n}$ (2)	Present value [(1) × (2)] (3)
1	$1,100	.917	$1,088.70
2	900	.842	757.80
3	700	.772	540.40
4	500	.708	354.00
5	300	.650	195.00
		Present value	$2,855.90

(Calculator solution = $2,856.41)

Lump-sum: $2,800

Conclusion: Alternative B in the form of a cash flow stream is preferred because its present value of $2,855,90 is greater than the other three values.

ST 6-4 $FVA_5 = \$8,000$; $FVIFA_{7\%,5yrs} = 5.751$; $PMT = ?$

$FVA_n = PMT \times (FVIFA_{k,n})$ [Equation 6.12 or 6.22]

$\$8,000 = PMT \times 5.751$

$PMT = \$8,000/5.751 = \underline{\$1,391.06}$

(Calculator solution = $1,391.13)

Judi should deposit $1,391.06 at the end of each of the 5 years to meet her goal of accumulating $8,000 at the end of the fifth year.

CHAPTER 7

ST 7-1   **a.** Expected return, $\bar{k} = \dfrac{\Sigma \text{Returns}}{3}$ (*Equation 7.2a in footnote 1*)

$$\bar{k}_A = \frac{12\% + 14\% + 16\%}{3} = \frac{42\%}{3} = \underline{14\%}$$

$$\bar{k}_B = \frac{16\% + 14\% + 12\%}{3} = \frac{42\%}{3} = \underline{14\%}$$

$$\bar{k}_C = \frac{12\% + 14\% + 16\%}{3} = \frac{42\%}{3} = \underline{14\%}$$

b. Standard deviation, $\sigma_k = \sqrt{\dfrac{\sum\limits_{i=1}^{n} (k_i - \bar{k})^2}{n-1}}$ (*Equation 7.3a in footnote 2*)

$$\sigma_{k_A} = \sqrt{\frac{(12\% - 14\%)^2 + (14\% - 14\%)^2 + (16\% - 14\%)^2}{3-1}}$$

$$= \sqrt{\frac{4\% + 0\% + 4\%}{2}} = \sqrt{\frac{8\%}{2}} = \underline{\underline{2\%}}$$

$$\sigma_{k_B} = \sqrt{\frac{(16\% - 14\%)^2 + (14\% - 14\%)^2 + (12\% - 14\%)^2}{3 - 1}}$$

$$= \sqrt{\frac{4\% + 0\% + 4\%}{2}} = \sqrt{\frac{8\%}{2}} = \underline{\underline{2\%}}$$

$$\sigma_{k_C} = \sqrt{\frac{(12\% - 14\%)^2 + (14\% - 14\%)^2 + (16\% - 14\%)^2}{3 - 1}}$$

$$= \sqrt{\frac{4\% + 0\% + 4\%}{2}} = \sqrt{\frac{8\%}{2}} = \underline{\underline{2\%}}$$

c.

	Annual expected returns	
Year	Portfolio AB	Portfolio AC
2001	$(.50 \times 12\%) + (.50 \times 16\%) = 14\%$	$(.50 \times 12\%) + (.50 \times 12\%) = 12\%$
2002	$(.50 \times 14\%) + (.50 \times 14\%) = 14\%$	$(.50 \times 14\%) + (.50 \times 14\%) = 14\%$
2003	$(.50 \times 16\%) + (.50 \times 12\%) = 14\%$	$(.50 \times 16\%) + (.50 \times 16\%) = 16\%$

Over the 3-year period:

$$\bar{k}_{AB} = \frac{14\% + 14\% + 14\%}{3} = \frac{42\%}{3} = \underline{\underline{14\%}}$$

$$\bar{k}_{AC} = \frac{12\% + 14\% + 16\%}{3} = \frac{42\%}{3} = \underline{\underline{14\%}}$$

d. AB is perfectly negatively correlated.

AC is perfectly positively correlated.

e. Standard deviation of the portfolios

$$\sigma_{k_{AB}} = \sqrt{\frac{(14\% - 14\%)^2 + (14\% - 14\%)^2 + (14\% - 14\%)^2}{3 - 1}}$$

$$= \sqrt{\frac{0\% + 0\% + 0\%}{2}} = \sqrt{\frac{0\%}{2}} = \underline{\underline{0\%}}$$

$$\sigma_{k_{AC}} = \sqrt{\frac{(12\% - 14\%)^2 + (14\% - 14\%)^2 + (16\% - 14\%)^2}{3 - 1}}$$

$$= \sqrt{\frac{4\% + 0\% + 4\%}{2}} = \sqrt{\frac{8\%}{2}} = \underline{\underline{2\%}}$$

f. Portfolio AB is preferred, because it provides the same return (14%) as AC but with less risk [$(\sigma_{k_{AB}} = 0\%) < (\sigma_{k_{AC}} = 2\%)$].

ST 7-2   **a.** When the market return increases by 10 percent, the project's required return would be expected to increase by 15 percent ($1.50 \times 10\%$). When the market return decreases by 10 percent, the project's required return would be expected to decrease by 15 percent [$1.50 \times (-10\%)$].

b. $k_j = R_F + [b_j \times (k_m - R_F)]$
$= 7\% + [1.50 \times (10\% - 7\%)]$
$= 7\% + 4.5\% = \underline{11.5\%}$

c. No, the project should be rejected, because its *expected* return of 11 percent is less than the 11.5 percent return *required* from the project.

d. $k_j = 7\% + [1.50 \times (9\% - 7\%)]$
$= 7\% + 3\% = \underline{10\%}$

The project would now be acceptable, because its *expected* return of 11 percent is now in excess of the *required* return, which has declined to 10 percent as a result of investors in the marketplace becoming less risk-averse.

CHAPTER 8

ST 8-1   **a.** $B_0 = I \times (PVIFA_{k_d,n}) + M \times (PVIF_{k_d,n})$
$I = .08 \times \$1,000 = \$80$
$M = \$1,000$
$n = 12$ yrs

(1) $k_d = 7\%$
$B_0 = \$80 \times (PVIFA_{7\%,12yrs}) + \$1,000 \times (PVIF_{7\%,12yrs})$
$= (\$80 \times 7.943) + (\$1,000 \times .444)$
$= \$635.44 + \$444.00 = \underline{\$1,079.44}$
(Calculator solution = $1,079.43)

(2) $k_d = 8\%$
$B_0 = \$80 \times (PVIFA_{8\%,12yrs}) + \$1,000 \times (PVIF_{8\%,12yrs})$
$= (\$80 \times 7.536) + (\$1,000 \times .397)$
$= \$602.88 + \$397.00 = \underline{\$999.88}$
(Calculator solution = $1,000)

(3) $k_d = 10\%$
$B_0 = \$80 \times (PVIFA_{10\%,12yrs}) + \$1,000 \times (PVIF_{10\%,12yrs})$
$= (\$80 \times 6.814) + (\$1,000 \times .319)$
$= \$545.12 + \$319.00 = \underline{\$864.12}$
(Calculator solution = $863.73)

b. (1) $k_d = 7\%$, $B_0 = \$1,079.44$; sells at a *premium*
(2) $k_d = 8\%$, $B_0 = \$999.88 \approx \$1,000.00$; sells at its *par value*
(3) $k_d = 10\%$, $B_0 = \$864.12$; sells at a *discount*

c. $B_0 = \dfrac{I}{2} \times (PVIFA_{k_d/2,2n}) + M \times (PVIF_{k_d/2,2n})$

$= \dfrac{\$80}{2} \times (PVIFA_{10\%/2,2\times12\text{periods}}) + \$1,000 \times (PVIF_{10\%/2,2\times12\text{periods}})$

$= \$40 \times (PVIFA_{5\%,24\text{periods}}) + \$1,000 \times (PVIF_{5\%,24\text{periods}})$

$= (\$40 \times 13.799) + (\$1,000 \times .310)$

$= \$551.96 + \$310.00 = \underline{\$861.96}$

(Calculator solution = $862.01)

ST 8-2 a. $B_0 = \$1,150$
$I = .11 \times \$1,000 = \$110$
$M = \$1,000$
$n = 18$ yrs
$\$1,150 = \$110 \times (PVIFA_{k_d,18\text{yrs}}) + \$1,000 \times (PVIF_{k_d,18\text{yrs}})$

Because if $k_d = 11\%$, $B_0 = \$1,000 = M$, try $k_d = 10\%$.
$B_0 = \$110 \times (PVIFA_{10\%,18\text{yrs}}) + \$1,000 \times (PVIF_{10\%,18\text{yrs}})$
$= (\$110 \times 8.201) + (\$1,000 \times .180)$
$= \$902.11 + \$180.00 = \$1,082.11$

Because $\$1,082.11 < \$1,150$, try $k_d = 9\%$.
$B_0 = \$110 \times (PVIFA_{9\%,18\text{yrs}}) + \$1,000 \times (PVIF_{9\%,18\text{yrs}})$
$= (\$110 \times 8.756) + (\$1,000 \times .212)$
$= \$963.16 + \$212.00 = \$1,175.16$

Because the $1,175.16 value at 9 percent is higher than $1,150, and the $1,082.11 value at 10 percent rate is lower than $1,150, the bond's yield to maturity must be between 9 and 10 percent. Because the $1,175.16 value is closer to $1,150, rounding to the nearest whole percent, the YTM is 9 percent. (By using interpolation, the more precise YTM value is 9.27 percent.)

(Calculator solution = 9.26%)

b. The calculated YTM of 9+ percent is below the bond's 11 percent coupon interest rate, because the bond's market value of $1,150 is above its $1,000 par value. Whenever a bond's market value is above its par value (it sells at a *premium*), its YTM will be below its coupon interest rate; when a bond sells at *par*, the YTM will equal its coupon interest rate; and when the bond sells for less than par (at a *discount*), its YTM will be greater than its coupon interest rate.

ST 8-3 $D_0 = \$1.80/\text{share}$
$k_s = 12\%$
a. *Zero growth:*

$P_0 = \dfrac{D_1}{k_s} = \dfrac{D_1 = D_0 = \$1.80}{.12} = \underline{\$15/\text{share}}$

b. *Constant growth, g = 5%:*

$D_1 = D_0 \times (1 + g) = \$1.80 \times (1 + .05) = \$1.89/\text{share}$

$P_0 = \dfrac{D_1}{k_s - g} = \dfrac{\$1.89}{.12 - .05} = \dfrac{\$1.89}{.07} = \underline{\$27/\text{share}}$

CHAPTER 9

ST 9-1   **a.** Book value = installed cost − accumulated depreciation

Installed cost = $50,000

Accumulated depreciation = $50,000 × (.20 + .32 + .19 + .12)

$$= \$50,000 \times .83 = \$41,500$$

Book value = $50,000 − $41,500 = $\underline{\$8,500}$

b. Taxes on sale of old equipment:

Capital gain = sale price − initial purchase price

$$= \$55,000 - \$50,000 = \$5,000$$

Recaptured depreciation = initial purchase price − book value

$$= \$50,000 - \$8,500 = \$41,500$$

Taxes = (.40 × $5,000) + (.40 × $41,500)

$$= \$2,000 + \$16,600 = \underline{\$18,600}$$

c. Initial investment:

Installed cost of new equipment		
Cost of new equipment	$75,000	
+ Installation costs	5,000	
Total installed cost—new		$80,000
− After-tax proceeds from sale of old equipment		
Proceeds from sale of old equipment	$55,000	
− Taxes on sale of old equipment	18,600	
Total after-tax proceeds—old		36,400
+ Change in net working capital		15,000
Initial investment		$58,600

ST 9-2   **a.** Initial investment:

Installed cost of new machine		
Cost of new machine	$140,000	
+ Installation costs	10,000	
Total installed cost—new (depreciable value)		$150,000
− After-tax proceeds from sale of old machine		
Proceeds from sale of old machine	$ 42,000	
− Taxes on sale of old machine[1]	9,120	
Total after-tax proceeds—old		32,880
+ Change in net working capital[2]		20,000
Initial investment		$137,120

---

[1]Book value of old machine = $40,000 − [(.20 + .32) × $40,000]

$$= \$40,000 - (.52 \times \$40,000)$$
$$= \$40,000 - \$20,800 = \$19,200$$

Capital gain = $42,000 − $40,000 = $2,000

Recaptured depreciation = $40,000 − $19,200 = $20,800

Taxes = (.40 × $2,000) + (.40 × $20,800) = $800 + $8,320 = $\underline{\$9,120}$

[2]Change in net working capital = +$10,000 + $25,000 − $15,000

$$= \$35,000 - \$15,000 = \underline{\$20,000}$$

b. Incremental operating cash inflows:

Calculation of Depreciation Expense for New Machine

Year	Cost (1)	Applicable MACRS depreciation percentages (from Table 4.7) (2)	Depreciation [(1) × (2)] (3)
With new machine			
1	$150,000	33%	$ 49,500
2	150,000	45	67,500
3	150,000	15	22,500
4	150,000	7	10,500
	Totals	100%	$150,000

Calculation of Depreciation Expense for Old Machine

Year	Cost (1)	Applicable MACRS depreciation percentages (from Table 4.7) (2)	Depreciation [(1) × (2)] (3)
With old machine			
1	$40,000	19% (year-3 depreciation)	$ 7,600
2	40,000	12 (year-4 depreciation)	4,800
3	40,000	12 (year-5 depreciation)	4,800
4	40,000	5 (year-6 depreciation)	2,000
		Total	$19,200[a]

[a]The total of $19,200 represents the book value of the old machine at the end of the second year, which was calculated in part a.

Calculation of Operating Cash Inflows

	Year			
	1	2	3	4
With new machine				
Profits before depr. and taxes[a]	$120,000	$130,000	$130,000	$ 0
− Depreciation[b]	49,500	67,500	22,500	10,500
Net profits before taxes	$ 70,500	$ 62,500	$107,500	−$10,500
− Taxes (rate = 40%)	28,200	25,000	43,000	− 4,200
Net profits after taxes	$ 42,300	$ 37,500	$ 64,500	−6,300
+ Depreciation[b]	49,500	67,500	22,500	10,500
Operating cash inflows	$ 91,800	$105,000	$ 87,000	$ 4,200
With old machine				
Profits before depr. and taxes[a]	$ 70,000	$ 70,000	$ 70,000	$ 0
− Depreciation[c]	7,600	4,800	4,800	2,000
Net profits before taxes	$ 62,400	$ 65,200	$ 65,200	−$ 2,000
− Taxes (rate = 40%)	24,960	26,080	26,080	− 800
Net profits after taxes	$ 37,440	$ 39,120	$ 39,120	−$ 1,200
+ Depreciation	7,600	4,800	4,800	2,000
Operating cash inflows	$ 45,040	$ 43,920	$ 43,920	$ 800

[a]Given in the problem.
[b]From column 3 of the first table.
[c]From column 3 of the preceding table.

Calculation of Incremental Operating Cash Inflows

	Operating cash inflows		
Year	New machine[a] (1)	Old machine[a] (2)	Incremental (relevant) [(1) − (2)] (3)
1	$ 91,800	$45,040	$46,760
2	105,000	43,920	61,080
3	87,000	43,920	43,080
4	4,200	800	3,400

[a]From final row for respective machine in the preceding table.

c. Terminal cash flow (end of year 3):

After-tax proceeds from sale of new machine		
Proceeds from sale of new machine	$35,000	
− Tax on sale of new machine[1]	9,800	
Total after-tax proceeds—new		$25,200
− After-tax proceeds from sale of old machine		
Proceeds from sale of old machine	$ 0	
− Tax on sale of old machine[2]	− 800	
Total after-tax proceeds—old		800
+ Change in net working capital		20,000
Terminal cash flow		$44,400

---

[1]Book value of new machine at end of year 3
= $150,000 − [(.33 + .45 + .15) × $150,000] = $150,000 − (.93 × $150,000)
= $150,000 − $139,500 = $10,500
Tax on sale = .40 × ($35,000 sale price − $10,500 book value)
           = .40 × $24,500 = $9,800
[2]Book value of old machine at end of year 3
= $40,000 − [(.20 + .32 + .19 + .12 + .12) × $40,000] = $40,000 − (.95 × $40,000)
= $40,000 − $38,000 = $2,000
Tax on sale = .40 × ($0 sale price − $2,000 book value)
                 = .40 × (− $2,000) = −$800 (i.e., $800 tax saving)

d.

Note: The year-4 incremental operating cash inflow of $3,400 is not directly included; it is instead reflected in the book values used to calculate the taxes on sale of the machines at the end of year 3 and is therefore part of the terminal cash flow.

CHAPTER 10

ST 10-1   a. Payback period:

$$\text{Project M:} \quad \frac{\$28,500}{\$10,000} = \underline{2.85 \text{ years}}$$

Project N:

Year (t)	Cash inflows (CF_t)	Cumulative cash inflows
1	$11,000	$11,000
2	10,000	21,000
3	9,000	30,000 ←
4	8,000	38,000

$$2 + \frac{\$27,000 - \$21,000}{\$9,000} \text{ years}$$

$$2 + \frac{\$6,000}{\$9,000} \text{ years} = \underline{2.67 \text{ years}}$$

b. Net present value (NPV):

Project M: NPV $= (\$10,000 \times PVIFA_{14\%,4\text{yrs}}) - \$28,500$

$= (\$10,000 \times 2.914) - \$28,500$

$= \$29,140 - \$28,500 = \underline{\$640}$

(Calculator solution $= \$637.12$)

Project N:

Year (t)	Cash inflows (CF_t) (1)	$PVIF_{14\%,t}$ (2)	Present value at 14% [(1) × (2)] (3)
1	$11,000	.877	$ 9,647
2	10,000	.769	7,690
3	9,000	.675	6,075
4	8,000	.592	4,736
	Present value of cash inflows		$28,148
	− Initial investment		27,000
	Net present value (NPV)		$ 1,148

(Calculator solution $= \$1,155.18$)

c. Internal rate of return (IRR):

Project M: $\dfrac{\$28,500}{\$10,000} = 2.850$

$PVIFA_{\text{IRR},4\text{yrs}} = 2.850$

From Table A-4:

$PVIFA_{15\%,4\text{yrs}} = 2.855$

$PVIFA_{16\%,4\text{yrs}} = 2.798$

IRR $= \underline{15\%}$ (2.850 is closest to 2.855)

(Calculator solution $= 15.09\%$)

Project N: Average annual cash inflow $= \dfrac{\$11,000 + \$10,000 + \$9,000 + \$8,000}{4}$

$$= \dfrac{\$38,000}{4} = \$9,500$$

$$PVIFA_{k,4\text{yrs}} = \dfrac{\$27,000}{\$9,500} = 2.842$$

$$k \approx 15\%$$

Try 16%, because there are more cash inflows in early years.

Year (t)	CF_t (1)	$PVIF_{16\%,t}$ (2)	Present value at 16% [(1) × (2)] (3)	$PVIF_{17\%,t}$ (4)	Present value at 17% [(1) × (4)] (5)
1	$11,000	.862	$ 9,482	.855	$ 9,405
2	10,000	.743	7,430	.731	7,310
3	9,000	.641	5,769	.624	5,616
4	8,000	.552	4,416	.534	4,272
	Present value of cash inflows		$27,097		$26,603
	− Initial investment		27,000		27,000
	NPV		$ 97		−$ 397

IRR = 16% (rounding to nearest whole percent)
(Calculator solution = 16.19%)

d.

	Project	
	M	**N**
Payback period	2.85 years	2.67 years[a]
NPV	$640	$1,148[a]
IRR	15%	16%[a]

[a]Preferred project.

Project N is recommended, because it has the shorter payback period and the higher NPV, which is greater than zero, and the larger IRR, which is greater than the 14 percent cost of capital.

e. Net present value profiles:

Data		
	NPV	
Discount rate	Project M	Project N
0%	$11,500[a]	$11,000[b]
14	640	1,148
15	0	—
16	—	0

[a]($10,000 + $10,000 + $10,000 + $10,000)
− $28,500 = $40,000 − $28,500 = $11,500

[b]($11,000 + $10,000 + $9,000 + $8,000)
− $27,000 = $38,000 − $27,000 = $11,000

From the NPV profile that follows, it can be seen that if the firm has a cost of capital below approximately 6 percent (exact value is 5.75 percent), conflicting rankings of the projects would exist using the NPV and IRR decision techniques. Because the firm's cost of capital is 14 percent, it can be seen in part **d** that no conflict exists.

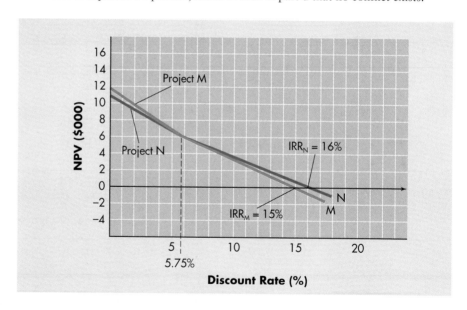

ST 10-2   **a.** $NPV_A = (\$7,000 \times PVIFA_{10\%,3yrs}) - \$15,000$
$= (\$7,000 \times 2.487) - \$15,000$
$= \$17,409 - \$15,000 = \underline{\$2,409}$
(Calculator solution = $2,407.96)

$$\begin{aligned}
\text{NPV}_B &= (\$10,000 \times PVIFA_{10\%,3\text{yrs}}) - \$20,000 \\
&= (\$10,000 - 2.487) - \$20,000 \\
&= \$24,870 - \$20,000 = \underline{\$4,870}^*
\end{aligned}$$

(Calculator solution = $4,868.52)

*Preferred project, because higher NPV.

b. Project A:

Year *(t)*	Cash inflows (CF_t) (1)	Certainty equivalent factors (α_t) (2)	Certain CF_t [(1) × (2)] (3)	$PVIF_{7\%,t}$ (4)	Present value at 7% [(3) × (4)] (5)
1	$7,000	.95	$6,650	.935	$ 6,218
2	7,000	.90	6,300	.873	5,500
3	7,000	.90	6,300	.816	5,141
			Present value of cash inflows		$16,859
		−	Initial investment		15,000
			NPV		$ 1,859*

(Calculator solution = $1,860.29)

Project B:

Year *(t)*	Cash inflows (CF_t) (1)	Certainty equivalent factors (α_t) (2)	Certain CF_t [(1) × (2)] (3)	$PVIF_{7\%,t}$ (4)	Present value at 7% [(3) × (4)] (5)
1	$10,000	.90	$9,000	.935	$ 8,415
2	10,000	.85	8,500	.873	7,421
3	10,000	.70	7,000	.816	5,712
			Present value of cash inflows		$21,548
		−	Initial investment		20,000
			NPV		$ 1,548

(Calculator solution = $1,549.53)

*Preferred project, because higher NPV.

c. From the CAPM-type relationship, the risk-adjusted discount rate for project A, which has a risk index of 0.4, is *9 percent;* for project B, with a risk index of 1.8, the risk-adjusted discount rate is *16 percent.*

$$\begin{aligned}
\text{NPV}_A &= (\$7,000 \times PVIFA_{9\%,3\text{yrs}}) - \$15,000 \\
&= (\$7,000 \times 2.531) - \$15,000 \\
&= \$17,717 - \$15,000 = \underline{\$2,717}^*
\end{aligned}$$

(Calculator solution = $2,719.06)

$$\begin{aligned}
\text{NPV}_B &= (\$10,000 \times PVIFA_{16\%,3\text{yrs}}) - \$20,000 \\
&= (\$10,000 \times 2.246) - \$20,000 \\
&= \$22,460 - \$20,000 = \underline{\$2,460}
\end{aligned}$$

(Calculator solution = $2,458.90)

*Preferred project, because higher NPV.

d. When the differences in risk were ignored in **a**, project B is preferred over project A; but when the higher risk of project B is incorporated in the analysis using either certainty equivalents (**b**) or risk-adjusted discount rates (**c**), *project A is preferred over project B.* Clearly, project A should be implemented.

CHAPTER 11

ST 11-1   **a.** Cost of debt, k_i (using approximation formula)

$$k_d = \frac{I + \dfrac{\$1,000 - N_d}{n}}{\dfrac{N_d + \$1,000}{2}}$$

$$I = .10 \times \$1,000 = \$100$$
$$N_d = \$1,000 - \$30 \text{ discount} - \$20 \text{ flotation cost} = \$950$$
$$n = 10 \text{ years}$$

$$k_d = \frac{\$100 + \dfrac{\$1,000 - \$950}{10}}{\dfrac{\$950 + \$1,000}{2}} = \frac{\$100 + \$5}{\$975} = 10.8\%$$

(Calculator solution = 10.8%)

$$k_i = k_d \times (1 - T)$$
$$T = .40$$
$$k_i = 10.8\% \times (1 - .40) = \underline{6.5\%}$$

Cost of preferred stock, k_p

$$k_p = \frac{D_p}{N_p}$$
$$D_p = .11 \times \$100 = \$11$$
$$N_p = \$100 - \$4 \text{ flotation cost} = \$96$$
$$k_p = \frac{\$11}{\$96} = \underline{11.5\%}$$

Cost of retained earnings, k_r

$$k_r = k_s = \frac{D_1}{P_0} + g$$

$$= \frac{\$6}{\$80} + 6.0\% = 7.5\% + 6.0\% = \underline{13.5\%}$$

Cost of new common stock, k_n

$$k_n = \frac{D_1}{N_n} + g$$
$$D_1 = \$6$$
$$N_n = \$80 - \$4 \text{ underpricing} - \$4 \text{ flotation cost} = \$72$$
$$g = 6.0\%$$
$$k_n = \frac{\$6}{\$72} + 6.0\% = 8.3\% + 6.0\% = \underline{14.3\%}$$

b. (1) Breaking point, BP

$$BP_{\text{common equity}} = \frac{AF_{\text{common equity}}}{w_{\text{common equity}}}$$

$$AF_{\text{common equity}} = \$225,000$$
$$w_{\text{common equity}} = 45\%$$

$$BP_{\text{common equity}} = \frac{\$225,000}{.45} = \$500,000$$

(2) WACC for total new financing < $500,000

Source of capital	Weight (1)	Cost (2)	Weighted cost [(1) × (2)] (3)
Long-term debt	.40	6.5%	2.6%
Preferred stock	.15	11.5	1.7
Common stock equity	.45	13.5	6.1
Totals	1.00		10.4%

Weighted average cost of capital = 10.4%

(3) WACC for total new financing > $500,000

Source of capital	Weight (1)	Cost (2)	Weighted cost [(1) × (2)] (3)
Long-term debt	.40	6.5%	2.6%
Preferred stock	.15	11.5	1.7
Common stock equity	.45	14.3	6.4
Totals	1.00		10.7%

Weighted average cost of capital = 10.7%

c. IOS data for graph

Investment opportunity	Internal rate of return (IRR)	Initial investment	Cumulative investment
D	16.5%	$200,000	$ 200,000
C	12.9	150,000	350,000
E	11.8	450,000	800,000
A	11.2	100,000	900,000
G	10.5	300,000	1,200,000
F	10.1	600,000	1,800,000
B	9.7	500,000	2,300,000

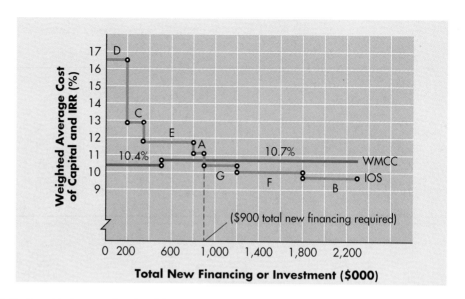

Total New Financing or Investment ($000)

d. Projects D, C, E, and A should be accepted because their respective IRRs exceed the WMCC. They will require $900,000 of total new financing.

CHAPTER 12

ST 12-1   **a.** $Q = \dfrac{FC}{P - VC}$

$$= \dfrac{\$250,000}{\$7.50 - \$3.00} = \dfrac{\$250,000}{\$4.50} = \underline{55,556 \text{ units}}$$

b.

		+20%
Sales (in units)	100,000	120,000
Sales revenue (units × $7.50/unit)	$750,000	$900,000
Less: Variable operating costs (units × $3.00/unit)	300,000	360,000
Less: Fixed operating costs	250,000	250,000
Earnings before interest and taxes (EBIT)	$200,000	$290,000

+45%

Less: Interest	80,000	80,000
Net profits before taxes	$120,000	$210,000
Less: Taxes ($T = .40$)	48,000	84,000
Net profits after taxes	$ 72,000	$126,000
Less: Preferred dividends (8,000 shares × $5.00/share)	40,000	40,000
Earnings available for common	$ 32,000	$ 86,000
Earnings per share (EPS)	$32,000/20,000 = $1.60/share	$86,000/20,000 = $4.30/share

+169%

c. $\text{DOL} = \dfrac{\% \text{ change in EBIT}}{\% \text{ change in sales}} = \dfrac{+45\%}{+20\%} = \underline{\underline{2.25}}$

d. $\text{DFL} = \dfrac{\% \text{ change in EPS}}{\% \text{ change in EBIT}} = \dfrac{+169\%}{+45\%} = \underline{\underline{3.76}}$

e. $\text{DTL} = \text{DOL} \times \text{DFL}$

$\quad\quad = 2.25 \times 3.76 = \underline{8.46}$

Using the other DTL formula:

$\text{DTL} = \dfrac{\% \text{ change in EPS}}{\% \text{ change in sales}}$

$8.46 = \dfrac{\% \text{ change in EPS}}{+50\%}$

$\% \text{ change in EPS} = 8.46 \times .50 = 4.23 = \underline{\underline{+423\%}}$

ST 12-2

Data summary for alternative plans		
Source of capital	**Plan A (bond)**	**Plan B (stock)**
Long-term debt	$60,000 at 12% annual interest	$50,000 at 12% annual interest
Annual interest =	.12 × $60,000 = $7,200	.12 × $50,000 = $6,000
Common stock	10,000 shares	11,000 shares

a.

	Plan A (bond)		**Plan B (stock)**	
EBIT[a]	$30,000	$40,000	$30,000	$40,000
Less: Interest	7,200	7,200	6,000	6,000
Net profits before taxes	$22,800	$32,800	$24,000	$34,000
Less: Taxes ($T = .40$)	9,120	13,120	9,600	13,600
Net profits after taxes	$13,680	$19,680	$14,400	$20,400
EPS (10,000 shares)	$1.37	$1.97		
(11,000 shares)			$1.31	$1.85

[a]Values were arbitrarily selected; other values could have been utilized.

Coordinates		
	EBIT	
	$30,000	$40,000
Financing plan	**Earnings per share (EPS)**	
A (Bond)	$1.37	$1.97
B (Stock)	1.31	1.85

b.

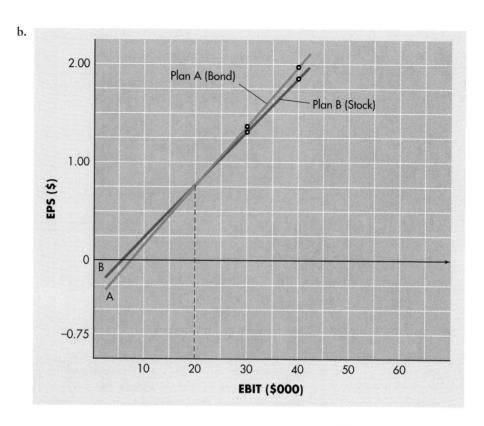

c. The bond plan (Plan A) becomes superior to the stock plan (Plan B) at *around $20,000* of EBIT, as represented by the dashed vertical line in the figure in **b**. (*Note:* The actual point is $19,200, which was determined algebraically by using a technique described in more advanced texts.)

ST 12-3   a.

Capital structure debt ratio	Expected EPS (1)	Required return, k_s (2)	Estimated share value [(1) ÷ (2)] (3)
0%	$3.12	.13	$24.00
10	3.90	.15	26.00
20	4.80	.16	30.00
30	5.44	.17	32.00
40	5.51	.19	29.00
50	5.00	.20	25.00
60	4.40	.22	20.00

b. Using the table in **a**:
  (1) Maximization of EPS: *40 percent debt ratio*, EPS = $5.51/share (see column 1).
  (2) Maximization of share value: *30 percent debt ratio*, share value = $32.00 (see column 3).

c. Recommend *30 percent debt ratio*, because it results in the maximum share value and is therefore consistent with the firm's goal of owner wealth maximization.

CHAPTER 13

ST 13-1   **a.** Earnings per share (EPS) $= \dfrac{\$2,000,000 \text{ earnings available}}{500,000 \text{ shares of common outstanding}}$

$= \underline{\$4.00/\text{share}}$

Price/earnings (P/E) ratio $= \dfrac{\$60 \text{ market price}}{\$4.00 \text{ EPS}} = \underline{\underline{15}}$

b. Proposed dividends = 500,000 shares × $2 per share = $1,000,000

Shares that can be repurchased $= \dfrac{\$1,000,000}{\$62} = \underline{16,129 \text{ shares}}$

c. *After proposed repurchase:*

Shares outstanding = 500,000 − 16,129 = 483,871

EPS $= \dfrac{\$2,000,000}{483,871} = \underline{\$4.13/\text{share}}$

d. Market price = $4.13/share × 15 = $\underline{\$61.95/\text{share}}$

e. The earnings per share (EPS) are higher after the repurchase, because there are fewer shares of stock outstanding (483,871 shares versus 500,000 shares) to divide up the firm's $2,000,000 of available earnings.

f. In both cases, the stockholders would receive $2 per share—a $2 cash dividend in the dividend case or an approximately $2 increase in share price ($60.00 per share to $61.95 per share) in the repurchase case. (*Note:* The $.05 per share ($2.00 − $1.95) difference is due to rounding.)

CHAPTER 14

ST 14-1   **a.**

	Cash Budget Carroll Company April–June					Accounts receivable at end of June	
	February	March	April	May	June	July	August
Forecast sales	$500	$600	$400	$ 200	$200		
Cash sales (.30)	$150	$180	$120	$ 60	$ 60		
Collections of A/R							
Lagged 1 month [(.7 × .7) = .49]		245	294	196	98	$ 98	
Lagged 2 months [(.3 × .7) = .21]			105	126	84	42	$42
						$140 +	$42 = $182
Total cash receipts			$519	$ 382	$242		
Less: Total cash disbursements			600	500	200		
Net cash flow			$ (81)	$(118)	$ 42		
Add: Beginning cash			115	34	(84)		
Ending cash			$ 34	$ (84)	$(42)		
Less: Minimum cash balance			25	25	25		
Required total financing (notes payable)			—	$109	$ 67		
Excess cash balance (marketable securities)			$ 9	—	—		

b. Carroll Company would need a maximum of $109 in financing over the 3-month period.

c.

Account	Amount	Source of amount
Cash	$ 25	Minimum cash balance—June
Notes payable	67	Required total financing—June
Marketable securities	0	Excess cash balance—June
Accounts receivable	182	Calculation at right of cash budget statement

ST 14-2 **a.**

Pro Forma Income Statement
Euro Designs, Inc.,
for the year ended December 31, 2001

Sales revenue (given)	$3,900,000
Less: Cost of goods sold (.55)[a]	2,145,000
Gross profits	$1,755,000
Less: Operating expenses (.12)[b]	468,000
Operating profits	$1,287,000
Less: Interest expense (given)	325,000
Net profits before taxes	$ 962,000
Less: Taxes (.40 × $962,000)	384,800
Net profits after taxes	$ 577,200
Less: Cash dividends (given)	320,000
To retained earnings	$ 257,200

[a]From 2000: CGS/Sales = $1,925,000/$3,500,000 = .55.
[b]From 2000: Oper. Exp./Sales = $420,000/$3,500,000 = .12.

b. The percent-of-sales method may underestimate actual 2001 pro forma income by assuming that all costs are variable. If the firm has fixed costs, which by definition would not increase with increasing sales, the 2001 pro forma income would likely be underestimated.

CHAPTER 15

ST 15-1   **a.**

Month	Total funds requirement (1)	Permanent funds requirement[a] (2)	Seasonal funds requirement [(1) − (2)] (3)
January	$7,400,000	$5,000,000	$2,400,000
February	5,500,000	5,000,000	500,000
March	5,000,000	5,000,000	0
April	5,300,000	5,000,000	300,000
May	6,200,000	5,000,000	1,200,000
June	6,000,000	5,000,000	1,000,000
July	5,800,000	5,000,000	800,000
August	5,400,000	5,000,000	400,000
September	5,000,000	5,000,000	0
October	5,300,000	5,000,000	300,000
November	6,000,000	5,000,000	1,000,000
December	6,800,000	5,000,000	1,800,000
Monthly average[b]		$5,000,000	$ 808,333

[a]Represents the lowest level of total funds required over the 12-month period.

[b]Found by summing the monthly amounts for 12 months and dividing the resulting totals by 12. For the permanent funds requirement, $60,000,000/12 = $5,000,000, and for the seasonal funds requirement, $9,700,000/12 = $808,333.

b. (1) *Aggressive strategy*—Applying this strategy would result in a perfect matching of long-term financing with the permanent funds requirement and short-term financing with the seasonal funds requirement. Therefore $5,000,000 of long-term financing and average monthly short-term financing of $808,333 would be used.

  (2) *Conservative strategy*—Applying this strategy would result in enough long-term financing to meet all projected funds requirements; short-term financing would be used only to meet emergency or unexpected financial needs. In this case, $7,400,000 of long-term financing would be used to meet the peak funds requirement (during January), and no short-term financing would be used.

c. (1) *Aggressive strategy:*

$$\text{Total cost} = (\$5,000,000 \times .16) + (\$808,333 \times .10)$$
$$= \$800,000 + \$80,833 = \underline{\$880,833}$$

  (2) *Conservative strategy:*

$$\text{Total cost} = (\$7,400,000 \times .16) + (\$0 \times .10)$$
$$= \$1,184,000 + \$0 = \underline{\$1,184,000}$$

d. The *aggressive strategy is more profitable,* because, as noted in **c,** its total cost is $880,833 compared to the total cost of $1,184,000 under the conservative strategy. This difference results because the aggressive strategy uses as much of the less expensive short-term (current liability) financing as possible, whereas the conservative strategy finances all needs with the more expensive long-term financing. Also, under the aggressive strategy, interest is paid only on necessary financing; under the conservative strategy, interest is paid on unneeded funds. (For example, under the conservative strategy, interest is paid on $7,400,000 in July when only $5,800,000 of financing is needed.)

The *aggressive strategy, on the other hand, is more risky,* because it relies heavily on the *limited* short-term financing, whereas the conservative strategy reserves short-term borrowing for emergency or unexpected financial needs. In addition, the aggressive strategy results in lower net working capital than the conservative strategy, thereby resulting in lower liquidity and a higher risk of technical insolvency.

ST 15-2   a.

Supplier	Approximate cost of giving up cash discount
X	$1\% \times [360/(55 - 10)] = 1\% \times 360/45 = 1\% \times 8 = 8\%$
Y	$2\% \times [360/(30 - 10)] = 2\% \times 360/20 = 2\% \times 18 = 36\%$
Z	$2\% \times [360/(60 - 20)] = 2\% \times 360/40 = 2\% \times 9 = 18\%$

b.

Supplier	Recommendation
X	8% cost of giving up discount < 15% interest cost from bank; therefore, *give up discount.*
Y	36% cost of giving up discount > 15% interest cost from bank; therefore, *take discount and borrow from bank.*
Z	18% cost of giving up discount > 15% interest cost from bank; therefore, *take discount and borrow from bank.*

c. Stretching accounts payable for supplier Z would change the cost of giving up the cash discount to

$$2\% \times \{360/[(60 + 20) - 20]\} = 2\% \times 360/60 = 2\% \times 6 = \underline{12\%}$$

In this case, in light of the 15 percent interest cost from the bank, the recommended strategy in **b** would be to *give up the discount,* because the 12 percent cost of giving up the discount would be less than the 15 percent bank interest cost.

CHAPTER 16

ST 16-1

Basic data		
Time component	Current	Proposed
Average payment period (APP)	10 days	30 days
Average collection period (ACP)	30 days	30 days
Average age of inventory (AAI)	40 days	40 days

Cash conversion cycle (CCC) = AAI + ACP − APP

$$\text{CCC}_{\text{current}} = 40 \text{ days} + 30 \text{ days} - 10 \text{ days} = 60 \text{ days}$$
$$\text{CCC}_{\text{proposed}} = 40 \text{ days} + 30 \text{ days} - 30 \text{ days} = \underline{40 \text{ days}}$$
$$\text{Reduction in CCC} \quad \underline{20 \text{ days}}$$

Annual operating cycle investment = $18,000,000

Daily expenditure = $18,000,000 ÷ 360 = $50,000
Reduction in financing = $50,000 × 20 days = $1,000,000
Annual profit increase = .12 × $1,000,000 = $\underline{\$120,000}$

ST 16-2   Time reduction:

Mailing time	$1\frac{1}{2}$ days
Processing time	$1\frac{1}{2}$ days
Clearing time	1 day
Total time reduction	4 days

Float reduction:

4 days × $300,000/day = $1,200,000

Gross annual benefit of float reduction:

.09 × $1,200,000 = $108,000

Because the annual earnings from the float reduction of $108,000 exceed the annual cost of $90,000, *the proposed lockbox should be implemented.* It will result in a net annual savings of $18,000 ($108,000 earnings − $90,000 cost).

CHAPTER 17

ST 17-1   **Tabular Calculation of the Effects of Easing Collection Efforts on Regency Rug Repair Company**

Additional profit contribution from sales			
[1,000 rugs × ($32 avg. sale price − $28 var. cost)]			$ 4,000
Cost of marginal investment in accounts receivable			
Average investment under proposed plan:			
$\dfrac{(\$28 \times 73{,}000 \text{ rugs})}{360/58} = \dfrac{\$2{,}044{,}000}{6.21}$		$329,147	
Average investment under present plan:			
$\dfrac{(\$28 \times 72{,}000 \text{ rugs})}{360/40} = \dfrac{\$2{,}016{,}000}{9}$		224,000	
Marginal investment in A/R		$105,147	
Cost of marginal investment in			
A/R (.24 × $105,147)			($25,235)
Cost of marginal bad debts			
Bad debts under proposed plan			
(.02 × $32 × 73,000 rugs)		$ 46,720	
Bad debts under present plan			
(.01 × $32 × 72,000 rugs)		23,040	
Cost of marginal bad debts			($23,680)
Annual savings in collection expense			$40,000
Net loss from implementation of proposed plan			($ 4,915)

Recommendation: Because a net loss of $4,915 is expected to result from easing collection efforts, *the proposed plan should not be implemented.*

ST 17-2 **a.** *Data:*

S = 60,000 gallons

O = $200 per order

C = $1 per gallon per year

Calculation:

$$EOQ = \sqrt{\frac{2 \times S \times O}{C}} = \sqrt{\frac{2 \times 60,000 \times \$200}{\$1}} = \sqrt{24,000,000} = \underline{4,899\ gallons}$$

b. *Data:*

Lead time = 20 days

Daily usage = 60,000 gallons/360 days

= 166.67 gallons/day

Calculation:

Reorder point = lead time in days $\times$ daily usage

= 20 days $\times$ 166.67 gallons/day

= $\underline{3,333.4\ gallons}$

Appendix C

Answers to Selected End-of-Chapter Problems

The following list of answers to selected problems and portions of problems is included to provide "check figures" for use in preparing detailed solutions to end-of-chapter problems requiring calculations. For problems that are relatively straightforward, the key answer is given; for more complex problems, answers to a number of parts of the problem are included. Detailed calculations are not shown—only the final and, in some cases, intermediate answers, which should help to confirm whether the correct solution is being developed. Answers to problems involving present and future value were solved by using the appropriate tables; calculator solutions are not given. For problems containing a variety of cases for which similar calculations are required, the answers for only one or two cases have been included. The only verbal answers included are simple yes-or-no or "choice of best alternative" responses; answers to problems requiring detailed explanations or discussions are not given.

The problems and portions of problems for which answers have been included were selected randomly; therefore, there is no discernible pattern to the choice of problem answers given. The answers given are based on what are believed to be the most obvious and reasonable assumptions related to the given problem; in some cases, other reasonable assumptions could result in equally correct answers.

1-1 **a.** Ms. Harper has unlimited liability: $60,000.
     c. Ms. Harper has limited liability and will not
             have to make any payments but
                 she will lose her $25,000 investment.

2-1 **b.** $1,002.50
     c. 2005
     e. 8 ¾% (8.75%)
     f. 8.73%
     g. ($6.25)
             $1,008.75

2-2 **b.** $81.75
     f. $1.32
     h. 1,243,200

2-3 **b.** $3.60

2-7 **b.** C: 10%
             E: 12%

3-1 **a.** Common stock (10,000 shares
                 @ $1 par) $ 10,000
             Paid in capital in excess of par   120,000
                 Common stock equity $130,000

3-4 **a.** $8.80
     c. $35.20

4-4 **b.** $27,050

4-5 **a.** $1.16

4-8 **a.** EPS = $1.94
     b. Total assets: $926,000

4-10 **a.** $19,700
     c. 21.30%

4-12 **a.** 15%; 25%; 34%; 39%; 34%; 34%; 35%

4-15 **a.** X: $250
             Y: $5,000
     b. X: $100
             Y: $2,000

4-17 $80,000

4-19 **a.** $70,680

5-2 **a.** Average age of inventory: 97.6 days

5-6 **a.** 1999 Johnson ROE = 22.13%
                   Industry ROE = 16.92%

5-8 **a.**
	Actual 2000
Current Ratio:	1.04
Average collection period:	56 days
Debt ratio:	61.3%
Net profit margin:	4.1%
Return on equity:	11.3%

6-3 **a.** Case C: 3 years $< n <$ 4 years

6-4 A: $530.60
     D: $78,450.00

6-6 **a.** (1) $15,456

6-9 **a.** (1) Annual: $8,810
                 Semiannual: $8,955
                 Quarterly: $9,030

6-10 **b.** B: 12.62%
             D: 16.99%

6-11 A: $1,197.22

6-14 B: $4,057.50
     E: $2,140,772

6-18 A: $3,862.50
     B: $138,450.00
     C: $6,956.80

6-21 A: $4,452.00
     D: $80,250.00

6-24 $63

6-26 **a.** A: $20,833.50
     c. B

6-29 **a.** PV of stream C = $52,410

6-30 **a.** PV of stream A = $109,890

6-32 E: $85,297.50

6-36 **b.** (D) $1,200,000

6-40 Future value of retirement home
         in 20 years = $272,595
     Annual deposit = $4,759.49

6-41 **b.** Deposit = $3,764.82

6-43
Year	Interest	Principal
2	$1,489.61	$4,970.34

6-48 $PVIFA_{k,10} = 5.303$
     $13% < k < 14%$

7-1 **a.** X: 12.5%
             Y: 12.36%

7-2 A: 25%

7-4 **a.** A: 8%
             B: 20%

7-5 **a.** R: 10%
             S: 20%
     b. R: 25.0%
             S: 25.5%

7-8 **a.** (4) Project 257 CV: .368
                 Project 432 CV: .354

7-9 **a.** F: 4%
     b. F: 13.38%
     c. F: 3.345

7-11 **a.** Alternative 2 return: 16.5%
     b. Standard deviation of 2: 0.0%

7-15 **a.** 18% increase
     b. 9.6% decrease
     c. No change

7-19 A: 8.9%
     D: 15%

7-20 **b.** 10%

8-2 C: $16,660
     E: $14,112

8-4 **a.** $1,156.88

8-5 A: $1,149.66
     D: $450.80

8-9 **a.** 12.685% using a financial calculator

8-11 $841.15

8-15 **a.** $68.82
     b. $7.87

8-17 **a.** $37.75
     b. $60.40

8-18 **a.** $236,111.11
     b. $386,363.64

8-19 **a.** $36.00
     b. $30.20

8-22 2.67

8-23 **a.** 14.80%
     b. $29.55

9-1 **a.** Current expenditure
     d. Current expenditure
     f. Capital expenditure

9-6 A: $275,500
     B: $26,800

9-8 **a.** Total tax: $49,600
     d. Total tax: ($6,400)

9-10   Initial investment: $22,680
9-11   a.   Initial investment: $18,240
        c.   Initial investment: $23,100
9-13   c.   Cash inflow, Year 3: $584,000
9-15   b.   Incremental cash flow, Year 3: $1,960
9-17   Terminal cash flow: $76,640
9-21   a.   Initial investment, Asset B: $51,488
        b.   Incremental cash flow, Year 2, Hoist A: $8,808
        c.   Terminal cash flow, Hoist B: $18,600
10-2   a.   Machine 1: 4 years, 8 months
              Machine 2: 5 years, 3 months
10-4   a.   (1) $2,675
              (2) Accept
10-6   a.   NPV = ($320); reject
10-8   a.   Project A: 3.08 years; Project C: 2.38 years
        b.   Project C: NPV = $5,451
10-9   Project A: 17%
        Project D: 21%
10-12   a.   NPV = $1,222
        b.   IRR = 12%
        c.   Accept
10-14   a.   Project A
              NPV = $15,245
        b.   Project B
              IRR = 18%
10-17   a.   Initial Investment: $1,480,000
        b.

Year	Cash Flow
1	$656,000
2	761,600
3	647,200
4	585,600
5	585,600
6	44,000

        c.   2.1 years
        d.   NPV = $959,289
              IRR = 35%
10-20   b.   Projects C, F, and G
10-25   a.   NPV = $22,320
        b.   NPV = ($5,596)
10-27   a.   Project E: NPV = $2,130
              Project F: NPV = $1,678
              Project G: NPV = $1,144
        c.   Project E: NPV = $834
              Project F: NPV = $1,678
              Project G: NPV = $2,138
11-2   a. $980
        c.   12.31%
        d.   Before-tax: 12.26%; after-tax: 7.36%
11-3   A: 5.66%
        E: 7.10%
11-5   A: 11.96%
        D: 12.24%
11-7   c.   15.91%
        d.   16.54%
11-10   a.   Weighted cost: 8.344%
        b.   Weighted cost: 10.854%
11-14   b. $500,000 and $800,000
        c.   WACC over $800,000: 16.2%
12-1   1,300
12-4   a.   21,000 CDs
        d. $10,500

12-7   a.   Q = 8,000 units
        e.   DOL = 5.00
12-9   a.   EPS = $0.375
12-11   a.   DFL = 1.5
        c.   DFL = 1.93
12-12   a.   175,000 units
        d.   DTL = 2.40
12-14

Debt ratio	Debt	Equity
40%	$400,000	$600,000

12-15   c.   Structure A is preferred if EBIT < $52,000
12-18   a.

Debt Ratio	Amount of Debt	Amount of Equity	# of Shares
30%	300,000	700,000	28,000
60%	600,000	400,000	16,000

        b.   At 45% annual interest = $58,500
13-1   b.   Monday, July 3 (due to the July 4 holiday)
        c.   Cash $170,000 Dividends payable $ 0
                          Retained earnings $2,170,000
13-3   a. $4.75 per share
        b. $0.40 per share
        d.   A decrease in retained earnings and hence
              stockholder's equity by $80,000
13-6   a.   1998 = $0.60
        b.   1998 = $0.50
        c.   1998 = $0.62
        d.   1998 = $0.62
13-7   a.   Retained earnings = $85,000
        b.   (1) Retained earnings = $70,000
              (2) Retained earnings = $40,000
13-9   a.   EPS = $2.00
        b.   1%
        c.   1%; stock dividends do not have a real value.
13-11   b.   Common stock   (400,000 shares @ $4.50 par)
              = $1,800,000
14-3

	(in $000)		
	Feb.	Mar.	Apr.
a. Ending cash	$37	$67	($22)
b. Required total financing			$37
Excess cash balance	$22	$52	

        c.   Line of credit should be at least $37,000 to cover
              borrowing needs for the month of April
14-6   a.   Net profit after taxes: $216,600
        b.   Net profit after taxes: $227,400
14-8   a.   Accounts receivable: $1,440,000
              Net fixed assets: $4,820,000
              Total current liabilities: $2,260,000
              External funds required: $775,000
              Total assets: $9,100,000
14-9   a.   Net profit after taxes: $67,500
        b.   Judgmental
              Total assets $697,500
              External funds required $ 11,250
15-1   b.   (1) $36,000
              (2) $10,333
15-2   Annual loan cost: $1,200
15-5   c.   January 9
15-7   Effective interest rate = 31.81%
15-9 $1,300,000

15-12	a.	12.94%
	c.	11.73%
15-15	a.	9.0%
	b.	13.06%
15-16	a.	Total: $80,000
	c.	$54,000
15-17	a.	Center City Bank: $1,000
16-1	a.	OC = 150 days
	b.	CCC = 120 days
	c.	$10,000,000
16-2	b.	CCC = 35 days
	c.	$97,222
16-4	Plan E	
16-7	a.	7 days
	b.	Opportunity cost = $21,450
16-9	a.	Maximum savings = $3,850
		Minimum savings = $1,100
16-12	Opportunity cost = $5,834	

16-14	$22,500 annual savings	
16-16	Total cost: $48,000	
17-1	a.	Credit score applicant B: 81.5
17-2	b.	$75,000
	c.	$9,000
17-4	a.	Present plan: $20,000
		Proposed plan: $48,000
17-6	The credit standards should not be relaxed, because the proposed plan results in a loss of $4,721	
17-7	Net profit on the proposal: $20,040	
17-9	a.	$14,000 additional profit contribution
	b.	$7,286
17-11	b.	$52,000 net savings
17-14	a.	(1) 10,541
		(2) 0
		(3) ∞
17-16	a.	200 units
	b.	122 units
	c.	33 units

Appendix **D**

Instructions for Using the *PMF* Brief CD-ROM Software

The *PMF Brief CD-ROM* contains three applications: the *PMF Tutor, PMF Problem Solver,* and the *PMF Excel Spreadsheet Templates.* These solutions are designed to run on any computer running Windows 3.1, 95 or 98 and Microsoft Excel version 5.0 or higher.

  The *PMF Tutor, PMF Problem-Solver,* and *PMF Excel Spreadsheet Templates* are arranged in the same order as the text discussions. For your convenience, text page references are shown on the screen for each associated computation in the *Problem-Solver* and the *Tutor.* As noted in the text preface as well as in Chapter 1, applicability of the software throughout the text and the study guide is keyed to related text discussions, end-of-chapter problems, and end-of-chapter and end-of-part cases by icons for all of the computational routines. Thus, you can integrate the procedures on the disk with the corresponding text discussions.

WHAT IS THE *PMF* TUTOR?

The *PMF Tutor* is an Excel workbook containing a collection of managerial finance problem types with the problem varied by random number generation. Its purpose is to give you an essentially unlimited number of problems to work through so that you can practice until you are satisfied that you understand a concept. In using the *Tutor,* the following sequence should produce the best results:

1. **Work the problem first yourself.** It is tempting to save time by letting the computer solve the problem for you and then studying the computer's answer. You won't learn much that way. Even if you make mistakes when you try the problem on your own, you will learn from those mistakes.
2. **Enter your answer.** The computer will check your answer against the correct answer.
3. **Check the solution.** If you do not get the same answer as the computer, check your work step by step against the correct solution displayed on the

computer screen. Doing so will help you to pinpoint your mistakes. Practice each type of problem until you have genuinely mastered it. Don't have false pride about your mastery. When you take the course exams, you won't be able to fake your knowledge level. So don't stop until you're sure that you have mastered the concepts.

The *Tutor* uses random number generation to choose the specific numbers, so it is unlikely that you will ever see a combination of numbers twice. This gives you an effectively unlimited number of practice rpoblems. The only limit is your willingness to practice.

WHAT IS THE *PMF* PROBLEM-SOLVER?

The *PMF Problem-Solver* is an Excel workbook containing a collection of financial computation worksheets. The purpose of the *PMF Problem-Solver* is to aid the student's learning and understanding of managerial finance by providing a fast and easy method for performing the often time-consuming mathematical computations required. It is not the intent of the *PMF Problem-Solver* to eliminate the need for learning the various concepts, but to assist in solving the problems once the appropriate formulas have been studied. The *PMF Problem-Solver* differs from the *Tutor* in that it solves for the answer, given the input data supplied by the user, whereas the *Tutor* supplies the input data and looks to the student to perform the calculations. The *Tutor* should be used to practice application of basic concepts; the *PMF Problem-Solver* should be used to save computational time once the concepts are understood.

WHAT ARE THE *PMF* EXCEL SPREADSHEET TEMPLATES?

The *PMF Excel Spreadsheet Templates* are preprogrammed Excel worksheets, with one file for each problem. The worksheets enable students to enter data and solve problems using Microsoft Excel—the most commonly used spreadsheet software. The worksheet files correspond to selected end-of-chapter problems, and the worksheet file names are based on the chapter number and the problem number. For selected problems, there are additional worksheets that are not tied to problems in the text. These worksheets can be used to provide additional opportunities for solving financial problems on their own.

HARDWARE AND SOFTWARE REQUIREMENTS

To use the *PMF Brief CD-ROM,* you must have the following:

- an IBM compatible PC
- Microsoft Windows 3.1, Windows 95, or Windows 98
- Microsoft Excel Version 5.0, 7.0, 97 or 2000

INSTALLING THE SOFTWARE

If you are using Windows 95 or 98 do the following:

1. Insert the *PMF Brief* CD-ROM into your CD-ROM drive.
2. An autorun will automatically lead you through the installation process. If your CD is configured to bypass this autorun, Select Start | Run | X:setup.exe where X:/ is the drive letter of your CD-ROM.
3. Follow the instructions on the screen to install the files to your hard drive.

You can also access spreadsheets directly on the CD-ROM. All of the individual files are available in folders for your respective version of Excel. The folder names are XL5, XL95, XL97, and XL2000.

If you are using Windows 3.1, there is no install—the files are available on the PMF Brief CD-ROM in a folder called XL5.

Be sure to store the CD-ROM in a safe place in the event that you need to install the software again at a later time.

THE *PMF* TUTOR

RUNNING THE PMF TUTOR

To run the *PMF Tutor,* follow these steps:

1. Start Excel.
2. Select File / Open.
3. Select the *PMF Brief* directory in which the *Tutor* is stored and then select the file Tutorial.xls.
4. Click the OK button and the *Tutor* will open, displaying its main menu.

When the *PMF Tutor* is loaded, the user sees the following introductory screen:

PRINCIPLES OF MANAGERIAL FINANCE
Tutorial Menu

> Valuation Models   > Analyzing Profitability

> Analyzing Liquidity   > Time Value of Money

> Analyzing Activity   > Cost of Capital

> Analyzing Debt   > Capital Budgeting

Copyright © 1999 Addison-Wesley. All Rights Reserved.
Developed by KMT Software, Inc.

FIGURE D–1

Excel *PMF Tutor* start-up screen showing the main menu

USING THE *PMF* TUTOR

From the *PMF Tutor* main menu, click the button of the problem category that you want to work with. When the category menu is displayed, select a specific problem type. Each tutorial will open with a new problem ready for you to solve. The following is an example *Tutor* problem:

Current Ratio

Cash	$11,100
Accounts Receivable	18,870
Inventory	22,200
Net Fixed Assets	58,830
Total Assets	111,000
Accounts Payable	12,210
Notes Payable (due in three months)	9,990
Long-term Liabilities	28,000
Retained Earnings	10,850

Enter the Current Ratio here -->
The correct answer is:

LEARNING OBJECTIVE

This problem tests you on the current ratio. Selected Balance Sheet data are given and you are asked to calculate this commonly used liquidity ratio.

See related text material on page 119.

FIGURE D–2

Excel *PMF Tutor* sample problem

There are five buttons at the top of the window for each tutorial:

- Solution—Click this to see the problem solution.
- New Problem—Click this to see new problem data.
- Prev—Click this to move to the previous tutorial problem.
- Main—Click this to return to the *PMF Tutor* main menu.
- Next—Click this to move to the next tutorial problem.

USING THE *PMF* TUTOR TOOLBAR

The *PMF Tutor* has a toolbar that also facilitates navigation and tasks. The twelve buttons of the toolbar are explained on the next page.

Click this button to go to the main menu

Click this button to go to the previous tutorial

Click this button to go to the next tutorial

Click this button to go to the summary sheet

Click this button to set the zoom factor for the tutorial

Click this button to make a new problem in the current tutorial

Click this button to check the solution to the current problem

Click this button to open the Windows calculator to facilitate your solution

Click this button to print the current tutorial sheets

Click this button to preview the printing of the current tutorial sheets

Click this button to view Help for *PMF Tutor*

Click this button to learn more about KMT Software, the developer of this application

When you are ready to solve a particular tutorial problem, you may want to follow these steps:

1. Review the learning objective. Each tutorial has a learning objective situated just below the problem. Learning objectives provide a brief description of what each problem is testing you on and note the associated pages in the textbook where the material is covered.
2. Review the problem data and calculate your answer.
3. Enter your answer in the yellow cell. Note: If the problem calls for a percentage, be sure to enter the percentage in decimal form (i.e., 20% as .2) or enter the number followed by the percent sign (i.e., type 20% and then press Enter).
4. Check your solution.
5. If you need more practice, click the New Problem button and begin with step 1.

THE *PMF* PROBLEM-SOLVER

RUNNING THE *PMF* PROBLEM-SOLVER

To run the *PMF Problem-Solver,* follow these steps:

1. Start Excel.
2. Select File / Open.
3. Select the *PMF Brief* directory in which the *Problem-Solver* is stored and then select the file Solver.xls.
4. Click the OK button and the *Problem-Solver* will open, displaying its main menu.

USING THE *PMF* PROBLEM-SOLVER

From the *PMF Problem-Solver* main menu, click the button of the calculation category that you want to work with. When the category menu is displayed, select a specific calculation. Here is the *PMF Problem-Solver* main menu:

FIGURE D–3

Excel *PMF Problem-Solver* start-up screen showing the main menu

Using a *PMF Problem-Solver* worksheet is simple. You enter your inputs in the yellow cells. You can move between these cells using your mouse or by pressing the Tab on your keyboard. If any of your inputs involve percentages (e.g., an interest rate of 10.5%), enter the percentage either in decimal form (i.e., enter .105 for 10.5%) or enter the percentage following the format number followed by the percent sign (i.e., type 10.5% and then press Enter).

The following is an example *Problem-Solver* problem:

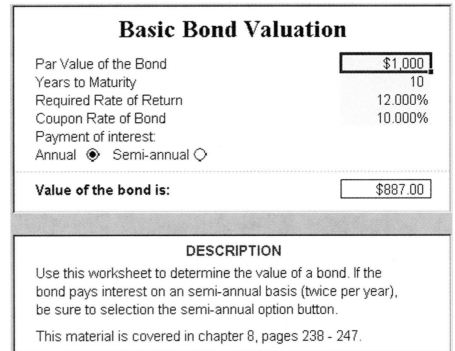

Basic Bond Valuation

Par Value of the Bond	$1,000
Years to Maturity	10
Required Rate of Return	12.000%
Coupon Rate of Bond	10.000%
Payment of interest:	
Annual ● Semi-annual ○	

Value of the bond is: $887.00

DESCRIPTION

Use this worksheet to determine the value of a bond. If the bond pays interest on an semi-annual basis (twice per year), be sure to selection the semi-annual option button.

This material is covered in chapter 8, pages 238 - 247.

FIGURE D–4

Excel *PMF Problem-Solver* sample problem

The *PMF Problem-Solver* has a toolbar that also facilitates navigation and tasks. The 10 buttons of the toolbar are explained below.

USING THE PROBLEM-SOLVER TOOLBAR

The *Problem-Solver* has a toolbar that performs a variety of functions depending on which button you select. The toolbar includes the following buttons and functions:

- Click this button to go to the main menu
- Click this button to go to the previous sheet
- Click this button to go to the next sheet
- Click this button to go to the summary sheet
- Click this button to set the zoom factor for the solver
- Click this button to open the Windows calculator to facilitate your solution
- Click this button to print the solver sheets
- Click this button to preview the printing of the current solverl sheets
- Click this button to view Help for *PMF Problem-Solver*
- Click this button to learn more about KMT Software, the developer of this application

THE *PMF* EXCEL SPREADSHEET TEMPLATES

RUNNING THE *PMF* EXCEL SPREADSHEET TEMPLATES

To run one of the *PMF Excel Spreadsheet Templates*, follow these steps:

1. Start Excel.
2. Select File / Open.
3. Select the *PMF Brief* directory in which the problems are stored and then select the appropriate file as described in the textbook (e.g. Ch02–15.xls).
4. Click the OK button and the problem will open.

USING THE *PMF* EXCEL SPREADSHEET TEMPLATES

The *PMF Excel Spreadsheet Templates* describe the problem from the chapter material. You then enter the inputs in the highlighted cells. If any of your inputs involve percentages (e.g., an interest rate of 10.5%), enter the percentage either in decimal form (i.e., enter .105 for 10.5%) or enter the percentage following the format number followed by the percent sign (i.e., type 10.5% and then press Enter).

Each of the *PMF Excel Spreadsheet Templates* has a description of the problem at the top of the worksheet and the answer is listed below. The screen shot below shows a typical problem description:

FIGURE D–5

Example *PMF Excel Spreadsheet Templates* sample problem description

---

PRINCIPLES OF MANAGERIAL FINANCE

Problem 4-14 Interest versus Dividend Expense

The Michaels Corporation expects earnings before interest and taxes to be $40,000 for this period, assuming an ordinary tax rate of 40%, compute the firm's earnings after taxes and earnings available for common stockholders (earnings after taxes and preferred stock dividends, if any) under the following conditions:

a. The firm pays $10,000 in interest.

b. The firm pays $10,000 in preferred stock dividends

Below the problem description, the answer is made available:

Answer:

a.	EBIT	$40,000
	Less: Interest expense	10,000
	Earnings before taxes	$30,000
	Less: Taxes (40%)	12,000
	Earnings after taxes	$18,000 *

* This is also earnings available to common stockholders

b.	EBIT	$40,000
	Less: Taxes (40%)	16,000
	Earnings after taxes	$24,000
	Less: Preferred Dividends	10,000
	Earnings available for common stockholders	$14,000

FIGURE D-6

Example *PMF Excel* Spreadsheet Templates sample answer

The data entry cells are clearly highlighted. When you enter your data, the worksheet automatically calculates the new answer.

USING THE *PMF* SPREADSHEET TOOLBAR

Each *PMF Spreadsheet* has a toolbar that performs a variety of functions depending on which button you select. The toolbar includes the following buttons and funcitons:

Click this button to set the zoom factor for the solver

Click this button to open the Windows calculator to facilitate your solution

Click this button to print the solver sheets

Click this button to preview the printing of the current tutorial sheets

Click this button to view Help for *PMF Spreadsheet*

Click this button to learn more about KMT Sofware, the developer of this application

PERSONAL FINANCE PERSPECTIVE SOURCES

Bold page numbers indicate location of features.

Chapter 4

90 *Depreciation Counts When Buying a Car* Ed Henry, "How to Get the Best Deal," *Kiplinger's Personal Finance Magazine* (December 1995), pp. 60–62; and Edward O. Welles, "Show and Sell," *Inc.* (October 1995), pp. 74–81.

Chapter 6

162 Karen Cheney, "Panic-Free Saving and Investing," *Money* (October 1995), pp. 82–87.

Chapter 7

217 Amey Stone, "Learning to Live with Risk—and Loving It," *Business Week* (May 22, 1995), pp. 142–143.

Chapter 8

247 Anthony Ramirez, "Dire News Rarely a Death Knell for Major Companies," *San Diego Union-Tribune* (July 23, 1995), p. I–7.

Chapter 11

360 Nancy Ann Jeffrey, "Debtor's Deals," *The Wall Street Journal* (December 8, 1995), p. R8.

Chapter 12

398 Lawrence J. Gitman and Michael D. Joehnk, *Fundamentals of Investing*, 6th ed., pp. 59–60, Addison Wesley Longman, Reading, Mass., 1996.

Chapter 13

455 Daniel Kadlec, "The Dumb Money," *Time*, February 22, 1999, downloaded from Electric Library Business Edition, **http://business.elibrary.com;** and Jim Rasmussen, "Investor-Pleasing Stock Splits Mostly an Exercise in Math," *Omaha World-Herald*, February 22, 1999, downloaded from **http://www.omaha.com.**

Chapter 14

462 Kristin Davis, "Financial Planning for Erratic Incomes," *Kiplinger's Personal Finance Magazine* (February 1994), pp. 57–66.

Chapter 15

511 *Choosing the Best Credit Card Pays Off* Georgette Jasen, "Ace in the Hole," *The Wall Street Journal* (December 8, 1995), p. R13.

Chapter 16

543 Gina Fann, "Banking in Your Bathrobe," *The Tennessean,* October 5, 1998, downloaded from Electric Library Business Edition, **http://busniess.elibrary.com;** Bill Wolf, "Online Banking: It's Convenient for User, But Banks Enjoy Biggest Savings," *The Courier-Journal* (Louisville, KY), January 5, 1998, downloaded from Electric Library Business Edition, **http://business.elibrary.com.**

Chapter 17

565 Lorrie Cohen, "Credit Card Lesson Can Carry High Price," *The Tucson Citizen,* February 2, 1998, downloaded from Electric Library Business Edition, **http://business.elibrary.com;** Jane Bryant Quinn, "Debt Counseling Can Be A Bulwark Against Bankruptcy," *Seattle Post-Intelligencer,* January 26, 1999, downloaded from Electric Library Business Edition, **http://business.elibrary.com;** and George Rodrigue, "FTC Targets 'Bogus' Credit Repair Firms," *The Dallas Morning News,* March 22, 1998, downloaded from Electric Library Business Edition, **http://business.elibrary.com.**

INDEX

Page numbers in *italics* indicate figures; page numbers followed by *n* indicate footnotes; page numbers followed by *t* indicate tables. Marginal terms are bold.